THE EMERGENCE
OF MODERN TURKEY

THE EMERGENCE
OF MODERN TURKEY

BERNARD LEWIS

Issued under the auspices of the
Royal Institute of International Affairs
OXFORD UNIVERSITY PRESS
LONDON   NEW YORK   TORONTO
1961

Oxford University Press, Amen House, London E.C.4

GLASGOW NEW YORK TORONTO MELBOURNE WELLINGTON
BOMBAY CALCUTTA MADRAS KARACHI KUALA LUMPUR
CAPE TOWN IBADAN NAIROBI ACCRA

DR
583
L 48

43601

Printed in Great Britain

To
Jill and Ercüment
in friendship and gratitude

PREFACE

THE theme of this book is the emergence of a new Turkey from the decay of the old. After an introductory examination of the sources and nature of Turkish civilization, the book falls into two parts. In the first the main events and processes are set forth in chronological sequence, not as a simple narrative history of Turkey, but rather as an attempt to trace and define the principal phases of change. The term of the study has been set in 1950, when the party of Atatürk was ousted from power in a free election which it had itself organized, and the country entered on a new phase in its history. In the second part of the book four aspects of change are examined in greater detail—the transformation of the corporate sense of identity and loyalty among the Turks, the transformation of the theory and practice of government, of religion and the cultural life which it dominated, and of the economic and social order. In a final chapter an attempt is made to draw some general conclusions on the nature of the Turkish Revolution and the measure of its accomplishment.

A separate note contains my thanks and acknowledgements to those who, in one way or another, have helped in the preparation of this book. Here I would like to express my gratitude to two scholars, neither of whom has been directly concerned with this book, yet both of whom have contributed largely to whatever merits it may possess. The first is my friend and colleague, Professor P. Wittek, whose conversation, over a period of many years, has enriched my understanding of Turkish history and civilization more deeply than any formal expression of thanks for help and guidance could indicate. The second is the late and deeply lamented Dr. A. Adnan Adıvar, to whose influence and teaching I owe my first acquaintance with Turkey and the Turks, my first knowledge of their language and literature, and an abiding concern that has shaped my life ever since.

London,   B. L.
January 1960

ACKNOWLEDGEMENTS

My grateful thanks are due to Miss Elizabeth Monroe, Professor Sir Hamilton Gibb, Professor A. T. Hatto, Dr. P. M. Holt, Mr. A. H. Hourani, Professor J. C. Hurewitz, and Professor D. A. Rustow for their careful reading of parts or all of my manuscript and for many helpful suggestions; to Dr. E. Atabay for taking photographs, and for aid and comfort throughout the preparation of this work; to Miss H. Oliver, for her painstaking and invaluable help in preparing the book for the press; to Professor D. A. Rustow for reading and correcting a set of proofs; to Mr. D. E. Pitcher for preparing the maps; to Miss M. Moyle for making the index; to Professor Franz Taeschner (editor of *Alt-Stambuler Hof- und Volksleben*, Hanover 1925), the Director of the Topkapı Sarayı Museum, and the Editor of *Hayat*, for their kind permission to reproduce illustrations. Parts of this book are based on matter previously published in the form of articles; I am greatly obliged to Professor G. E. von Grunebaum and the Chicago University Press (the editor and publishers of *Unity and Variety in Muslim Civilization*, Chicago 1955), and to the editors of the *Journal of World History*, *Middle Eastern Affairs*, *International Affairs*, the *Encyclopaedia of Islam*, and *Studia Islamica*, for their consent to this. Finally I should like to express my thanks to the Royal Institute of International Affairs for grants to cover the cost of my journeys to Turkey between 1954 and 1959, and for help and encouragement in the preparation of this study.

CONTENTS

PLATES

Between pages 272 and 273

ABBREVIATIONS

Ank. Univ. Dil ve Tar.- Cog. Fak. Derg.	Ankara Üniversitesi Dil ve Tarih-Coğrafya Fakültesi Dergisi.
BSOAS . . .	Bulletin of the School of Oriental and African Studies.
C. Or. contemp. . .	Cahiers de l'Orient contemporain.
EI¹, EI² . . .	Encyclopaedia of Islam, 1st and 2nd editions.
IA	Islam Ansiklopedisi.
Int. Aff. . . .	International Affairs.
Ist. Univ. Iktisat Fak. Mec. . . .	Istanbul Üniversitesi Iktisat Fakültesi Mecmuası.
J. As. . . .	Journal Asiatique.
JRAS . . .	Journal of the Royal Asiatic Society.
Jäschke, Kalender .	G. Jäschke and E. Pritsch, 'Die Türkei seit dem Weltkriege; Geschichtskalender 1919-28'. Welt des Islam, x (1927-9), &c. (see Bibliography).
MEA . . .	Middle Eastern Affairs.
MEJ . . .	Middle East Journal.
Mitt. Aus. Hoch. Univ. Berlin	Mitteilungen der Ausland-Hochschule an der Universität Berlin.
MSOS . . .	Mitteilungen des Seminars für orientalische Sprachen
OM . . .	Oriente Moderno.
R.C. As. J. . .	Royal Central Asian Society Journal.
R. Ét. islam. . .	Revue d'Études islamiques.
R. Fac. Sci. Éc. Univ. Ist.	Revue de la Faculté des Sciences Économiques de l'Université d'Istanbul.
RMM . . .	Revue du monde musulman.
R. hist. . . .	Revue historique.
RIIA, Survey . .	Royal Institute of International Affairs, Survey of International Affairs.
Tar. Derg. . .	Tarih Dergisi.
Tar. Ves. . .	Tarih Vesikaları.
TM . . .	Türkiyat Mecmuası.
TOEM . . .	Tarih-i Osmani Encümeni Mecmuası.
Türk Huk. ve Ikt. Tar. Mec. . . .	Türk Hukuk ve Iktisat Tarihi Mecmuası.
Vak. Derg. . .	Vakıflar Dergisi.
WI . . .	Welt des Islam.
ZDMG . . .	Zeitschrift der deutschen morgenländischen Gesellschaft.

NOTES ON TRANSCRIPTION

MANY different systems have been used for the transcription of Turkish in Latin letters. That used in the following pages is based on the official modern Turkish orthography. Some notes on pronunciation may be useful to readers unacquainted with Turkish. The descriptions given below are approximate and non-technical.

c —*j* as in *John*

ç —*ch* as in *church*

b, d —as in English, except that at the end of a syllable they are usually pronounced and sometimes written *p, t* (e.g. Recep, Rağıp, Ahmet, Mehmet for Receb, Rağıb, Ahmed, Mehmed). In transcribing Ottoman texts, I have retained the *b* and *d* as being nearer to the original.

ğ —after e, i—roughly as *y* in *saying*; after o, ö, u, ü—roughly as *w* in *sowing*; after a, ı—hardly sounded, but has the effect of lengthening the preceding vowel

ı —something between *i* as in *will* and *u* as in *radium*

ö —French *eu* as in *seul*, or German *ö* as in *öffnen*

ş —*sh* as in *shut*

ü —French *u* as in *lumière*, or German *ü* as in *schützen*

CHAPTER I

Introduction: The Sources of Turkish Civilization

Quis unquam tam sapiens aut doctus audebit describere prudenciam, miliciam et fortitudinem Turcorum? Qui putabant terrere gentem Francorum minis suarum sagittarum, sicut terruerunt Arabes, Saracenos et Hermenios, Suranos et Grecos.

GESTA FRANCORUM, *c.* 1100.

It is one of the strange things of Constantinople that for one copper coin one can be rowed from Rumelia to Frangistan or from Frangistan to Rumelia.

TURSUN BEG, *'Tarih-i Ebu'l-Fetih', c.* 1500.

'The Turks are a people who speak Turkish and live in Turkey.' At first glance, this does not seem to be a proposition of any striking originality, nor of any very revolutionary content. Yet the introduction and propagation of this idea in Turkey, and its eventual acceptance by the Turkish people as expressing the nature of their corporate identity and statehood, has been one of the major revolutions of modern times, involving a radical and violent break with the social, cultural, and political traditions of the past.

The name Turkey has been given to Turkish-speaking Anatolia almost since its first conquest by the Turks in the eleventh century—given, that is, by Europeans.[1] But the Turks themselves did not adopt it as the official name of their country until 1923. When they did so, they used a form—*Türkiye*—that clearly revealed its European origin. The people had once called themselves Turks, and the language they spoke was still called Turkish, but in the Imperial society of the Ottomans the ethnic term Turk was little used, and then chiefly in a rather derogatory sense, to designate the Turcoman nomads or, later, the ignorant and uncouth Turkish-speaking peasants of the Anatolian villages. To

---

[1] The first occurrence of the name Turkey for the Anatolian lands conquered by the Turks is in a chronicle of the Crusade of Barbarossa, of 1190. By the thirteenth century the term is already in common use among western authors. See Claude Cahen, 'Le Problème ethnique en Anatolie', *J. Wld. Hist..* ii (1954), 360.

apply it to an Ottoman gentleman of Constantinople would have been an insult.[2]

Even the term Ottoman was understood not in a national but in a dynastic sense, like Umayyad, Abbasid, and Seljuk, and the Ottoman state was felt to be the heir and successor, in the direct line, of the great Islamic Empires of the past. The concepts of an Ottoman nation and an Ottoman fatherland, as foci of national and patriotic loyalty, were nineteenth-century innovations under European influence. They were of brief duration.

Until the nineteenth century the Turks thought of themselves primarily as Muslims; their loyalty belonged, on different levels, to Islam and to the Ottoman house and state. The language a man spoke, the territory he inhabited, the race from which he claimed descent, might be of personal, sentimental, or social significance. They had no political relevance. So completely had the Turks identified themselves with Islam that the very concept of a Turkish nationality was submerged—and this despite the survival of the Turkish language and the existence of what was in fact though not in theory a Turkish state. They had not even retained to the same degree as the Arabs and Persians an awareness of their identity as a separate ethnic and cultural group within Islam.

The Turkish national idea, in the modern sense, first appears in the mid-nineteenth century. Many factors contributed to its development—European exiles in Turkey, and Turkish exiles in Europe; European Turcological research, and the new knowledge which it brought of the ancient history and civilization of the Turkish peoples; the Russian Turks and Tatars, who encountered Russian pan-Slavism and reacted against it with a growing national consciousness of their own, nourished—by an odd paradox—by Russian Turcological discoveries; the influence of the subject peoples of the Ottoman Empire, who as Christians were more open to national ideas coming from the West, and who in time helped to transmit the infection to their Imperial masters.

At first these ideas were limited to a small circle of intellectuals, but gradually they spread far and wide, and their victory was

---

[2] A text studied by Cahen shows that already in the thirteenth century a bourgeois of Konya 'uses the designation "Turk" exclusively for the "barbarous" and "unbearable" Turkoman frontier population' (Cahen, in G. E. von Grunebaum, *Unity and Variety in Muslim Civilization* (1955), p. 330).

finally symbolized by the official adoption, for the first time, of the names of Turkey and Turk for the country and people of the Republic. The growth of the sentiment of Turkish identity was connected with the movement away from Islamic practice and tradition, and towards Europe. This began with purely practical short-term measures of reform, intended to accomplish a limited purpose; it developed into a large-scale, deliberate attempt to take a whole nation across the frontier from one civilization to another.

After the nationalist and modernist movements had established themselves, an interesting new development appeared—the assertion of identity with earlier, pre-existing local civilizations. This movement has its parallels in some other Islamic countries, and is of course a consequence of the importation of the European idea of the secular and territorial fatherland and of a mystical and permanent relationship between the land and the people who inhabit it. In Turkey it gave rise to the so-called Anatolianist movement and to the theories, fathered by Atatürk, of the Turkish origin of such ancient peoples as the Sumerians, the Trojans, and, above all, the Hittites.[3]

This movement was partly political, with the purpose of encouraging the Turks to identify themselves with the country they inhabit—and thus at the same time of discouraging dangerous pan-Turanian adventures. But despite its politically inspired excesses and absurdities, Atatürk's Anatolian theory contained, or rather brought to light, important elements of truth.

We may then distinguish three main streams of influence that have gone to make modern Turkey: the Islamic, the Turkish, and a third, composite one that for want of a better name we may call local.

1. Local

The Muslim Turks who came to Turkey were marked by a complex and diverse pattern of tradition and culture. One strain is the Anatolian, the importance of which was stressed in the Turkish official thesis. The Hittites have left the most striking remains and have been the subject of the most publicized theorizing,

---

[3] It is interesting that while the Turks claimed to be kinsmen and descendants of the ancient Anatolians, they made no such claim concerning the Byzantines, who had the threefold disadvantage, for this purpose, of being Greek, Christian, and above all, extant.

and the other ancient peoples of Anatolia have no doubt also left their mark. The Anatolian is, however, not the only strain. The Ottoman Empire from its first century was a Balkan as well as an Anatolian power, and Rumelia was for long the main centre. Only in our own day has it lost its central position, together with that of Constantinople-Istanbul, the Imperial city with its millennial traditions of state and civilization, the ancient link between the European and Asian territories of the Empire.

Any visitor to Turkey, especially one entering from the south or the east, must at once be struck by the vigorous survival of these local traditions within Turkish Islam. Many things will bring them to his attention—the Anatolian village house and mosque, so different in style and structure from those of Syria and Iraq; the Balkan, almost European tonalities of Turkish music of the kind called popular, as against the 'classical' music in the Perso-Arabic manner; the Byzantine-looking cupolas on the mosques and the Greek and south-east European decorative motives in both formal design and peasant handicrafts.

The survival of Anatolian elements in modern Turkey is now beyond dispute. There is no need to assert that the Turks are Hittites or that the Hittites were Turks—but it is clear that there was a large measure of continuity. This becomes clearer with the parallel progress of archaeological and anthropological work in Anatolia today. It is true that there was large-scale Turkish colonization in Antolia, but the indigenous population was neither exterminated nor entirely expelled. The Greek upper class and the Greek cultural layer were replaced—and in time the inhabitants were reassimilated, this time to Islamic and Turkish patterns. They carried over much of their own culture, especially in what pertains to agriculture and village life—the alternation of the seasons, sowing and reaping, birth, marriage, and death. With these things the newly imported Islamic culture, here as elsewhere essentially urban, had less concern.

The Rumelian influence, after the conquest, came from the top rather than from the bottom. Unlike Anatolia, most of Rumelia was never assimilated either to Islam or to the Turkish language. The peasant masses remained Christian, alien in language and culture as well as religion, outside the cultural horizon of the Turks. But the Balkan peoples had an enormous influence on the Ottoman ruling class. One of the most important channels was the *devşirme*,[4] the levy of boys, by means of which countless Balkan Christians entered the political and military *élites* of the Empire. Nor was that all. Even the local Christian landed ruling class was not wholly destroyed, as was once thought, but survived to some extent on its lands, and was incorporated in the Ottoman system. In the fifteenth century there were still Christian Timariots— military fief-holders—in Albania.[5] Then and later, Rumelian Christian troops served with the Ottoman forces, both as feudal cavalry and as common soldiers, while converted Rumelians were to be found holding fiefs and commands all over the Asiatic provinces of the Empire. The great role of the Albanians and Bosniaks in the Ottoman Empire is well known. Together with other Rumelians, they continued to play an important part in the reforms and revolutions of the nineteenth and twentieth centuries.

The Byzantine heritage of Turkey was at one time much exaggerated. Some historians attributed almost everything in Ottoman state and society to one or other source in Byzantium, and spoke of massive borrowings of Byzantine institutions and practices after the capture of Constantinople in 1453. It is now generally agreed that much of this is erroneous, and that in fact the Byzantine elements in Ottoman civilization are very much smaller than had previously been supposed. Moreover, these elements date from before the conquest of Constantinople, in most cases indeed from before the establishment of the Ottoman state. Some borrowings can be traced back to the time of the Anatolian Seljuks—others even to the Abbasid Caliphate, from which they came to Turkey as part of classical Islamic civilization itself. It was natural for the Seljuks to borrow during their long cohabitation with Byzantium, at a time when that state had not yet dwindled into the pale shadow that the Ottomans encountered.[6]

Yet, if the Byzantine elements have been exaggerated and

---

[4] On this term, and the practice that it denotes, reference may be made to the article 'Dews̲h̲irme' in *EI*. The compulsory levy of boys, originating in early Ottoman times, died out in the seventeenth century.

[5] See Halil Inalcık, 'Timariotes chrétiens en Albanie, au XV siècle, d'après un registre de timars ottoman', *Mitt. des Österreichischen Staatsarchivs*, iv (1952), 118–38.

[6] Köprülüzade Mehmet Fuat (=M. F. Köprülü), 'Bizans Müesseselerinin Osmanlı Müesseselerine Te'siri hakkında bazı Mülâhazalar', *Türk Huk. ve İkt. Tar. Mec.*, i (1931), 165–313.

misdated, they are nevertheless there. Though perhaps fewer, they are at the same time older and more deeply rooted—older perhaps than the Byzantine Empire. The survival of Byzantine motives in architecture has already been mentioned. But something as central and as typical in a society as its religious architecture cannot be an isolated phenomenon. The Byzantine elements in the Turkish mosque—so universal and so persistent—must express some deeper social and cultural affinity, all the more so in a society like Islam, where all is under the sign of religion. To suggest but one possible line of thought: perhaps we may associate the domed basilica type of mosque with the appearance—for the first time in Islam, and under Turkish rule—of an ecclesiastical hierarchy, with muftis presiding over territorial jurisdictions, under the supreme authority of the *Şeyh-ül-Islâm*, the Chief Mufti of the capital, whom we may describe, perhaps a little fancifully, as the Archbishop-primate of the Ottoman Empire. And here we may recall that hierarch and cupola are both oriental invaders even in Byzantium.

One other aspect of local influence may perhaps be considered here. Rumelia and Constantinople are part of Europe, and the Ottomans have from an early stage in their history been in contact with Europe—longer and more closely than any other Islamic state, not excluding North Africa. The Empire included important European territories, in which it absorbed European peoples and institutions. It also maintained contact with the West through trade, diplomacy, war, and—not least—immigration.

Mehmed the Conqueror had a knowledge of Greek and a library of Greek books. His entourage included the Italian humanist Ciriaco Pizzocolli of Ancona; his biographer was the Greek Critoboulos, his portraitist the Venetian Bellini.[7] Though unusual, this was not an isolated phenomenon. Not a little knowledge of the West was brought by the many renegades and refugees who sought a career in the Ottoman service, as well as by European diplomats and merchants. In the fifteenth century the Ottoman Sultans were quick to adopt the European device of artillery—often with European gunners and gun-founders. By the sixteenth and seventeenth centuries Ottoman soldiers and sailors were trying, with varying success, to adopt European techniques of warfare, while Ottoman scholars were making their first tentative

---

[7] E. Jacobs, 'Mehemmed II, der Eroberer, seine Beziehungen zur Renaissance, und seine Büchersammlung', *Oriens*, ii (1949), 6–30.

inquiries into European geography, history, and medical science.[8] Before the nineteenth century Ottoman borrowings from Europe were mainly of a material order, and were restricted in both scope and effect. But today it is almost a truism that there can be no limited and insulated borrowing by one civilization of the practices of another, but that each element introduced from outside brings a train of consequences. We should perhaps reconsider the significance and effects of such early Ottoman importations from Europe as cartography, navigation, shipbuilding, and artillery, followed in the eighteenth century by printing, military engineering, and an Italianate style in Turkish architecture, exemplified in the Nuruosmaniye mosque in Istanbul.[9]

2. *Turkish*

A visitor to Turkey will encounter at once the first and unmistakable sign of Turkishness—the Turkish language, which, despite long subjection to alien influences, survives triumphantly. Scholars have noted the remarkable capacity of Turkish to resist, displace, and even supplant other languages with which it has come in contact. With the Turkish language, as a sign of Turkish tradition, the visitor may perhaps associate the habit of authority and decision, and therefore of self-reliance, which the Turks have retained from their historic role in the Islamic world. And perhaps, with a little effort of imagination, he may sense a feeling of purpose and direction in the air, that sometimes jars, but more often stimulates.

Language was indeed the main—or at any rate the most readily identifiable—contribution of the Turks to the diversified culture of the Ottoman Empire. As once the Arabic language and the Islamic faith, so now the Turkish language and the Sunni Islamic faith were necessary qualifications of membership of the dominant social class. In Ottoman Turkish was created a rich and subtle means of expression, a worthy instrument of an Imperial civilization. The Ottomans had no racial arrogance or exclusiveness, no insistence on 'pure' Turkish descent—nothing equivalent to the segregation on a lower level of the *Mawālī*—the non-Arab

---

[8] A. Adnan, *La Science chez les Turcs ottomans* (1939). A more extensive treatment of the subject by the same author in Turkish will be found in A. Adnan-Adıvar, *Osmanlı Türklerinde İlim* (1943). See further below, ch. iii.

[9] See below, p. 434.

converts to Islam—by the Arab masters of the early Caliphate.[10] Islam and the Turkish language were the entry requirements which opened the door both to real power and to social status, to Albanian, Greek, and Slav as well as to Kurd and Arab.

For a time the Turks showed little national consciousness—far less, for example, than the Arabs or Persians. The pre-Islamic Turks were after all no savages, but peoples of a certain level of civilization, with their own states, religions, and literatures. Yet, save for a few fragments, all was forgotten and obliterated in Islam, until its partial recovery by European scholarship in the eighteenth and nineteenth centuries. There is no Turkish equivalent to Arab memories of the heathen heroes of old Arabia, to Persian pride in the bygone glories of the ancient Emperors of Iran, even to the vague Egyptian legends woven around the broken but massive monuments of the Pharaohs. Save for a few fragments of folk poetry and of genealogical legend, all the pre-Islamic Turkish past was forgotten, and even a newly Islamized Turkish dynasty like the Karahanids in the tenth century forgot their Turkish antecedents and called themselves by a name from Persian legend—the House of Afrāsiyāb.[11] Even the very name Turk, and the entity it connotes, are in a sense Islamic. Though the word Turk occurs in pre-Islamic inscriptions, it refers only to one among the related steppe peoples. Its generalized use to cover the whole group, and perhaps even the very notion of such a group, dates from Islam and became identified with Islam; and the historic Turkish nation and culture, even in a certain sense the language, in the forms in which they have existed in the last millennium, were all born in Islam. To this day the term Turk is never applied to non-Muslims, though they be of Turkic origin and language like the heathen Chuvash and Christian Gagauz, or citizens of a Turkish state, like the Christians and Jews of Istanbul.[12]

But the real Turkish element in Ottoman society and culture, if unselfconscious and unarticulated, is nevertheless profoundly important. It was revived in the late fourteenth century, when the

[10] cf. B. Lewis, *The Arabs in History* (1958), pp. 70 ff.

[11] In Iranian legend, re-echoed in Persian heroic poetry, Afrāsiyāb was king of Turan, a term which was later arbitrarily applied to the Turks.

[12] cf. P. Wittek, 'Türkentum und Islam. I', *Archiv für Sozialwissenschaft und Sozialpolitik*, lix (1928), 489–525; Osman Turan, 'Türkler ve Islâmiyet', *Ank. Univ. Dil ve Tar.-Coğ. Fak. Derg.*, v (1945–6), 457–85.

Ottomans, expanding from western into eastern Anatolia, encountered large groups of Turkish nomads, with their tribal organization and traditions intact—not yet scattered, disintegrated, and affected by local influences as in the western part of the peninsula.

During the first half of the fifteenth century there are a number of signs of the rise of a kind of Turkish national consciousness. It was at this time that the Ottoman Sultan assumed the old Turkish title of Khan; the cattle-brand of the Oğuz Turkish tribe of Kayı, from whom the Ottomans claimed descent, appeared as an emblem on Ottoman coins, and Ottoman historians and poets elaborated the Oğuz legend, which linked the Ottoman ruling house with a quasi-mythical Turkish antiquity and became the official account of the origins of the dynasty.[13] At the court of Murad II (1421–51) and his successors, Turkish poetry flourished and the study of Turkish antiquities was greatly in vogue. Even the Central Asian Turkish language and literature were for a while cultivated, and towards the end of the fifteenth century a literary school tried to write in pure and simple Turkish, without excessive use of the Persian and Arabic words and expressions that were already a part of the Turkish literary language.[14] This movement was limited and in many respects transitory, but it had an important effect in reaffirming the position of the Turkish language and thus of all that accompanies and is contained in language in the life of a people. It is significant too as the first major appearance, in the Ottoman state, of the nomadic Turkish element, which was now an important part of the Turkish population.

It is primarily as an ethnic reservoir that the Turkish nomadic tribes are important in the Ottoman Empire.[15] They were not a ruling element as such, but were rather treated with alternating mistrust and contempt by the state and the ruling groups. They were, however, the reserve on which the ruling class drew. The movement of the tribesmen into Ottoman society took place in several ways. One was the process of sedentarization, by which the nomads were settled on an increasing scale in different parts of

[13] P. Wittek, 'Le Rôle des tribus turques dans l'empire ottoman', *Mélanges Georges Smets* (1952), 665–76.
[14] Köprülüzade Mehmed Fuad (=M. F. Köprülü), *Milli Edebîyatın ilk Mübeşşirleri* (Ist., 1928).
[15] Wittek, in *Mél. G. Smets.*

Anatolia, and became peasant cultivators. This was partly due to the operation of normal economic processes, partly to deliberate government policy. The Ottoman Sultans from early times made extensive use of the method known as *sürgün*—the transfer of populations from one place to another for settlement and colonization.[16] Sometimes these deportations were penal, sometimes they were intended to serve political, economic, and military ends, as, for example, transfers of populations to newly conquered provinces or to disaffected areas. In all these movements the nomadic element played an important part. Nomadic settlement was not limited to the countryside. Evidence in both documentary and literary sources shows that there were tribal quarters in many towns. Such a process was inevitable in view of the close economic connexion between the town on the one hand and the peasants and tribes on the other—the two latter increasingly Turkish.

This seepage, so to speak, of Turks into the town and country population, and thus eventually into the governing *élite*, preserved and reinforced the Turkish character of Ottoman society, so that even the revolution of our time has been described with some justice as the emergence of a by now Turkish Anatolia, asserting itself against the cosmopolitan civilization of Constantinople and Rumelia—in other words, as a victory of Turks over Ottomans, typified by the transfer of the capital and the change of name of the country.

The conscious effort in modern Turkey to return to Turkism is important politically, as it affects the basis of polity and direction of policy of the state, but it is limited in its effects in other fields. The old Turkish civilizations were too thoroughly obliterated by Islam for any real revival of ancient Turkish culture to be possible. There have of course been attempts to revive it, the most noteworthy and most discussed being the language reform, the aim of which was to rid the language of the Persian and Arabic borrowings acquired during a thousand years of Islamic influence, and to return to a pure and unadulterated Turkish. There have also been some rather self-conscious but sometimes quite effective

---

[16] These transfers have been studied in a series of important articles by Ömer Lûtfi Barkan. See for example his 'Les Déportations comme méthode de peuplement et de colonisation dans l'Empire ottoman', *R. Fac. Sci. Éc. Univ. Ist.*, xi (1949–50), 67–131; Turkish section, 524–69.

adaptations of folk material—as for example the use of stressed verse in place of the quantitative Perso-Arabic prosody, and the employment of Turkish melodies in modern orchestral and operatic compositions.[17] But modern Turkish literature and art owe far more to Europe than to any such deliberate experiments with old or popular material. The real importance of the Turkish strain in Turkey must be sought in uninterrupted survivals in the deeper layers of society—and these layers are now coming to the surface, with results yet to be seen.

3. *Islam*

We come now to the third factor—to Islam, which despite a period of eclipse has recently shown renewed vigour in Turkey, and is still clearly a major, if not the major element in the collective consciousness of a large proportion of the Turkish nation.

The Turks first encountered Islam on the frontiers—and their faith has from then till now retained some of the peculiar quality of frontier Islam, of the militant and uncomplicated religion of the frontiersmen.[18] The Turks were not forced into Islam, as were so many other peoples, and their Islam bears no marks of constraint or subjection. On the frontiers of the Caliphate, in East and West, the march-warriors had still maintained the simplicity, militancy, and freedom of early Islam, which elsewhere had been lost in the transformation of the old Islamic theocracy into an Oriental Empire. From all over that Empire, those who could not adapt themselves to the new order, those who for spiritual or material reasons felt the call of the frontier, joined the bands of the borderers and waged war for God, glory, and booty against the infidel and the heathen. In Central Asia, one of the two most important frontiers, the Turks, converted for the most part by wandering missionaries and mystics, joined in the struggle against their cousins who were still heathen, and, as the military classes of the Caliphate came to be more and more exclusively Turkish, began to play a predominant part in it. In the early eleventh century the first great independent Turkish sovereign in Islam, Mahmud of Ghazna, used his power to lead an army of Turks

[17] See below, p. 435.

[18] The significance of the frontier and of the frontier warrior (*gazi*) in the evolution of Turkish Islam has been studied by Professor Wittek in a series of notes, articles, and monographs beginning in 1925 (*ZDMG*, lxxix, 288 ff.). For a general survey see his *The Rise of the Ottoman Empire* (1938), where references to earlier studies are given.

to a frontier war on the grand scale, for the conquest of Hindu India. Later in the same century the Seljuks released a new wave of Turkish invaders across South West Asia, who wrested new territories for Islam from the Byzantine Empire, and infused into the Islamic Orient the martial and religious vigour which enabled it to withstand and eventually throw back the great European offensive of the Crusades.

The Islam of the Turkish frontiersmen was thus of a different temper from that of the heartlands of Islam. Unlike their brothers who had gone to Iraq or Egypt as Mamluks, and been brought up in the cosmopolitan atmosphere of the old Islamic capitals, the free Turks were Islamized and educated in the borderlands, and their Islam was from the first impregnated with the special characteristics of the frontier. Their teachers were dervishes, wandering ascetics and mystics, usually Turkish, preaching a very different faith from that of the theologians and the seminaries of the cities. Not for them was the subtlety—or the laxness—of Abbasid Baghdad, the easy-going tolerance and diversity of a mixed urban civilization—or the meticulous and exclusive orthodoxy of the schools. Theirs was a militant faith, still full of the pristine fire and directness of the first Muslims; a religion of warriors, whose creed was a battle-cry, whose dogma was a call to arms.

This was the faith—and the preaching—which the first Turks brought to Anatolia. And then, as the gazi, the dervish, and the nomad conquered, converted, and colonized the peninsula, the old Islamic traditions of government and civilization established themselves in what became the cities of a new sultanate, and the frontiersmen and dervishes moved on to seek new adventures on western fringes, by the Aegean, and in Europe. Anatolia became a province of the Middle Eastern Empire of the Seljuks, and the traditional pattern of Islamic life was gradually impressed on the country. Muslim bureaucrats and literati, jurists and theologians, merchants and artisans moved into the newly acquired territory, bringing with them the old, high, urban civilizations of classical Islam. The border moved farther westwards, and in time the new territories won by the Ottoman borderers in western Anatolia and in the Balkans were also transformed into a new Muslim Empire. Like Sivas and Konya under the Seljuks, so now under the Ottomans, first Brusa, then Adrianople, finally Constantinople

became Muslim cities, centres of Muslim life and culture, decked
with all the panoply of orthodox Islam.

From its foundation until its fall the Ottoman Empire was a
state dedicated to the advancement or defence of the power and
faith of Islam. For six centuries the Ottomans were almost
constantly at war with the Christian West, first in the attempt—
mainly successful—to impose Islamic rule on a large part of
Europe, then in the long-drawn-out rearguard action to halt or
delay the relentless counter-attack of the West. This centuries-long
struggle, with its origins in the very roots of Turkish Islam, could
not fail to affect the whole structure of Turkish society and
institutions. For the Ottoman Turk, his Empire, containing all the
heartlands of early Islam, was Islam itself. In the Ottoman
chronicles the territories of the Empire are referred to as 'the lands
of Islam', its sovereign as 'the Padishah of Islam', its armies as
'the soldiers of Islam', its religious head as 'the *şeyh* of Islam'; its
people thought of themselves first and foremost as Muslims. Both
Ottoman and Turk are, as we have seen, terms of comparatively
recent usage, and the Ottoman Turks had identified themselves
with Islam—submerged their identity in Islam—to a greater
extent than perhaps any other Islamic people. It is curious that
while in Turkey the word Turk almost went out of use, in the
West it came to be a synonym for Muslim, and a Western convert
to Islam was said to have 'turned Turk', even when the conversion
took place in Fez or Isfahan.

A counterpart of this identification may be seen in the high
seriousness of Turkish Islam, the sense of devotion to duty and of
mission, in the best days of the Empire, that is unparalleled in
Islamic history, not excluding that of the Caliphate. Which of the
Abbasid Caliphs, for example, can show anything to compare with
the loyalty, the intensity of moral and religious purpose, that
clearly impelled the early Ottoman Sultans—the inexorable
devotion to duty that made the ageing and dying Sultan Süleyman
the Magnificent face the hardships of yet another Hungarian
campaign, and go from the comforts of his capital to the rigours
of the camp and a certain death?

It is perhaps in the realm of law that one can see most clearly
the seriousness of the Ottoman endeavour to make Islam the true
basis of private and public life. The Ottoman Sultans gave to the
Şeriat, the holy law of Islam, a greater degree of real efficacy than

it had had in any Muslim state of high material civilization since early times.[19]. In a sense it may even be said that the Ottomans were the first who really tried to make the *Şeriat* the effective law of the state, to apply it throughout the land, and to give full recognition and authority to the courts and judiciary that administered it. The medieval Muslim Kadi cuts a miserable figure beside his Ottoman colleague. Appointed by and answerable to the central authorities, he was compelled to abandon to them important fields of jurisdiction, and was wholly dependent on their rather dubious co-operation for the execution and enforcement of his judgments. The Ottoman Kadi on the other hand *was* the central authority in the area of his jurisdiction, which in the Ottoman system of provincial administration was known, significantly, as a kaza—the area governed by a Kadi, as a vilayet was governed by a Vali. Moreover, he was one of a proud and powerful hierarchy of juridical and theological authorities, ready to support him in any clash with the military and political institutions, and presided over by the *Şeyh-ül-Islâm* (or Chief Mufti) and the two Kazıaskers in the capital, so great and revered, that the Sultan himself rose to his feet to receive them when they came to offer him their greetings at the Bayram festival.[20] The old Caliphs were theoretically subject to the Holy Law, and could be deposed for violating it—but this rule was a dead letter in the absence of any authority or machinery for enforcing it. The Ottomans, however recognized a supreme religious authority—the highest instance of the *Şeriat*—with power to authorize the deposition of the sultan. The actual role of this authority, the *Şeyh-ül-Islâm*, was of course determined in the main by the play of politics and personalities. The significant thing from our point of view is that such an authority, with such a jurisdiction, should have existed at all and have been recognized.

Another characteristic of Turkish Islam, of a rather different kind but of similar significance, is the social segregation of the non-Muslim communities. The Ottoman Empire was tolerant of other religions, in accordance with Islamic law and tradition, and its Christian and Jewish subjects lived, on the whole, in peace and security. But they were strictly segregated from the Muslims, in their own separate communities. Never were they able to mix

[19] J. Schacht, *Esquisse d'une histoire du droit musulman* (1952), p. 79.
[20] *Kanunname*, quoted in Köprülü, in *Türk Huk. ve İkt. Tar. Mec.*, i, 196.

freely in Muslim society, as they had once done in Baghdad and Cairo—nor to make any contribution worth the mention to the intellectual life of the Ottomans. There are no Ottoman equivalents to the Christian poets and Jewish scientists of the Arabic Golden Age. If the convert was readily accepted and assimilated, the unconverted were extruded so thoroughly that even today, 500 years after the conquest of Constantinople, neither the Greeks nor the Jews in the city have yet mastered the Turkish language—though neither people is lacking in linguistic versatility. One may speak of Christian Arabs—but a Christian Turk is an absurdity and a contradiction in terms.[21] Even today, after thirty-five years of the secular Republic, a non-Muslim in Turkey may be called a Turkish citizen, but never a Turk.

The first characteristic of Turkish Islam that we have noted is then—paradoxically—the extent to which the Turks have effaced themselves in Islam. We may find others. It is natural to look first to the popular, mystical, and more or less heterodox forms of religion which in Turkey, as in most other Muslim countries, flourish at the side of the formal, dogmatic religion of the theologians, and correspond to a far greater degree to the real religious beliefs and practices of the people. The different orders—*tarikats*[22]—that between them have commanded and perhaps still command the allegiance of the great majority of Turkish Muslims, certainly preserved much that is pre-Islamic in their beliefs, and still more in their traditions and observances. Turkish scholars have drawn attention to the Central Asian survivals—the elements of Shamanism, even of Buddhism and Manichaeism retained by the Central Asian Turks after their conversion to Islam and brought by them in various disguises to the West.[23] No less important are the many examples of Muslim-Christian (or Turco-Greek) syncretism in popular religious life.[24]

This kind of survival on the popular level is almost universal in Islam, and has its parallels in the persistence of old Celtic, Germanic, and Slavonic customs in a Christianized form in

[21] The use of the expression 'Christian Turk' to describe Christian populations of Turkish speech such as the Gagauz of the Dobrudja is of course restricted to the professional jargon of scholarship, and to very recent Turkish adaptations of it.

[22] See below, p. 398.

[23] See for example Köprülüzade Mehmed Fuad, *Influence du Chamanisme Turco-Mongol sur les ordres mystiques musulmans* (Ist., 1929).

[24] cf. F. W. Hasluck, *Christianity and Islam under the Sultans* (1928).

Europe. Popular Islam has always been looked upon with suspicion by the theologians and the state, perhaps more so in Turkey than elsewhere, and it is significant that even today the government of the Turkish Republic, though according tolerance and even encouragement to a limited revival of orthodoxy, has so far severely repressed all manifestation of activity by the *tarikats*.

It is, however, not on the popular, but on the formal level that we encounter one of the most characteristic qualities of Islam in the Ottoman Empire—that almost architectonic quality to which allusion has already been made. Here for the first time in Islamic history is created an institutional structure—a graded hierarchy of professional men of religion, with recognized functions and powers, worthy of comparison with the Christian priesthoods or those of the ancient Empires. The dictum that there is no priesthood in Islam remains true in the theological sense, in that there is no ordination, no sacrament, no priestly mediation between the believer and God—but it ceases to be true in the sociological and political sense. The origins of the great Ottoman religious institution can no doubt be traced back to the Sultanate of the Great Seljuks, when schools and schoolmen were organized to counter the threat of revolutionary heresy. But only in the Ottoman state did the religious institution reach maturity and fulfil its function as the guardian of the faith and the law.

We have now passed in review the three main trends in Turkish life and culture. In modern times there has been a fourth—Western civilization, which in Turkey as everywhere else in the world has struck with devastating impact against the existing order.

There are two concepts in relation to which we may consider those features and characteristics which set modern Turkey apart from her Muslim neighbours, and bring her nearer to both the merits and the faults of the Western world. One is the notion of process—the tendency to view a sequence of events not as a simple series but as a process in time, or, in organic terms, as a development; the second, related to it, is the notion of organism, of organic structure—the ability to conceive a whole made up of interrelated and interacting parts, rather than a mere congeries of separate, disjunct entities. These qualities are central to the modern Western form of civilization. They are the prerequisites of our physical and natural sciences; they determine our vision of the individual and the group, of man and the universe, and thus shape our institutions and our thought, our government and our arts, our industry, our science, and—save the mark—our religion. They make, to name but a few examples, the difference between the Western novel and the Oriental tale, Western portraiture and Oriental miniature, Western history and Oriental annals, Western government and Oriental rule—and perhaps between Western restlessness and Oriental repose.

For better or worse, these qualities have, in the course of the last century and a half, become more and more effective in Turkish public life—in the structure of state and law, in the formulation and direction of aspiration and policy, in the re-organization of social and even private life. They are already discernible in certain manifestations of the arts and sciences, where these go beyond the purely imitative. In the present forms in which these qualities appear in Turkey, they are certainly of Western and indeed recent provenance, and seem at times to be of but precarious tenure. But we may try, however tentatively, to see if they can be brought into relation with qualities in Ottoman or Turkish civilization which created, shall we say, a predisposition to accept them. The capacity for analysis and synthesis of the modern historian and the feeling for the development of character and plot of the modern novelist may have their precedents in the Ottoman chroniclers and memoranda writers, with their discussion of causes and analysis of effects. Even the modern constitutional republic is not entirely an importation. The Ottoman state, based on law and hierarchy, is in some ways nearer to it than to the amorphous and shifting society of classical Islam. The problem of the possible deeper affinities between Turkey and the West is of more than passing interest. In recent years the achievements and hopes of the whole reform movement have once again been brought into dispute and even, so it seemed for a while, into jeopardy. In the long run it will be the deeper rhythm of Turkish life, rather than the rapid surface movement of our time, which will determine the future relationship of Turkey with Islam, with the West, and with herself.

PART I

The Stages of Emergence

CHAPTER II

The Decline of the Ottoman Empire

For it has been well observed, that the arts which flourish in times while virtue is in growth, are military; and while virtue is in state, are liberal; and while virtue is in declination, are voluptuary: so I doubt that this age of the World is somewhat upon the descent of the wheel.

FRANCIS BACON, 'The Advancement of Learning', 1605.

The social condition of man corresponds to his individual condition, and in most matters the one is parallel to the other. . . . First of all, the natural life of man is reckoned in three stages, the years of growth, the years of stasis, and the years of decline. Though the times of these three stages are ordained in individuals, nevertheless these times vary according to the strength or weakness of individual constitutions . . . and these stages also vary in different societies . . . when the reckoning from the migration of the Prophet (upon him the best of greetings) had reached the year 1063, and the lofty Empire of Osman had attained its 364th year, in accordance with God's custom and the natural laws of civilization and human societies, signs of indisposition appeared in the complexion of this lofty Empire, and traces of discord in its nature and its powers. . . .

HACI HALIFA, 'Düstur ül-Amel', 1653.

THE decline of great empires has always been a subject of fascinated interest, and in our own day has a new poignancy, both for those who rejoice and for those who weep at the passing of Imperial greatness. The decline of the Ottoman Empire has also received its share of attention. though not of serious study.[1] The half-millennium of Ottoman history is still one of the most neglected of fields of study. Whereas recent research, both in Turkey and in the West, has increased our knowledge of the beginnings and of the end of the Empire, it has shed but little light on the processes of its decline. The modern Turkish historians, naturally enough, have devoted most of their attention to the early greatness and recent revival of their people, while such Western scholars as have discussed the subject have been content, in the main, to

---

[1] An exception is the essay on the decay of the Ottoman 'Ruling Institution', incorporated in H. A. R. Gibb and Harold Bowen, *Islamic Society and the West*, I/i (1950), 173 ff.

follow the analysis of the Ottoman historians themselves. Often, too, they have been influenced by the national historiographical legends of the liberated former subject peoples of the Empire in Europe and Asia. These have tended to blame all the defects and shortcomings of their societies on the misrule of their fallen Imperial masters, and have generalized the admitted failings of Ottoman government in its last phases into an indictment of Ottoman civilization as a whole.

'The decline and fall of the Roman Empire', Professor Jones has recently remarked, 'was the result of a complex of interacting causes which the historian disentangles at his peril.'[2] The peril is all the greater when, as with the Ottoman Empire, the essential preliminary work of detailed historical research is so little advanced. The great mass of Ottoman records for the seventeenth and eighteenth centuries are unpublished, almost untouched; even the chronicles have received only slight attention. The internal economic and social history in that period has hardly been studied at all, while the study of political history has progressed very little beyond the point to which it was brought by Hammer and Zinkeisen in the nineteenth century.

In what follows no attempt is made to cut through the complex web of cause, symptom, and effect. What is offered is a broad classification and enumeration of some of the principal factors and processes which led to, or were part of, or were expressions of the decline of Ottoman government, society, and civilization. They will be considered in three main groups—those relating to government, to economic and social life, and to moral, cultural, and intellectual change.

In the first group we may include the familiar changes in the apparatus of government—the court, the bureaucracy, the judiciary, the armed forces, which form the main burden of the famous memorandum of Koçu Bey, presented to Murad IV in 1630.[3] If the first ten Sultans of the house of Osman astonish us

[2] A. H. M. Jones, 'The Decline and Fall of the Roman Empire', *History*, xl (1955), 226.

[3] Koçu Bey, an Ottoman official of Macedonian or Albanian birth, was recruited by the *devşirme* and joined the palace staff, where he became the intimate adviser of Sultan Murad IV (1623–40). The memorandum which he composed for the Sultan in 1630 on the state and prospects of the Ottoman Empire has been greatly admired both in Turkey and among Western scholars, and led Hammer to call Koçu Bey 'the Turkish Montesquieu'. On the editions and translations of his treatise see F. Babinger,

with the spectacle of a series of able and intelligent men rare if not unique in the annals of dynastic succession, the remainder of the rulers of that line provides an even more astonishing series of incompetents, degenerates, and misfits. Such a series as the latter is beyond the range of coincidence, and can be explained by a system of upbringing and selection which virtually precluded the emergence of an effective ruler. Similarly, the Grand Vezirate and other high offices, both political and religious, were filled and administered in such a way that what must surprise us is that they produced as many able and conscientious men as they did.

The breakdown in the apparatus of government affected not only the supreme instruments of sovereignty but also the whole of the bureaucratic and religious institutions all over the Empire. These suffered a catastrophic fall in efficiency and integrity, which was accentuated by the growing change in methods of recruitment, training, and promotion. This deterioration is clearly discernible in the Ottoman archives, which reflect vividly and precisely the change from the meticulous, conscientious, and strikingly efficient bureaucratic government of the sixteenth century to the neglect of the seventeenth and the collapse of the eighteenth centuries.[4] The same fall in professional and moral standards can be seen, though perhaps in less striking form, in the different ranks of the religious and judicial hierarchy.

Most striking of all was the decline of the Ottoman armed forces. The Empire could still draw on great reserves of loyal and valiant subjects, said Koçu Bey, writing in 1630. The Turkish soldier had suffered no loss of courage or morale, said Ali Paşa writing after the disastrous treaty of Küçük Kaynarca of 1774.[5] Yet the Ottoman armies, once the terror of Europe, ceased to frighten

Die Geschichtsschreiber der Osmanen und ihre Werke (1927), 184–5. A new edition was published in Istanbul in 1939. A German translation by W. F. Behrnauer appeared in *ZDMG*, xv (1861), 272 ff.

[4] In the sixteenth century the records are careful, detailed, and up to date; in the seventeenth and eighteenth centuries they become irregular, inaccurate, and sketchy. Even the quality of the paper becomes poorer. In this general picture of falling standards, the carefully kept registers of the Köprülü interlude stand out the more significantly.

[5] Ali Paşa had served as governor of Trebizond, where he founded a *derebey* dynasty. Two questions, he tells us, had profoundly occupied his thoughts: why the Empire from being so strong, had become so weak, and what was to be done to recover her former strength. His memorandum, still unpublished, is preserved in manuscript in Uppsala. A Swedish paraphrase was included by M. Norberg in *Turkiska Rikets Annaler* (Hernösand) v (1822), 1245 ff. See *EI*², 'Djānikli 'Alī Pasha' (by B. Lewis).

anyone but their own sovereigns and their own civil population, and suffered a long series of humiliating defeats at the hands of once despised enemies.

In the sixteenth century the Ottoman Empire reached the limits of its expansion, and came up against barriers which it could not pass. On the eastern border, despite the victories in the field of Selim I and Süleyman, the Ottoman armies could not advance into Persia. The new centralized monarchy of the Safavids, then at the peak of their power; the high plateau of Iran, posing new problems of logistics and calling for new and unfamiliar techniques; the difficulties of leading against a Muslim adversary an army whose traditions since its birth were of the holy war against the infidels—all these combined to halt the Ottoman forces at the frontiers of Iran, and cut them off from overland expansion into Central Asia or India.

In Eastern waters they encountered the stout ships of the Portuguese, whose shipbuilders and navigators, trained to meet the challenge of the Atlantic, were more than a match for the calm-water ships of the Ottomans. Stouter vessels, more guns, better seamanship were what defeated the successive attempts of the Ottomans to break out of the ring, and swept Muslim shipping from the waters of the Indian Ocean.

In the Crimea and the lands beyond it they were halted by Russia. In 1475 the Ottomans had conquered Kaffa. Part of the Crimean coast passed under direct Ottoman rule, the Giray Khans of the Tatars became Ottoman vassals, and in 1569 the Ottomans even launched a plan to open a canal between the Don and Volga and thus, by acquiring a shipping route to Central Asia, to break out of the Portuguese noose.[6] But here too the Ottomans found their way blocked. At the same time as Western Europe was expanding by sea round Africa and into Asia, Eastern Europe was expanding by land across the steppe, southward and eastward towards the lands of Islam. In 1502 the once mighty Khanate of the Golden Horde was finally extinguished, and much of its territory absorbed by Russia. The successor Khanates of Kazan, Astrakhan, and Crimea lingered on for a while, but before

---

[6] On this project see the article of Inalcık, 'Osmanlı-Rus rekabetinin menşei ve Don-Volga kanalı teşebbüsü (1569)', *Bell.* no. 46 (1948), 349–402. English version: 'The Origins of the Ottoman-Russian Rivalry and the Don-Volga Canal 1569', *A. Univ. Ank.*, i (1946–7), 47–107.

long the Russians were able to conquer the first two, and to exercise a growing pressure on the third. The way was open to the Black Sea and the North Caucasus, the Caspian and western Siberia, where the advance of Russia barred and enclosed the Ottomans as did the Portuguese and their successors in the Eastern seas.

In Africa, desert, mountain, and climate offered obstacles which there was no incentive to surmount, while in the Mediterranean, after a brief interval, naval supremacy was lost to the maritime countries of the West.[7]

But the classical area of Ottoman expansion had been in none of these. Since the first crossing of the Bosporus in the mid-fourteenth century, Europe had been the promised land of the Ottomans—the 'House of War' par excellence, in which the power and the glory of Islam were to be advanced by victorious battle against the infidel. On 27 September 1529, after conquering Hungary, the armies of Süleyman the Magnificent reached Vienna—and on 15 October they began to withdraw from the still unconquered city. The event was decisive. For another century and a half inconclusive warfare was waged for Hungary, and in 1683 yet another attempt, the last, was made against Vienna. But the cause was already lost. The Ottoman Empire had reached the line beyond which it could not advance, from which it could only withdraw. The valour of the Habsburg, as of the Safavid armies, no doubt played its part in stemming the Ottoman onslaught, but is insufficient as an explanation of why the defenders of Vienna were able to halt the victors of Kossovo, Varna, Nicopolis, and Mohacs. There too we may perhaps find an explanation in the problems of a new and different terrain, calling for new techniques of warfare and especially of supply and transport.

It was after the halting of the Ottoman advance that the lag began to appear between the standards of training and equipment of Ottoman and European armies. Initially, the backwardness of

---

[7] Lûtfi Paşa, writing after 1541, could already see the danger to Turkey of the growing naval power of Europe. He quoted with approval a remark by Kemalpaşazade (d. 1533–4) to Selim I: 'My Lord, you dwell in a city whose benefactor is the sea. If the sea is not safe no ships will come, and if no ship comes Istanbul perishes.' He himself had said to Sultan Süleyman: 'Under the previous Sultans there were many who ruled the land, but few who ruled the sea. In the conduct of naval warfare the infidels are ahead of us. We must overcome them' (Lûtfi Paşa, *Asafname*, ed. and tr. R. Tschudi (1910), text 32–33, trans. 26–27).

the Ottomans was relative rather than absolute. Once in the forefront of military science, they began to fall behind. The great technical and logistic developments in European armies in the seventeenth century were followed tardily and ineffectively by the Ottomans—in marked contrast with the speed and inventiveness with which they had accepted and adapted the European invention of artillery in the fifteenth century. One possible contributory factor to this change is the fall in the flow of European renegades and adventurers to Turkey—but to state this is to raise the further question of why Turkey had ceased to attract these men, and why the Turks made such little use of those who did come.

The decline in alertness, in readiness to accept new techniques, is an aspect—perhaps the most dangerous—of what became a general deterioration in professional and moral standards in the armed forces, parallel to that of the bureaucratic and religious classes, which we have already noted. It led directly to what must be accounted, in the Ottoman as in the Roman Empire, one of the principal causes of decline—the loss of territory to more powerful foreign enemies. Modern historians have rightly tended to put the loss of territory to invaders among the symptoms rather than the causes of weakness, but the effect of the steady draining away of manpower, revenue, and resources should not be underrated. For Koçu Bey and his successors, the causes of these changes for the worse lay in favouritism and corruption. The different presuppositions of our time may incline us to regard these less as causes than as symptoms, and to seek their motives and origin in vaster and deeper changes.

During the sixteenth century three major changes occurred, principally of external origin, which vitally affected the entire life of the Ottoman Empire. The first of these has already been mentioned—the halting of the Ottoman advance into Europe. This was an event comparable in some ways with the Closing of the Frontier in the United States—but with far more shattering impact. The Ottoman state had been born on the frontier between Islam and Byzantine Christendom; its leaders and armies had been march-warriors in the Holy War, carrying the sword and the faith of Islam into new lands. The Ottoman gazis and dervishes, like the pioneers and missionaries of the Americas, believed themselves to be bringing civilization and the true faith to peoples sunk in barbarism and unbelief—and like them reaped the familiar rewards of the frontier warrior and the colonist. For the Ottoman state, the frontier had provided work and recompense both for its men of the sword and its men of religion and, in a deeper sense, the very *raison d'être* of its statehood. True, by the sixteenth century that state had already evolved from a principality of march-warriors into an Empire, but the traditions of the frontier were still deeply rooted in the military, social, and religious life of the Ottomans, and the virtual closing of the frontier to further expansion and colonization could not fail profoundly to affect them. The Ottoman systems of military organization, civil administration, taxation, and land tenure were all geared to the needs of a society expanding by conquest and colonization into the lands of the infidel. They ceased to correspond to the different stresses of a frontier that was stationary or in retreat.[8]

While the great Ottoman war-machine, extended beyond its range, was grinding to a standstill in the plains of Hungary, the life and growth of the Ottoman Empire were being circumvented, on a far vaster scale, by the oceanic voyages of discovery of the Western maritime peoples, the ultimate effect of which was to turn the whole Eastern Mediterranean area, where the Empire was situated, into a backwater. In 1555 the Imperial ambassador in Constantinople, Ogier Ghiselin de Busbecq, one of the acutest European observers of Turkey, could still comment that the Western Europeans basely squandered their energies 'seeking the Indies and the Antipodes across vast fields of ocean, in search of gold', and abandoning the heart of Europe to imminent and almost certain conquest.[9] But in about 1580 an Ottoman geographer, in an account of the New World written for Murad III, gave warning of the dangers to the Islamic lands and the disturbance to Islamic trade resulting from the establishment of Europeans on the coasts of America, India, and the Persian Gulf; he advised the Sultan to open a canal through the isthmus of Suez and send a fleet 'to capture the ports of Hind and Sind and drive away the infidels'.[10]

[8] The significance of the frontier and of the frontiersman in Ottoman government and society has been demonstrated by Paul Wittek. The whole question of the frontier as a cultural entity, with some reference to F. J. Turner's famous thesis on the significance of the frontier in American history, has been re-examined by Owen Lattimore in his 'The Frontier in History' (published in *Relazioni*, i, 105–38, of the Tenth International Congress of Historical Sciences, Rome 1955).

[9] *The Turkish letters of Ogier Ghiselin de Busbecq*, tr. by C. T. Forster and F. H. B. Daniell (1881), i, 129–30.

[10] *Tarih al-Hind al-Garbi* (Constantinople, 1142/1729), fol. 6b ff.

By 1625 another Ottoman observer, a certain Ömer Talib, could
see the danger in a more pressing form:

> Now the Europeans have learnt to know the whole world; they send
> their ships everywhere and seize important ports. Formerly, the goods
> of India, Sind, and China used to come to Suez, and were distributed
> by Muslims to all the world. But now these goods are carried on
> Portuguese, Dutch, and English ships to Frangistan, and are spread all
> over the world from there. What they do not need themselves they
> bring to Istanbul and other Islamic lands, and sell it for five times the
> price, thus earning much money. For this reason gold and silver are
> becoming scarce in the lands of Islam. The Ottoman Empire must
> seize the shores of Yemen and the trade passing that way; otherwise
> before very long, the Europeans will rule over the lands of Islam.[11]

The effects on Middle Eastern trade of the circumnavigation of
Africa were by no means as immediate and as catastrophic as was
at one time believed. Right through the sixteenth century
Eastern merchandise continued to reach the Ottoman Empire,
coming by ship to Red Sea ports and Basra and overland across
Persia, and European merchants came to Turkey to buy. But the
volume of international trade passing this way was steadily
decreasing. From the seventeenth century, the establishment of
Dutch and British power in Asia and the transference of the routes
of world trade to the open ocean deprived Turkey of the greater
part of her foreign commerce and left her, together with the
countries over which she ruled, in a stagnant backwater through
which the life-giving stream of world trade no longer flowed.[12]

The European voyages of discovery brought another more
immediate blow, as violent as it was unexpected. The basic unit
of currency of the Ottoman Empire had been the silver *akçe*, or
asper, in which all the revenues and expenditures of the state had
been calculated. Like other Mediterranean and European states,
the Ottoman Empire suffered from a recurring shortage of
precious metals, which at times threatened its silver-based monetary system. To meet these difficulties, the Ottoman Sultans
resorted to such well-tried measures as controlling the silver mines,

---

[11] The observations of Ömer Talib, written on the margins of a manuscript of the
Tarih al-Hind al-Garbi in Ankara (Maarif Library 10024), were published by A. Zeki
Velidi Togan, *Bugünkü Türkili (Turkistan) ve Yakın Tarihi*, i (1947), p. 127.

[12] On these questions see the important studies of Köprülü (in his additional notes
to the Turkish translation of Barthold's *Muslim Culture* (*Islam Medeniyeti Tarihi*, 1940),
pp. 255 ff.) and Inalcık in *Bell.*, no. 60 (1951), pp. 661 ff.

discouraging the export and encouraging the import of coin and bullion, extending the non-monetary sector of the state economy, and alternately debasing and reissuing the currency.

This situation was suddenly transformed when the flow of precious metals from the New World reached the Eastern Mediterranean. American gold, and, to a far greater extent, American silver had already caused a price revolution and a financial crisis in Spain. From there it passed to Genoa and thence to Ragusa, where Spanish coins of American metal are first reported in the 1580's.[13] Thereafter the financial impact on Turkey of this sudden flow of cheap and plentiful silver from the West was immediate and catastrophic. The Ottoman rulers, accustomed to crises of shortage, were quite unable to understand or meet a crisis resulting from an excess of silver, and the traditional measures which they adopted only served to worsen the situation. In 1584 the asper was reduced from one-fifth to one-eighth of a dirham of silver—a measure of devaluation which unleashed a continuous financial crisis with far-reaching economic and social consequences. As the price of silver fell by 70 per cent., that of gold rose by 100 per cent.; cheaply bought silver coin by the million flowed from Europe to Turkey for quick and profitable re-sale, crowding out the traffic in commodities, draining the Turkish Empire of gold, and accentuating the steep rise in the level of prices, which brought distress and then ruin to whole classes of the population. Before long there was a vast increase in coining, coin-clipping, and the like; the rate of the asper fell from 60 to the ducat to over 200, and foreign coins, both gold and silver, drove the debased Ottoman issues even from the internal markets. Twice in the seventeenth century the Ottoman government tried to stem the inflationary tide by the issue of a new silver currency; first, the *para*, which appeared as a silver coin in the 1620's, then the piastre, or *kuruş*, which appeared in the 1680's, in imitation of the European dollar. Both followed the asper into debasement and devaluation.[14]

[13] I am informed by Professor R. B. Serjeant that cheap silver of Portuguese provenance is reported slightly earlier in Southern Arabia, where it caused a drop in the rate of silver to gold.

[14] The effects on wages, prices, and currencies of the flow of American bullion, first studied for Spain in the classic monograph of Earl J. Hamilton (*American Treasure and the Price Revolution in Spain, 1501–1550*, 1934), were examined on a larger scale for the whole Mediterranean area in the great work of F. Braudel, *La Méditerranée et le monde méditerranéen à l'époque de Philippe II* (1949). Braudel's pointers on events in Turkey

Precisely at this time of monetary and financial crisis, the government was compelled to embark on a great expansion in its salaried personnel and a great increase in expenditure in coin. When Mehmed the Conqueror had faced a monetary crisis, he had reduced the numbers of paid soldiers and increased the numbers of cavalry sipahis, whose services were rewarded with fiefs and not coin.[15] But in the changed conditions of warfare of the sixteenth and seventeenth centuries this had ceased to be possible. The greatly increased use of firearms and artillery necessitated the maintenance of ever larger paid professional armies, and reduced the relative importance of the feudal cavalryman. Both Koçu Bey and Hacı Halifa note and deplore the decline of the sipahis and the increase in the paid soldiery which, says Hacı Halifa, had increased from 48,000 in 1567 to 100,000 in about 1620.[16] Both writers are aware of the harmful financial and agrarian effects of this change. Understandably, they miss the point that the obsolescence of the sipahi had become inevitable, and that only the long-term, professional soldier could serve the military needs of the time.

The price was appalling. Faced with a growing expenditure and a depreciating currency, the demands of the treasury became more and more insatiable. The underpaid and over-sized salaried personnel of the state—civil, military, and religious—had growing difficulties in making ends meet, with the inevitable effects on their prestige, their honesty, and their further recruitment. Though the feudal cavalryman was no longer needed by the army, his disappearance was sorely felt in the countryside, as the old Ottoman agrarian system, of which he had once been the foundation, tottered and collapsed. In place of the sipahi, who resided in or near the fief in which he had a hereditary interest, palace favourites, parasites, and speculators became the recipients of fiefs, sometimes accumulating great numbers of them, and thus

(especially pp. 393–4, 419–20, 637–43) were taken up and developed by Inalcık in his illuminating study, 'Osmanlı Imparatorluğunun Kuruluş ve Inkişafi devrinde Türkiye' nin Iktisadi Vaziyeti üzerinde bir tetkik münasebetile', *Bell.*, no. 60 (1951), 656 ff. See further the review of Braudel's book by Barkan in *R. Fac. Sci. Éc. Univ. Ist.*, xi (1949–50), 196–216.

[15] Inalcık, in *Bell.*, no. 60, 656 ff.

[16] *Düstur al-'Amal li-Islah al-Halal* (Ist., 1280/1863, as an appendix to the *Kavanin-i Al-i Osman* of Ayn-i Ali), pp. 131–2; German trans. by Behrnauer in *ŽDMG*, xi (1857), 125. In this little treatise, written in about 1653, Hacı Halifa examines the causes of the financial and other troubles of the Ottoman Empire.

becoming, in effect, absentee owners of great latifundia. Other fiefs reverted to the Imperial domain.[17] But the growing inefficiency and venality of the bureaucracy prevented the formation of any effective state system for the assessment and collection of taxes. Instead these tasks were given to tax-farmers, whose interposition and interception of revenues became in time a prescriptive and hereditary right, and added to the number of vast and neglected latifundia.

The shrinking economy of the Empire thus had to support an increasingly costly and cumbersome superstructure. The palace, the bureaucracy, and the religious hierarchy, an army that in expenditure at least was modern, and a parasitic class of tax-farmers and absentee landlords—all this was far more than the medieval states or even the Roman Empire had tried to support; yet it rested on an economy that was no more advanced than theirs. The technological level of agriculture remained primitive, and the social conditions of the Turkish countryside after the sixteenth century precluded the appearance of anything like the English gentleman-farmers of the seventeenth century whose experiments revolutionized English agriculture.

These developments are not peculiar to Turkey. The fall in money and rise of prices, the growing cost of government and warfare, the sale of offices and farming of taxes—all these are known in other Mediterranean and adjoining states, where they contributed to the rise of a new class of capitalists and financiers, with a growing and constructive influence on governments.

In Turkey too there were rich merchants and bankers, such as the Greek Michael Cantacuzenos and the Portuguese Jew Joseph Nasi—the Fugger of the Orient, as Braudel called him.[18] But they were never able to play anything like the financial, economic, and political role of their European counterparts. Part of the cause of this must undoubtedly be found in the progressive stagnation of Ottoman trade, to which allusion has already been made. But that is not all. Most if not all of these merchants were Christians or Jews—tolerated but second-class subjects of the Muslim state. However great their economic power, they were politically

---

[17] From the late sixteenth century onwards the cadastral registers in the Ottoman archives show a steady decrease in the number of *timars*, and a corresponding increase in the extent of Imperial domain.

[18] Braudel, p. 567.

penalized and socially segregated; they could obtain political power only by stealth, and exercise it only by intrigue, with demoralizing effect on all concerned. Despite the scale and extent of their financial operations, they were unable to create political conditions more favourable to commerce, or to build up any solid structure of banking and credit, and thus help the Ottoman government in its perennial financial straits. In England too finance and credit were at first in the hands of alien specialists, who have left their name in Lombard Street. But these were ousted in time by vigorous and pushful native rivals. In Turkey no such rivals arose, and in any case, in the general decline of the seventeenth century, even the Greek and Jewish merchant princes of Constantinople dwindled into insignificance. Fortunes were still made in Turkey, but their origin was not economic. Mostly they were political or fiscal in origin, obtained through the holding of public office. Nor were they spent on investment or development, but consumed or hoarded, after the fashion of the time.

Reference has often been made to the technological backwardness of the Ottoman Empire—to its failure not only to invent, but even to respond to the inventions of others. While Europe swept forward in science and technology, the Ottomans were content to remain, in their agriculture, their industry, and their transport, at the level of their medieval ancestors. Even their armed forces followed tardily and incompetently after the technological advances of their European enemies.

The problem of agriculture in the Ottoman Empire was more than one of technical backwardness, however. It was one of definite decline. Already during the reign of Süleyman the Magnificent, Lûtfi Paşa gave warning of the dangers of rural depopulation, and urged that the peasantry be protected by moderation in taxation and by regular censuses of village population, as a control on the competence of provincial government.[19] Koçu Bey reinforces these arguments; but by 1653 Hacı Halifa reports that people had begun to flock from the villages to the towns during the reign of Süleyman, and that in his own day there

---

[19] Lûtfi Paşa, *Asafname*, ch. 4. Lûtfi Paşa's treatise, written after his dismissal from the office of Grand Vezir in 1541, sets forth rules on what a good Grand Vezir should do and, more urgently, on what he should avoid. In this booklet, written at a time when the Ottoman Empire was still at the height of its power and glory, the writer shows deep concern about its fate and welfare, and is already able to point to what, in later years, became the characteristic signs of Ottoman decline.

were derelict and abandoned villages all over the Empire.[20]

Much of this decline in agriculture can be attributed to the causes named by the Ottoman memorialists: the squeezing out of the feudal sipahis, the mainstay of the early Ottoman agrarian system, and their replacement by tax-farmers and others with no long-term interest in peasant welfare or land conservation, but only an immediate and short-term interest in taxes. Harsh, exorbitant, and improvident taxation led to a decline in cultivation, which was sometimes permanent. The peasants, neglected and impoverished, were forced into the hands of money-lenders and speculators, and often driven off the land entirely. With the steady decline in bureaucratic efficiency during the seventeenth and eighteenth centuries, the former system of regular land surveys and population censuses was abandoned.[21] The central government ceased to exercise any check or control over agriculture and village affairs, which were left to the unchecked rapacity of the tax-farmers, the leaseholders, and the bailiffs of court nominees. During the seventeenth century some of the more permanently established lease-holders began to coalesce with the landowners into a new landed aristocracy—the *ayan-i memleket* or country notables, whose appearance and usurpation of some of the functions and authority of government were already noted at the time.[22]

While agriculture declined, industry fared little better. The corporative structure of the guilds fulfilled a useful social function in expressing and preserving the complex web of social loyalties and obligations of the old order, and also, though to a diminishing extent, in safeguarding the moral level and standards of craftsmanship of the artisan. Their economic effects, however, were restrictive and eventually destructive. A man's choice of profession was determined by habit and inheritance, the scope of his endeavour limited by primitive techniques and transport, his

[20] Hacı Halifa, ch. 1.

[21] See for example the list of *tapu* registers for the Arab provinces, given in B. Lewis, 'The Ottoman Archives as a Source for the History of the Arab Lands', *JRAS* (1951), pp. 149 ff. The great majority of the registers listed there are of the sixteenth century. After 1600 the surveys become less and less frequent, and the resulting registers more and more slipshod.

[22] cf. the remarks of Hüseyin Hezarfenn, writing in 1669 (R. Anhegger, 'Hezarfen Hüseyin Efendi'nin Osmanlı devlet teşkilâtına dâir mülâhazaları', *TM*, x (1951–3), 372, 387. The *ayan-i vilayet* already appear occasionally in *Kanuns* of the sixteenth century (Barkan, *XV ve XVI inci asırlarda . . . Kanunlar*, i (1943), index).

D

manner and speed of work fixed by guild rule and tradition; on the one hand a sufi religious habit of passivity and surrender of self, on the other the swift fiscal retribution for any sign of prosperity, combined to keep industrial production primitive, static, and inert, utterly unable to resist the competition of imported European manufactures.[23]

Some have sought the causes of this backwardness in Islam or in the Turkish race—explanations which do not satisfy, in view of the previous achievements of both. It may, however, be possible to find part of the explanation of Ottoman lack of receptivity— perhaps even of Ottoman decline—in certain evolving attitudes of mind, inherited by the Ottomans along with the classical Islamic civilization of which they had been the heirs and renovators.

Classical Islamic civilization, like others before and after it, including our own, was profoundly convinced of its superiority and self-sufficiency. In its earliest, primitive phase, Islam had been open to influences from the Hellenistic Orient, from Persia, even from India and China. Many works were translated into Arabic from Greek, Syriac, and Persian.[24] But with the solitary exception of the late Latin chronicle of Orosius, not a single translation into a Muslim language is known of any Latin or Western work until the sixteenth century, when one or two historical and geographical works were translated into Turkish. For the Muslim of classical times, Frankish Europe was an outer darkness of barbarism and unbelief, from which the sunlit world of Islam had nothing to learn and little to fear. This view, though becoming outdated towards the end of the Middle Ages, was transmitted by the medieval Muslims to their Ottoman heirs, and was reinforced by the crushing victories of Ottoman arms over their European opponents. On the warlike but open frontier one could still exchange lessons with one's counterpart on the other side; through renegades and refugees new skills could still reach the Islamic Empire. But the willingness to learn these lessons was not there, and in time the sources also dried up. Masked by the still imposing military might of the Ottoman Empire, the peoples of

[23] Sabri F. Ülgener, *Iktisadî Inhitat Tarihimizin Ahlak ve Zihniyet Meseleleri* (1951). Much light is thrown on these questions by Professor Ülgener's attempt to apply the methods of Weber and Sombart to the study of Ottoman social and economic history.

[24] See further B. Lewis, 'The Muslim Discovery of Europe', *BSOAS*, xx (1957), 415.

Islam continued to cherish the dangerous but comfortable illusion of the immeasurable and immutable superiority of their own civilization to all others—an illusion from which they were slowly shaken by a series of humiliating military defeats.

In the military empire, at once feudal and bureaucratic, which they had created, the Muslims knew only four professions—government, war, religion, and agriculture. Industry and trade were left to the non-Muslim conquered subjects, who continued to practise their inherited crafts. Thus the stigma of the infidel became attached to the professions which the infidels followed, and remained so attached even after many of the craftsmen had become Muslim. Westerners and native Christians, bankers, merchants, and craftsmen, were all involved in the general contempt which made the Ottoman Muslim impervious to ideas or inventions of Christian origin and unwilling to bend his own thoughts to the problems of artisans and vile mechanics. Primitive techniques of production, primitive means of transportation, chronic insecurity and social penalization, combined to preclude any long-term or large-scale undertakings, and to keep the Ottoman economy at the lowest level of competence, initiative, and morality.[25]

This apathy of the Ottoman ruling class is the more striking when contrasted with the continuing vigour of their intellectual life. An example of this may be seen in the group of writers who memorialized on the decline of the Empire, which they saw so clearly but were powerless to stop. We may point also to the brilliant Ottoman school of historiography, which reaches its peak of achievement in the work of Naima (1655–1716); to the Ottoman traditions of courtly and religious poetry, two of the greatest exponents of which, Nedim and Şeyh Galib, lived in the eighteenth century; to the Ottoman schools of architecture, miniature, and music. It is not until the end of the eighteenth century and the beginning of the nineteenth that we can speak of a real breakdown in the cultural and intellectual life of Turkey, resulting from the utter exhaustion of the old traditions and the absence of new creative impulses. And even then, behind the battered screen of courtly convention, the simple folk arts and folk poetry of the Turks continued as before.

In the late Middle Ages, the Ottoman Empire was the only state in Europe which already possessed the territory, the cohesion,

[25] Ülgener, pp. 193 ff.

the organization, the manpower and the resources to carry the new apparatus of warfare, the crushing cost of which was out-moding the city states and feudal principalities of medieval Europe, as surely as modern weapons have outmoded the petty sovereignties of Europe in our own day. In part perhaps because of that very primacy, it failed to respond to the challenge which produced the nation-states of sixteenth-century Europe, and the great commercial and technological efflorescence of which they were the scene.

Fundamentally, the Ottoman Empire had remained or reverted to a medieval state, with a medieval mentality and a medieval economy—but with the added burden of a bureaucracy and a standing army which no medieval state had ever had to bear. In a world of rapidly modernizing states it had little chance of survival.

The stages in the decline of Ottoman power and grandeur are well marked by public, international treaties. The first was the treaty of Sitvatorok, signed with Austria in November 1606. For the first time, this was not a truce dictated in Istanbul to the 'King of Vienna', but a treaty negotiated on the frontier and agreed with the 'Roman Emperor'. The Ottoman Sultan had at last consented to concede the Imperial title to the Habsburg monarch, and to treat with him as an equal.

The seventeenth century began with a concession of equality; it ended with a clear admission of defeat. In 1682 the Ottoman Empire, temporarily restored to health and vigour by the reforms of the Köprülü Vezirs, had launched one more major offensive, in the grand style, against its European enemies. The second failure before the walls of Vienna, in 1683, was decisive and final. The Austrians and their allies advanced rapidly into Ottoman territory in Hungary, Greece, and the Black Sea coast, and the Austrian victories at the second battle of Mohacs in 1687 and at Zenta in 1697 sealed the defeat of the Turks. The peace treaty of Carlowitz, signed on 26 January 1699, marks the end of an epoch and the beginning of another. This was the first time that the Ottoman Empire signed a peace as the defeated power in a clearly decided war, and was compelled to cede extensive territories, long under Ottoman rule and regarded as part of the House of Islam, to the infidel enemy. It was a fateful opening to the eighteenth century.

By the treaty of Passarovitz of 1718, Turkey made further

cessions of territory. Though the mutual suspicions of her enemies enabled her to recover some ground during the war of 1736–9, the recovery was of slight duration. A new humiliation came with the treaty of Küçük Kaynarca of 1774, after a war in which Russian troops had carried all before them and a Russian fleet had entered the Mediterranean and threatened the very coasts of Anatolia. By this treaty, the Sultan renounced not only conquered lands inhabited by Christian populations, but old Muslim territory in the Crimea;[26] he also conceded to the Russian Empress what became a virtual protectorate over his own Orthodox Christian subjects.

Thereafter there was a halt. Apart from the loss of Bukovina to Austria in 1775 and of Bessarabia to Russia in 1812, the Ottoman Empire made no important cessions to foreign powers until a century later, when the process was resumed with the loss of Bosnia and Herzegovina to Austria and of Batum and Kars to Russia in 1878. During this period the main threat to the unity and integrity of the Empire came from within.

The humiliations of Carlowitz, Passarowitz, and later treaties further weakened the already waning authority of the central government over the provinces. Significantly, it was in the old Islamic territories in Asia and Africa that provincial independence first appeared and went farthest. These movements were in no sense expressions of popular or national opposition to Ottoman rule. Except in a few remote desert and mountain areas, such as Arabia, the Lebanon, and Kurdistan, neither the leaders nor the followers were local, but were drawn from either the Ottoman or the Mamluk military classes. In neither case had they any roots in local soil—in neither could they count on any serious local support. Most of them were rebellious and adventurous pashas and officers, profiting from the remoteness and weakness of the Sultan's authority to intercept a larger share of the revenues of their provinces and to transform them into virtually independent principalities. Such were Ali Bey in Egypt, Ahmed Jezzar in Syria, and the Mamluk lords of Baghdad and Basra. They were no more concerned with the language and sentiments of their subjects than

[26] By the terms of the treaty, the Sultan renounced his suzerainty over the Tatar Khanate of the Crimea, which became independent. The second stage was completed in 1783, when Russia annexed the Crimea, and the Khanate was extinguished. On the Turkish reactions see below, p. 49 and n. 24.

was a medieval European feudal magnate; far less with their welfare.

Rather different was the position in Anatolia, where the independent *derebeys*—valley-lords, as they were called—won virtual autonomy about the beginning of the eighteenth century. These too began as officers or agents and became vassals of the Sultan. Unlike the pashas in the Arab lands, however, they struck root among the peoples whom they ruled and from whom they had sprung, and formed genuine local dynasties, with strong local traditions and loyalties. Their financial and military obligations to the Porte came to be well defined and regulated, and evolved into a regular system of suzerainty and vassalage. Their close and intimate relationship with their territories and peoples seem to have had a beneficial effect on both.

In Rumelia, still the main centre and stronghold of the Empire and the home of its governing *élites*, the central government was able to maintain some measure of direct control. But there too the *ayan*, the new aristocracy of 'notables', were steadily taking over the functions of government, and by the end of the eighteenth century the notables of Rumelia, with their private armies, treasuries, and courts of law, had rivalled the independence of the Anatolian valley-lords.

After each of the great military defeats of the eighteenth century, Ottoman statesmen and historians discussed with brutal frankness the decrepit state of the Empire and the abject performance of its armies. The treaty of Küçük Kaynarca and the subsequent annexation of the Crimea in particular gave rise to much heart-searching and discussion. Then, in 1787, a new war broke out between Turkey and Russia, joined in the following year by Austria. This time, distracted by events in Poland, Prussia, and France, the Russians and Austrians did not press the campaign as vigorously as previously, and in 1791–2 Turkey was able to make peace with Austria, at Sistova, and with Russia, at Jassy, on comparatively lenient terms.

During the war a new Sultan, Selim III, had been invested with the sword of Osman. Thirty-eight years of age at his accession, he was a man of greater ability and wider knowledge and experience than any who had emerged from the cage of princes in the Saray for a long time. Already as a young man he had entered, through his personal emissary Ishak Bey, into direct correspondence with the king of France, and showed a growing interest in European affairs. He was well aware that the respite of 1792 was due to difficulties elsewhere in Europe, and that there would be little time before Austria and Russia returned to the assault.

Selim's first problem was the modernization of the armed forces, and he began, reasonably enough, by setting up new military and naval schools. For these, however, he had to rely on foreign instructors. Such attempts at Westernizing the armed forces as had been made during the eighteenth century had all relied on French instruction, and it was natural for Selim, when he had prepared the list of foreign instructors and technicians whom he needed to recruit, to send that list to Paris. The time was the autumn of 1793.

CHAPTER III

The Impact of the West

It is certainly a good Maxim for an Embassadour in this Country, not to be over-studious in procuring a familiar friendship with Turks; a fair comportment towards all in a moderate way, is cheap and secure; for a Turk is not capable of real friendship towards a Christian.

PAUL RYCAUT, 'The History of the Present
State of the Ottoman Empire', 1668.

Familiar association with heathens and infidels is forbidden to the people of Islam, and friendly and intimate intercourse between two parties that are to one another as darkness and light is far from desirable.

ASIM EFENDI, 'History', c. 1809.

. . . sans perdre de temps je m'appliquai à l'étude de la langue française, comme la plus universelle, et capable de me faire parvenir à la connoissance des auteurs qui ont écrit sur les belles sciences.

SEID MUSTAFA, 'Diatribe de l'Ingenieur', 1803.

THE French Revolution was the first great movement of ideas in Western Christendom that had any real effect on the world of Islam. Despite the long confrontation of Christendom and Islam across the Mediterranean, and their numberless contacts, in peace and in war, from Syria to Spain, such earlier European movements as the Renaissance and the Reformation woke no echo and found no response among the Muslim peoples. It may at first sight seem strange that Islamic civilization, which in its earlier stages was so receptive to influences from Hellenism and Iran, even from India and China, nevertheless decisively rejected the West. But an explanation is not hard to find. When Islam was still expanding and receptive, the Christian West had little or nothing to offer, but rather flattered Islamic pride with the spectacle of a culture that was visibly and palpably inferior. Furthermore, by the very fact that it was Christian, it was discredited in advance. The Muslim doctrine of successive revelations, culminating in the final mission of Muhammad, enabled the Muslim to reject Christianity as an earlier and imperfect form of something which he alone possessed in its entirety, and to discount Christian thought and Christian civilization. After the initial impact of eastern Christianity on Islam in its earliest years, Christian influence, even from the high civilization of Byzantium, was reduced to a minimum. Later, when the advance of Christendom and the decline of Islam created a new relationship, Islam was crystallized—not to say ossified—and had become impervious to external stimuli, especially from the millennial enemy in the West.

Earlier Western Influences

All this does not mean that there was no Western influence in Turkey before the eighteenth century. On the contrary, the Turks, while rejecting Christianity, Christian ideas, and Christian civilization, still found many things in Christian Europe that were useful enough and attractive enough to borrow, imitate, and adapt.

No nation in the world [wrote the Imperial ambassador Busbecq in 1560] has shown greater readiness than the Turks to avail themselves of the useful inventions of foreigners, as is proved by their employment of cannons and mortars, and many other things invented by Christians. They cannot, however, be induced as yet to use printing, or to establish public clocks, because they think that the Scriptures, that is, their sacred books—would no longer be *scriptures* if they were *printed*, and that, if public clocks were introduced, the authority of their muezzins and their ancient rites would be thereby impaired.[1]

Firearms could be accepted, since they would be of service in the Holy War for Islam against the infidels; printing and clocks could not be accepted, since they served no such purpose, and might flaw the social fabric of Islam. The attitude of mind described by Busbecq is attested by many examples. When a Sultan wished to imitate the construction and armament of a captured Venetian galley, and some voices were raised in objection to this aping of infidel ways, the ulema ruled that for the sake of the Holy War it was permissible to learn from the infidels new ways of waging war against them. But when Jewish refugees from Spain asked Bayezid II for permission to set up printing presses in Turkey, he consented on condition that they did not print any books in Turkish or Arabic, and confined themselves to Hebrew and European languages.[2]

---

[1] Busbecq, i. 255 (pp. 213–14 of the Latin text in the Elzevir edition, Leiden, 1633).

[2] cf. the interesting observations of Nicolas de Nicolay, who visited Turkey in 1551, on the role of the Spanish and Portuguese Marranos: 'Oultre ce ilz ont entre eulx des couriers en tous arts & manufactures tres-excellens, specialement des Marranes n'as pas longs temps bannis & deschassez d'Espagne & Portugal, lesquelz au grand detriment & dommage de la Chrestienté ont apprins au Turc plusieurs inuentions,

The Ottoman state was born on the frontier between Islam and Christendom. For centuries the Ottomans and other Turkish principalities of march-warriors in Anatolia cohabited with Byzantium in the tense intimacy of frontier warfare—imitating and influencing one another in tactics and weapons, in clothing and diet, drawing closer to one another through the subtler workings of conversion, of assimilation, and of marriage by capture. Not a few of the Turkish frontiersmen were suckled and weaned by Greek mothers—not a few of the noble families of the early Empire were descended from converted Greeks. In the popular religion of both Greek Christians and Turkish Muslims, there are countless common saints, common festivals, and common holy places, which each group reinterpreted in its own way. Jalal ad-Din Rumi (1207-47), the great mystical poet of Konya— no Anatolian but an immigrant from Central Asia—tried his hand at Greek verse;[3] even Sultan Mehmed the Conqueror had Greek books and a Greek biographer, and the Sultans more than once called on the services of Greek architects for their mosques and Greek shipwrights for their fleet.[4]

Byzantine influence on the Ottomans was limited in the main to material things, and to the popular level of religious belief and practice. It died out in the course of the fifteenth century, under the impact of two events: the incorporation of the former frontier lands into the sphere of the old, classical Islamic civilization, and the decay and disappearance of Byzantium itself. Thereafter the general adoption of traditional Islamic institutions, attitudes, and conceptions served to reduce and to neutralize any influences emanating from the conquered House of War.

It is often overlooked that Western influence on the Turks is in a sense almost as old as that of Byzantium. Constantinople, two

---

artifices & machines de guerre, comme à faire artillerie, hardquebuses, pouldres à canon, boulets & autres armes. Semblablement y ont dressé Imprimerie, non iamais au parauant veue en ces Regions: par laquelle en beaux caracteres ilz mettent en lumiere plusieurs liures en diuerses langues, Grecque, Latine, Italienne, Espagnolle, & mesmement Hebraique, qui est la leur naturelle. Mais en Turc, ny en Arabe, ne leur est permis d'imprimer' (*Les Navigations, peregrinations et voyages, faicts en la Turquie*, Antwerp, 1576, p. 246). On the early history of printing in the Middle East, see L. Cheikho, 'Ta'rīkh Fann al-Ṭibāʻa,' in *Mashriq*, iii (1900), 78 ff., 174, &c.

[3] Abdülbâki Gölpınarlı, *Mevlânâ Celâleddin* (1952), pp. 254 ff.; cf. P. Burguière and R. Mantran, 'Quelques vers grecs du XIIIᵉ siècle en caractères arabes', *Byzantion*, xxii (1952), p. 75.

[4] See above, p. 6 and n. 7; also Babinger, *Mehmed der Eroberer* (1953), p. 502.

and a half centuries before its conquest by the Turks, had suffered a more shattering conquest by Western invaders, and both the city and many of the provinces had been subjected to Western European government and institutions. Late Byzantine feudalism, which helped to shape the Ottoman system of military fiefs, had itself been reshaped under the impact of the Frankish feudalism of the Latin Empire of Constantinople and its dependent and successor principalities. When the Ottomans conquered the Morea, most of it had been ruled for the previous two centuries by French barons, Catalan adventurers, or Florentine financiers; its law was the feudal *Assises de Romanie*, based on the *Assises de la Haute Cour de Jérusalem*, a purely Western system of feudal law elaborated by the Crusaders in Palestine and later imposed by them on other countries which they conquered.

Once established in their new Imperial role, the Ottoman Turks found many points of contact with the West. What the Byzantine Empire had once been to the medieval Caliphate, Western Europe now was to the Ottomans—a rival empire and a rival civilization, the seat of a rival religion which it was the sacred duty of the Islamic Empire to subjugate and convert. Just as the Ottomans had succeeded the Caliphs as the sovereigns of Islam, so the Kings of Frangistan had succeeded the Emperors of Constantinople as Lords of the House of War. And as Baghdad had borrowed Greek fire from Constantinople, Istanbul might borrow artillery from Europe.

But in the intervals of war there was peace, and commerce; European diplomats sat in Istanbul; European merchants and scholars travelled in the Ottoman realms. Many came to stay; renegades and adventurers seeking a career in the Ottoman service, refugees from political or religious persecution, seeking shelter under the Ottoman power. Such was the mass migration of Jews from Spain and Portugal in the late fifteenth and early sixteenth centuries, bringing with them printing, and some medical and technological knowledge.

It was chiefly in the arts of war that the Turks were ready to turn to Europe for instruction. There are some rather dubious references to the use of firearms by the Ottomans as early as the fourteenth century. Their use of siege artillery is well attested in the early fifteenth century, and by the middle of the century they were already using field-guns at the second battle of Kossovo

(1448). Hand-guns were introduced at about the same time, and before very long gunners, musketeers, bombardiers, and sappers begin to play a central role in the Ottoman armed forces.[5]

The Ottomans showed equal readiness in adopting European techniques of naval construction and warfare. In the fifteenth century Venice was their model in shipbuilding, and improvements made by Venetian shipyards in the design and construction of galleys were closely watched and imitated. In the same way, in the course of the seventeenth century the Barbary Corsairs were followed by their Turkish overlords in building and operating large, square-rigged sailing ships, mounting twenty guns and capable of making long voyages on the open seas.[6]

With European naval construction, they also acquired a working knowledge of European maps and navigation. During the sixteenth century many European charts and portulans fell into Turkish hands. Of the theory of cartography they knew little enough, but they were soon able to copy and to use European sailing charts, and to make coastal charts of their own. Piri Reis (d. *c.* 1550), the first noteworthy Ottoman cartographer, seems to have known Western languages and made use of Western maps and geographical books. Hacı Halifa (1608-57) was acquainted with the *Atlas Minor* of Mercator, which he translated into Turkish with the help of a French renegade in 1653-5. He incorporated data from this and from other standard European geographical works of the time, by Ortelius, Cluverius, and others, in his *Cihannüma*, or World-Mirror, for long the standard Ottoman geographical work. Another indication of Ottoman interest in Western geographical science at that time was the invitation issued by Murad IV (1623-40) to the Dutch Orientalist Golius to make a map of the Ottoman dominions. The invitation was not accepted.[7]

---

[5] On the Ottoman adoption of firearms and artillery see V. J. Parry, 'Bārūd', in *EI²*.

[6] On the Ottoman fleet see I. H. Uzunçarşılı, 'Bahriyya iii' in *EI²*, and the excellent survey by J. W. Zinkeisen in his *Geschichte des osmanischen Reiches in Europa*, iii (1855), 279 ff.

[7] Fr. Taeschner, 'Die geographische Literatur der Osmanen', *ZDMG*, n.s. 2, lxxvii (1923), 31–80; J. H. Kramers, 'Djughrafiya', in *EI¹*, suppl. For further appreciations of these and subsequent changes from special points of view see Mümtaz Turhan, *Kültür Değişmeleri* (1951) (social psychology), Ahmet Hamdi Tanpınar, *XIX Asır Türk Edebiyatı Tarihi*, i (1956) (literature and ideas); and Enver Ziya Karal, 'Tanzimattan evvel garplılaşma hareketleri', in Turkey, Min. of Ed., *Tanzimat* (1940), pp. 13–30. In this article Professor Karal gives a general survey of movements of Westernization before the *Tanzimat*.

The First Attempts at Westernization [8]

The first deliberate attempt at a Westernizing policy—the first conscious step, that is, towards the imitation and adoption of certain selected elements from the civilization of Western Europe —came in the early eighteenth century. The treaties of Carlowitz (1699) and Passarowitz (1718) had given formal expression and recognition to two humiliating defeats of the Ottoman Empire by the Austrian and Russian Empires. On the other hand the example of Russia under Peter the Great suggested that a vigorous programme of Westernization and modernization might enable the Empire to throw off its weakness and once again become the terror of its enemies.

A Turkish document, written about the time of the treaty of Passarowitz, contains an imaginary conversation between a Christian and an Ottoman officer, in which they discuss the military and political situation. The purpose of the document appears to have been to prepare Ottoman ruling circles to accept defeat, by depicting as darkly as possible the unfavourable situation of the Empire. The conversation also, however, makes a comparison between the two armies, to the great disadvantage of the Ottomans, and would appear to embody a plea for military reform. [9]

The statesman chiefly responsible for the first attempt at reform was Damad Ibrahim Paşa, who became deputy Grand Vezir in 1716 and was Grand Vezir from 1718 to 1730. As soon as peace was restored he sent an Embassy to Vienna, in 1719, and in 1721 sent Yirmisekiz Mehmed Said Efendi as ambassador to Paris, with instructions to 'make a thorough study of the means of civilization and education, and report on those capable of

[8] Information on these projects, from Turkish sources, will be found in the standard history of the Ottoman Empire by J. von Hammer-Purgstall, *Geschichte des Osmanischen Reiches* (1st ed. 1827–35, 2nd ed. 1835–40; French trans., *Histoire de l'Empire ottoman*, 1835–43). This may be supplemented by the later histories, written from European sources only, of Zinkeisen, and N. Jorga, *Geschichte des osmanischen Reiches* (1908–13). A useful outline will be found in C. von Sax, *Geschichte des Machtverfalls der Türkei* (1913). On the penetration of Western scientific knowledge to Turkey, see the pioneer works of Adnan, *La Science chez les Turcs ottomans*, and the fuller treatment by the same author in Turkish, Adnan-Adıvar, *Osmanlı Türklerinde Ilim*.

[9] Faik Reşit Unat, ed., 'Ahmet III devrine ait bir islâhat takriri', *Tar. Ves.*, i (1941), 107–21.

application' in Turkey.[10] One of these, as we shall see, was print-ing. As early as 1716 a French officer, de Rochefort, submitted a project for the formation of a corps of foreign engineer officers in the Ottoman army, which, however, came to nothing.[11] In 1720 another Frenchman, the convert David known as Gerçek, organized a fire brigade in Istanbul—the first of the long series of reforms in municipal services that were to follow in the nineteenth and twentieth centuries.[12] In the admiralty and navy too the new mood was felt. The admiralty offices were reorganized, and an important change made in ship construction. The three-decker galleon was first built in Turkish dockyards in 1682, but few were made. Under Ahmed III the construction of these ships was resumed and improved, and the galley began to disappear from the Ottoman fleets.[13]

These exchanges with Europe began to produce, for the first time, some slight impact on cultural and social life. The wave of *Turquerie* started by the Turkish Embassy in Paris in 1721 had its counterpart in a rather smaller wave of Frankish manners and styles in Istanbul. French gardens, French decorations, French furniture acquired a brief vogue in palace circles. The Sultan him-self built a fountain outside the palace gates which shows a distinctly rococo style.[14] The Flemish painter van Mour (1671–1737) enjoyed some success in the Turkish capital, where he painted the portraits of the Sultan, the Grand Vezir, and other dignitaries.[15]

Towards the end of Ahmed III's reign the unwonted interval of peace which the Empire had enjoyed after the treaty of Passarowitz was disturbed by the outbreak of war on the eastern frontier, against Persia. In 1730 an Ottoman defeat at the hands of Nadir Khan, who had just risen to power in Persia, touched off a popular revolt in Istanbul, where resentment had been growing

---

[10] Cited by Karal, in *Tanzimat*, p. 19; Mehmed Said Efendi's report on his embassy (*Sefâretnâme*) was several times printed in Istanbul, and appeared in a French transla-tion by J. C. Galland (*Relation de l'Ambassade de Mehémet Effendi . . .*) in Constantinople and Paris in 1757.

[11] Hammer, 2nd ed., iv. 397.

[12] Osman Nuri [Ergin], *Mecelle-i Umur-i Belediye*, i (1922), 1170 ff. cf. below, pp. 387 ff.

[13] I. H. Uzunçarşılı, *Osmanlı Devletinin Merkez ve Bahriye Teşkilâtı* (1948), pp. 465 ff.

[14] On Turkish taste and fashions in this period see Ahmet Refik, *Lâle Devri* (1932). Passages from this book were published in French translation in E. Saussey, *Prosateurs turcs contemporains* (1935).

[15] A. Boppe, *Les Peintres du Bosphore au dix-huitième siècle* (1911).

against the extravagance of the court and the 'Frankish manners' of the palace circles. The Sultan was forced to abdicate, and the Grand Vezir and other dignitaries were put to death.[16]

The setback was only temporary. The most important Western innovations of the preceding reign—printing and naval reforms—were maintained, and soon a new start was made on the larger and more pressing problem of military reform. Already before the revolt Ibrahim Müteferrika, the director of the printing press, had presented a memorandum to Ibrahim Paşa; at the beginning of 1732 he printed it, and presented it to the new Sultan Mahmud I (1730–54). The memorandum, forty-nine pages long, is divided into three parts. In the first the author points out the importance, to all states and peoples, of a well-ordered system of government, and describes and comments on the various kinds of régime existing in other countries. In the second, he urges on his reader the importance of scientific geography, as a means of knowing one's own lands and those of one's neighbours, as a useful adjunct to the military art, and as an aid to provincial and military administration; in the third, he examines the different kinds of armed forces maintained by the kings of Christendom, their training, organization, and discipline, in camp and in the field, their methods of waging war, and their military laws. Ibrahim, himself a convert, was careful to speak with proper disgust and contempt of the Frankish infidels, but at the same time makes clear the superiority of the Frankish armies, and the importance for the Ottomans of imitating them.[17]

Another convert was conveniently at hand to help in taking the first steps. The Count de Bonneval, a French nobleman, had, after a somewhat chequered career, arrived in Turkey in 1729. Apparently to avoid being extradited, he adopted Islam, took the name Ahmed, and entered the Ottoman service. In September 1731 he was summoned by the Grand Vezir Topal Osman Paşa, who gave him the task of reforming the Bombardier Corps on European lines. In 1734 a new training centre, the *Hendesehane*, or school of geometry, was opened in Üsküdar, and in the following

---

[16] On these events see Münir Aktepe, *Patrona Isyanı* (Ist., 1958); M. L. Shay, *The Ottoman Empire from 1720 to 1734* (Urbana, 1944).

[17] *Usūl al-Hikām fī Nizām al-Umam* (1144 A.H.). For discussions of this book see G. Toderini, *Letteratura turchesca* (1787), iii. 97–108; Babinger, *Stambuler Buchwesen im 18 Jahrhundert* (1919), p. 15; Niyazi Berkes, 'Historical Background of Turkish Secularism' in R. N. Frye, ed. *Islam and the West* (1957), p. 51.

year de Bonneval was made a pasha of two tails and given the rank and title of Chief Bombardier.[18]

This school, and the 'corps of mathematicians' established under the command of de Bonneval's adopted son Süleyman, were not of long duration. The Janissaries were of course bitterly opposed to any such new-fangled notions, and despite an apparent attempt to keep the project secret from them, they found out about the school and forced its closure.[19]

The effort was not, however, entirely wasted. One of the teachers of the school, a certain Mehmed Said, the son of a Mufti from Anatolia, invented a 'two-arc quadrant' for the use of artillerymen and wrote a treatise illustrated with geometrical diagrams. Other writings of the time include a treatise on trigonometry, apparently based in part on Western sources, an anonymous Turkish translation of a treatise on military science by Count Montecuccoli, some medical works, and a few writings on European history and affairs.[20] Some interest in Westernization was also shown by the Grand Vezir Rağıb Paşa, an admirer of European science who is credited with having desired the translation into Turkish of a treatise of Voltaire on the philosophy of Newton.[21] It is reported by some sources that in 1759 he reopened the school of geometry, which functioned secretly in a private house at Karaagaç, near Sütlüce.[22]

A more serious effort began in 1773, with the opening of a new school of mathematics for the navy. In this and related projects the Turks were helped by the Baron de Tott, an artillery officer of French nationality and Hungarian origin, who had come to Turkey some years previously to study Turkish. He helped to form and train new corps of engineers and artillery, reorganized the gun-foundry, and for the first year or two taught rectilinear

---

[18] Tayyarzade Ata, *Tarih-i Ata* (1291–3 A.H.), i. 158. On Bonneval see H. Bowen, 'Ahmed Pasha Bonneval', in *EI²*; Mehmed Arif, 'Humbaracı-başı Ahmed Paşa Bonneval', *TOEM*, pts. 18–20; Osman Ergin, *Türkiye Maarif Tarihi* (1939 ff.), i. 44 ff.

[19] On the role and position of the Janissaries at this time see Gibb and Bowen, I/1. 56 ff.

[20] Adnan, *Science*, pp. 142 ff.   [21] Toderini, i. 130.

[22] Ergin, *Maarif*, i. 50; Adnan, *Ilim*, pp. 182–3. Another Turk who showed an interest in the West at this time was the diplomat Ahmed Resmi Efendi (1700–83), who went on embassies to Vienna in 1757, and to Berlin in 1763. Beside accounts of his embassies, he wrote an analysis of the causes of Turkey's defeat in the war of 1769–74, in which he urged the need for reform and reorganization. On him see Babinger, *Geschichtsschreiber*, pp. 309–12.

trigonometry and other subjects at the school of mathematics In these tasks he was assisted by some other foreigners, notably a Scottish renegade called Campbell, who after his conversion to Islam was known by the doubly incongruous name of Ingiliz Mustafa. It was he who replaced de Tott as chief instructor after the latter's return to France in 1775.

The nucleus of the student body was provided by the surviving pupils of the earlier schools, who were transferred to the new centre, as well as of serving naval officers. De Tott in his memoirs speaks of his 'white-bearded captains' and of 'sixty-year-old pupils'. In the following years the naval school of mathematics was expanded and developed, and provided the model for the military engineering, medical, and other schools set up by Selim III and his successors. We have a description of it by the Venetian priest Toderini, who was in Istanbul between 1781 and 1786. He found it well equipped with European maps and appliances, and with a library of European books, some with Turkish translations. There were over fifty pupils, sons of captains and Turkish gentlemen.[23]

The Russian annexation of the Crimea in 1783 gave the impetus to a new programme of reform, in which the Ottoman government was encouraged by the French, who were apprehensive of a possible Russian threat to their interests in the Levant. In October 1784, at the initiative of the Grand Vezir Halil Hamid Paşa and with the assistance of the French Embassy, a new training course was instituted, with two French engineer officers as instructors, working with Armenian interpreters.[24] After the outbreak of war with Austria and Russia in 1787 the French instructors were recalled, as their continued presence was regarded as a breach of

---

[23] On the history of the navy school see Ergin, *Maarif*, ii. 264 ff.; Mehmed Esad, *Mirât-i Mühendishane* (1312 A.H.), and the contemporary accounts of Toderini (i. 177 ff.) and de Tott, *Mémoires* (1785), *passim*.

[24] On the Turkish reactions to the Russian annexation of the Crimea, see Mustafa Nuri Paşa, *Netaic ül-Vukuat*, iv (1327 A.H.), 97: 'There [in Hungary] the Muslims had lived only in the towns and had had the character of visitors, while the mass of the population was Christian; Crimea, on the other hand, had a Muslim population of close on two million. Its loss therefore naturally affected the people of Islam far more, and its liberation became a prime objective.'

On the military reforms of the 1780's see Ahmed Cevdet Paşa, *Tarih* (1301–9 A.H.), iii-iv, *passim*; Nuri, *Netaic*, iv. 4 ff.; Uzuncarşılı, 'Sadrazam Halil Hamit Paşa', *TM*, v (1936), 213–67; Boppe, 'La France et le "militaire turc" au XVIIIe siècle', *Feuilles d'Hist.* (1912), pp. 386–402 and 490–501. See further Adnan, *Science*, p. 155 and *Ilim*, pp. 183–5.

E

neutrality. This, and the strains of the war itself, hampered the development of the new schools, which remained inactive until the restoration of peace in 1792 gave the new Sultan, Selim III, the opportunity to make a new start.

Non-Military Innovations

The most important technical innovation from Europe outside the military field was undoubtedly printing. In a sense this had been known to the Turks for centuries. In the fourteenth century the Mongol rulers of Persia had printed and issued paper money, in obvious imitation of Chinese models, and it is not impossible that the Turkic peoples of the Chinese borderlands had encountered some form of block-printing, common in the Far East. But all this had long since been forgotten, and the Ottoman Turks, like other Middle Eastern Muslim peoples, had no knowledge of book printing until it was introduced from Europe. This happened at the end of the fifteenth century, when Jewish refugees from Spain set up printing presses on Ottoman soil. The first Jewish press was established in Constantinople about 1493 or 1494, and others followed in various cities, notably in Salonika, which became the main Jewish publishing centre.

The Jews were followed by the other religious minorities. In 1567 an Armenian press was established in Constantinople by Apkar of Sivas, a priest who had studied typography in Venice, and a Greek press in 1627 by Nicodemus Metaxas, with machinery and type imported from England.

The ban on printing in Turkish or Arabic[25] remained effective until the early eighteenth century, when its relaxation was due largely to the efforts of two men. One of them was Said Çelebi, son of the famous Yirmisekiz Mehmed Said, who had gone to Paris as Turkish ambassador in 1721. Said Çelebi had accompanied his father on his journey, and during his stay in France seems to have acquired an interest in the art of printing and a conviction of its usefulness. On his return to Turkey he attempted to secure the support of the Grand Vezir for the setting up of a Turkish printing press in Constantinople. In this, despite the opposition of religious conservatives and the strong vested interest of the scribes and calligraphers, he was successful.

He found a kindred spirit in Ibrahim Müteferrika, the true

[25] See above, p. 41.

founder and director of the first Turkish printing press. Ibrahim was of Hungarian origin, born in Kolosvar in 1674, and destined for the Calvinist ministry. In 1693 he became a Turkish prisoner of war, and was sold as a slave in Constantinople. He became a convert to Islam, and made a career in the Ottoman service. In collaboration with Said Çelebi, he drafted a memorandum on the usefulness of printing, which was submitted to the Grand Vezir. Support came from an unexpected quarter when the *Şeyh-ül-Islâm* Abdullah Efendi was persuaded to issue a *fetva* authorizing the printing of books in Turkish on subjects other than religion. The printing of the Koran, of books on Koranic exegesis, traditions, theology, and holy law was excluded as unthinkable. Finally, on 5 July 1727, an Imperial ferman was issued giving permission for the establishment of a Turkish press and the printing of Turkish books 'in the high, God-guarded city of Constantinople'.

Presses and types were at first obtained from the local Jewish and Christian printers already working in the city, and recourse was also made to Jewish type-founders and compositors. Later, presses and types were imported from Europe, especially from Leiden and Paris. Some specialists in different aspects of typography were also brought from Germany and other European countries.

The first book appeared in February 1729. By the time the press was closed in 1742, seventeen books had been printed. Most of them were in Turkish, and dealt with history, geography, and language. They included, however, a Turkish grammar in French, an account by Mehmed Said Çelebi of his Embassy in France in 1721, and a short treatise by Ibrahim Müteferrika himself on the science of tactics as practised by the European states. The press was reopened in 1784, since when the development of printing in Turkey proceeded rapidly.[26]

Turning from gunnery and typography to knowledge and ideas, we find far fewer traces of Western influence, for it is here that

[26] On the early development of printing in Turkey see Babinger, *Stambuler Buchwesen*, and Selim Nüzhet Gerçek, *Türk Matbaacılığı*, I: *Müteferrika Matbaası* (1939). The first book published from the Müteferrika press, the dictionary of Vankuli, appeared in Rejeb 1141, corresponding to February 1729. The first volume opens with an introduction by the editor, followed by the full texts of the fermans authorizing the establishment of the press, the *fetva* of the *Şeyh-ül-Islâm* declaring printing licit, and certificates of approval from the two chief judges and other dignitaries. These in turn are followed by a treatise on the usefulness of printing.

the Muslim rejection of Christianity and all that came from it was most effective. Though clever with their hands in making useful devices like guns, clocks, and printing presses, the Europeans were still benighted and barbarous infidels, whose history, philosophy, science, and literature, if indeed they existed at all, could hold nothing of value for the people of the universal Islamic Empire. During the reign of Mehmed II there was indeed the beginning of a scientific renaissance, but under his successors, in the words of a modern Turkish writer, 'the scientific current broke against the dikes of literature and jurisprudence'.[27]

In these dikes there were, however, a few small leaks, through which some knowledge of the West percolated into the circles of Muslim scholarship. Among the many thousands of historical manuscripts of the sixteenth and seventeenth centuries found in the libraries of Istanbul, none deal with Christian Europe, for the Muslim, like other civilizations before and after it, equated universal history with its own. But there are a few signs of interest. Ottoman chroniclers occasionally report events in darkest Frangistan, and one of them, Ibrahim Peçevi (1574–c.1650), even went so far as to use, through a translator, Hungarian Latin chronicles for his history of the Turkish campaigns in Hungary. Hacı Halifa, whose interest in European maps has already been mentioned, is also credited with having prepared, probably in collaboration with a Frankish colleague, a history of the Franks, and Hüseyin Hezrafenn, whose observations on the state of the Empire have already been cited, sought out the company of such European visitors to Istanbul as Galland, Marsigli, and Prince Kantemir, and made a study of European history. A little later Ahmed ibn Lûtfullah, known as Müneccimbaşı (d. 1702), wrote a universal history which includes a brief account of the principal monarchies of Europe—the second, it would seem, in Islamic historiography.[28] In the course of the eighteenth century, no doubt in connexion with the military training schools, a small number of books on European affairs were prepared or translated.

The occasional Ottoman interest in European geography has already been mentioned. In addition there was some slight interest in European medicine. In the seventeenth century a

[27] Adnan, *Science*, p. 57.

[28] On all these see B. Lewis, 'The Use by Muslim Historians of Non-Muslim Sources', in B. Lewis and P. M. Holt, eds. *Historians of the Middle East* (in the press).

Turkish translation appeared of a European treatise on syphilis, and one or two passages in other medical works suggest an acquaintance with European writings.[29] In general, however, Ottoman medicine remained faithful to Galen and Avicenna, as Ottoman science to Aristotle, Ptolemy, and their commentators. The discoveries of Paracelsus and Copernicus, Kepler and Galileo were as alien and irrelevant to the Ottomans as were the arguments of Luther and Calvin.

Of the aesthetic life of the West little or nothing was known in Turkey. Of Western art there was some slight influence; several of the Sultans called on the services of Western portrait painters, and Western influences undoubtedly affected Turkish architecture and decoration in the early eighteenth century. Of Western literature and music practically nothing was known. The great Western movements of ideas passed without even an echo in the lands of Islam.[30]

The Ideas of the French Revolution [31]

With the French Revolution, for the first time, we find a great movement of ideas penetrating the barrier that separated the House of War from the House of Islam, finding a ready welcome among Muslim leaders and thinkers, and affecting to a greater or lesser degree every layer of Muslim society.

The success of Western ideas in the Islamic world in the nineteenth century is often attributed to the advance of the material might of the West—to the establishment of European economic, political, and eventually, military supremacy in much of the Islamic world. The Muslim, no less than other men, is inclined to listen with greater sympathy and respect to the beliefs of those whom God has favoured with power and wealth in *this* world, and the visible success of the West was certainly a contributory factor, if not indeed a prerequisite, in making Western ideas acceptable

[29] Adnan, *Science*, p. 98.

[30] One solitary exception to the general lack of interest in Western literature may be mentioned. Ali Aziz Efendi, an eighteenth-century diplomat and man of letters, was appointed ambassador to Berlin, where he died in 1798. He knew French and some German, and adapted some tales from French into Turkish. They were not entirely alien, being taken from Pétis de la Croix's Oriental collection, *Les Mille et un Jours* (Paris, 1710–12). See A. Tietze, 'Aziz Efendis Muhayyelat', *Oriens*, i (1948), 248–329 and 'Ali Aziz', in *EI²*.

[31] A more extensive treatment of this subject will be found in B. Lewis 'The Impact of the French Revolution on Turkey', *J. Wld. Hist.*, i (1953), 105–25.

to him. But this is not a sufficient explanation. The age of the Renaissance and the Discoveries saw great Christian advances in the western Mediterranean and in Asia, which, if to some extent offset by the still formidable power of the Ottomans, might nevertheless have produced some effect on the Muslims of the invaded areas, had might alone been sufficient to impel acceptance. Nor do European wealth and power explain why the ideas of the French Revolution, rather than any other of the competing Western modes of thought, should have won such wide acceptance. The initial attraction of these ideas—which were later modified to respond to the political needs of the time and place—is rather to be found in their secularism. The French Revolution is the first great social upheaval in Europe to find intellectual expression in purely non-religious terms. Secularism as such has no great attraction for Muslims, but in a Western movement that was non-Christian, even anti-Christian, and whose divorce from Christianity was stressed by its leading exponents, the Muslim world might hope to find the elusive secret of Western power without compromising its own religious beliefs and traditions.

During the century or so that followed the first percolation of these new ideas from Europe, the channels of transmission became broader and more numerous, the trickle grew to a river and then to a flood. While Western material culture transformed the structure and aspect of Islamic society, often for the worse, ideas from the West were affecting the very basis of group cohesion, creating new patterns of identity and loyalty, and providing both the objectives and the formulation of new aspirations. These new ideas may be summarized in three words: liberty, equality, and—not fraternity, but what is perhaps its converse, nationality.

Before 1800 the word liberty in the languages of Islam was primarily a legal term, denoting the opposite of slavery. In the course of the nineteenth century it acquired a new political connotation from Europe, and came to be the war-cry of the struggle against both domestic despotism and foreign imperialism. Organized liberty required constitutions, representative government, the rule of law—and these in turn involved secular authority and legislation, with a new class of lawyers and politicians, different from the Doctors of the Holy Law and the agents of autocratic rule of former times.

Equality tended to take on a different meaning. Social and

economic inequality were not major grievances. Islamic society did not know the rigid social barriers and caste privileges of pre-revolutionary Europe; its undeveloped economy limited the opportunities both of acquiring and of spending wealth, and thus prevented the growth of glaring disparities between rich and poor. To some extent the gulf between the two was still bridged by the corporative structure of society and the moral and charitable traditions of Islam. But if appeals to the individual had little effect, appeals to the group struck a more responsive chord. Soon the demand was raised for equality between nations, in time linked with the new Western principle of national self-determination.

The Western concept of the nation as a linguistic, racial, and territorial entity was not unknown to the Islamic Orient, but was never the primary basis of group identity. This was the brotherhood of faith within the religious community, reinforced by common dynastic allegiance. To this day the Western notions of patriotism and nationality have never entirely superseded the older pattern—indeed, though dynastic loyalties have faded, religious loyalty is in our own day showing renascent vigour. The history of the reform movements in the nineteenth and early twentieth centuries is largely concerned with the attempt by Western-educated intellectuals to impose a Western pattern of secular political classification and organization on the religious community of Islam.

The crucial period in the transmission of the ideas of the French Revolution to the Muslim Turks was the years 1792–1807, beginning with the military reforms of Selim III and ending with his deposition. During these years, while the Revolution itself was still in progress, the first vital penetration of ideas took place, opening the way to the great flood which, in the course of the last century and a half, has transformed the outlook, thought, and self-awareness not only of Turkey but of all Islam. It is therefore necessary to give close attention first to the channels through which these ideas were transmitted from France to Turkey, second to the immediate response to these ideas of the Turks of that time.

The Channels of Transmission

By far the most important of these was military instruction. From Renaissance times onwards Islam had been the pupil of

Christendom in the arts of war, especially in the more technical branches such as engineering, navigation, and artillery. For some time the imposing military façade of the Ottoman Empire masked the growing internal decline in skill and inventiveness, which found expression in the prominence of Western renegades or employees among the gun-founders and gunners of the Ottoman armies and the shipwrights and navigators of the Ottoman fleets. By the eighteenth century the rulers of the Empire, stimulated by a series of defeats at the hands of their despised Christian adversaries, began to give intermittent attention to the need for modernizing the equipment and training of their armies.

The restoration of peace in 1792, and the preoccupation of Europe with the problems of the French Revolution, gave the new Sultan Selim III the opportunity to plan and in part execute a large-scale reform of the Ottoman armed forces, intended to bring them up to the level of contemporary Western armies in technical equipment, training, and skill.

Such attempts at reform as had been made during the eighteenth century had all been under the guidance of French instructors, usually working in the French language. The latest was that of 1784, while Selim was still heir-apparent.[32] In this project both the initial impulse and the main guidance came from the government of France, and Selim himself had entered into correspondence with Louis XVI, who had given him good if somewhat patronizing advice.[33] Such nuclei of trained officers as were available in Istanbul had been taught by French teachers and with French textbooks. The only treatises available in Turkish were translations from French, printed at the press of the French Embassy—the best equipped press in the city.[34] What little knowledge of European languages the Turks possessed was of French.

It was therefore natural that the Sultan should turn once again to France for help in preparing his New Order—*Nizam-i Cedid*—in the armed forces. There was an additional reason for him to do

[32] See above, p. 49.

[33] Uzunçarşılı, 'Selim III' ün Veliaht iken Fransa Kralı Lüi XVI ile muhabereleri', *Bell.*, no. 5–6 (1938), 191–246; Tahsin Öz, 'Fransa Kıralı Louis XVI ci'nin Selim III' e Namesi', *Tar. Ves.*, i/3 (1941), 198–202 (with the French text of a letter from Louis XVI to Selim III); cf. Karal, *Selim III' ün Hat-ti Hümayunları; Nizam-i Cedit* (1946), pp. 11 ff.

[34] On the French Embassy press in Constantinople see Babinger, *Stambuler Buchwesen*, pp. 27–28, and Gerçek, *Türk Matbaacılığı*, pp. 99 ff. In the latter work reproductions will be found of the title-pages of these translations.

so. In an exchange of notes written on the eve of the launching of the military reforms, the Grand Vezir reported to the Sultan the arrival of letters from the King of France on the New Order— *Nizam-i Cedid*—that had arisen in France as a result of the recent upheaval, and the Sultan expressed interest in this New Order.[35] It is not without significance that in these notes the same term is applied to the 'New Order' in France as was shortly afterwards applied to the whole programme of reform in Turkey.

At the same time Selim sent a special envoy, Ebu Bekir Ratib Efendi, to make direct inquiries in Europe. Ratib Efendi went to Vienna in 1791, with instructions to study Austrian conditions and also to gather information on other European countries. On his return in May 1792, he presented a detailed report on the military systems of the European states, and especially of Austria, as well as on government, society, and political thought. One of his informants in Vienna seems to have been the Austrian apprentice dragoman Joseph Hammer, later famous as the author of the *Geschichte des osmanischen Reiches* and other standard works on Turkey.[36]

In the autumn of 1791, while the returning Ottoman army was still at Silistria, the Sultan issued a command to twenty-two civil, military, and religious dignitaries requesting them to set forth their views on the causes of the weakness of the Empire, and their proposals for its reform. The twenty-two included two Christians, a French officer called Bertrand or Brentano, serving with the Ottoman army, and the famous Mouradgea d'Ohsson, the Armenian dragoman of the Swedish Embassy in Istanbul. They presented their replies in the form of *Lâyiha*—memorials, perhaps an echo of the French *cahiers* of 1789. Whether intentional or not, the resemblance was a portentous one.[37]

All agreed in laying the main stress on the need for military reform, but differed as to how best to accomplish it. On the one

[35] Karal, *Selim III*, p. 30.

[36] Ratib Efendi's report, of some 500 pages, deals with military and administrative institutions in Austria and elsewhere, and quotes the views of European political philosophers on the need for a disciplined army, orderly finances, loyal and competent statesmen, and a prosperous population (ibid. pp. 31 ff.; cf. Cevdet, *Tarih*, vi. 19 ff.; Von Hammer-Purgstall, *Erinnerungen aus meinem Leben* (Vienna, 1940), 25–27; idem, *Geschichte der osmanischen Dichtkunst* iv (Pest, 1838), 418 ff., and Babinger, *Geschichtsschreiber*, p. 330). Ratib was *Reis-ül-Küttab* from 1794 to 1796, and was executed in 1799.

[37] Cevdet, *Tarih*, vi. 5 ff.; Ahmed Asım, *Asım Tarihi* (n.d.), i. 34; Karal, *Selim III*, pp. 34 ff. and 'Nizam-i Cedide dair Lâyihalar', *Tar. Ves.*, i (1942), 414–25; ii (1942–3), 104–11, 342–51, 424–32; Berkes, in Frye, pp. 56–58.

hand were the conservatives, who sought to recover the military glories of the Ottoman golden age by reverting to its military methods. Then there were the romantics and compromisers, who sought various ways of insinuating Frankish training and weapons into the existing military order by claiming that this was in fact a return to the pure Ottoman past. Finally there were the radicals, who believed that the old army was incapable of reform, and urged the Sultan to set up a new one, trained, equipped, and armed from the start along European lines. It was to this view that the Sultan himself inclined.

From the first these proposals for reform aroused the bitterest opposition, and the reformist memorials were attacked with spite and ridicule even in the palace. But the Sultan proceeded with resolution and energy. Setting up a small committee of reform supporters to assist him, he promulgated, in 1792 and 1793, a whole series of new instructions and regulations which came to be known collectively as the *Nizam-i Cedid*. They included new regulations on provincial governorships, on provincial taxation, on the control of the grain trade, and other administrative and fiscal matters. By far the most important, however, were those providing for a new corps of regular infantry, trained and equipped on European lines. To finance this experiment, a special new treasury was set up, with revenues from escheated and forfeited fiefs and from newly imposed taxes on spirits, tobacco, coffee, and other commodities. It is both interesting and significant that the term *Nizam-i Cedid*, originally applied to the regulations of the new system, came to be used almost exclusively of the new, regular troops established under it. Just as centuries earlier the Arabic abstract noun *sulṭān*, authority, had come to designate a man, so now did *Nizam-i Cedid*, new order, become the name of a body of men.[38]

A central place in Selim's projects was assigned to his new military and naval schools, which provided training in gunnery, fortification, navigation, and ancillary sciences. In these schools Selim relied, very heavily, on French help. French officers were

---

[38] On the financial arrangements see Cevdet, *Tarih*, v. 289 ff. (on the reorganization of the military fiefs), and vi. 61 ff.; Karal, *Selim III*, pp. 134 ff. On the military reforms see Cevdet, vi; Hammer, and Zinkeisen, v–viii *passim*, where further references are given. Turkish documents are published and analysed in: Ergin, *Maarif*, ii, *passim*; Karal, *Selim III*, pp. 43–94; Uzunçarşılı, *Merkez ve Bahriye*, pp. 507 ff. (on the navy), as well as numerous other Turkish works.

recruited as teachers and instructors, French was made a compulsory language for all students, and a library of some 400 European books acquired, most of them French, and including, significantly, a set of the *Grande Encyclopédie*.[39]

The change of régime in France in no way discouraged the Sultan from seeking French aid. In the autumn of 1793 the Ottoman government sent to Paris a list of officers and technicians whom it wished to recruit from France; as late as 1795 the *Reis-ül-Küttab*, Ratib Efendi, addressed a similar but longer list to the Committee of Public Safety.[40] In 1796 the French ambassador General Aubert Dubayet brought a whole body of French military experts to Constantinople with him.[41] French co-operation in the Ottoman military reform was interrupted by the Franco-Turkish war of 1798–1802, but was later resumed, and reached its peak with the mission to Turkey of General Sébastiani in 1806–7. Though the pure wine of revolution was by now diluted with Caesarism, this more familiar flavour, with the added spice of victory, can only have made it more palatable.

The result of all this was to create a new social element— a class of young army and naval officers, familiar with some aspects of Western civilization through study, reading, and personal contact, acquainted with at least one Western language —usually French[42]—and accustomed to look up to Western experts as their mentors and guides to new and better ways. These men could not, like most of their contemporaries, despise the infidel and barbarous West from an altitude of comfortable and unassailable ignorance—on the contrary, for reasons both of inclination and of interest they were aligned with the Westernizers against the reactionaries. But these neophytes of Western culture, filled with an often naïve enthusiasm for things Western,[43]

---

[39] A. de Juchereau de Saint-Denys, *Révolutions de Constantinople en 1807 et 1808*, i (1819), 76.

[40] See H. von Sybel, 'La Propagande révolutionnaire en 1793 et 1794', *R. hist.*, xi (1879), 107–8; A. Debidour, *Recueil des Actes du Directoire*, ii (1911), 630 ff.; Karal, 'Osmanlı Tarihine dair Vesikalar', *Bell.*, no. 14–15 (1940), 175 ff.

[41] Juchereau, i. 68 ff.; ii. 12 ff.

[42] Italian too was fairly well known, however, especially in commerce and in the navy. Many of the earlier European loanwords in Turkish are Italian in form.

[43] An example of the outlook of these people will be found in the *Diatribe de l'ingénieur sur l'état actuel de l'art militaire, du génie et des sciences à Constantinople*, printed in Scutari in 1803, and reprinted in Paris in 1810. The author, Seid Mustafa, was a graduate and later a teacher of engineering. He was killed in the reactionary rising of

soon found that the West had more to offer than mathematics and
ballistics, and that their knowledge of French enabled them to
read other things besides their textbooks. Some of these other
things were available to them in their own college library. We
may assume that others were brought to their notice by French
instructors who, after 1792, were chosen and appointed by the
government of the French Republic.[44]

During the same period, another of the reforms of Selim III
opened a second window to the West—that of diplomacy. Until
the end of the eighteenth century the Ottoman Empire maintained no permanent diplomatic representation in foreign
countries. From time to time a special mission was sent to one or
another foreign capital, for a specific purpose—but barely a score
of these are recorded in the whole period up to 1792. For its
normal dealings with foreign powers the Empire preferred to rely
on the foreign ambassadors resident in Constantinople. Even with
those, business was carried on chiefly through the intermediary of
local Christian dragomans. Very few even of the highest officials
of the state had any knowledge of a Western language or any
direct experience of Europe.[45] In earlier times a very important
role had been played by renegades, men of European birth and
education, who often rose to the highest positions in the Ottoman
service, and brought with them invaluable skills and knowledge.
These were, however, rarely transmitted, and in any case by the
eighteenth century ex-Christians had ceased to play any significant role in the councils of state, which were now more and more
monopolized by the Muslim Turks.

It was no doubt with the intention of securing more direct and
reliable information on European countries and affairs, as well as
bringing Turkey into line with the normal practice of Western
states, that in 1792 Selim III resolved to establish regular and

1807–8 (see Adnan, *Science*, pp. 156–7). Mustafa describes his early enthusiasm for
European science, and remarks: 'aussi je me suis formé l'idée de m'en rapprocher; et
sans perdre de temps je m'appliquai à l'étude de la langue française, comme la plus
universelle, et capable de me faire parvenir à la connoissance des auteurs qui ont
écrit sur les belles sciences' (*Diatribe*, Paris ed., pp. 16–17).

[44] cf. the chronicle of Asım Efendi, quoted below, p. 71.

[45] In 1770, when a Russian fleet under Admiral Spiridov sailed round western
Europe into the Mediterranean and attacked the Turks in the Aegean, the Porte,
apparently still using medieval maps, protested to Venice against their permitting the
Russians to sail from the Baltic into the Adriatic. See Kramers, 'Djughrāfiya', in *EI*[1],
suppl.

permanent Ottoman Embassies in the major European capitals.
The first was in London in 1793, followed by Vienna (1794),
Berlin (1795), and later Paris, where in 1796 Seyyid Ali Efendi
arrived as the first Ottoman ambassador to the French Republic.[46]
Among other duties, these ambassadors were instructed to study
the institutions of the countries to which they were accredited, and
to acquire 'languages, knowledge, and sciences useful to servants
of the Empire'.[47] Most of these first diplomats were Ottoman
palace or chancery officials of the old school, ignorant of Western
languages and conservative in outlook. Most of them, to judge by
their dispatches, learned little about the countries to which they
were sent, and were not greatly impressed by what they did
learn.[48] But they did not travel alone. Besides the inevitable Greek
dragomans, they took with them young Turkish secretaries, whose
duty it was to study the languages of Europe—and especially
French—and to learn something of the ways of Western society.

These missions thus gave an opportunity to a number of young
men to reside for a while in a European city, master a European
language, and make the acquaintance of some of the revolutionary ideas current among their European contemporaries.
Some of them, on their return, became officials at the Porte,
where they formed a Westward-looking minority among the
bureaucratic hierarchy similar to that created among the officers
by the military and naval reforms.

So far we have spoken only of Muslims—but there were of course
other elements in the Empire, Christian and also Jewish. The
Jews seem to have been surprisingly little affected by Western
influences in this period, and with one or two exceptions played
no significant role. The Christians on the other hand—especially
the Greek and Armenian *élite* of the capital—had for long been on

---

[46] His general report on his mission was published by Ahmed Refik in *TOEM*, iv
(1329/1911), 1246 ff., 1332 ff., 1378 ff., 1458 ff., 1548 ff. A selection of his dispatches
was edited by Karal in *Fransa-Mısır ve Osmanlı Imparatorluğu, 1797–1802* (1940).
The choice of London for the first resident Embassy is explained in Cevdet, *Tarih*,
vi. 257–60. (cf. Uzunçarşılı, 'Ondokuzuncu Asır başlarına kadar Türk-Ingiliz
Münasebatına dair Vesikalar', *Bell.*, no. 51 (1949), 581 ff., and Karal, *Fransa-Mısır*,
pp. 169 ff.

[47] Karal, *Selim III*, p. 79.

[48] On these embassies see Zinkeisen, vii. 55; Cevdet, *Tarih*, vi. 88 ff.; 231 ff.; and
257 ff.; Karal, *Selim III*, pp. 163 ff.; Babinger, *Geschichtsschreiber*, pp. 331–2, where a
bibliography of published documents is given. Many of the dispatches and reports of
these ambassadors have since been published and examined by Karal, Uzunçarşılı,
and other Turkish scholars.

terms of familiarity with the West, and thanks to their monopoly of the knowledge of Western languages had managed to gain an important position in the Ottoman state and economy. In the late seventeenth century the Phanariot Greeks gradually ousted the renegades and Levantines who had hitherto served as interpreters in dealings with foreign embassies. The Greeks, and to a lesser extent the Armenians, were familiar enough with Western culture—many of the wealthier families had for long been in the habit of sending their sons to be educated in Italian universities, especially in Padua. They were thus prepared, both linguistically and intellectually, to receive the new Western ideas of their time.

On the whole, however, the influence of the ideas of the Revolution on the Christians of Constantinople was not considerable. The churches of course used their authority against it; the wealthy and conservative Greek aristocracy too, recognizing the danger to the existing Ottoman order, preferred at first to preserve a régime in which they had so considerable an interest. Some converts to French ideas were found, however, among the Christians, more especially when the French began to address themselves directly to Greek and other national aspirations. Some Ottoman Christians—as for example Mouradgea d'Ohsson —may have played some small part in influencing Ottoman policy towards the French Republic; later they certainly played a vital role in bringing the ideas of the Revolution, with explosive effect, to the peoples of the Balkans. But their role in bringing Western ideas to the Muslim Turks is small and indirect, and is in the main limited to their functions as interpreters, language teachers, and translators. As Christians and as subject peoples they were doubly discredited, and unlikely to gain much of a hearing for any new ideas they might attempt to convey— the more so since their own secular and religious leaders were opposed to them. If anything, the minorities acted as a cushion— absorbing the impact of regular Western commercial and diplomatic activities in Turkey, and thus protecting the Turks from direct contact and contamination. What they did do, however, was to provide a nucleus of people familiar, on the one hand, with Turkish, on the other, with French or Italian, and thus able, when required, to translate Western books, to act as interpreters for Western instructors, and to teach Western languages to aspiring Turks.

If the channels through which the ideas of the Revolution might flow into Turkey existed, their use was not left to chance, but was the subject of sustained efforts by the French. Partly out of general missionary enthusiasm, partly in order to secure the support of the still not negligible Ottoman power at a critical time, the French devoted much attention to winning sympathy in the Ottoman capital and provinces. From the first an important section of the French community in Constantinople adhered to the Revolution, and aroused the ire of the Austrian and Prussian embassies by the wearing of revolutionary emblems and the holding of revolutionary meetings.[49] In June 1793 citizen Descorches (*ci-devant* Marquis de Sainte-Croix) arrived in Istanbul as emissary of the French Republic, with the double mission of winning Ottoman support for French policy and Ottoman sympathy for the French Revolution. The 14th July was made the occasion of a public celebration, culminating in a salute from two French ships moored off Seraglio Point. They flew the colours of the Ottoman Empire, of the French and American republics, 'and those of a few other powers that had not sullied their arms in the impious league of tyrants'.[50] In a solemn ceremony a tree of liberty was planted in the soil of Turkey.

The French government also took further steps to encourage its growth. In April 1795 the Foreign Ministry in Paris informed Descorches that the Committee of Public Safety had decided to re-establish the French printing press in Constantinople, and announced the dispatch of Louis Allier, director of the French *Imprimerie Nationale*, to take charge of it. Three other assistants were sent, together with two presses and a quantity of French type. The ambassador was instructed to use this press to the best advantage of the Republic.[51]

[49] E. de Marcère, *Une Ambassade à Constantinople*, i (1927), 45; Zinkeisen, vi. 861 ff.; Cevdet, *Tarih*, vi. 119 ff.

[50] Marcère, ii, 12–15. See further Sybel, in *R. hist.*, xi, 107 ff. on French propaganda in Turkey in this period. The published proceedings of the Committee of Public Safety contain several references to the expenditure of large sums of money in Turkey, for the purposes of the Republic. For further details, see B. Lewis, in *J. Wld. Hist.*, i. 114 ff.

[51] Ibid. pp. 116 ff.; L. Lagarde, 'Note sur les journaux français de Constantinople à l'époque révolutionnaire', *J. As.*, ccxxxvi (1948), 271 ff.; Gerçek, *Türk Gazet.*, pp. 10 ff. In the latter work a reproduction is given of an entire issue of the *Gazette française de Constantinople*, dated 1 Floréal, year 5 (20 Apr. 1797). In July 1795 Descorches reported that he had distributed a bulletin in Turkish on the victories of the republican armies (J. Sorel, *L'Europe et la Révolution française*, iv (1909), 248).

Far more important, however, than any pamphlets, bulletins, or newspapers was the effect of the unrecorded efforts of individual Frenchmen in Istanbul and elsewhere, who abandoned the mutually agreed exclusiveness that had kept Franks and Muslims from all but formal contacts in the past, and for the first time sought the intimacy and cultivated the friendship of Muslim Turks. Turkish-speaking Frenchmen and French-speaking Turks formed a new society in the capital, in which the ideas of the time were freely discussed, and the enthusiastic optimism of revolutionary France found a ready response among a new generation of Turks that looked to the West for guidance and inspiration.

The Turkish Reaction [52]

The Revolution seems to have made little immediate impression on the Turks, who, like other contemporary observers, at first regarded it as a purely internal affair of no great consequence. Even when the Revolution spread by war to the neighbouring countries and convulsed Western Europe, the Turks still regarded it as an internal affair of Christendom, having no relevance to the Ottoman Empire, which as a Muslim state was immune to this contagion. Diplomatically, the preoccupation of the Christian powers with the revolutionary wars was even of benefit to the Porte. Ahmed Efendi, the Privy Secretary of Selim III, noted this in his journal in January 1792, and concluded: 'May God cause the upheaval in France to spread like syphilis to the enemies of the Empire, hurl them into prolonged conflict with one another,

[52] The contemporary Turkish historians are discussed in Babinger, *Geschichtsschreiber*, and in O. M. von Schlechta-Wssehrd, 'Die osmanischen Geschichtsschreiber der neueren Zeit', *Denkschriften der phil. hist. Classe der Kgl. Ak. der Wissenschaften*, viii (1856), 1 ff. The most important published chronicle is that of Ahmed Asım Efendi (? 1755–1819), who wrote the official annals of the Empire for the years 1791–1808 (*Asım Tarihi*. On Asım see Babinger, *Geschichtsschreiber*, pp. 339–40, Schlechta-Wssehrd, pp. 10–11, and the article on Asım in the *IA*, by Köprülü.) A far profounder treatment is that of Ahmed Cevdet Paşa (1822–95), whose 12-volume history of the Ottoman Empire from 1774 to 1826 must rank as one of the greatest achievements of Ottoman historiography. Cevdet's history is based to a very large extent on archive documents, many of which he quoted *in extenso*. Since the foundation of the Ottoman (later Turkish) Historical Society in 1910, Turkish historians have published an increasing number of studies and of editions of documents from the State Archives, which have meanwhile been rehoused and reorganized. (For a brief account see B. Lewis, 'The Ottoman Archives as a Source for the History of the Arab Lands', *JRAS*, Oct. 1951, pp. 139 ff.)

and thus accomplish results beneficial to the Empire, amen.'[53]

A new phase began with the partition of the territories of the Republic of Venice by the treaty of Campo Formio of 17 October 1797. By the fifth article of this treaty, the Ionian islands, together with the former Venetian possessions on the adjoining coasts of Albania and Greece, were annexed to the French Republic. France, the traditional ally of the Ottoman Empire, had become her neighbour—and ancient friendship could not stand the shock. Soon alarming reports began to come in from Morea—of liberty and equality on the borders of the Empire, of speeches and ceremonies recalling the ancient glories and liberties of Hellas and promising their restoration—of French intelligence with rebels and dissidents in Ottoman Greece and French plans to annex Morea and Crete.[54] French reassurances failed to comfort the Divan, and when General Tamara, the new Russian ambassador, repeated the warnings of his predecessor against the dangers of revolutionary France, he was listened to with greater attention.[55] Before long still more alarming reports began to arrive of French naval preparations in Toulon, and of a projected French attack on the Ottoman dominions. In the spring of 1798 the *Reis-ül-Küttab*, Ahmed Atıf Efendi, was instructed to prepare a memorandum for the Divan on the political situation, and on the invitation extended by the Allies to the Porte to join an anti-French coalition. His report is worth quoting at some length. He begins with a general account of the French Revolution, presented, in accordance with Ottoman politeness, as something well known to his readers, but clearly intended to remove their illusions as to the real purport of the events in France.

It is one of the things known to all well-informed persons that the conflagration of sedition and wickedness that broke out a few years ago in France, scattering sparks and shooting flames of mischief and tumult in all directions, had been conceived many years previously in the minds of certain accursed heretics, and had been a quiescent evil

---

[53] Tahsin Öz, ed., 'Selim III ün Sırkatibi tarafından tutulan Ruzname', *Tar. Ves.*, iii (May 1949), 184. cf. Cevdet, *Tarih*, vi. 130. In Turkish syphilis is called Frengi.

[54] On the reports of Hasan Paşa, the Vali of Morea, see Karal, *Fransa-Mısır*, pp. 113 ff.; cf. Cevdet, vi. 248–9 and 282–4. Karal, 'Yunan Adalarının Fransızlar tarafından işgalı ve Osmanlı-Rus münasebâtı 1797-8', *Tar. Semineri Derg.*, i (1937), 103 ff.

[55] Karal, *Tar. Sem. Derg.*, pp. 116 ff., where the official Ottoman record of the conversation with Tamara is given.

F

which they sought an opportunity to waken. In this way: the known and famous atheists Voltaire and Rousseau, and other materialists like them, had printed and published various works, consisting, God preserve us, of insults and vilification against the pure prophets and great kings, of the removal and abolition of all religion, and of allusions to the sweetness of equality and republicanism, all expressed in easily intelligible words and phrases, in the form of mockery, in the language of the common people. Finding the pleasure of novelty in these writings, most of the people, even youths and women, inclined towards them and paid close attention to them, so that heresy and wickedness spread like syphilis to the arteries of their brains and corrupted their beliefs. When the revolution became more intense, none took offence at the closing of churches, the killing and expulsion of monks, and the abolition of religion and doctrine: they set their hearts on equality and freedom, through which they hoped to attain perfect bliss in this world, in accordance with the lying teachings increasingly disseminated among the common people by this pernicious crew, who stirred up sedition and evil because of selfishness or self-interest. It is well known that the ultimate basis of the order and cohesion of every state is a firm grasp of the roots and branches of holy law, religion, and doctrine; that the tranquillity of the land and the control of the subjects cannot be encompassed by political means alone; that the necessity for the fear of God and the regard for retribution in the hearts of God's slaves is one of the unshakeably established divine decrees; that in both ancient and modern times every state and people has had its own religion, whether true or false. Nevertheless, the leaders of the sedition and evil appearing in France, in a manner without precedent, in order to facilitate the accomplishment of their evil purposes, and in utter disregard of the fearsome consequences, have removed the fear of God and the regard for retribution from the common people, made lawful all kinds of abominable deeds, utterly obliterated all shame and decency, and thus prepared the way for the reduction of the people of France to the state of cattle. Nor were they satisfied with this alone, but, finding supporters like themselves in every place, in order to keep other states busy with the protection of their own régimes and thus forestall an attack on themselves, they had their rebellious declaration which they call 'The Rights of Man' translated into all languages and published in all parts, and strove to incite the common people of the nations and religions to rebel against the kings to whom they were subject.[56]

In this document the French Revolution is clearly regarded as a danger which threatened the Ottoman Empire as well as

[56] Cevdet, *Tarih*, vi. 311 ff.

the Christian states. The need to overcome it overrode both the traditional enmity between the Porte and her neighbours and the traditional friendship between the Porte and France.

The French landing at Alexandria on 1 July 1798, and the subsequent activities of the French in Egypt and Palestine confirmed Atif's reasoning. The long-term effects of the impact of revolutionary France on the Arab peoples are well known. But even the immediate effects were disturbing enough to induce the Ottoman government to embark on what in our time is called ideological warfare. In a proclamation distributed in Arabic in Syria, Egypt, and Arabia, a detailed refutation of revolutionary doctrines was offered:

In the Name of God, the Merciful and the Compassionate.

O you who believe in the unity of God, community of Muslims, know that the French nation (may God devastate their dwellings and abase their banners) are rebellious infidels and dissident evildoers; they do not believe in the unity of the Lord of Heaven and Earth, nor in the mission of the intercessor on the Day of Judgment, but have abandoned all religions, and denied the after-world and its penalties . . . so that they have pillaged their churches and the adornments of their crucifixes and attacked their priests and monks. They assert that the books which the prophets brought are clear error, and that the Koran, the Torah and the Gospels are nothing but lies and idle talk . . . that all men are equal in humanity, and alike in being men, none has any superiority or merit over any other, and every one himself disposes of his soul and arranges his own livelihood in this life. . . . With lying books and meretricious falsehoods they address themselves to every party and say: 'We belong to you, to your religion and to your community', and they make them vain promises, and utter fearful warnings. They are wholly given up to villainy and debauchery, and ride the steed of perfidy and presumption, and dive in the sea of error and impiety and are united under the banner of Satan. . . .[57]

It is interesting to note which characteristics of the French Revolution were most shocking to Atıf Efendi and to the author of the proclamation, or were regarded by them as most likely to shock their readers. Neither makes any reference to the execution of Louis XVI, which had such an effect on Christian Europe.

[57] The Turkish text, from a document in the Istanbul archives, is given by Karal, *Fransa-Mısır*, pp. 108 ff. The Arabic text, as brought to Acre by Sir Sidney Smith, is given in an Arabic biography of Jazzar Paşa, attributed to Haydar Aḥmad Shihāb, *Ta'rīkh Aḥmad Bāshā al-Jazzār* (Beirut, 1955), pp. 125 ff.

Von Knobelsdorf, the Prussian chargé d'affaires in Constantinople, reported in a dispatch of 11 March 1793 that 'le Grand Seigneur, instruit jusqu'aux moindres détails de ce crime affreux, en fut si affecté, qu'il en a été malade; tout le Divan, tout le peuple en est saisi d'horreur'.[58] That the Sultan was sick with horror at the execution of his royal brother is likely enough, but the violent death of a sovereign was too familiar a feature of political life in Constantinople to arouse much comment. Nor did even the abolition of the monarchy attract much attention. The Ottomans had been familiar for centuries with republican institutions in Venice and Ragusa, and there was nothing in the mere establishment of a republic to alarm them. What was by now disturbing ruling circles in Constantinople was the secularism of the Revolution—the separation of State and Church, the abandonment of all religious doctrines, the cult of reason. At first the attempt of the French to curry favour with the Muslims by stressing their rejection of Christianity and affecting a sympathy for Islam awoke some response, but soon—with Russian and Austrian assistance—the rulers of the Empire realized the dangers that this proffered friendship held for the traditional Islamic order and principles. Their fears were well grounded—the whole subsequent history of the Middle East has shown how great is the seductive power of a Western revolutionary ideology divorced from Western religion. Some indication of the degree of French success in this propaganda may be gathered from the frequent hostile allusions to it in Ottoman sources. At the same time they began to appreciate the explosive content of the ideas of equality and liberty, though it seems that the latter was at first regarded as a danger to the Christian subjects of the Porte rather than to the Turks themselves.

While France and Turkey were at war, the communication of French ideas to the Turks was at a disadvantage. Nevertheless, the swift and easy success of an army of less than 30,000 Frenchmen in conquering and ruling Egypt for over three years did not fail to impress, nor did the tolerance and sympathy shown by the French rulers of Egypt. By the terms of the peace, France withdrew from the Ionian islands as well as from Egypt, and thus terminated her brief tenure as a neighbour of the Porte. The voice of France, no longer shouting in Greek and in Arabic, became more audible in Istanbul.

[58] Zinkeisen, vi. 858–9 n. 2.

While Brune, Ruffin, and Sébastiani worked to restore French influence at the Porte, a new Turkish ambassador, Mehmed Said Halet Efendi, served in Paris from 1802 to 1806. Halet was a convinced reactionary, and a hater of all things Western. But even his strictures on Frangistan, as he calls it, reveal how strong French influence was. Some extracts from his letters may illustrate the point:

I ask you to pray for my safe return from this land of infidels, for I have come as far as Paris, but I have not yet seen the Frangistan that people speak of and praise; in what Europe these wonderful things and these wise Franks are, I do not know . . .

Glory be to God, the minds and beliefs of these people! It is a strange thing that this Frangistan, with the praises of which our ears have for so long been filled, we found to be not only unlike what was said, but the reverse. . . .

If anyone, with the intention either of intimidating you or of leading you astray, praises Frangistan, then ask him this question: 'Have you been to Europe, or have you not?' If he says: 'Indeed I have been there, and I enjoyed myself awhile', then assuredly he is a partisan and a spy of the Franks. If he says, 'No, I have not been, I know it from history books', then he is one of two things—either he is an ass, who takes heed of what the Franks write, or else he praises the Franks out of religious fanaticism. . . .[59]

Despite Halet's encouragement of the reactionary party in Istanbul, French influence continued to grow. The French victories of 1805 and the humiliation of Austria and Russia delighted the Sultan, and decided him to recognize Napoleon as Emperor. In August 1806 Sébastiani returned to Constantinople, and was soon able to involve the Porte in war with both Russia and England. The repulse of an English naval squadron from Constantinople, thanks in no small measure to the energetic intervention of Sébastiani and a number of French officers and volunteers, gave the French ambassador a position of unparalleled ascendancy at the Porte. But it was this very victory of French influence and the prominence of Frenchmen in the defence of Istanbul that outraged Muslim sentiment, and helped to provoke the reactionary rebellion

[59] Karal, *Halet Efendinin Paris Büyük Elçiliği, 1802–6* (1940), 32 ff.

that culminated in the deposition of Selim III in May 1807.[60]

The first trial of strength with the opponents of reform had already come in 1805, when the Sultan, hard pressed for troops, had ordered a general levy to provide men for the *Nizam-i Cedid* regiments, in place of the system of voluntary recruitment maintained until then. The levy was required from the Janissaries as well as from the general population. This bold measure brought to a head the smouldering resentment of the Janissaries and the ulema at the new order. Some brushes with Janissary regiments had already occurred in previous years. They now broke out in open revolt in Rumelia. A regiment of *Nizam-i Cedid* troops sent against them from Anatolia was crushingly defeated, and in the face of this crisis the reactionaries and the mob in the capital were able to enforce a suspension of the reforms. To avoid a general revolt, the Sultan was induced to dismiss his reformist advisers, send the *Nizam* troops back to Anatolia, and entrust the Grand Vezirate to the Aga of the Janissaries.

This capitulation postponed but did not avert the debacle. In May 1807 the *Yamaks*—auxiliary levies—mutinied against an order to put on European-style uniforms. The leader of the mutineers, Kabakçıoğlu Mustafa, was soon able to command powerful support in high quarters. He marched with his henchmen to Istanbul, where he set up headquarters in the Hippodrome and entered into close relations with the kaymakam of the Grand Vezir, Musa Paşa, and with the Chief Mufti. Armed with a list of the chief partisans of reform, he and his mutineers, with the help of a maddened mob, set to work to round them up and kill them. Some they killed in their own houses, others they dragged to the Hippodrome and slaughtered them there.

A decree by the Sultan abolishing the *Nizam-i Cedid* came too late to save his throne. On 29 May 1807, after a turbulent meeting at the Hippodrome, a deputation of Janissary officers called on the Chief Mufti to ask 'whether a Sultan, who by his actions and enactments had worked against the religious principles sanctified by the Koran, could continue to reign?' The Mufti, with a becoming show of surprise and reluctance, then authorized the Sultan's deposition, in the interests of the Muslim religion and the house of Osman. Selim was accordingly deposed, and his cousin Mustafa was proclaimed Sultan. The *Nizam* forces were at

[60] Zinkeisen, vii. 455 ff.

once dissolved, and the chief of the mutineers became commandant of the fortresses of the Bosporus. In the capital the real
rulers were the kaymakam and the Chief Mufti.[61]

It was a year or so after these events that Ahmed Asım Efendi,
Imperial Historiographer, wrote his chronicle of the years 1791–
1808. From his narrative we can draw a clear impression of the
general effect of French influences in Turkey during these years.
Asım approves of the reforms, which he hoped would restore the
military strength of the Empire, and in an interesting passage he
describes how Russia emerged from weakness and barbarism
to the status of a great power by borrowing the sciences and
techniques of the West.[62] But he is bitterly anti-Christian, considering all Christian powers as inveterate enemies of Islam, and
foreseeing nothing but evil consequences from agreements with
them. In particular he detests the French, and reviles the pro-
French party in Turkey as deluded fools.[63] His reference to the
internal affairs of France are few and hostile. The republic was
'like the rumblings and crepitations of a queasy stomach',[64]
its principles consisted of 'the abandonment of religion and the
equality of rich and poor'.[65]

Of French activities in Turkey he has more to say. In a lengthy
discussion of the successes and failures of the reforms of Selim III
and the causes and circumstances of his fall, Asım Efendi devotes
a great deal of attention to French influence. The French had
presented themselves as friends and even as prospective converts to
Islam, assuring the Turks of their hostility to Christianity and
their intention of following the teachings of Muhammad. By
intensive propaganda they had confused the minds 'not only of the
great ones of the state but also of the common people'. To spread
their pernicious ideas, they had sought the society of Turks,
beguiling them with protestations of friendship and goodwill,
and thus, through familiar and intimate social intercourse, had
found many victims.

Certain sensualists, naked of the garment of loyalty, from time to
time learned politics from them; some, desirous of learning their
language, took French teachers, acquired their idiom and prided

---

[61] Zinkeisen, vii. 461 ff.; Juchereau, ii. 104 ff.; Cevdet, *Tarih*, viii. 139 ff.; Asım,
ii. 178 ff.; Ata, iii. 44 ff.

[62] Asım, i. 265.   [63] Ibid. pp. 76, 175, &c.

[64] Asım, i. 78.   [65] Ibid. p. 62.

themselves . . . on their uncouth talk. In this way they were able to insinuate Frankish customs in the hearts and endear their modes of thought to the minds of some people of weak mind and shallow faith. The sober-minded and far-sighted and the ambassadors of the other states foresaw the danger of this situation; full of alarm and disapproval, they reviled and condemned these things both implicitly and explicitly, and gave forewarning of the evil consequences to which their activities would give rise. This malicious crew and abominable band were full of cunning—first sowing the seed of their politics in the soil of the hearts of the great ones of the state, then, by incitement and seduction to their ways of thought, undermining—God preserve us— the principles of the Holy Law.[66]

By the summer of 1807 the Emperor Napoleon was in alliance with his Imperial brother in Russia; the Sultan Selim III was dethroned and the party of reaction in power in Constantinople. The French Revolution seemed dead in the land of its birth, and its influence stifled in Turkey. But the cutting from the tree of liberty had struck root in the soil of Islam. It was to bear both sweet and bitter fruit.

[66] Asım, i. 374–6; cf. Cevdet, *Tarih*, viii. 196 ff., where an account is given of the influence of European instructors and experts, the exaggerated respect for European ideas and practices among young Turks, the aping of European manners and customs, and the appearance of 'heresy and materialism' in Istanbul.

CHAPTER IV

The Ottoman Reform

Moi-même, ivre de joie de voir ma patrie dans l'état que je desirois si ardemment, éclairée tous les jours davantage du flambeau des sciences et des arts. . . .

SEID MUSTAFA, 'Diatribe', 1803.

In scanning over the riches of civilization, spread out before him for acceptance, he contemptuously rejects those calculated to benefit his people, and chooses the modern scientific governing machine, result of ages of experiments, with its patent screws for extracting blood and treasure, conscription and taxation.

ADOLPHUS SLADE, R.N., 'Record of Travels in Turkey, Greece, &c.', 1831.

IN the summer of 1807 the reform movement in Turkey seemed to be extinguished. The reforming Sultan was deposed, his new-style army disbanded, his reformist ministers dead or in hiding. In their place the Chief Mufti and the Janissaries ruled the city—the two forces most bitterly opposed to social and military change.

But the reform, though young, was a vigorous plant—vigorous enough to survive both the violence of the Hippodrome mutineers and the subtlety of the Chief Mufti. The latter began to have difficulties with his governmental colleagues. In September 1807, after mounting disagreements, he procured the dismissal of the kaymakam Musa Paşa, who was replaced by another well-known reactionary, Tayyar Paşa. In June 1808 he too was dismissed. Swallowing his convictions, he took refuge with Bayrakdar Mustafa, the Pasha of Silistria and military commander of the Danube frontiers—the only important partisan of reform still alive, at large, and in a position of power.

Bayrakdar Mustafa Paşa [1]

Mustafa the Standard-bearer (Bayrakdar) was born in Ruschuk, the son of a Janissary. After distinguished service in the war against Russia in 1767–74, he lived on his estates near Ruschuk, where he acquired the status of *ayan*. In 1805 he took part in the revolt of the Janissaries at Edirne against the *Nizam-i Cedid*.

---

[1] On the Bayrakdar (also called Alemdar, with the same meaning) there are two modern monographs based on original sources: Uzunçarşılı, *Alemdar Mustafa Paşa* (1942); and A. F. Miller, *Mustafa Pasha Bayraktar* (1947). Detailed accounts will also be found in Cevdet, Zinkeisen, &c.

Afterwards, however, he was won over, became an enthusiastic partisan of reform, and was given high military rank and his appointment in Rumelia.

His headquarters in Ruschuk now became the rallying-point of the surviving reformers, as well as of other opponents of the new régime in the capital. In the summer of 1808 he was ready to take the offensive. The Grand Vezir, Çelebi Mustafa Paşa, was still at Edirne with the army of Rumelia, and was virtually excluded from power by the ruling group in Istanbul. Bayrakdar Mustafa and his associates now moved from Ruschuk to Edirne, joined forces with the Grand Vezir, and together marched on Istanbul, where they obtained control of the city. The Sultan Mustafa IV, learning of their intention to restore Selim III, took the precaution of having him murdered. He himself was immediately after deposed, and his brother Mahmud became Sultan.

The Grand Vezirate of Bayrakdar Mustafa Paşa lasted only a few months, until November 1808, when he was overthrown and killed by a revolt of Janissaries. During that time, however, he began a most ambitious programme. He reconstituted the *Nizam* troops under a new name, revived and extended the reforming edicts, and convened a great Imperial assembly, to which he invited high officials, governors, pashas, and *ayan* from all over the Empire. Among those who came were the Beylerbeys of Rumelia and Anatolia, the governors of the provinces adjoining the capital, the heads of several of the powerful *derebey* families of Anatolia, and of course the high dignitaries of the capital. By the beginning of October some two-thirds of the invited guests had reached Istanbul, and the Bayrakdar, accompanied by the highest officers of state as well as by a number of the ulema, formally inaugurated the assembly in the Imperial palace. In a rousing address, he set before the assembled pashas a programme of reform, including a thoroughgoing reorganization of the Janissary corps, which would have removed a whole series of long-cherished abuses, and, at the same time, confirmed the rights and privileges of the *derebeys* and *ayan*, the new provincial *élite* to which the Bayrakdar himself belonged.[2]

---

[2] Şanizade, i. 66–73. Cevdet, *Tarih*, ix. 3–7 and 278–83. On the significance of this 'deed of agreement' (*sened-i ittifak*) see Inalcık, 'Tanzimat Nedir' in *Tarih Araştırmaları* (1941), p. 249 (a brief restatement in English by the same author in 'Land Problems in Turkish History', *Muslim Wld.*, xlv (1955), 225; also below, p. 441.

All those present signed the project, which was also blessed with an approving *fetva* from the Chief Mufti. But attempts to put it into force soon alienated all but a few devoted friends, and in the following month all was ended by a rising of the infuriated Janissaries. Bayrakdar Mustafa died in the flaming ruins of his residence, and the Sultan himself, tarred with the brush of reform, owed his throne and perhaps his life only to the fact that he was the sole surviving prince of the house of Osman. Once again the reactionaries were in control. Only the Sultan watched and waited the opportunity to resume the reform, by first destroying the forces that opposed it.

Mahmud II [3]

Mahmud II, sometimes described as the Peter the Great of the Ottoman Empire, was born in the Saray in July 1784. There is a story, of dubious authenticity, that his mother was

---

[3] There is a vast literature on the Ottoman reforms inaugurated under Mahmud II and his successors, though as yet no comprehensive monographic treatment. The most recent general survey, by a Turkish historian using both Turkish and Western sources, is that given by Karal in his three volumes contributed to the large-scale Ottoman history published in Ankara by the Turkish Historical Society: *Osmanlı Tarihi* v (1789–1856), 1947; vi (1856–61), 1954; vii (1861–76), 1956. A collection of studies and surveys on various aspects of the reforms, by different authors, will be found in the volume *Tanzimat*, published in 1940 by the Turkish Ministry of Education on the occasion of the 100th anniversary of the first great reforming edict. Among Turkish historians of an earlier generation, Abdurrahman Şeref, the last Imperial Ottoman Historiographer and first president of the Ottoman Historical Society, is particularly illuminating. Of special value are his *Tarih Musahabeleri* (1340 A.H.) (a collection of essays on personalities and events in nineteenth-century Turkey) and his *Tarih-i Devlet-i Osmaniye* (1309 A.H.), a general history, including excellent surveys of administrative and institutional changes. General accounts of the period will also be found in the historical writings of Ahmed Rasim, *Osmanlı Tarihi* (1326–30 A.H.) and *Istibdaddan Hakimiyet-i Milliyeye* (1923–5). A brief outline of the reforms, using Turkish sources, was written by J. H. Kramers for *EI*[1] (*s.v.* 'Tanzimat') where numerous other articles will be found on Turkish personalities and institutions. Useful material will also be found in certain works by Western historians, although these are based exclusively or almost exclusively on Western sources. These include both contemporary and near contemporary works such as G. Rosen, *Geschichte der Türkei . . . 1826 . . . 1856* (1866–7) and Ed. Engelhardt, *La Turquie et le Tanzimat* (1882–4) (this work was translated into Turkish and much used by Turkish historians); and also more modern works like von Sax, *Geschichte des Machtverfalls der Türkei*, Vienna 1913; Jorga, *Geschichte des osmanischen Reiches*; H. W. V. Temperley, *England and the Near East, I: The Crimea* (1936); F. E. Bailey, *British Policy and the Turkish Reform Movement* (1942). Among the many contemporary Western observers of the reforms, some are of special interest. The period of Mahmud II is well described by the Prussian soldier Helmut von Moltke, *Briefe über Zustände und Begebenheiten in der Türkei aus den Jahren 1835 bis 1839* (1891), and the English sailor Adolphus Slade, *Record of Travels in Turkey, Greece, &c.,* . . . *in*

French.[4] He himself certainly had no knowledge of French, nor of any other Western language.[5] His father was Abdülhamid I, during whose reign the first modern training schools were established in Turkey. His cousin, Selim III, seems to have exercised a profound influence on him, especially in the last year of joint seclusion, between Selim's deposition and his death. His education was that normal to an Ottoman prince—Turkish and the classical Islamic languages, religion and law, poetry and history. He had no direct knowledge of the West, nor any means of access to it save through intermediaries, since he knew no Western language, and little or nothing was available in Turkish translation.

After the violent end of Bayrakdar Mustafa Paşa, it was eighteen years before the Sultan could return to his projects of military reform. These years were not, however, spent in idleness. His first task was the war against Russia. After its conclusion in 1812, he set to work to restore or establish the authority of the central

---

the years 1829, 1830, and 1831 (1832). For Turkey in the 1840's and 1850's, there are excellent accounts in Charles White, *Three Years in Constantinople* (1846), and A. Ubicini, *Lettres sur la Turquie* (1853–4). The final phase of the *Tanzimat*, and the brief interlude of the first constitution, are described with knowledge and insight by the German consul and scholar A. D. Mordtmann, in his book published anonymously under the title *Stambul und das moderne Türkenthum* (1877). The major published Turkish chroniclers of the period are Şanizade, Cevdet, and Lûtfi. Şanizade (on whom see below, p. 84) was an Imperial Historiographer whose chronicle (n.d.) covers the years 1808–20. Cevdet Paşa's history (see above, p. 64 n. 52) goes only as far as 1826, but his observations and memoranda (*Tezakir*, i–xii, ed. Cavid Baysun (1953); *Maruzat*, published in *TOEM*, nos. 78–93) tell us much about the events of his own time. Ahmed Lûtfi, who succeeded Cevdet as Imperial Historiographer in 1865, wrote a chronicle covering the period 1825–68, of which only the first eight volumes, as far as 1847, have been printed (*Tarih-i Lûtfi*, 1290–1328 A.H.). Among other Turkish historians of the time, mention may be made of Tayyarzade Ata, whose chronicle (*Tarih-i Ata*) is especially informative on court affairs and personalities; Mustafa Nuri Paşa, whose *Netaic ül-Vukuat* includes valuable surveys and analyses of development and reform in the government, armed forces, and finances; Mehmed Süreyya, to whom we owe an invaluable biographical dictionary of Ottoman worthies (*Sicill-i Osmani* (1308–15); and the Grand Vezir Kâmil Paşa, whose political history (*Tarih-i Siyasî-i Devlet-i Aliye-i Osmaniye*, 1327 A.H.) goes as far as about the mid-century. Besides these and other works of historiography, there are Turkish newspapers, periodicals, and pamphlets of the period, as well as a vast documentation in the state archives that has only to a very limited extent been examined or exploited by scholars. On these archives see B. Lewis, 'Başvekalet Arşivi', in *EI²*.

[4] For a brief bibliographic note on the 'abundant literature' on this story, see J. Deny, 'Wālide Sultān', in *EI¹*, iv. 1118.

[5] Moltke, p. 408: 'so viel ist gewiss, dass der Grossherr nicht eine Silbe Englisch, Französisch oder Deutsch verstand'.

government in the provinces, most of which had a considerable measure of autonomy.[6]

All these powers and privileges Mahmud II was determined to suppress. In his view, with which many subsequent observers have agreed, no real progress towards reform would be possible until all power other than that emanating from him had been eliminated, and the Sultan's will made the sole source of authority in the provinces as well as in the capital. In two areas he failed—in Egypt, where he was forced to concede autonomous status to an Ottoman military adventurer who had made himself master of that country; and in the Morea, where he was compelled by the intervention of the powers to recognize the freedom of the Greeks. Elsewhere in the Empire, however, especially in Rumelia and Anatolia, he was largely successful in overcoming the rebellious pashas and local dynasts and notables, and in bringing the provinces under the effective control of the government in Istanbul.

The Suppression of the Janissaries [7]

In 1826, immediately after the surrender by the Greek insurgents of the fortress of Missolonghi, the Sultan was encouraged to resume the favourite project of his forerunners on the path of reform, and order the formation of a new-style army, with European training and equipment. A *Hatt-i Şerif* of 28 May 1826 established a new corps. The corps of Janissaries was to be maintained, but each battalion stationed in the capital was to provide 150 men for the new force. Though this new force was in effect a revival of the *Nizam-i Cedid* of Selim III, the Sultan was careful in his order establishing it to avoid any reference to the reforms or the reformers. On the contrary, he blandly presented the new force as a restoration of the military order of Süleyman the Magnificent, which since the days of Koçu Bey had been the panacea of all who sought to revive the strength of the Empire by reverting

---

[6] See above, pp. 37–38.

[7] The official Turkish account of the 'Auspicious Incident', is the *Üss-i Zafer* of Mehmed Esad (1243/1827); French translation by A. P. Caussin de Perceval, *Précis historique de la destruction du corps des janissaires . . .* (1833). cf. Nuri, *Netaic*, iv. 76 ff.; Kâmil Paşa, *Tarih-i Siyasî*, iii. 100 ff.; Rasim, *Osmanlı Tarihi*, iv. 1805 ff. There are also numerous descriptions and comments by Western writers, e.g. Rosen, i. 8 ff. For brief critical accounts of the episode see Temperley, pp. 15–21 and 402 n. 22; Bailey, pp. 34–35. The military reforms that followed are described in Lûtfi, i. 191–202 and 252–59; Ata, iii. 108 ff.; Nuri, *Netaic*, iv. 109 ff., and in Ubicini, letter 19.

to the practices of her golden prime. The Sultan even specified that the new force would not be instructed by Christians or foreigners, but only by Muslim officers familiar with modern military methods. The whole was approved by the Chief Mufti and the ulema, as being justified by the overriding needs of the Holy War against the infidels.

But the Janissaries, as Mahmud had no doubt anticipated, would not be persuaded. On 15 June, ten days after the formal inauguration of the new corps, they mutinied for the last time. Overturning their soup-kettles in the traditional gesture of revolt, the five Janissary battalions assembled in the Hippodrome and soon gathered a furious mob, bent on repeating the massacre of 1807. But this time most of the populace was against them—and Mahmud was ready for them. His military commander, Kara Hüseyin, had arrived at the palace with troops and guns, and against the heavy cannon the Janissaries were helpless. Not a whiff, but thirty minutes of grape-shot fired into the packed square and barracks sufficed to exterminate the Janissaries and to destroy a centuries' old institution, once the terror of Europe, lately the terror of the Sultans and their law-abiding subjects. A proclamation, issued the same day, abolished the corps of Janissaries, and set up in their place a new army, to be known as the *Asakir-i Mansure-i Muhammediye*, the victorious soldiers of Muhammad. A month later, on the pretext that they had stirred up revolts of protest against the destruction of the Janissaries, the Sultan dissolved the dervish brotherhood of the Bektaşis, for centuries intimately associated with the corps of Janissaries. With the support of the Chief Mufti and the chief ulema, he outlawed the brotherhood, destroyed its convents, publicly executed three of its leaders, and exiled the rest.[8]

The massacre of the Janissaries, known to the reformers as the *Vak'a-i Hayriye*—the Auspicious Incident—completed the preparatory work which the Sultan had already begun with his campaigns to end provincial autonomy. The valley-lords and notables in the provinces, the Janissaries and dervishes in the capital, all those who restricted the arbitrary power of the Sultan, had been crushed and destroyed. Now no group remained that could challenge the Sultan's will from entrenched positions of ancient and accepted privilege; no armed force survived, other than the Sultan's own new-style soldiery—equipped with guns and

[8] Rasim, iv. 1830 ff.

gunners who no longer needed to fear the anger of the city populace. Even the ulema, the guardians of the Holy Law, with neither the Janissaries nor the crowd to appeal to, were gravely weakened in their task of moderating the despotism of the Sultan. The way was now clear to that radical reorganization for which Mahmud had been waiting for so many years.

Between the destruction of the Janissaries in 1826 and his death in 1839, Mahmud II embarked on a great programme of reforms; in them he laid down the main lines along which later Turkish reformers, in the nineteenth and to some extent even in the twentieth century, were to follow. In each field of reform, the creation of a new order was preceded by the destruction of an old one—and all these preliminary demolitions were made possible by the destruction of the Janissary corps, the central repository of military power of the traditional order.

Military Reforms

With the Janissaries safely out of the way, Mahmud was able to proceed more rapidly with his plans for a new-style army, the creation of which had been the prime objective of his less fortunate predecessors. In place of the Aga of the Janissaries he created a new office, that of Serasker. The title was an old one, given to army commanders in former times. As used by Mahmud, it came to connote an officer who combined the functions of commander-in-chief and Minister of War, with special responsibility for the new-style army. In addition, he inherited from the Aga of the Janissaries the responsibility for public security, police duties, fire-fighting, and the like, in the capital. In a period of growing centralization and enforced change, the police function came to be of increasing importance, and the maintenance and extension of the police system one of the chief duties of the Serasker. Husrev Paşa, during his term as Serasker (1827–36), was particularly successful in this part of his work. The police were taken from the jurisdiction of the Serasker and placed under a separate *Zabtiye Muşiriyeti* in 1845.[9]

At the end of 1826 a code of regulations for the new-style army was prepared. It provided for a force of 12,000 men, to be stationed in Istanbul, and divided into eight sections. Orders were also to be issued for the recruitment of new-style troops in the provinces. The soldiers were to serve for twelve years.[10]

[9] B. Lewis, 'Bāb-i Ser'askerī' and 'Ḍabṭiyya' in *EI²*.   [10] Ubicini, letter 19.

The restoration of peace, with the signing of the treaty of Adrianople in 1829, gave the Sultan leisure to take up more actively the training and equipment of his new troops, for whom there were still many tasks within the Empire. The most important of these was the impending reckoning with Muhammad Ali, the refractory Pasha of Egypt, whose strikingly successful efforts at Westernizing his army and navy had provided the spur that drove Mahmud and his ministers forward in the same direction. In the competition for the support and goodwill of the West, it was necessary to show that the Sultan could be as progressive and as liberal as his vassal. In the battle for Syria, it was necessary to put in the field forces capable of meeting the modern army of the Pasha of Egypt.

The Egyptian forces had acquitted themselves well in the campaign against the Greek insurgents, and provided a model of successful reform. It was to Cairo, therefore, that, in 1826, the Sultan sent his first appeal for help—a request to the Pasha of Egypt for twelve expert instructors.[11] It was, needless to say, refused with somewhat specious excuses, and the Sultan, like the Pasha before him, had to look to Europe for help. France, hitherto the source of military guidance and instructors, was compromised, first by her sympathy for the Greek insurgents, and later by her support for Muhammad Ali. The Sultan therefore looked elsewhere. Britain was tarred with the brush of philhellenism, and an offer from Palmerston in 1834 to send officers to train the Turkish army was turned down. In the following year some further attempts were made to arrange for British assistance to the Turkish forces. Some Turkish cadets were accepted at Woolwich, and three officers went to Istanbul to assist and advise in the reorganization of the army. They accomplished little, and a naval mission sent in 1838 fared no better. One of the reasons for their failure was no doubt the growth of Russian influence in Istanbul, which worked against any British connexion with the Turkish armed forces. Another was the resentment of the officers at the slighting way in which they were received, and the quasi-menial status offered to them.[12]

[11] Lûtfi, i. 196.

[12] Bailey, pp. 146 ff. On British policies towards the Ottoman reform see further F. S. Rodkey, 'Palmerston and the Regeneration of Turkey 1830–41', *J. Mod. Hist.*, i (1929), 570–93, ii (1930), 193–225, and H. Temperley, 'British Policy towards Parliamentary Rule and Constitutionalism in Turkey (1830–1914)', *Camb. Hist. J.*, iv (1932–4), 156–191.

The same attitude was noted by another European officer, who spent four years in Turkey. The Prussian Lieutenant, later Field-Marshal Helmuth von Moltke, reached Istanbul towards the end of 1835, on a private visit. While there he made a deep impression on the Sultan, who engaged his services as adviser in the training of his new army. The Sultan now turned to Prussia and Austria with requests that they send officers to Turkey and accept Turks in their military academies. Five Prussian officers were sent, and a few Turkish cadets accepted in Vienna. Though this was much less than had been asked for, it was an important beginning, and initiated a strong German influence and tradition in the Turkish army which later became very strong and has lasted to our own day.[13]

Moltke set to work on the inspection of the defences of the Empire and the preparation of plans for military reorganization. His letters show that he was far from satisfied with the results of his work. This lack of success he attributes in part to the failings of Mahmud II, whom he compares very unfavourably with Peter the Great of Russia; still more to the invincible contempt of the Turks for the European advisers:

. . . in Turkey even the least gift becomes suspect, as soon as it comes from the hand of a Christian . . . in Russia the foreigners may have been hated; in Turkey they are despised. A Turk will concede without hesitation that the Europeans are superior to his nation in science, skill, wealth, daring and strength, without its ever occurring to him that a Frank might therefore put himself on a par with a Muslim . . .

Few Europeans, he writes, had entered Turkey in as favourable circumstances as he and his colleagues. They had been received with the greatest solicitude by the first dignitaries of the Empire, who came to greet them, handed them pipes, and gave them seats of honour by their sides. But respect for them decreased lower in the social scale. 'The Colonels gave us precedence, the officers were still tolerably polite, but the ordinary man would not present arms to us, and the women and children from time to time followed us with curses. The soldier obeyed but did not salute.' Even the Turkish command did not dare to demand of the Turkish soldier that he show respect to a Gâvur.[14]

---

[13] Rosen, i. 234–5; Sax, p. 265. On the translation into Turkish of a Prussian military manual about this time see Ata, iii. 126 ff.

[14] Moltke, pp. 412–13.

Education[15]

One of the most serious defects of the new army was its lack of officers. Soldiers could be found and drafted easily enough, and the teaching of new drill and new weapons did not offer insuperable difficulties. The production of a competent officer corps was, however, another matter. There were a few Western renegades and adventurers in the artillery and engineers, who provided a nucleus of technically trained officers. Otherwise all branches of the new army were desperately short of competent officers.

It was partly to fill this need, partly to meet the parallel need for competent civil servants, that Mahmud devoted increasing attention to education. Without adequate cadres of men able and willing first to receive and then to impart instruction, the whole edifice of reform was doomed to collapse.

Two schools were already in existence—the naval and military engineering schools established in 1773 and 1793 respectively. These had gone through some difficult days, but were now revived and functioning again. In 1827, in the teeth of strong opposition, the Sultan took the revolutionary step of sending student missions to various European countries.[16] This step, like so many of Mahmud's other reforms, followed a precedent set by Muhammad Ali, who had sent a large batch of students to Paris in 1826, and individuals in previous years. Mahmud began with a batch of military and naval cadets, for whom places were found in various European capitals. They were the first outriders of a great procession of Turkish students to Europe, who on their return played a role of immense importance in the transformation of their country.

In the same year, 1827, a medical school was opened in Istanbul—this time less than a month after the opening of Muhammad Ali's medical school at the Abu Za'bal hospital in Cairo. Its purpose was to train doctors for the new army. Physicians for the civil population were still trained at more traditional establishments, such as the medical division of the Süleymaniye *Medrese*,

[15] Turkish histories of education in this period will be found in Mahmud Cevad, *Maarif-i Umumiye Nezareti Tarihçe-i Teşkilât ve Icraatı* (1339 A.H.) (an official history of the Ministry of Education with many documents); Ergin, *Maarif*, ii. For a contemporary Western impression see Ubicini, letter 9.

[16] Karal, *Selim III*, v. 166. A picture of the first group of students, taken in Paris in 1830, is reproduced in *Tanzimat*, facing p. 737.

where the syllabus was still based substantially on the writings of Galen and Avicenna. The medical school included a preparatory section, giving an approximation to a secular primary and secondary education—the first in Turkey. The school was several times reorganized, the most notable reorganization being that of 1838, when it was transferred to Galatasaray, the seat of the old palace school of pages and a famous educational centre dating back to the reign of Bayezid II (1481–1512). The teaching was given partly in Turkish, partly in French, and the instructors included several brought from Europe.

In 1831–4 two further schools were opened, both directly military in purpose. One was the Imperial Music School (*Muzika-i Humayun Mektebi*), the function of which was to provide the new army with drummers and trumpeters to match its tunics and breeches. One of the instructors was Donizetti Paşa—a brother of the composer.[17] More important was the School of Military Sciences (*Mekteb-i Ulum-i Harbiye*). This school, which was planned for some years before its inauguration in 1834, was intended to serve as the St. Cyr of the Ottoman army, and was modelled as closely as circumstances permitted on its French original. Here too foreigners played a dominant role in the teaching, and the mastery of a foreign language, usually French, was the first need and prerequisite of all studies. As in the medical school, there was a preparatory division for children.

So far Mahmud's educational measures had been mainly concerned with the army. In 1838, however, he took up the question of primary and secondary education for civilian purposes, and planned the creation of what he named *rüşdiye* schools— from *rüşd*, adolescence. Little progress was made during Mahmud's lifetime, but two new grammar schools were set up, at the Sultan Ahmed and Süleymaniye mosques, for boys up to the age of about eighteen. Their syllabus was traditional and mainly grammatical and literary. Their purpose was to prepare candidates for the civil service, and, as with the military schools, their pupils were supported out of public or endowment funds.

In an address to the students of the medical school at the inauguration of the new building in 1838, the Sultan remarked:

You will study scientific medicine in French . . . my purpose in having you taught French is not to educate you in the French language;

[17] See below, p. 435.

it is to teach you scientific medicine and little by little to take it into our language . . . work to acquire a knowledge of medicine from your teachers, and strive gradually to take it into Turkish and give it currency in our language. . . .[18]

With these words the Sultan had touched on a central problem of the educational and indeed of the entire reform project—the language barrier. The number of Muslim Turks with an adequate knowledge of a European language was still fantastically small. Some had been trained during the reign of Selim III, but most of them had perished during the Hippodrome massacre of 1807. Instructors, advisers, even technical officers in the army were Europeans, and their instruction, advice, and commands had to pass through the prism of translation and interpretation. For a while recourse was had to native Christian interpreters, but these had many drawbacks. The instruction of a Frankish teacher, repellent enough in itself, did not gain by the mediation of an Armenian or Greek interpreter, whose appearance and accent would, for Turkish hearers, add to its alien grotesqueness a ridiculous familiarity.

There was thus an urgent need for Muslims with a knowledge of languages—to learn and to teach the sciences of the West, to translate textbooks into Turkish, and, as part of this task, to create in the Turkish language the technical and scientific vocabulary needed to express the many new objects and concepts imported from the West.

In these tasks two men made a contribution of outstanding importance. The first was Ataullah Mehmed, known as Şanizade (1769–1826).[19] By education one of the ulema, he was a man of encyclopaedic knowledge, and in 1819 was appointed Imperial Historiographer. He was dismissed and exiled in 1826, after the suppression of the Janissaries, because of his connexion with the Bektaşi fraternity. He was, however, no reactionary. He seems to have learnt several European languages, and made a study of European medicine and other sciences. His major work was a Turkish translation, probably made from an Italian version, of an Austrian medical textbook. It was accompanied by an explanatory treatise by Şanizade on physiology and anatomy, and by another translation of an Austrian work on vaccination. Şanizade's medical

---

[18] Quoted by Suheyl Ünver in *Tanzimat*, pp. 940–1.

[19] On Şanizade see Babinger, *Geschichtsschreiber*, pp. 346–7; Adnan, *Ilim*, pp. 192–5.

textbook marks the end of traditional and the beginning of modern medicine in Turkey; in it he created, for the first time, a modern medical vocabulary in the Turkish language, which remained in use until the linguistic reform of recent years.

The other major pioneer of modern science and terminology was Hoca Ishak Efendi (1774–1834), a Balkan convert to Islam.[20] A native of Narte, near Yannina, and a Jew by birth, he is said to have known French, Latin, Greek, and Hebrew as well as Turkish, Persian, and Arabic. By 1815 he was a teacher at the school of mathematics, and during the following years became the chief instructor and guiding spirit of that institution. His most important work was a four-volume compendium of the mathematical and physical sciences, which brought to the Turkish student, for the first time, some knowledge of European mathematics, physics, and mechanics. Like Şanizade, he had to create new terms to express new concepts, and ranks with him as the creator of most of the scientific terminology in use in Turkey until recent times. Besides this work, Hoca Ishak produced a number of others, chiefly translations, on military science and engineering. He died in Suez in 1834, on his way back from a trip to Arabia where he had combined a pilgrimage to Mecca with the restoration of some installations in Medina.

Reforms in Government and Administration: the Language Question

A knowledge of Western languages was also needed in the conduct of public affairs, and especially in foreign relations. In the past, Ottoman sovereigns and ministers had felt no need to demean themselves by learning the barbarous idioms of Europe. Such contact as was indispensable was maintained through the European embassies in Istanbul, and conversations were held through the medium of dragomans, who were usually local Christians. Every Embassy employed one, and the Ottoman government itself maintained a functionary known as the Dragoman of the Sublime Porte or of the Imperial Council, who conducted both its conversations and its correspondence. This post,

---

[20] On Ishak Efendi see Adnan, *Ilim*, pp. 196–7; Esad, *Mirât-i Mühendishane*, pp. 34–42; Lûtfi, iii. 167; M. Franco, *Essai sur l'histoire des Israélites de l'Empire ottoman* (1897), pp. 141–2. For a rather unfavourable contemporary impression of Ishak and his school see [J. E. de Kay], *Sketches of Turkey in 1831 and 1832, by an American* (1833), pp. 138 ff. (later referred to as *Sketches*). Many of Ishak Efendi's neologisms are still in use in the Arab countries at the present time.

which lasted for over three centuries, was usually held by Christians, and in the course of the eighteenth century had become the preserve of a small group of patrician Greek families of the Phanar district of Istanbul.

It will be obvious that the holder of the post was in a position to exercise considerable influence on the foreign policy of the Empire. Nevertheless, the Greek monopoly was not challenged until 1821, when the Greek revolt raised obvious and serious difficulties. In that year the last Greek dragoman, Stavraki Aristarchi, was dismissed and executed, and the decision taken to entrust the post to a Muslim.[21]

It was not easy to find one. Selim's young men, few enough to start with, had for the most part perished or lost their proficiency and there were few others. As late as 1844, when Charles White was in Istanbul, he was able to name only a bare dozen of educated Turks with a competent knowledge of a Western language and some reading in Western books.[22]

After two or three weeks, says Şanizade, when papers in Greek or 'Frankish' were accumulating at the Sublime Porte, the Sultan transferred Yahya Efendi, a teacher at the school of mathematics, to the office of dragoman, first with a temporary and then with a permanent appointment. Şanizade rightly insists on the importance of this nomination, which placed this crucial post in safe, Muslim hands, and emancipated the professional use of foreign languages from the stigma of a gâvur trade.[23]

Yahya Efendi was himself a convert to Islam, and is variously reported as having been of Bulgarian, Greek, or Jewish origin. He was the founder of a dynasty in what became a new and vital official career. His son, Ruhuddin Mehmed Efendi, also educated at the school of mathematics, went to Paris in 1834 as dragoman to the Embassy of Mustafa Reşid Paşa; his grandson, Ahmed Vefik Paşa, entered the same service, which led him to a distinguished career as diplomat, statesman, and scholar.[24]

---

[21] Şanizade, iv. 20; Cevdet, *Tarih*, xi. 166.   [22] White, ii. 176.

[23] Şanizade, iv. 33–35; Cevdet, xii. 43. cf. *Sketches*, pp. 281 ff.

[24] See the biography of Ahmed Vefik Paşa in Mahmud Kemal Inal, *Osmanlı Devrinde Son Sadrıazamlar* (1940–53), pp. 651–738; also the articles by H. Bowen, 'Aḥmad Wafīḳ Pasha' in *EI*[2], and by Tanpınar in *IA*. Some interesting personal impressions of Vefik Paşa will be found in Nassau W. Senior's *Journal Kept in Turkey and Greece in the Autumn of 1857 and the beginning of 1858* (1859); in Mordtmann's *Stambul*, and other Western authors. On Yahya Efendi see Esad, *Mirât-i Mühendishane*, pp. 33–34.

On Yahya's death in 1823 or 1824, he was succeeded by his colleague Hoca Ishak, from the school, who held the office until 1830, when he returned to his teaching.[25] In 1833 the Sultan took the problem more seriously in hand, and created a 'translation chamber' (*tercüme odası*) at the Sublime Porte, which was later followed by similar 'chambers' in the Seraskerate and other departments of state.[26] In 1834 he reopened the permanent Embassies in the major European capitals, which had been allowed to lapse after the deposition of Selim III. The young diplomats and dragomans who staffed these missions thus had an opportunity to undergo in person the direct impact of the West. The significance of that impact may be gauged from the fact that almost every one of the reforming leaders and statesmen of the next half-century had served in these embassies. Of the three chief architects of the *Tanzimat*, Mustafa Reşid Paşa went to Paris in 1834; Âli Paşa went to Vienna in 1836; Fuad Paşa went to London in 1840. Among their outstanding collaborators Sadık Rifat Paşa was minister in Vienna in 1837, Mehmed Şekib was there in 1841, and Ibrahim Sarim Paşa served in London in 1834. Even the sons of these first diplomats, profiting from the opportunities of a stay in Europe in childhood or youth, filled a disproportionate number of high offices of state in the next generation. An outstanding example was Ahmed Vefik Paşa, the grandson and the son of interpreters, who went with his father to Paris in 1834 and spent the three years from 11 to 14 as a pupil at the Lycée St. Louis. Later he was ambassador in Paris, twice Grand Vezir, and President of the first Ottoman parliament of 1876. His literary and scholarly achievements were of at least equal significance. His Turkish dictionary, the first serious attempt at one by a Turk, had an importance analagous to that of Dr. Johnson's Dictionary in England; his translations of *Télémaque*, *Gil Blas*, and above all his brilliant adaptation of a group of plays by Molière, opened new paths and revealed new vistas in Turkish literature.[27]

[25] Cevdet, *Tarih*, xii. 91.

[26] Lûtfi, iv. 99. On the dragomans of the Sublime Porte, in general, see Kramers, 'Tardjumān', in *EI*[1]; Gibb and Bowen, I/i. 123; Ergin, *Maarif*, pp. 613–17 (n.1.); Uzunçarşılı, *Merkez ve Bahriye*, pp. 71–76. For a biographical survey of the Greek Chief Dragomans from 1661 to 1821, see Epaminondas I. Stamatiadis, Βιογραφίαι των Ἑλλήνων Μεγάλων Διερμηνέων τοῦ Ὀθωμανικοῦ Κράτους (1865).

[27] On Sadık Rifat Paşa see below, p. 129; on Ahmed Vefik Paşa see above, p. 86.

Centralization

Mahmud II lavished special care on his foreign service and on the training of young diplomats and civil servants in the use of foreign languages. This did not, however, help him very much in the larger, more difficult, and more complicated task of reorganizing and modernizing the internal administration of the Empire. The first essential of this task, as Mahmud saw it, was the centralization of all power in his own hands, and the elimination of all intermediate authorities, both in the capital and in the provinces. All power deriving from inheritance, from tradition, from usage, or from popular or local assent was to be suppressed, and the sovereign power alone was to remain as the sole source of authority in the Empire. Mahmud therefore continued his campaign in Rumelia and Anatolia, and succeeded in establishing direct central control over most areas. Only against the Pasha of Egypt was he ultimately unsuccessful.

At the same time as he extended the powers of the central government, he tried to improve the apparatus through which they were exercised. An ancient complaint of Ottoman officialdom had been its insecurity of tenure and exposure to confiscation which, according to Koçu Bey and his fellow memorialists, had led to a decline in competence and a weakening of moral fibre. Mahmud tried to improve the status of his civil officials, and to raise their standards both of proficiency and of honesty. In June 1826, two weeks after the destruction of the Janissaries, he issued a *Hatt-i Şerif* abolishing the office of Confiscation and Escheat and renouncing some of the previous reversionary rights of the treasury to heirless property and to the property of persons banished or condemned to death. This measure was no doubt costly to the treasury: it did, however, give to civil servants and indeed to others a measure of security of life and property such as they had not known before, and greatly facilitated the transaction of both public and private business.[28]

Census and Survey

Two further measures of centralization came in 1831. One was the first Ottoman census and survey in modern times. The immediate objectives were conscription and taxation—men for

[28] Lûtfi, i. 59; White, i. 109; Ubicini, letter 19.

the new army, and money to support it. Careful preparations were
made, and a committee appointed, which conducted a census of
the male population of Anatolia and Rumelia. Females and the
Arabian peninsula were omitted since neither were subject to
conscription. To forestall popular resentment and fear at this
unprecedented step, members of the ulema were included among
the census-takers.

At the same time as the census, a land survey was made, to
register landholdings and thus make possible a more efficient and
accurate system of tax assessment and collection.[29]

'*The Abolition of Feudalism*'

This prepared the way for the second major change of the year
—the abolition of the *timars*. The *timar*, or military fief, had been
the basis of the distinctively Ottoman type of feudalism since the
very beginnings of the Empire. The *timar* was a grant of land, in
return for which the sipahi, a feudal cavalryman, was bound to
render military service in person and with as many men-at-arms
as were required by the size and income of his fief. From the end
of the sixteenth century the system had begun to decay. In the
army the paid regular troops grew in importance at the expense
of the feudal cavalry; in the countryside more and more *timars*
were converted into crown lands and appanages and then leased
out (*iltizam* or *mukataa*) to tax-farmers with purely financial and
no military obligations. The decline of the sipahis as a class, and
the gradual replacement of *timar* by *iltizam* in the country, are
among the most frequently cited causes of Ottoman decline.

At the beginning of the nineteenth century, however, neither
the sipahi nor the *timar* had yet disappeared. Extensive lands,
especially in Anatolia, were still classed and held as *timar*, and in
the armed forces there were still many who were paid by fief
instead of, or as well as, from the treasury. The cavalry was still
predominantly feudal, as were also many of the local levies raised
in the provinces. The distinction between the different kinds of
troops was not rigid, and it was not infrequent for Janissaries and
other regulars to receive *timars*.

The policy of converting *timar* into domain and then leasing it as
iltizam was adopted in a more rigorous form by Selim III, who

---

[29] Lûtfi, iii. 142; Karal, *Tarih*, v. 159. Karal has also written a monograph on the
census of 1831, entitled *Osmanlı Imparatorluğunda ilk nüfus sayımı* (1943).

needed ready money for his New Army and was not averse to weakening the basis of the old one. As Asım said:

> Since the ancient revenues of the exalted Dynasty were not adequate to its present expenditure, and since it was a present necessity to organize an adequate income to cover the cost of the New Army, *timars* in the *eyalet* of Anatolia were to be taken over by the treasury. Though a group of ignorant people considered this to be manifest tyranny, it is obvious to people of sound judgement ... that the martyred Sultan had acted in a way very far from tyranny.[30]

Indeed, Asım implies, considering the cowardly and miserable performance of the sipahis in the war against Russia, it was generous of the Sultan merely to divert the revenues of their *timars* to the use of the New Army, and to leave them to enjoy life and repose in their countries.

Mahmud's revocation of all remaining *timars* in 1831 was thus a logical continuation of the policies of his predecessors. The military aspect of the change was of secondary importance. The old-style cavalry had been dissolved at the same time as the Janissaries, the new army was growing, and the dissolution of the last of the sipahis made no great difference in the military forces of the Empire. Those of the sipahis whose services were worth retaining were formed into four squadrons of cavalry, which provided the nucleus of a new regular cavalry arm. The remaining sipahis were given pensions.

What was more important was the liquidation of the last vestiges of feudalism. Even at this stage, the extent of *timar* land must have been fairly considerable, for the amount assigned for pensions came to 120,000 purses, or 60 million piastres (at that time about £750,000). The cost of maintaining the New Army, 12,000 men strong, was estimated in 1827 at 34,000 purses. There are reported to have been about 1,500 *timars* in Anatolia, and under 1,000 in Rumelia. These now became crown domains and were mostly leased out to tax-farmers. From the point of view of the revenue, the seizure of the *timars* seems to have been disappointing; by it, however, the Sultan tightened his hold on the provinces, and carried his policy of centralization an important step forward.[31]

---

[30] Asım, i. 40–41; cf. Cevdet, *Tarih*, v. 289–90 and vi. 57 ff.

[31] On the *timar* system, see Deny, 'Tīmār', in *EI*[1]. On the abolition of the fiefs see Inalcık's study, 'Tanzimat Nedir', pp. 244 ff., and sources cited there; also Bailey, pp. 36–37.

Vakf[32]

The pensioning off of the sipahis and the seizure of the *timars* was a comparatively easy matter; it was an obvious corollary to the destruction of the Janissaries, and was, in a sense, the culmination of a process that had been going on for a long time. Far more dangerous and controversial was the subordination to the Sultan's control of another category of lands and estates— the *evkâf*, or pious foundations.

The *vakf* was an old Islamic institution,[33] well established in the Ottoman Empire. Originally it was a dedication of land or other revenue-producing property to pious purposes. In time the practice grew up of establishing family *evkâf*, for the benefit of the founder's family and descendants, as a safeguard against the general insecurity of property rights. Except by a Sultan, *vakf* could only be made out of *mülk*, or freehold property, and not out of land held as fief, tax-farm, appanage, and the like. It was therefore comparatively rare in agricultural areas, and most frequent in and around the cities. In Istanbul and other cities most *mülk* had in the course of time become *vakf*, and almost all the building sites, fruit and vegetable gardens, orchards and vineyards in the city and its immediate environs had become, in fact or in name, inalienable and irrevocable pious endowments. The effective control and disposition of these *evkâf* and their revenues was usually in the hands of administrators and collectors (*mütevelli* and *cabi*), who belonged to, or were appointed by, members of the class of ulema. The Chief Mufti and other dignitaries, both religious and lay, had their own groups of *evkâf* under their control, each with his own arrangements for supervision. The most important were directly or indirectly under the control of the Muftis and Kadis, and thus constituted a major source of economic power for the religious institution.

In 1826, with the Janissaries out of the way, Mahmud was able

---

[32] On the *vakf* reform, see Lûtfi, i. 205; Ubicini, letter 12; White, i. 236; Köprülü, 'Vakıf müessesesinin hukukî mâhiyeti ve tarihî tekâmülü', *Vak. Derg.*, ii. 23 ff. of Turkish text, pp. 31 ff. of translation; Temperley, pp. 31 and 405. Reference may also be made to the official history of the Ministry of Vakf, *Evkâf-i Humâyûn Nezaretinin Tarihçe-i Teşkilâtı* (1335). In this too Mahmud seems to have been following an example set by Muhammad Ali in Egypt, in 1812.

[33] Turkish *vakf* or *vakıf* (plural *evkâf* or, in the new Turkish, *vakıflar*), from Arabic *waqf* (plural *awqâf*). On the institution in general see *EI*[1] ('Wakf', by W. Heffening).

to strike at this power. Ostensibly with the intention of ending the existing anarchy in *evkâf* administration and bringing them all under a single jurisdiction, he created a new Directorate (later Ministry) of *Evkâf*, into which the existing agencies of supervision were incorporated. But, in the words of the historian Mustafa Nuri Paşa, himself for a while a Minister of *Evkâf*, 'since some of the ministers were of tyrannical disposition and some of them were ignorant of important matters of law, the *vakf* administration brimmed over with abuses'.[34] Mahmud's aim was nothing less than to centralize the collection and expenditure of *Evkâf* revenues in his own hands, receiving them from the collectors and administrators and paying out what was necessary for the upkeep of religious buildings, the salaries of religious personnel, and other pious purposes. Mustafa Nuri's description of Mahmud II's *vakf* policy amounts to a charge of malversation, and concludes that the Ministry of *Evkâf*, 'which should have been the protector of the *evkâf*, became their destroyer'.[35] Mahmud, it would seem, was not only the Peter the Great but also the Henry VIII of Turkey. From a different point of view, Charles White was of the same opinion, at least as regards the Sultan's intentions:

Sultan Mahmoud II . . . seriously contemplated carrying this plan into effect, and would probably have done so had his life been spared. The government in this case would have paid the salaries of all sheikhs, priests, and persons attached to the sacred edifices, together with all repairs and expenses of their dependent institutions, and would have converted the surplus to state purposes. Various plans were suggested to Sultan Mahmoud's predecessors; but during the existence of the Janissaries, no one dared to interfere with the institutions, whence the oolema, intimately connected with the Janissaries, derived invariable benefit.[36]

Mahmud's attempt to divert *evkâf* revenues was not entirely successful. He did, however, initiate a process which gravely weakened the power of the ulema to oppose him. Under his successors, the diversion of *evkâf* revenues to state purposes was standard practice, so much so that many mosques and other genuinely religious endowments were starved of funds for their upkeep.

[34] Nuri, *Netaic*, iv. 100.   [35] Ibid. p. 101.   [36] White, i. 236.

Communications

Another group of reforms that helped the Sultan in his policy of centralization was that concerned with the improvement of communications. In 1831 the first issue appeared of the *Takvim-i Vekayi*, the Ottoman official gazette.[37] This was not the first newspaper in Turkey. Between 1796 and 1798 the French Embassy in Constantinople had published a newspaper in French for distribution to the French colony and such others as knew the French language. In the 1820's some further French newspapers appeared, this time in Izmir. The most important of them was *Le Spectateur oriental*. The real spur, however, was the publication in Egypt in 1828, by Muhammad Ali, of the *Waḳā'i'Miṣriyya*, the Egyptian gazette—the first indigenous newspaper published in the Middle East.

What the Pasha could do, the Sultan could do better, if later. In 1831 the first issue appeared of the *Moniteur ottoman*, in the French language, under the editorship of a Frenchman called Alexandre Blaque, the former editor of *Le Spectateur oriental*. A Turkish version, called *Takvim-i Vekayi*, followed a few months later. It was the first newspaper in the Turkish language, and is well described by Charles White: 'The contents of this journal were at first strictly limited to a reproduction of official appointments, extracts of judicial trials, and pompous descriptions of the Sultan's progress on state occasions.'[38] It remained the only newspaper in Turkish until 1840, when an Englishman called William Churchill published the first non-official Turkish newspaper, the *Ceride-i Havadis*. The second did not appear until 1860.

The *Takvim-i Vekayi* was required reading for public officials. Its efficacy as a means of making the Sultan's policies and purposes better known to his servants was greatly increased by the inauguration of a postal system in 1834. The first post road, from

[37] On the development of the press see White, ii. 218 ff.; Ubicini, letter 11; Temperley, pp. 244–5; Slade, i. 273 ff.; Mahmud Kemal in *TOEM*, no. 96–97 (on the contributors to the *Ceride-i Havadis*), and the histories of the Turkish press by Ahmed Emin [Yalman], *The Development of Modern Turkey as Measured by its Press* (1914); Gerçek, *Türk Gazeteciliği, 1831–1931* (1931); Server R. Iskit, *Türkiyede Matbuat Rejimleri* (1939); and Vedad Günyol in *IA*, vii. 367 ff. On the French papers: L. Lagarde, 'Note sur les journaux français de Constantinople', *J. As.* (1948), pp. 271–6 and 'Note sur les journaux français de Smyrne à l'époque de Mahmoud II', ibid. (1950), pp. 103–44.

[38] White, ii. 218 ff.

Üsküdar to Izmit, was formally opened by the Sultan, riding in a phaeton, followed by his suite in post-carts. They travelled as far as Kartal, where the Sultan received a petition in a local dispute arising out of the conversion of a Christian girl to Islam. A second postal route was opened from Istanbul to Edirne, and later others linked the main centres of the Empire. The purpose of the new postal system is indicated in the *Hatt-i Humayun* establishing it:

> Since it is obligatory to secure the safety and procure the revenues of my Imperial realm, and since disorder has arisen and appeared in the matter of correspondence, on account of its not being known from whom and to whom the letters that are sent from my Gate of Felicity to the country and that come from the country to my Gate of Felicity come and go; therefore, in order to set this matter aright, it has occurred to my Imperial mind to deal with it in this way: as is the practice in other countries, so also in my lofty Empire, a responsible official being appointed to supervise the matter, and a suitable place assigned to it, men shall be established by him at appropriate places in Anatolia and Rumelia, so that henceforth no person shall despatch letters of his own accord, but both the people of Islam and the Raya and Frankish communities shall bring the letters and objects which they wish to send to the superintendent; these being registered in the book, shall be sent, &c., &c.[39]

There were other improvements in communications besides the post. New roads were built, and the introduction of a quarantine system facilitated movement between Turkey and Europe, which had previously been subject to vexatious delays. With the coming of the telegraph in 1855 and the first railways in 1856, the administrative centralization initiated by Mahmud was enormously strengthened.

Committees and Ministries

At the same time as he extended and strengthened the control of the central government over the provinces, the Sultan made a number of significant changes in the structure and organization of the central government staff. One purpose of these was to give to the apparatus and personnel of Ottoman government the nomenclature and outward appearance of their European

[39] Karal, *Tarih*, v. 160–1; Lûtfi, iv. 162 ff. On ports and other communications see further Bailey, p. 136; Ubicini, letter 18.

equivalents, and thereby to impress European observers with the modernity and progressiveness of Turkey, and perhaps also to win for Turkey something of the elusive secret of Western power and efficiency. The change had very little success in either respect. European observers both contemporary and subsequent were contemptuous of a change that affected only externals and appearances, leaving the realities as they were before.

Clearly, to call the Grand Vezir and his colleagues ministers, dress them in frock-coats, provide them with offices, desks, and newly frock-coated staffs, did not change them overnight into the administration of a modern state. Mahmud's administrative reforms were, however, by no means ineffective—though their effects were understood by but few contemporaries, either Turkish or Western.

The most important was the breakdown of old traditions, of established rights and privileges, of institutions with powers and prestige deriving from the past instead of from the Sultan, and their replacement by a new set of institutions which, since they had neither inherited dignity nor acquired esteem, depended entirely on the sovereign power.

The first changes came immediately after the destruction of the Janissaries, which here too cleared the way for the extension of the Sultan's control. Of the two chief limiting authorities in the capital, the old army was crushed and the ulema cowed. The Sultan hastened to make use of his opportunity. The Serasker and his staff at the Seraskerate became the nucleus of the civilian Ministry of War which, until the Young Turk Revolution, was able to maintain the control of the central government over the armed forces and prevent the recurrence of anything like the constant Janissary uprisings that had terrorized the Sultans of the preceding period.[40]

The former residence of the Aga of the Janissaries, near the Süleymaniye mosque, was turned over to the Chief Mufti, who thus for the first time acquired an office and department. Until 1826 the Chief Muftis had held courts and issued rulings from their own residences. Their revenues, their employees, their establishments had been entirely independent of the palace, subject only to the final power of dismissal. The creation of an office and department of the Chief Mufti (known as *Bab-i Meşihat* or

[40] B. Lewis, 'Bāb-i Ser'askerī', in *EI*². See also above, p. 79.

Fetvahane) was the first step towards the bureaucratization of the ulema, which undermined their popular and effective power and gravely weakened their ability—and at times even their desire— to resist change. Another, of no less importance, was the subjection to government control of the *evkâf*.[41]

Deprived of both their financial and their administrative autonomy, the ulema were weakened as against the sovereign power, and were unable to resist successive diminutions of their competence, authority, and status. The appointment of teachers and control of schools and colleges was later transferred to a Ministry of Education; the appointment of judges and the administration of the law to a Ministry of Justice; and in time even the drafting of *fetvas* was entrusted to a committee of legal specialists in the Chief Mufti's office under the Fetva Emini, the commissioner of *fetvas*. The Chief Mufti himself became a government office-holder, with some consultative and advisory functions, and with only such effective influence as his own personal character could win for him.

The Sultan's first new departments of state—war, *evkâf*, and the Mufti's office—were thus not so much measures of modernization as attempts to consolidate the gains won from the forces of the old order by the destruction of the Janissaries, and to render the army and the ulema incapable of reviving their ancient authority against the Sultan. A few years later Mahmud felt strong enough to attack the Sublime Porte itself—the office of the Grand Vezir, which for nearly two centuries had been the real seat of Ottoman Government. In 1835 two departments, those of the Kâhya and of the Reis Efendi, were constituted as separate ministries—though remaining in the same building and performing the same duties— and named Ministries of Civil and Foreign Affairs respectively. Two years later the old office of the Defterdar was renamed Ministry of Finance, and the Defterdar himself joined the Grand Vezir and the Reis Efendi as a minister. The Ministry of Civil Affairs was renamed Ministry of the Interior in 1837, and in the following year the title of Grand Vezir was abolished and the incumbent was named Prime Minister. Later the title of Grand Vezir was restored.[42]

A Grand Vezir turned Prime Minister, with a couple of other

[41] B. Lewis, 'Bāb-i Mas̲h̲ī̲k̲h̲at', in *EI²*, and above, pp. 91–92.

[42] On the new ministries in general see Karal, *Tarih*, vi. 123 ff.; Şeref, *Tarih-i Devlet-i Osmaniye*, ii. 464 ff. and Lûtfi, iii. 145. See further B. Lewis, 'Başvekil' and 'Daftardār' in *EI²*.

new holders of ministerial titles, do not yet make cabinet government. Mahmud was, however, preparing the way for a system of government based on malleable and interchangeable groups instead of powerful and entrenched individuals. Some consultative committees had already existed in earlier times. Mahmud now created a Privy Council or Council of Ministers (*Meclis-i Hass* and *Meclis-i Vükela*) presided over by the Prime Minister. As the number of ministers increased under his successors, this body gained in importance. Of more immediate significance were two other bodies, created in 1836 and 1837: the Council for Military Affairs (*Meclis-i Dar-i Şura-yi Askeri*) and the High Council for Judicial Ordinances (*Meclis-i Vala-i Ahkâm-i Adliye*). These were small, executive groups, each consisting of a chairman, five members, and one or two secretaries. They were to play an important role in planning and executing the reforms of the immediately following period. In 1838 Mahmud also established committees for agriculture, trade, industry, and public works. [43]

While these changes in nomenclature brought little or no immediate change in the conduct of affairs, they did mark the first step towards the break-up of old, well-entrenched institutions and their replacement by others of foreign provenance. The changes became more of a reality when the old officials of the Porte were replaced by a new generation of civil servants different in education, outlook, and social background from their predecessors.

Social and Cultural Change

The medieval Egyptian chronicles tell us that after the great Mongol conquests of the thirteenth century, even the Muslim Sultans and Emirs of Egypt began to wear their hair long in the Mongol style. But in 1315 the Sultan decided to return to the Muslim practice of shaving his head. In the words of Maqrīzī (d. 1442): 'He went to the bath and shaved his whole head, and there did not remain one of the Emirs and Mamluks that failed to do likewise; and from that time the soldiers ceased to wear their hair long, and so it has continued until today.' [44]

[43] Ata, iii. 121 ff., 137 ff., 294 ff.; Lûtfi, v. 70, 106, 128, &c.; Karal, *Tarih*, vi. 116 ff.

[44] *Sulūk*, II/1 (Cairo, 1941), p. 148; L. A. Mayer, *Mamluk Costume* (1952), pp. 17–18; cf. Maqrīzī, *Khitat*, ii (Bulaq, 1270 A.H.), pp. 216–17 on the introduction of Mongol-style dress by Qala'un in the thirteenth century (D. S. Rice, *Le Baptistère de St. Louis* (1951), p. 13).

H

From the rise of Islam until the coming of the European, the Mongol was the only infidel invader to establish an empire in the heartlands of Islam—and Mongol methods of warfare, Mongol laws and customs as well as Mongol styles of dress were for a while imitated and adopted even in such lands as Egypt, which remained beyond the reach of the Mongol sword.

After the decline of the Mongol power, these influences decreased and eventually disappeared, and the older Muslim customs were once again supreme. It is a measure of the impact of European power and prestige on Selim III and Mahmud II that they should once again have attempted to breach the defences of sartorial conservatism and clothe their troops in European-style uniforms—in a costume to which was attached the aura of success and victory.

In the code of regulations issued in 1826 for the new-style army, it was laid down that their uniforms were to consist of European-style tunics and trousers. Twenty years previously an attempt to put the auxiliary troops into Frankish dress had launched the mutiny of 1807 and led directly to the deposition of Selim III. This time the reform was accepted, though not without rumbles of opposition, and the troops were issued with 'a *şubara*, a drill-coat, a short tunic and vest of broadcloth, tight-fitting serge breeches, and frontier-boots'.[45]

The question of Frankish uniforms raised larger issues than could be settled in the quartermaster's stores. Since early times, dress and above all head-gear were the means by which a man indicated his religious allegiance and his social status. Apart from a ban on silk, the Muslim law does not actually prohibit any kind of garment, but there are countless traditions urging the Muslims to distinguish themselves, even in appearance, from the infidels and to avoid imitating their habits in dress as well as in all else. 'God and the angels give their blessing at the Friday prayer to those who wear the turban.' 'Two prostrations with the turban outweigh seventy without the turban.' 'The turban is the barrier separating belief and unbelief.' 'Distinguish yourselves from the idolators; let your beards grow and trim your moustaches.' 'He who imitates a people, becomes one of them.'[46]

---

[45] Lûtfi, i. 191–3.

[46] Cited in M. Canard, 'Coiffure européenne et Islam', *A. l'Inst. d'Ét. or.* (Algiers), viii. (1949–50), 200 ff. Slade's comments on some aspects of the reform in dress, written

These and many other similar sayings attributed to the Prophet helped to reinforce the general feeling that to abandon one's own form of dress and adopt another was an act of treason and of apostasy. Non-Muslims were forbidden to adopt Muslim dress; Muslims would not dream of adopting Christian or Jewish dress. Even within the Muslim camp, each order of society had its own distinctive head-gear; the different shaped head-gear of the ulema, the Janissaries, and the men of the pen distinguished them during their lifetimes, and were carved in stone on their tombs after their death.

It was thus no easy matter to persuade ordinary Muslim Turkish soldiers to accept what for them were the distinguishing marks of the infidel, the stigmata of inferiority. Most difficult of all to accept was the hat, and even at the present time, in many Muslim countries, the head-covering is the last refuge of conservatism. The fez and the sidara remain as the final symbol of religious identification and allegiance, while the rest of the body has accepted the fitted garments of the West.

The *şubara* was a wadded cap, made of cloth, with a roughly cylindrical crown ending in a flap. It was worn in former times by the Bostancıs and then by the *Nizam-i Cedid* troops of Selim III. Its use by Mahmud's new-style army was of short duration. In 1828 a new head-gear, of North African origin, was shown to the Sultan, and won his approval. It was called the Fez. A meeting was convened at the office of the Chief Mufti, and presided over by the Grand Vezir, to discuss the problem of military head-gear. It was agreed that the *şubara* was in every way unsatisfactory, and a fez was examined and approved, despite hesitation on the part of some of those present as to whether it could properly be considered an Islamic head-covering. Strong measures were taken to forestall and, if necessary, to suppress

from quite another point of view, are worth citing: 'In no one thing did Sultan Mahmoud make a greater mistake, than in changing the mode of mounting the Turkish cavalry, which before had perfect seats, with perfect command over their horses, and only required a little order to transform the best irregular horse in the world into the best regular horse. But Mahmoud, in all his changes, took the mask for the man, the rind for the fruit.—European cavalry rode flat saddles with long stirrups; therefore he thought it necessary that his cavalry should be the same. European infantry wore tight jackets and close caps; therefore the same. Were this blind adoption of forms only useless, or productive only of physical inconvenience, patience; but it proved a moral evil, creating unbounded disgust' (ii. 210–11). For a contrasting comment see *Sketches*, p. 237.

popular opposition to this new head-gear, and orders were given
for its issue to the army. A century later it had become so well
acclimatized that it was attacked—and defended—as the emblem
of Ottoman and Islamic traditionalism and orthodoxy.[47]

A modification to the fez, of the year 1845, may be related in
the words of the Imperial Historiographer Lûtfi:

Until this time, the tassels which the regular troops, as well as the
generality of Imperial servants and subjects, attached to their fezzes
were made of unspun silk. The damage that befell their threads from
the wind, the rain, and other vile things made it an urgent necessity
to have the tassels combed every day. To comb the tassels, there were
people, mostly Jewish boys, who, like the bootblacks today, cried 'Let
us comb your tassels' in the streets and market-places, and made a
living by this. The women too, arranging things somehow, used to
attach combed tassels to flat-topped fezzes; to make them rest more
easily on their heads, they used to put wires inside the fez, and plates
of silver instead of paper at the top. These silken tassels rightly came to
be called by the people 'the tasselled curse'. This being so, and since
it was a matter involving much trouble both for the military and for
civilians, the principle was adopted that for the commanders, officers,
and men of the army, plaited tassels of a designated and indicated
weight were to be attached; that for military ceremonies badges of
rank in the form of circular metal plates were to be attached to the
crown of the fez, and that for other ranks plaited tassels were to be
adopted instead of tassels of silk thread.[48]

In 1829 the clothing reform was extended to civilians.[49] A
decree of that year sets forth in great detail the costume to be
worn by different classes of officials on different occasions. In
general, the robe and the turban were permitted only to the
ulema. For other civilians the fez compulsorily replaced all other
forms of head-gear, and robes and slippers gave way to frock-
coats and capes, trousers, and black leather boots. Jewels, pelisses,
and other adornments were to go, and even beards were trimmed.
The Sultan himself set an example which spread from the court
to the pashas and then through the various grades of officials.
At the same time European chairs and tables began to appear

[47] On the introduction of the fez see the study by Uzunçarşılı in *Bell.*, no. 70 (1954),
223–30. On the vestimentary reforms see further Lûtfi, i. 255–6; Rasim, *Osmanlı Tar.*,
iv. 1826 n. 280; White, ii. 50 ff.; Slade, ii. 210 ff.; Temperley, p. 21; Bailey, p. 37;
Karal, *Tarih*, v. 154, 161–2.

[48] Lûtfi, viii. 69–70; Karal, *Tarih*, vi. 279.   [49] Lûtfi, ii. 148, 269.

beside the divans and cushions of the old order, and European
social manners were adopted. The Sultan began to receive foreign
diplomats according to European and not Ottoman protocol,
gave receptions and chatted with his guests, and even went so far
as to show deference to ladies. The Thursday day of rest—
religiously neutral—was borrowed from France and introduced in
government offices, and, still more startling, the Sultan's portrait
was hung on their walls.[50]

These changes were as yet still only on the surface. The Holy
Law of Islam was still unchallenged, above all in social and
family matters. Marriage and divorce, property and inheritance,
the status of women and of slaves—all these were substantially
unchanged, and at this stage the reformers do not seem to have
thought of any kind of reform in religious institutions. 'In political matters', said Sadık Rifat Paşa to Stratford Canning in
1844, 'we shall defer entirely to the advice of Europe. In religious
matters we need all our liberty. Religion is the basis of our laws.
It is the principle of our government; His Majesty the Sultan
can no more touch it than we can.'[51]

The Men of the Reform [52]

In the thirteen years between the destruction of the Janissaries
in 1826 and his death in 1839, the Sultan attempted to carry out a
programme of reform as extensive as that of Peter the Great in
Russia and far more difficult. Peter was already an autocrat;
Mahmud had to make himself one, overcoming the resistance of
the old, deeply-rooted Ottoman Islamic tradition of society and
government, the opposition of well-entrenched and popularly
supported classes both in the capital and the provinces, and, most
of all, the ancient and profound contempt of Islam for the infidel
and its rejection of anything bearing the taint of infidel origin.

The example of Peter the Great was not unknown in Turkey;
it was cited by the chronicler Asım as an illustration of how a weak

[50] Lûtfi, v. 50 (portrait); iv. 100 and v. 55 (Thursday day of rest).

[51] Cited by P. Graves, *Briton and Turk* (1941), p. 23; cf. the observations of Fuad
Paşa, cited by Cevdet, *Tezakir*, p. 85.

[52] The most comprehensive biographical data will be found in Inal, *Sadrıazamlar*,
a series of biographies of the Ottoman Grand Vezirs from Mehmed Emin Âli Paşa
(appointed 1852) to the end. See also *EI¹*, *EI²*, and *IA*, where biographies of many
personalities will be found, with further bibliographical indications. Appreciations of
some of the literary figures of the time—including many politicians—will be found
in E. J. W. Gibb, *A History of Ottoman Poetry*, iv (1905), and Tanpınar, i.

and backward country could win power and greatness by borrowing Frankish devices.[53] It was not to Peter, however, that Mahmud looked for a model; it was to his admired predecessor Selim, whose work he was determined to complete, and to his hated rival the Pasha of Egypt, whose example he was resolved to better.

But the task was appallingly difficult. Even when the forces of reaction had been beaten into submission, there was still the problem of finding suitable men to devise and apply the reforms. The Sultan himself, strong-willed and violent, was profoundly ignorant of everything Western. There were still lamentably few of his countrymen who were any better placed. Peter had invited great numbers of West Europeans to help him in his reforms. Muslim fanaticism prevented Mahmud from inviting more than a small number of foreigners, and from making much use of those who did come. Even a knowledge of European languages was still a rarity; and this gap was only gradually filled by the missions abroad and the Translation Office in Istanbul.

The men at Mahmud's disposal were thus poorly equipped to carry out the tasks assigned to them. Still worse was the growth and spread of corruption in the new civil service. Complaints of corruption were often heard under the old régime. They became more frequent under the new one. The increased cost of a Westernized style of living; the continuing insecurity of tenure and property; the chronic financial disorders of the reformist ministries, and above all the breakdown, without replacement, of traditional moral standards, all helped to make the new civil servants cynical and venal. In the old order there had been an accepted set of social loyalties and obligations, to which most men had tried to conform. With the destruction of the old order this complex web of social relationships and loyalties was torn asunder, and in its place came a new set of imported and alien institutions, with little meaning for the new officialdom and none at all for the people whom they ruled. There had always been a gulf between the rulers and the ruled. It now became fantastically wide, as the progress of Westernization added to the differences of power and wealth those of education and outlook, home and furnishings, even food and dress.

Reşid Paşa, Mahmud's chief instrument in the establishment of direct Imperial control in Eastern Anatolia, Armenia, and Kurdistan, was by no means well-disposed to the reforms. Husrev

[53] See above, p. 71.

Paşa (1756–1853), who was Serasker from 1827 to 1836, was, however, a fanatical supporter of the reforms, and was able both to train and present to the Sultan a body of new-style troops, and to maintain order by rigorous police methods. Though he later became Grand Vezir, he never learnt to read or write, and his contributions to reform, if vigorous, were often ignorant and violent. His successor as Serasker, Hafiz Paşa, was also favourable to modern military methods, and took Moltke with him on a campaign in Mesopotamia.

On the civilian side, the most powerful man in the early years of Mahmud's reign was Halet Efendi, a convinced reactionary who had been ambassador in Paris from 1802 to 1806 and had returned to Turkey with a reinforced hatred of Europe and everything European. He defended the Janissaries and opposed military reform until his fall and execution in 1822. Another ex-ambassador to Paris, Galib Paşa (1763–1828), who had served in France in 1801, was far more positive in his attitude to the West. He held various offices under Mahmud II and became Grand Vezir in 1823, holding the office for only nine months. He is credited with having had a fine understanding of Turkish and European political problems, and with having exercised a formative influence on the rising generation of reformist statesmen.

In the 1820's and 1830's the rival poets Akif Paşa (1787–1845) and Pertev Paşa (d. 1837) alternated in the high offices of state. Though both were thoroughly conservative and traditional in their upbringing and political outlook, Akif nevertheless made a contribution of some importance to the progress of the reforms by casting off the cumbersome and convoluted chancery style until then current in Ottoman official usage, and initiating the development of a simpler and more direct prose style better suited to the needs of a modern state.[54]

Mustafa Reşid Paşa [55]

Far more important than any of these, however, was Mustafa Reşid Paşa (1800–58), in many ways the real architect of the

[54] On Halet, see Şeref, *Tar. Mus.*, pp. 27–38 and Karal, *Tarih*, vi. 279; on Husrev Paşa, *EI*[1] and *IA*, *s.v.*; on Galib Paşa, Babinger, *Geschichtsschreiber*, p. 331, and Uzunçarşılı in *Bell.*, no. 2 (1937), 357 ff.; on Akif and Pertev, Gibb, *Ottoman Poetry*, iv. 323 ff. and Tanpınar, pp. 60 ff.

[55] On Mustafa Reşid Paşa: Reşat Kaynar, *Mustafa Reşit Paşa ve Tanzimat* (1954); Cavid Baysun, 'Mustafa Reşit Paşa' in *Tanzimat*, pp. 723–46; Şeref, *Tar. Mus.*, pp. 75–87; and the general works on the period, by Karal, Şeref, Temperley, Rasim, &c.

nineteenth-century Ottoman reforms. He was born in Istanbul, the son of a *vakf* official who died when he was only ten years old. He was taught to read by his father, and then attended the mosque school, but did not complete a formal higher education in the *medrese*, of the type customary at that time. He was protected by a relative by marriage, Ispartalı Seyyid Ali Paşa, with whose help he entered government employment at an early age. His talents soon won him advancement, and in 1832 he was appointed *Amedi*, a post which made him in effect chief secretary to the Reis Efendi, the official in charge of foreign affairs.

In 1834 he was sent as ambassador to Paris—the first of a series of diplomatic appointments. Among those who accompanied him was Ruhuddin Efendi, the dragoman—the son of Yahya Efendi, who had been a teacher at the naval school and later dragoman of the Porte, and the father of the more famous Ahmed Vefik Paşa. On his way to Paris he passed through Vienna, where he had a conversation with Prince Metternich. Soon after his arrival in Paris, he set to work to master the French language, and by 1839, when on another visit to France he was received by Louis Philippe, he was able to converse with the king without an interpreter. While in Paris he became friendly with the venerable Orientalist Silvestre de Sacy, who helped him in learning French and in meeting important people.

After holding various other diplomatic and official appointments, he became Minister of Foreign Affairs, and was on a special mission to London when the news arrived, in 1839, of the death of Mahmud II and the accession of his son Abdülmecid.

Abdülmecid: the Rescript of the Rose Chamber [56]

The new Sultan was determined to continue his father's work, and was supported in this by his mother, the Valide Sultan Bezm-i Alem, a remarkable woman who exercised considerable influence over her son and consequently over the government of the Empire. The moment was a critical one. Muhammad Ali, the rebellious

[56] On Abdülmecid see *EI*[2] and *IA*, *s.v.* On the Rescript of 1839, see the important comments of Cevdet Paşa (*Tezakir*, pp. 7 ff.) and of Prince Metternich (Engelhardt, i. 47–51; cf. Metternich's *Mémoires*, Paris, 1884, vi. 378–86). Further discussions and comments in Lûtfi, vi. 59 ff.; Nuri, *Netaic*, iv. 97 ff.; Ata, iii. 203 ff.; Kâmil Paşa, *Tarih-i Siyasî*, iii. 191 ff.; White, i. 110–20; Ubicini, letter 2; Rosen, ii. 16 ff.; Engelhardt, i. 35 ff.; Şeref, *Tar. Mus.*, pp. 48 ff.; Jorga, v. 390; Sax, pp. 278 ff.; Temperley, p. 157; Bailey, pp. 193 ff.; Kaynar, pp. 164 ff.; Karal, *Tarih*, v. 173 ff.

Pasha of Egypt, had resumed hostilities against the Porte, and on 24 June his armies had inflicted a crushing defeat on the Ottoman forces at the battle of Nezib. It was no doubt in part to demonstrate to Europe that the Sultan's government, as well as that of the Pasha of Egypt, could produce a liberal and modern régime, that the new Ottoman ministers produced the famous Noble Rescript of the Rose Chamber (*Hatt-i Şerif* of Gülhane), promulgated on 3 November 1839.[57]

Husrev Paşa had become Grand Vezir after the succession of the new Sultan, but Reşid Paşa, who had returned post-haste from London to direct foreign affairs in the new ministry, took the main initiative in drafting and promulgating the first of the great reforming edicts which are collectively known in Turkish history as the *Tanzimat*—the Reorganization.

The Noble Rescript proclaimed such principles as the security of life, honour, and property of the subject, the abolition of tax-farming and all the abuses associated with it, regular and orderly recruitment into the armed forces, fair and public trial of persons accused of crimes, and equality of persons of all religions in the application of these laws. It was this last that represented the most radical breach with ancient Islamic tradition, and was therefore most shocking to Muslim principles and good taste.

The laws and traditions of Islam, the policy and practice of the Ottoman Empire, agreed in prescribing tolerance and protection for the non-Muslim subjects of the state, and in granting them a large measure of autonomy in their internal communal affairs. This toleration, however, was predicated on the assumption that the tolerated communities were separate and inferior, and were moreover clearly marked as such. To give up this principle of inequality and segregation required of the Muslim no less great an effort of renunciation than is required of those Westerners who are now called upon to forego the satisfactions of racial superiority. Of the two prejudices, that of the Muslim against the infidel had stronger roots both in tradition and in morality. The Muslim could claim that he assigned to his inferiors a position of reasonable comfort and security; he could moreover claim that his

---

[57] The text of this, and of other Turkish laws of the nineteenth and early twentieth centuries, will be found in the *Düstur* (Ist., 1871–1928); translations of some of them in G. Aristarchi, *Législation ottomane* (1873–88) and G. Young, *Corps de droit ottoman* (1905–6).

discrimination related not to an accident of birth but to a conscious choice on the most fundamental questions of human existence. Infidel and true believer were different and separate; to equalize them and to mix them was an offence against both religion and common sense.

Another striking feature of the Noble Rescript is its frank reference to 'new rules'. In traditional Muslim usage the word *Bid'a*, innovation, was the converse of *Sunna*, the accepted practice of the orthodox, and it came to be in effect a synonym for heresy. This attitude is well summed up in a saying attributed to the Prophet that 'the worst things are those that are novelties, every novelty is an innovation, every innovation is an error, and every error leads to Hell-fire'.[58] It was in this spirit that earlier reforms were often presented not as something new, but as a reversion to ancient practice. The Noble Rescript also begins with a pious allusion to the mighty and honoured past, but goes on to speak frankly of the creation of 'new institutions' to secure for the Empire the benefits of good administration.

The most important of these was the Council of Judicial Ordinances (*Meclis-i Ahkâm-i Adliye*), more commonly known as the Council of Justice. This body had been set up two years previously by Sultan Mahmud II.[59] It was presided over by the Serasker Husrev Paşa, and consisted of the president, five members, and two secretaries. The Noble Rescript laid down that this body was to be enlarged by the addition of new members, and to exercise a supervisory and quasi-legislative function.

A few months later, in March 1840, a new Imperial Rescript (*Hatt-i Humayun*) gave details of the reorganization of the Council of Justice, which, in various forms, played a central role throughout the period of the *Tanzimat*.[60] At about the same time Reşid Paşa introduced a completely new system of centralized provincial administration, modelled on the French system of prefectures and *départements*, with salaried officials in charge of them, to replace the loose-knit, quasi-feudal association of pashas and tax-farmers of earlier times. It was, however, some time before this ambitious project could be put into effect.[61]

Other reforms, foreshadowed in the Noble Rescript, followed

---

[58] cf. B. Lewis, 'Some Observations on the Significance of Heresy in the History of Islam', *Studia Islamica*, i (1953), pp. 52 ff.

[59] Lûtfi, v. 106 ff.   [60] Lûtfi, vi. 92 ff. cf. Bailey, p. 199.   [61] See below, pp. 378 ff.

rapidly, relating principally to two matters—justice and finance. Both involved radical breaches with the past.

Legal Reform [62]

In the strict theory of the Muslim jurists, there could be no legislative power in the state, since law came from God alone and was promulgated by revelation. Theoretically, therefore, there was no law other than the Şeriat, the unchangeable, God-given law of Islam, and no judiciary other than that which administered it. In earlier Islamic Empires legal practice had made some compromise with reality, recognizing custom and the will of the ruler as legally effective, and applying them in administrative or customary tribunals outside the system of the Şeriat courts. The Ottoman Sultans, down to Mahmud II, had issued *Kanuns*, which are sometimes described as laws. The description is not, however, accurate. The Ottoman *kanun* is in no sense a legislative enactment, but rather a codification of existing law— a tabulation of legal rules. In fact the Ottomans went further than any previous Muslim régime in establishing the sole authority of the Şeriat and its exponents, and in eliminating or reducing the operation of such other systems of law and judicature as were in existence. The administrative, commercial, military, and equity courts which had existed under the Caliphate disappeared, and the Muftis and Kadis, organized in a hierarchy under the supreme control of the Şeyh-ül-Islâm in Istanbul, achieved an exclusive competence in all matters of law and justice concerning Muslims.

The promulgation in May 1840 of a new penal code did not at first appear to be a revolutionary step. The name given to it— *Kanun-i Ceraim*—indicated a desire to remain within the existing tradition of *Kanun*-making, and the provisions of the code, though influenced by French law, are mainly within the framework of the penal law of the Şeriat itself. There are, however, one or two significant changes, which prepared the way for the more radical legal reforms that were to follow. One of these is the affirmation of the equality of *all* Ottoman subjects before the law. Another is the preparation and promulgation of a legal code, consisting of a preamble and fourteen articles, by a corporate body

---

[62] On the penal and commercial codes see Engelhardt, i. 40; Ubicini, letter 7; Lûtfi, vi. 102–4; *Tanzimat*, pp. 176, 214, 226; Temperley, p. 163; Bailey, p. 200; Karal, *Tarih*, v. 177.

entrusted with that task. Though the code was confused in thought and expression and ineffective in application, it marks the first tentative appearance, in the Ottoman state, of the legislative principle and of a legislative body.

The significance of this innovation seems to have escaped the ulema, who offered no resistance. They were, however, more perturbed by the creation, in the same year, of a new *ad hoc* court of justice, in the newly created Ministry of Commerce, to hear commercial disputes, and still more by the preparation, under the inspiration of Reşid Paşa, of a new commercial code based on French models. This raised an ancient dispute of the Muslim jurists, who recognized the new code as a derogation from the *Şeriat*, and forced its suspension. Dealing with partnerships bankruptcies, bills of exchange, and similar matters, it was derived almost entirely from French commercial law. When Reşid had introduced it to the High Council in 1841, he was asked whether it was in conformity with the Holy Law. ' "The Holy Law has nothing to do with the matter", said Reşid. "Blasphemy", protested the *Ulemas* present. The young Sultan promptly dismissed his minister of enlightenment.'[63]

Finance [64]

One of the provisions of the Noble Rescript had stated that: 'it is our belief that banks should be opened in order to raise the prestige of the finances of the Empire by adjusting and protecting the value of money, that capital funds should be created to augment the sources of material wealth'.

The point was a crucial one. From first to last finance was the Slough of Despond of the Turkish reformers, in which their brightest hopes were bemired, their cleverest plans befouled and engulfed. Two basic requirements were never met—a full treasury and a sound currency; and in their absence the apparatus of government was clogged and neglected, its servants became cynical and corrupt.

The reforming Sultans inherited from their predecessors the unfortunate practice of meeting a deficit by debasing the currency. During the reign of Mahmud II the form and name of the

---

[63] Temperley, p. 163.

[64] On the Ministry of Commerce, see Lûtfi, vi. 28 and 145; on the finance committee, ibid. p. 125; on the banknote issue, ibid. p. 127; White, ii. 71; Ubicini, letter 14.

Ottoman coinage was changed 35 times for gold and 37 for silver issues, and the rate of the Turkish piastre or its equivalent to the pound sterling, fell from 23 in 1814 to 104 in 1839. The effects of this inflation on the trade of the Empire and on the standard of living and integrity of salaried officials will be obvious.

In April 1840 an Imperial ferman authorized the establishment of an Ottoman bank, to be formed along European lines, with a guaranteed subvention from the government of 30 million piastres a year for fifteen years. In the following year the Turkish government made its first issue of paper money. These papers, though sometimes described as banknotes, should more properly be termed treasury bonds. They were to carry interest at the lavish rate of 12 per cent., payable twice yearly, and the total issue was not to exceed 60 million piastres. There were no guarantees, and no date of redemption was specified. In the following year the interest rate was halved, and a part of the issue redeemed, but new issues soon followed, and within ten years the original amount was trebled. For a while these bonds remained fairly steady, and in 1844 the government, together with the new bank, was able to introduce a set of new measures for the safeguarding of the currency. These involved the withdrawal of the old coinage and the issue of a new currency on European lines, consisting of a gold pound of 100 piastres. For the moment all was well, but in banking and finance the reformers had an explosive device which was beyond their capacity to handle. By the time of the Crimean War the circulating treasury bonds had become a menace, notably in their effect on prices. A foreign loan was therefore negotiated in 1858, for the purpose, only partially accomplished, of withdrawing them; it was the first of a series which led directly to the bankruptcy and collapse of 1875.

The Fall of Reşid: Interruption of Reform

At the beginning of 1841 the reforms suffered a setback. Reşid Paşa was dismissed, and in the following year the new system of provincial administration and taxation was dropped and the old partnership of military governors and tax-farmers restored.[65] Even under the reactionaries, however, the process of reform did not entirely cease. In 1842 the Council was reconstituted and a more moderate régime emerged; in the following year an

[65] Engelhardt, i. 50; Temperley, p. 165.

important change was made in the organization of the army, which was now reorganized in five army corps, with a period of five years' service for regular soldiers, followed by seven in the reserves (*Redif*). Recruitment was by a form of conscription, with the drawing of lots, and all matters of training, equipment, weapons, and organization were on Western lines.[66]

Reşid Paşa: the Second Phase

In 1845 a new phase of reform began, and Reşid Paşa returned to the Ministry of Foreign Affairs. In the following year he was appointed to the Grand Vezirate, an office which he held six times.

The Sultan had meanwhile made his own preparation. In January 1845 he issued a *Hatt-i Humayun*, in which he said that apart from the military reform, with which he was fully satisfied, all his other proposals for the benefit of his subjects had been misunderstood and misapplied by his ministers; the main reason for this lamentable fact was the general ignorance of the population. This should be remedied by the establishment of good schools throughout the Empire, so as to disseminate useful knowledge and thus make possible the introduction into other branches of the government of the improvements already tried in the Ministry of War.[67]

The Assembly of Provincial Notables[68]

It was no doubt with the same idea of associating the population with the reforms that a little later in the same year the Sultan took the unprecedented and potentially dangerous step of consulting his people. From each province of the Empire two men were to be sent to Istanbul 'from among those who are respected and trusted, are people of intelligence and knowledge, who know the requisites of prosperity and the characteristics of the population', in order to consult with the High Council. They were to be sent at the expense of the local treasuries, and lodged in Istanbul as 'honoured guests in the *konaks* of the great'. When these instructions arrived in the provincial capitals, 'persons were elected from among the prominent and respected people' and travelled to Istanbul, where they were given a document

[66] Lûtfi, vii. 74; Engelhardt, i. 71; Ubicini, letter 19.   [67] Lûtfi, viii. 8.
[68] Ibid. pp. 15–17; cf. Engelhardt, i. 76.

explaining the purpose for which they had been convened, and were asked their views on the present state and further needs of the reform.

The delegates seem to have been confused by this new and unfamiliar procedure, and, not knowing what they were expected to say, preferred to say nothing. The Sultan then resorted to the method of sending roving commissions to the provinces in both Europe and Asia, to investigate and report on the state of the reforms. They travelled for about seven or eight months, and in accordance with their instructions reported their findings to the Sublime Porte by every post. These were considered by the High Council, which occasionally took action on them. Some officials were dismissed or transferred, some army officers and naval engineers set to work to prepare maps and inspect some roads and ports, but for the most part, in Lûtfi's words, 'the orders of most of them were pawned to neglect and incoming papers were locked in the box of abrogation'.

Education [69]

Of rather more effect were the educational measures that followed the *Hatt-i Humayun* of 1845. In March of the same year a circular of the Porte appointed a committee of seven, 'of men well-versed in the judicial, military, and civil sciences',[70] to investigate the existing schools and prepare places for new ones. Among its members were Âli Efendi, Under-Secretary of Foreign Affairs and director of the chancery of the Divan, and Fuad Efendi, Chief Dragoman of the Divan.

The committee reported in August 1846. Its report, as was normal, was elaborate and unrealistic, providing for an Ottoman state university, a system of primary and secondary schools, and a permanent Council of Public Instruction. The creation of a university and of a network of schools was a difficult task, the accomplishment of which stretched over many years and encountered many obstacles. The foundations of the University were laid, and a medal struck depicting the completed building, but work on the building was abandoned when the walls were only a few feet high. The secondary schools, called *rüşdiye*, came slowly,

[69] Ubicini, letter 9; Engelhardt, ii. 7; Rosen, ii. 86; Bailey, p. 214; Temperley, p. 234.

[70] Translation of the circular in Ubicini, doc. XIII.

and by the mid-century there were six of them, with 870 pupils; a poor result if compared with the programme, but creditable in relation to reality. The Council of Public Instruction was created immediately, and in 1847 became a Ministry.

The change, though perhaps unimpressive in terms of the number of schools and pupils provided, was nevertheless significant. Both the Sultan and his committee had been careful to pay lip-service to the primacy of religion in education—'the first of the necessities of this life', said the circular of March 1845, 'is to know the duties and obligations which religion imposes on man'. The effect of the change, however, was to set up new schools, with teachers and curricula outside the scope of the ulema and the religious sciences which they cultivated, and thus prepare the way for a system of secular education. The creation of a separate Ministry of Education confirmed the removal of this important matter from the sole jurisdiction of the ulema.

Law and Justice

Even more delicate than the question of education was that of law and justice, which to an even greater extent had been a preserve of the ulema. So far the reformers had not dared to set up any formal legislative organs, any system of courts and judges outside those of the Şeriat. There had, however, been a few tentative moves in that direction. The cautiously named Council of Judicial Ordinances had been given, by the edict of 1839, what were in effect legislative and quasi-judicial functions. In 1847 mixed civil and criminal courts were constituted, with European and Ottoman judges in equal numbers, and with rules of evidence and procedure drawn from European rather than Islamic practice.[71]

In 1850 a more radical step was taken—the promulgation of Reşid Paşa's Commercial Code, prepared some years previously, and delayed by his fall from power in 1841. It was to be administered in the tribunals of commerce.[72] The promulgation of this Code was the first formal recognition in Turkey of a system of law and of judicature independent of the ulema, dealing with matters outside the scope of the Şeriat. Such a recognition was by

[71] Lûtfi, vi. 102; Engelhardt, i. 83

[72] *Düstur*, i. 375 ff.; Young, vii. 55 ff.; Aristarchi, i. 275 ff.; *Tanzimat*, p. 196; Temperley, pp. 163, 232.

no means new in Islam. It was, however, a radical departure from previous Ottoman practice, and the harbinger of a complete legal and social revolution.

The Fall of Reşid Paşa: 1852

More than once Reşid Paşa was unseated by the reactionaries. The most serious setback was in 1852, when, after his dismissal from the Grand Vezirate, his new system of provincial administration was abrogated and the whole movement of reform came to a standstill. Already in the previous year the British ambassador Stratford de Redcliffe had written in a private letter: 'The *great* game of improvement is altogether up for the present.'[73]

There is no doubt that one of the compelling motives that had led Reşid Paşa to promulgate this high-sounding programme of reform had been the need to win the goodwill and support of the European powers against that other and, in his time, more successful Westernizer, Muhammad Ali of Egypt. In view of this, some Western observers, seeing the appalling discrepancy between the Noble Rescript of the Rose Chamber and the ignoble realities of less fragrant purlieus, concluded that the whole reform was no more than window-dressing, intended only to deceive the Western powers, without making any real change in the state of affairs in Turkey. To adopt such a view, however, is to disregard the long course of events which, since the eighteenth century, had prepared the way for the reform; the long working out, in the century that followed, of the principles and beliefs contained in it, and, at the moment of its promulgation, the deeper convictions and aspirations of Mustafa Reşid Paşa and other men of his generation.

Âli and Fuad Paşas: the Imperial Rescript of 1856

A new phase began in 1854. The poor performance of the new-style army against the Russians had revealed the hollowness of the reforms, and it was once again urgently necessary to convince Europe of the sincerity and good intentions of the Ottoman government. The Sultan's government therefore again offered Europe the only evidence she would accept of progress and improvement—that is, a movement towards a greater resemblance to herself.

The reformers returned to power, and the Grand Council of

[73] March 1851, cited in Temperley, p. 242.

I

Justice was reorganized, being divided into two bodies, one more strictly concerned with legal matters, the other, known as the High Council of Reform (*Meclis-i Āli-i Tanzimat*), with general responsibility for the whole programme of reform.[74]

For most Europeans the touchstone of Turkish sincerity was the treatment of non-Muslims. On 7 May 1855, therefore, a ferman was issued abolishing the two principal measures of discrimination against them. The poll-tax, which had been demanded from the protected non-Muslim subjects of the Muslim state since the beginnings of Islamic government, was solemnly abolished, and the privilege of bearing arms—i.e. of military service—which had been restricted to Muslims for almost as long, was thrown open to all. However, since after centuries of exemption the non-Muslim subjects had developed a disinclination or were found unsuitable to serve in the army, which in any case offered them few attractions as a career, they were required, instead of serving, to pay an exemption tax called the *bedel*. This was levied in the same way as the abolished poll-tax.[75]

On 18 February 1856 a new reform charter, the Imperial Rescript (*Hatt-i Humayun*), was promulgated by the Sultan, as part of the preliminaries of the treaty of Paris and the acceptance of Turkey as a participant in that concatenation of discords known as the Concert of Europe. The Rescript reaffirmed the principles of the edict of 1839, again abolished tax-farming and other abuses, and laid down, in terms more specific and categorical than previously, the full equality of all Ottoman subjects irrespective of religion. The Turkish government had once again declared its good intentions. The West had concerned itself more directly with their fulfilment.[76]

In the preparation and promulgation of this new charter Reşid Paşa, for long the leader of the reformers, had no part. Though he was twice again Grand Vezir, for short periods, before his death in 1858, the leadership of the reform had passed into

[74] Young, i. 2.

[75] Aristarchi, ii. 14 ff.; *EI*² ('Badal' by H. Bowen); *IA* ('Bedel-i Askeri' by S. S. Onar). On this question generally see Roderic H. Davison, 'Turkish Attitudes concerning Christian-Muslim Equality in the Nineteenth Century', *Am. Hist. R.*, lix (1953–4), 844–64.

[76] Cevdet's comments on the edict of 1856 are contained in *Tezakir*, pp. 67 ff., where some memoranda of Reşid Paşa are also given. See also Engelhardt, i. 139 ff.; Rosen, ii. 239 ff.; Jorga, v. 482; Sax, pp. 342 ff.; Rasim, iv. 2048 ff.

the hands of his former disciples and present rivals, Âli Paşa and Fuad Paşa. These two men led the reform for the next fifteen years.[77]

Âli Paşa (1815–71) was born in Istanbul, the son of a shop-keeper. Like Reşid Paşa, he entered the civil service as a boy, and rose through the ladder of official promotions. In 1833, having acquired some knowledge of French, he was attached to the Dragoman of the Porte, whose staff was increased in that year from two to four assistants to cope with the increasing volume of translation work. While in this employment he made good progress in French, under a French teacher, and in 1836 went to Vienna on the staff of the special envoy Ahmed Fethi Paşa. This was the first of a series of diplomatic appointments, which culminated in his nomination as ambassador in London in 1840. On his return to Turkey in 1844, he became a member of the Council of Justice, and thereafter held a number of high positions, mostly in association with Reşid Paşa. In 1852, when Reşid Paşa was dismissed, Âli Paşa succeeded him as Grand Vezir. Though on this occasion he held the post only for two months, he remained at the centre of events. In 1854 he became president of the newly formed High Council of Reform, and a little later returned to the Grand Vezirate, in time to preside over the promulgation of the *Hatt-i Humayun*. Thereafter he held the Grand Vezirate and other offices at various periods, and played a dominating role in the reform movement until his death in 1871.

His closest associate and collaborator during this period was Fuad Paşa (1815–69). He too was born in Istanbul, but with a very different background and education. He was the son of Keçecizade Mehmed Izzet Efendi (d. 1830), a well-known Ottoman poet, scholar, and statesman, who had for a while enjoyed high rank and favour under Mahmud II, and who played a role of some importance in the movement for linguistic and literary reform. Fuad himself entered the medical school which Mahmud had established at Galatasaray in 1827, and after graduating entered the new army medical corps. His knowledge of French, however, was of more immediate use than his medical training. In 1837 he joined the Translation Office and in 1840 went to London as First Secretary of the Embassy. Thereafter he held many diplomatic appointments, and in 1852 became Minister

[77] On Âli and Fuad Paşas see *EI¹*, *EI²*, *IA*, and Inal, *s.vv.*

of Foreign Affairs under Âli Paşa. He too was a member of the High Council of Reform, of which he later became president, and was actively concerned in the preparation of new projects and the drafting of new laws. Besides his work as statesman and diplomat, he was a scholar of some quality, and collaborated with the historian Ahmed Cevdet in composing the *Kavaid-i Osmaniye* (1851), the first Turkish work on Turkish grammar to be printed, and a landmark in the linguistic reform.

Together with Reşid Paşa, Âli and Fuad were the chief architects and executants of the *Tanzimat*. Like him, they owed their first steps towards advancement to their knowledge of a foreign language. For the shopkeeper's son, as for the others, French was the talisman that made the clerk a translator, the translator an interpreter, the interpreter a diplomat, and the diplomat a statesman. At a time when the Ottoman Empire was obsessed with the sheer problem of survival in a world dominated by an aggressive and expanding Europe, the positions of trust and decision inevitably went to those who knew something of Europe, its languages, and its affairs. The new *élite* of power came not from the army, not from the ulema, but from the Translation Office and the Embassy secretariats. What had once been a despised and quasi-menial task, contemptuously left to Greek dragomans whose services helped to preserve their Ottoman masters from the defilement of contact, now became the school of statecraft and the battlefield of power.

Legal Reforms

The reforms of Âli and Fuad continued along the lines laid down by their predecessors. The legal reform was carried a few steps further, with the introduction of a land code[78] and a new penal code[79] in 1858, a reorganization of the commercial tribunals, which were amalgamated with the mixed courts in 1860,[80] and further commercial[81] and maritime[82] codes, all of French origin, in 1861 and 1863.

[78] Text in *Düstur*, i. 165; trans. in Young, vi. 45 ff. and Aristarchi, i. 57 ff.; studied by [F.A.] Belin ('Étude sur la propriété foncière . . . en Turquie', *J. As.*, 1862) and Barkan ('Türk Toprak Hukuku Tarihinde Tanzimat ve 1274 (1858) Tarihli Arazi Kanunnamesi', in *Tanzimat*, pp. 321–421). See also Inalcık, 'Tanzimat Nedir'.

[79] *Düstur*, i. 527 ff.; Young, vii. 1 ff.; Aristarchi, ii. 212 ff.

[80] *Düstur*, i. 445; Young, i. 226.   [81] *Düstur*, i. 780; Young, vii. 155.

[82] *Düstur*, i. 466; Young, vii. 103; Aristarchi, i. 344.

The commercial codes were a logical development from Reşid Paşa's first initiative. The penal code marked a more considerable advance. It was more elaborate and more carefully devised than its predecessor of 1840. The main part of it derived from French law, but with several significant omissions, additions, and emendations.

In many ways more important than either the commercial or the criminal codes was the new land law of 1858. This, like the Egyptian land reform of the same year, was basically an attempt to apply to the problems of the countryside the panacea of formal Westernization. Western villages were populous, Western agriculture was prosperous—therefore the system of land tenure and occupancy must be amended so as to make it more European. The last *timars* had been abolished by Mahmud; the abolition of the system of tax-farming had for some time been one of the objectives of the reformers, and some progress had been made in accomplishing it. The general trend of the reforms was to abrogate the earlier agrarian relationships and progressively to extend and confirm the rights of use, of possession, and of ownership. Leaseholders and tax-farmers acquired freehold ownership, with full rights of disposal and succession, confirmed by the possession of documents issued by the Survey Department. The actual cultivators, their rights and status much diminished, became share-croppers or hired labourers, at the mercy of a reinforced landlord class which was the principal beneficiary of the reform. The harmful effects of the new law were modified only by the inefficiency of its application.

Âli and Fuad Paşas were men of the second generation of reform. Much that for their predecessors was strange and new was already part of their normal lives. More secure than Reşid Paşa both in their convictions and in their personal positions, they could afford to be more cautious and practical. To European observers, their rate of progress seemed lamentably slow, and in October 1859 the representatives of the European powers presented a joint memorandum complaining to the Grand Vezir of the lack of progress in applying the charter of 1856.[83]

[83] Engelhardt, i. 161 ff.; Rasim, iv. 2092 ff.

Financial Troubles [84]

The disagreements of the powers, however, prevented them from taking any effective action to follow up the protest, and before very long the Ottoman Empire was concerned with more pressing matters—with the growing financial crisis. Finance had always been the weak point of the reformers. Now the treasury was empty, the army unpaid, and the populace, feeling the pinch, increasingly hostile to both Europeans and reformers. Turkey had obtained loans, for war expenditure, from her British and French allies during the Crimean War. A further loan in 1858 produced only temporary relief, and by 1860 the Ottoman government was sending out urgent appeals for help. A new loan in 1861 brought some improvement, but did not long postpone Turkey's career towards bankruptcy and foreign financial control.

Abdülaziz: Reaction [85]

On 20 June 1861 the Sultan Abdülmecid died, and was succeeded by his brother Abdülaziz. Abdülmecid had been a mild well-intentioned ruler, and personally well disposed to the reform movement. He knew some French—the first of his line to use a Western language; he read the Paris newspapers, and introduced or accepted many European practices at his court.[86] His successor was a man of a different temper. Capricious and violent, obstinate and irascible, he soon fell foul of the reformers, whose work was impeded and often nullified by his interference. There had been tyrants before in the house of Osman—though far fewer than is sometimes thought; but the abrogation of the traditional restraints on the one hand, and the introduction of a new, Westernized apparatus of surveillance and repression on the other, had given to the Imperial absolutism of the Sultan a scope and an impact unknown in earlier times.

Âli and Fuad Paşas did, however, manage to make some

[84] On Ottoman finances see A. du Velay, *Essai sur l'histoire financière de la Turquie* (1903); Belin, 'Essai sur l'histoire économique de la Turquie', *J. As.*, 1885; and Rasim's note on the loans (iv. 2028 ff.).

[85] On Abdülaziz see Haluk Y. Şehsuvaroğlu, *Sultan Aziz* (1949); also the relevant articles in *EI²* and *IA*, and sources quoted there. Comments from British diplomatic sources are cited by Temperley in *Camb. Hist. J.*, 167 ff.

[86] On some of these, see Rasim, iv. 2009 ff., n. 289.

progress, and in 1864 a new Law of Vilayets regulated the provincial administration along lines that were to remain effective to the end of the Empire and beyond.[87]

The French Note of 1867: New Reforms [88]

In February 1867 the French government, supported by England and Austria, presented a note to the Porte urging a more active policy of reform, and setting forth detailed suggestions. The Sultan was violently opposed to the idea, but gave way to the pressure of events. For the next three years Âli and Fuad Paşas ran the state and a stream of new laws and institutions followed.

Later in 1867 an invitation from Napoleon III to visit the Paris International Exhibition gave the Sultan the occasion to make a journey to Europe—the first made by an Ottoman Sultan for any purpose but war. He was received at the courts of Paris, London, and Vienna, and also met the King of Prussia.[89]

Justice and Education

The reforms of the next two years were once again concerned with the two major topics of law and education. In April 1868 the High Council was reorganized, and two new bodies created from it; a Divan of Judicial Ordinances (*Divan-i Ahkâm-i Adliye*) and a Council of State (*Şura-yi Devlet*). The former was a revised version of the earlier Council of Justice, with quasi-legislative and some judicial functions. The latter, modelled on the French *Conseil d'État*, was in effect a high court of appeal in administrative cases.[90]

The same year saw the opening of the Imperial Ottoman Lycée at Galatasaray.[91] In this school the language of instruction was French (except for purely Turkish subjects), and a serious attempt was made to give a modern and Western curriculum of

---

[87] *Düstur*, i. 4; Young, i. 29. See further Engelhardt, i. 193–8; Karal, *Tarih*, vii. 153; Temperley, p. 237; Sax, pp. 372 ff.; cf. below, p. 381.

[88] Engelhardt, i. 237 ff.; ii. 1 ff.; Sax, pp. 380 ff.

[89] On this visit, see the account written by Halimi Efendi, chief court secretary, who accompanied the Sultan as interpreter: ed. Necib Asim in *TOEM*, no. 49–62 (1337 A.H.), pp. 90–102. Also Ali Kemali Aksüt, *Sultan Aziz'in Mısır ve Avrupa Seyahatı* (1944).

[90] *Düstur*, i. 703 ff.; Young, i. 3 ff., 159 ff.; Aristarchi, ii. 38 ff. On the high hopes entertained of the Council of State by the Turkish liberals, see Tanpınar, p. 190.

[91] Engelhardt, ii. 10; Ergin, *Maarif*, ii. 400; Ihsan Süngü, 'Galatasaray Lisesi'nin Kuruluşu', *Bell.*, no. 28 (1943), pp. 315–47.

secondary education. A few such schools had already been established by foreign missions, notably the American Protestant Robert College (1863); the Galatasaray school was, however, the first serious attempt by a Muslim government to provide modern education at secondary level in a Western language. Another new feature was the teaching of Muslim and Christian pupils side by side—a step towards religious de-segregation.

The influence of the Galatasaray school on the rise of modern Turkey has been enormous. As the need for administrators, diplomats, and others with a Western education and a capacity to handle Western administrative apparatus became more and more pressing, the graduates of Galatasaray came to play a preponderant role in the politics and administration of the Ottoman Empire and, after it, of the Turkish Republic. The Imperial Ottoman Lycée had no playing-fields, but not a few of the victories of modern Turkey were won in its classrooms.

Probably the most important legal reform of the nineteenth century was the promulgation of the new civil code, known as the *Mecelle*, the first section of which appeared in 1869.[92] It was completed in 1876. The code was very largely the work of Ahmed Cevdet Pasha (1822–95), a scholar, historian, and jurist of genius who was a leading figure in the intellectual life of his time. After holding various official posts, he was appointed president of the Divan of Judicial Ordinances in 1868. As such, he was in effect Minister of Justice, and was later officially confirmed in this title when a separate Ministry of Justice was recognized. His achievements include the institution of courses in law, at the Ministry, for judges, the elaboration of a new set of secular courts, the *Nizami* courts, with their own judiciary and procedure and with Courts of Appeal at the 'Divan of Judicial Ordinances'.

Cevdet Paşa had, during an earlier tenure of office on the Committee of Justice, played some part in producing the penal and land codes. He was now called upon to deal with the vaster problem of a new civil code, to replace the existing confusion.

---

[92] Many editions and translations of the *Mecelle* are available. For a brief general account by a Turkish lawyer see S. S. Onar, 'The Majalla', in Majid Khadduri and Herbert J. Liebesny, eds., *Law in the Middle East*, i (1955), 292–308. On the legal work of Ahmed Cevdet Paşa see Ebul'ulâ Mardin, *Medenî Hukuk Cephesinden Ahmet Cevdet Paşa* (1946), and, more briefly, H. Bowen, 'Aḥmed Djawdat Pasha' in *EI²*. Cevdet's own views are given briefly in *Tezakir*, pp. 62–64.

Âli Paşa was anxious to follow the precedent of the commercial code, and to adopt the French *Code Civil* as the civil law of the Empire. Cevdet, however, preferred to remain within the Islamic tradition, and to prepare a code which, while modern in form and presentation, would be firmly based on the *Şeriat*. He and his committee had their way; the result of their endeavours, a digest rather than a code of *Şeriat* law of the Hanafi school, must rank as one of the great achievements of Turkish jurisprudence. It remained in force in Turkey until abrogated by the Republic in 1926, and still forms the basis of the legal systems of several of the Ottoman successor states in Asia.

In 1869 the partnership of the two reform leaders was dissolved by the death of Fuad Paşa.[93] Âli Paşa, probably the abler of the two, but the less popular among his countrymen, was left to cope with a renewed financial crisis, and soon made himself still more disliked by raising the tithe rate. The Franco-Prussian war of 1871 reduced the prestige of France and therefore of the reform, and Âli Paşa was already weakened and isolated when he died, after a three-month illness, in September 1871.

The reformers were dead; France, their patron and guide, was defeated, and a mood of reaction set in against any foreign intervention. Even Ottoman Christians were dismissed from public office, and greater stress was laid on the Islamic character of the Empire and the need for Islamic unity, in a form foreshadowing the pan-Islamic doctrines current in the next decade. Under Abdülaziz the doctrine was advanced for the first time that the Ottoman Sultan was not only the head of the Ottoman Empire but also the Caliph of all Muslims and the heir, in a sense not previously accepted, of the Caliphs of early times. At a time when most Muslim lands in Africa and Asia were falling under European colonial rule, this new claim quickly won considerable support, and the Ottoman Caliphate provided a rallying point for the forces opposed to Westernization and to the West.[94]

The death of Âli Paşa and the triumph of the reaction provide a

---

[93] For a useful survey of the documents and problems relating to the so-called political testament of Fuad Paşa, see Davison, 'The Question of Fuad Paşa's "Political Testament" ', *Bell.*, no. 89 (1959), 119–36.

[94] See below, pp. 317 ff. and 334–7.

convenient halt at which to consider the efforts of the reformers, and the effects and limitations of their achievement.

Conclusions

In European writings on the nineteenth-century Turkish reforms it has become a commonplace that the reforms were stillborn. 'The *Tanzimat* stopped at the doorstep of the Sublime Porte.'[95] Yet a comparison of Turkey in 1800 with Turkey in 1871 will reveal many profound changes—soon enough to show that, for better or worse, the *Tanzimat* were more than a sop to Europe or a pious expression of good intentions by naïve would-be reformers.

The general feeling of Europe was that the ancient institutions and structure of the Empire were barbarous and irretrievably bad, and that only the adoption, as rapidly as possible, of a European form of government and way of life would admit Turkey to the rank and privileges of a civilized state. This view was urged on Turkish statesmen with considerable vigour by the governments and embassies of the European powers, and eventually came to be accepted, at least tacitly, by a larger and larger proportion of a Turkish ruling class, which was deeply aware of the power, wealth, and progress of Europe as compared with their own backwardness, poverty, and weakness. Their attitude is well expressed in a famous poem by Ziya Paşa (1825–80) one of the outstanding intellectual figures of nineteenth-century Turkey:

> I passed through the lands of the infidels, I saw cities and mansions;
> I wandered in the realm of Islam, I saw nothing but ruins.[96]

But in questioning the common assumption that the reforms were ineffectual, we may also question the related assumption that what effect they did have was beneficial, and represented an improvement on what had gone before.

Already in the first half of the nineteenth century some voices were raised in doubt. Perhaps the most penetrating comments are those of Adolphus Slade, a British naval officer who visited

---

[95] Cited in Geoffrey Lewis, *Turkey* (1955), p. 35.

[96] This poem, written in Geneva in 1870, will be found in many Turkish anthologies. It appears on p. 29 of the very useful collection of 'Turkish poetry under Western influence' ed. by Kenan Akyüz, *Batı Tesirinde Türk Şiiri Antolojisi* (1953). For discussions of Ziya Paşa and his work see Gibb, *Ottoman Poetry*, v. 41–111, and below, pp. 134 ff.

Turkey many times from 1829 onwards, and acquired an intimate knowledge of the language, the country, and the people. His basic criticism is that the reformers destroyed an old order which was not in itself evil, but on the contrary contained much that was enviable:

Hitherto the Osmanley has enjoyed by custom some of the dearest privileges of freemen, for which Christian nations have so long struggled. He paid nothing to the government beyond a moderate land-tax, although liable, it is true, to extortions, which might be classed with assessed taxes. He paid no tithes, the vacouf sufficing for the maintenance of the ministers of Islamism. He travelled where he pleased without passports; no custom-house officer intruded his eyes and dirty fingers among his baggage; no police watched his motions, or listened for his words. His house was sacred. His sons were never taken from his side to be soldiers, unless war called them. His views of ambition were not restricted by the barriers of birth and wealth: from the lowest origin he might aspire without presumption to the rank of pasha; if he could read, to that of grand vezir; and this consciousness, instilled and supported by numberless precedents, ennobled his mind, and enabled him to enter on the duties of high office without embarrassment. Is not this the advantage so prized by free nations? Did not the exclusion of the people from posts of honour tend to the French revolution? I might infinitely extend the parallel existing between nations removed by ages of knowledge. One more example, rather burlesque, however, than correct. The Janizzaries of Constantinople somewhat resembled a chamber of deputies, for they often compelled their sovereign to change his ministers, and any talented, factious member among them, with the art of inflaming men's passions, was sure to obtain a good employment in order to appease him.[97]

This order Mahmud destroyed, and in its place offered nothing but his own unbridled will:

For this freedom, this capability of realizing the wildest wishes, what equivalent does the Sultan offer? It may be said none. I do not think that the Osmanleys would have objected to a uniform system of government, with the burthen of a standing army which would have defended their honour, provided their liberties had been respected. But instead of engrafting his plans on the old system, which—embracing a respected hierarchy, an hereditary noblesse, and a provincial magistracy—offered such facilities, with a studious care not to shock prejudices, idle, but sanctified; to make it appear that he aimed at

[97] Slade, i. 275–6 (2nd ed. p. 145).

rendering European subservient to Asiatic, rather than Asiatic to European, manners, he rejected all subterfuge, and prematurely disclosed his schemes of self-aggrandizement and appropriation which disgusted his subjects, and changed their respect for him into something less than honour.[98]

Moltke passes a similar judgement:

For the accomplishment of his purpose it was indispensable for him to raze to the ground any other authority within the compass of the Empire and to unite the whole plenitude of power in his own hand; to clear the site before setting up his own building. The first part of his great task the Sultan carried through with perspicacity and resolution; in the second he failed.[99]

After Mahmud, the men of the *Tanzimat* tried to erect a new structure on the terrain which he had levelled with such violent and destructive haste. But they were working in a style and with materials that were unfamiliar to them, with unskilled and resentful workmen, and alien and therefore mistrusted foremen— or none at all.

Nevertheless they accomplished a great deal. In the world of the nineteenth and twentieth centuries, Turkey had to modernize herself or perish, and the men of the *Tanzimat*, with all their failings, laid the indispensable foundation for the more thorough modernization that was to follow. Their legal and administrative reforms were often ill judged and incompetently applied—but in a world of railways and telegraphs the old feudal structure of the Empire could not survive, and there was in reality little freedom of choice. Perhaps their greatest achievement was in education. In the schools and colleges set up during the nineteenth century, slowly and painfully a new educated *élite* was evolved, with a new spirit, and a new and clearer perception of realities. The problems of moral and spiritual adjustment were enormous, and there were many, far too many, who fell into frustration, cynicism, and corruption. The new class of officials emerging from the schools were often ignorant, superficial, corrupt, and separated from those over whom they ruled by a widening gulf; but even this was better than the ignorant self-assurance of those whom they replaced. And among these new officials there was a high proportion of men of loyalty, integrity,

[98] Slade, i. 276–7 (2nd ed. p. 146).   [99] Moltke, pp. 409–10.

and responsibility, with a real understanding of the problems and difficulties of their country, and a determination to face and overcome them. The infusion of this new spirit into the dominant classes of the Empire was a slow, often a heart-breaking business, but by the twentieth century it had produced a ruling *élite* with the knowledge, the capacity, and above all the sense of responsibility and decision to carry through the great social and political revolution that made modern Turkey. The value of that *élite* to Turkey is strikingly confirmed by the penalties of its absence in other countries with a similar legacy and similar problems.

The difficulties facing the nineteenth-century reformers were enormous. The forces opposing them, even though pursuing objectives which were ultimately unrealizable, were none the less truculent and menacing. There was much about the reforms to arouse resentment and dislike. The political, social, and economic changes they involved seemed to offer some kind of threat to the interests of almost every group in Turkish society; to almost all they appeared as a triumph over Islam of the millennial Christian enemy in the West. For the reforms were basically the forcible imposition, on a Muslim country, of practices and procedures derived from Europe, with the encouragement, if not the insistence, of European powers, and with the help of European experts and advisers. Military defeat and political humiliation had indeed shaken the torpid and complacent trust of the Turks in their own invincible and immutable superiority, but the ancient contempt for the barbarian infidel, where it yielded, often gave place to rancour rather than emulation. The reforms were not endeared to the Muslim population by the obvious and active interest of the Christian powers in furthering them; the granting of equal status to non-Muslims within the Empire was to many the final insult and outrage.

By 1871 the reform had already gone far enough to make a simple policy of reversion to the past impracticable. The destruction of the old order had been too thorough for any restoration to be possible; for better or for worse, only one path lay before Turkey, that of modernization and Westernization. She could move fast or slowly, straight or deviously; she could not go back.

CHAPTER V

The Seeds of Revolution

In front of the central gate one encounters a statue of freedom; she has a staff in her hand and is seated on a chair. Her appearance and manner convey this meaning to spectators: 'O worthy visitors! When you look upon this fascinating display of human progress, do not forget that all these perfections are the works of freedom. Under the protection of freedom do peoples and nations attain happiness. Where there is no freedom there can be no security; where there is no security there can be no endeavour; where there is no endeavour there can be no prosperity; where there is no prosperity there can be no happiness! ...

SADULLAH PAŞA, 'The Paris Exhibition', 1878.

The substance of the ideas of 1789 is not the limitation of the sovereign power, but the abrogation of intermediate powers.

LORD ACTON, 'Nationality', 1862.

THE Turkish word *hürriyet*, freedom, derives from the Arabic *ḥurriyya*, an abstract noun formed from *ḥurr*, free. In classical Islamic usage it is employed commonly in a legal and social, occasionally in a philosophic sense. In the former it denotes the converse of slavery, of the servile status, sometimes also exemption or privilege; in the latter freedom of will—the converse of pre-destination.[1] At no time does it seem to have had the meaning which Cicero, in imitation of Aristotle, gave to the Latin *libertas* —that of citizenship, of the right to share in the conduct of government.

It was at the end of the eighteenth century that the word first began to acquire a new significance in Turkish. Reports from France, translations of French manifestoes, helped to familiarize the new notion.[2] The first reception was not favourable. In 1798

---

[1] See the dictionaries of classical Arabic by Freytag, Lane, Dozy, &c. The social meaning is noted especially in Muslim Spain (cf. the Spanish *Vocabulista aravigo en letra castellana* of Pedro de Alcala, Granada 1505, *hurr* ='franco previlegiado': Dozy, i. 262).

[2] The term first used for political freedom was the now obsolete *serbestiyet*, a pseudo-Arabic abstract formation from *serbest*, free. This is a Turkish corruption of *serbaz*, a Persian word meaning bare-headed, and applied in Turkey to soldiers, i.e. those who make free with their lives. *Serbestiyet* was only gradually replaced by the now common *hürriyet*. In Ruphy's Arabic word list, prepared for the French expedition in Egypt at the beginning of the nineteenth century, *hurriyya* is given as equivalent to *liberté*, but with the restriction 'opposé à l'esclavage' (J. F. Ruphy, *Dictionnaire abrégé François-arabe* (Paris, An X [1802], p. 120). In the sense of 'pouvoir d'agir' Ruphy prefers the

the Reis Efendi Atıf, reporting on the proceedings of the French in the areas they had occupied on the Adriatic coast, remarks that 'their action in recalling the form of government of the ancient Greeks and installing a régime of liberty in these places reveals beyond any need for comment or explanation the evil intentions in their minds'.[3]

Nationalism and liberalism—Atıf had correctly diagnosed the two forces that in the nineteenth century were to do so much to destroy the Empire. Later in the same year the Sultan tried to refute these dangerous new ideas, describing French liberty as mere libertinism and anarchy:

In this vain belief and preposterous opinion they have erected new principles and set new laws, and established what Satan whispered to them, and destroyed the bases of religions, and made lawful to them-selves forbidden things, and permitted themselves whatever their passions desire, and have enticed into their iniquity the common people, who are as raving madmen, and sown sedition among religions, and thrown mischief between kings and states. . . .[4]

But despite these and other efforts to destroy it, the slip from the tree of liberty planted in the soil of Turkey struck root. Before long another development heightened the interest of thoughtful Turks in liberty, equality, and the rule of law. During the first half of the nineteenth century growing numbers of Turks, especi-ally among those who had had the opportunity to travel in the West, were becoming disagreeably aware of the backwardness and poverty of their own country, as contrasted with a Europe which was rich and powerful beyond belief, and which, in its limitless self-confidence and aggressiveness, seemed to be bringing the whole world within its grasp. The old question: 'Why is the Empire declining?' had now to be restated: 'Why is the Empire declining while Europe advances and progresses, and what is the secret of European success?'

For a while the secret was believed to lie in European manu-factures and technical devices, which were the sole merits of an

Arabic term *sarāḥ*). As late as 1841 Handjeri, in his *Dictionnaire français-arabe-persan et turc*, 3 vols. (Moscow, 1840–1) renders 'liberté civile' and 'liberté politique' by *ruhsat-i şeriye* and *ruhsat-i mülkiye* respectively, and it is only about the mid-century in the new newspapers and periodicals that we begin to find *hürriyet* in the sense of political freedom.

[3] Cevdet, *Tarih*, vi. 400–1; cf. B. Lewis in *Slav. R.*, xxxiv (1955), 232–5.

[4] Ferman of 1798; cf. above, p. 67.

otherwise contemptible crew of barbarians. The redoubtable Halet Efendi, who was ambassador in Paris from 1802 to 1806, expresses this view in its crudest form:

God knows, their minds and their comprehension are such, that the difference between them and the people of Islam is like the difference between boatmen and scribes among us. Their strategems and policies are crude; before they even formulate an intention one can understand what they are going to do; these successes they have won arise only from our own lack of zeal, for they have no soldiers as brave as ours, no ministers like our ministers, and our artillery officers are more competent than theirs. Their capital consists of nothing but talk. God knows, I am of the opinion that if, as an emergency measure once every three or four years, 25,000 purses of aspers were to be set aside, and five factories for snuff, paper, crystal, cloth and porcelain, as well as a school for languages and geography set up, then in the course of five years there will be as good as nothing left for them to hold on to, since the basis of all their current trade is in these five commodities. May God bestow some zeal on our masters, Amen.[5]

Industry and science—factories and schools; these were the talismans by which both Mahmud II in Turkey and Muhammad Ali in Egypt tried to conjure up the wealth and power of Europe, and thus maintain the European-style armies which were their prime concern. The same basic ideas have underlain the work of many subsequent reformers and innovators.

But once a door had been opened in the wall separating Islam from Christendom, it was no longer possible to control and select the traffic in ideas that passed through it. Young Turks were learning European languages, studying with European teachers travelling in Europe—it was inevitable that they should extend their reading and their interests somewhat beyond the acquisition of the technical skills assigned to them.

The talisman did not seem to be working too well; some further secrets concerning its correct application must be discovered. To the eager young Turkish visitor to Europe, in search of the elusive source of European strength, it seemed natural to seek it in those features of European life and government which were most different from his own. Liberalism, in the 1830's and 1840's, was the sacred cause of enlightenment and progress, combining the hopes both of the noblest of idealists and the most practical of

[5] Karal, *Halet*, pp. 32–33; cf. above, p. 69.

business men and technicians—and what, to the visiting Oriental, could be more peculiar, more distinctive of the West, than constitutional and parliamentary government?

One of the first to argue along these lines was Sadık Rifat Paşa (1807–56), who went to the Turkish Embassy in Vienna in 1837 and later held a number of senior appointments in Istanbul.[6] One of his writings is a twelve-page essay entitled 'Concerning the Condition of Europe' of which a first draft was prepared during his embassy in Vienna.

In this essay he sets forth some ideas on the essential differences between Europe and Turkey, and those respects in which the latter should seek to imitate the former. Like many of his generation, Sadık Rifat was deeply impressed by the wealth, industry, and science of Europe, and saw in these the chief means of regenerating his country. But he also links European progress and prosperity to certain political conditions. The basis of the prosperity of European states, he explains, is the steady increase in numbers of the population, the improvement in cultivation of the country, and the maintenance of tranquillity and security. But these in turn depend on

the attainment of complete security for the life, property, honour, and reputation of each nation and people, that is to say, on the proper application of the necessary rights of liberty. This being so, this kind of security and these rights of liberty are maintained with exceeding care and concern; since individual subjects and likewise countries are not made and created for states, but on the contrary, by the wisdom of the Almighty King, the sovereigns of the world were only vouchsafed the grace of God in order to protect and safeguard the welfare and prosperity of countries, therefore in the conduct of the affairs of government they act in accordance with the rights of the nation and the laws of the state, and no kind of arbitrary or violent action occurs. . . . Since these matters occupy, for the civilised states of Europe, the position of the alphabet of their basic policy, it is a matter of urgent necessity to strive with the utmost exertion of will and endeavour to secure the conditions by which they may also be attained for the Empire. . . .[7]

[6] On Sadık Rifat Paşa see Tanpınar, i. 88 ff.; Şeref, *Tar. Mus.*, pp. 115 ff.; Ali Fuat, 'Ricali Tanzimattan Rifat Paşa' in *TTEM*, n.s. i/2 (1930), 1–11.

[7] A version of Sadık Rifat's memorandum was published by Şeref, pp. 125 ff. A somewhat variant text will be found in Sadık Rifat's collected writings, *Müntehabât-i Asar* (n.d.) which includes a brief biography of the pasha.

K

Rifat's basic ideas are well within the framework of traditional Islamic political thought. His concern is with justice rather than liberty—with the obligation of rulers to rule according to law and to treat their subjects justly and benevolently. But the idea that the subject has a *right* to such treatment is a new one, in marked contrast to the older conception summed up in an Arab dictum: 'If the Caliph is just, his the reward and yours to be thankful. If he is unjust, his the sin and yours to be patient.'[8]

When Rifat speaks of 'the rights of the people' and 'the rights of liberty', he is expressing new ideas, derived from France, and still imperfectly understood. We find them again in the Essay on Europe of Seyyid Mustafa Sami, a former chief secretary of the Turkish Embassy in Paris. In this essay, published in 1840, the author speaks with admiration of the European form of government, of freedom of religion, of equality and security before the law, of liberty and progress.[9]

Both writers stress the importance of science in creating prosperity, and are aware of a connexion between science and freedom. But freedom for them still means equality and security before the law—the security of the subject from arbitrary and illegal actions by the government, and not his right to share in it. The statesmen of the *Tanzimat* held the same opinion, and tried, by making new laws and establishing new courts, to protect the subject from arbitrary action by the government or its agents. The triumph of science, the rule of law, and the spread of education are jointly celebrated in the somewhat ponderous ecstasies of Sadullah Paşa's (1838–91) ode on 'The Nineteenth Century':[10]

> The rights of person and possession are protected from attack,
> A new order has been given to the world of civilization.

[8] Ibn 'Abd Rabbihi, *Kitāb al-'Iqd al-Farīd*, i (Cairo, 1940), 10; cf. B. Lewis, 'The Concept of an Islamic Republic', *WI*, i (1955), 7.

[9] Tanpınar, pp. 93 ff. Another work of the time, of great importance in the spread of liberal and constitutional ideas, is the account written by the Egyptian Azhari Shaykh Rifā'a Rāfi' al-Tahtāwī of his stay in Paris during the years 1826–31. Rifā'a's book, which appeared in Bulaq in Arabic in 1834 and in a Turkish version in 1839, includes a translation, with comments, of the French constitution, a discussion of the 1830 revolution, which the author witnessed, and an eloquent plea for constitutional and representative government, as the best safeguard against tyranny.

[10] Akyüz, *Antoloji*, pp. 66 ff. The poem will also be found in other anthologies. For other examples of his writings see Ebüzziya Tevfik, *Nümûne-i Edebiyat-i Osmaniye* (1306 A.H.), pp. 280 ff.

Amr is not Zeyd's slave, nor is Zeyd Amr's master,[11]
A clear and indubitable rule establishes the basis of equality.

The spread of science has enlightened the minds of men,
The printing press has completed what was lacking.

Alas, the Western lands have become the daysprings of knowledge,
Nothing remains of the fame of Rūm and Arab, of Egypt and Herat.

The time is a time of progress, the world is a world of science,
Is the survival of societies compatible with ignorance?

Even the Sultans and their ministers gave some recognition to the new ideas on the relationship between sovereign and subject. The Noble Rescript of the Rose Chamber of 1839 lays down that the new institutions, to be set up for the better government of the Empire, must cover three major points, the first of which is 'the guarantees ensuring to our subjects perfect security for life, honour and fortune'. The Imperial Rescript of 1856 goes still further, and reaffirms in its very first article that

the guarantees promised on our part by the Imperial Rescript of the Rose Chamber and the laws of the *Tanzimat* to all the subjects of my Empire, without distinction of class or religion, for the security of their persons and their property and the preservation of their honour, are today being confirmed and consolidated, and efficacious measures shall be taken in order that they may have their full and entire effect.

These guarantees are impressive enough on paper, and led some observers to describe the reforming edicts as the Charters of the Ottoman Empire. The reformers themselves were no doubt sincere in their intentions, and Sultan Abdülmecid had, in 1845, gone so far as to convene an assembly of provincial notables for consultation. But in fact the autocratic authority of the sovereign power was not decreasing but increasing throughout the nineteenth century. The old and well-tried checks on the Sultan's despotism had all gone: the corps of Janissaries, with its ancient privileges and its deep conviction of corporate identity and prerogative; the feudal sipahis; the local dynasties of the valley-lords and the provincial magistracy of the *ayan*; the separate power of the ulema, controllers of the law, religion, and education, buttressed by an independent hierarchy of dignitaries and underpinned by vast independent revenues. These, and all other intermediate powers, had been abrogated or enfeebled, leaving the

[11] Amr and Zeyd are Arab personal names, traditionally used in Islamic law books—the John Doe and Richard Roe of the Holy Law.

sovereign power with nothing but the paper shackles of its own edicts to restrain it. These edicts, alien in their conception and irrelevant in their application to the problems of an Islamic Empire, had little chance of success. Their purpose and purport were meaningless or suspect to the mass of the Sultan's subjects; the men entrusted with their enforcement were inept and half-hearted; nor was there any group, any force among the different classes of the population which might, in its own interest, have impelled their effective application.

But the growth of autocracy, if unchecked, did not pass un-noticed—and in the Europe of the mid-nineteenth century there was no lack of ideologies of revolt. Islam was no longer insulated. Young France, Young England, Young Germany, were an inspiration to Young Turkey also. Turkish students and diplomats witnessed—may even have shared in—the heart-lifting events of 1848. After the suppression of the Polish and Hungarian risings of that year, a number of Polish and more especially Hungarian revolutionaries sought refuge in Turkey.[12] As rebels against Russia and Austria they could be sure of a sympathetic welcome, and this time they brought new ideas against which their hosts were no longer immune.

The growing economic difficulties of the country on the one hand, and the replacement of the easy-going Sultan Abdülmecid by the more despotic Abdülaziz on the other, brought matters to a head, and during the 1860's a new phase began in which the argument was no longer whether to accept or reject the Western-izing reforms, but whether—and how—to limit the autocracy of the sovereign power. The new phase of reform was opened not by government enactments but by literary manifestoes, and the first leaders of Young Turkey were not politicians but poets and writers.

The Literary Movement [13]

From about the middle of the century the spread of Western ideas and the acclimatization of Western social and political

---

[12] See below, p. 339.

[13] By far the most illuminating account of Turkish literary and intellectual move-ments in the nineteenth century is that given by Tanpınar, in the work already cited. Among works in Western languages, the most up to date is Alessio Bombaci, *Storia della letteratura turca* (1956), where further references are given. A very useful series of selections will be found in the *Türk Klasikleri*, published by Varlık Yayınları, Ist., 1952 ff.

attitudes among the Turks was greatly accelerated by the rise of a new Turkish literature, differing both in form and in content from classical Ottoman writings. In it the literature of France had begun to replace the classics of Iran as the source of inspiration and the model for imitation.

Three men are usually credited with being the pioneers of this new literature; Ibrahim Şinasi (1826–71), Ziya Paşa (1825–80), and Namık Kemal (1840–88). Ibrahim Şinasi was a poet, dramatist, and journalist.[14] The son of an artillery officer, he received his first instruction in French from one of his father's colleagues, a French renegade in the Ottoman service, and himself obtained a post in the artillery office. Thanks to the protection of Reşid Paşa he was able to join one of the Turkish student missions to Paris, where he stayed for four or five years. According to Turkish literary tradition he took part in the revolution of 1848, and hung a republican flag on the Pantheon. Certainly he was a young student in Paris during or shortly after those heroic days, and cannot but have been marked by them. While he was there, he is said to have been befriended by Samuel de Sacy, the son of the famous Orientalist Silvestre de Sacy, and to have made the acquaintance of the poet Lamartine, by whose writings he was much influenced.

On his return to Turkey he re-entered the government service, and became a member of the newly created Council of Education. He was, however, viewed with disfavour because of his Westernized manners. A particular grievance was his shaving of his beard —a practice due, according to one source, to a skin infection, according to another, to Frankish influence. A beardless official was as much an oddity at that date as a bearded one would be today, and before long Âli Paşa himself ordered Şinasi's dismissal from the Council of Education, in a document demanding 'the abrogation of his rank, the cancellation of his appointment, the cessation of his salary'.[15]

Âli Paşa's objection to Şinasi was not confined to his bare chin; there was the more serious matter of his being a protégé of Reşid Paşa. Other nominees of Reşid Paşa, impeccably bearded,

[14] On Şinasi see *EI*[1] ('Shināsī', by J. Deny); Gibb, *Ottoman Poetry*, v. 22–40; Tanpınar, pp. 155–88; Şinasi (*Türk Klas.*, xxv); Ebüzziya, *Nümûne*, pp. 220–48; Akyüz, *Antoloji*, pp. 1–15; and the relevant passages in the general literary histories and anthologies.

[15] Şinasi, *Türk Klas.*, p. 6.

were also removed by the great reformer's disciples and rivals. On Reşid Paşa's return to the Grand Vezirate, Şinasi was reinstated in his former appointment. The death of Reşid in 1858 deprived him of his protector, but also took the sting out of Âli and Fuad Paşas' antagonism, and for some time Şinasi was untroubled by official hostility.

From this time onwards he became increasingly occupied with literature and with journalism—a new profession and a new form of expression in Turkey. From 1862 he edited his own journal, the *Tasvir-i Efkâr*, which came to play a role of great importance in the intellectual life of the country. In 1865, for reasons that are not quite clear, he seems to have feared official anger, and left once again for Paris, from where he did not finally return until after the death of the Grand Vezir Fuad Paşa in 1869. He himself died in Istanbul in 1871.

Şinasi's political ideas were cautious and tentative, and contained no radical criticisms of the existing order. The general line of his thought is, however, indicated in an ode which he wrote to Mustafa Reşid Paşa at the time of the promulgation of the Imperial Rescript of 1856—that is, shortly after his own return from his studies in France:

> Life, property and honour are the candles of our hearts,
> Your justice is a lantern to guard us from the blast of oppression.
>
> You have made us free, who were slaves to tyranny,
> Bound as if in chains by our own ignorance.
>
> Your law is an act of manumission for men,
> Your law informs the Sultan of his limits.[16]

The radical implications of the last couplet will be obvious. Also a protégé of Reşid Paşa was Ziya Paşa, the second of the three pioneers of the new literature.[17] The son of a clerk in the customs house at Galata, he was educated at the grammar school which Sultan Mahmud II had opened by the Süleymaniye mosque, and entered the civil service at the age of seventeen. In 1854, thanks to the influence of Reşid Paşa, whose goodwill he had won, Ziya was appointed third secretary to the Sultan, and

[16] Ibid. pp. 42-43; Akyüz, *Antoloji*, p. 8; Bombaci, p. 426.
[17] On Ziya Paşa see Gibb, *Ottoman Poetry*, v. 41–111; Tanpınar, pp. 279–321; Ziya Paşa (*Türk Klas.*); Ebüzziya, *Nümûne*, pp. 249–79; Akyüz, *Antoloji*, pp. 16–41, &c.

embarked on a new career in the Imperial household. It was at this stage that he began to study French, and soon acquired sufficient mastery of the language to translate French books into Turkish.

Like Şinasi and other protégés of Reşid Paşa, he was not viewed with favour by Âli and Fuad Paşas, the more so since he seems to have used his position in the palace to warn the Sultan against Âli Paşa. Eventually Âli Paşa secured his removal from the Imperial household. Ziya then held various minor posts, and at the same time joined with Namık Kemal and other young men in forming the Young Ottoman Movement. In 1867, faced with virtual banishment as titular governor of Cyprus, he fled to Europe together with a number of his Young Ottoman associates.

Between 1867 and 1872 Ziya remained an exile, first in Paris, then in London, and finally in Geneva. During these years he wrote some of his most vigorous criticisms of the régime of Âli and Fuad Paşas, and of the changes they were making in Turkey. After the death of Âli Paşa, he was authorized to return to Turkey, when in 1876 he was made governor of Syria, with the rank of vezir and pasha, by Sultan Abdülhamid. He died in Adana in May 1880.

Ziya Paşa was by no means a consistent Westernizer. While urging the importance of learning Western languages, he disapproved of the imitation of Western literary models, since each civilization had its own genius:

> Is there not a difference of climate?
> Is the situation of East and West the same?
> Could Racine or Lamartine adorn a Kasida like Nefi?
> Could Senai or Farazdak write plays like Molière?[18]

He is by no means enthusiastic about the granting of equal status to non-Muslims, and in his famous satire against Âli Paşa he criticizes the minister's moves in that direction:

> If but the help of God assist in his purpose clear,
> Full soon will these gypsies sit on the couch of the Grand Vezir;
> It is but the Jews alone that form the exception here,
> For of Greeks and Armenians both doth he make Bey and Mushir;
> The equality of rights to perfection brought hath he.[19]

[18] Ziya Paşa, *Türk Klas*, p. 68 (from *Harabât*, Introduction, sect. 15).
[19] Tr. by E. J. W. Gibb, *Ottoman Poetry*, v. 105–6.

In a bitter attack on the fashions of his time, he observes:

> To impute fanaticism to men of zeal
> To ascribe wisdom to men without religion is now the fashion.
>
> Islam, they say, is a stumbling-block to the progress of the state
> This story was not known before, and now it is the fashion.
>
> Forgetting our religious loyalty in all our affairs
> Following Frankish ideas is now the fashion.[20]

But Ziya, despite his cultural and religious conservatism, did not himself disdain to follow Frankish ideas, suitably disguised. The most potent of these was constitutional government. His views on this matter are contained in two works, both written during his exile. The first, entitled 'Dream',[21] describes a vision which Ziya saw while sleeping on a bench in Hampstead Heath, and is curiously reminiscent of the visionary dialogue of the seventeenth-century poet Veysi,[22] and similar works. In his dream Ziya has a conversation with Sultan Abdülaziz, and warns the Sultan of the parlous state of the country. The Sultan accuses Ziya of having tried to undermine his authority by recommending the formation of a national assembly, and Ziya replies that the creation of such an assembly would bring Turkey into line with the practice of civilized states without infringing the lawful rights of the sovereign.

> Now condescend to look at the states of this continent of Europe. Apart from Russia, does arbitrary government remain anywhere? And is not even Russia gradually trying to imitate the systems of government of the other European states? Are the Emperors of France and Austria, the Kings of Italy and Prussia, the Queen of England less than the Russian in might and majesty? . . . Since the lofty Dynasty is also considered one of the family of Europe, it is not within the bounds of possibility for us to remain in this way at variance with all the world.[23]

The Sultan, in Ziya's dream, is still not satisfied, and points out that while these other states each rule over one nation, his subjects

[20] Akyüz, *Antoloji*, p. 38 (*Terkib-i Bend*, no. x).

[21] An abridged text of *Rüya* (Dream) will be found in Ziya Paşa, *Türk Klas.*, pp. 111–19.

[22] On Veysi see Gibb, *Ottoman Poetry*, iii. 208 ff.

[23] Ziya Paşa, *Türk Klas.*, p. 115.

are of various religions, and since each group would pursue its own interests, a national assembly would only provide a platform for conflict and give rise to dissension and disunity. Ziya agrees, and says: 'Yes, Sire, if the national assembly to be created here were to begin with the privileges of the French or English parliaments, this observation would indeed be in place.'[24] But this is not what he has in mind. The Ottoman assembly, for the reasons noted, must begin with limited powers, which may, however, be extended when this can be done with safety. The dream ends when Ziya is awakened by a park-keeper.

In another essay written during his exile Ziya takes as his text the tradition attributed to the Prophet that 'difference of opinion within my community is an act of divine mercy'.[25] This saying, which was usually cited to legitimize the coexistence of different schools of Holy Law, was given a new meaning by Ziya, and used by him to justify the creation of an assembly where truth would emerge from the clash of different opinions, and in which responsible statesmen would have to submit their actions to the test of criticism and opposition.

The same tradition is cited in a famous ode to freedom by the third and by far the most gifted of the trio of literary innovators. Namık Kemal was born in Rhodosto in 1840, to an aristocratic family.[26] His father was the court astronomer, and the descendant of a line of senior Ottoman officials. His mother, of Albanian birth, was the daughter of a governor. He was educated at home, and was taught French as well as Persian and Arabic. Following the normal course of young men of his class and time, he entered the civil service at the age of seventeen and found a niche in the Translation Office of the Sublime Porte—Turkey's open window to the West.

He soon came under the influence of Şinasi, and collaborated with him on the journal *Tasvir-i Efkâr*, of which he took over the

[24] Ibid. p. 116.

[25] Text in Ebüzziya, *Nümûne*, pp. 257–61; *Türk Klas.*, ed., pp. 138–41.

[26] On Namık Kemal see *EI*[1] ('Kemal', by Th. Menzel); Tanpınar, pp. 322–432; Namık Kemal (*Türk Klas.*); Ebüzziya, *Nümûne*, pp. 294–493; Akyüz, *Antoloji*, pp. 42–65; Berkes, in Frye, pp. 65 ff., &c. Among many modern Turkish works on Namık Kemal, special mention may be made of Mithat Cemal Kuntay, *Namık Kemal* (1944–56); and Mehmed Kaplan, *Namık Kemal*; *Hayatı ve Eserleri* (1948). A useful selection of his journalistic writings will be found in Mustafa Nihat Özön, *Namık Kemal ve Ibret Gazetesi* (1938).

editorship when Şinasi fled to France in 1865. At first his contributions consisted exclusively of translations, but then the need to deal with such events as the second Polish revolution of 1863–4 and the American Civil War sharpened his perceptions and improved his skill as a political journalist and essayist. His essays on Ottoman affairs brought him into trouble with the authorities, and in 1867, together with Ziya and the other Young Ottomans, he fled to Europe.

The next three years were spent in exile, in London, Paris, and Vienna. There he occupied himself with the publication of opposition journals, with the study of law and economics, and with the translation of a number of French works into Turkish.

On his return to Turkey in 1871 he resumed his journalistic activities, and in 1873 produced the patriotic drama *Vatan*.[27] This aroused such dangerous enthusiasms that the author was exiled to Cyprus, where he remained for over three years. After the deposition of Sultan Abdülaziz in 1876, he was allowed to return to Istanbul, and took some part in the preparation of the constitution, though, like Ziya, he was debarred from offering himself as a candidate. Later he fell foul of Sultan Abdülhamid, and spent most of his remaining years in detention or exile. He died in Chios in 1888.

Namık Kemal is best known in Turkey as the apostle of two ideas: freedom and fatherland. In a long series of articles, essays, novels, plays, and poems he brought to the Turkish Muslim reader these two characteristic ideas of the French Revolution, but in a form adapted to Muslim traditions and attitudes.

Despite his fervent patriotism and liberalism, Namık Kemal was a sincere and devoted Muslim, and the Fatherland of which he speaks, though he uses a term denoting territory and not community, is Islamic no less than Ottoman. Throughout his life he remained firmly attached to traditional Muslim values and beliefs, and was often sharply critical of the men of the *Tanzimat* for their failure to safeguard and preserve the best of the old Islamic traditions, and to let them inspire and direct the new institutions which had to be imported from Europe. He upheld Islamic values and defended Islamic achievements against European belittlers, and even advanced the idea of a pan-Islamic unity, under Ottoman leadership, to accept, adapt, and

[27] See below, p. 154.

diffuse modern civilization through Asia and Africa, and thus create an Eastern balance of power to counter that of Europe.

He was profoundly impressed by the achievements of European civilization. The backwardness of Islam, however, was in his view relative rather than absolute; it was not due to any inherent defect in Islam itself, but to the domination of the West, which had deprived the East of the opportunity of self-advancement. The Islamic state had to modernize itself, but in doing so it should not slavishly imitate Europe and abandon its own laws, beliefs, and traditions. On the contrary, he argued, all that is best in European civilization derived from or could be paralleled in classical Islamic civilization, and the Muslim, in adopting these things, was returning to what was deepest and most authentic in his own tradition. Here Namık Kemal used a line of argument that was to become typical of a certain trend of romantic and apologetic writing among Muslims. Sometimes its purpose was to win the respect of Westerners or Westernizers for traditional Islamic values. More frequently, in this period, it was intended to make the ideas of the reformers more palatable to orthodox Muslims.

Namık Kemal's political theory derives largely from Montesquieu and Rousseau, his ideas on the practice of government from the parliaments of London and Paris. One of the deepest and most lasting influences on his political thinking was Montesquieu's *Esprit des Lois*, of which he began to publish a translation in 1863. In later essays he tried to make the ideas of Montesquieu compatible with the principles of the Şeriat—a task which, like the earlier Muslim attempt to marry Aristotelian philosophy and Koranic theology, involved some reinterpretation of both. For Kemal, the wise and just rules of the Şeriat are none other than the natural law of which Montesquieu speaks, and 'the nature of things', from which law arises, could therefore be identified with a somewhat sufistic conception of God Himself.

According to the law-makers, there is no greater task than striving, from the point of view of abstract good, to bring to light origins and consequences. With us the Şeriat determines good and evil. Among the people of our country the compatibility of these consequences with abstract good can be known by testing the case against this touchstone of justice.[28]

[28] 'Hukuk', from *Ibret*, no. 5 of 1872, reprinted in Özön, *Ibret*, p. 51.

One of the basic rules of natural—i.e. of divine—law is freedom. Kemal was not the first to speak of human rights and parliamentary government in Turkey, but he was the first to correlate them, and to achieve a clear vision of freedom and self-government under law. Sadık Rifat Paşa had spoken of the natural human right to freedom, but had seen no way of safeguarding it except by exhorting the sovereign to rule justly. Ziya Paşa spoke of constitutions and assemblies—but saw in them only a device of government, a means of giving the Ottoman Empire the appearance, and perhaps also some of the perquisites, of a Western state. For Kemal too the primary duty of the state is still to act justly; but he also has a clear idea of the political rights of the citizen, which justice requires the state to respect, and also of the means by which they may be safeguarded. Typically, these ideas, of French and British origin, are equated with principles of Islamic law:

Every book treats the subject of political rights with different subdivisions. However, the points on which the greatest measure of agreement exists among authors are such general principles as the sovereignty of the nation, the separation of powers, the responsibility of officials, personal freedom, equality, freedom of thought, freedom of the press, freedom of association, enjoyment of property, sanctity of the home.

The sovereignty of the people, which means that the powers of the government derive from the people, and which in the technical language of the *Şeriat* is called *Baya*, is not an authority which has happened to become attached to the abstract meaning expressed by the word 'public' or 'people'; it is a right necessarily arising from the personal independence that each individual by nature possesses.

'Everyone is Emperor in his own world'. . . .

To keep the government within the limits of justice, there are two basic devices. The first of them is that the fundamental rules by which it operates should no longer be implicit or tacit, but should be published to the world. . . . The second principle is consultation, whereby the legislative power is taken away from the government. . . .[29]

For these ideas Namık Kemal tried valiantly to find precedents in the Islamic past. The sovereignty of the people he identified with the *Baya*, the formal oath of obedience which was given to a new Caliph after his appointment, and which completed the

[29] 'Hukuku Umumiye', from *Ibret*, no. 18, of 1872; reprinted in Ebüzziya, *Nümûne*, pp. 357–8 and Özön, *Ibret*, pp. 96–97.

contract between the new sovereign and his subjects. For the principle of government by consultation and representation he was able to find justification in the Koran itself, notably in the verse in the third *Sura* when the Prophet is commanded to be lenient with his followers and to take counsel with them.[30] This verse was frequently quoted by Namık Kemal, Ziya Paşa, and their friends and became one of the favourite texts of the nineteenth-century Turkish and other Muslim liberals. Kemal went further, and tried to show that the Ottoman Empire itself, before the beginning of the reforms, had practised a form of representative government. Even the Janissaries, until their abolition, served as a kind of 'armed consultative assembly of the nation'.[31]

These attempts to identify European parliamentary institutions with traditional Islam are no doubt open to damaging criticisms from the point of view of Muslim law, theology, and history. They did, however, succeed in winning acceptance far beyond the Ottoman frontiers, and in convincing a generation of Muslim intellectuals who were no longer wholly satisfied with traditional Islam, but were sufficiently attached to it to feel a need to restate and justify their Islamic faith and heritage in terms of their newly acquired Western values. The effects of their ideas can be seen after the Young Turk Revolution when, in the speech from the throne at the opening of the Ottoman parliament on 14 November 1909, the Sultan began with a reference to 'the parliamentary form of government prescribed by *Şeriat*'.[32]

For the actual form of representative government to be adopted even Namık Kemal could find no model in Islamic law and history, but was compelled to look abroad. His choice fell on London. Although his Western knowledge and reading were fundamentally French, the Paris Chamber under Napoleon III was too authoritarian for his taste. In his view, the Ottomans

could very well be governed under a more liberal constitution than that of France. . . . Since the French are of a very fiery disposition, they

[30] Koran, iii. verse 153.

[31] Kaplan, p. 107. This idea, which Kemal expresses in a number of places, might possibly derive from Slade (*Travels*, i. 276; cf. above p. 123). That Slade was read in Turkey is attested by N. W. Senior (p. 36), who found Vefik Paşa 'reading Captain Slade's "Turkey", of which he praised the fidelity'.

[32] I. Goldziher, *Vorlesungen über den Islam* (1925), p. 380 n. 20, and Turkish press, 15 Nov. 1909.

are always inclined to change. The basis of their actions is reason, but, under the impulsion of one specious sophism they spoil the result of a thousand sound deductions. . . . Since the great republic, they have constituted thirty or forty different forms of government. . . . The Ottoman people, on the other hand, thanks to their innate gravity and calm, are in no danger of running to extremes. . . . In the course of six centuries we have made hundreds of revolts; in all of them the men who governed were changed, but the form of government remained. . . .[33]

Namık Kemal is thus very far from agreeing with Ziya Paşa's view that the Ottomans would be wise to begin with restricted parliamentary powers.

In an article entitled 'Progress', and published in the *Ibret* in November 1872, Kemal speaks in glowing terms of London. 'What need is there to wander through all the civilized countries? If a man will but stroll about London with an attentive eye, he will be bewildered by the wonders that he sees. If London be called the model of the world, it would be no exaggeration!' He goes on to speak in rapturous terms of the schools and colleges, libraries, theatres, hospitals, and factories of the English capital, above all of its parliament, 'the cradle of most of the political principles that we see in the world . . . and the embodiment in stone of the indomitable power of public opinion against authority'.[34]

This was the form of government, these the resources and methods, that were needed to save the Ottoman Empire from destruction. Could they be won? To this question Kemal answers with true Victorian optimism:

It took Europe two centuries to reach this condition, and while they were the inventors in the paths of progress, we find all the means ready to hand . . . can there be any doubt that we too, even if it takes us two centuries, can reach a stage when we would be counted as one of the most civilized countries?[35]

[33] Kaplan, p. 108, quoting *Hürriyet*, no. 12.
[34] 'Terakki', from *Ibret*, no. 45 of 1872, reprinted in Ebüzziya, *Nümûne*, pp. 308 ff. and Özön, *Ibret*, pp. 176 ff.
[35] Ibid.; Özön, p. 187.

New Media: the Press [36]

Namık Kemal and his friends had, however, no intention of waiting two centuries to catch up with a Europe which, it is inferred, would meanwhile remain stationary. Their plans called for a more immediate programme of modernization and of social and political reform, the difficulties of which they grievously underestimated. Progress depended on free institutions, and free institutions were maintained by public opinion. The Ottoman liberals therefore set to work to create and instruct a Turkish public opinion which, they hoped, would play the same role in Turkey as its counterparts in Paris and London.

One of their chief media in this was the press, the importance of which, in the Western world, they were quick to realize. The first non-official periodical in Turkish, the weekly *Ceride-i Havadis* (Journal of News) had been started in 1840 by William Churchill, and was continued by his son after his death in 1846.[37] This journal, which in its form and style was moulded on the official gazette, devoted rather more space than the latter to international affairs. In its early years it encountered some difficulties, and in 1843 was forced to close down for a while, possibly as a result of Russian pressure. Later it resumed publication, and seems to have been given a government subsidy. This, and a growing revenue from advertisements, kept the journal going, though, like the official gazette, it did not achieve regularity of publication.

The outbreak of the Crimean War brought new opportunities. The younger Churchill covered the fighting for English newspapers, and his reports, which were also published in special supplements by the *Ceride-i Havadis*, gave the news-hungry Turkish reader a new insight into the function and value of the newspaper in the modern state. To keep in touch with this growing circle of readers, the editors of the *Ceride-i Havadis* began to simplify the language in which the journal was written, gradually abandoning the cumbersome chancery style which they had previously shared with the official gazette, and adopting a simpler and more direct form of language. Turkish journalese

[36] On the early history of the press in Turkey see Emin, *Press*; Gerçek, *Türk Gazet.*; Iskit, *Türkiyede Matbuat Rejimleri*; *IA* ('Matbuat II/I' by Vedad Günyol); Tanpınar, pp. 224 ff.; above, p. 93 n. 37.

[37] Gerçek, pp. 35 ff.

was born in their columns. As well as news, they published articles and features, often in serial form, and thus gave a first apprenticeship in literary journalism to a number of Ottoman men of letters, perhaps including Şinasi.

Apart from the colourless official gazette, the *Ceride-i Havadis* enjoyed a virtual monopoly of journalism in the Turkish language for twenty years. During that time it played an important pioneer role, accustoming the Turkish reader to news and features, and training a generation of journalists, as well as of printers, distributors, and other necessary adjuncts of the newspaper trade. In 1860 it had to encounter another aspect of the world of Western journalism—competition. In that year Çapanzade Agah Efendi, a scion of an aristocratic *derebey* family and a senior member of the Translation Chamber of the Sublime Porte, took the initiative in founding a new weekly, the *Tercüman-i Ahval* (Interpreter of Conditions). Associated with him as editor and writer was Ibrahim Şinasi, the poet and modernist. The opening paragraphs of his first leader are a good example of the mixture of styles, ideas, and traditions of the first journalists and liberals:

Since people who live in a social body are thereby charged with legal obligations, the expression of one's ideas by word and by pen concerning the interests of one's country must assuredly be reckoned as one of the acquired rights. If written proof of this contention be sought, it may suffice to point to the political newspapers of the civilized nations whose minds have been opened by the power of knowledge.

This argument is also in a sense confirmed as regards the Exalted Dynasty, in that when the High Council of Reform was constituted, official permission was given to the public to submit, in writing, proposals concerning the laws and regulations. And moreover, the newspapers which, with the permission of the Exalted Government, the non-Muslim subjects in the Ottoman realms still publish in their own languages, have perhaps more freedom than is their right. But when we come to discuss truly Ottoman newspapers, for some reason no member of the dominant nation has up to now been willing to trouble himself with the regular publication of a non-official newspaper. Now at last, thank God, under just Imperial auspices, it has become possible to make good the deficiency of the past. So that in this way, upon a report given from the General Council of Education, which approved the purport of a recently submitted memorandum concerning a petition for the publication of a newspaper in Turkish, the Privy

Council of Noble Ministers also approved the matter and, in this connexion, the Imperial consent was also vouchsafed.[38]

Churchill responded to this challenge by publishing a daily version of his paper five days a week, and for a while there was keen rivalry between the two publications. Before long, however, the new weekly ran into difficulties. In the increasingly authoritarian mood of the 1860's there were some who thought that Şinasi and his friends were exercising 'perhaps more freedom than is their right'. As a result of an article probably written by Ziya Paşa, the *Tercüman-i Ahval* was closed by government order for two weeks—the first precedent in Turkey for government suppression of a newspaper.

Şinasi himself, finding his freedom of expression restricted, left the *Tercüman-i Ahval* after only twenty-five issues, and in June 1862 began to publish his own paper, the *Tasvir-i Efkâr* (Illustration of Opinion). This paper adopted a slightly more advanced position, though its radicalism was cultural rather than political. Şinasi did, however, devote some attention to political matters, and spoke from time to time of the need for financial and legal reform. In this he was followed by his more famous disciple Namık Kemal. Kemal made his journalistic debut in the *Mirat* (Mirror), a journal which appeared in March 1863 and of which only three issues were published. Significantly, he began with an annotated translation of parts of Montesquieu's *Considérations sur les causes de la grandeur et de la décadence des Romains*. A little later he began to contribute to the *Tasvir-i Efkâr*, and when Şinasi went to Paris in 1865 took over the editing of the paper. By temperament far less circumspect than Şinasi, he began to give the paper a more outspokenly political character, and his trenchant editorials on foreign and internal questions soon began to attract the attention of authority.

Still more radical in tone and content was the *Muhbir* (Informer), the first issue of which appeared on 1 January 1867, the last on 8 March. This was edited by Ali Suavi Efendi (1838–78).[39] Unlike most of the liberals and intellectuals of the time, he had not emerged from the landowning and official classes, but

---

[38] Reprinted in Şinasi (*Türk Klas.*), pp. 72 ff.

[39] On Ali Suavi see Kuntay, *Sarıklı İhtilâlci Ali Suavi* (1946); Tanpınar, pp. 204–23; and a rather impressionistic account by Falih Rıfkı Atay, *Başveren İnkılâpçı* (n.d., preface dated 1951).

was the son of a villager who had come to Istanbul and made a poor livelihood by polishing paper. Ali Suavi received a traditional education in the *Medrese*. A schoolmaster by profession, he taught in the new *ruşdiye* schools in Bursa and Filibe, and was dismissed from the latter for his alleged demagogy. His vigorous and somewhat sensational articles in the *Muhbir* aroused the ire of the Grand Vezir, who exiled him to Anatolia. From there he escaped to Europe where for a short time he continued to publish the *Muhbir* in London. In the meantime several other papers had begun to appear in Istanbul, among which mention may be made of the *Ayine-i Vatan* (Mirror of the Fatherland). This publication, the first issue of which appeared on 14 January 1867, was—apart from the short-lived *Mirat*—the first illustrated Turkish paper, and also the first to bear the name of Fatherland.

This rapid increase in the numbers and vigour of the press began to cause concern to the government, which, after the accession in 1861 of Sultan Abdülaziz, was becoming more and more autocratic. On 1 January 1865 a press law entered into force—the first of its kind in Turkey.[40] This laid down strict rules for the conduct of the press, and provided for the establishment of a Press Commission, to sit at the Sublime Porte and supplement the police courts in the enforcement of the law. A 'notification' of 12 March 1867 made the intentions of the government clear:

A part of the local press, not recognising the spirit by which journalism should be inspired in the East, has made itself the passionate organ of all the extreme parties and of tendencies essentially hostile to the general interests of the country . . . the Sublime Porte therefore reserves the right, whenever the general interest of the country may require it, to act through administrative channels and independently of the law of the press, against those newspapers which do not recognise the above-stated principles, whose observance is an essential condition of a national press. . . .[41]

These measures introduced a period of severe pressure, culminating in the suppression of several newspapers and the departure for Europe of their more prominent contributors. For the next few years the most significant Turkish newspapers were published in exile in London, Paris, and Geneva. In the words

[40] *Düstur*, ii. 220; Young, ii. 321 ff.; Aristarchi, iii. 320 ff.
[41] Young, ii. 326; Aristarchi, iii. 325–6.

that introduce the first London issue of one of them: '*Muhbir* has found a country where it is not forbidden to tell the truth, and appears again.'[42]

Turkish officials, faced with a new problem, were learning the techniques of influence and control of the press. But Turkish journalists had also completed, in a remarkably short time, the evolution from report to comment, from comment to criticism, from criticism to opposition, and from opposition to defiance.

Organized Opposition: the Young Ottomans [43]

The reforms of Mahmud II and his successors had created a new administrative and governing *élite* in the Empire, literate, idealistic, and ambitious. The transformation of Ottoman government and society had given them new opportunities and appetites; the translation and imitation of European writings had filled their minds with new beliefs and ideas. When therefore, in the second half of the nineteenth century, the growing autocracy of the Sultan and his ministers began to weigh on their shoulders,

---

[42] *Muhbir*, no. 1, 31 Aug. 1867 (the front page is reproduced in Gerçek, *Türk Gazet.*).

[43] The only detailed history of the Young Ottoman movement was that written by Ebüzziya Tevfik, and published serially in the *Yeni Tasvir-i Efkâr*, 1909. Most subsequent versions are based on this. Useful brief accounts will be found in Akçuraoğlu Yusuf [=Yusuf Akçura], 'Türkcülük', in *Türk Yılı*, 1928, pp. 294 ff.; Tarık Tunaya, *Türkiyede Siyasî Partiler*, *1859–1952* (1952), pp. 91 ff.; Kaplan, pp. 54 ff.; Ahmed Bedevi Kuran, *Osmanlı Imparatorluğunda Inkılâp Hareketleri ve Millî Mücadele* (1956), pp. 57 ff.; and Karal, *Tarih*, vii. 299 ff. The most detailed documentation on the movement with special reference to the role of Namık Kemal is contained in Kuntay's biography, vol. i. On the connexion of Ottoman princes with the Young Ottomans see the notes of Abdülhamid, published in *TTEM*, nos. 90–92 (1926). A survey of the political ideas of the movement, with many illustrative quotations from their writings, was contributed by Ihsan Süngü to the *Tanzimat* anniversary volume ('Tanzimat ve Yeni Osmanlılar', in *Tanzimat*, pp. 777–857). Finally, among the Turkish sources, mention must be made of two excellent interpretative essays, the first historical, the second literary, by Şeref, *Tarih Musahabeleri*, pp. 172 ff., and Tanpınar, pp. 189 ff. The earliest Western accounts were those of the Turcophiles Léon Cahun and Arminius Vambéry (see below, p. 340), who met the Young Ottomans in Paris and London. Cahun wrote a brief account of them in the *Histoire générale* of Lavisse and Rambaud (xi. 543 ff.), while Vambéry described them in an article in the *Deutsche Rundschau* of October 1893 (cited by Paul Fesch, *Constantinople aux derniers jours d'Abdul-Hamid*, 1907, p. 323. For further Western notices see Gibb, *Ottoman Poetry*, v. 60 ff.; Engelhardt, ii. 3 f.; Sax, pp. 383 f.; G. L. Lewis, *Turkey*, p. 36; E. Rossi, 'Dall' Impero ottomano alla Repubblica di Turchia, Origine e Sviluppi del Nazionalismo Turco sotto l'Aspetto politico-culturale', *OM*, xxiii (1943), 361 ff.; Davison, in *Am. Hist. R.*, 1954, pp. 851 ff. The only monographic treatment of the Young Ottomans is that of Yu. A. Petrosian, '*Novye Osmani*' *i Borba za Konstitutsiyu 1876 g. v Turtsii* (1958). (I owe my knowledge of this work to Professor A. Tietze.)

they did not lack instruction either in the ideology or in the technique of opposition and revolution.

It is customary to begin the history of the Turkish liberal protest against absolutism with what is known as the Kuleli Incident, of 1859. In that year a small group of conspirators plotted to depose and if need be assassinate Sultan Abdülmecid. The plot was discovered, and the leaders were deported to Asia as prisoners. Several European writers describe this unsuccessful plot as the first attempt to introduce constitutional and parliamentary government. More recent research, however, would seem to indicate that the conspirators had no such aim or programme in mind—on the contrary, they disapproved of the concessions already made to the Christians. They were acting *against* the Sultan and his ministers rather than *for* any particular principles, and were thus concerned with an *attentat* and coup d'état on orthodox lines.[44]

Liberal and constitutional ideas had of course been known in the Ottoman Empire for some years. They appear, if faintly, in the writings of Sadık Rifat Paşa, and had some influence on the reforms of Sultan Abdülmecid and Mustafa Reşid Paşa. As far back as 1808 the reformist Grand Vezir Bayrakdar Mustafa Paşa had convened an Imperial assembly in Istanbul to approve his programme of reform,[45] and in 1829 Muhammad Ali Pasha in Egypt had gone a step further in nominating a consultative council of 156 members, which met for a few days each year.[46] In 1845 Abdülmecid himself had experimented, without success,

---

[44] The Kuleli Incident has been discussed by many authors, and variously interpreted. For Engelhardt (i. 158–9), followed by Jorga (v. 517), Vambéry, and some others, it was a liberal movement, the first attempt to establish constitutional government. V. I. Shpilkova, in a recent article in *Problemy Vostoka*, i (1959), 100–4 (summarized in *MEJ*, xiii (1959), 347), goes even further, and describes it as a 'progressive and anti-monarchist plot' that failed through lack of mass support. The Turkish historian Uluğ İğdemir, whose book *Kuleli Vakası hakkında bir Araştırma* (1937) is the only monograph on the subject based on Turkish documentary evidence, regards it as a petty *attentat* on traditional lines, devoid of any liberal ideological content but expressing rather a reaction against the trend of Westernization and the neglect of the Holy Law. İğdemir's findings, based on documents in the Turkish archives, are reinforced by Roderic Davison with evidence from Western diplomatic records ('European Archives as a Source for Later Ottoman History', in *Report on Current Research on the Middle East 1958*, pp. 38–41). See further Karal, *Tarih*, vi. 95–97; Tunaya, *Partiler*, pp. 89–90; Kuran, pp. 49 ff.

[45] See above, p. 74.

[46] J. Landau, *Parties and Parliaments in Egypt* (New York, 1954), p. 7.

with an assembly of provincial notables.[47] More recently, in 1861, the Bey of Tunis had proclaimed the first constitution of European type in a Muslim country. While reserving executive power to the Bey, it shared the legislative power between him and a Grand Council of sixty members, who were, however, nominated.[48] Finally, in 1866 the Khedive Ismail in Egypt made the first experiment with an elected assembly, by setting up a consultative body with a restricted electorate and still more restricted functions.[49]

It is in the 1860's in Turkey that we find for the first time an unmistakable liberal critique of government action, and a programme of constitutional reform. These ideas first appear in the circle of Şinasi, Namık Kemal, and their friends, and find a somewhat guarded expression in the journals of that time.

The first attempt to organize a definite group seems to have come in 1865. In June of that year a small group of six, one of whom was Namık Kemal, held a meeting and established a secret society. Little is known of its original programme, though we are told that one of the founder members, Ayetullah Bey, came to the first meeting with 'two important books, concerning the Carbonari and a secret society in Poland'.[50] Later a programme based on that of the Carbonari seems to have been adopted. The society grew rapidly, and at a later date was able to claim 245 members. Two princes of the Ottoman house, Murad and Abdülhamid, showed interest in the society, though it later became clear that Abdülhamid's intentions were from the first hostile.

Another prince who played a role of far greater significance in the movement was Mustafa Fazıl, of the Egyptian ruling house.[51] A son of the redoubtable Ibrahim Paşa, he was the brother of the Khedive Ismail and had been his heir until June 1866, when he was ousted by a change in the law of succession, obtained from the Sultan by the Khedive. Prince Mustafa Fazıl therefore had some reason to oppose the Sultan and the Grand Vezir, and is believed to have cherished the ambition of becoming the first

---

[47] See above, p. 110.   [48] *EI*², *s.v.* 'Dustūr'.   [49] Landau, p. 7.

[50] Ebüzziya Tevfik, in *Yeni Tasvir-i Efkâr*, issue of 20 June 1909; cf. Akçuraoğlu p. 295; Kaplan, p. 58.

[51] On Mustafa Fazıl see Ebüzziya Tevfik in *Yeni Tasvir-i Efkâr*, issues of 31 May, 1 June, &c., 1909; M. Colombe, 'Une Lettre d'un prince égyptien du XIXᵉ siècle au Sultan Ottoman Abd al-Aziz', *Orient*, v (1958), 23–38; Kuntay, *Namık Kemal*, i. 311 ff.

minister of a constitutional empire, instead of or as well as Khedive of Egypt. It would, however, probably be unjust to ascribe his interest in reform purely to pique or private ambition, though these no doubt had their effect. The prince took an active interest in the Ottoman liberals, and from Paris sent an open letter to the Sultan, in French, telling a few hard truths about the state of the Empire and proposing constitutional and other reforms. This document caused great excitement among the liberals; it was translated into Turkish by Namık Kemal, Ebüzziya Tevfik, and Sadullah, and printed and distributed in great numbers by the staff of the *Tasvir-i Efkâr*.[52]

The government, though informed by spies of the formation of the group, had hitherto taken no measures against it. This last act, however, provoked Âli Paşa, who in February 1867 had become Grand Vezir again, to swift if disguised action. Of the leaders of the group, Ali Suavi was exiled to Kastamonu, in Anatolia, while Kemal and Ziya were given official postings in the provinces which amounted to decrees of banishment.

It was at this time that the first revolutionary committee received its name. At the beginning of February 1867 the Belgian newspaper *Nord* had published a report that Prince Mustafa Fazıl had formed a money-changing business in Turkey. In a letter correcting this mis-statement, the prince referred to his supporters in Turkey as 'jeunes Turcs', a phrase that was no doubt inspired by the Young England, Young France, Young Germany of earlier decades in Europe. This *démenti* was copied from the Belgian paper by the *Courrier d'Orient* of Pera, the editor of which was on friendly terms with the Ottoman liberals, and thence translated into Turkish in the *Muhbir* of 21 February 1867. The name appealed to Ali Suavi and Namık Kemal, who tried various Turkish equivalents for it, eventually deciding on *Yeni Osmanlılar*—New or Young Ottomans. This, together with the French *jeunes Turcs*, appeared as the heading of the publications of the group.[53]

---

[52] Text in Colombe, pp. 29 ff.; Turkish in *Yeni Tas. Ef.* 1–5 June 1909. cf. Kuntay, pp. 277 ff.

[53] *Yeni Tas. Ef.* of 31 May 1909; Colombe, p. 25; Süngü, in *Tanzimat*, p. 777 n.1; Kuntay, *Namık Kemal*, i. 289–90. Among those concerned with the distribution of the letter in Istanbul, Kuntay mentions two Europeans—the French lithographer J. Kayol (*sic*), a convert settled in Turkey, and the Hungarian bookseller Daniel Silâki (*sic*), a political refugee.

When Âli Paşa's orders became known, Prince Mustafa Fazıl, a man of considerable wealth, invited the leaders of the 'Young Turks' to Paris, and in the middle of May they left Istanbul on a French steamer. Ali Suavi, escaping from his Anatolian exile, joined them in Paris, and then went on to London, where on 31 August 1867 he published the newspaper *Muhbir*. Ali Suavi, however, soon fell foul of his colleagues. A man of strong religious convictions and a pilgrim to Mecca, he is described by a modern Turkish writer as a liberal theologian, by another, perhaps more accurately, as a turbanned revolutionary. Namık Kemal and Ziya were also sincere and devoted Muslims, but they were not prepared to support him in his insistence on a religious reform as the starting-point of a revived Islamic state and law, nor in his attacks on the Christians. Ali Suavi's ambition and obstinacy soon led to a break, and in 1868 the Young Ottomans produced their own paper, the first issue of which appeared on 29 June. Its name was *Hürriyet* (freedom).[54] From the first Namık Kemal and Ziya Paşa were closely associated with this journal, and seem to have been responsible for editorial policy. The first issue contained two leading articles, probably both by Kemal, which laid down the two main points in the Young Ottoman programme. One of them, entitled 'Love of One's Country is Part of the Faith',[55] speaks of patriotism, and puts forward the idea of an Ottoman patriotism similar to that of the European countries. The other, headed, 'And Consult with Them in the Matter',[56] uses this Koranic quotation as a peg on which to hang a plea for consultative and representative government. These two themes were developed in most of the subsequent issues of the journal, and are linked with more detailed and specific criticisms of the domestic, foreign, and especially the financial policies of Âli Paşa.

Meanwhile, Ali Suavi's *Muhbir* had closed down in London, and Ali Suavi himself moved to Paris, where he began to publish a new journal called *Ulum* (Science). The breach between him and the Young Ottomans grew wider, and when they returned to Turkey after the death of Âli Paşa, he, with perhaps a more accurate assessment of conditions in Turkey, elected to stay in

---

[54] The front page of the first issue is reproduced in Gerçek, *Türk Gazet.* On Kemal's stay in London see Kuntay, i. 533 ff.

[55] 'Ḥubb al-Waṭan min al-Īmān', an Arabic dictum attributed to the Prophet.

[56] See above, p. 141.

France. He continued to publish in Paris and then, during the Franco-Prussian War, in Lyons. It was at this period that he began to express, for the first time, the idea of a *Turkish* as distinct from an Islamic or Ottoman loyalty. His publication, which reached Turkey through various channels, aroused some interest. Speaking of the *Muhbir*, the official historiographer Lûtfi says:

> The said journal, appearing every week in London, was in numerous ways, sometimes through the letters of merchants, sometimes by unknown means, distributed in many copies, so that few were unacquainted with its purport. The ultimate purpose of this was to deride the principles of the state, to enumerate and elaborate the errors of the ministers, and perhaps to frighten the minds of Europe. So great was the demand for it among the people that copies were heard to have been sold for up to one pound.[57]

Ali Suavi did not return from exile with the rest of the Young Ottomans after the amnesty of 1871; he did, however, return to Istanbul in time to perish in a dramatic but ineffective intervention in the events of 1876.

Another seceder of some interest was Mehmed Bey (1843–74).[58] Unlike Ali Suavi, he was not a man of the people, but a member of the palace and governing circle to which most of the Young Ottomans belonged. His father was a Minister of Posts, his father-in-law the former Grand Vezir Mustafa Naili Paşa, and his uncle the notorious Mahmud Nedim Paşa, several times Grand Vezir under Sultan Abdülaziz. Mehmed Bey had been one of the founder members of the original secret committee in Istanbul, and, according to some, its moving spirit. More radical than the Young Ottomans, he parted from them and published a paper called *Ittihad* (Union) in Turkish, Greek, Arabic, and Armenian. Then, moving to Geneva, he joined with Hüseyin Vasfi Paşa in publishing a journal called *Inkılâb* (Revolution). A new and portentous word had entered the Turkish political vocabulary. Mehmed Bey is said to have had some connexion with the Carbonari, and contributed to French radical newspapers. In the Franco-Prussian War he fought as a volunteer with the French army, returning to Turkey shortly before his death in 1874.

[57] Quoted in Kaplan, p. 65.

[58] On Mehmed Bey see Kuntay, *Namık Kemal*, i. 414 ff.; Şeref, *Tar. Mus.*, pp. 173 ff.; Kaplan, p. 67.

Not a great deal is known of the European connexions of the Young Ottomans. Their headquarters were the Paris residence of Prince Mustafa Fazıl, who put them in touch with French political circles and more especially with French Foreign Office officials. According to the historian Abdurrahman Şeref, one of those whom they met in Paris was Léon Cahun, whose ideas on Turkish nationality and history, expressed in his book *Introduction à l'histoire de l'Asie* (1896), were later to have so great an effect on Turkish political thought.[59]

In June 1867 Sultan Abdülaziz went on a state visit to France. Prince Mustafa Fazıl, who still cherished the hope of achieving high office in Istanbul, seized this opportunity of restoring himself in the Sultan's good graces. When the Sultan landed at Toulon, the liberal prince was there to greet him and 'at the moment of the august arrival of the august and imperial person, to pay homage as a faithful slave'.[60] He was now able to ingratiate himself with the Sultan, and accompanied him to Paris, London, Vienna, and Budapest. From there he returned to Paris on 10 August, by permission of the Sultan, to settle his affairs before following him to Istanbul.

These 'affairs' included the Young Ottomans. When the Sultan reached Paris, the Young Ottomans, as a result of pressure from the Ottoman Embassy, were asked to leave, and went to Britain —Reşad, Nuri, and Mehmed to Jersey, Ziya, Namık Kemal, Ali Suavi, and Agah, to London. The prince now made financial arrangements for the Young Ottomans, assigning them living allowances and also funds to cover their publications. He then left for Istanbul to become a minister.

The defection and departure of their princely patron threw the Young Ottomans into disarray. In protest against what they regarded as a betrayal, Ali Suavi and Mehmed Bey refused to accept the allowances assigned to them by the prince. The others accepted his money, and, though Ziya Paşa later included some unkind remarks about him in his satirical *Zafername*, they seem to have regarded his appointment as a success for their cause rather than as a betrayal of it. Deprived, however, of his guiding and authoritative hand, they began to break up as a group, and gave way to the internal squabbles that are so often the fate of *émigré* politics. Towards the end of 1870 Namık Kemal, through intermediaries, managed to make his peace with the Grand Vezir Âli Paşa, and returned to Istanbul.

In February 1871 Âli Paşa died, and the Young Ottomans, who had always tended to take a naïvely personal view of the causes they were defending and opposing, prepared to return home. The arch-enemy, the ruthless autocrat, was at last out of the way, and now all would be well.

Namık Kemal, after spending a few months in Vienna, had already arrived in Istanbul on 25 November 1870. The rest, encouraged by the death of Âli Paşa, followed in the course of 1871 and 1872. Only Mehmed and Suavi remained abroad, the former fighting for France, the latter still mistrustful of the régime that followed the death of Âli Paşa.

Events proved him wholly right. Âli Paşa may have been authoritarian; he may have despised such new-fangled notions as constitutional government and freedom of the press. He was however, an able and honest ruler, and a sincere partisan of reform, which he did something to advance. None of these things can be said of his immediate successors, under whose fumbling rule the Empire slid into a downward slope of bankruptcy, rebellion, repression, war, and defeat. More and more the Sultan, headstrong and wilful, became the effective ruler of the Empire; the Grand Vezir, Mahmud Nedim Paşa, did little but pander to his costly and destructive whims.

Immediately after his return to Turkey Namık Kemal resumed his journalistic activities, and in June 1872 took over the newspaper *Ibret*. By this time there was quite a number of Turkish newspapers and magazines in Istanbul, but Kemal's articles and essays in the *Ibret* gave it an importance unequalled in the annals of the Turkish press.[61] His editorship, however, lasted less than a year, for in April 1873 a new crisis resulted in a second exile, this time to Cyprus. The crisis was touched off by the performance, at the Gedik Paşa theatre, of Kemal's play *Vatan yahut Silistre* (Fatherland or Silistria). The first original Turkish play, Şinasi's *Marriage of a Poet*, had been a brief comedy of manners, commenting on the status of women and the practice of marriage among the Turks—and published in a magazine. The second dealt in a

---

[61] A selection of his editorials will be found in Özön, *Namık Kemal*.

more violent manner with a more explosive subject—and was performed before an enthusiastic audience. Its theme was patriotism, the doctrine, new to a Muslim people, of the love and loyalty men owe to their country. The four acts of the drama deal with an episode in the defence of the Turkish fortress of Silistria against the Russians in 1854. The play burns with fervent patriotic sentiment, and is full of rousing appeals to the Ottomans—not the Turks—to love their country and defend it against its enemies. In it the ideas formulated in Kemal's leading articles in *Hürriyet* and *Ibret* find dramatic and poetic expression.

The play was first performed on 1 April 1873, amid scenes of wild enthusiasm; the next and following days letters of rapturous praise and support were published in the *Ibret*.

All this was not viewed with favour by authority. Namık Kemal, recently permitted to return from exile in Europe, was still under a cloud. Any manifestation of popular enthusiasm was suspect, all the more so when it was associated with the alien and subversive idea that the people owed loyalty not to the Sultan and his ministers, not to the Islamic community and its authorized exponents, but to an abstract and unfamiliar entity called the Fatherland. A lively and pointed report in the *Ibret* on the scenes at the performance of the play provided the occasion for government action. On 5 April an order was published closing the newspaper, on the grounds of irresponsibility, sedition, and impudence. A defiant farewell editorial was promptly followed by the arrest and deportation of Kemal and several of his associates. No doubt his other activities and associations had helped to bring this about.[62] When Ziya and Kemal had fled to Europe in 1867, they had been threatened with nothing worse than provincial governorships, in such remote places as Cyprus and Erzurum. But by 1873 conditions had become harder. Ziya, it is true, having no further grievance after the death of Âli Paşa, had provisionally made peace with authority, and held various government offices. Kemal, however, continued to think, write, and agitate. These activities, coupled with his probable contacts with the heir-apparent Prince Murad, made him too dangerous to leave at large.

---

[62] Accounts of these events will be found in the biographies of Namık Kemal, notably in Kuntay, ii/1, chs. 1–16. A lucid summary, with quotations from the contemporary sources, will be found in the appendix to Özön's edition of the play *Vatan yahut Silistre* (1943).

This time, therefore, he was deported under close arrest, and kept in Famagusta, in Cyprus, for thirty-eight months, during the first part of which he was in solitary confinement. This imprisonment ended only with the deposition of Sultan Abdülaziz in 1876.

After the death of Âli Paşa in 1871 the condition of the Empire deteriorated rapidly. The mad extravagance of the Sultan, the reckless borrowing of his ministers, combined to bring the finances of the state into complete chaos. In October 1875 the Grand Vezir Mahmud Nedim Paşa announced the suspension of interest payments on the Ottoman Debt—in effect a declaration of bankruptcy, with catastrophic effects on the standing and credit of the Ottoman government in Europe. Nor was the situation in the provinces such as to give hope of improvement. In July 1875 an insurrection had broken out in Bosnia and Herzegovina. This had spread to Bulgaria, where its bloody repression by Ottoman irregular forces led to a cry of outrage all over Europe. The murder, on 6 May 1876, of the French and German consuls at Salonika by a mob further embroiled the Porte with the European powers, leaving it bankrupt, discredited, and alone to face the war that was looming on the northern horizon.

Midhat Paşa and the Constitution [63]

On 10 May 1876 the Softas, or theological students, of the Fatih, Bayezid, and Süleymaniye *medreses* rioted outside the

---

[63] The dramatic events of 1876–8 have formed the subject of an extensive literature, of which only a few items can be mentioned here. Turkish memoirists of the period include Ismail Kemal (*The Memoirs of Ismail Kemal Bey*, ed. by Sommerville Story, 1920), Ali Haydar Midhat (*The Life of Midhat Pasha*, 1903, and, in Turkish, *Hatıralarım 1872–1946*, 1946), and even the Sultan Abdülhamid, some of whose dictated notes were edited, after the Revolution, in the journal of the Turkish Historical Society (*TTEM*, nos. 90–92, 1926). Among contemporary Western observers, some are of special interest; A. D. Mordtmann, whose *Stambul* was published anonymously; Sir Henry Elliot, *Some Revolutions and other Diplomatic Experiences* (1922); and Sir Edwin Pears, *Forty Years in Constantinople* (1916) and *Life of Abdul Hamid* (1917); G. Washburn, *Fifty Years in Constantinople* (1909); Paul Fesch, *Constantinople aux derniers jours d'Abdul-Hamid*. Among earlier Turkish historians, mention may be made of Ahmed Midhat, whose *Üss-i Inkılâb* (1294/1877) presents the official justification of Abdülhamid's accession; Osman Nuri, *Abdülhamid-i Sani ve Devr-i Saltanatı* (1327/1909, published after his deposition); Rasim, *Istibdaddan Hakimiyet-i Milliyeye*; Şeref, *Tar. Mus.*, pp. 187 ff. Among modern Turkish writers, the following deal with various aspects of the period: Kuran, pp. 82 ff.; Kuntay, *Namık Kemal*, ii. pts. 1 and 2; Kaplan, pp. 96 ff.; Karal, *Tarih*, vii. 352 ff.; Haluk Y. Şehsuvaroğlu, *Sultan Aziz; Hayatı Hal'ı Ölümü* (1949); for monographic treatments of the first constitutional period see Bekir Sitki Baykal, '93 Meşrutiyeti', *Bell.* nos. 21–22 (1942), 45–83; Petrosian, *Novye Osmani*, pp. 71 ff.; Temperley, in *Camb. Hist. J.*, pp. 169 ff.

Sublime Porte, demanding the dismissal of the Grand Vezir Mahmud Nedim Paşa and the Chief Mufti Hasan Fehmi Efendi. Some of them, it is said, measured the railings outside the Porte, to see if they were high enough to hang the Grand Vezir on them.[64] The evidence indicates that these riots were not wholly spontaneous. Sultan Abdülhamid—admittedly not an impartial witness—says that the riots were arranged and paid for by Midhat, whose fellow plotters behind the scenes included Rüşdi Paşa, Damad Mahmud, Halim Paşa, Hayrullah Efendi, and Murad.[65] There is also other evidence that the riots were organized, if not by Midhat Paşa and Prince Murad, then at least by others favourable to their interests. Riots by theological students were nothing new in Turkey; since the sixteenth century at least they had played an important and sometimes dangerous role in Ottoman affairs, and are a phenomenon of some significance in the social history of the country.[66] The prearranged and prepaid student demonstration for the purpose of procuring a change of ministry was, however, something new. It introduced into Turkey a tradition well established in parts of Europe, and set a precedent that was followed many times, especially in the successor states.

The Sultan gave way to their pressure, and two days later dismissed both Mahmud Nedim Paşa and Hasan Fehmi Efendi. Mütercim (Translator) Rüşdi Paşa now became Grand Vezir, with Hüseyin Avni Paşa as War Minister, Hasan Hayrullah Efendi as Chief Mufti, and Midhat Paşa as a kind of minister without portfolio. Between the Sultan and his new ministers, however, there was a complete lack of confidence, and a show-down could not long be delayed. On 25 May the British ambassador, Sir Henry Elliot, reported in a dispatch that

the word 'Constitution' was in every mouth; that the Softas, representing the intelligent public opinion of the capital, knowing themselves to be supported by the nation—Christian as well as Mahometan—would not, I believed, relax their efforts till they obtained it, and that,

---

[64] Şeref, *Tar. Mus.*, pp. 192 ff.; Kuran, pp. 82 ff.; Ismail Kemal, p. 108; Midhat, *Life*, p. 81; Şehsuvaroğlu, 60 ff. pp.; 'Abdülhamid-i Sani'nin Notları', *TTEM*, pp. 92 ff.; Tunaya, *Partiler*, pp. 96–97; Ismail Hami Danişmend, *Izahlı Osmanlı Tarihi Kronolojisi*, iv (1955), 253–4.

[65] *Notlar, passim*, espec. pp. 93–94.

[66] See for example Mustafa Akdağ, 'Türkiye Tarihinde . . . Medreseli Isyanları', *Ist. Üniv. Iktisat Fak. Mec.*, xi (1949–50), 361–87.

should the Sultan refuse to grant it, an attempt to depose him appeared almost inevitable; that texts from the Koran were circulated proving to the faithful that the form of government sanctioned by it was properly democratic, and that the absolute authority now wielded by the Sultan was an usurpation of the rights of the people and not sanctioned by the Holy Law; and both texts and precedents were appealed to, to show that obedience was not due to a Sovereign who neglected the interests of the State. . . .[67]

Sir Henry was perhaps a trifle naïve with his talk of 'public opinion', 'the bulk of the Nation', and the like, but he was accurate enough in his assessment of the trend of events. The arguments he cites, and the purpose for which they were adduced, were the logical culmination of the teachings of the Young Ottomans, the influence of whose ideas will readily be recognized.

On 30 May 1876, armed with a ruling from the Chief Mufti authorizing the deposition of the Sultan, and fortified with suitable military preparations, the ministers formally declared that Abdülaziz had ceased to reign, and installed Murad as Sultan in his place. The old Sultan went quietly, writing a letter of abdication in favour of his successor; the new one at once issued a decree confirming all the ministers in their posts.

The accession of Murad V seemed like a victory for the liberals. He had for some years been both in contact and in sympathy with the Young Ottomans, several of whom now received palace appointments. Namık Kemal, recalled from Cyprus, and Ziya became his private secretaries; Sadullah was given the key position of chief of the palace secretariat.

The satisfaction of the liberals with their new sovereign was, however, of short duration. Murad had been a prince of high intelligence, widely read in both Western and Turkish writings, with a keen and informed interest in European literature, science, and affairs. In 1867 he had accompanied Abdülaziz on his European tour, and had made an excellent impression. This, and the knowledge of his secret contacts with the exiled liberals, had led the Sultan to treat him with increasing suspicion, and to force upon him a life of virtual seclusion under surveillance. The strains of this life, and the solace of alcohol, were too much for a nature already subject to nervous disorder, and by the time of his

[67] Elliot, pp. 231–2; also cited, with slight variations, by Midhat, *Life*, p. 81; cf. Temperley, in *Camb. Hist. J.*, p. 172.

accession Murad was already well on the way to mental derangement.

Two unfortunate shocks, following immediately on that of accession to the throne, completed his mental collapse. The first was the violent death of Abdülaziz, who was found in the Çırağan palace with his wrists slashed a day or two after his deposition. The second was the murder of Hüseyin Avni Paşa and several other ministers by Çerkes Hasan, a Circassian infantry captain who had been *aide-de-camp* to Prince Izzeddin, the son of Abdülaziz, and who ran amok at a cabinet meeting. Shocked out of his wits by these events, the new Sultan became incapable of making any public appearance or attending to any public business. A Dr. Leidesdorff of Vienna, who had previously examined the Sultan, was called in again, and pronounced his condition incurable.[68]

In the midst of foreign war and domestic crisis such a situation soon became intolerable, and the ministers, however reluctantly, began to consider the possibility of a second deposition. The next heir was Murad's younger brother Abdülhamid. On 27 August 1876 Midhat went to see him at his mother's palace at Nişantaş, to obtain his prior promise of sympathy for the liberal cause. The prince was shown a draft of the constitution which the ministers proposed to introduce; he gave it his approval and the pledge of his support. This preliminary having been completed, the Grand Vezir obtained from the Chief Mufti a ruling authorizing the deposition of the Sultan on grounds of mental incapacity, and on 31 August the unhappy Murad was deposed and Abdülhamid proclaimed Sultan in his place. Namık Kemal is said to have begged Midhat, with tears in his eyes, to postpone the deposition of Murad, but without avail.[69] The deposed Sultan was taken to the Çırağan palace, where he died in 1904 after twenty-eight years of captivity.

Twice within four months the Sultan had been deposed and replaced by the decision of his ministers. These events were not without precedent in the annals of the house of Osman, and many of the ministers, as well as the public, would no doubt have been content with a simple exercise of armed force, initiated by the

[68] On the Çerkes Hasan incident, see Uzunçarşılı, 'Çerkes Hasan Vakası', *Bell.* no. 33 (1945); on Murad's medical condition, idem, 'Beşinci Sultan Murad . . .' ibid. no. 38 (1946).

[69] Ismail Kemal, p. 118. On Murad V see *IA* and *EI¹*, *s.v.*, where further references are given.

political and ratified by the religious authority, along traditional lines. Midhat, however, had other ideas.

Midhat Paşa was born in Istanbul in 1822, the son of a Kadi from Ruschuk.[70] While still in his teens he obtained a post in the office of the Grand Vezir, and thereafter rose rapidly in the service of the Porte. In 1858 he spent six months' study leave in Europe, visiting London, Paris, Vienna, and Brussels. After his return he held various governorships and won a reputation as an able and conscientious administrator. In 1864 he was summoned to the capital to advise on the new law of provincial administration of that year, and in 1865 he was made governor of the newly constituted vilayet of the Danube, formed by combining the former vilayets of Silistria, Vidin, and Nish. In this office, and in the governorship of Baghdad to which he was transferred in 1869, Midhat showed outstanding ability, giving the provinces security and prosperity such as they had long not known. In August 1872, after the fall of Mahmud Nedim Paşa, he was appointed Grand Vezir by Sultan Abdülaziz. He was not, however, the man to serve as the instrument of Abdülaziz's capricious absolutism, and was dismissed after a tenure of only two and a half months. During the next few years the manœuvres of rival cliques at the Sublime Porte brought him in and out of various ministerial offices, none of which he held for very long and in none of which he made any great impression.

As early as the winter of 1875, Midhat Paşa explained to the British ambassador Sir Henry Elliot that the object of his group was to obtain a constitution:

The Empire [he said] was being rapidly brought to destruction. . . . The only remedy that he could perceive, lay, first, in securing a control over the Sovereign by making the Ministers, and especially as regarded the finances, responsible to a national popular Assembly; secondly in making this Assembly truly national by doing away with all distinctions of classes and religions . . . thirdly, by decentralisation and by the establishment of provincial control over the governors. . . .[71]

Plans for the new constitution seem to have been set on foot immediately after Midhat joined the government in May 1876.

[70] There are biographies of Midhat Paşa by his son Ali Haydar (see above, p. 156 n. 63) and by Inal, in his *Sadrıazamlar*, pp. 315–414. See further *EI*[1] and *IA s.v.*

[71] Elliot, p. 228.

A committee of statesmen and ulema, presided over by Server Paşa, was given the task of drafting the text, which was completed towards the end of the year. Like so many other constitutions of the nineteenth and early twentieth centuries, it was largely based on the Belgian constitution of 1831. Unlike the Belgian constitution, however, it was not passed by a constituent assembly, but promulgated by the sovereign power. This happened on 23 December 1876, a few days after Midhat had been reappointed to the Grand Vezirate by Sultan Abdülhamid.[72]

The promulgation of the Ottoman constitution in 1876 has been the subject of much debate in Europe between Turcophiles and Turcophobes, whose arguments and judgements in Turkish matters are often determined by considerations quite independent of the merits or shortcomings of the Turks. The criticism has often been made that the constitution of 1876 did not represent any real desire to reform or change the government of the Empire, but was simply a piece of window-dressing, a manœuvre intended to throw dust in the eyes of the Western powers and to circumvent their plans of intervention in the interest of the subject peoples.

The circumstances in which the constitution was promulgated and the manner in which it was applied would seem, at first sight, to confirm the validity of this criticism. The ruthless suppression of the rebellions in the Balkan provinces, followed by the defeat of the Serbs in the war they had begun against the Empire in June, had precipitated an international crisis. By November Russia was already preparing for war, and Disraeli had made it clear that the British government would not acquiesce in a partition of the Ottoman Empire. In December, as a last attempt to avert war, a conference of the powers was convened in Istanbul, to discuss peace terms between Turkey and Serbia, and the reorganization of the Balkan provinces with reforms under the supervision and guarantee of the powers. The day before the conference was due to open, Midhat became Grand Vezir;

---

[72] On the constitution see Baykal; G. Jäschke, 'Die Entwicklung des osmanischen Verfassungsstaates', *WI*, v (1918), 5 ff.; *IA* ('Kanun-i Esasi' by Hüseyin Nail Kubali); *EI*² ('Dustūr' by B. Lewis). The Turkish text will be found in the various editions of the *Düstur* and is reprinted, in the new Turkish script, in A. S. Gözübüyük and S. Kili, *Türk Anayasa Metinleri* (1957), pp. 25 ff.; among the numerous translations the most useful is the scholarly German version of F. von Kraelitz-Greifenhorst, *Die Verfassungsgesetze des osmanischen Reiches* (1919).

M

while the plenipotentiaries were engaged upon the initial formalities, the thunder of cannon announced to the capital the proclamation of a new Turkish constitution of the most elaborate kind, so framed as to provide an excuse for the argument that the Porte was now actively embarking upon far-reaching reforms and could dispense with the proffered assistance of the Powers.[73]

The inference is perhaps excusable. This was not the first time that a major reform had come at a moment when the goodwill of the Western powers was needed. The Noble Rescript of the Rose Chamber, of 1839, came soon after the disastrous defeat of the Ottoman army at Nezib, when European support was needed against the victorious Muhammad Ali of Egypt; the Imperial Rescript of 1856 had followed immediately on the Crimean War, when Western goodwill was required in securing a peace treaty favourable to Turkey; and now the appointment of a reformer as Grand Vezir and the proclamation of a liberal constitution were perfectly timed to circumvent plans for intervention and protection, and to rally Western support in the war with Russia that was looming ahead.

These considerations were no doubt well to the fore in Midhat's mind in 1876, as in the minds of the earlier reformers in 1839 and 1856. The timing of the reforms, and the dramatic manner of their presentation, were no doubt influenced by the desire to secure political advantage from them. But it would be a grave error to conclude from this that the constitution and the earlier reforms were nothing but diplomatic subterfuges, intended to deceive foreigners but to change nothing at home. Certainly both the reformers and the liberals, no less than their conservative opponents, were loyal Muslims and Osmanlis, concerned to defend the integrity and sovereignty of the Empire from whatever threat. But the best of them were hardly less serious in their devotion to reform and to liberalism, which they believed to be in the best interests of the Empire. By 1876 the cause of reform was a century old in Turkey, and already had a tradition, an impetus, and indeed an achievement of its own. The liberal cause was much younger, but already it had produced a not inconsiderable ideological literature, and had won firm and ramified support within the Ottoman governing *élite*. When Midhat spoke to Elliot in 1875 of the need in Turkey for responsible

[73] R. W. Seton-Watson, *Disraeli, Gladstone, and the Eastern Question* (1935), p. 122.

and popular government, he no doubt hoped to please the ambassador and incline his government in Turkey's favour; but he was also quoting arguments and ideas that had become commonplace in the publications of the Young Ottomans during the preceding decade, and were accepted by many hopeful young men in the service of the Sublime Porte. In the same way when he asserted, in an article in the *Nineteenth Century*, that 'in Islam the principle of government rests upon bases essentially democratic, inasmuch as the sovereignty of the people is therein recognized' he was not, as one historian has suggested, trying to pull the wool over the eyes of the gullible English reader,[74] but was reproducing an argument which was familiar from the writings of Namık Kemal and Ziya, and which has since become an article of faith with Muslim liberals, reformists, and romantics.

There was one, however, among the prime movers in 1876 who had no sympathy whatever for liberalism or democracy, and whose use of the constitution and the constitutionalists was purely cynical and opportunistic. That one was the Sultan, Abdülhamid II.

It was not long before the new Sultan began to show his hand. Midhat's appointment as Grand Vezir had been timed to coincide with the meeting of the ambassadors' conference in Istanbul. On 20 January 1877 the conference ended—and on 5 February Midhat was ignominiously dismissed and ordered to leave the country. In a statement to the powers, the Sultan justified this action by reference to article 113 of the new constitution, which authorized the Sultan 'to expel from the territory of the Empire those who, as a result of trustworthy information gathered by the police administration, are recognized as dangerous to the security of the state'.

The moment, as usual, was well chosen. At home, Midhat was being attacked on two sides, by the conservatives, who disliked the whole programme of reform, and by the liberals, led by Namık Kemal and Ziya, who found his measures entirely inadequate. During the ambassadors' conference the Sultan had already been at work undermining Midhat's position; when the conference ended there was no further obstacle to his dismissal.[75]

[74] Seton-Watson, p. 123, citing the *Nineteenth Century* of June 1878.

[75] On the dismissal and banishment of Midhat see, *inter alia*, Seton-Watson, pp. 146–7; Ismail Kemal, pp. 136 and 149; Haydar, *Life*, p. 145; Inal, *Sadrıazamlar*, pp. 350 ff.; Baykal, pp. 67 ff.

The constitution itself lasted a little longer. It had already been publicly proclaimed, with much pomp and circumstance. As well as diverting the European powers, the promises it contained had aroused such a response among sections of the population of Istanbul that it would have been inexpedient and perhaps dangerous to abrogate it at once. The Sultan therefore proceeded with arrangements for a general election—the first in Ottoman and indeed in Islamic history.[76]

The first Ottoman parliament met on 19 March 1877. It was not an impressive spectacle. A Senate of twenty-five nominated officials; a chamber of 120 deputies elected under official pressure and amid general indifference with a franchise and by a procedure that were already in conflict with the new constitution—these seemed to meet the Sultan's need for a puppet assembly which would give his régime a façade of liberal and democratic government, and provide a semblance of popular support and legal validity for whatever he found it expedient to do.

But even this assemblage of tame and inexperienced deputies began to develop a life of its own. It has been well described by Sir Edwin Pears, who was at that time correspondent in Istanbul of the *Daily News*:

It was the first time that representatives from such distant places as Baghdad, Albania, Armenia and Syria met together. Their discussions were singularly full of interest and even surprises. Though most of the members spoke of serious grievances which required redress in their own district, they were surprised to learn that their own constituencies were not alone as spheres of misgovernment. When the members for Jerusalem, Baghdad, Erzerum and Salonika met together, they found that the administration throughout all the country was corrupt, and they set themselves honestly to discuss their grievances and the changes in the system which were necessary to secure a remedy. Amongst the deputies were several able and thoughtful men. They had no traditions of parliamentary government, and some of the speeches were banal, speeches which would have been brought to an end by the Speaker had they been delivered in the Legislative Chamber either of England, America, or a British colony. They often had a tendency to personalities unconnected with public affairs, but more usually they attacked this pasha or that for abuses, for receiving bribes and refusing to do what

---

[76] For a record of the proceedings of the Ottoman parliament see Hakkı Tarık Us, *Meclis-i Meb'usân, 1293-1877* (1940). Western impressions of the Ottoman chamber will be found in the works, already cited, of Mordtmann, Pears, Fesch, &c.

was right unless he was paid for it. Had the Sultan been as wise as his sycophants represented him to be, he would have seen the value of such statements and would have allowed the deliberations of the Chamber to continue. There were at first absolutely no attacks whatever upon him, though many of his Ministers were personally charged with specific irregularities and misconduct. The discussions were a revelation to Turkish subjects. They showed that the government from one end of the country to the other required radical reform. The Chamber had at its head a President, Ahmed Vefyk, who had been Ambassador of Turkey at the Court of Napoleon III, was an excellent French scholar, and in education was no doubt the superior of nearly all the deputies. But in public and private life he had become despotic, and his superior, school-masterly manner as Chairman of the House was arrogant and sometimes amusing. He frequently stopped deputies in the midst of speeches, telling them that they knew nothing about the subject and were talking nonsense. Dr. Washburn, the President of Robert College, was present when a white-turbanned deputy, who was making a long and prosy statement, was suddenly pulled up by a stentorian shout from the President of 'Shut up, you donkey!' (*Sus eshek*).[77] The orator sat down as if he were shot.

Meantime the accusations brought by members against the corruption of individual Ministers became more serious and definite in form. The claim that certain of the Ministers should be brought before the Chamber in order to answer charges against them was naturally opposed by the accused Ministers and was distasteful to Abdul Hamid. The hostility between the Chamber and the pashas became serious, and various correspondents predicted that within a short time the Chamber would upset the rule of the pashas, or the pashas would get rid of the Chamber.[78]

In the event it was the Sultan who got rid of the chamber. On 13 February 1878 the deputies went so far as to demand that three ministers, against whom specific charges had been brought, should appear in the chamber to defend themselves. The next day the Sultan dissolved the chamber, and ordered the deputies to return to their constituencies. The chamber had sat for ten months and twenty-five days. It did not meet again for thirty years.

---

[77] cf. Washburn, p. 119, for a slightly different version, in which Vefik Paşa deals in this way not with a white-turbanned speaker but with a green-turbanned interruptor.

[78] Pears, *Abdul Hamid*, pp. 49–51.

The End of the Young Ottomans

For the Young Ottomans, this was the end. They had been sharply critical of Midhat, suspecting him, not without some justification, of being another authoritarian reformer in the tradition of Mustafa Reşid, Fuad and Âli Paşas, willing to modernize and Westernize the administrative structure of the Empire, but without sympathy for their liberal and patriotic aspirations. Now, in the personal autocracy of the Sultan, the causes both of reform and of liberty seemed to be lost. The great age of the *Tanzimat* had come to an end—and the liberals, who had been its keenest critics, were silenced.

At this point it may be opportune to review briefly the chief arguments used by the liberals against the Sultans, statesmen, and edicts of the *Tanzimat*. Their criticisms are far removed from those of the simple reactionaries, and, though they probably expressed the outlook of a far smaller body of opinion in Turkey, were far more significant for the understanding of what followed. These opinions are first adumbrated in the Istanbul press of the early 1860's, clearly and vigorously expressed in the newspapers published in exile, and developed, with greater circumspection, in those published after their return to Turkey.[79]

Some two years after his return to Istanbul from exile, Namık Kemal published an article in the *Ibret* under the heading 'Tanzimat'. In it he speaks eloquently of the high hopes that had been raised by the Rescript of the Rose Chamber, and of the belief that at last the age of bloody and arbitrary rule was coming to an end.

Indeed [he says if] one looks at its external aspect, one would think it to have been made as a surety for the life, property, and honour of every individual. But the truth of the matter is that it was proclaimed for the purpose of securing the life of the state.[80]

[79] The best sources of information of the ideas of the Young Ottomans are the articles published by them in Turkey and especially abroad. Some of these articles were later reprinted in various collections and anthologies. A useful survey of their ideas, with lengthy quotations, will be found in Süngü's article in *Tanzimat*, already cited. There are also excellent surveys of their political and social ideas in Tanpınar, pp. 189 ff.; Kaplan, pp. 105 ff. For an examination of the influence of the political philosophy of Montesquieu, Rousseau, and Voltaire, see Kâmiran Birand, *Aydınlanma Devri Devlet Felsefesinin Tanzimatta Tesirleri* (1955).

[80] *Ibret*, no. 46 of 1872, cited by Süngü, p. 778.

The *Tanzimat*, in other words, was less a reform than a manœuvre, intended to accomplish a political, rather than a legal or
social purpose. Thus far, the Young Ottomans seem to be in
agreement with those European critics who saw in the *Tanzimat*
no more than a piece of window-dressing designed to deceive the
West—a paper reform which 'never passed the threshold of the
Sublime Porte'. But the Young Ottomans saw farther than that.
They knew that the successive reforms had indeed made many
real changes in Turkey—and despite their own devotion to
progress and reform, there was much in these changes that they
disliked.

The fundamental charge which they brought against the
statesmen of the *Tanzimat* was that of arbitrary and absolutist
government. The old safeguards, the old balances provided by
law, custom, and established interests had been abrogated or
eliminated. The limiting power of the Janissaries, in which
Namık Kemal affected to see a kind of armed popular assembly,
had been destroyed; the Holy Law itself had been disregarded or
violated, and replaced by a caricature of Western laws which
was in fact neither Western nor Islamic, and which, being unreal
and ineffectual, left the sovereign power free from any check at all.
The reforming edicts had brought some changes in administrative
procedures, but had done nothing to protect the subject against
arbitrary rule. The point is well made by Namık Kemal in an
article in *Ibret*.

The Rescript of the Rose Chamber is not, as some have supposed,
a fundamental charter for the Lofty Empire. It consists of a declaration
which, while reiterating some of the principles of the Holy Law which
is our only true Charter, sanctions a number of administrative measures
in the line of European thought.

Had the Rescript not confined the general precepts of law set forth
in its preamble to personal freedom alone, which it interpreted as
security of life, property, and honour, but also proclaimed such other
basic principles as freedom of thought, sovereignty of the people, and
the system of government by consultation, then only could it have
taken the character of a fundamental Charter for the Islamic
Caliphate.[81]

In fact, said the Young Ottomans, they had done none of these
things. They had taken away the rights which the people enjoyed

[81] *Ibret*, no. 46 of 1872, cited by Süngü, pp. 844-5.

under the old, Islamic order, and had given them none of the rights which belonged to the European system of government that they were introducing. By their actions they were discrediting Islamic government in the West, and Western government among Muslims.

In introducing a foreign form of goverment, under foreign pressure or advice, the men of the *Tanzimat* had thrown the country wide open to foreign influence and interference of every kind. Foreigners had been given the right to own land in Turkey, and were acquiring positions of control in every branch of the economic and public life of the Empire. To domestic tyranny, the men of the *Tanzimat* had added foreign exploitation.

A direct result of these policies was the economic ruination of the Empire. In an article published in *Hürriyet* in 1868, Namık Kemal reviews the economic situation. 'In this world wealth is obtained from three sources, agriculture, industry, and trade.' Ottoman agriculture was potentially one of the richest in the world, but was being crushed by reckless conscription and taxation. 'The second is industry. Industry is a product of intelligence. This being so, is it not a pity that a nation endowed, like the Ottomans, with extraordinary quickness of mind should be obliged to import from abroad even the clothes that it wears? . . .' The reason was a suicidal fiscal policy which, under the specious name of free trade, had stifled Ottoman industry and thrown the country into the hands of European exporters. The same causes, aggravated by the lack of roads and of educational facilities, had led to the backwardness and poverty of Ottoman trade.[82]

A subject of frequent and violent attack by the Young Ottomans was the government policy of borrowing money from abroad. Until the time of the Crimean War Turkey had incurred no foreign debts. From 1854, however, the Sultan's government began to raise loans in Europe, on terms that were ruinous to the Empire and that led to complete financial collapse.

For these and other reasons, the men of the *Tanzimat*, far from lightening the burdens that weighed on the Empire in the days of its decay, had greatly added to them. In the words of Ziya Paşa, 'if from 1000 to 1255 [1592 to 1839] the Empire had advanced on the road to decline at the pace of a two-horse carriage, from 1255

[82] Cited in Süngü, pp. 825–7.

to 1285 [1839 to 1869] it had rushed with the speed of a railway-train'.[83]

The remedy for all these ills was constitutional and parliamentary government. The Holy Law must be restored, for it alone corresponded both to the traditions and to the needs of a Muslim people. This would not, however, mean a simple rejection of Westernization and a return to the immediately preceding past; what was needed was a return to the true spirit of early Islam, which recognized the sovereignty of the people and the principle of government by consultation. These could best be ensured by a constitutional apparatus of an assembly and a supreme court which, though imitated from European models, would be adapted to the needs of a Muslim people living under the God-given law of Islam.

The ideas of the Young Ottomans are clearly derivative, and it is easy to recognize the sources from which they were drawn. The jurisprudence of Montesquieu, the politics of Rousseau, the economics of Smith and Ricardo provided their theoretical foundations, while many even of their specific criticisms of *Tanzimat* policies are influenced by the comments of European observers. The judgements of Slade, in particular, seem to have had a marked influence on them. Their ideas are often confused and naïve, as for example when they ascribe the economic backwardness of Turkey simply to the incompetence of Turkish ministers and the rapacity of European merchants, or when, on a different level, they discuss the problems of law, power, and democracy.

Nevertheless, despite these gaps and obliquities in their vision, they saw more and further than most other Turks of their time. Their understanding of the problems of change in Ottoman society was deeper than that of the mechanicians of the *Tanzimat* and their ideal, if vague, was not an ignoble one. Many new and significant ideas first found Turkish expression in their writings, and their influence on the thought and action of the generations that followed was very great indeed.

In 1876 their ideal of constitutional liberty under Holy Law seemed about to be realized. A new constitution—the first in Islam—promised all those rights and liberties of which they had learned from their European teachers, and did so in the

[83] *Hürriyet*, no. 36 of 1869; cited in Süngü, p. 816.

name of the Sultan-Caliph, the guardian of the Holy Law.

The collapse of the constitution, and the squalid despotism that followed it, were bitter blows. Some of the Young Ottomans, abandoning their ideals, found employment in the Sultan's service. Others suffered banishment, imprisonment, and death. Namık Kemal, the most brilliant among them, was imprisoned for nearly six months as a common criminal in Istanbul, and then exiled to Chios, where he was detained for two years. Later he was given minor government posts in the Aegean islands, where he spent the rest of his days until his death on 2 December 1888. It occurred the night after he received an Imperial order forbidding him to print or continue the history of the Ottomans on which he was then working.

In a poem written not long before his death, Namık Kemal gives expression to the mood of desperation that held Young Turkey in those days:

> Let us truly renounce all ambition and all desire
> Let us break the cage of flesh, if it trammels our resolve
> As long as every breath of our motherland moans with sorrow,
> 'Come to my help!' she says. See, this is the voice of God.
> Zeal becomes us; mercy is God's,
> The verdict of the future belongs neither to beggar nor Emperor,
> Listen to her anguish that is told in her sigh
> See, what says the breath of our motherland as she moans.
>
> .   .   .   .   .
>
> Our country is no more; yet still it is, while you and I are there,
> In this condition we can have no greater enemy than ourselves.
> We are in the hands of the foe; for the sake of God, O countrymen,
> Enough! Let us indeed renounce every personal wish and desire![84]

[84] 'Murabba'; Akyüz, *Antoloji*, pp. 58–59.

CHAPTER VI

Despotism and Enlightenment

In any scheme of reform, I believe your attention will be far more usefully directed to persons than to paper institutions. Good officers, well selected for a length of time, will create suitable traditions of administration which will gradually harden into institutions, and, made this way, reformed institutions will regenerate a people. But if they are merely written in a pretentious law, they will have no other effect but to disturb the few traditions that are left and to give perpetual subject-matter for diplomatic wrangling.

LORD SALISBURY TO SIR HENRY LAYARD, 25 June 1878.

Since present circumstances are unfavourable to the full discharge of the duties of the general assembly, and since, according to the constitution, the limitation or curtailment of the period of session of the said assembly in accordance with the needs of the time form part of the sacred Imperial prerogatives, therefore, in accordance with the said law, a high Imperial order has been issued . . . that the present sessions of the Senate and Chamber, due to end at the beginning of March . . . be closed as from today . . .

PROCLAMATION OF 14 FEB. 1878.

Government by a chief who is obeyed from custom, and who is himself restrained by custom from mere tyranny, may at certain stages of culture be better than anything else which can be substituted for it. And representation, even when it is possible, is not an unchanging entity, but an expedient capable of an infinite number of variations.

GRAHAM WALLAS, 'Human Nature in Politics', 1929.

THE last of the Young Ottomans to make his peace with the government and return from exile was Ali Suavi, the turbanned revolutionary and man of the people. He was also the first to try and overthrow Abdülhamid.

After the deposition of Abdülaziz, Ali Suavi at last returned to Turkey. By the time he reached Istanbul, Murad had been deposed, and Abdülhamid had taken his place. The Sultan and the revolutionary seem at first to have been on good terms, and Ali Suavi was given the important appointment of director of the Galatasaray school. In December 1876 he and his English wife acted as hosts to H. A. M. Butler-Johnstone, a British member of parliament who was visiting Turkey, probably as a personal emissary of Disraeli.[1] Soon, however, he formed a political committee, the so-called Üsküdar committee, which met in his house.

Relations between Ali Suavi and the new Sultan deteriorated rapidly. On 19 August 1878, when the Russians were almost at the gates of Istanbul, an advertisement appeared in the daily *Basiret*, signed by Ali Suavi, announcing that in the next day's issue he would expound and explain the remedy for the country's difficulties. This seems to have been a prearranged signal, for on the next day, at about 11 in the morning, some 500 men assembled in front of the Çırağan Palace, most of them Muslim refugees from the lost provinces. Led by Ali Suavi, about 100 of them forced their way into the palace, where they tried to release Murad and proclaim him Sultan. A police contingent, summoned by the palace staff, soon arrived, and dealt rapidly with the movement. Hasan Paşa, the police commandant of Beşiktaş, boasted to the end of his days of how he had felled and killed Ali Suavi with a blow of his cudgel. Twenty others were killed, and thirty wounded. A court martial pronounced one sentence of death, later commuted to life imprisonment, and several of deportation. The first rising against Hamidian rule was at an end.[2]

The deposed Sultan was still not without friends, and now sought them in a new direction. When, after the ignominious failure of the Suavi attempt, Murad was confined in the Malta Pavilion in the Yıldız palace grounds, he smuggled a note to one of them, saying: 'If you do not save me from this place, the Malta Pavilion will be my grave.'

The recipient of this dramatic appeal for help was Cleanthe Scalieri, a Greek subject living in Istanbul. His importance lay in his position as master of the Prodos masonic lodge, and the exalted European connexions to which this admitted him. Scalieri at once wrote an open letter to Abdülhamid, and sent it to the English-language newspaper *Eastern Express* with a demand, backed by threats, that it be published. The editor of the paper, Whittaker, referred the letter to the Palace counsellor Said Paşa, 'who shrugged his shoulders and said "publish" '. The publication of the letter provoked the Sultan to immediate reprisals

[1] Seton-Watson, p. 129.

[2] A detailed study of this first rising, based on archive documents, was published by Uzunçarşılı, 'Ali Suâvi ve Çırağan Vak'ası', *Bell.*, no. 29 (1944), 71–118. See further Kuntay, *Ali Suavi*, pp. 160 ff.; Tunaya, *Partiler*, pp. 98–100; Kuran, pp. 119–21; Ismail Kemal, pp. 120–1, 145–6; Pears, *Abdul Hamid*, p. 48.

against the newspaper, its editor and even, it is said, against Said Paşa; but the publicity achieved its effect, and Murad was restored to relative security in the Çirağan palace.[3]

Scalieri and his masonic friends did not leave the matter at that. From a report submitted to Sultan Abdülhamid, it seems that an attempt was made to persuade the German and English lodges, the heads of which were the Emperor Wilhelm and the Prince of Wales, to use their influence and secure the intervention of the German and British ambassadors in Istanbul in favour of Murad.

Nothing came of this suggestion. Scalieri then became associated with a group of Turkish conspirators, led by Nakşibend Kalfa, a palace servant of Murad's mother, Aziz Bey, a high official of the Inspectorate of *Evkâf*, and Ali Şefkati Bey, an official of the Council of State. The aim of this group, like that of Suavi, was to depose Abdülhamid and restore Murad to the throne. Members swore an oath 'to strive to work to the best of my ability for the safety of the nation (*millet*)' and a plan was prepared for a coup d'état.[4]

A traitor denounced them to the Sultan, who ordered police action. The members of the committee were besieged in Aziz Bey's house, where they had their headquarters. Some of them, including Scalieri himself, Nakşibend Kalfa, and Ali Şefkati, managed to escape abroad. The rest were arrested, tried by court martial, and sentenced to varying terms of imprisonment, or confinement to a fortress.[5]

This attempt to restore Murad, like that of Ali Suavi, had little effect, except perhaps to reinforce the autocratic tendencies of the new Sultan. But the Scalieri–Aziz Bey committee, insignificant as it was, revealed several new and interesting features. However incompetently, they did organize a group of conspirators to plan and execute a coup d'état; their purpose was not merely to replace one prince by another, but to depose an autocrat and enthrone in his place one whom they believed to be more liberal and progressive in his views. This belief was based on Murad's past connexion with freemasonry, and it was through masonic channels that the conspirators directed some of their efforts.

[3] Uzunçarşılı, 'V Murad tedâvîsine ve ölümüne dair', *Bell.*, no. 38 (1946), 320 n.6.

[4] Uzuncarsılı, 'V Murad'i tekrar padişah yapmak isteyen K. Skaliyeri-Aziz Bey Komitesi', *Bell.*, no. 30 (1944), 264.

[5] For a monographic study of the Scalieri plot see Uzunçarşılı's article cited in the preceding note. Further, Tunaya, *Partiler*, pp. 100-2; Kuran, pp. 121-4.

Finally—and this is perhaps the most remarkable feature—the conspiracy united a Christian with Muslims in a common cause, the safety of the 'nation', which for some of them at least must have had a secular and no longer a purely religious meaning.

The revolt of the returned exile Ali Suavi and the conspiracy of the Greek freemason Cleanthe Scalieri deepened the suspicion with which the Sultan regarded new and liberal ideas, and made him still less willing in any way to relax or divide his authority. The constitution remained in abeyance, the constitutionalists were either exiled or, if willing, incorporated in the apparatus of despotism. In 1881 Midhat Paşa, who, under British pressure, had been allowed to return to Turkey, was arrested and brought to Istanbul, where he was tried and found guilty of having caused the assassination of Sultan Abdülaziz. Under foreign pressure, the death sentence imposed on this trumped up charge was commuted to life banishment, and in April 1883 he was murdered in his prison in Arabia.[6] The Sultan was again an autocratic ruler, unrestrained by any legal or social checks, unchallenged by any opposition movement—and with his rule vastly reinforced by a new and immensely improved apparatus of repression.

The new Sultan, though bitterly hostile to liberal or constitutional ideas, was by no means entirely opposed to reform and Westernization in which, judiciously selected and applied, he saw the means of reinforcing both the Ottoman Empire and his own position in it. Abdülhamid was far from being the blind, uncompromising, complete reactionary of the historical legend; on the contrary, he was a willing and active modernizer, the true heir of Sultan Abdülaziz and the statesmen of the *Tanzimat*, against whose autocratic reformism the Young Ottomans had levelled the first Turkish liberal critique of despotic government. Politics apart, the first decades of Abdülhamid's reign were as active a period of change and reform as any since the beginning of the century, and saw the accomplishment of much that had been only started or sketched under earlier rulers, more famous for their reforming zeal. It would not be an exaggeration to say that it was in these early years of the reign of Abdülhamid that the

---

[6] On the arrest and subsequent fate of Midhat Paşa, see Uzunçarşılı, *Midhat ve Rüştü Paşaların Tevikflerine dair Vesikalar* (1946) and *Midhat Paşa ve Taif Mahkûmları* (1950).

whole movement of the *Tanzimat*—of legal, administrative, and educational reform—reached its fruition and its climax. And so, too, did the tendencies, already discernible under the *Tanzimat* régimes, towards a new, centralized, and unrestrained despotism.

A key figure in the Sultan's reforms was Mehmed Said Paşa (1838–1914), sometimes known as Küçük (little) Said or, no doubt because of his Anglophile tendencies, as Ingiliz Said.[7] Said was born in Erzurum, the son of a diplomat and the descendant of a family of ulema.[8] After a successful career in the government service, he became Grand Vezir for the first time in October 1879, and held the office almost continuously until 1885. He was Grand Vezir again in 1895 and in 1901–3, as well as on three occasions after the revolution of 1908.

A good indication of Said Paşa's ideas and policies can be obtained from the lengthy memorandum on the reforms needed by the Empire which, in accordance with what had become an established Ottoman custom, he submitted to the Sultan in 1880.[9]

In a lengthy historical preamble, that clearly owed much to a study of earlier memorialists, Said Paşa demonstrates that 'the advancement of a state can only be secured through knowledge and uprightness',[10] and that it was through the decay or disappearance of these qualities that the Ottoman Empire fell into a decline. The remedy is to restore them, and the means are education and justice.

Educational reform is the first prerequisite to any further improvement.

In order to remedy this situation, first and foremost a serious and powerful effort must be made to improve public education. As long as public education is not disseminated, there will be no leaders capable

[7] On Said Paşa, see *EI*[1] *s.v.* (by Th. Menzel). His memoirs were published in three volumes—*Said Paşanın Hâtırâtı* 1328 A.H. (analysed by K. Süssheim, 'Die Memoiren Küçük Said Paša's . . .' in *Orientalische Studien Fritz Hommel*, ii (1916), 295–312). Said Paşa seems to have been the first Turkish statesman to publish his memoirs. He was followed by many others, and to this day the flow of memoirs from retired statesmen and generals is one of the features of the Turkish scene that link Turkey with the West.

[8] It is interesting that Said Paşa prided himself on his authentically Turkish descent—one of the earliest appearances of this theme in Turkish politics. See Süssheim, p. 301 n.4.

[9] The memorandum appears in *Hâtırât*, i. 418–36. A translation of this, with some other documents from the memoirs, was made by the late Mr. Harold Bowen and awaits publication.

[10] *Hâtırât*, i. 423.

of directing the internal and external affairs of the Empire soundly, no judges who can administer the public laws justly, no commanders who can run the Army efficiently, and no finance officers who can show how to manage and increase the sources of revenue in accordance with economic principles. None of the institutions and operations that serve public prosperity and wellbeing can be brought into existence as long as education is not disseminated. . . .[11]

In short, Said Paşa goes on to explain, education is necessary for the efficient conduct of public affairs, for the life of a civilized community, for defence against foreign enemies, 'and even, henceforth, in order to keep under control the Christian populations, whose minds are now being opened by education. . . .'

Education is not, however, sufficient in itself; there is also a need for uprightness, the absence of which produces hypocrisy, falsehood, and a lack of patriotism (*hubb-i vatan*). To prevent the ruination of the Empire by the spread of these vices, the state must stamp out corruption, and must itself set a better example than hitherto of honest and upright behaviour. 'Though the Islamic religion defends justice, the government's neglect, for some time past, of this stern duty has reached a point when it can no longer be denied.'[12] To remedy this, there must be a reorganization of the law courts and a revision of legal procedures; in addition, there must be law schools to train a new generation of lawyers and judges.

Said Paşa then goes on to discuss a number of civil, military, and administrative matters, and finally comes to what he calls 'the fundamental and vital problem of the Empire . . . that of finance'.[13] He has no objection to further loans, provided that the terms are equitable, that there is no infringement of Ottoman rights, and that the money is spent on capital improvements and not on covering a budgetary deficit. But the real answer is financial reorganization and reform, the main points being the rationalization of the currency, the publication of proper annual budgets and balances, the adoption of an equitable and efficient tax system, and the introduction of a proper system of accountancy for government financial transactions. This will also help to make possible the urgently needed public works for the improvement of agriculture, industry, and trade, and for the extension of communications.[14]

[11] *Hâtırât*, i. 423   [12] Ibid. p. 424.   [13] Ibid. p. 433.   [14] Ibid. p. 434.

Educational Reform [15]

Educational reform, in Said Paşa's view, was the essential prerequisite to all further improvements, and it was in this field that the Hamidian régime made its first and greatest effort.

Its most impressive achievement was in higher education, where the number of schools and the number of students were both considerably increased. The *mülkiye* school, established in 1859 as a training centre for civil servants, was in 1877 reorganized and expanded, especially in the senior classes, and the curriculum revised to include modern subjects. Boarding facilities were also added for students from the provinces.[16] From a first graduation, in 1861, of 33 students, the numbers rose by 1885 to 395 of whom 295 were boarders. This school, the first purely civilian institution among the new modern centres of higher education in Turkey, remained, even under the pressures of the later Hamidian régime, an important intellectual centre and a forcing-ground of new ideas. Its teachers included such men as Murad Bey (d. 1912), later a leader among the Young Turks, Recaizade Mahmud Ekrem (1846–1913), a poet and literary reformer and a disciple of Namık Kemal, Abdurrahman Şeref (1835–1925), a historian— all of them men of high calibre and profound influence.[17]

Like the *Mülkiye*, the *Harbiye*, or War College at Pangalti was maintained and extended, as were also the military and civil medical schools and a few other foundations, such as the artillery, naval and military engineering schools, inherited from the earlier reformers. But that was not all. To the existing schools, Abdülhamid added no less than eighteen new higher and professional schools. Though some of them were of short duration, their influence as a whole was considerable. They included the schools of finance (1878), law (1878), fine arts (1879), commerce (1882), civil engineering (1884), veterinary science (1889), police (1891), customs (1892), and an improved new medical school (1898).

Most ambitious of all was the founding of a Turkish university.

[15] The most detailed account of educational developments in this period will be found in Ergin, *Maarif*. For a brief British account of Turkish education, extracted from the Embassy Annual Report for 1907, see C. P. Gooch and H. W. V. Temperley, *British Documents on the Origins of the War*, v (1928), 29–31.

[16] And abolished in 1902 (Ergin, *Maarif*, p. 516).

[17] Ibid. pp. 510 ff., and Ali Çankaya, *Mülkiye ve Mülkiyeliler* (1954).

N

This project, first mooted in 1845, had run into many difficulties, and suffered from several false starts. It was not until August 1900 that, after long preparation, the Darülfünun, later known as the University of Istanbul, opened its gates. Turkey had at last acquired a university—the first truly indigenous modern university in the Muslim world.[18]

To provide students for all these new colleges, a large-scale expansion of the primary and secondary schools became necessary, as well as of teachers' training colleges to provide their staffs. The earliest training college had been opened in 1848; the first statistical statement published after the 1908 revolution shows 31 in operation, in vilayet and sanjak centres as well as in the capital.

Modern elementary education was provided in the *rüşdiye* schools, the first of which had been opened in Istanbul in 1847. From 1875 separate military *rüşdiye* schools were established, to prepare for admission to military high schools and colleges. Under Abdülhamid *rüşdiye* schools were set up in the centres of all the 29 vilayets and 6 independent *mutasarrıflıks* of the Empire, as well as in many kaza centres in Turkey proper. These led to the *idadiye* schools, which provided middle and early secondary education. The first *idadiye* was opened in Istanbul in 1875. A special education tax imposed in 1884 made it possible to establish seven-class schools in vilayet centres and five-class schools in sanjak centres all over the Empire. At the same time the network of military schools was extended, and in 1904, military schools were opened in Damascus, Baghdad, Erzincan, Edirne, and Manastir.

The apex of the system of secondary education was provided by the two great public schools of Galatasaray and Darüşşafaka.[19] Both were inherited from the *Tanzimat* period, the former an Imperial, the latter a private foundation. In the Hamidian period the Galatasaray school, originally a Franco-Turkish enterprise, became more Turkish in character. Latin was dropped from the curriculum, the proportion of Turkish pupils increased, and the school became more and more the favourite place of education for the sons of the ruling classes—the landowning, military, and bureaucratic families of the capital. Its teachers included some of

---

[18] Ergin, *Maarif*, pp. 997 ff.

[19] Ibid. pp. 400 ff. and 743 ff.; Süngü, in *Bell.*, no. 28 (1943), 315–47.

the leaders of Turkish scholarship and letters—its pupils were the sons of the ruling *élite*, preparing to succeed them.

Judicial and Legal Reform [20]

A whole generation of schoolboys and students were toiling in the schools of Turkey to achieve the first of Said Paşa's remedies —knowledge. The second, justice, on which would largely depend the use they made of their knowledge, proved more difficult of access.

The most important legal reforms of the Hamidian era occurred during the first few years of the Sultan's reign, and were in reality the completion of a process begun under the *Tanzimat*. These were a group of four laws, promulgated in May and June 1879, of which two dealt with the organization of justice and the courts and two with legal procedure. A Ministry of Justice had been established by ferman and given authority over the commercial courts. It was now reorganized, and given control over all non-religious courts. Another law provided for the regulation of the *nizamiye* courts—the mixed courts established some years previously to try lawsuits between Muslim and non-Muslim litigants.[21] At the same time two further laws dealt with procedural matters—the first providing for the execution of judgements, the second embodying a code of civil procedure.

One of the main purposes of these changes was to meet foreign criticisms of Ottoman justice, and thus prepare the way for the abrogation or limitation of the foreign judicial privileges recognized by the capitulations. In this the Ottoman legislators were unsuccessful. The laws on execution of judgements and on civil procedure were not recognized by the foreign missions, and were in consequence never actually applied in mixed law suits.[22] The extraterritorial privileges of the foreign communities remained firmly established, and the Ottoman courts, limited in their competence to cases involving Ottoman subjects only, were untroubled by foreign observation or criticism.

The failure to meet foreign criticism seems to have put an end to legal reform; domestic criticism, at the time, seemed less

---

[20] On the legal and judicial reforms of this period, see Engelhardt, ii. 237–4; *EI*[1] s.v. 'Tanzimat' (by J. H. Kramers); Nuri, *Abdülhamid-i Sani*, ii. 700 ff.; Mardin, *Ahmet Cevdet*.

[21] Karal, *Tarih*, vi. 167 ff.   [22] *EI*[1], iv. 658.

important. In 1888 the official drafting committee, which was set up in 1869 and which had produced the *Mecelle* code of civil law and the code of civil procedure, was dissolved by order of the Sultan. Work on the revision and codification of other branches of law was not resumed until after the revolution of 1908.[23]

The Ministry of Justice continued to function, and under the leadership of such able men as Ahmed Cevdet Paşa, made some progress in extending and rationalizing the system of non-religious courts for civil, commercial, and criminal cases. But in a time of increasing autocracy and repression, justice was an early casualty, and the high hopes of the reformers were bitterly disappointed.

Communications

The Sultan's repressions bred discontent and resentment, which the young men being educated in the Sultan's schools found ways of expressing. New communications provided the means for the rapid dissemination of new ideas and movements.

The best known development was in the railways.[24] At the accession of Abdülhamid there were only a few hundred miles of railway line in Turkey. The first line, a British concession, linked Izmir with Aydın, through the Menderes valley; 80 miles long, it was opened to traffic in 1866, and helped to develop south-western Anatolia. The others included a 58-mile line from Haydarpaşa to Izmit, completed in 1873, and a link between Istanbul and Edirne of 198 miles—the first stage of the Orient Express.

From about 1885 a burst of railway construction, most of it by foreign concession-holders, increased the railways of Turkey from several hundred to several thousand miles of track. The figures are not in themselves impressive; as late as 1913 the Ottoman Empire in Europe and Asia possessed a total of 3,882 miles of line—less than the kingdom of Belgium.[25] But the importance of these lines cannot be judged only by their mileage. When, on 12 August 1888, the first direct train left Vienna on its way to Istanbul, a new breach was opened in the crumbling wall that

[23] Mardin, pp. 151 ff.

[24] There is a vast literature on the Turkish railways. For brief accounts, from different points of view, see R. Hüber, *Die Bagdadbahn* (1943); E. M. Earle, *Turkey, the Great Powers, and the Bagdad Railway* (1923); Nuri, *Abdülhamid-i Sani*, ii. 715 ff.

[25] E. G. Mear, and others, *Modern Turkey* (1924), p. 222. According to Nuri, ii. 717, there were 1,145 km. (=711 miles) of track in 1878.

separated Turkey from the West. It grew steadily wider. Hitherto, communications between Istanbul and the European capitals had been by slow and indirect sea routes, via Marseilles or Odessa. Henceforth there was a regular and direct railway service. The traffic on the new line increased every year, still more so after the introduction of a special international train known as the Orient Express. The name reflects the viewpoint of the Europeans who planned, built and operated it—but for a whole new generation of Turks it was the express to Europe, and the Sirkeci railway terminus in Istanbul the ante-room to freedom and modernity.

The building of roads lagged behind that of railways, and in some areas there was even a retrogression, when the old roads were supplanted by the new railway lines and allowed to fall into disrepair. The ports, too, suffered from neglect and inefficiency. One of the reforms suggested by Lord Salisbury in 1877 was an improved postal service, and an official from the British General Post Office, Mr. Scudamore, was sent to Turkey to help organize a modern, central, postal service. His efforts had only a very limited success, and most people still preferred to patronize the extraterritorial post offices maintained, under cover of the Capitulations, by the foreign diplomatic missions.[26]

More striking was the spread of the telegraph—a service of direct value to the government for defence and home security, and not merely an amenity for the public.[27] Like so many other innovations and inventions, the telegraph was first brought by the impetus of war. The first lines in Turkey were laid by the British and French during the Crimean War; the first message—sent in September 1855, from Shumna via Edirne to Istanbul and from Istanbul to Europe—stated that 'Allied forces have entered Sevastopol'.

The Turks were quick to realize the value of this new medium of communication. When the war was over, the Frenchman Dolaro, who had laid the Edirne–Istanbul line, was given a concession to extend the service to other parts of the Empire. By 1864 there were already 76 telegraph stations, with 267 leagues of

[26] Pears, *Abdul Hamid*, pp. 189–91.

[27] The best history of the telegraph in Turkey is that given by Ergin in his account of the telegraph schools (*Maarif*, pp. 517 ff.). See further Karal, *Tarih*, vii. 273. For a medieval parallel, the use of the postal system by the Caliphs, see *EI*[2] ('Barīd', by D. Sourdel).

line in use and 304 more under construction.[28] By the accession of Abdülhamid, the greater part of the Empire was linked to the capital by a network of telegraphic communications.

At first the telegraph was operated by foreigners, using the Latin alphabet and the French language.[29] But the conduct of vital internal communications by foreign officials in a foreign language was obviously unsatisfactory, and a truly impressive effort was made to put this right.

Two men share the credit of founding Turkish telegraphy; Feyzi Bey, a member of the Translation Office of the Sublime Porte, who became the first Turkish communications officer, and Mustafa Bey, the inventor of the Turkish morse code and the trainer of the first group of Turkish telegraph operators. In 1861 Mustafa Bey, who had been appointed director of the Edirne telegraph office, sent the first telegram in Turkish, 128 words long, to Istanbul.

The government now took the question of telegraph personnel seriously in hand, and in the same year decided to set up a school for telegraph operators in Istanbul. The course was of two years duration, and included theoretical, technical, and practical instruction. The school seems to have been closed down in about 1880, but other provision for the training of telegraphists was made. In the 1870's and 1880's instruction in telegraphy was even included in the curricula of the Galatasaray and Daruşşafaka schools, and from 1883 specially selected students were sent to Paris for more advanced instruction. This ceased in 1892, when all the Turkish students in Paris were recalled after a number of them had taken part in a Young Turk political demonstration. Instruction continued in the Turkish schools, notably the Daruşşafaka, and in the early years of the twentieth century a centre for practical instruction appears to have been established. The telegraphic network was under the control of a separate ministry—the Ministry of Posts and Telegraphs.[30]

It is not difficult to see the reasons for this wide expansion of telegraphy, in which the Ottoman authorities showed a speed and efficiency in striking contrast with most of their other activities. The point was well made by Sir Charles Eliot, in a book published in 1900:

[28] Karal, *Tarih*, vii. 273. The Ottoman league (*fersah*) was a little over 3 miles.
[29] Ergin, *Maarif*, p. 518.   [30] Ibid. pp. 517–23.

little as the Turks like railways, they are great patrons of the telegraph, because it is the most powerful instrument for a despot who wishes to control his own officials. It is no longer necessary to leave a province to the discretion of a governor, and trust that he will come home to be beheaded when that operation seems desirable. With the telegraph one can order him about, find out what he is doing, reprimand him, recall him, instruct his subordinates to report against him, and generally deprive him of all real power.[31]

In other words, the telegraph was a potent instrument of centralized and autocratic rule, and Abdülhamid, following the example of his predecessors, made the most of it. Already at the end of the century there was a vast network of telegraphic communications, covering the whole of the Empire, and centred on Istanbul. And in each station, however remote, there was an operator, usually young, with enough modern education to read his manual, and enough science to do his job,—a natural recruit for the Young Turk committees.

Press and Publications[32]

Yet another of the media of communication underwent a considerable development during the reign of Abdülhamid—the printed word. And here, too, the results were in many ways far removed from the Sultan's purposes and intentions.

The censorship, already well established in the time of Abdülaziz, was maintained and reinforced, and extended from newspapers to almost all printed matter. At first, newspapers and periodicals were allowed some measure of freedom of comment —but this was rapidly reduced, and a censorship of often farcical strictness imposed.[33] The name of the deposed Sultan Murad V might not be mentioned—so a newspaper report of the restoration, in 1904, of the fifteenth-century mosque of Murad II in Bursa, spoke of 'the mosque of the heaven-dwelling father of his majesty Sultan Mehmed the Conqueror'.[34] Regicide was an even more dangerous subject—so the Turkish newspapers attributed the

---

[31] Odysseus [Sir Charles Eliot], *Turkey in Europe* (1900), pp. 158–9.

[32] The main works on the history of the Turkish press are cited above, p. 93 n. 37. On the press under Abdülhamid see especially Fesch. A useful survey of the movement of publication in Turkey will be found in Iskit, *Türkiyede Neşriyat Hareketleri Tarihine bir Bakış* (1939). For a survey of the Turkish press in 1906–7 by G. H. Fitzmaurice see Gooch and Temperley, v. 24–29.

[33] cf. Fesch, p. 36.   [34] Gerçek, *Türk Gazet.*, p. 77.

sudden and simultaneous deaths of the king and queen of Serbia in 1903 to indigestion.[35] In the same way the Empress Elizabeth of Austria died of pneumonia, President Carnot of apoplexy, President McKinley of anthrax.[36] The position of the press in Turkey was well summed up by Paul Fesch in a work published on the eve of the Young Turk Revolution:

> For thirty years, the press has ceased to exist in Turkey. There are indeed newspapers, many of them even, but the scissors of the censor-ship cut them in so emasculating a manner that they no longer have any potency. If I dared, I would call them gelded newspapers—or rather, to keep the local colour, eunuchs. Far be it from me to mock at an infirmity which they are the first to deplore and which they cannot in any way remedy. They are to be pitied. I can understand that they prefer this diminished life to total death—I would do the same—with a patience the more resigned in that their virility will sprout again of its own accord the day their persecutor disappears and that they are only waiting for that day to prove it.[37]

Even the emasculated and ineffectual newspapers of the Hamid-ian era, however, made some contribution to the modernization of Turkey, if only by increasing their numbers and readership and thus accustoming more Turks to the European habit of reading the news every day. No less important than the newspapers were the periodicals and books that were issuing in growing numbers from the printing presses, to satisfy—and again arouse—the appetites of the new literate classes. At the time of the accession of Abdül-hamid, there were still only a few printing presses in Istanbul. The official Ottoman yearbook of 1883 lists 54 presses in the city; that of 1908, no less than 99.[38]

Book printing, like the newspaper press, was under strict censorship. Nevertheless, the output increased steadily, and a biblio-graphy, prepared in 1890 by the Young Turk leader Murad,[39] lists some 4,000 books published in Turkish during the first fifteen years of Abdülhamid's reign. Of these, some 200 dealt with religion, nearly 500 were language primers, readers, grammars, dictionaries, &c., 1,000 dealt with scientific and scholarly subjects, over 1,000 consisted of fiction, poetry, drama, &c., and over 1,200 contained laws and rules and regulations of various kinds.[40]

[35] Ibid. p. 78.   [36] Fesch, p. 54.   [37] Ibid. p. 50.
[38] Iskit, *Neşriyat*, pp. 97 f. and 113 f.   [39] See below, p. 189.   [40] Iskit, pp. 100 ff.

Of these, the most important are the literary works, and works of popular science and scholarship. Turkish intellectuals, debarred from politics and from political thought, turned either to 'pure literature' or to scholarship. In both fields the Hamidian period, thanks to the energies and talents thus diverted, is one of rapid and significant development.

A characteristic figure of the period is Ahmed Midhat (1844–1912), journalist, novelist, historian, and popularizer.[41] The son of a poor Istanbul draper and a Circassian mother, he was educated at the *rüşdiye* school in Nish, where his elder brother held a government appointment. Ahmed himself entered the civil service by the usual method of recommendation and apprenticeship, and continued his studies privately, also studying French and 'Western knowledge' under the guidance of a Christian colleague. He enjoyed the patronage of Midhat Paşa, and served under him in both the Danube province and Iraq.

In 1871 he left the state service, and devoted himself entirely to writing and printing. In the course of his journalistic activities he seems to have become associated in some way with the Young Ottomans, and in 1872 was exiled to Rhodes. In 1876, after the deposition of Abdülaziz, he was permitted to return to Istanbul, where he resumed his work as writer, printer, and publisher. His circumspection during the critical months that followed enabled him to win and retain the goodwill of Abdülhamid; in 1877 the publication of a book justifying the Sultan's accession and title to the throne won him the directorship of the official gazette and state printing press. Thereafter, he held a number of official appointments.

All this led inevitably to a permanent breach with the Young Ottomans and with their liberal and revolutionary successors. After the revolution of 1908 he was retired from his various official positions, ostensibly under the age-limit, and was subjected to sharp criticism. An attempt to resume the literary work which he had long since sacrificed to his official career was abandoned in the face of hostile opinion and altered tastes, and his last years were spent in teaching at the University and elsewhere.

---

[41] See *EI²* ('Ahmed Midhat', by B. Lewis); *IA* ('Ahmed Midhat Efendi', by Sabri Esat Siyavuşgil); Tanpınar, pp. 433–66. A selection of his writings was published in the *Türk Klas.*

Ahmed Midhat was a man of no great literary talent; his close association with the Hamidian régime brought him the dislike and contempt of the new generation of Turkish intellectuals. Yet this acquiescent mediocrity was able to make a contribution of no small importance to the intellectual and cultural development of Turkey.

The most important of his variegated journalistic activities was the publication of the daily newspaper *Tercüman-i Hakikat* (the Interpreter of Truth), which he edited with a small group of associates. This paper, founded by Ahmed Midhat in 1878, continued for many years, and was one of the most important of the Hamidian period.[42] For a while the newspaper included a literary supplement, which from 1882 to 1884 was edited by the well-known author Muallim Naci[43] (1850–93), and engaged in violent literary controversies. Another, perhaps more significant, supplement was a weekly for schoolboys, distributed among the pupils in the *rüşdiye* schools.[44] The greater part of the copy of the *Tercüman-i Hakikat* was provided by Ahmed Midhat himself, who poured out an unceasing flow of stories, articles, serials, and features, original, adapted, and translated. In addition, he published an enormous number of books, estimated at more than 150. These fall into two main groups, fiction and popular knowledge. The former were widely read, and played a great part in developing new tastes and interests among a public still almost entirely unacquainted with Western literary forms and themes. The latter include a vast number of works on history, philosophy, religion, ethics, science, and other subjects, through which Ahmed Midhat was able to bring some idea of modern European knowledge to the Turkish reader in a simple and attractive form. Of special interest among these are a universal history in three volumes (1880–2) and a series of separate histories of European countries, in fourteen volumes (1871–81), which were among the first works to give the Turkish reader some insight into the history of the world outside the Islamic œcumene.[45]

A contemporary of Ahmed Midhat, whose career followed a

---

[42] Emin, *Press*, p. 63.

[43] On Muallim Naci see *EI*[1] ('Nādjī', by Th. Menzel) and Tanpınar, pp. 596 ff.

[44] Gerçek, pp. 75–76; *IA*, vii. 370.

[45] cf. B. Lewis, 'History-writing and National Revival in Turkey', *MEA*, iv (1953), 218–27.

slightly different line, was Ebüzziya Tevfik (1849–1913).[46] Acquainted at an early age with Şinasi and Namık Kemal, he became associated with the Young Ottomans, whose historian he later became, and in 1872 was exiled to Rhodes with the others. He too made his peace with Abdülhamid, in whose reign he became a member of the Council of State and Director of the School of Arts. He proved, however, less compliant than Ahmed Midhat, and was in due course exiled again, first to Rhodes and then to Konya. Thanks to this he was able, after his return to Istanbul in 1908, to play some role in the parliament and press of the Young Turk period.

Under Abdülhamid Ebüzziya's activities were, of necessity, literary. They consisted chiefly of the publication of a fortnightly magazine (1879 onwards) and the editing of a series of well over a hundred books, written or translated by various authors, and known as the Ebüzziya library. His own writings, besides Turkish literary and historical matters, deal also with such topics as Gutenberg, Buffon, and Napoleon. All these works were widely disseminated and read, and helped to form the opinions and outlook of the new generation.

More ambitious, intellectually, were the efforts of Ahmed Ihsan [Tokgöz] (1869–1942), a graduate of the *mülkiye* school who gave up a promising official career in order to become a journalist.[47] While employed as a translator on an Istanbul evening paper, the *Servet* (Treasure), he brought out an illustrated scientific supplement, called *Servet-i Fünun* (Treasure of Science) which a year later he was able to publish as an independent periodical, owned and edited by himself. The first issue, which appeared on 27 March 1891, described itself as an 'illustrated Ottoman journal', devoted to literature, science, art, biography, travel, and fiction. In its first phase, it was modelled on the French *L'Illustration*, and was a kind of pictorial news magazine relying chiefly on foreign sources for both pictures and text. From the first it had a certain literary interest, with a Westernizing tendency, and published translations from Daudet and other French writers.

This new journal rapidly attracted the interest and support of the young writers of the time. In January 1895 one of the most

---

[46] *IA s.v.* (by Fevziye Abdullah).

[47] *EI*[2] ('Aḥmad Iḥsān', by K. Süssheim—G. L. Lewis).

distinguished among them, the poet Tevfik Fikret[48] (1867–1915) took over the editorship, and from that time onwards the character of the journal changed radically. He remained in control until 1901, when he resigned after a disagreement with Ahmed Ihsan. About the same time the journal fell foul of the censors, who condemned as seditious an article translated from the French by the journalist Hüseyin Cahid [Yalçın][49] containing a passing reference to the 'régime of 1789'.[50] After a few weeks of suppression the journal was permitted to reappear, with Ahmed Ihsan again in charge, but the best contributors had gone, and the journal lost its interest and its influence. After the 1908 Revolution it appeared for a while as a daily newspaper.

It was during the six years of Tevfik Fikret's editorship that the *Servet-i Fünun*,[51] with the collaboration of the most gifted writers of the time, really made its impact on Turkish opinion. In a sense the *Servet-i Fünun* group and the 'New Literature'—*Edebiyat-i Cedide*—which they propounded were conservative, even reactionary. Rejecting the tendencies towards the simplification of the language that had appeared in the preceding period, they wrote in a style that was deliberately recondite and obscure, laden with learned Persian and Arabic words and expressions, and addressed only to a highly educated *élite*.

Even this, however, was in part an expression of the Western influence that appears so strongly in the Turkish literature of the time. The men of the 'New Literature' were rejecting simplicity, despising words 'worn out in the mouth of the common people'.[52] They were not rejecting the literature of the West; there, on the contrary, under the prevailing influence of the French symbolists, they were able to find an aesthetic justification for that retreat into the ivory tower which the Hamidian censorship had imposed upon them. Despite their linguistic conservatism, Tevfik Fikret and his associates went much farther than their predecessors in imitating and adapting French models. Though political criticism was barred, social comment could be and was made through the

---

[48] On Tevfik Fikret, see *EI*[1] ('Tewfīḳ Fikret', by Th. Menzel); Akyüz, *Tevfik Fikret* (1947); Bombaci, pp. 449–54. For a selection of his writings see *Türk Klas.*

[49] Hüseyin Cahit Yalçın, selected works (ibid. xlix).   [50] Ibid. p. 4.

[51] On the *Servet-i Fünun*, see 'Serveti Fünun Edebiyatı Antolojisi', in the *Türk Klas.*; Bombaci, pp. 447 ff.

[52] U. Heyd, *Language Reform in Modern Turkey* (1954), p. 15.

fictional analysis of the social life of the time. One of the main tasks of the *Servet-i Fünun* was to make known to the Turkish reader something of the intellectual and cultural life of Europe, especially of France. Such a message, even in a parnassian, symbolist literary form, still held a profoundly revolutionary content; there is a symbolic quality in the suppression of the journal for a passing allusion in a translated article to the French Revolution—and perhaps also in the subsequent career of the translator.[53]

The *Servet-i Fünun* avoided politics, even though many of its authors held strong political opinions and Tevfik Fikret himself was more than once in trouble with the authorities. A bolder line was taken by the weekly *Mizan* (Balance), founded in 1886.[54] It was suppressed in 1890, and later restarted in exile. In the first issue, the editor discussed the importance, form, and proper contents of the press in civilized countries, and promised his readers to supply them with news, to discuss political questions, and to correct European misapprehensions about Turkey.

The editor, Murad Bey (1853–1912), known as Mizancı, was a person of some interest.[55] A native of Daghistan, in the Caucasus, he completed his education, perhaps including a university course, in Russia before settling in Turkey in 1873. Like so many Muslim emigrants from the Russian Empire, Murad found a ready opening for his talents and qualifications, and was employed for some time in the Council of the Public Debt. Later he became a teacher of history at the *Mülkiye*, where, according to the testimony of some of his pupils, he exercised a profound influence on the rising generation. Through his books, and still more through the weekly *Mizan*, he was able to extend that influence far beyond his classroom. Ahmet Emin [Yalman], the historian of the Turkish press, describes him as 'the leading figure in the press of the time . . . the idol of the intellectual classes'.[56] Under Hamidian rule the next stages—the suppression of the *Mizan*, and, after an interval, the flight to Egypt and Europe of its editor—followed inevitably. Among the Young Turks abroad he won a position of authority and leadership which ended only when he yielded to the Sultan's

[53] See his selected works in *Türk Klas.*   [54] *IA*, vii. 371.

[55] On Murad Bey see E. E. Ramsaur, *The Young Turks* (1957), index; Fevziye Abdullah, 'Mizancı Mehmed Murad Bey', *Tar. Derg.*, iii–iv. 67–88.

[56] Emin, *Press*, p. 65.

blandishments and returned to Istanbul to take up an official appointment in 1887.

With the increasing severity of the censorship from about 1890-1 onwards, the most significant and interesting productions of Turkish journalism were the newspapers and periodicals published, in growing numbers, by the Young Turk exiles in France, Switzerland, England, Egypt, and elsewhere. Nevertheless, even the press in Istanbul, though debarred from any serious political comment or even news reporting, continued to form its readers in new ways of thought, to inculcate, no doubt unconsciously, European social ideas and attitudes, and to bring to them some notion, however garbled, of the larger, modern world of which Turkey was now a part.

In 1891, when the growth of Young Turk activities abroad led to a worsening of the position of the press at home, there were six Turkish daily newspapers. Within a few years the pressure from above had reduced their number to three, all in receipt of government subsidies and under strict palace control. The *Tercüman-i Hakikat* has already been mentioned. The other two—the *Ikdam* (Effort) and *Sabah* (Morning)—both had fairly substantial circulations, the former about 15,000 and the latter about 12,000.[57] These numbers may seem small in comparison with the present-day circulations of 100,000-200,000 of some of the Istanbul papers. At that time, however, they were sufficient to keep the papers going even when the subsidies ceased, to reach and influence the members of the numerically small educated *élite*, and to provide a training, an outlet, and a livelihood for the followers of a new profession—journalism. It is significant that both papers managed to survive the revolution of 1908, and to play a role of some importance under the régimes that followed it.

The First Revolutionaries [58]

In spite of these changes, the government of Turkey was still the accepted and recognized prerogative of an *élite* of professionals, who retained all the rights and duties of politics, including that of opposition. It was, therefore, among the servants of the state that

[57] Emin, *Press*, p. 78.

[58] A detailed monographic study of the opposition movements under Abdülhamid, based on both Turkish and Western sources, will be found in Ramsaur's *Young Turks*. Additional material from Turkish sources not used by Ramsaur will be found in several more recent Turkish works, notably Tunaya, *Partiler*, and Kuran.

the pioneers of revolutionary change emerged; it was in the schools
—those nurseries of the civil and military *élite*, so carefully tended
by the Sultan himself—that the seeds of revolution were sown.

Many Turkish writers have described the atmosphere of discontent and revolutionary ferment in the Hamidian schools,
especially in the provincial centres, less subject to the immediate
control of the palace. Even in the Imperial Lycée of Galatasaray
in Istanbul, feeling against the Sultan was very strong. Hikmet
Bayur, who graduated from the Lycée in 1909, has described how,
two years before the Young Turk Revolution, the pupils were
assembled on various festivals for the distribution of sweets and
ordered to shout 'Padişahım çok yaşa'—long live the Emperor!

We, however, or at least the great majority of us, used to shout
'Padişahım başaşağıya'—down with the Emperor. Among those who
shouted in this way were the sons of ministers and even of such close
associates of the Emperor as the palace chamberlains . . . the youth
even of the circles nearest to the Emperor neither loved nor respected
him. . . .[59]

This universal disgust no doubt took some time to reach the
level described by Hikmet Bayur. But already in the first decades
of Abdülhamid's rule there was discontent and frustration in the
schools, where teachers and students alike read the forbidden
writings of Namık Kemal and Ziya Paşa, talking and dreaming of
freedom and fatherland. Niyazi Bey, the hero of the revolution
of July 1908, describes in his memoirs how, already as a young
schoolboy in the 1880's, he imbibed from the teachers of French
and history—the choice is significant—the ideas of

loyalty, progress, humanity, and love of country. . . . They used to tell
us stories about the patriotism of the old Ottomans and the French. . . .
When we used to talk about the affairs of the world, with schoolmates
and other people . . . the name of [Namık] Kemal Bey, of that great
and respected writer, . . . and his works were mentioned.
. . . Would it not be our duty to defend the fatherland and repel the
attacks of the enemy? Why then is there no trace, in our courses and
syllabuses, of fatherland or of training of the mind? Why do they force
us to conceal a whole set of feelings that by religion, reason and logic
are sacred to us? Why do they not give us books to read that would
serve to develop and elevate these feelings? . . .

[59] Hikmet Bayur, 'Ikinci Meşrutiyet devri üzerinde bazı düşünceler', *Bell.*, no. 90
(1959), p. 269. Bayur is a grandson of Kâmil Paşa.

In fact, however, Niyazi and his friends were introduced by a teacher to such writings, including the poems of Kemal, under whose influence 'an intoxicating patriotism prepared my heart, my innocent heart, for revolutions . . .'

When Niyazi went to the War College at Pangaltı in 1882, he found that Kemal, whose works placed him 'among the greatest men of the nation, the greatest leaders of politics, the zealots of the community' was proscribed, together with the rest of the liberals. 'Even to mention their names or their works was considered a mortal sin.'[60]

There were, however, many sinners. Ali Kemal, Rıza Tevfik, and others have described how the teachers of the *mülkiye* and other schools talked to them of freedom, and introduced them to the writings of the proscribed Young Ottoman authors. The authorities were aware of this, and tried to replace them with safer and more submissive teachers. Ali Kemal remarks: 'At that time teachers like Murad Bey and even Ekrem Bey were removed from the *mülkiye* school because of their intellectual freedom. In their place dull and stupid men were brought.'[61]

An order of the time forbids teachers to diverge from the syllabus and provides for the 'exemplary punishment of teachers acting in a way contrary to the principles of loyalty'.[62] These measures, however, had only limited effect, and failed to prevent the spread of subversive views among the cadets and schoolboys. These young men, the future soldiers and administrators of the Empire, were given the most advanced and most modern education that the state could offer; it was inevitable that they and their teachers should, sooner or later, reach some radical conclusions on the conduct of the state which they were to serve.

Organized Opposition

The first organized opposition group was formed in 1889—the centenary, as a Turkish historian has pointed out, of the French Revolution.[63] Its founders were four medical students, meeting in May in the garden of the military medical college,

---

[60] *Hâtırât-i Niyazi* (1326 A.H.), pp. 14–15. The influence of Namık Kemal is attested by other Young Turk memoirists. See, for example, Kâzım Nami Duru's account of how he read Namık Kemal while still a cadet at the military *idadi* school at Manastir, and secretly made a copy of one of them which reached him in manuscript form (*Ittihat ve Terakki Hatıralarım* (1957), p. 6).

[61] Cited in Ergin, *Maarif*, pp. 504 ff.   [62] Ibid. p. 513.   [63] Tunaya, *Partiler*, p. 104.

halfway between the old Imperial palace and the new railway terminus. The founders were Ibrahim Temo, an Albanian from Ohri, Mehmed Reşid, a Circassian from the Caucasus, Abdullah Cevdet and Ishak Sükûti, two Kurds from Arabkir and Diyarbakır respectively. Some accounts add a fifth name—that of Hüseyin-zade Ali, from Baku, in the Russian Empire.[64]

The new society grew rapidly, winning adherents among the cadets in the civil, military, naval, medical, and other higher schools in Istanbul. Like their predecessors, the Young Ottomans of 1865, these new conspirators seem to have taken the Italian Carbonari as their model, and formed themselves into numbered cells, in which each member also had a number. Temo, the first member of the first cell, was 1/1.

By means of the French post office in Galata, the conspirators were able to maintain contact with Paris, where in the meantime the first organized group of exiles had constituted itself. A small group of Ottoman liberals had been living there since the closing of parliament by Abdülhamid, and one of them, a Lebanese Maronite and former member of the Ottoman parliament called Khalil Ghanim,[65] had started a journal, in France, called *La Jeune Turquie*. The name was no doubt a conscious evocation of the memory of the Young Ottoman exiles of the 1860's.

In 1889 the director of education of Bursa, Ahmed Rıza Bey, obtained permission to visit Paris to see the exhibition. Arriving there, he joined the group of exiles, and soon became a dominant figure among them.

Ahmed Rıza (1859–1930), one of the most consistent and fearless of the Young Turks, is in many ways a key figure among them.[66] He was born at Istanbul, the son of Ali Rıza Bey, nick-named 'Ingiliz Ali' because of his knowledge of English and his friendship with Englishmen during the Crimean War; his mother was an Austrian or Hungarian lady converted to Islam. Ingiliz Ali had been a member of the first parliament, and had been

---

[64] Ramsaur, p. 14; Tunaya, *Partiler*, p. 104; Kuran, pp. 134 ff. Biographical notes on these personalities will be found in Ibrahim Alâettin Gövsa's useful compendium, *Türk Meşhurları Ansiklopedisi* (n.d.). On Abdullah Cevdet see further *EI¹* suppl. ('Djewdet', by K. Süssheim).

[65] The role of this Ottoman Syrian Christian seems to have been overlooked by the historians both of Turkish and Arab nationalism. See Ramsaur, p. 22.

[66] On Ahmed Rıza, see Ramsaur, Tunaya, Kuran, *passim*. Surprisingly, he is missing from both the Turkish and Leiden Encyclopaedias of Islam.

o

exiled to Ilgin, where he died. Ahmed Rıza went to school at Galatasaray, and was then sent to study agriculture in France. It was on his return to Turkey, from his studies, that he was appointed director of education in Bursa. This post he abandoned in order to undertake a vaster project of re-education from abroad.

In Paris Ahmed Rıza fell under the influence of Pierre La Fayette, a disciple of Auguste Comte who instructed him in the positivist philosophy that was to dominate his thinking. In 1895, in association with other exiles, he began to publish a fortnightly journal, the *Meşveret*. The name—a word of Arabic origin meaning consultation—is an echo of earlier arguments, drawn from the Koran, for consultative government.[67] The device under it— *Intizam ve Terakki*—Order and Progress, is that of the Positivists. It is probably through this positivist influence that the group in Istanbul now changed its name from *Ittihad-i Osmani*, Ottoman Union, to *Ittihad ve Terakki*, Union and Progress.[68]

The *Meşveret*, smuggled through the foreign post offices and other channels, began to circulate in Istanbul, helping both to increase the numbers of the society and, as an inevitable consequence, to bring it to the attention of the authorities. At about the same time Murad Bey presented a memorandum on necessary reforms to the Sultan and then, feeling no doubt that his point could be made more effectively from beyond the Sultan's reach, fled to British-occupied Egypt, where he began to publish his *Mizan*, this time in a form openly critical of the Sultan and his régime.

The Sultan retaliated by arresting some of Murad's friends in Istanbul, and arresting or exiling the known leaders of the opposition groups. Far from being crushed, the conspirators were now driven from theory to practice, and prepared a coup d'état which was to depose the Sultan in August 1896. The plot was, however, betrayed to the Sultan, and swift police action led to the arrest of almost all the conspirators. Although the charge was virtually one of rebellion or treason, the court martial that tried the plotters imposed no sentences of death. Instead, the unsuccessful conspirators were exiled, in accordance with the old Ottoman practice, to remote provinces of the Empire—to Anatolia, Mosul, and Syria, and, for the most dangerous, to Fezzan in Libya. Kâzım Paşa, the general commanding the first division in

[67] See above, pp. 141 and 151.   [68] Ramsaur, pp. 23 ff.

Istanbul, and leader designate of the coup d'état, was punished with nothing worse than the governorship of Scutari in Albania.[69]

In spite of the failure of this first attempt to overthrow the Sultan, the Young Turk agitation continued to grow in Istanbul, notably among the students. It was actively encouraged by the exiles in Egypt and Europe, whose publications circulated in Turkey, and who managed, chiefly through the foreign post offices, to keep in touch with their friends at home. Çürüksulu Ahmed, a former teacher at the War College who had fled to France, corresponded secretly with some of his former pupils, and had a hand in the formation of two cells or committees at the War College. They were known, significantly, as the Hüseyin Avni and Süleyman Paşa groups—after the Minister of War and the War College commandant who took part in the deposition of Sultan Abdülaziz.[70]

At the beginning of June 1897 a special court martial was set up, presided over by Major-General Reşid Paşa, 'the tormentor of the country's youth'.[71] Its purpose was to crush the freedom movements among the cadets, and a grim, slow procession of arrests, detentions, and deportations filled the bleak corridors of the Taşkışla barracks. Political prisoners previously held at the Arsenal (Tersane) and elsewhere were transferred to Taşkışla for examination and trial, and then sent on their road to exile. On 28 August a party of seventy-eight prisoners—army, navy, medical officers, cadets from the military academies—emerged after 102 days at Taşkışla, and proceeded to the Kabataş quay, where they were put on board a steamer appropriately named the *Şeref* (Honour). They arrived on Wednesday 3 September at Tripoli, and were dispatched to military prisons.[72]

In spite of these repressions, the Young Turk movement continued to grow alarmingly, and the Sultan, feeling that the main impulse came from the exiles abroad, tried a new approach—that of reconciliation.

The situation among the exiles was not entirely happy. They were split up among a number of centres—the most important in Paris, Geneva, and Cairo, with smaller groups in Naples, Folkestone, London, and elsewhere. Differences, both personal and ideological, had begun to appear among them. These were

[69] Ibid. pp. 31–34. [70] Ramsaur, p. 45; Fesch, p. 341; Tunaya, *Partiler*, p. 104.
[71] Kuran, p. 143. [72] Tunaya, *Partiler*, p. 105; Kuran, pp. 144 ff.

aggravated when, towards the end of 1896, Murad Bey moved from Egypt to Europe, where he soon emerged as a successful rival of Ahmed Rıza for the leadership of the Young Turks. Murad became the leader of the Geneva branch of the Committee of Union and Progress, and his *Mizan*, now appearing in Geneva, rivalled and surpassed Ahmed Rıza's *Meşveret* as an organ of Young Turk opinion.[73]

It was at this juncture that the Sultan began to make approaches to the leaders in exile. A first mission, consisting of Yusuf Ziya Paşa and Ebüzziya Tevfik, produced no results, but in August 1897 Major-General Ahmed Celâleddin Paşa, a Circassian confidant of the Sultan, succeeded in persuading Murad, in Geneva, to accept a truce and return to Istanbul.

This defection was a shattering blow to the Young Turks. For a while the attempt was made to present this as a genuine negoti-ated, armed, truce. Murad, said a report of the time, 'without accepting any personal favour, will go alone to Constantinople as hostage. It is a new sacrifice on his part, for in the event of a resumption of hostilities, he will undoubtedly pay for this move-ment with his life.'[74]

Murad did not, in fact, pay with his life; instead, he became a member of the Council of State. That his intentions were honour-able at the moment of his return to Istanbul is generally conceded; but his defection, its exploitation by the Sultan, and the more flagrant betrayals of some of his associates, spread a wave of demoralization through the movement, especially inside Turkey. What was worse, Murad, the hero and idol of the movement, had set an example of compromise and submission that others were to follow. Two of the original four members of the Committee at the Medical School, Ishak Sükûti and Abdullah Cevdet, arrived in Europe about this time, and started a new journal, the *Osmanlı*, in Geneva. They were joined by another of the founders, Mehmed Reşid, as well as by other Young Turk militants, and succeeded once again in reviving the Geneva centre of the movement. Then, in 1899, they too ceded to the Sultan's blandishments and struck a bargain whereby he agreed to release political detainees in

---

[73] Ramsaur, pp. 37–39; Fesch, p. 338.

[74] Ramsaur, pp. 49–50; Fesch, p. 343; Fevziye Abdullah, p. 84. For a very detailed account of the mission of Ahmed Celâleddin Paşa and the defection of Murad, see Kuran, pp. 151 ff.

Tripoli and they to silence the *Osmanlı*. For this settlement Süküti and Cevdet may have had good humanitarian reasons; they can have had none for accepting salaried appointments as medical officers to the Ottoman Embassies in Rome and Vienna respectively. Abdullah Cevdet, despite his intellectual pre-eminence and his undoubted contributions to the ideology of Young Turkism, never really succeeded in living down this defection.[75]

Meanwhile, Ahmed Rıza and his friends in Paris remained impervious to both the blandishments and the threats of the Sultan and his emissaries, and continued to publish and distribute the *Meşveret*, now almost the sole organ of the Young Turk cause. And then, in December 1899, when Young Turk prospects seemed to be at their lowest ebb, both in Turkey and in Europe, the movement was suddenly galvanized into life again by the dramatic flight, from Istanbul to France, of a small group of new recruits from an unexpected source—from the Imperial family itself.

Damad Mahmud Celâleddin Paşa (1853–1903) was the son of a Vezir and the grandson, by his mother, of Sultan Mahmud II.[76] His wife was a daughter of Abdülmecid and a sister of Abdülhamid, to whom he was thus doubly related. His departure, with his sons Sabaheddin and Lûtfullah, was a heavy blow to the Sultan.

The arrival of the royal rebels was of course a great addition of strength and prestige to the Young Turks. It also had the effect of accentuating the divisions among them. Murad and Abdullah Cevdet had both successfully challenged for a while the leadership of Ahmed Rıza—and had then surrendered themselves into insignificance. Now a new and more enduring rival appeared, high in prestige and firm of principle, to confront the positivist prophet of the *Meşveret*. Between the two there followed a polarization of opinion, that split the Young Turks in exile until the Revolution, and in office until the end of the Empire.

This new leader was Prince Sabaheddin (1877–1948) who rapidly emerged as the chief personal and, later, ideological rival of Ahmed Rıza.[77] The cleavage between the two wings of the movement became apparent and was made permanent in 1902, at a

---

[75] Ramsaur, p. 53; Fesch, p. 346. cf. Kuran, pp. 204 ff.

[76] On the intervention of the Damad and his sons, see Ramsaur, pp. 54 ff.; Fesch, p. 356; Kuran, pp. 228 ff.

[77] On Sabaheddin, see Ramsaur, pp. 81–89; Kuran, pp. 317 ff. and 400 ff. &c.; Fesch, *passim*.

Young Turk congress convened in Paris to restore and confirm the unity of the movement. The idea of such a congress was first mooted by the two princes, in an appeal put out by them during a visit to Egypt in 1900.[78] The congress finally assembled on 4 February 1902, at the private house of a French well-wisher, under the presidency of Prince Sabaheddin.[79]

According to reports that have been published, two important questions came up during and after the congress. One was the argument, put forward by Ismail Kemal, that 'by propaganda and publications alone a revolution cannot be made. It is therefore necessary to work to ensure the participation of the armed forces in the revolutionary movement.'[80] Ismail Kemal, in his memoirs, describes how with Prince Sabaheddin's approval, he set to work to organize a military coup, and actually succeeded in interesting the British government in his plans. They came, however, to nothing.[81]

It was on the other question, that of intervention, that a serious split developed. The Armenian participants were anxious to seek the intervention of the European powers, as a guarantee of effective reform in the Ottoman Empire. Ahmed Rıza and most of the Turks in the Committee of Union and Progress were opposed to this; the problem was, in their view, a purely internal one, and any outside intervention would be unnecessary and even harmful. Prince Sabaheddin agreed on this occasion with the Armenians, and a resolution was passed including a reminder to the Europeans

that is is their duty in the general interest of humanity to ensure that the clauses in the treaties and international agreements concluded between themselves and the Sublime Porte are put into effect in such a way as to benefit all parts of the Ottoman Empire.[82]

Ahmed Rıza and his friends remained implacably opposed to this policy, and the difference between his party and that of Prince Sabaheddin begins to crystallize from now onwards as one

[78] Ramsaur, p. 65; Kuran, pp. 267 ff.

[79] On the Paris congress of 1902 see Ramsaur, pp. 66 ff.; Fesch, pp. 364 ff.; Kuran, pp. 317 ff.; Tunaya, *Partiler*, pp. 106 ff.

[80] Kuran, p. 321.

[81] Ismail Kemal, *Memoirs*, pp. 308 ff.; cf. Ramsaur, p. 76 ff. For a somewhat different version see Kuran, pp. 326 ff.

[82] Fesch, p. 371; Ramsaur, p. 71

between Turkish nationalism and Ottoman liberalism. The
minority statement makes interesting reading.

. . . We, the minority, convinced that the Powers are guided by interest
and that this interest is not always in accord with that of our country,
therefore utterly reject an action which infringes the independence of
the Ottoman Empire. Nevertheless we are not, as has been claimed,
hostile to Europe; on the contrary, one of our chief desires is to see
European civilization spread in our country, notably its scientific
progress and its useful institutions. We follow the path traced by
Europe and, even in our refusal to accept foreign intervention, we
draw inspiration from the patriotic resolution of which all the
European peoples, jealous of their independence, have shown themselves rightly proud.[83]

The Prince now proceeded to found a new society in Paris, with
the princely name of 'the League for Private Initiative and
Decentralization'. Like its rival the Committee of Union and
Progress, the League set up branches among the Turkish diaspora,
as well as in various parts of the Ottoman Empire. They seem to
have concentrated on Asiatic Turkey, and branches are mentioned in Erzurum, Trabzon, Izmir, Alanya, as well as in
Damascus and Latakia in Syria.[84] In Istanbul the League seems
to have been represented by the 'Revolutionary Society'
(*Cemiyet-i Inkılabiye*), founded in September 1904 by a group of
students and schoolboys.[85]

The somewhat ponderous name of the League derives from the
writings of Edmond Demolins, a French writer by whom Prince
Sabaheddin was profoundly influenced.[86] Demolins's book *À Quoi
tient la supériorité des Anglo-Saxons?* was published in 1897, and
translated into English immediately after. It attracted a good deal
of attention at the time, and in particular aroused the interest of
Muslim reformers, liberals, and modernists looking for an explanation of the backwardness of their own societies. The book was
quickly published in an Arabic version in Egypt,[87] and seems to
have had no small impact on Arab and Turkish thinking.
Demolins's thesis, briefly, was that the superiority of the Anglo-
Saxons rested on their superior education, which developed

---

[83] Fesch, pp. 372-3; Ramsaur, p. 69.   [84] Tunaya, *Partiler*, pp. 142 ff.

[85] Ibid. pp. 149 ff.   [86] Ramsaur, pp. 82 ff.

[87] Tr. by Aḥmad Zaghlūl Pasha; see C. C. Adams, *Islam and Modernism in Egypt*
(1933), p. 312.

personality and individual initiative—confidence in oneself, instead of the confidence in the collectivity usual in other human societies. Within this framework of historical and educational theories, Prince Sabaheddin developed his idea of a federalized, decentralized Ottoman state. A constitutional monarchy, on British lines, would provide a minimum of central government; for the rest, the different peoples and communities of the Empire could satisfy their aspirations and safeguard their rights in regional and local government and in a public life emancipated from collective or governmental control. The German Orientalist C. H. Becker, writing in 1916, grimly commented on this doctrine:

one may imagine what would have resulted if such theorists had been able to put their ideas into practice, if English individualism had been introduced in a country, millions of whose inhabitants are still in a state of ethnic collectivism, not to mention the irredeemable dissolution of Turkey into various European spheres of influence.[88]

Prince Sabaheddin's ideas, despite some initial success, were in fact foredoomed to failure. The Armenians and other Christian nationalities, whom he tried so hard to conciliate, found little to attract them in an Ottoman federation, and preferred to seek the fulfilment of their political aspirations outside the Empire altogether. For the Turks, already irritated by the clashes and arguments with the Armenian committees, private initiative and decentralization seemed a much less satisfying slogan than union and progress. The growing menace, from dissident nationalism and foreign imperialism, to the integrity of the Empire made decentralization seem a dangerous if not suicidal formula. The growing pre-eminence of the army in the revolutionary movement gave the direction of the latter to an institution and a profession that were inevitably imbued with a spirit of authoritarian centralism. Neither private initiative nor decentralization held much appeal for the Prussian-trained officers of the Turkish army.

Between 1902 and 1906 the Young Turk movement continued to expand and to ramify. New groups appeared in Geneva and Cairo. Even in Istanbul, apparently for the first time since the defection of Murad, revolutionary groups began to appear once

---

[88] C. H. Becker, *Islamstudien*, ii (1932), p. 355.

more among the cadets and students of the military and civil schools.[89]

Then, in 1906, came the really important development—the establishment of revolutionary cells among serving officers in field formations. The first of such organizations seems to have been the 'Fatherland and Freedom Society' established by a small group of officers in Damascus, among them Mustafa Kemal, in the autumn of 1906. Branches were formed in Jaffa and Jerusalem, among the officers of the Fifth Army Corps.

Of more permanent significance was the committee formed in Salonika, at about the same time, among the officers of the Third Army Corps. The early history of this group is obscure, but it seems that Mustafa Kemal and the Damascus group played some role in getting it started. The vital phase began in September 1906, with the foundation of the 'Ottoman Freedom Society' by Ismail Canbulat and Midhat Şükrü [Bleda]. Its first supreme committee, of ten men, included Bursalı Tahir, headmaster of the military *rüşdiye* school in Salonika and a well-known scholar, Talât, chief clerk in the correspondence division of the Salonika directorate of posts and telegraphs, and a number of army officers.[90]

Events now moved rapidly. The cadets had by now become captains and majors, with men and arms under their command; the parlous state of the armed forces, and the increasing dangers of secession and aggression, made a change of régime an urgent necessity obvious to any patriotic and aspiring young officer. These were not of the kind that was to be familiar in subsequent Middle Eastern revolutions—ambitious young subalterns, drawn from new and rising social classes, using the discipline and cohesion of the army to destroy an old social order and initiate a revolutionary upheaval. They were members of a ruling *élite*, prepared by education to command and to govern; their complaint was that they were not permitted to do so effectively. The army, mistrusted by the Sultan, was starved of money and equipment, its pay in arrears and its weapons obsolete. Smart, young officers, with up-to-date training for an out-of-date army, could not but be painfully aware of the inadequacy of the defences of the Empire, in the face of the

[89] Tunaya, *Partiler*, p. 107. This revival of activity in Istanbul is not mentioned by Ramsaur.

[90] Ramsaur, pp. 95 ff.; Tunaya, *Partiler*, pp. 113 ff. and 150–2; Kuran, pp. 377 ff. There is some conflict of evidence on the personal role of Mustafa Kemal in these events.

dangers that were looming. Their political ideas were simple and rudimentary—freedom and fatherland, the constitution and the nation.

In December 1907 the Armenian Tashnak society took the initiative for a second attempt at the unification of the anti-Hamidian forces. A congress was again held in Paris, at which both Ahmed Rıza and Prince Sabaheddin were present; the latter was elected chairman.[91] This time the congress was held partly *in camera*, and seems to have been concerned with immediate practical decisions. Theoretical and ideological questions were left aside, and a large measure of agreement reached on an immediate programme of action. Only on one ideological matter did the opposing wings come together; on a proposal of the positivist Ahmed Rıza Bey, the liberals and the nationalists agreed to confirm the rights of the Caliphate and Sultanate.[92]

The real centre of events, however, was no longer among the exiles, but among the officers in Turkey, where new groups were being formed in Macedonia and Anatolia. In September 1907 the Salonika group had merged with the old Union and Progress organization in Paris, which thus acquired new vigour and prestige.[93] The Salonika officers seem, however, to have remained very independent in their affairs, using the committee in Paris as they used the masonic lodges in Turkey—because it was convenient to do so—but without paying much attention to the ideologies in either place.

By 1908 there was much to encourage the conspirators in Turkey. In the Far East, an Oriental but constitutional Japan had a few years previously defeated a European but autocratic Russia —and both Russia and Persia had accepted this demonstration of the superiority of democratic institutions, and had introduced, the one by precaution, the other by revolution, constitutional and parliamentary régimes. In Europe, the meeting of the English and Russian sovereigns at Reval on 9–10 June 1908 portended the obsequies of the Sick Man of Europe, and suggested an urgent need for the constitutional nostrum. And in the Empire, a wave of mutinies or rather strikes spread from Anatolia to Rumelia as Abdülhamid's unpaid, underfed, and ragged soldiery rose in

[91] On the second Paris congress see Ramsaur, pp. 124 ff.; Tunaya, *Partiler*, pp. 107–8; Kuran, pp. 408 ff.

[92] Tunaya, *Partiler*, p. 108.   [93] Ramsaur, pp. 121 ff.

desperation to demand the satisfaction of a few basic, minimum human needs.

The Constitutional Revolution[94]

In the early months of 1908 these troubles seemed to be spreading to the Third Army Corps, stationed in Macedonia. Alarming reports began to reach the Sultan's government in Istanbul, and in the late spring a commission was sent to Salonika to investigate the situation. The Sultan had accumulated vast archives of alarming reports from his spies over a period of many years, and seems at first to have seen no reason for precipitancy. This time he was mistaken. The Young Turk officers, by now seriously concerned at the growing threat to the Empire from inside and outside, were ready to overthrow a régime so incompetent in its defence. By the time the Sultan was ready to take action, it was too late.

The appointment of two successive commissions, to investigate and to punish, brought matters to a head. One young officer, attached to the staff of Hilmi Paşa, seems to have aroused suspicion and, characteristically, was invited to visit Istanbul in order to 'explain the situation and receive a promotion'. The officer in question, wisely mistrusting the motives behind the invitation, preferred to disappear into the Resne hills. His name was Enver Bey.[95]

On 4 July another officer, Major Ahmed Niyazi—at that time far more important in the councils of the Young Turks—followed him into the hills. Niyazi, however, did not go alone and in secret. He went with a substantial body of men, and with arms, munitions, and money seized from the company stores. At the same time, he addressed a declaration to the Palace Secretariat, the Inspectorate-General of Rumelia, the vilayet of Manastir, as well as letters of accusation to the commandant of the gendarmerie at Manastir and the gendarme officer at Resne.[96] His attitude is

---

[94] There are many political, personal, and journalistic accounts of the revolution of 1908. Much useful material is given in the relevant parts of Kuran (*Inkılâp*) and of Hikmet Bayur's comprehensive history of the Turkish revolution—*Türk Inkılâbı Tarihi* (1940 ff.). An excellent summary of political developments will be found in Tunaya, *Partiler*, pp. 161 ff. For a recent documentary study see Uzunçarşılı, '1908 yılında ikinci Meşrutiyetin ne Surette İlân Edildiğine dair vesikalar', *Bell.* no. 77 (1956), 103–74.

[95] Ramsaur, p. 134; Kuran, pp. 425 ff.   [96] Niyazi, pp. 83 ff.

summed up in a note written, on the eve of his departure, to his brother-in-law, Ismail Hakkı Bey, kaymakam of the kaza of Manastir, to whose care he entrusted his family:

I shall set out, with the help of God, in about an hour, and will therefore write briefly. . . . I see no point in lengthy explanations. The cause is known. Rather than live basely, I have preferred to die. I am therefore going out now, with two hundred patriots armed with Mausers, to die for our country. As to my family, please send them to Istanbul, as I explained to you yesterday, with my nephew Şevki, tomorrow if possible, otherwise Sunday. For the rest, either death or the salvation of the fatherland![97]

In the event, it was not Niyazi who died. That fate was reserved for Şemsi Paşa, the general appointed by the Sultan to suppress the mutineers and rebels. On 7 July Şemsi Paşa was shot in broad daylight as he was coming out of the telegraph office in Manastir; his assassin, one of the officers of the force that he commanded, walked calmly and unmolested away.[98]

The mutiny now spread rapidly among the different units of the Third Army Corps in Macedonia, and began to affect the Second Army Corps in Edirne. The Committee of Union and Progress came out into the open, adopting the mutineers and rebels and formulating a clear political demand—for the restoration of the constitution.

The Sultan at first attempted to resist this demand, and to deal with the leaders of the movement by the time-dishonoured alternatives of espionage, bribery, and repression. But this time all of them failed.[99] The spies despatched by the Sultan to report on the loyalty of the officers in Macedonia were detected, and added to the resentment of the army at this kind of insult and humiliation. The shower of decorations, promotions, and warrants for arrears of pay evoked no response from the dissident officers; the generals entrusted with repressions were fired on by their own men.[100]

The armies of Salonika and Manastir were now openly opposed to the Sultan, and were assured of the support of the Second Army Corps at Edirne. Even the faithful Anatolians, dispatched from Izmir to Salonika, were infected by Young Turk propaganda. The

[97] Ibid. p. 73; cf. Uzunçarşılı, in Bell., no. 77, 107 ff.

[98] Pears, Forty Years, p. 229; Ramsaur, p. 135; Y. H. Bayur, Türk. Ink. Tar., i. 219; Kuran, p. 427. Uzunçarşılı, pp. 109 ff.

[99] Pears, Forty Years, p. 234. 	[100] Ibid. pp. 231–2.

crisis came on 21 July 1908, when a telegram arrived at the Yıldız Palace from Serez, demanding the immediate restoration of the constitution. If the Sultan refused, the heir-apparent would be proclaimed as Sultan in Rumelia, and an army of 100,000 men would march on Istanbul. After two days of hesitation and discussion, the Sultan gave way, and on 24 July announced that the constitution was once again in force. The mutiny had become a revolution, and the revolution had achieved its goal. Only the details of the millennium remained to be arranged.

CHAPTER VII

Union and Progress

In order to warn our Muslim and Christian countrymen against the system of government of the present régime, which violates such human rights as justice, equality, and freedom, which withholds all Ottomans from progress and surrenders our country to foreign domination, an Ottoman Society of Union and Progress has been formed, composed of men and women all of whom are Ottomans.

PROGRAMME OF THE OTTOMAN SOCIETY OF UNION AND PROGRESS, *c.* 1890.

And although time has only partially fulfilled so many generous hopes, or has turned them to bitterness, I refuse to believe that they were totally insincere. I shall always count on it, on the contrary, among the most enlarging experiences of my life to have been in Constintinople in 1908, and to have seen a people at one of those rare moments when it really lives.

H. G. DWIGHT, 'CONSTANTINOPLE, SETTINGS AND TRAITS', 1926.

SOME ten years before the revolution, the poet Tevfik Fikret had written a famous ode—*Sis* (Mist)—describing the decay of Istanbul under the tyranny of Abdülhamid:

> Once more a stubborn mist has swathed your horizons . . .
> A dusty, fearsome darkness, which the eye
> Takes care not to pierce, for it is afraid.
> But for you this deep, dark veil is right and fitting,
> This veiling becomes you well, O scene of evil deeds . . .
> Yes, veil yourself, O tragedy, veil yourself, O city;
> Veil yourself and sleep forever, whore of the world![1]

In 1908 the triumphant optimism of the revolution was given words by the same poet:

> Now we are far from that accursed night,
> The night of calamity has joined the nights of oblivion,
> Our eyes have opened to a radiant morning.
> Between you, O world of renewal, and that ill-omened night
> There is no kinship; you are noble and great.
> There is no mist or shade about your face, only splendour and majesty,
> A bursting brightness like the dawning sun.[2]

The long night of Hamidian despotism was over; the dawn of freedom had come. The constitution had once again been proclaimed and elections ordered. Turks and Armenians embraced

[1] Akyüz, *Antoloji*, p. 236.

[2] Ibid. p. 239. The poem, entitled 'Rücu' (Return) is dated 24 July 1908.

in the streets; the age of freedom and brotherhood had come. The writings of that time reflect an almost delirious joy, which found its echoes even in the sceptical European press.

The second Turkish constitutional régime lasted longer than the first, but it too ended in failure, bitterness, and disappointment. The dangers and difficulties, at home and abroad, were too great; the defenders of the constitution were too few, too weak, too inept. Though the constitution remained in force and elections were still held, the régime degenerated into a kind of military oligarchy of the Young Turk leaders, which ended only with the defeat of the Ottoman Empire in 1918.

A Turkish historian of the Turkish Revolution, in a book published in 1940, has remarked that 'there are very few movements in the world that have given rise to such great hopes as the Ottoman Constitutional Revolution; there are likewise very few movements whose hopes have been so swiftly and finally disappointed.[3]

Even at the time, and still more later, there were many foreign observers who, out of prejudice, misunderstanding, or disappointment were ready to write off the whole Young Turk movement and revolution as mere window-dressing, as yet another attempt to mislead the West with a show of change while leaving the basic realities of Turkish life unchanged, perhaps unchangeable. Others went even farther, and tried to explain the Young Turks as something alien and irrelevant, an interlude by foreign players, unconnected with either the preceding or the following acts. In this way various writers, mostly adherents of the conspiratorial conception of history, have attributed the revolution of 1908 to the Jews, the Freemasons, the Roman Catholic Church, the positivists, the house of Orléans, the German General Staff, and the British Foreign Office.[4]

[3] Y. H. Bayur, *Türk Ink. Tar.*, i. 225.

[4] On these various stories, see Ramsaur, pp. 88 ff., 103 ff., 107 ff., 140 ff. The story of a Jewish Masonic plot, because of special circumstances, received for a while a wide circulation outside the circles in which this approach to history usually flourishes, and therefore requires a brief notice. Originating in a line of clerical and nationalist thought familiar on the Continent, it was taken up in some British circles, and a few years later was seized upon by Allied propagandists as a means of discrediting their Turkish enemies. The Young Turks, since the revolution, had been remarkably successful in their propaganda among non-Ottoman Muslims, both with pan-Turkish and pan-Islamic appeals (see below, p. 337). It seemed therefore a good idea to demonstrate that they themselves were neither Turks nor Muslims. A characteristic

The Young Turk Revolution was in fact none of these things; it was a patriotic movement of Muslim Turks, mostly soldiers, whose prime objective was to remove a fumbling and incompetent ruler and replace him by a government better able to maintain and defend the Empire against the dangers that threatened it. Ottoman non-Muslims played a small and diminishing role in the movement and the régimes that grew out of it; foreigners hardly any at all. The young officers were little interested in ideologies and social panaceas as such. The fundamental question that concerned them was survival, the survival of the Ottoman state which they and their fathers had for generations served, and both their actions and their discussions revolved around this central problem. *Bu devlet nasıl kurtarılabilir?*—How can this state be saved?

It is, perhaps, through the different solutions that were sketched and attempted for this problem, that the Young Turk Revolution, despite its disappointments and its failures, was so profoundly

statement will be found in R. W. Seton-Watson's *Rise of Nationality in the Balkans* (1917, pp. 135–6): 'The main fact about the Committee of Union and Progress is its essentially un-Turkish and un-Moslem character. From the very first hardly one among its true leaders has been a pure-blooded Turk. Enver is the son of a renegade Pole. Djavid belongs to the Jewish sect of Dunmehs. Carasso is a Sephardim Jew from Salonika. Talaat is an Islamised Bulgarian gipsy. Achmet Riza, one of the group's temporary figureheads, is half Circassian and half Magyar, and a Positivist of the school of Comte.' An admittedly fictionalized picture of the Young Turks will be found in John Buchan's famous romance *Greenmantle*, where for good measure Enver Paşa is made a Polish Jew. This curious story of Enver Paşa's Polish origin is probably due to a confusion with Enver Celâleddin Paşa, a general staff officer who was the son of the Polish renegade Count Constantine Bozęcki (on whom see below, p. 339).

The Turks of the Young Turk period were very far from thinking in such terms as 'pure-blooded Turks', and no doubt Turkish-speaking Ottoman Muslims of Balkan, Caucasian, and other origin played a considerable part in the movement. There seems, however, to be no evidence at all, in the voluminous Turkish literature on the Young Turks, that Jews ever played a part of any significance in their councils, either before or after the Revolution, or that the Masonic lodges were ever more than an occasional cover for their secret meetings. The Salonika lawyer Carasso, whose name is frequently mentioned by European opponents of the Young Turks, was a minor figure. Cavid, who did play a role of great importance, was a *dönme* (a Judaeo-Islamic syncretist sect founded in the seventeenth century) and not a real Jew; he seems in any case to have been the only member of his community to reach front rank. (For some interesting observations on the role of the *dönme* and the Turkish reaction to it see Leskovikli Mehmed Rauf, *Ittihad ve Terakki Cemiyeti ne idi?* (1327 A.H.), pp. 79 ff. In November 1911 Ebüzziya Tevfik, who had several times expressed concern about Zionism, for the first time connects the masonic lodges with Jewish purposes. He is careful to exonerate the Unionists, whose use of the lodges for their own purposes was justifiable when the need for secrecy was paramount. See 'Italyan Farmason Locaları ve Siyonizm', *Mecmua-i Ebüzziya*, no. 121 (1329 A.H.), pp. 129–34.)

important in the development of modern Turkey. In the few years of freedom that followed the ending of Abdülhamid's autocracy, there was an opportunity for discussion and experiment such as the country had never known before. In a spate of periodicals and books, the basic problems of religion and nationality, of freedom and loyalty in the modern state, were discussed and examined; in the new parliamentary and administrative apparatus that followed the Revolution, new methods of government were devised and put to the test. And even though the discussions ended in silence and the experiments in dictatorship, new hopes and new appetites had been created which could not be indefinitely denied.

The Young Turks in Power [5]

From the first, the Young Turks in power were divided between the two tendencies that had already appeared during the phase of opposition and exile. On the one hand were the liberals, in favour of some measure of decentralization and of some autonomous rights for the religious and national minorities; on the other, the nationalists, coming out more and more clearly for central authority and Turkish domination. The instrument of the latter was the Committee of Union and Progress, at first as the silent and self-effacing power behind the throne, later as an unashamed contender for supreme authority. The liberals, divided into many different groups, formed a series of ephemeral parties, the most important being the *Ahrar*, or liberal party of 1908 and the so-called Liberal Union of 1911.[6] Neither was able to accomplish very much.

At first it seemed that liberal and moderate ideas were indeed

[5] The years 1908–18 are well documented, in both Turkish and foreign sources. From the time of the Revolution onwards, there was a flood of memoirs, reports, journalistic, diplomatic, and political accounts, &c., often containing important material. A few major and many minor Turkish figures of the time have left memoirs, which have so far hardly been touched by Western scholarship. The only extensive historical treatment is that given by Y. H. Bayur in his large-scale history of the Turkish Revolution. Among shorter treatments, mention may be made of the useful if somewhat wilful chronology of events prepared by Danişmend, *Kronoloji*, iv. 356–455; Sax, pp. 545–654 (the best informed, on Turkish internal developments, of those who treat Turkish history in terms of the 'Eastern Question'); Emin, *Turkey in the World War* (1930); and Tunaya, *Partiler*, pp. 161–398 (for an invaluable account, with documents, of political parties and ideologies). Finally, mention should be made of the detailed and documented biographies of the Grand Vezirs given by Inal in his *Sadrıazamlar*.

[6] On these parties see below, pp. 372 ff.

P

about to prevail. Said Paşa and Kâmil Paşa,[7] the first two Grand Vezirs of the constitutional era, were elder statesmen who enjoyed both the support of the Ottoman liberals and the respect of most others. But whatever the intentions of the Young Turks, they were almost at once subjected to a series of blows, from inside and outside the Empire, that threw them into a mood of anger, bitterness, and frustration. It is difficult to judge how sincere the Young Turks may have been in their promises and proclamations of freedom and equality; it is, however, undeniable that the immediate response of Europe and of the Balkan Christians to the heart-lifting events of July 1908 was what, in Turkish eyes, could only be described as aggression and betrayal. Austria seized the opportunity to proclaim the annexation of Bosnia and Herzegovina; Bulgaria declared her independence; Crete announced her union with Greece. The precedents had been set which were to be followed by Italy, in her attack on Ottoman Tripolitania in September 1911, and by the Balkan States, in their combined attack on Turkey in October 1912.

While the Christian subjects and neighbours of the Turks were demonstrating the unworkability of a multi-national Ottoman state, the Turks themselves vividly illustrated some of the dangers of weakened central control. On 13 February 1909 the Committee, dissatisfied for various reasons with Kâmil Paşa's government, secured his fall and replacement, as Grand Vezir, by Hüseyin Hilmi Paşa,[8] another survivor of the old régime, but more acceptable for the moment to the nationalist Young Turks.

Both the Sultan and the liberals were now opposed to the régime, and both have been accused, not without some colour, of complicity in the events that followed. During the preceding months, the constitutional revolution had been sadly tarnished, in the public eye, by the immediate loss of territory and prestige, and by the failure of the millennium, in general, to make its appearance. Anger was mounting against the Committee, too, because of the cavalier way in which, while remaining in the background, they manipulated government appointments. They were also accused of using intimidation and murder against

---

[7] On Said Paşa, see above, p. 175 n. 7. Kâmil Paşa is missing in both *EI*[1] and *IA*. There are, however, biographies by his grandson H. K. Bayur, *Sadrazam Kâmil Paşa Siyasî Hayatı* (1954), and Inal, *Sadrıazamlar*, pp. 1347–472. Kâmil's own memoirs, published in 1911, refer to the period of Abdülhamid.

[8] On Hüseyin Hilmi Paşa, see Inal, *Sadrıazamlar*, pp. 1654–703.

political opponents, and when, on 7 April, Hasan Fehmi, the liberal editor of the *Serbesti*, was mysteriously murdered on the Galata bridge in Istanbul, the Committee was widely believed to be responsible, and became the object of much criticism and abuse.[9]

On 12 April, after a week of mounting tension, the Committee of Union and Progress published a statement in the press saying that it was no longer a secret association, but had become an ordinary political party.[10] The same night, only one month after the fall of Kâmil Paşa, an armed, reactionary rising broke out. Some part in this rising was played by the so-called Muhammadan Union, an extremist religious organization founded on 5 April at a meeting in the Santa Sophia mosque.[11] Its journal, the *Volkan*, edited by a Bektaşi dervish called Vahdetî, posed as a champion of Muslim orthodoxy and of a 'revolutionary Islamic internationalism'.[12] Another exponent of these ideas was none other than Murad Bey,[13] the erstwhile radical and renegade—now a purveyor of militant pan-Islamism, and a stalwart of the Muhammadan Union. The actual rising took the form of a mutiny by the soldiers, largely Albanian, of the First Army Corps stationed in Istanbul. It began on the night of the 12–13 April, when some *chasseur* and infantry units mutinied in their barracks, crossed the Galata bridge in the early morning, and assembled in the Santa Sophia Square outside the parliament building. They encountered little resistance, and were joined by mutineers from other units as well as by some mollahs and theological students. Other bands gathered in the main centres of the city. The demands of the mutineers were simple—'The *Şeriat* is in danger, we want the *Şeriat*!' Some of them added that they did not want college-trained officers.

The government floundered helplessly in the crisis; the Sultan obliged with the time-honoured response to violent dissatisfaction —a change of Grand Vezir. Further, he promised protection for the Holy Law and an amnesty for the soldiers who had mutinied to defend it. On 15 April a circular went out to all provincial

---

[9] For contemporary Western accounts of these events, see Francis McCullagh, *The Fall of Abd-ul-Hamid* (1910), pp. 23 f., 71 ff.; Pears, *Forty Years*, pp. 274–5.

[10] McCullagh, p. 74.   [11] Tunaya, *Partiler*, p. 261.

[12] Ibid. pp. 226–3; cf. Lowther's comments in Gooch and Temperley, v. 319.

[13] See above, p. 189 n. 55, and Fevziye Abdullah, pp. 85 ff.

governors, instructing them to safeguard the *Şeriat*. In the Chamber, the positivist Ahmed Rıza was deposed from the speaker's chair, where he had reigned since the Revolution, and Ismail Kemal elected in his place.[14]

The counter-blow was not long delayed. News of the reactionary rising was soon telegraphed to Salonika, and an 'Army of Deliverance',[15] commanded by General Mahmud Şevket Paşa, advanced on Istanbul. With him were Niyazi and also Enver, who had returned post-haste from the Turkish Embassy in Berlin on hearing the news. The deliverers reached the capital on 23 April, and occupied it, after some clashes with the mutineers, on the following day.[16]

The reactionary movement was by no means limited to Istanbul. With suspicious simultaneity a wave of outbreaks spread across Anatolia. Particularly bad were the events in the Adana district, which culminated in the massacre of thousands of Armenians. Responsibility for this was variously allocated. While Europe was appalled by Turkish brutality, Muslim opinion was shocked by what seemed to them the insolence of the Armenians and the hypocrisy of Christian Europe.

The Turks were, however, well aware of the painful effects produced by these massacres in Europe, which had not yet forgotten the horrors of Hamidian repression. They were at some pains to remove it. On the Sunday after the entry of the deliverers into Istanbul, some fifty men who had fallen in the fighting were solemnly buried, with a public ceremony, in a common grave.

[14] Ismail Kemal, *Memoirs*, p. 335.

[15] This is the common European designation. In Turkish it is simply called *hareket ordusu*—Route Army.

[16] The mutiny is known in Turkish annals as the '31 March Incident', following the old-style Greek calendar then in use for various purposes. Contemporary accounts will be found in McCullagh; A. Sarrou, *La Jeune-Turquie et la Révolution* (1912), pp. 77 ff.; Pears, *Forty Years*, pp. 257 ff. D. W. Dwight, *Constantinople; Settings and Traits* (1926), pp. 425 ff.; Sir W. M. Ramsay, *The Revolution in Constantinople and Turkey* (1909), pp. 11 ff. as well as in the reports of foreign diplomats, e.g. Gooch and Temperley v. 313–19). Among Turkish accounts are those of Ismail Kemal (*Memoirs*, pp. 329 ff.); Ali Fuad Türkgeldi (1867–1935—a former palace Chief Secretary and Counsellor to the Grand Vezirate, whose memoirs cover events in the palace and cabinet from the Young Turk Revolution to the end of the Empire), *Görüp İşittiklerim* (1951), pp. 25 ff.; Hasan Amca (pseud.), *Doğmayan Hürriyet* (1958), pp. 67 ff.; and a very detailed one by Yunus Nadi, *İhtilâl ve İnkılâb-i Osmani* (1325 A.H.) (an abridged paraphrase of this was published in the newspaper *Cumhuriyet*, in twenty instalments, in Mar.–Apr.1959). The fullest accounts are those of McCullagh and Yunus Nadi. See further Kuran, pp. 460 ff.; Y. H. Bayur, *Türk İnk. Tar.* i. 295 ff.; Danişmend, iv. 370

In a speech delivered over the grave, Enver Bey 'emphasized . . . that Moslems and Christians were lying side by side in token that they, living or dying, were henceforward fellow-patriots who would know no distinction of race or creed'.[17]

The Committee of Union and Progress were now firmly in the saddle, and took care not to be unseated again. Their first task was to depose Sultan Abdülhamid who, having managed to survive the 1908 revolution, was now sent into ignominious exile in Salonika.[18] The new Sultan, Mehmed Reşad, was at the mercy of the Committee, who made a clean sweep of the palace and put their own nominees into key positions there.[19] From now on, the Committee of Union and Progress were the undisputed masters of Turkey. What they meant by 'no distinction of race or creed' became clearer a few months later, with the publication of the new 'Law of Associations' on 16 August and the 'Law for the Prevention of Brigandage and Sedition' on 27 September.[20] The first of these prohibited the formation of political associations based on or bearing the name of ethnic or national groups, and was followed immediately by the closure of the Greek, Bulgarian, and other minority clubs and societies in Rumelia. The second authorized the formation of special 'pursuit battalions' from the army, and prescribed strong measures for the disarming and repression of armed bands and of the famous Balkan *komitadjis*. Severe penalties were imposed for failure to report *komitadji* activities to the authorities and for the unauthorized possession of

[17] Pears, *Forty Years*, p. 282.

[18] The deposition of Abdülhamid has been described by many writers, most of whom have concentrated on the final phase—the unanimous vote of parliament to depose him, and the sending of a delegation of four, two deputies and two senators, to convey the decision of parliament to the Sultan. Interesting information on an earlier phase is given in the memoirs of Ali Fuad Türkgeldi, who describes the pressures used by Talât Bey to extract a *fetva* authorizing the Sultan's deposition from the reluctant religious authority. When Talât demanded that the *Şeyh-ül-Islâm* accompany him to parliament, the latter objected that he was too ill. 'What is the matter with you?' asked Talât. 'I can't hold my water,' said the *Şeyh-ül-Islâm*. 'Then bring a bed-pan with you, and come', said Talât (Türkgeldi, p. 36). See further Pears, *Forty Years*, pp. 284 ff. and *Abdul Hamid*, pp. 295 ff.; McCullagh, pp. 265 ff.; Danişmend, iv. 376 ff.

[19] Halid Ziya Uşaklığil, who was appointed palace Chief Secretary at this time as a nominee of the Committee of Union and Progress, gives a lively picture of the fear and apprehension with which he was awaited by the palace staff and even by the Sultan himself. (*Saray ve Ötesi*, i (1940), 12 ff.)

[20] Y. H. Bayur, *Türk. Ink. Tar.*, i. 306.

weapons. To complete the pattern, steps were taken, for the first time, to conscript non-Muslims into the armed forces.

Whatever the measure of sincerity that lay behind the promises of the Ottoman constitution, the march of events soon made those promises unrealizable. The spread of nationalism among the subject peoples of the Empire, and the final contamination, by the nationalist virus, of even the Turkish masters of it, ended for ever the 'Ottomanist' dream of the free, equal, and peaceful association of peoples in a common loyalty to the dynastic sovereign of a multi-national, multi-denominational empire.[21] In August 1910 the British acting Consul in Manastir reported a speech made by Talât Bey to a 'secret conclave' of the Salonika Committee of Union and Progress, in these terms:

You are aware that by the terms of the Constitution equality of Mussulman and Ghiaur was affirmed but you one and all know and feel that this is an unrealizable ideal. The Sheriat, our whole past history and the sentiments of hundreds of thousands of Mussulmans and even the sentiments of the Ghiaurs themselves, who stubbornly resist every attempt to ottomanize them, present an impenetrable barrier to the establishment of real equality. We have made unsuccessful attempts to convert the Ghiaur into a loyal Osmanli and all such efforts must inevitably fail, as long as the small independent States in the Balkan Peninsula remain in a position to propagate ideas of Separatism among the inhabitants of Macedonia. There can therefore be no question of equality, until we have succeeded in our task of ottomanizing the Empire—a long and laborious task, in which I venture to predict that we shall at length succeed after we have at last put an end to the agitation and propaganda of the Balkan States.

In a comment written a few days later, the British ambassador, Sir Gerald Lowther, remarked to Sir Edward Grey:

That the Committee have given up any idea of Ottomanizing all the non-Turkish elements by sympathetic and Constitutional ways has long been manifest. To them 'Ottoman' evidently means 'Turk' and their present policy of 'Ottomanization' is one of pounding the non-Turkish elements in a Turkish mortar. . . .[22]

[21] Yorgi Bosho, a Christian deputy from the Balkans in the Young Turk parliament, infuriated the Turks by his ironic remark 'I am as Ottoman as the Ottoman Bank' (Talât, *Hatıralar* (1946), p. 15; Duru, *Hatıralarım*, p. 3).

[22] Gooch and Temperley, ix 1. 207–9 (cited by Z. N. Zeine, *Arab-Turkish Relations and the Emergence of Arab Nationalism* (1958), p. 75).

The repressive and centralist policies of the Young Turks were by no means limited to the Christian subjects of the Empire. In both Rumelia and the Asian provinces, they followed a policy of Turkification, and attempted to impose the Turkish language on Arabs, Albanians, and other non-Turkish Muslims. Even in the capital, a new ferocity and ruthlessness appear in the treatment of the opposition elements. Whatever brutalities he condoned in the treatment of humble unbelievers in remote provinces, Sultan Abdülhamid had always hesitated to impose the death penalty on Turks and Muslims; at times he had gone to the limit of leniency in dealing even with armed sedition against himself, rather than shed the blood of members of the governing *élite*. The Young Turks—young, patriotic, soldierly, and efficient—had no such scruples. The suppression of the reactionary mutiny in April 1909 was followed by a court martial, and the public hanging of a number of mutineers and reactionaries. The first to be hanged was Nadir Ağa, the chief Eunuch of the Imperial household.[23] Mahmud Şevket Paşa, the commander of the Army of Deliverance, proclaimed a state of siege in the city, which was extended for two years.[24]

From 1909 till 1911 the Committee, through its men in and behind the government, remained in effective control of the Empire. Its supremacy was by no means unchallenged, and rival factions, dissenting for personal or policy reasons from the dominant group, appeared inside as well as outside the Committee organization. Opposition was of more than one kind, as was shown by the discovery, in July 1910, of a reactionary conspiracy headed by the gendarme officer, Ali Kemal.[25]

The domination of the Committee was, however, not seriously shaken until 1911, when for the first time they had to face a serious internal threat. The first signs of a parliamentary opposition had begun to appear in the first parliament after the restoration of the constitution. The crises that followed, however, and the imposition and maintenance of martial law after the failure of the mutiny, had impeded the development of any very effective constitutional opposition. At the beginning of 1911 the growing dissatisfaction in many quarters with the trend of events found expression in the first major split in the Unionist ranks. A group called the 'New Party' (*Hizb-i Cedid*) was formed, under the leadership of Colonel

[23] Pears, *Forty Years*, pp. 302–3.   [24] Sax, p. 573.   [25] Ibid. pp. 574–5.

Sadık and Abdülaziz Mecdi Bey, which offered serious criticisms of the political and social policies followed by the Committee.[26] On 23 April the group, which rapidly mustered considerable support in the party, published a ten-point memorandum, setting forth its demands.[27] Most of these were concerned with the better observance of democratic and constitutional procedures, and with similar improvements. Some, however, indicate another line of thought. Thus no. 6 seeks, 'while preserving general religious and national ethics and morals, to make use of the advances and products of Western civilization for the development of the Ottoman Empire': no. 7 demands 'the maintenance and safeguarding, within the framework of the constitution, of historic Ottoman traditions'; while no. 9 goes even farther, and demands the amendment of certain clauses in the constitution so as to reinforce the 'sacred rights of the Caliphate and Sultanate'. In a speech, Mecdi Bey made the point clearer.[28] There were, he said, three tendencies in the country—reactionary fanaticism, recklessly fast progress, and the movement for cultural progress with the preservation of existing customs and traditions. It was the third that he and his friends desired. The appearance of this rather right-wing group was paralleled by the emergence of a left-wing splinter group, the Progress Party (*Hizb-i Terakki*) which, however, remained more closely attached to the Committee and its programme.[29]

These matters were all thrashed out at a party congress held in August–September 1911. This, incidentally, was the last party congress held secretly in Salonika, which was shortly afterwards lost to the Ottoman Empire. The remaining congresses of the Committee of Union and Progress, those of 1912, 1913, 1916, 1917, and the final congress of 1918, assembled in Istanbul.[30] The 1911 congress—the first, according to a Turkish author, 'with heat and argument'—met in an atmosphere of great tension, generated by the threatening international situation.[31] After thundering against the Italian aggression at Tripoli, which occurred while the congress was in session, the delegates managed to reach a compromise declaration covering the points of policy raised by the dissident groups.

[26] Tunaya, *Partiler*, p. 186; Sax, p. 588.   [27] The text is given by Tunaya.

[28] Sax, p. 589.   [29] Tunaya, *Partiler*, p. 187.

[30] Ibid. p. 189.   [31] Ibid. p. 191.

These resolutions did little more than paper over the cracks. Some of the seceders remained outside the party, and other resignations followed, weakening the authority and diminishing the prestige of the once all-powerful Committee. On 21 November 1911 a new party was formed, the so-called Liberal Union,[32] by the merging of almost all the groups, parties, and personalities opposed to the Committee of Union and Progress.

Most of the founders of the Liberal Union were already members of parliament, and they were thus able immediately to form a parliamentary opposition. Their first real contest with the Unionists came when the party was only twenty days old. The appointment of the Foreign Minister Rifat Paşa as ambassador to London left a vacant seat in Istanbul. In the resulting by-election, there were two candidates; the Minister of the Interior, Memduh Bey, for the Unionists, and the liberal journalist Tahir Hayreddin[33] for the Liberal Union. The liberal candidate was elected by a majority of a single vote of the electoral college.

This by-election, held on 11 December 1911, was the first genuine electoral contest between two candidates, each representing a different party and programme. The victory of the opposition candidate created a new and unprecedented situation, and to many at the time seemed almost as important a victory as the 1908 revolution itself. After the constitutional millennium, the democratic redemption was coming, and the Liberal Union leader, Damad Ferid Paşa, prepared with vigour for the role.[34]

Public opinion in the capital had asserted itself in a striking form against the Unionist régime. Another voice was now raised— that of the venerable Kâmil Paşa, one of the two most eminent elder statesmen of the country, and a keen supporter of the liberals against the Unionists. On 20 December 1911 Kâmil Paşa, then wintering in Egypt, sent a letter to the Sultan, in which he blamed the Unionists for the misfortunes of the Empire, and demanded the raising of the state of siege and the dissolution of the Committee of Union and Progress. At the same time he

[32] In Turkish *Hürriyet ve Itilaf* (Freedom and Association). The official name in French was *Entente libérale*.

[33] He was the son of the liberal Grand Vezir Tunuslu Hayreddin Paşa (d. 1889) on whom see Inal, *Sadrıazamlar*, pp. 894–960 and *EI¹ s.v.* 'Khair al-Din'.

[34] On Damad Ferid Paşa, see Inal, *Sadrıazamlar*, pp. 2029–94 and *EI²*, *s.v.* (by D. A. Rustow).

proposed an alliance with England as the best means of preventing further disasters.[35]

Faced with this dangerous combination, against them, of freedom and authority, the Committee acted swiftly against both. Kâmil Paşa's memorandum was denounced in the press, and used to discredit him; the tone was set by Hüseyin Cahid [Yalçın], who discussed it in a leader entitled 'A Voice from the Grave'.[36] In January 1912 the Unionists procured the dissolution of parliament, and in April held a general election so well prepared and conducted that, out of a total of 275, only six opposition members managed to slip through into the chamber. The first opposition victory in a by-election had been followed by the first general election held under the pressure of the ruling party. A second precedent had been established. This election is known in Turkish history as 'the big-stick election'.[37]

The Unionists now finally transferred their headquarters from Salonika to Istanbul, where, with an obedient parliament and a submissive Sultan, they seemed to be in full and undisputed control. But difficulties were growing; the war against Italy was going badly, and there were troubles in many of the provinces, notably in Salonika. The Committee had crushed the liberal parliamentary opposition by dissolving the old chamber and packing the new one through a shamelessly dishonest election. By thus illegally removing the legal opposition, the Committee inevitably called into being a new opposition, not democratic or parliamentary, but military and conspiratorial—a ghost from its own past. The Committee of Union and Progress had gone to Istanbul and become the oppressors—so once again young officers in Rumelia took to the hills, where they could now count on a welcome from the Albanian rebels.

In May–June 1912 a group of 'Saviour Officers' (*Haláskâr Zabitân*) was formed in Istanbul, apparently in relation with the rebel officers in Rumelia.[38] Their objective was to remove an illegal government and parliament, to break the power of the Committee of Union and Progress, to hold new and free elections, and to return to constitutional legality. Like all the opposition

[35] H. K. Bayur, *Kâmil Paşa*, pp. 307–12; Sax, pp. 589–90.

[36] H. K. Bayur, *Kâmil Paşa*, p. 308 and n.1.

[37] Tunaya, *Partiler*, p. 322. cf. Kuran, pp. 496–7.

[38] Tunaya, *Partiler*, pp. 345 ff.; Sax, p. 590.

parties of the Young Turk period, this group of military conspirators demanded the withdrawal of the army from politics. The
army would of course have to mend what the army had marred;
after that it could return to its proper task of defending the
Empire, leaving its government to the politicians and officials.
Faithful to this principle, the group accepted no civilian recruits,
and allowed its numbers to accept no governmental appointments.[39]

By the end of June the situation in Albania was causing serious
alarm, and criticism of the Unionist government headed by Said
Paşa grew rapidly. On 14 July the Minister of War Mahmud
Şevket Paşa resigned. This sacrifice failed to appease the critics,
and on 16 July the government felt it necessary to seek a vote of
confidence from the Chamber. After speeches by the Grand Vezir
and the Foreign Minister making light of the troubles in Albania,
they obtained their vote with only four dissentients.[40]

The 'Saviour Officers' now went into action. A manifesto in the
press, a declaration sent through the Army Council to the Sultan
and, above all, certain ominous military movements and preparations, brought swift results. On 17 July, less than twenty-four hours
after receiving their overwhelming vote of confidence from the
Chamber, Said Paşa and his cabinet resigned. When the Sultan
asked him a few days later 'Why did you resign? They still have
confidence in you', Said Paşa replied: 'They have confidence in
me, but I have no confidence in them.'[41] On the day of the
resignation the Saviours held a meeting at Bostancı, to which
came a delegation of three pashas from the resigning government, to discover the Saviours' terms. These were simple:
Nazım Paşa to be Minister of War, Kâmil Paşa to be a member
of the government. The choice of Grand Vezir was left to the
Sultan.

After a brief stop-gap ministry of Tevfik Paşa, the new cabinet
was constituted on 21 July 1912. The Grand Vezir was the scholar
and soldier Gazi Ahmed Muhtar Paşa (1839–1918);[42] Nazım
Paşa and Kâmil Paşa became Ministers of War and Foreign
Affairs respectively. At the end of October Kâmil Paşa again took
over the Grand Vezirate.

With the formation of Gazi Ahmed Muhtar Paşa's government,

[39] Ibid. p. 347.   [40] Ibid. pp. 348–9.   [41] Türkgeldi, p. 35.
[42] See Inal, *Sadrıazamlar*, pp. 1803–68.

known among the Turks as 'the great cabinet',[43] the first and basic demand of the opposition was met—the ousting from power of the C.U.P. Other steps soon followed. The state of siege was lifted the very next day, the Committee-dominated parliament was dissolved on 15 August, and an oath exacted from all serving officers not to interfere in politics, as well as a written undertaking to the same effect: '. . . I swear by God and guarantee by my honour that I will not enter any political society, secret or public, nor interfere in any way whatsoever in the internal or external affairs of the state'.[44]

The government was already fully occupied with the Italian war when, in October 1912, a new blow fell: the attack of the Balkan allies. The 'Saviour Officers' were now fully occupied with the waging of war, and the C.U.P., ousted but by no means destroyed, prepared for its return to power.

Kâmil's cabinet, struggling with a desperate situation, seemed to many to be weak and incompetent, and, as the Balkan armies approached the walls of Istanbul, the Committee completed its plans for a return to power.

On 23 January 1913, when the cabinet was believed—wrongly, as it appears—to be considering a proposal to cede Edirne to the Bulgarians, the Unionists launched their surprise assault on the Sublime Porte. Led by Enver Bey, a small party of officers forced their way into the cabinet room, shooting the Minister of War Nazım Paşa dead as they did so. At the point of their guns, the aged Kâmil Paşa wrote out his resignation, which Enver triumphantly took to the palace and presented to the Sultan.[45]

The Committee had made their preparations in the army, the police, the government offices. They were now firmly in power again, and secured the appointment of Mahmud Şevket Paşa as Grand Vezir. His murder, on 11 June 1913, provided them with

---

[43] Also as the 'Father-and-son cabinet (*Baba-oğul Kabinesi*)', because of the presence of the Grand Vezir's son, Mahmud Muhtar Paşa, as Minister of Marine (Y. H. Bayur, *Türk. Ink. Tar.* iv/4, 219 ff.; Danişmend, iv. 388; Sax, p. 591).

[44] Tunaya, *Partiler*, p. 350 n. 30.

[45] On the coup d'état see Sax, p. 591; Kuran, pp. 519 ff.; Danişmend, iv. 398 (where different versions of events are discussed). Y. H. Bayur, *Türk. Ink. Tar.*, ii/4, pp. 271 ff.; Inal, pp. 1411 ff. and 1874 ff.; H. K. Bayur, *Kâmil Paşa*, pp. 386 ff. Contemporary accounts in Türkgeldi, pp. 77 ff.; Cemalüddin Efendi (*Şeyh-ül-Islâm*, 1891–1908, 1908–9, 1912–13; he was deposed after the coup d'état and left for Egypt where he wrote his memoirs), *Hâtırât-i Siyasiye* (1336/1917), pp. 52 ff.; Pears, *Forty Years*, p. 331; Cemal Paşa, *Memoirs*, pp. 1 ff.

the pretext for removing the last shreds of freedom and democracy. From then until 1918 Turkey was governed by a virtual military dictatorship, dominated by three men—Enver, Talât, and Cemal Paşas. Mahmud Şevket's immediate successor as Grand Vezir was Mehmed Said Halim Paşa (1863–1921), a member of the Egyptian Khedivial house and the author of a number of works pleading for an Islamic revival. He was, however, a captive of the Unionist leaders; finally in February 1917 he retired to the Senate, leaving Talât as Grand Vezir and the triumvirs openly in control.[46]

Enver Paşa[47] was born in Istanbul in 1881, the son of a father variously described, by his friends or enemies, as a railway official or a porter. A graduate of the War College in Istanbul, he soon joined the Young Turks, and first achieved fame as a 'hero of freedom' by his role in the revolution of 1908. After serving as military attaché in Berlin and then as a highly popular field officer, he returned to Istanbul and led the raid on the Sublime Porte. In 1913 he became Minister of War, general, and pasha; In 1914, by marrying an Ottoman princess, he even acquired the title of Damad.

Cemal Paşa,[48] born in Istanbul in 1872, to a military family, was a man of a very different stamp from the flamboyant, reckless, and self-indulgent Enver. He too was a product of the War College and an early recruit to the Young Turks. After the coup d'état of January 1913 he became military governor of Istanbul, and showed great skill in organizing the police forces and directing their work for the preservation of the régime. He later became Minister of Marine and army commander in Syria. He was known as a man of high professional competence in military matters, of personal authority and responsibility, and of a cold, fanatical ruthlessness when he judged it necessary for the cause he served.

The third, and by far the ablest of the triumvirate was Talât

---

[46] On Mehmed Said Halim Paşa see Inal, *Sadrıazamlar*, *s.v.* Some of Said Halim's works, written in French, were translated into Turkish by the poet Mehmed Akif. A group of his writings was reprinted under the title *Buhranlarımız* (1330 A.H.).

[47] Enver Paşa, alone among the Young Turk triumvirs, has left no published memoirs. He is missing from both *EI*[1] and *IA*, but a brief biography appears in Gövsa, *s.v.*

[48] Cemal Paşa's memoirs were published in Turkish (*Hâtırât, 1913–22*, 1922), German, French, and English (Ahmed Djemal Pasha, *Memories of a Turkish Statesman 1913–1919*, 1912. (cf. the Turkish volume, Cemal Paşa, *Hatıralar ve Vesikalar*, 1933). A modernized and annotated version was edited by Behcet Cemal (*Hatıralar*, 1959).

Paşa,[49] born in a poor home in Edirne in 1874. After attending
the local schools, he joined the staff of the telegraph office in
Edirne, and in due course was promoted chief secretary of
the directorate of posts and telegraphs in Salonika, where his
position enabled him to render great service to the Young Turk
cause. After the Revolution he rose rapidly in the councils of the
C.U.P., and held various appointments, including that of Minister
of the Interior for a while. In 1916 he became Grand Vezir. He
was a man of swift and penetrating intelligence, forceful when
necessary, but never fanatical or vengeful—'The Danton of the
Turkish Revolution', according to a contemporary European
observer.[50]

Under these three men the mechanism of state power was
wound tighter and tighter. The opposition parties were broken up,
their leaders exiled or made innocuous, and a ruthless repression
applied which for a time approached the proportions of a reign of
terror.

Their rule ended only with the defeat of Turkey in 1918, when
the Committee of Union and Progress disbanded itself, its leaders
fled abroad, and the liberal spokesmen emerged from exile, con-
cealment, or insignificance to quarrel for the privilege of presiding
over the dissolution of the Ottoman Empire.

The Achievements of the Young Turks

From 1908 until the final defeat of the Ottoman Empire in 1918,
the Unionists were, except for brief intervals, in control. Even
though they preferred, for much of the time, to leave the nominal
leadership of the government to ageing survivors of the past like
Said Paşa, Hüseyin Hilmi Paşa, or Ibrahim Hakkı Paşa, or, later,
to an intermediate figure like Said Halim Paşa, it was the Young
and not the old Turks who were the real masters.[51]

They have been harshly judged by history, and not without some
cause. They have been blamed for many things—the brutalizaton
of public life by violence, repression and terror; the intrusion of
the army into politics, leading to the twin evils of a militarized
government and a political command; the pursuit of policies, at

[49] The memoirs of Talât Paşa were edited by Huseyin Cahit Yalçın, *Talât Paşa'nın
Hatıraları* (1946). Having attained to the Grand Vezirate, he qualified for a biography
by Inal, *Sadrıazamlar*, pp. 1933–72.

[50] J. Østrup, *Det Nye Tyrki* (1931), pp. 77–78.

[51] Y. H. Bayur, in *Bell.*, no. 90 (1959), 272.

home and abroad, that led directly to the destruction of the Empire.

The record of the ten years from 1908 to 1918 is indeed, at first sight, a black one. The high hopes of the Revolution were swiftly disappointed, and the orderly progress of constitutional government was ended in the wretched cycle of plot and counterplot, repression and sedition, tyranny, humiliation, and defeat.

Yet there is another theme in the story, one that is often overlooked amid the alarums and excursions of the Young Turk drama. The ultimate and desperate concern of all the Young Turk factions and committees was the survival of the Empire, by now in manifest danger; like their predecessors, both reformers and revolutionaries, they believed that certain radical improvements in Ottoman state and society were needed to save them from inner decay and foreign attack. Behind all the hectic struggles of those years, the Committee and the government found time to give their attention to some of these problems, and to try and solve them by legislative and by administrative action. Though their work was often ill conceived, incomplete, and frustrated by events, they did nevertheless help to prepare the way, in many important respects, for the new Turkey that was to emerge after their disappearance.

One matter needing urgent attention was provincial and local administration. New difficulties had been added to old in the provinces and had, if anything, been aggravated rather than improved by reformist legislation. A new system of provincial and municipal government was now worked out and put into effect which, with only minor changes, provided the legal and administrative framework of the local and provincial government of the Turkish republic.

In Istanbul too the Young Turks made important and lasting changes. A new municipal organization provided for the more effective government of the capital of the Empire; an energetic programme of public works immensely improved the amenities of the city. The Young Turks may have failed to give Turkey constitutional government. They did, however, give Istanbul drains. Other improvements included the reorganization of the police, fire brigades, public transport services, and utilities. The famous packs of dogs that for centuries had patrolled the streets of the city were, by a decision of the municipal council, collected and shipped to a waterless island, to perish. They were replaced by relays of dustmen and scavengers.[52]

It was not only in Istanbul that the police were reorganized. The new-style gendarmerie, initiated in Macedonia under Abdülhamid, was now extended to many parts of the Empire, and training schools set up in Izmir and Beirut as well as Salonika. By a law of February 1912, the control of the gendarmerie was transferred from the Ministry of War to the Ministry of the Interior, and provincial gendarme posts placed at the disposal of the governors. A number of foreign, chiefly British officers and inspectors served in the Ottoman gendarmerie.[53]

The Young Turks, like most governments of their time, gave less attention to economic than to political and administrative problems. They did, however, attempt to tackle, with mixed results, one major economic problem—that of land[54] and also took the first steps in the policy of economic nationalism that was to develop under the Republic; in neither respect did they achieve any great success.

In social life, the movement of Westernization begun in the previous century gathered momentum. The old method of reckoning time gave way to the European twenty-four hour day. The Westernization of costume and manners went far enough to bring an anxious rejoinder from the religious authorities; in April 1911 the *Şeyh-ül-Islâm* issued a warning to Muslim women not to wear European dress, and in September of the same year the cabinet actually voted an order authorizing the arrest and fining of Muslims who publicly violated the fast of Ramazan.[55]

These measures, however, did little to halt the increasing modernization of society. An important factor was education, in which the Young Turks achieved their greatest successes. Building on the work of their predecessors, they created a new system of secular primary and secondary schools, teachers' training colleges and specialized institutes, with the reorganized University of Istanbul at the apex. A major change was the extension of educational opportunities for girls. Women of the highest classes of society had always had access to a good, private education; the

---

[52] Nuri, *Mec. Um. Bel.*, i. 960 ff.   [53] Pears, *Forty Years*, pp. 318–19; Sax, p. 606.

[54] On the land laws see E. Nord, *Die Reform des türkischen Liegenschaftsrechts* (1914); cf. below, pp. 442 ff.

[55] Sax, p. 589

Tanzimat reformers had added a few girls' schools, women's training colleges, and arts schools. The Young Turk régimes opened the doors first of the middle and secondary schools, then of the university, to girl students, thus preparing the way for their entry into the professions and into public life. The drain of men to the army during the war years created an urgent need for their services, and Turkish women, whose only possible professions had been nurse, midwife, or teacher, now appeared as doctors, civil servants, lawyers, and business women.

To women thus trained and employed, the seclusion of earlier times and the garments that symbolized it were an irritating and humiliating anachronism. Educated women were still few in numbers, but they enjoyed the sympathy and support of most men among the Young Turks; as a result the cause of female education and emancipation made noteworthy progress. In 1917 a new Family Law was approved, which marked an important step forward in the achievement of women's rights. The religious courts, which dealt with matters of family and personal status, were put under the jurisdiction of the Ministry of Justice—that is, of a modern, secular authority, above the religious hierarchy. Though, in an Islamic state, it was not possible to remove the two chief disabilities of women, polygamy and repudiation, the law did contain a number of revisions in favour of women, giving them the right to insert and enforce certain stipulations in marriage contracts, including the right of divorce and monogamy. This law, which could probably never have secured a parliamentary majority, was enacted by emergency order, and a small number of educated women actually took advantage of it.[56]

Intellectual and Cultural Movements [57]

It is perhaps in its intellectual and cultural life that the Young Turk period is most interesting and most significant. The

[56] On the Ottoman Family Law see Jäschke, 'Der Islam in der neuen Türkei', *WI*, n.s., i (1951), 13; Halide Edib, *Turkey Faces West* (1930), pp. 130–1. On social and cultural developments, valuable insights may be obtained from the writings of European Orientalists who visited or studied Turkey during the Young Turk period, notably M. Hartmann, *Der islamische Orient*, iii; *Unpolitische Briefe aus der Türkei* (1910); C. Snouck-Hurgronje, *Verspreide Geschriften*, iii (1923) (espec. no. 37); Becker, *Islamstudien*, ii (espec. nos. 37 and 38).

[57] By far the most comprehensive and illuminating studies of the ideological movements and conflicts in the Young Turk period are those of Tarık Tunaya on the Westernizing and pan-Islamic tendencies in the political thought of the second

proclamation of the constitution released a vast surge of ideas and self-expression that the seal of the Sultan's censorship had for so long contained. On 25 July 1908 the *Ikdam* published 60,000, the *Sabah* 40,000 copies; by the afternoon copies were changing hands at forty times the marked price.[58] A whole series of new literary, political, and other periodicals began to appear, and some of the major Young Turk organs were transferred from their places of exile to Istanbul. Voices that had long been silenced or muted spoke loud and clear; ideas long pent up now swirled into print. Although, after the mutiny of April 1909, repression and press control returned again to Turkey, even the coercion and bullying of the Unionists and the harshening conditions of the war years could never really quench the flow of new thought, expression, and argument.

In the literature of this period, foreign teachings once again provide the theoretical foundations of political and social criticism. The main source of these foreign intellectual influences is still France, but in place of the Enlightenment of the eighteenth century, the social science of the nineteenth century has come to dominate the thinking of Turkish reformers and revolutionaries. The first influence to emerge was that of Auguste Comte, whose positivist sociology inspired Ahmed Rıza to the first expositions of Union and Progress, and profoundly influenced the subsequent development of secularist radicalism in Turkey. Prince Sabaheddin, seeking a philosophy for his own rival school, found it in the teachings of Le Play and more especially of Demolins, whose ideas formed the basis of Sabaheddin's doctrines of individual

constitutional period, from the point of view of public law ('. . . Garpçılık Cereyanı', *Ist. Univ. Hukuk Fak. Mec.*, xiv (1948), 585–630, and '. . . Islamcılık Cereyanı', ibid. xix (1954), 1–41, and of Y. H. Bayur, *Türk Ink. Tar.*, ii/4, pp. 1 ff. Briefer and broader surveys by Tunaya will be found in his 'Türkiyenin Siyasi Gelişme Seyri içinde Ikinci "Jön Türk" Hareketinin Fikrî Esasları', in the volume presented by the Istanbul Law Faculty to Professor Tahir Taner (*Prof. Tahir Taner'e Armağan*, 1956), and in his *Partiler*, pp. 167 ff. Among other Turkish works see also Peyami Safa, *Türk Inkılabına Bakışlar* (c. 1938), and among earlier works, Ziya Gökalp, *Türkleşmek, Islamlaşmak, Muasırlaşmak* (1918) and reprints. For brief accounts in Western languages see Emin, *Press*, pp. 86 ff.; Rossi, 'Dall'Impero ottomano . . .', *OM*, xxiii (1943), 371 ff.; K. H. Karpat, *Turkey's Politics* (1959), 19 ff.; and three anonymous articles in the *RMM*, xxii (1913): 'Doctrines et programmes des partis politiques ottomans', pp. 151–64; 'Les Rapports du mouvement politique et du mouvement social dans l'Empire ottoman', pp. 165–78; and 'Le Panislamisme et le Panturquisme', pp. 179–220. According to Mlle A. M. Goichon (Jamâl ad-Din al-Afghânî, *Réfutation des matérialistes* (1942), p. 9), the last-named were written by S. H. Taghizade.

[58] Emin, *Press*, p. 87.

initiative and decentralization. Finally, it was in sociology, especially that of Émile Durkheim, that Ziya Gökalp found the conceptual framework within which he constructed the first elaborate theoretical formulation of Turkish nationalism.

A common feature of all these schools is their tendency to treat sociology as a kind of philosophy, even of religion, and as a source of quasi-revealed authority on moral, social, political, and even religious problems.

The Young Turks seem to have been less concerned with political theory than their nineteenth-century predecessors. In the period of opposition, their view of the power they were opposing was often naïvely personal. Abdülhamid was a tyrant; he must repent or retire. Various definitions were given of his tyranny. Sometimes it lay in his violation of the Holy Law and of the traditional standards of conduct of the good Muslim sovereign. More often—and perhaps more sincerely—the Young Turks condemned him for suspending the constitution and arresting the development of parliamentary government. In either case, it was his personal autocracy that was corrupting the political life of the country, excluding the 'light of civilization', and keeping the people backward, ignorant, and impoverished.

Our sovereign and our government [wrote Abdullah Cevdet in Geneva in 1897] do not want the light to enter our country: they want all the people to remain in ignorance, on the dunghill of misery and wretchedness; no torch of awakening may blaze in the hearts of our compatriots. What the government want is for the people to remain like beasts, submissive as sheep, fawning and servile as dogs. Let them hear no word of any honest lofty new idea. Instead, let them languish under the whips of ignorant gendarmes, under the aggressions of shameless, boorish, oppressive officials. . . . [59]

Against such a régime, revolt was both legitimate and necessary. The new régime to be established was still that of the earlier liberals—constitutional monarchy and parliamentary government. This would win for Turkey the respect of the West—always an important point with the Young Turks—and open the way to the political, social, and economic reforms that the country needed.

After the revolution of 1908 political discussion, naturally enough, became more concerned with current problems than with

[59] *Iki Emel* (1906), p. 4; Tunaya, in *Prof. Taner'e Armağan*, p. 3.

general principles. Political comment and criticism, though often wrapped up in imperfectly understood political terms and phrases borrowed from the European press, were basically concerned with one question—for or against the Committee of Union and Progress; and as the Committee became increasingly intolerant of criticism, the discussion of current issues became superficial and evasive.[60]

The Committee had no general objection to criticism; only to criticism of itself, and of its current actions. The discussion of the larger social, philosophic, and even—for the first time—religious issues was unimpeded, and the great debate about Turkey's future, begun by the Young Turks in exile, was now engaged with renewed vigour and extended scope.

Fundamentally the questions were the same as had been occupying Turkish statesman and memorialists since the sixteenth century—what is wrong with the Empire, why is it falling behind in the race with its infidel rivals, what must be done to save it? Many answers were offered and argued, some of them on lines already well known in the nineteenth century or earlier, some of them strange and new.

The problem of how to save the Empire from collapse or overthrow was old and familiar, even when the formulations and the solutions propounded bore a sociological and unfamiliar aspect. In discussing it, however, the writers and thinkers of this time found themselves face to face with a new and radical question, barely considered in earlier times; what was the nature of this entity that was to be saved? Official spokesmen and others continued to speak piously of 'the union of elements'[61]—the common Ottoman citizenship that was to unite all the Sultan's subjects, irrespective of race, creed, or language, in a single nationality and loyalty. Already during the Hamidian period, there were some among the Young Turks with sufficient perception—and sufficient frankness—to reject Ottomanism as an impossible fantasy. Their judgement was amply confirmed by the conduct both of the Turks and of their subjects during the years following the revolution. What existed was not a nation but a domination, the hegemony of the conquerors of an empire over the peoples they had conquered. The task of loyal members of the dominant group was to defend that group—its supremacy, or,

---

[60] Emin, *Press*, p. 95.   [61] In Turkish *ittihad-i anasır.*

failing that, its very existence—against the dangers that threatened it.

One of the most pressing of these dangers was uncertainty as to the very nature of that group. Were they Muslims, or were they Turks? Most of them, clearly, were both, but the question of whether the Muslim community or the Turkish nation was to be the basis of identity and focus of loyalty was one of the most hotly debated of the time. Much would depend on the answer— the social and cultural policies of the state, its international friendships and alignments, even, it might be, its territorial limits.

Linked with this question of corporate political identity were the deeper and vaster problems of civilization. To what civilization did the Turks belong—and in what civilization did their future lie? For the past millennium the Turkish peoples had formed a part—for long the dominant part—of the community of Islam, and their whole culture—religion and politics, law and art, society and government—was shaped in Islamic moulds and stamped with the imprint of the common Islamic past. For the past century they had been imitating the West, in an attempt— mainly unsuccessful—to save the Empire from collapse and win the respect of Europe by conforming to European patterns of culture and organization. With all its failures and disappointments, however, the movement of Westernization was continuing, and the Turkish people had come to a crisis of civilization—a turning-point in their history comparable, in its way, with that remote and half-forgotten time when their Central Asian ancestors had hesitated between China and Islam, and, then, too, had chosen the Western alternative.

Among the many solutions propounded in the writings of the Young Turk period to this crisis of culture, two general trends may be discerned—the Islamists and the Westernizers, with a wide range of compromise and confusion between them. Among the Islamists there were the four-square fundamentalists, for whom the faith and the Holy Law were the beginning and end of all wisdom, and derogation from them the cause of all Turkey's troubles. This view, commoner among the silent masses and the lower religious functionaries than among the articulate intellectuals, also found expression in the writings of such figures as the *Şeyh-ül-Islâm* Musa Kâzım Efendi (1858–1919).[62]

---

[62] On Musa Kâzım's writings, see Y. H. Bayur, *Türk Ink. Tar.*, ii/4, pp. 377 ff.; Tunaya, 'Islamcılık Cereyanı', *passim*.

More important were the moderate Islamists, most of them men with some Western education, who saw the need for some measures of reform in Islam, and sought desperately for ways of achieving it, without endangering the religious and cultural heritage of Islam or the unity of the Islamic world. In their insistence on pan-Islamic unity, their anxious insistence that Islam is not an obstacle to modern civilization, that it is indeed the source and origin of European culture, they are strongly reminiscent of the apologetic and romantic writers of nineteenth-century Muslim India, by whom, indeed, they were influenced to no small extent. For them, the decline of the Ottoman Empire was due to the abandonment of Islam—and by this they did not mean, as did the orthodox ulema, the historic Islam of the law and the traditions, but an ancient and authentic Islam, which they themselves had rediscovered and reinterpreted. There was no need to go to the West for guidance in political and social matters, for all the elements of political and social progress could be found in the Islamic past, from which the West itself had borrowed. Science and technology could be taken from the West—Islam offered no obstacle to their adoption or their progress—but in government, in law, in social usage, in education, in basic loyalty, Islam must remain dominant.[63]

The moderate wing of the Westernizers differed from the moderate Islamist more in mood and emphasis than in real content. Civilization, says one of their outstanding spokesmen, Celâl Nuri [Ileri][64] (1877–1939) is of two kinds, technical and real. The West had reached the highest peak of technical civilization, but had not achieved and never would achieve any 'real' civilization. Technical civilization could be transferred and borrowed from one country to another; real civilization could not, and the Ottoman reformers had made a great mistake in confusing the two. Instead of limiting their borrowings to technical matters, they had tried to copy the West in a field in which Islam was, in fact, superior.[65]

The same charge of superficiality, of blind and senseless copying

---

[63] The writings of Mehmed Said Halim Paşa (see above, p. 221) may serve as examples of this trend.

[64] On this important author there is still no monographic treatment. Some account of his ideas will be found in the works cited above (p. 225 n. 57).

[65] Tunaya, 'Garpçılık', pp. 594–5.

of everything European, is brought against the *Tanzimat* reformers by other writers of this period.

The fallacy that everything seen in Europe can be imitated here [says Ismail Hami] has become a political tradition among us. For example—by simultaneously introducing Russian uniforms, Belgian rifles, Turkish headgear, Hungarian saddles, English swords, and French drill—we have created an army that is a grotesque parody of Europe.[66]

For the extreme Westernizers, the remedy was not less, but more Westernization. The trouble with the earlier reforms, they said, was that they had not gone far enough. Westernization was not a matter of choice but of survival. 'Either we Westernize, or we are destroyed,' wrote Ahmed Muhtar, in 1912.[67] The most consistent exponent of this view was Abdullah Cevdet, whose opinions were summed up in the phrase 'There is no second civilization; civilization means European civilization, and it must be imported with both its roses and its thorns'.[68] To borrow was pointless, to copy superficial and dangerous. The only answer was the complete acceptance of European civilization—the incorporation of Turkey as part of civilized Europe.

There were not many, at that time, who were prepared to go as far as that. When they did, and drew the logical inferences as to the place of Islam in such a Westernized Turkey, they aroused the bitter hostility of both pietists and patriots, and sometimes even the rigour of the law.

In 1912 the periodical *İçtihad*, edited by Abdullah Cevdet, published two articles entitled 'A Very Wakeful Sleep', describing a vision, seen in a dream, of the future of Westernization in Turkey. It was a wild and fantastic vision indeed. The Sultan would have one wife and no concubines; the princes would be removed from the care of eunuch and harem servants, and given a thorough education, including service in the army; the fez would be abolished, and a new headgear adopted; existing cloth factories would be expanded, and new ones opened, and the Sultan, princes, senators, deputies, officers, officials, and soldiers made to

---

[66] In the periodical *İçtihad*, no. 69 (1329 A.H.), p. 1508; cited in Tunaya, 'Garpçılık', p. 591.

[67] *Ikdam*, no. 5716 (1328 A.H.), pp. 3-4; cited in ibid. p. 590 n. 18.

[68] *İçtihad* no. 89 (1329 A.H.), pp. 1890-1984; cited in ibid. p. 590.

wear their products; women would dress as they pleased, though not extravagantly, and would be free from dictation or interference in this matter by ulema, policemen, or street riff-raff; they would be at liberty to choose their husbands, and the practice of match-making would be abolished; convents and *tekkes* would be closed, and their revenues added to the education budget; all *medreses* would be closed, and new modern literary and technical institutes established; the turban, cloak, &c., would be limited to certificated professional men of religion, and forbidden to others; vows and offerings to the saints would be prohibited, and the money saved devoted to national defence; exorcists, witch-doctors, and the like would be suppressed, and medical treatment for malaria made compulsory; popular misconceptions of Islam would be corrected; practical adult education schools would be opened; a consolidated and purified Ottoman Turkish dictionary and grammar would be established by a committee of philologists and men of letters; the Ottomans, without awaiting anything from their government or from foreigners would, by their own efforts and initiative, build roads, bridges, ports, railways, canals, steamships, and factories; starting with the land and *Evkâf* laws, the whole legal system would be reformed.[69]

To his contemporaries, the vision of the wakeful sleeper must have seemed a more than usually exuberant piece of fantasy; yet there is no document of the time that more accurately foreshadows the subsequent course of events.

The disputes between conservatives and radicals, between moderates and extremists, are well summed up in an exchange of views on the subject of education. Should there be more schools, or more *medreses*; should the latter be maintained, reformed, or suppressed? An Islamist journal, after arguing that instead of opening new schools and colleges it would have been better to reform the *medreses* and modernize their curricula, goes on to remark that 'the two greatest universities of the world today, Oxford and the Sorbonne, were in their time nothing but a couple of *medreses*. It was by developing according to the needs of the time that they achieved their present state of perfection.'

In reply to this argument the radical *İçtihad* reminded its readers that this transformation of the Western universities had taken place by a slow and gradual evolution, extending over four

[69] Cited by Safa, pp. 51–55; cf. Tunaya, 'Garpçılık', pp. 493, 601–3, 606, 622.

or five centuries, and asked in conclusion: 'Have we the time to wait so long?'[70]

It was while they were still discussing this question that, in October 1914, the Turks stumbled into a major European war, as allies of one group of European great powers against another. By 1918 it was clear that their time had run out.

[70] Safa, p. 33.

CHAPTER VIII

The Kemalist Republic

The basis of liberty, equality, and justice is the sovereignty of the nation.

MUSTAFA KEMAL.

The Turkish nation is ready and resolved to advance, unhalting and undaunted, on the path of civilization.

MUSTAFA KEMAL, 1924.

Revolutions are inevitable in the lifetime of nations. They may result in despotism, but they also launch nations on paths previously blocked to them.

MILOVAN DJILAS, 'The New Class', 1957.

AT the end of 1918 it seemed that the Sick Man of Europe was about to die at last. Resentment against the dictatorship of the Young Turk leaders had been mounting for some time; the advance of the Allied armies lent it a force that could no longer be resisted. In July a new Sultan, Mehmed Vahideddin, a younger brother of Abdülhamid, had succeeded to the throne of Osman. In October the Young Turk ministers resigned, and the Sultan appointed Ahmed Izzet Paşa as Grand Vezir, with the task of seeking an armistice.[1]

After three days of preliminary negotiation, on 29 October a Turkish delegation led by the Minister of the Navy Rauf Bey[2] went on board H.M.S. *Agamemnon*, at anchor off Mudros, in the island of Lemnos, and signed an armistice next day.[3] The Young Turk pashas, Talât, Enver, and Cemal, fled across the Black Sea on a German gunboat. An allied fleet of sixty ships sailed past the

[1] On Izzet Paşa, see Inal, *Sadrıazamlar*, pp. 1973–2028.

[2] Hüseyin Rauf [Orbay], born in 1881, was a naval officer who had become a national hero through his exploits as commander of the cruiser *Hamidiye*. He later played a role of some importance in the national struggle.

[3] On the armistice see Jäschke, 'Die Vorgeschichte des Waffenstillstandes von Mudros', *Or.-Rund.*, xviii (1936), 49–51, and sources quoted there, and *WI*, n.s., ii (1952), 126-8. Türkgeldi, *Mondros ve Mudanya Mütarekelerinin Tarihi* (1948), pp. 23 ff. For the period from the armistice onward, Jäschke's historical calendar, based in the main on Turkish press and official sources, is invaluable (Jäschke and E. Pritsch, 'Die Türkei seit dem Weltkriege; Geschichtskalender 1918–28' *WI*, x (1929), with continuations in subsequent issues, in the *MSOS*, and in separate publications (cited as Jäschke, *Kalender*, with date reference). The Ottoman chronology of Danişmend (above, p. 209 n.5) will also be found useful for the last years of the Ottoman Empire.

silent guns of the Dardanelles, and on 13 November anchored in the port of Istanbul.

General Izzet Paşa's tenure of office lasted only twenty-five days. Having achieved the armistice for which he was appointed, he gave place to Ahmed Tevfik Paşa, a former Grand Vezir and ambassador in London who would, it was hoped, be able to win the goodwill of the British. In the meantime, on 8 December, an Allied military administration was set up in Istanbul. Allied troops occupied various quarters of the city, strict Allied control was established over the port, tramways, defences, gendarmerie, and police, and on 8 February 1919 the French General Franchet d'Espérey, like Mehmed the Conqueror centuries before, rode into the city on a white horse, the gift of the local Greeks. The Arab provinces of the Empire were already in Allied possession, and had been promised independence. Allied forces now began to threaten even the Turkish provinces themselves. French troops advanced from Syria into Cilicia and the Adana district. British forces occupied the Dardanelles, Samsun, Ayntab, and other strategic points, as well as the whole length of the Anatolian railway. On 29 April 1919 Italian troops landed at Antalya, to take possession of some of the areas assigned to them by the secret wartime agreements of the Allies.

In Istanbul the new Sultan showed a disposition to follow in the footsteps of his elder brother and take over personal control of affairs. The Committee of Union and Progress had collapsed; its leaders had fled abroad. On 21 December the Sultan dissolved the Chamber of Deputies, and on 4 March 1919 appointed his brother-in-law Damad Ferid Paşa as Grand Vezir. Except for an interval of six months, from October 1919 to March 1920, Damad Ferid Paşa remained in power until October 1920, when Ahmed Tevfik Paşa returned to the Sublime Porte to hold office for just over two years, as the last Grand Vezir of the Ottoman Empire.

One of the first tasks of the Sultan and his ministers was to crush the remnants of the Young Turks. On 26 November court martial proceedings were opened against Enver and Cemal Paşas, *in absentia*. On 1 January 1919 they were dismissed from the army, and at the end of the month a new series of arrests and prosecutions began against the former leaders and supporters of the

Committee of Union and Progress.[4] Among the new leaders in
the capital even the will to independent survival seemed to have
failed and political discussion centred on the form which Turkish
subjection was to take, and on the relative merits of an American
or a British mandate.

There was indeed little room for hope. Exhausted by eight
years of almost continuous warfare, the once great Ottoman
Empire lay supine in defeat, its capital occupied, its leaders in
flight. The country was shattered, impoverished, depopulated,
and demoralized. The Turkish people, beaten and dispirited,
seemed ready to accept almost anything that the victors chose to
impose on them.

Almost, but not quite—for when, under cover of Allied warships, a Greek army landed at Izmir in May 1919, the smouldering anger of the Turks was at last kindled into an inextinguishable
blaze. The cession of remote provinces inhabited by alien peoples
could be borne, even the occupation of the capital could be
suffered, for the occupiers were the victorious great powers of
the invincible West, and their soldiers would sooner or later return
whence they came. But the thrust of a neighbouring and former
subject people into the heart of Turkish Anatolia was a danger—
and a humiliation—beyond endurance.

The city and district of Izmir contained an important Greek
population, and already in February 1919 Venizelos, the Greek
Prime Minister, had presented a formal claim to them at the
Peace Conference in Paris. The Italians, too, had a claim to
Izmir, based on the superseded treaty of St. Jean de Maurienne,
and it was largely in order to forestall the Italians that the
Allies agreed to a Greek landing. On 15 May 1919, protected
by British, French, and American warships, a Greek army
landed at Izmir; after systematically occupying the town and
surrounding district, they began to advance eastwards into the
interior.

The Greeks made it clear from the first that they had come, not
for a temporary occupation, but for a permanent annexation—to
incorporate western Anatolia in a greater Greece on both shores
of the Aegean, and thus bring nearer the 'Great Idea'—the restor-

---

[4] Danişmend, iv. 455–6; Jäschke, *Kalender*, Nov. 1918–Feb. 1919. For a transcript
report of the trial of the Young Turk leaders, which opened on 27 April 1919, see
Tarihî Muhakeme, i (1919).

ation of the departed glories of the Greek Christian Empire of Constantinople.

The ultimate menace of the Byzantine 'Great Idea' to the Ottoman Turkish state was clear enough to those who could see; the immediate blow of the Greek occupation to the Turkish people was felt in all the areas that they occupied. The Turkish reaction was violent and instantaneous. In Istanbul, under the guns of the occupying armies, there were great protest meetings, and the first beginnings of a secret resistance movement. In Anatolia, the first armed clash occurred on 28 May at Ödemiş, where a small body of Turks fought unsuccessfully to halt the Greek forces, and guerrilla warfare flared up along the line of Greek advance. The Turks were ready to rise against the invader—only the leader was awaited.

Mustafa Kemal [5]

On 19 May 1919, four days after the Greek landing at Izmir, Mustafa Kemal Paşa landed at Samsun, on the Black Sea coast of

[5] Mustafa Kemal, later Kemal Atatürk, is the hero of many popular biographies, but still awaits a serious scholarly monograph. A bibliography of Turkish and foreign works on Kemal and the Kemalist revolutions was published by M. Orhan Durusoy and M. Muzaffer Gökman, *Atatürk ve Devrimleri Bibliyografyası* (1957; 926 items). The best short biography is that contributed by a group of authors to *IA*, *s.v.* 'Atatürk'. Of special interest are a group of Kemal's reminiscences, of which a French adaptation was published by Jean Deny, 'Les "Souvenirs" du Gazi Moustafa Kemal Pacha', *R. Ét. islam.*, i (1929), 117–36, 145–222, 459–63 The received version of the War of Independence and the subsequent struggles is that given by Kemal himself in his famous six-day speech, delivered in October 1927. (The Turkish text, simply entitled *Nutuk*, has been printed several times. Here reference is made to the two-volume edition published by the Ministry of Education, 1950–2. An English version, called *A Speech Delivered by Ghazi Mustapha Kemal*, was published in Leipzig in 1929; this version, though apparently authorized, is not satisfactory.) The account of events given in this speech, supplemented by Kemal's other speeches and by such Turkish official publications as the *Histoire de la République turque* (1935), has inspired most subsequent accounts of the Turkish Revolution and Republic. Kemal's speech, though a remarkable achievement, inevitably reflects the powerful personality of its author and the struggles in which he was then and later engaged. Some other Turkish sources are available, which, presenting independent testimony, make it possible to amplify and occasionally rectify the received version. Mehmed Arif's account of the struggle in Anatolia, *Anadolu İnkılabı*, was published in Istanbul in 1923. More recently General Ali Fuat Cebesoy has published an important series of memoirs on the War of Independence (*Millî Mücadele Hatıraları*, 1953), on his embassy to Moscow in 1920–2 (*Moskova Hatıraları*, 1955), and on the political struggle after his return (. . . *Siyasî Hatıraları* 1957). Many other memoirs and documents have appeared in Turkey in recent years including those of Kâzım Karabekir *İstiklâl harbimizin Esasları* (1951; suppressed in 1933). A work of great literary merit markedly different from the mass of autobiographic sagas by political and military veterans of the

Anatolia, with orders from Istanbul to supervise the disbanding of the remaining Turkish forces. Instead, he set to work at once on the double task of organizing a movement and raising an army. Mustafa, later known as Kemal Atatürk, was born in Salonika in 1881, in a modest home. His grandfather had been an elementary school-teacher in Salonika; his father was a minor official who later became a timber merchant. Orphaned at the age of seven, Mustafa was brought up by his mother Zübeyde Hanim. In 1893, against her wishes, he entered the military *rüşdiye* school in Salonika; it was there that, in accordance with a common Turkish custom, he was given a second name by his teacher, and thus became Mustafa Kemal. In 1895 he went on to the military academy (*idadi*) in Manastir, and on 13 March 1899 entered the War College (*Harbiye*) in Istanbul as an infantry cadet. In 1902 he was assigned to a staff course, and in January 1905 graduated with the rank of staff-captain.

Mustafa Kemal's years at the War College coincided with some of the harshest repressions of Abdülhamid—and the College was one of the main centres of secret opposition. Despite all disciplinary measures, the cadets read the works of Namık Kemal and the Young Turk exiles secretly in their dormitories, and exchanged opinions on the ills of their country and the means of remedying them. Speaking of his years as a cadet, Mustafa Kemal later remarked:

I worked well at the usual lessons. On top of this, new ideas emerged among some of my companions and myself. We began to discover that

struggle for independence, is Yakup Kadri Karaosmanoğlu's *Vatan Yolunda, Millî Mücadele Hatıraları* (1958). A full critical study of the mass of Turkish and foreign documentation now available on the national struggle and the early years of the Turkish Republic is a task still to be undertaken. Among general studies of the Turkish War of Independence, mention may be made of two early ones by Jäschke ('Der Freiheitskampf des türkischen Volkes', *WI*, xiv (1932), 6–21) and A. J. Toynbee in RIIA, *Survey, 1925*, and of a recent work by Elaine D. Smith, *Origins of the Kemalist Movement 1919–23* (1959). Useful information on particular problems and periods will be found in Jäschke, 'Beiträge zur Geschichte des Kampfes der Türkei um ihre Unabhängigkeit', *WI*, n.s., v (1957), 1–64; Dankwart A. Rustow, 'The Army and the Founding of the Turkish Republic', *Wld. Polit.* xi (1959), 513–52. Tevfik Bıyıklıoğlu *Atatürk Anadolu'da, 1919–21*, i (1959); idem, *Trakya'da Millî Mücadele* (1955–6) M. Tayyib Gökbilgin, *Millî Mücadele Başlarken* (1959). A recent work by a Turkish author, Irfan Orga, *Phoenix Ascendant* (1959), diverges from the received version in its presentation of the roles of Kazım Karabekir and Rauf. Finally, for the course of events in Turkey since the Revolution, reference may be made to the regular surveys in *OM*, *WI*, and the RIIA *Survey*.

there were evils in the administration and politics of the country, and we felt the urge to communicate this discovery to the thousands of students of the College. We founded a handwritten newspaper for them to read. We had a small organization in the class. I was in the committee, and I used to write most of what appeared in the paper.[6]

Inevitably, the apprentice conspirators were denounced and arrested. After a few months' detention Mustafa Kemal was released and given orders—half-posting, half-exile—to join the staff of the Fifth Army in Damascus. It was then that he had his first taste of active service, against Druze rebels. In 1906, together with a few friends, he founded a secret opposition group, and may have had some part in the Young Turk movement in Salonika. In 1907 he was promoted Major and posted to the Third Army in Macedonia. Then he got in touch with the secret Committee of Union and Progress, and took part in their work. His relations with the Young Turk leaders do not, however, seem to have been very cordial, and the revolution of 1908 did not bring him greatly to the fore. After the revolution he abandoned politics for a while, and devoted himself to his military career, publishing translations of General Litzmann's manuals on platoon combat drill (1909) and company combat drill (1910).[7] In 1910 he went on his first visit to Europe, to attend the great French military manœuvres of that year in Picardy. In the Italian and Balkan wars he served with distinction on several fronts, and during the uneasy peace that followed was posted to Sofia as military attaché. At the beginning of 1915, at his own urgent request, he was recalled to Turkey to take part in the war, and was given the command of the 'almost imaginary' 19th Division, then in process of formation at Tekirdağ, on the European shore of the Sea of Marmara. From there he and his division went to the Gallipoli peninsula, where he played a vital role in the successful defence of the Straits against the great British assault in 1915. This victory, which saved the capital from invasion, was the only really striking success won by Ottoman arms during the war. To Mustafa Kemal it brought promotion, fame—and a posting to the remote eastern battle-front, many hundreds of miles from Istanbul, where a victorious national hero might be disagreeably conspicuous.

On 27 February 1916 he assumed a command at Diyarbakır, with the rank of general. A swift campaign against the Russians

---

[6] *IA*, i. 720.   [7] *Atatürk'ün Askerliğe dair Eserleri* (1959).

enabled him to recover Bitlis and Muş for Turkey (7–8 August 1916), and to win new honours for himself.

After further service in Syria and the Caucasus, he was on 5 July 1917 appointed to the command of the newly constituted Turkish Seventh Army, forming part of the so-called 'Yıldırım Army Group' under the German General Falkenhayn, in Syria. Disagreements with Falkenhayn led to his resignation and return to Istanbul in October 1917. Two visits to Europe followed, the first to Germany with the heir-apparent Mehmed Vahideddin, the second to Austria for medical treatment. In July 1918, still weak from illness, he returned to Istanbul, and on 7 August resumed command of the Seventh Army in Palestine. Six weeks later, on 17 September, Allenby began his final offensive south of Jerusalem, and the Turkish and German forces were driven out of Palestine and Syria. It was while Mustafa Kemal was preparing a last desperate struggle north of Aleppo that he heard of the signature of the armistice at Mudros. The next day, on 31 October, he was appointed commander of the Yıldırım Army Group, in succession to Liman von Sanders. Two weeks later his Army Group was dissolved and he himself summoned to the capital. He reached Istanbul on 13 November—the day of the arrival of the Allied fleets.

Despite his prestige as the only remaining victorious general in Turkey, Mustafa Kemal was not able to do very much in Istanbul. The Sultan and his friends were strongly opposed to all nationalist ideologies, which they held responsible for the misfortunes that had befallen the Empire; they were therefore anxious to discourage any popular movement of revolt which might, they felt, threaten the existing order as much as it threatened the invader. And so they continued the disarming of the Turkish forces, accepted successive Allied violations of the Armistice terms, ordered the Turkish troops in Izmir to offer no resistance to the Greeks, and suppressed any tendency to oppose or resist in the city. In the opening phrases of his historic speech on the revolution, delivered in 1927, Mustafa Kemal described the situation with characteristic vigour:

Those who had dragged the nation and the country into the Great War had thought only of saving their own lives and had fled abroad. Vahideddin, who occupied the position of Sultan and Caliph, was a degenerate who, by infamous means, sought only to guard his own person and throne. The cabinet, headed by Damad Ferid Paşa, was weak, cowardly, and without dignity, subservient to the will of the Sultan, and ready to agree to anything that might protect him as well as their own persons.[8]

Realizing the hopeless condition of the capital, Mustafa Kemal decided to go to Anatolia, where some signs of revival were already noticeable. In December 1918 the first resistance groups had been formed, the so-called 'Societies for the Defence of Rights' (*Mudafaai Hukuk*). The first to appear were in Thrace and Izmir; others followed in Manisa and elsewhere in Anatolia, and set the pattern for national resistance movements in areas menaced or occupied by the enemy.[9]

The problem of how to leave the occupied capital and reach Anatolia proved unexpectedly simple. The Sultan, unaware of his intentions, was induced to give him an appointment as Inspector-General of the Ninth Army (in June 1919 renumbered Third Army), based on Samsun, on the Black Sea coast of Anatolia. His instructions were to restore order, to settle Muslim-Christian disturbances, to disarm and disperse the semi-military bands that had been operating in the area, and in general to supervise the disarmament and demobilization of the remaining Ottoman forces. Instead he set to work to establish links between existing resistance groups, to form new ones, and to prepare for the armed defence of the Turkish heartlands against invasion.[10]

Meanwhile, in the West, the victorious Allies were at last completing their arrangements for the disposal of the Sick Man's worldly goods. After a series of conferences in London and San Remo, a treaty was drawn up, and was signed by the representatives of the Allies and of the Sultan at Sèvres on 10 August 1920.

The treaty of Sèvres was very harsh, and would have left Turkey helpless and mutilated, a shadow state living on the sufferance of the powers and peoples who were annexing her richest provinces. It was far more severe than that imposed on a defeated

---

[8] *Nutuk*, i. 1; cf. *Speech*, p. 9.

[9] On these societies, see Rustow, in *Wld. Polit.*, xi. 541–2; Tunaya, *Partiler*, pp. 481 ff.; Jäschke, in *WI*, n.s., v. 19 ff.

[10] On the semi-legendary pre-history of the Kemalist movement—the activities of Kemal in Istanbul from November 1918 to May 1919—see the remarks of Jäschke, ibid. pp. 27 ff. and Rustow, pp. 537–8. See further Jäschke, 'Mustafa Kemals Sendung nach Anatolien', in F. Taeschner and G. Jäschke, *Aus der Geschichte des islamischen Orients* (1949), pp. 17 ff.

Germany, and was received in Turkey with a national day of mourning.

It was, however, never implemented. While the Allies were imposing their terms on the docile government of the Sultan, a new Turkish state was emerging in Anatolia, led by men who rejected outright the treaty and the principles that underlay it, and condemned as traitors those Turks who had accepted it.

From the moment of his landing at Samsun, Mustafa Kemal had been hard at work in Anatolia, organizing the cadres of a national army, and preparing the ground for a war of liberation. In June he had a secret meeting in Amasya with Ali Fuad Paşa [Cebesoy], Hüseyin Rauf [Orbay], and Colonel Refet [Bele], and communicated with General Kâzım Karabekir Paşa, commanding the 15th Army Corps at Erzurum.[11] Soon afterwards he sent a circular telegram, in cypher, to a number of civil and military authorities in the country, setting forth his views. The opening phrases strike the keynote of the nationalist programme during the next few years:

1. The integrity of the country, the independence of the nation are in danger.
2. The central government is unable to discharge the duties for which it is responsible. As a result the nation is regarded as non-existent.
3. Only the will and resolution of the nation can save the independence of the nation.

The telegram then goes on to demand the convening of a congress, free from any influence or interference, to assert the rights of the nation before the world, and calls on each district to send delegates, in secret, to Sivas 'which is the safest place in Anatolia for that purpose'.[12] At the same time Kâzım Karabekir

[11] Karabekir (pp. 35ff.) describes in his memoirs how, before leaving Istanbul early in April 1919 to take up his command in Erzurum, he called on Mustafa Kemal at his house in Şişli, and declared his intention of using the Army Corps at Erzurum as an instrument of national resistance, and thus preparing the ground for Kemal's own arrival and activities in Anatolia (cf. Gökbilgin, p. 79; Orga, pp. 73–74). In general, Karabekir's memoirs indicate a larger role in the movement in Anatolia than is allowed to him in Mustafa Kemal's historic speech, written, it will be remembered, after the break between the two men.

[12] *Nutuk*, i. 30–31; *Speech*, p. 31. Documents (*Die Dokumente zur Rede*, 1927), no. 12. For Cebesoy's rather fuller account of proceedings at Amasya, see his memoirs, i. 69 ff.; further Orga, p. 77; Gökbilgin, p. 145; Smith, pp. 14 ff., and *WI*, n.s., ii (1952), 130.

sent out invitations for a meeting of delegates from the eastern provinces in Erzurum in July.

News of Mustafa Kemal's activities reached Istanbul, bringing joy to some quarters and alarm to others. The Minister of War called on him to return to Istanbul, and, when he omitted to do so, obtained an *irade* from the Sultan terminating his appointment. Mustafa Kemal, anxious to avoid any open act of rebellion against the legitimate Ottoman government, resigned his commission and put on civilian clothes.[13] He now turned to the Association for the Defence of the Rights of Eastern Anatolia, founded in Erzurum on 3 March 1919; this society, later registered in proper legal form at the vilayet of Erzurum, provided both an element of legal continuity and an instrument of organization.

On 23 July 1919 a congress of delegates from the eastern provinces, convened by the Association, assembled in Erzurum. Mustafa Kemal was elected chairman on the first day. The most important achievement of the congress, which continued until 17 August, was the drafting of the first version of the declaration which later came to be known as the National Pact (*Millî Misak*).[14] During the congress Kâzım Karabekir received orders from Istanbul to arrest Kemal and Rauf, and to take over Kemal's post as Inspector-General. He refused to obey.

On 4 September the second and more important congress opened at Sivas, attended by delegates from all over the country. Once again Mustafa Kemal was elected chairman, and directed the discussions of the meeting. The main business of the congress was to extend to the whole country the decisions taken at Erzurum, and to modify the organization established there accordingly. The 'Association for the Defence of the Rights of Eastern Anatolia' now became the 'Association for the Defence of the Rights of Anatolia and Rumelia', with a permanent Representative Committee headed by Mustafa Kemal, and this new organization became the instrument of the political struggle ahead.

[13] On his resignation see Unat, 'Atatürk'ün Askerlikten İstifası . . .', *Tar. Ves.*, n.s., i (1955), 3–8; further Rustow, p. 546; Smith, p. 16.

[14] On the Erzurum congress see Cevat Dursunoğlu, *Millî Mücadelede Erzurum* (1946); *Nutuk*, i. 64 ff.; *Speech*, pp. 57 ff.; Arif, *Anadolu Inkılabı*, pp. 30 ff.; Cebesoy, i. 110 ff.; Karabekir, pp. 66 ff.; Gökbilgin, pp. 167 ff.; Orga, pp. 78 ff.; Smith, pp. 17 ff. On the history of the National Pact see Jäschke, 'Zur Geschichte des türkischen Nationalpakts', *MSOS*, xxxvi/2 (1933), 101–16.

The political aims expressed at the Sivas congress were neither clear nor united. The delegates began by taking an oath never to revive the Committee of Union and Progress, and sending an address to the Sultan; they then went on to consider whether they should concern themselves with politics or not, and were by no means unanimous in agreeing to do so.[15] Even there, the idea of an American mandate, popular in some circles in Istanbul, was raised by some delegates, only to be rejected by the great majority.[16] The congress instead reaffirmed the principles of the Erzurum manifesto, and indeed strengthened the wording at some points, demanding the preservation of territorial integrity and national independence, and envisaging armed action against the occupying powers if necessary.

The congress lost no opportunity of reaffirming its loyalty to the Sultan, laying the blame on the Grand Vezir and the cabinet. On 10 September Mustafa Kemal telegraphed to Adil Bey, the Minister of the Interior:

You are preventing the nation from submitting their case to their sovereign. Cowards, criminals! You are engaged in treasonable conspiracies with the enemy against the nation. I did not doubt that you would be incapable of appreciating the strength and will of the nation; but I did not want to believe that you would act in this traitorous and murderous way against the fatherland and the nation. Think what you are doing. . . .'[17]

The next day a telegram was sent to the Sultan from the army commanders, reaffirming their loyalty to the throne and the sovereign, and begging him to 'deign to order the formation of a new government, loyal and respectful of the privileges of Your Majesty and of the Caliphate'.[18] Another telegram, signed by the 'General Assembly of the Congress', was sent to the Grand Vezir Damad Ferid Paşa, accusing him both of trampling on the rights of the nation and of outraging the dignity and honour of the Sultanate.

---

[15] *Nutuk*, i. 88; cf. *Speech*, p. 76.

[16] The *Nutuk* glosses over the fact, revealed by Cebesoy, that a telegram was actually sent from Sivas to the President of the Senate in Washington, asking for a fact-finding mission. The text of the telegram was later published in Washington. See Rustow, in *MEJ*, x (1956), 325–6.

[17] *Nutuk*, i. 131; cf. *Speech*, p. 114.   [18] *Documents*, no. 82.

The nation has no confidence left in any of you other than the Sultan, to whose person alone therefore it must submit its reports and petitions. Your cabinet . . . is coming between the nation and the sovereign. If you persist in this obstinacy for one hour longer, the nation will consider itself free to take whatever action it thinks fit, and will break off all relations between your illegal cabinet and the whole country. This is our last warning. . . . [19]

The immediate cause of these outbursts was the attempt by the Istanbul government, with some British help, to stir up the Kurdish tribes in the east against Kemal. These efforts had little effect, and precipitated the rupture between the Kemalists and Istanbul.

At first, however, relations with the capital showed signs of improvement. On 2 October Damad Ferid Paşa resigned, and was replaced by Ali Rıza Paşa, who, if not in favour of the Kemalists, was not actively opposed to them. He did go so far as to open negotiations with Mustafa Kemal, and on 20–22 October conversations were held at Amasya between representatives of the Kemalists and of the government, the latter led by the Minister of the Navy, Salih Paşa. Some measure of agreement was reached, involving the virtual recognition of the Kemalists by the government, and the acceptance by Istanbul of the main political principles of the Kemalist programme. In December 1919, as a result of nationalist persuasion and pressure, new elections were held for the Ottoman parliament, which assembled in Istanbul on 12 January 1920.[20] The Kemalists and their sympathizers had won a majority, and among the new members were some from the nationalist camp in Anatolia, including Rauf Bey. A fortnight later Parliament voted the National Pact, based on the declarations of Erzurum and Sivas, and formulating the basic demands for territorial integrity and national independence.

Mustafa Kemal and the 'Representative Committee', now established in Ankara, seemed in a strong position, with a sympathetic parliament in Istanbul and some measure of recognition from the government. Nationalist sympathizers in the capital became more active, and helped the Kemalists not only with

[19] *Nutuk*, i. 137; cf. *Speech*, p. 121. On the Sivas congress see further Arif, *Anadolu Inkılabı*, pp. 31 ff.; Cebesoy, i. 156 ff.; Karabekir, pp. 94 ff.; Smith, pp. 19 ff.

[20] See below, pp. 372 ff, where parliamentary and constitutional developments are more fully discussed.

words, but also by raiding Allied arms depots and sending their booty to Anatolia. The Allies, alarmed at these developments, reacted sharply. On 3 March Ali Rıza Paşa was forced to resign, and was replaced on 8 March by his Minister of the Navy, Salih Paşa. The same day the Allied Supreme Council decided on a reinforced occupation of Istanbul. On 16 March British forces entered the Turkish quarters of the city of Istanbul, and General Wilson, the Allied Commander, ordered the arrest and deportation of Young Turk and other suspected nationalist sympathizers. Some 150 were arrested in all, and a number of deputies, among them Rauf, deported to Malta. They were released late in 1921, in exchange for British officers arrested in Anatolia and held as hostages by the nationalists.

On 18 March 1920 the last Ottoman parliament in Istanbul held its last session. After unanimously voting a resolution of protest against the arrest of some of its members, it prorogued itself indefinitely. It did not meet again, and was finally dissolved by the Sultan on 11 April.

Matters now came rapidly to a head. On 19 March, the day after the prorogation of parliament in Istanbul, Mustafa Kemal called for elections to a new emergency assembly. It was to meet in Ankara, where the 'Representative Committee' had established itself on 27 December 1919. This small Anatolian hill town now became the headquarters of the nationalist resistance—the virtual capital of Turkish independence.

On 23 April a body of delegates, known as the Grand National Assembly, met in Ankara. Even now, the delegates were very reluctant to take any steps that might be construed as rebellious, and tried desperately to maintain legal continuity. So long as it was possible to do so, the nationalists proclaimed their loyalty to Mehmed Vahideddin, Sultan of the Empire and Caliph of Islam, and reaffirmed their desire to rescue him from enemy hands.

It soon ceased to be possible. On 5 April 1920 the Sultan had recalled Damad Ferid Paşa to the Grand Vezirate, and opened a new and bitter attack on the nationalists. On 11 April the *Şeyh-ül-Islâm* Dürrizade Abdullah Efendi issued a *fetva* declaring that the killing of rebels, on the orders of the Caliph, was a religious duty; the Grand Vezir published a proclamation denouncing 'the false representatives of the nation'; the Circassian Anzavur, who had been fighting against the nationalists since September, was given the title of pasha. On 18 April 'Disciplinary Forces' (*Kuvva-i Inzıbatiye*) were formed to fight the nationalists, and on 11 May Mustafa Kemal and other nationalist leaders were solemnly sentenced to death, *in absentia*, by a court martial in Istanbul. The Sultan and his government were preparing to use all weapons —religious, political, military—in their last desperate assault on the new power rising in Anatolia.

The nationalists replied in kind. On 5 May the Mufti of Ankara, Börekcizade Mehmed Rifat Efendi, issued a *fetva*, endorsed by 152 other Muftis in Anatolia, declaring that a *fetva* issued under foreign duress was invalid, and calling on the Muslims to 'liberate their Caliph from captivity'. On 19 May the Grand National Assembly in Ankara declared Damad Ferid Paşa a traitor.[21]

These measures had, however, only limited effect in counteracting the immense prestige of such ancient and venerated offices as those of the Sultan, the Grand Vezir, and the *Şeyh-ül-Islâm*. Anti-nationalist riots broke out in many places, and irregular forces of various kinds, encouraged and sanctified by the authority of Istanbul, harried the nationalists even in the neighbourhood of Ankara.

The nationalists, already militarily engaged against the Greeks, the Armenians, and the French, were hard put to it to defend themselves against the 'Army of the Caliphate'. In late 1920 and in 1921, however, events took a turn in their favour. The signing of the treaty of Sèvres caused an immense revulsion of feeling in Turkey against the régime that had accepted it; the growing dissensions of the former allies made it possible for Kemal to strengthen his position by judicious separate negotiation. In Istanbul, on 17 October 1920, Damad Ferid Paşa, under strong Allied pressure, resigned for the last time and gave place to Tevfik Paşa. Above all, the progress of the struggle against the Greeks identified the Ankara régime with the national cause, and made opposition to it, rather than support for it, seem like treason and impiety in Turkish eyes.

The Greco-Turkish war falls into three stages, corresponding roughly with the campaigns of 1920, 1921, and 1922. In the first, the Turks, hopelessly outmatched in numbers and material, were

---

badly defeated, and Greek forces advanced in both Anatolia and Rumelia. The second Greek campaign, in 1921, also opened well for the invaders, who made several important gains. The Turks, however, rallied, and in April a Turkish force under Colonel Ismet drove back the Greeks near Inönü. It was from this engagement that Ismet Inönü, the collaborator and successor of Mustafa Kemal, later took his surname.

A new Greek advance began in July, and continued until the Greeks met the Turks on the Sakarya river. Then, on 24 August, a great battle took place, and the Turkish forces, under the personal command of Mustafa Kemal, won a decisive victory. The Greeks withdrew to a new line farther west. The victorious general was greeted by the Grand National Assembly with the title of 'Gazi'—victor in the holy war.[22]

The effects of the victory by the Sakarya were considerable. The nationalists were now internationally recognized as a powerful factor; by some as the real government of Turkey. The Soviets had already signed an agreement with them in March 1921, fixing the frontier and establishing friendly relations.[23] The French now did the same. In October a new Franco-Turkish treaty was signed with the nationalists, drawing up a new Turco-Syrian frontier far more favourable to Turkey than that laid down in the treaty of Sèvres, and providing for the French evacuation of Cilicia. The Italians too withdrew from their zone in southern Anatolia, stipulating only the retention by them of the Dodecanese islands. These withdrawals and agreements greatly strengthened the military position of the nationalist forces, who now in addition began to acquire large quantities of arms.

While the Turks had been growing in strength, the Greeks were weakened by dissension and changes of régime and policy at home. In August 1922 the third and final phase of the war began. The Turks drove back the Greeks in headlong retreat and at last, on 9 September, reoccupied Izmir, thus completing the reconquest of Anatolia.

Mustafa Kemal now prepared to continue the struggle in European Turkey, and to drive the Greeks out of eastern Thrace.

[22] On the significance of this title in earlier Turkish history see above, pp. 11 ff.

[23] On the history of the Russian treaty, see Jäschke, in *WI*, n.s., v. (1957), 44 ff. Among others, Jäschke quotes the important testimony of Cebesoy on the supply of arms and money by the Soviets to the Kemalists.

To do so, he had to cross the Dardanelles, still occupied by an inter-Allied force. The French and Italian contingents withdrew, but the British remained, and for a while an Anglo-Turkish clash seemed imminent. Finally, the British gave way to Kemal's demands, and on 11 October, 1922 an armistice was signed at Mudanya. By its terms, the Allied governments agreed to a restoration of Turkish sovereignty in Istanbul, the Straits, and eastern Thrace, and merely delayed full Turkish reoccupation pending the signature of a peace treaty. The Greeks acceded to the armistice on 14 October; on the 19th Refet Paşa, with a special commission from the Grand National Assembly in Ankara, crossed by the S.S. *Gülnihal* from Mudanya and entered the city of Istanbul.

The Treaty of Lausanne

The peace conference opened at Lausanne on 20 November 1922. Many months of diplomatic wrangling followed, until the treaty was finally signed on 24 July 1923. Its chief significance for Turkey was the re-establishment of complete and undivided Turkish sovereignty in almost all the territory included in the present-day Turkish Republic. At the same time the Capitulations, long resented as a symbol of inferiority and subservience, were abolished. Thus Turkey, alone among the defeated powers of the First World War, succeeded in rising from her own ruins and, rejecting the dictated peace imposed on her by the victors, secured the acceptance of her own terms. For the treaty of Lausanne was substantially an international recognition of the demands formulated in the Turkish National Pact.

The military battle was won; the political programme of the nationalists had been achieved, and had been recognized by the world in an international treaty. What was to be done next? It was in his answer to this question that Mustafa Kemal showed his true greatness.

The point was well made by the Turkish journalist Falıh Rıfkı Atay, in his comparison between Mustafa Kemal and the Young Turk leader, Enver Paşa:

Enver's special quality was boldness, Mustafa Kemal's was insight. . . . Had Mustafa Kemal been Minister of War in 1914, he would not have pushed the country into the First World War; had

Enver entered Izmir in 1922, with the same *élan* he would have turned back, marched on Syria and Iraq, and lost all that had been won.[24]

There were indeed many distractions, which at that time might have enticed a warrior-hero. There were the lost Ottoman provinces in Europe and Asia, where the growing difficulties of the successor régimes might have favoured a reassertion of Turkish claims.[25] Nearer to the heart of Turkish nationalists, there were the 20 odd million Turkish-speaking Muslims of the fallen Russian Empire, which in the throes of revolution, intervention, and civil war might have offered a tempting field for political adventure.

But Kemal did none of these things. Once the war was over, he made peace with the Greeks, settling the ancient disputes between them by the brutal but effective method of an exchange of populations. He accepted the demilitarization of the Straits, to be ended only many years later and then by negotiation and agreement. Renouncing all foreign ambitions and all pan-Turkish, pan-Ottoman, or pan-Islamic ideologies, he deliberately limited his actions and aspirations to the national territory of Turkey as defined by treaty, and devoted the rest of his life to the grim, laborious, and unglamorous task of reconstruction. In a speech in 1923 he warned the people of Turkey:

> The successes which our army has gained up to now cannot be regarded as having achieved the real salvation of our country. These victories have only prepared the ground for our future victories. Let us not be puffed up with military victories. Let us rather prepare for new victories in science and economics.[26]

The Political Reform

The first problem to be settled was, however, political—the form and structure of the Turkish state. The nationalists had from the first insisted on their loyalty to the sovereign; his actions against them and against what they regarded as the national cause were attributed to evil advisers and foreign control, from both of which they proposed to rescue him. But at the same time they had also formulated and adopted certain political principles

---

[24] Atay, *Niçin Kurtulmamak* (1953), p. 6.

[25] On Kemal's refusal even to attempt the recovery of his birthplace, Salonika, see Orga, pp. 131–2.

[26] . . . *Millî Eğitimle ilgili Söylev ve Demeçleri,* i (1946), 10.

which, in the long run, would prove incompatible with the survival of the Sultanate. As early as July 1920 Mustafa Kemal declared to the National Assembly in Ankara, amid applause: 'I think that the fundamental reality of our present-day existence has demonstrated the general tendency of the nation, and that is populism and people's government. It means the passing of government into the hands of the people.'[27] In August of the same year he made the same point again: '. . . Our point of view, which is populism, means that power, authority, sovereignty, administration should be given directly to the people, and should be kept in the hands of the people'.[28] It was about this time that the Assembly, with obvious reluctance, began to discuss constitutional questions. On 20 January 1921 it passed a 'Law of Fundamental Organizations', which began with the uncompromising declaration that 'sovereignty belongs without reservation or condition to the nation; the system of administration rests on the principle that the people personally and effectively directs its own destinies'. The subsequent articles went on to establish the position of the Grand National Assembly in Ankara as 'the only real representative of the people, and as the holder of both legislative and executive power'.[29]

With the Greeks and Allies at last out of the way, two forces remained, face to face, in Turkey; on the one hand a populist, nationalist government and Assembly, flushed with military victory and popular support; on the other the ancient supreme offices of the Muslim state and faith, still able to confer on their holders, however discredited by defeat and collaboration, an immense prestige and authority in the eyes of Muslim Turks of all classes.

The final clash between the two was precipitated by the Allied powers, who still insisted on recognizing the Sultan's government in Istanbul, and invited them as well as the nationalists to the

[27] *Atatürk'ün Söylev ve Demeçleri* (collected speeches), i (1945), 87.

[28] Ibid. pp. 97–98.

[29] The text will be found in the useful collection of constitutional documents by Gözübüyük and Kili, pp. 85–87, and of the laws and debates relating to the War of Independence and the Revolution by Kemal Arıburnu, *Millî Mücadele ve Inkılaplara ilgili Kanunlar* . . . i (1957), 11 ff. It is of interest that in late April 1921, when the Ottoman prince Ömer Faruk attempted to join the nationalists in Anatolia, he was politely but firmly advised by Kemal to stay in Istanbul (Jäschke, 'Auf dem Wege zur Türkischen Republik', *WI*, n.s., v (1958), 215–16, from a private communication).

peace conference at Lausanne. This twofold invitation and the prospect which it opened of divided Turkish authority at a crucial time, decided Kemal to terminate, once and for all, the political power of the throne.

The task was not easy. Kemal himself tells how he sounded some of his closest associates, and found them still loyal to the Sultanate. Rauf Bey, for example, when asked his views on this question, replied:

> I am bound by conscience and sentiment to the Sultanate and Caliphate. . . . It is my duty to remain loyal to the sovereign: my attachment to the Caliphate is imposed on me by my education. Besides this, I would make a general observation. It is hard for us to control the general situation. This can only be secured by an authority that everyone is accustomed to regard as unapproachably high. Such is the office of Sultanate and Caliphate. To abolish this office and to try and set up an entity of a different character in its place, would lead to failure and disaster. It is quite inadmissible.

Refet Paşa, who was sitting near-by, agreed, and added that 'in fact, there can be no question of any form of government other than the Sultanate and Caliphate'.[30]

Mustafa Kemal had, however, reached his decision. The Sultanate and Caliphate were to be separated, and the former abolished. There would henceforth be no Sultan, but an Ottoman prince would hold office as Caliph only, with religious but not political powers. By this compromise Mustafa Kemal hoped to disarm the opposition of the religious elements to political change, to retain the advantages of a legitimate and revered authority above politics, and at the same time to end the personal autocracy of the Sultan.

On 31 October Kemal put his proposals to a meeting of the association for the Defence of Rights. The next day they were submitted to the Assembly, where they formed the subject of long and heated arguments. Strong opposition to the proposals at once appeared, and the members of the Assembly's committee on *Şeriat*, mostly men of religion, raised all kinds of legal and theological objections. Kemal, sitting in a corner of the crowded committee room, saw that nothing very satisfactory to him was likely to emerge from these debates. The rest of the story is best told in his own words:

[30] *Nutuk*, ii. 684; cf. *Speech*, p. 573.

Finally, I asked the Chairman of the joint committee for permission to speak, and, jumping on the bench in front of me, I made this statement, in a loud voice: 'Gentlemen,' I said, 'Sovereignty and Sultanate are not given to anyone by anyone because scholarship proves that they should be; or through discussion or debate. Sovereignty and Sultanate are taken by strength, by power and by force. It was by force that the sons of Osman seized the sovereignty and Sultanate of the Turkish nation; they have maintained this usurpation for six centuries. Now the Turkish nation has rebelled, has put a stop to these usurpers, and has effectively taken sovereignty and sultanate into its own hands. This is an accomplished fact. The question under discussion is not whether or not we should leave Sultanate and sovereignty to the nation. That is already an accomplished fact—the question is merely how to give expression to it. This will happen in any case. If those gathered here, the Assembly, and everyone else could look at this question in a natural way, I think they would agree. Even if they do not, the truth will still find expression, but some heads may roll in the process.

'As regards the theological aspect of the matter, there is no need for alarm or anxiety on the part of the reverend gentlemen. Let me give you a scholarly explanation.'

Having said this, I went on to give a lengthy explanation. Thereupon one of the deputies for Ankara, Hoca Mustafa Efendi said: 'I beg your pardon, sir, we were looking at the matter from another point of view. We have been enlightened by your explanations.'

The question was settled in the mixed committee. The draft law was quickly drawn up, and read on the same day at the second sitting of the Assembly. On a proposal to take a nominal vote, I mounted the tribune and said: 'There is no need for this. I believe that the Assembly will unanimously adopt the principles which will for ever preserve the independence of the country and nation!' Cries of 'Vote!' were raised, and finally the chairman put it to the vote and announced that it had been unanimously accepted. Only one opposing voice was heard saying: 'I am against it', but was drowned by cries of 'Silence!'

In this way, gentlemen, the final obsequies of the decline and fall of the Ottoman Sultanate were completed.[31]

The resolution passed on 1 November 1922 contains two articles. The first declared that 'the Turkish people consider that the form of government in Istanbul resting on the sovereignty

---

[31] *Nutuk*, ii. 690 ff.; cf. *Speech*, pp. 577 ff. Cebesoy's version of the abolition of the Sultanate is given in the third volume of his memoirs, pp. 110 ff. On the question in general see Jäschke, 'Das Ende des osmanischen Sultanats', *Studien zur Auslandskunde, Vorderasien*, I/i.

of an individual had ceased to exist on 16 March 1920 [i.e. two and a half years previously] and passed for ever into history'; the second recognized that the Caliphate belonged to the Ottoman house but laid down that the Caliphate rested on the Turkish state, and that the Assembly would choose as Caliph 'that member of the Ottoman house who was in learning and character most worthy and fitting'.[32]

Mehmed VI Vahideddin did not wait for the Assembly's judgement of his learning and his character. On 12 November news was received that he had slipped out of the palace and boarded a British warship, on which he fled to Malta. Next day the Grand National Assembly in Ankara declared him deposed, and elected his cousin Abdülmecid as Caliph.

Mustafa Kemal now prepared for the next stages of the political struggle. His first need was for a political instrument. The Association for the Defence of the Rights of Anatolia and Rumelia had served well enough during the struggle for national liberation. It was not, however, adequate to the needs of a country enjoying peace and independence. Mustafa Kemal now set to work to transform it into a real political party. As early as 6 December 1922 he made his first announcement to the press about the formation of a new party, to be called the People's Party, and invited the educated classes of the country to communicate their views to him directly. In the new year he went on extensive journeys in Anatolia, and on 8 April 1923 published a manifesto with nine articles.[33] These reiterate his views on popular sovereignty, representative government, and the abolition of the Sultanate, and then go on to sketch a number of necessary reforms, especially in fiscal and administrative matters. In his 1927 speech, Kemal remarked of this manifesto:

This programme contained essentially all that we have accomplished and applied until today. There were, however, certain important and fundamental questions that were not included in the programme, such as the proclamation of the Republic, the abolition of the Caliphate, the suppression of the Ministry of *Şeriat*, the closing of the *medreses* and *tekkes*, the introduction of the hat. . . . I did not think it right, by prematurely introducing these questions into the programme, to give the ignorant and the reactionary the opportunity to poison the whole

---

[32] Text in Gözübüyük and Kili, pp. 90–91; Arıburnu, pp. 311–12.

[33] Text in Tunaya, *Partiler*, pp. 580–2.

nation. For I was quite sure that at the proper time these questions would be solved and the people would in the end be satisfied. . . .[34]

In spite of some complaints that the programme was brief and inadequate, it served as the starting-point of a new political development. On 16 April the Grand National Assembly, which in three years had grown from a rebel band to a national parliament, dissolved itself in preparation for new elections—the first real general election in many years. The elections, held in June, returned a new chamber of 286 deputies, which opened its proceedings on 11 August 1923. Two days earlier, on 9 August, the inaugural congress of the People's Party began its deliberations, under the presidency of Mustafa Kemal.[35]

The first major political act of the new Assembly was the ratification, on 23 August 1923, of the treaty of Lausanne, securing the international status of the new Turkey. At home, too, important consequences followed. On 2 October the last Allied contingents left Istanbul; on 6 October Turkish troops under the command of Şükrü Naili Paşa marched into the Imperial city, where they were coldly received. By a strange coincidence Damad Ferid Paşa died on the same day in Nice.

The Ankara government now faced a decision of fundamental importance. Its answer was not long delayed. On 9 October Ismet Paşa, at a meeting of the People's Party, moved a constitutional amendment, in the form 'Ankara is the seat of government of the Turkish state'. Four days later the Assembly formally decided on its adoption.

The decision meant a new breach with the past—a logical sequel to the abolition of the Sultanate. The Emperor had gone; the Imperial city was ill adapted to house the government of revolutionaries that had overthrown him. For nearly five centuries Istanbul had been the capital of an Islamic Empire; the pallid ghosts of a splendid past still flitted unhappily through the halls of the Saray and the Sublime Porte. Turkish Istanbul, with its mosques and palaces, its divines and courtiers; Pera, the Levantine suburb, with its cosmopolitan merchant community of concessionaires and compradors—these were too intimately associated with the past, in fact and in the mind of the Turkish people, to provide a centre for the new Turkey that Kemal wanted to build.

[34] *Nutuk*, ii. 718 ff.; cf. *Speech*, p. 598. [35] See below, p. 375.

And so a new capital was chosen, symbolizing and accentuating the changes that were taking place. The new state was based not on a dynasty, an empire, or a faith, but on the Turkish nation —and its capital was in the heart of the Turkish homeland.[36]

In the meantime Kemal had been preparing a still more radical change—the proclamation of the Republic. The abolition of the Sultanate and retention of a separate Caliphate had created a dangerous ambiguity in the headship of the state. There were many, in the Assembly and elsewhere, who saw in the Caliph the legitimate sovereign and head of state—a kind of constitutional monarch and, more especially, defender of the faith. Kemal, however, had other ideas. At the beginning of October reports began to circulate that he was going to proclaim a Republic, and they gave rise to impassioned opposition and discussion. At the end of October, after a series of carefully planned political manœuvres, Kemal came to the Chamber and proposed certain constitutional amendments which, he said, would remove the ambiguities and confusions in their political system. The draft amendment, prepared the previous night, included the phrases

The form of government of the state of Turkey is a Republic . . . the President of Turkey is elected by the Grand National Assembly in plenary session from among its own members. . . . The President of Turkey is the head of the state . . . and appoints the Prime Minister. . . .

At 8.30 in the evening, after hours of debate, the resolution was carried by 158 votes, with many abstentions but no dissentients. Fifteen minutes later, at 8.45, the deputies elected Mustafa Kemal as first President of the Republic. He appointed Ismet Paşa as his first Prime Minister. The news was published all over the country the same night, and greeted after midnight in all parts by a salute of 101 guns.[37]

The Attack on the Theocracy

Among those who took part in the debate on the constitutional amendment was the distinguished historian Abdurrahman Şeref, the last Imperial Ottoman Historiographer, the first

---

[36] G. J[äschke], 'Ankara wird Hauptstadt der neuen Türkei', *WI*, n.s., iii (1954), 262–7; cf. below, pp. 371–2.

[37] *Nutuk*, ii. 815 ff.; cf. *Speech*, pp. 657 ff. Texts and discussions in Gözübüyük and Kili, pp. 95 ff. and Arıburnu, pp. 32 ff. See also Orga, pp. 140 ff.

president of the Turkish Historical Society, and, at that time, a deputy for Istanbul in the Grand National Assembly.

There is no point [he said] in enumerating all the different forms of government. 'Sovereignty belongs unconditionally to the people!' Once you have said that, you can ask whoever you like, and they will tell you that it means a Republic. That is the name of the new-born child. It seems, however, that some people dislike this name. Let them —it will make no difference. [38]

Not all the Sultan's former subjects were able to view the march of events with the same historical realism. In many quarters the proclamation of the Republic was received with enthusiasm, as the beginning of a new era. In others, it brought shock and grief, and profound anxieties as to the future. What did it mean? Would it merely replace the autocracy of the Sultan by that of Mustafa Kemal? How would it affect the Caliphate, and, with it, Turkey's standing as the leader of the Islamic world?

No great intelligence is necessary [said an editorial in *Tanin*, on 11 November 1923] to understand that if we lose the Caliphate, the state of Turkey, with its five or ten million inhabitants, would lose all importance in the world of Islam, and in the eyes of European politics we would sink to the rank of a petty and insignificant state. . . . The Caliphate was acquired by the Ottoman dynasty and its retention in Turkey thus assured for ever; deliberately to create a risk of losing it is an action totally incompatible with reason, loyalty, and national feeling. [39]

The question of the Caliphate aroused interest far beyond the borders of Turkey, and brought anxious inquiries, especially from India, about the intentions of the republican régime. These last invoked the sharp comment from Kemal that 'those who had attacked the Caliphate were not strangers . . . they were Muslim peoples, who fought against the Turks under the British flag at the Dardanelles, in Syria, and in Iraq'. [40]

The main objection to the Republic, on the part of its conservative opponents in Turkey, was that it endangered the links of the Turkish people both with their own Islamic and Imperial past, and with the larger Muslim world of which they had for so long been the leaders. It was inevitable that the forces of tradition

[38] *Nutuk*, ii. 812; cf. *Speech*, p. 655.   [39] *Nutuk*, ii. 830; cf. *Speech*, p. 669.
[40] *Nutuk*, ii. 829; cf. *Speech*, p. 668.

should rally around the person of the Caliph, the living symbol of their attachment to both. The Caliph Abdülmecid, by all accounts a mild and scholarly man, nevertheless lent himself to this role, and in January 1924 was subjected to a stinging reproof from the President of the Republic:

> In his domestic establishment and more especially in his public appearances the Caliph seems to be following the path of his ancestors the Sultans. . . . We cannot sacrifice the Republic of Turkey for the sake of courtesy or sophistry. The Caliph must know exactly who he is and what his office is, and must content himself with it. . . . [41]

It was, it seems, the interest of Indian Muslims in the Caliphate that touched off the crisis which ended with its abolition. On 24 November 1923 three of the major Istanbul daily papers published the text of a letter to Ismet Paşa, signed by two distinguished Indian Muslim leaders, the Aga Khan and Ameer Ali. The two signatories pointed out that the separation of the Caliphate from the Sultanate had increased its significance for the Muslims in general, and begged the Turkish government to place the Caliphate 'on a basis which would command the confidence and esteem of the Muslim nations, and thus impart to the Turkish state unique strength and dignity'. [42]

Mustafa Kemal agreed with his opponents in seeing in the Caliphate the link with the past and with Islam. It was precisely for that reason that he was determined to break it.

Once again, the preparation was carefully planned. At the beginning of 1924 Mustafa Kemal went to Izmir, to preside over large-scale military manœuvres, and stayed there for two months. With him were Ismet Paşa, the Prime Minister, Kâzım Paşa, the Minister of War, and Fevzi Paşa, the Chief of the General Staff. 'We were agreed on the need to abolish the Caliphate. At the same time we decided to suppress the Ministry of *Şeriat* and *Evkâf* and to unify public education.' [43]

On 1 March 1924 Mustafa Kemal opened the new session of the Assembly. In his speech, he emphasized three main points: the safeguarding and stabilization of the Republic, the creation of a unified national system of education, and the need to 'cleanse and elevate the Islamic faith, by rescuing it from the position of a

---

[41] *Nutuk*, ii. 847–8; cf. *Speech*, pp. 682–3.   [42] RIIA, *Survey*, 1925, p. 571.
[43] *Nutuk*, ii. 848; cf. *Speech*, p. 683. See also *WI*, x (1924), 81.

political instrument, to which it has been accustomed for centuries'.[44]

The meaning of this third point was clarified next day at a meeting of the People's Party group. The President's proposals were discussed, and agreement reached on a series of motions, which were read to the Grand National Assembly on 3 March. They provided for the deposition of the Caliph, the abolition of the Caliphate, and the banishment of all members of the Ottoman house from Turkish territory. The next morning at daybreak the unhappy Abdülmecid was packed into a car and driven to a railway station to board the Orient Express—not the main Sirkeci station, where his departure might have provoked demonstrations, but a small one outside the city. The last of the Caliphs had followed the last of the Sultans into exile.[45]

In abolishing the Caliphate, Kemal was making his first open assault on the entrenched forces of Islamic orthodoxy. The traditional Islamic state was in theory and in the popular conception a theocracy, in which God was the sole legitimate source of both power and law, and the sovereign His vice-gerent on earth. The faith was the official credo of the established political and social order. The same Holy Law, coming from the same source and administered through the same judicature, embraced civil, criminal, and constitutional as well as ritual and doctrinal rules. The sovereign was the supreme embodiment of the Holy Law, maintained by it, and maintaining it. The ulema were its authorized defenders and exponents.

Since the beginning of the Ottoman reforms, great inroads had been made into the power of the ulema, who had been forced by successive reformers to surrender large areas of jurisdiction in legal, social, and educational matters. They still retained, however, great power and greater influence. A large part of the educational facilities of the country were under their control; the laws relating to family and personal matters were still dominated by the code which they administered; since the disappearance of

---

[44] *Nutuk*, ii. 849; cf. *Speech*, p. 684.

[45] On the final phase of the Ottoman Caliphate, and its abolition, see Jäschke, 'Das osmanische Scheinkalifat von 1922', *WI*, n.s., i (1951), 195–217, 218–28; C. A. Nallino, 'La fine del così detto califfato ottomano', *OM*, iv (1924), 137–53 (reprinted in *Raccolta di Scritti*, iii (1941), pp. 260–83. Texts in Gözübüyük and Kili, pp. 98 ff., and Arıburnu, p. 329. Ismet Paşa's speech on this occasion is included in his collected speeches, *İnönü'nün Söylev ve Demeçleri*, i (1946), 87–93.

the Sultanate and all the other institutions of the old régime, they remained the only power in Turkish society with the cohesion, the organization, and the authority to be able to challenge the leadership of the new régime.

More than once in the past, the ulema had delayed or frustrated the work of the reformers; Mustafa Kemal was determined that they should not hinder his revolution. The abolition of the Caliphate was a crushing blow to their whole hierarchic organization. It was accompanied by a series of others, abolishing the ancient office of *Şeyh-ül-Islâm* and the Ministry of *Şeriat*, closing the separate religious schools and colleges, and, a month later, abolishing the special *Şeriat* courts in which theologian-judges had administered the Holy Law. The new order was confirmed in the republican constitution, adopted by the Grand National Assembly on 20 April 1924, which affirmed the legislative authority of the Assembly and reserved the judicial function to independent courts acting 'in the name of the nation'.[46]

Radical changes of this kind inevitably aroused active and widespread resentment. In addition, opposition to Kemal's personal ascendancy was growing among those who had been most closely associated with him in the early phases of the national struggle. In the capital, a number of Kemal's former supporters broke away and began to form an opposition group, called the 'Progressive Republican Party'. Its leaders included Rauf and Generals Ali Fuad and Refet, who had been with him at the secret meeting in Amasya in June 1919, as well as General Kâzım Karabekir and other prominent civilian and military members of the nationalist old guard. On 21 November 1924 Mustafa Kemal appointed his old friend Fethi [Okyar], regarded as a liberal, as Prime Minister in place of Ismet.[47]

Political insurrection in the party was one thing; armed insurrection was another, and when, in February 1925, a Kurdish revolt broke out in the eastern provinces, Kemal acted swiftly and vigorously. The leader of the rebels was Şeyh Said of Palu, the hereditary chief of the Nakşbendi dervishes. By the beginning of March the rebellion had spread to much of the south-east, and

---

[46] On the constitution see below, pp. 256 ff.

[47] See Rustow, pp. 547–8; Orga, pp. 153 ff., and below, p. 375. Cebesoy's fourth volume, which will presumably deal with his role in the Progressive Republican Party, has at the time of writing not yet appeared.

seemed to offer a serious threat to the republican régime. In Ankara the experiment in government by the President's loyal opposition was abandoned. On 3 March Fethi was dismissed and Ismet Paşa resumed the premiership, and on the following day a drastic 'Law for the Maintenance of Order' was rushed through the Assembly, giving extraordinary and, in effect, dictatorial powers to the government for two years.[48] They were renewed again in 1927 and did not finally expire until March 1929. At the same time special 'independence tribunals' were set up, in the east and in Ankara, the former with summary powers of execution. On the report of the tribunal in Ankara, the Progressive Republican Party was outlawed on 3 June. Fethi had meanwhile been appointed, on 11 March, as ambassador to France.

In the east swift military action crushed the rebellion; the 'independence tribunals' administered swift justice to the rebel leaders. Şeyh Said was captured in April and sentenced to death, together with forty-six of his followers, by an 'independence tribunal' in Diyarbakır, on 29 June. The sentences were carried out next day.

The Kurdish rebellion had been led by dervish *şeyhs*, who had urged their followers to overthrow the godless Republic and restore the Caliph. Kemal now reacted against the dervishes, closing their convents, disbanding their associations, and banning their meetings, ceremonies, and special garb.

It was at this time, and in this context, that Kemal made the first of his great symbolic revolutions—those dramatic changes of outward forms which expressed, in a manner at once vivid and profound, the forcible transference of a whole nation from one civilization to another. To the Westerner, the enforced replacement of one form of headgear by another may seem comic or irritating, and in either case trivial; to the Muslim it was a matter of fundamental significance, expressing—and affecting—his relations with his neighbours and his ancestors, and his place in society and in history. Islam was a faith and a civilization, distinct from other faiths and civilizations, uniting the Muslim to other Muslims, and separating him both from his heathen forefathers and his infidel neighbours. Dress, and especially headgear, was the visible and outward token by which a Muslim indicated his

[48] Text and discussion in Arıburnu, pp. 174 ff.

allegiance to the community of Islam and his rejection of others. During the past century modernization and reform had made great inroads into Muslim exclusiveness in matters of dress, and had created a new social gulf between the Westernized and the un-Westernized—the former comprising the male and secular elements of the ruling *élite*, the latter the rest of the population. But even among the immaculately trousered and jacketed dandies of the capital, one badge of distinctness had remained—the fez. This headgear, introduced a bare century earlier and fiercely resisted as an infidel innovation,[49] had been adopted and accepted by Muslims in Turkey and in many other countries, and had become the last symbol of Muslim identification. The rest of the Muslim's body might be Westernized, but his head remained Islamic—with the tall, red, challenging fez proclaiming at once his refusal to conform to the West and his readiness to abase his unimpeded brow before God.

Already in the Young Turk period there were some more consistent Westernizers who dismissed the possibility of a separate Islamic civilization, modern yet distinct. 'Civilization means European civilization', Abdullah Cevdet had written in 1911.[50] Mustafa Kemal was entirely of the same opinion. Speaking to the Assembly in November 1924, after the laws against the theocracy had gone into force, he remarked: 'The Turkish nation has perceived with great joy that the obstacles which constantly, for centuries, had kept Turkey from joining the civilized nations marching forward on the path of progress, have been removed.'[51] 'Uncivilized people', he said on another occasion, 'are doomed to remain under the feet of those who are civilized.'[52] And civilization meant the West, the modern world, of which Turkey must become a part in order to survive. 'The nation has finally decided to achieve, in essence and in form, exactly and completely, the life and means that contemporary civilization assures to all nations.'[53]

The events of 1925 had shown that the forces of reaction were still powerfully entrenched, and able to offer serious resistance to the progress of Westernization. The removal of the Caliphate had not sufficed; a further shock was necessary—a traumatic impact that would shake every man in the country into the realization

---

[49] See above, p. 99.   [50] See above, p. 231.   [51] *Söylev*, i. 320.

[52] Mustafa Baydar, *Atatürk diyorki* (1957), p. 46.   [53] *Söylev*, i. 325.

that the old order had gone, and a new one come in its place. The fez was the last bastion of Muslim identification and separateness. The fez must go.

In his speech of October 1927 Kemal explained his action in these terms:

> Gentlemen, it was necessary to abolish the fez, which sat on the heads of our nation as an emblem of ignorance, negligence, fanaticism, and hatred of progress and civilization, to accept in its place the hat, the headgear used by the whole civilized world, and in this way to demonstrate that the Turkish nation, in its mentality as in other respects, in no way diverges from civilized social life.[54]

The operation was carried through with characteristic speed and efficiency. In the last week of August 1925, on a visit to Kastamonou and Inebolu, Mustafa Kemal launched the first attack on the fez and the traditional garments still worn in provincial Anatolia. In a series of speeches he ridiculed them as wasteful, uncomfortable, and, above all, barbarous—unworthy of a civilized people. Addressing a crowd in Inebolu on 28 August he said:

> Gentlemen, the Turkish people who founded the Turkish republic are civilized; they are civilized in history and in reality. But I tell you as your own brother, as your friend, as your father, that the people of the Turkish Republic, who claim to be civilized, must show and prove that they are civilized, by their ideas and their mentality, by their family life and their way of living. In a word, the truly civilized people of Turkey . . . must prove in fact that they are civilized and advanced persons also in their outward aspect. I must make these last words clear to you, so that the whole country and the world may easily understand what I mean. I shall put my explanations to you in the form of a question.
>
> Is our dress national? (Cries of no!)
>
> Is it civilized and international? (Cries of no, no!)
>
> I agree with you. This grotesque mixture of styles is neither national nor international. . . . My friends, there is no need to seek and revive the costume of Turan. A civilized, international dress is worthy and appropriate for our nation, and we will wear it. Boots or shoes on our feet, trousers on our legs, shirt and tie, jacket and waistcoat—and, of course, to complete these, a cover with a brim on our heads. I want to make this clear. This head-covering is called 'hat'.[55]

[54] *Nutuk*, i. 895; cf. *Speech*, pp. 721–2.   [55] *Söylev*, ii. 212–13; *Hist. Rép. turque*, p. 230.

The secret was out. Mustafa Kemal drove his point home two days later, in Kastamonu:

I see a man in the crowd in front of me [he said, pointing to a citizen]; he has a fez on his head, a green turban on the fez, a smock on his back, and on top of that a jacket like the one I am wearing. I can't see the lower half. Now what kind of outfit is that? Would a civilized man put on this preposterous garb and go out to hold himself up to universal ridicule?[56]

On 2 September a group of new decrees directed against the theocracy included a ban on the wearing of religious vestments or insignia by persons not holding a recognized religious office,[57] and an order to all civil servants to wear the costume 'common to the civilized nations of the world'—that is, the Western suit and hat. At first ordinary citizens were free to dress as they pleased, but on 25 November 1925 a new law required all men to wear hats, and made the wearing of the fez a criminal offence.[58]

The reaction of Muslim conservatives to this revolution can best be seen in a declaration issued in March 1926, on behalf of the 'Islamic Religious Presidency of the Kingdom of Egypt', and signed by the Rector of the al-Azhar university and the Chief Mufti of Egypt.

It is clear [they said] that a Muslim who seeks to resemble a non-Muslim by adopting the latter's distinctive form of dress, will also come to take the same way as he in his beliefs and actions. That is why he who wears the hat because of an inclination to the religion of another and a contempt for his own is an infidel, according to the unanimous opinion of the Muslims. He who wears the hat in order to resemble non-Muslims, if he also adopts some of the practices of their religion, such as entering a church, is an infidel; if he does not do this, he is still a sinner. . . . Is it not folly to abandon one's own national way of dressing in order to adopt that of other people, when this desire for imitation can lead to the disappearance of our nationality, the annihilation of our own identity in theirs, which is the fate of the weak. . . .[59]

[56] *Söylev*, ii. 219 ff.; *Hist.*, pp. 231–2.

[57] In December 1934 a further law prohibited the wearing of religious dress of any kind by clergy (*ruhaniler*) of all faiths, except in places of worship and during religious ceremonies. Exemptions from this law were granted to eight recognized religious chiefs.

[58] Jäschke, in *WI*, n.s., i (1951), 45–46. For Kemal's speeches on his trip to Kastamonu and Inebolu see also Mustafa Selim Imece, *Atatürk'ün Şapka Devriminde Kastamonu ve Inebolu Seyahatları 1925*, (1959).

[59] Quoted by Canard, in *A. l'Inst. d'Ét. or.*, viii. 219–23.

Statements of this kind, for obvious reasons, are not found in Turkey, but there can be little doubt that the pronouncement of the Egyptian divines substantially expressed the views of the Turkish opponents of the reform. The Caliph had, after all, been a remote and semi-mythical figure; the hat law affected every Turk in his own person, and the response was correspondingly greater. There were new disturbances in the east, and ominous stirrings elsewhere. The emergency 'Law for the Maintenance of Order', passed in March 1925 to deal with the Kurdish rebellion, was still in force, and the government was able to impose and enforce its will through the armed forces and the 'independence tribunals'. As Kemal grimly remarked:

We did it [i.e. the abolition of the fez] while the Law for the Maintenance of Order was still in force. Had it not been, we would have done it all the same, but it certainly is true that the existence of the law made it much easier for us. Indeed, the existence of the Law for the Maintenance of Order prevented the large-scale poisoning of the nation by certain reactionaries.[60]

Together with the fez, Mustafa Kemal changed some other symbols. The Turkish finance (*maliye*) calendar, based on a combination of the Greek months with the *hijri* year, had been in increasing use in Ottoman administration since the late eighteenth century, and in 1917 had been adjusted to the Gregorian months, though still with a modified *hijri* year. On 26 December 1925 it was abolished, and the Gregorian calendar and era officially adopted. At the same time the twenty-four-hour 'international' clock was confirmed as the only legally valid method of measuring time.

Another, and more delicate matter, was that of female clothing. In his speech at Kastamonu on 30 August 1925, Mustafa Kemal had attacked the veil as well as the fez.

In some places I have seen women who put a piece of cloth or a towel or something like it over their heads to hide their faces, and who turn their backs or huddle themselves on the ground when a man passes by. What are the meaning and sense of this behaviour? Gentlemen, can the mothers and daughters of a civilized nation adopt this strange manner, this barbarous posture? It is a spectacle that makes the nation an object of ridicule. It must be remedied at once.[61]

60 *Nutuk*, ii. 895; cf. *Speech*, p. 722.   61 *Söylev*, ii. 220; *Hist.*, p. 234.

Even the great reformer, buttressed as he was by the Law for the Maintenance of Order and the 'independence tribunals', did not venture to legislate against the veil. The unveiling of women, already accepted among the educated classes in the big towns, made only slow progress elsewhere. It was not until 1935 that a ban on the veil was proposed at a congress of the People's Party, and even then no action was taken.[62]

The Law Reform[63]

The 'outward aspect' of the Turkish people, or at least of its accessible male members, had been changed. There remained the more difficult task of transforming its 'family life and way of living' to accord with the 'common practice of civilized nations'. For this a radical reorganization of the entire legal system of the country was necessary.

The nineteenth-century reforms had already removed large areas of law from the domination of the Şeriat and the jurisdiction of its exponents. On 8 April 1924 Mustafa Kemal had gone still further, and had abolished the separate Şeriat courts. But even after all these changes, the Şeriat still remained in force in most fields of family and personal law, and was still administered by judges who, though they sat in secular courts, were still to a large extent, by training and outlook, doctors of the Holy Law.

Throughout the periods of the reforms, the exclusive competence of the Şeriat lawyers in matters of family and personal status had been left intact. Kemal was determined to end it. At the beginning of 1924 the Minister of Justice, Seyyid, proposed the restoration, in an improved form, of the liberal Family Law of 1917. Kemal, however, was not interested in a law based on the Şeriat, however much it had been liberalized and modernized by interpretative ingenuity.

I wish to declare categorically [he said, in a speech at Dumlupinar on 30 August 1924][64] that the basis of civilization, the foundation of progress

---

[62] Jäschke, in *WI*, n.s., i. 47. There were, however, municipal orders against the veil in some places.

[63] The best account and interpretation of the transformation of the legal system will be found in Count Léon Ostrorog, *The Angora Reform* (1927). See further Ali Fuad Başgil and others, *La Turquie* (1939), (no. vii in *La Vie juridique des peuples*, ed. H. Levy-Ullmann and B. Mirkine-Guetzevitch); Jäschke, in *WI*, n.s., i and Bülent Daver, *Türkiye Cumhuriyetinde Lâyiklik* (1955; on laicism).

[64] Or on 26 Aug. according to the *Hist*.

and power, are in family life. A bad family life leads inevitably to social, economic and political enfeeblement. The male and female elements constituting the family must be in full possession of their natural rights, and must be in a position to discharge their family obligations.[65]

A few days later, on 11 September 1924, a commission of twenty-six lawyers set to work on the task of adapting the Swiss civil code to Turkish needs. The completed code was voted by the Assembly on 17 February 1926, and entered into force on 4 October.

It is difficult to exaggerate the significance of this change in the development of Turkey. There had been many previous legal reforms, under the *Tanzimat* and Young Turk régimes, and not a few of the prescriptions of the *Şeriat* had been tacitly dropped, chiefly in the fields of administrative, commercial, and criminal law. But this was the first time that a reformer had dared to invade the intimacies of family and religious life, the inviolate preserve of the doctors of the Holy Law—and to do so, not by stealth, but by head-on attack. The God-given *Şeriat* was repealed by the Assembly, and its rules declared null and void, superseded by the new Turkish civil code.[66] Polygamy, repudiation—all the ancient bars to the freedom and dignity of women—were abolished. In their place came civil marriage and divorce, with equal rights for both parties. Most shocking of all, to Muslim opinion, the marriage of a Muslim woman to a non-Muslim man became legally possible, and all adults were given the legal right to change their religion at will.

The voting of the Swiss civil code by the Turkish Assembly did not, of course, transform Turkey overnight into a Middle Eastern Switzerland. In the towns and in the villages near to the main roads and railway lines, the new laws of marriage, divorce, and inheritance were, in the main, enforced. In the countless villages that made up the rest of the country, the old ways survived. A marriage was usually registered with the civil authorities, to ensure legitimacy and legal inheritance. The 'legal' wife was then credited with the offspring of other wives, bound to their husbands by the bonds of religion and custom, though without the consecration of the secular state. Even though the law gave them new and extensive rights, there were few village women who dared—

[65] *Söylev*, ii. 183; *Hist.*, p. 223.   [66] Jäschke, in *WI*, n.s., i. 36–37.

or cared—to assert them against their husbands, fathers, and brothers. Even in the provincial towns, though polygamy disappeared, the women of the un-Westernized classes for a long time enjoyed very little real improvement in their status.

The citadel had, however, been breached. The authority of the state, always so important in a Muslim country, was now unmistakably on the side of reform, and the defenders of tradition were forced into the difficult and unfamiliar role of clandestine resistance. Following on a series of other defeats, the ulema had been driven from their last stronghold of power and influence; the apparatus of the law and the coercive agencies of its enforcement were being used in a determined effort to break their power for ever. Mustafa Kemal's purposes were made clear in his speech at the opening of the new law school in Ankara, on 5 November 1925:

Gentlemen, when I speak to you of legal foundations, of the laws required by our new needs, I am not merely referring to the dictum that 'every revolution must have its own special sanctions'. While restraining myself from useless recriminations, I must at the same time observe, with the deepest regret, how the efforts made by the Turkish nation for at least three centuries to profit from the means and benefits of modern civilization have been frustrated by such painful and grievous obstacles.

The negative and overwhelming force that has condemned our nation to decay, that has ultimately broken and defeated the men of initiative and drive whom our fecund nation has in no period failed to produce, is the law that has hitherto been in your hands, the law and its faithful followers. . . .

Think of the Turkish victory of 1453, the capture of Istanbul, and its place in the course of world history. That same might and power, which in defiance of a whole world made Istanbul for ever the property of the Turkish community, was too weak to overcome the ill-omened resistance of the men of law and to receive in Turkey the printing press, which had been invented at about the same time. Three centuries of observation and hesitation were needed, of effort and energy expended for and against, before the old laws and their exponents would permit the entry of printing into our country. Do not think that I have chosen a remote and ancient period, incapable of resuscitation, to illustrate the old law and the old lawyers. If I were to start giving you examples of the difficulties caused during our new revolutionary era, to me personally, by the old law and its exponents, I would run the risk of overburdening you. . . . All these events show that the greatest and at the same time the most insidious enemies of the revolutionaries are rotten laws and their decrepit upholders. . . .

It is our purpose to create completely new laws and thus to tear up the very foundations of the old legal system. . . .[67]

The most important of these new laws was undoubtedly the civil code. At the same time committees of jurists worked on others too, borrowing and adapting various Western systems of law to Turkish needs. Within a few years Turkey had new codes of obligations, commerce, maritime law, criminal law, and civil and criminal procedure, and a new system of judicature to administer them.

Conspiracy and Repression [68]

These reforms brought a renewal of activity by the opponents of the régime, who had been quiescent since the crushing of the Kurdish rebellion. On 15 June 1926, thanks to an informer, the police discovered a conspiracy in Izmir. Its leader was Ziya Hurşid, a former deputy who had opposed the abolition of the Caliphate in 1924; its purpose was to assassinate Mustafa Kemal by throwing a bomb into his car when he came to Izmir.

The conspirators were arrested, and on 16 June the Gazi entered Izmir unharmed. Two days later the 'independence tribunal', hastily transferred from Ankara, assembled in Izmir, and the Gazi issued a message to the nation, saying: 'One day I shall die, but the Republic will live on!'

The trial began on 20 June, in the Alhambra cinema in Izmir; the presiding judge was Ali [Çetinkaya], better known as Kel Ali, Bald Ali—an old soldier, a deputy, and a veteran of the Kemalist cause from the beginning. On 13 July sentences of death were pronounced against the accused, and carried out next day. The 'independence tribunal' now returned to Ankara, and began a new trial on 1 August, of a new batch of prisoners. On 26 August sentence of death was pronounced against a number of the accused, and carried out the same day.

The 'Law for the Maintenance of Order' had given Kemal the

---

[67] *Millî Eğ. Söylev*, i. 29–30; cf. *Hist.*, pp. 207–8.

[68] On these events, details will be found in Jäschke's *Kalender*, the RIIA, *Survey, OM, WI*, &c.; the Turkish official version in the *Hist.* Among the participants, Kılıç Ali has had his memoirs published (*Istiklâl Mahkemesi Hatıraları* and *Kılıç Ali Hatıralarını Anlatıyor*, 1955). For recent discussions see Karpat, pp. 46 ff., and Orga, pp. 165 ff.

legal authority to deal not only with the insurgents in the east but also with political opponents in Ankara, Istanbul, and elsewhere. After the Kurdish rebellion, the Progressive Republican Party was outlawed, and a strict control clamped down on the opposition press. The Izmir conspiracy provided the opportunity to deal with its leaders as well as other opposition figures.[69] The 'independence tribunals' at Izmir and Ankara soon extended their inquiries far beyond the original conspiracy and conspirators, and, with scant concern for legal rules and procedure, embarked on what was, in effect, a prosecution of all the major political opponents of Mustafa Kemal. Some were acquitted—the four generals, Kâzım Karabekir, Refet, Ali Fuad, and Cafer Tayyar Paşas, all concerned in the proscribed Progressive Party, were too respected to be condemned, and were released, to the great and ominous satisfaction of the army and a good many civilians. Other prisoners were less fortunate. Among those executed were prominent survivors of the Young Turk movement, such as the former Finance Minister, Cavid Bey, and even intimate associates of the Gazi during the war of independence, such as Colonel Arif. Rauf Bey, described as the arch plotter, had left for Europe before the plot was discovered, and was condemned *in absentia* to ten years' banishment.

By 1927 all opposition to the régime—military, religious, or political—had been silenced, and when elections were held in August and September 1927 for a third Assembly of the Turkish Republic, only one party, the Republican People's Party of Mustafa Kemal, was there to take part in them. It was after this election, from 15 to 20 October, that Mustafa Kemal delivered his famous speech to the Congress of the People's Party. Taking thirty-six hours to deliver, the speech contains the Gazi's description and justification of his proceedings from the moment when he landed at Samsun on 19 May 1919. It is still the classic account of the Kemalist Revolution.

Secularization: the Romanization of the Script [70]

The new session of the Assembly began unremarkably, with the re-election of Mustafa Kemal as President and the reappointment

---

[69] Whether the Progressive Republican leaders were in any way implicated in the Kurdish rising or in the Izmir conspiracy is still a matter of argument in Turkey. See, for example, Karpat, p. 47 n. 47.

[70] See further, pp. 419 ff., below.

of Ismet as Prime Minister. Further projects were, however, in preparation, with the purpose of giving the Turkish state and people a more secular, more national, more modern—and less Islamic character.

The first step was little more than a formal ratification of the changes already accomplished. The second article of the 1924 constitution had begun with the words 'The religion of the Turkish state is Islam'—a formula retained, with appropriate modifications, since the first Ottoman constitution of 1876. On 5 April 1928 the People's Party resolved to delete this clause from the constitution, and five days later, on 10 April, the Assembly voted a law to that effect. At the same time three other clauses were amended to remove religious expressions and allusions.

The disestablishment of Islam was completed, and Turkey was now, legally and constitutionally, a lay state, secular and modern in her constitution, her laws, and her aspirations. But there remained one symbol, potent and universal, that bound her to the Orient and set her apart from the Western community of nations —the Arabic script. It was this final badge of Muslim identity that was now to follow the Caliphate and the Holy Law into oblivion.

Reform of the alphabet was not a new topic. There had been proposals for an improvement of the Arabic script since the time of the *Tanzimat*, though nothing very much had come of them. The more radical idea of abandoning the Arabic script entirely and replacing it by the Latin alphabet was put forward and discussed in Turkey in 1923 and 1924, but was decisively rejected.

By 1927, however, the situation had changed. The Kemalist régime was now firmly in the saddle, and in possession of virtually dictatorial powers; the religious opposition was cowed and disheartened by a series of crushing blows. A new factor of some importance was the decision of the Soviet authorities to adopt the Latin alphabet in place of the Arabic for the Turkic languages of the USSR, thus providing both an example and an incentive to the government of the Turkish Republic.

Already in March 1926, immediately after the Soviet decision, the Minister of Education Necati had spoken of the political significance of romanization. Preparations went on during 1927, but nothing was heard in public until January 1928, when the first ranging shots of the preliminary barrage were fired. On 8 January the Minister of Justice, Mahmud Esad, a radical reformer who had played a major role in the repeal of the Holy Law, made a speech in which he praised the merits of the Latin script. A fortnight later the Minister of Education Hamdullah Subhi went further; 'The adoption of the Latin letters', he said, 'is for us a necessity. The old literature is doomed to moulder away.'[71] On 24 May the first legislative step was taken—the adoption, by law, of the 'international' numerals in place of the Arabic figures which Turkey had previously shared with other Muslim countries. On 26 June a special commission met at the Dolmabahçe palace in Istanbul, with the task of 'examining the possibility and the manner of adopting the Latin letters'. Kemal, in Istanbul for the summer, personally led and directed the discussions, and was no doubt responsible for the quick and expeditious way in which the commission conducted its business.

In six weeks the new alphabet was completed, and Kemal was ready to present it to the nation. On 9 August 1928 the sometime Gazi Paşa, now President of the Republic, appeared in a new role—that of schoolmaster. The Republican People's Party was holding a fête that night, in the park at Seraglio Point, and many of its leading figures were present. Towards eleven o'clock the President himself appeared, and after a while he rose to address them.

My friends [he said], our rich and harmonious language will now be able to display itself with new Turkish letters. We must free ourselves from these incomprehensible signs, that for centuries have held our minds in an iron vice. You must learn the new Turkish letters quickly. Teach them to your compatriots, to women and to men, to porters and to boatmen. Regard it as a patriotic and national duty . . . and when you perform that duty, bear in mind that for a nation to consist of 10 or 20 per cent. of literates and 80 or 90 per cent. of illiterates is shameful. . . . The fault is not ours; it is of those who failed to understand the character of the Turk and bound his mind in chains. Now is the time to eradicate the errors of the past. We shall repair these errors, and in doing so I want the participation of all our compatriots. . . . Our nation will show, with its script and with its mind, that its place is with the civilized world.[72]

[71] Jäschke, *Kalender*, 21 Jan. 1928.
[72] *Millî Eğ. Söylev*, i. 32–33; variant versions in *Söylev*, ii. 254–5; *Hist.*, pp. 248–9.

PLATE I

Nuruosmaniye Mosque, Istanbul, completed 1755.
Turkish baroque; Ottoman plan with Italianate details

PLATE II

a Dolmabahçe Mosque Istanbul 1850: Tanzimat eclectic

b Vakıf Han Istanbul 1918: Yeves Tank neo-classical

PLATE III

ATABAY

a. Şişli Mosque, Istanbul, completed 1949

b. Atatürk Mausoleum, Ankara

PLATE IV

a. Sultan Mahmud II, before the destruction of the Janissaries. (Paintings in the Topkapı S...

b. Sultan Mahmud II, after the destruction of the Janissaries. (Paintings in the Topkapı S...

PLATE V

President Kemal Atatürk

PLATE VI

Ladies in Sultan Ahmed Square, 1907 (from *L'Illustration*, reprinted in *Hayat*, 4 January 1957)

PLATE VII

b. Günseli Başar ('Miss Turkey'), elected Miss
Europe, 1951

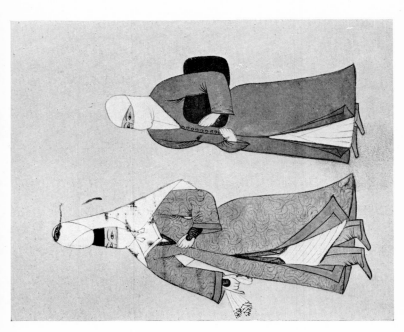

a. Lady going to the bath, with a servant; (from
a seventeenth-century Turkish miniature album)

PLATE VIII

a. Dance of the Mevlevi Dervishes (from a seventeenth-century Turkish miniature album)

b. Turkish football team

After this call to mobilization, the Gazi set out on a tour of the country, teaching and examining the populace in village squares, schoolrooms, town halls, and cafés. The Prime Minister and other dignitaries followed his example, and soon all Turkey was a school-room, with the nation's intellectuals, armed with blackboard and easel, teaching the people to read and write the new script. On 1 November 1928 the Assembly, on the first day of its new session, resolved to present the new alphabet to Mustafa Kemal on a golden tablet; on 3 November they passed a law establishing the new Turkish script and prohibiting the public use of the Arabic alphabet for the Turkish language after the end of the year. A few days later examinations were held to test the literacy of civil servants in the new script, and on 11 November a cabinet decision laid down the regulations of the 'School of the Nation'. Articles 3 and 4 read: 'Every male and female Turkish citizen is a member of this organization'; 'The chief instructor of the School of the Nation is His Excellency the President of the Republic, Gazi Mustafa Kemal.'[73]

Various arguments have been put forward to explain and justify the revolution in the alphabet. The Arabic letters were ill suited to express the sounds of the Turkish language; they were difficult to teach and troublesome to print, and thus constituted a barrier to education and cultural expansion. These charges are not without foundation, and it is certain that the new script, clear, simple, and phonetic, showed the way to a great increase in literacy and a vast expansion of publications. But the basic purpose of the change was not so much practical and pedagogical, as social and cultural—and Mustafa Kemal, in forcing his people to accept it, was slamming a door on the past as well as opening a door to the future. The way was now clear to the final break with the past and with the East—to the final incorporation of Turkey into the civilization of the modern West. This desire, with the danger inherent in it, is well expressed by the distinguished Turkish writer Mme Halide Edib Adıvar:

We can conceive of modern civilization as an entirety. That is to say, we cannot put on Western civilization as a whole the label English, or French, or Italian. Therefore, even a nation that is a late-comer to this civilization is not simply their follower, but is also part of Western civilization. Total and slavish imitation of a model is the very

[73] Jäschke, *Kalender*, 11 Nov. 1928.

T

opposite of the spirit of Western civilization. This point needs special attention from late-comers to this civilization. [74]

Experiment with Democracy

The law authorizing emergency powers was renewed in 1927 for a further period of two years. On 4 March 1929 it was allowed to run out, and the government announced that it would not be extended. At first there was no response to this relaxation of administrative control. Then, in December 1929, a new newspaper, *Yarın* (Tomorrow), began to appear and attracted attention by its criticisms of the government. As in 1924, the attack was not levelled against Kemal but against the Prime Minister Ismet and especially against his economic policies. In April the paper was suppressed for one day, and on 17 May its editor, Arif Oruç, was sentenced to a month's imprisonment on a charge of writing provocative articles. Before long he was back at work, and continued his criticisms of the government and of individual government officials. [75]

This mild reaction presaged a second experiment with a tolerated opposition. The first hint came from Mustafa Kemal himself, who mentioned at a ball in Yalova that a new party was about to be formed. On 9 August 1930 Fethi, back in Turkey from his embassy in Paris, wrote a letter to Mustafa Kemal complaining of the failure of the government's fiscal and economic policies, of the lack of free criticism in the Assembly, and of the resulting irresponsibility of the cabinet. What was needed, he said, was an opposition, and he therefore requested the President's views on his proposal to found a new party. Kemal replied reaffirming his belief in freedom of discussion, and expressing his gratification at Fethi's acceptance of the basic principles of the secular Republic. The letter and reply were duly published, and on 12 August Fethi submitted the constitution of the Free Republican Party to the acting Vali of Istanbul with the request that it be registered in accordance with the law of associations. The programme included greater freedom, lower taxes, better and less government. [76]

The short and unhappy life of the Free Republican Party remains an obscure episode in the history of the Turkish Republic,

[74] Halide Edib Adıvar, *Türkiye'de Şark* . . . (1946), p. 11.
[75] Jäschke, *Kalender*, and *OM*, under the relevant dates.
[76] Tunaya, *Partiler*, pp. 622 ff.

and has given rise to many different explanations. Some believe that Mustafa Kemal really wished to create a multi-party democracy in Turkey, and abandoned the attempt only when reactionary violence proved that it was premature. Others have said that he aimed only at a tame, manageable opposition to release tension during a time of economic crisis, and crushed it when it seemed to be getting out of hand. Others again have interpreted the episode as a disagreement between Kemal and Ismet, the former seeking a counterweight to Ismet and the People's Party, the latter finally convincing him that the experiment was too dangerous. Certainly the Free Republican Party, founded by the authority of Mustafa Kemal and operating under his close supervision, was far less independent than the Progressive Party of 1924, and looked even less like a serious alternative to the party in power.[77]

Whatever the truth of the matter, it soon became clear that the experiment was both premature and dangerous. Fethi and Ismet were careful to maintain the fullest courtesy and friendliness towards one another, but the appearance of a licensed opposition provoked an explosion of accumulated hatreds and resentments from many different quarters. Fethi's speeches were followed by riots and disturbances, and there were ominous stirrings in the eastern provinces. Finally, in November, the Gazi's loyal opposition was disbanded. On 15 November Fethi accused the government, in the Assembly, of electoral malpractices, and shortly afterwards announced his decision to dissolve the Free Republican Party 'because struggle against the Gazi was impossible'.[78] This decision was made known to the Ministry of the Interior in a letter of 17 November 1930. Two other minor parties that had appeared at about the same time, the Popular Republican Party and the minute Workers' and Peasants' Party, were dissolved by government order.[79]

Economic Development [80]

In October 1929 the crash on the New York Stock Exchange ushered in the great depression, which swiftly spread across the

[77] Ibid.   [78] Jäschke, *Kalender*, 17 Nov. 1930.   [79] Tunaya, *Partiler*, p. 635.

[80] For a critical assessment of Kemalist economic policies see Z.Y. Hershlag, 'Turkey: Achievements and Failures in the policy of economic development during the inter-war period 1919–1939', *Kyklos* (1954), pp. 323–50, and the same author's book, *Turkey; an Economy in Transition* (n.d., preface dated 1958).

world, bringing trade stagnation and falling prices, unemployment and ruin. Turkey, though still very imperfectly assimilated into the Western world of capitalist free enterprise, was badly hit by the fall in the prices of agricultural produce, on which she depended very largely for her export trade. Substantially self-sufficient in foodstuffs, she was able to feed her own people and shield them from the most terrible consequences of the depression. But her economic position in other respects was very vulnerable. The economic clauses in the treaty of Lausanne had restricted her power to impose certain tariffs, and had left her with a backward and undeveloped industry and a dangerously unfavourable balance of trade. For many vital supplies she was dependent on imports from the more advanced industrial countries, for which she paid with exports of raw materials. With the fall in prices, the Turkish leaders were soon faced with a grave economic crisis, caused by events beyond their reach or control, but demanding from them immediate remedial action.

The first measures taken by the Turkish government—as by most other governments affected by the crisis—were orthodox and restrictive, palliative rather than remedial in their effects, and intended to reduce the volume of foreign trade and to cut down government expenditure. Already in June 1929, following the expiration of the restrictions imposed by the Lausanne treaty, the Assembly had approved a new tariff law; it was intended to give necessary protection to the nascent Turkish industries which the Kemalist régime had been trying almost since its inception, but without much success, to foster. The new tariff came into force on 1 October 1929, just before the beginning of the depression, and the emphasis of Turkish fiscal policy was inevitably shifted from the original objective of fostering industry to the immediate need for restriction and protection. On 4 December restrictions were imposed on currency dealings and purchases abroad, and the rate of the Turkish pound dropped to TL11.10 to the pound sterling.

These, and other measures that followed, transformed the balance of trade in Turkey's favour, and gave some measure of protection to local products; in time they placed the whole foreign trade of the country under government control. The Turkish leaders were, however, well aware that these restrictions, though helpful in their immediate effects, did nothing to bring about what the country most needed—an economic expansion that would develop her resources, endow her with industry, raise the standard of living of the people, and make her less vulnerable to the vagaries of international trade. But how was such an expansion to be accomplished?

The depression of 1929, and the hardships that resulted from it, brought a revival of anti-Western and anti-capitalist feeling. Once again, as in the early days of the struggle for independence, it seemed to many Turks that capitalism and imperialism—the two were more or less identified—were the real enemies, that it was the West, at once greedy and inefficient, that was enslaving the backward nations, by preserving and exploiting their backwardness. The Ottoman Debt, the Lausanne restrictions, the trade deficit—and now a terrible crisis which the fumbling and stricken West seemed utterly unable to control or remedy and in which the Turks, innocent bystanders, had become painfully involved.

Capital and initiative were urgently needed for development; who could provide them? After the struggle to end foreign control and interference, the new republican régime did not look kindly on foreign capital, nor for that matter did foreign investors show any great desire to put money into Turkey.[81] Local capitalist enterprise was lacking in both capital and enterprise, and such people as still possessed wealth after the long years of war, occupation, and revolution were reluctant to venture it in undertakings of a new and unfamiliar kind. The government for their part did little to encourage local private enterprise. A régime of soldiers and officials, they had retained much of the traditional contempt for trade and traders, all the more so since the commercial class in the large towns still consisted very largely of Christians and Jews.

The West had failed; it was inevitable that many eyes should turn to another part of the world, where a rival, totally different system of economic organization was being tried. Soviet Russia, with all her difficulties, had been little affected by the crisis of capitalism. Her state-directed, state-operated economy seemed immune to the depression, and even the governments of the

[81] Apart from short-term business credits, only one foreign loan was accepted by the Turkish Republic before 1933. That was a loan of $10 million negotiated by Ivar Kreuger in 1930, in return for a monopoly of match production in Turkey. This one experiment was not encouraging (Hershlag, *Turkey,* pp. 121–2. Orhan Conker and Émile Witmeur, *Redressement économique et industrialisation de la nouvelle Turquie,* 1937, pp. 198–200).

capitalist West, in apparent defiance of their own principles, were trying to solve the crisis by increasing state intervention in economic matters. Turkey was soon to follow—and surpass—their example.

Russian Influences

The suggestion has often been made that the introduction of the Turkish policy of etatism was inspired by the example and precept of the Soviet Union. Certainly, there were points of resemblance, and even of direct contact. Since the early days of the Kemalist movement, when the two outlaw, revolutionary régimes were drawn together by 'the common struggle which both peoples have undertaken against the intervention of imperialism',[82] relations between the Turkish and Soviet Republics had been friendly. After a temporary chill during the Lausanne period, they grew warmer in 1924–5, when a clash with Britain over the Mosul question again inclined Turkish sentiments away from the West and towards the Soviets, and led to the signature of a Russo-Turkish treaty of friendship on 17 December 1925.

This diplomatic friendship brought no ideological influences. Kemal had made it clear from the start that, whatever might be the arguments for Communism in Russia, he had no use for it in Turkey. On more than one occasion he specifically disavowed any affinity between Kemalist and Communist ideologies, and as early as January 1921 took steps to counter Communist activities in Turkey. In 1922 Rauf's government banned Communist propaganda; in 1925 the last semi-legal vestiges of the Turkish Communist Party were finally outlawed.[83] In Russia, these affronts to the Communist cause were swallowed for political reasons, and the ideologists of the Comintern were busy explaining that Kemal, though anti-Communist, could be regarded as progressive, and even revolutionary, since he was destroying the remnants of feudalism, pursuing liberal agrarian policies, initiating industrial development, and resisting the encroachments of the capitalist West.[84]

[82] Turco-Russian treaty of friendship, 16 Mar. 1921. Text in J. C. Hurewitz, *Diplomacy in the Near and Middle East*, ii (1956), 95. cf. Jäschke, 'Der Weg zur russisch-türkischen Freundschaft', *WI*, xvi (1934), 23–28; Hershlag, *Turkey*, pp. 77 ff., and above, p. 248.

[83] Tunaya, *Partiler*, p. 552; W. Z. Laqueur, *Communism and Nationalism* (1956), pp. 210–11 and *The Soviet Union and the Middle East* (1959), pp. 25–29.

[84] Laqueur, *Soviet Union*, pp. 87–88.

In 1928–9, in the course of a general ideological reorientation in Moscow, a new line of interpretation was adopted, and Kemal was abruptly transformed from a revolutionary hero to a reactionary tyrant.

Kemalism had ceased to be a mass movement, and was on the way to total capitulation. It had destroyed some, but by no means all, of the feudal vestiges in the Turkish villages, and its social basis was an alliance between the top layers of the bourgeoisie and the big landowners, plus the 'kulaks'. Kemal was said to rule by means of a unique mixture of terror and social demagogy, a special Turkish brand of 'national fascism' or 'agrarian Bonapartism'.

Kemal was a fascist; under his rule Turkey was falling back into Imperialist domination and social reaction.[85] These changes inevitably affected relations between the two governments. The Russian reassessment of the Kemalist régime led to a renewal of Turkish Communist activity against it, which in turn led to new and more forceful repressive measures by the Turkish authorities. In the summer of 1929 these were reported in the Soviet press, which condemned, in strong language, the actions of the Turkish government and its economic policies. The Turkish press replied defending them, and drawing the attention of the Russians to some of their own shortcomings. When the newspapers on both sides are government organs, press polemics easily become international disputes.[86] In these circumstances, it is the more remarkable that there should have been such a dramatic improvement in Turco-Russian relations a few months later. The first sign came in November 1929, when a commercial agreement with the USSR was initialed. On 11 December a company for trade with the USSR, founded by the Agricultural Bank and the Bank of Industry and Mines, began work. On 13 December the Soviet Deputy Commissar for Foreign Affairs, Karakhan, arrived in Ankara, where he was received by Mustafa Kemal, and on 17 December a 'Russo-Turkish Protocol' was signed, renewing the agreement of 1925. Relations became still closer in September 1930, when the Turkish Foreign Minister Tevfik Rüştü [Aras] went on a visit to Moscow. This was followed by other visits— Litvinov in Ankara in October 1931, Ismet Paşa in Moscow in April–May 1932, Voroshilov in Ankara in October 1933, Celâl

[85] Ibid. p. 105.   [86] Ahmet Şükrü Esmer, *Siyasî Tarih, 1919–39* (1953), pp. 204–5.

Bayar in Moscow in July 1935. The most important of these visits
was that of the Turkish Prime Minister and Foreign Minister to
Moscow in 1932, where on 8 May they signed an agreement with
the USSR for a loan of $8 million. Most of it was used for the
development of the textile industry, through the Soviet-guided
kombinat at Kayseri.

At a time when the West was still in the grip of the depression,
the Soviets were thus able to offer a method of economic expansion, capital to initiate it, and experts to assist in its application.
The Kemalist adoption of etatism was not due to any political
or ideological leanings to the Soviet Union or to Communism, but
to the sheer practical necessities of the moment. The country, still
not fully recovered from the ruin and impoverishment brought by
earlier struggles and upheavals, was now again stricken by the
consequences of a world-wide crisis in which the Turkish leaders
had neither responsibility nor control. Help was urgently needed;
it must be taken where it could be found.

Etatism

The first hint of the new economic policy came in a speech of
Ismet Paşa at Sivas in 1930, when he stressed the need for greater
economic activity by the state. Then, on 20 April 1931, Mustafa
Kemal published his famous manifesto, in which he set forth, for
the first time, the six 'fundamental and unchanging principles'
which were adopted the following month by a general conference
of the Republican People's Party, and later incorporated in the
constitution. They are still represented by the six arrows of the
party crest. 'The Republican's People's Party', says the first article
of the manifesto, 'is republican, nationalist, populist, etatist,
secularist, and revolutionary.'

Of these principles, only one was new—that of *devletcilik*,
usually translated etatism. It was defined in the third article of
the manifesto in these words:

Although considering private work and activity a basic idea, it is
one of our main principles to interest the State actively in matters
where the general and vital interests of the nation are in question,
especially in the economic field, in order to lead the nation and the
country to prosperity in as short a time as possible.[87]

[87] *OM*, May 1931, pp. 225–6; official English version, from the 1935 programme,
in J. Parker and C. Smith, *Modern Turkey* (1940), p. 238. Cf. Hershlag, *Turkey*, p. 86.

Further definitions of etatism were given, in the following years, by the party, the government, and Kemal himself. The spokesmen of etatism were at some pains to point out that they were not socialists. They had no intention of collectivizing the economy or establishing state monopolies; they would not touch agriculture at all, and had no desire to eliminate private enterprise from industry and commerce. Their purpose was to initiate and develop projects in fields which were of vital concern to the strength and well-being of the nation, and in which private capital was incapable, inactive, or dilatory.

In 1933 the first Turkish five-year plan was prepared, for the expansion of Turkish industry; it was approved on 9 January 1934, and completed in 1939. This plan was no doubt inspired by the Russian precedent, and was certainly helped by the Russian loan and Russian advice. Its aim was the simultaneous development of consumer industries, chiefly textiles, and also paper, glass, and ceramics, and of the basic industrial potential, especially iron, steel, and chemicals. The most important achievements were the Soviet-planned textile factory (the *kombinat*) at Kayseri, with 33,000 spindles, and the British-constructed iron and steel works at Karabük.[88]

As the five-year plan developed, the Turkish economic planners, though still reaffirming their respect for private enterprise, showed little interest in its expansion or even survival. Once again, the reasons were not doctrinal.

The system of etatism applied in Turkey [said Mustafa Kemal at the Izmir Fair in August 1935], is not a system copied and translated from the ideas that socialist theoreticians have been putting forward since the 19th century; our etatism takes as its basis the private initiative and personal aptitudes of individuals, but at the same time, taking account of all the needs of a great nation and a broad land, and of the fact that so much still remains to be done, it rests on the principle that the state must take charge of the national economy.[89]

Economists have on the whole been severe in their judgement of the economic achievements of Turkish etatism. Undoubtedly, it endowed the country with many new industrial enterprises. There were factories for textiles at Kayseri, Eregli, Nazilli,

---

[88] See the comments in M. W. Thornburg and others, *Turkey, an Economic Appraisal* (1949), pp. 109 ff.

[89] Baydar, p. 87; cf. Hershlag, *Turkey*, p. 89, and below, pp. 463 ff.

Malatya, and Bursa; paper and cellulose at Izmir, artificial silk at Çemlik, glass and bottles at Paşabahçe, china-ware at Kütahya, sulphur at Keçiborlu, cement at Sivas. In heavy industry there were the great anthracite works at Zonguldak, and the iron and steel works at Karabük. But the efforts of the Turkish planners— and of their foreign advisers—were all too often inept, confused, and misdirected, and there are many tales of wasteful and in-efficient factories, producing shoddy products at high prices.

What we see in Turkey [says the Thornburg report] looks, not like a planned economy, but like a poorly managed capitalist economy in which most of the capital happens to be supplied by the government. . . . The result [of Russian influence] is a hybrid which does not embody the best potentialities of either of its parents.[90]

The Thornburg report accuses the etatist planners not only of botching their own work, but also of preventing the expansion of private enterprise which might otherwise have taken place. 'Private enterprise did not fail; it was deliberately discouraged.'[91] The report of the International Bank for Reconstruction and Development, on the other hand, concedes that 'under etatism Turkey has made substantial progress. It is doubtful whether comparable accomplishment would have taken place in this period under domestic private enterprise with the handicap of the Ottoman heritage.'[92]

Perhaps the most serious defect of the whole operation was the almost complete neglect of agriculture. 'Consequently', says Hershlag, 'the greatest natural asset of the country remained unexploited, agricultural production did not increase and only a limited labour force was released for urban industries.'[93]

The Last Years

During the 1930's the government of the Republic was mainly concerned with economic matters and, later, with the looming menace of Axis aggression. Mustafa Kemal did, however, find time for a few further measures of Westernization and reform. A second experiment, in 1930, with Western-style democratic govern-ment had been abandoned after a short time, and the attempt

---

[90] Thornburg, p. 39.   [91] Ibid. p. 34.
[92] *The Economy of Turkey* (1951), p. 9.
[93] *Kyklos*, p. 324; cf. his *Turkey*, pp. 143 ff.

was not renewed until 1945.[94] But other forms of Westernization continued. In December 1934 women were given the right to vote in parliamentary elections and to be elected as deputies, and in the election of 1935 seventeen women were elected.

The same year 1935 brought two other notable innovations. The first was the compulsory adoption, by all Turks, of surnames; the second was the introduction, in all government and public offices, of a weekly holiday from 1 p.m. Saturday until Monday morning.

Both these measures involved radical departures from Islamic custom, albeit minor in comparison with those already accomplished. The weekly day of rest is a Jewish and Christian, but not a Muslim custom; the Muslim Friday is a day of public worship, but not a Sabbath, and traditionally it was the day of greatest activity in the markets centred round the mosque. The weekly day of rest, on Friday, was first introduced by the Assembly for railway workers in 1920, and in 1924 was made general for all towns with more than 10,000 inhabitants. The transfer of the weekly day of rest from the Muslim Friday to the Christian Sunday had obvious economic and administrative advantages, and followed logically on the adoption of the Western clock and the Western calendar.[95]

The Turks, like most other Muslim peoples, were not in the habit of using family names. A man would be known by his personal or birth-name (*göbek adı*) supplemented by a second name given in childhood, or by his father's name. Surnames existed, but were rare, and not in common usage. The more complex and extensive relationships of a modern society made a system of family names desirable; the adoption of the new civil code made it immediately necessary. A law of 28 June 1934 imposed on every Turkish citizen the obligation to adopt a surname with effect from 1 January 1935.[96] At the same time all non-military ranks and titles surviving from the old régime were abolished, and replaced by the new words *Bay* and *Bayan*—Mr. and Mrs. The Prime Minister, Ismet Paşa, chose the name of the place where he had won a military victory and became Ismet İnönü. The President renounced his titles of Gazi and Paşa, and assumed the name Atatürk—father-Turk. At the same time he dropped the

[94] See above, p. 274, and below, pp. 375-6. [95] Jäschke, in *WI*, n.s., i. 50 ff.
[96] Ibid. p. 53.

excessively Arabic 'Mustafa' thus becoming Kemal Atatürk, the name by which he was known for the rest of his life, and after.[97]

In the early months of 1938, during a journey in Anatolia, Kemal Atatürk was taken ill.

After a brief recovery his condition worsened rapidly, and on 5 September he thought it advisable to make his will. On 1 November, when the new session of the Assembly opened its proceedings, the President's message was, for the first time, read for him by the Prime Minister, and on 10 November a stunned and anguished nation learned that the great leader who had guided it for nearly twenty years was dead. 'The Turkish fatherland', said the government communiqué, 'has lost its great builder, the Turkish nation its mighty leader, mankind a great son.'[98] On 16 November his coffin, on a catafalque draped with the Turkish flag, was placed in the great reception hall of the Dolmabahçe Palace in Istanbul, where for three days and nights an endless stream of mourners passed to pay their last respects. On the 19th Professor Şerefeddin Yaltkaya, head of the Department of Religious Affairs, recited the Muslim funeral prayers over his body, and twelve generals carried the catafalque to a gun-carriage waiting outside the Palace. A mighty funeral cortége followed it to the Gülhane park, where the coffin was placed on board a torpedo boat and then transferred to the battleship *Yavuz*, the former *Göben*. From there it was landed at Izmit and taken by a special train to Ankara, where it was consigned, with full military honours, to a temporary tomb in the Ethnographical Museum. In 1953 it was transferred to its final resting place in the newly completed mausoleum at Rasat Tepe, on the outskirts of the capital.

Kemal Atatürk was a man of swift and decisive action, of sudden and often violent decision. A tough and brilliant soldier, a hard drinker and wencher, he was in all things a man of immense will and abounding vitality. By his contemporaries he was often called a dictator, and in a sense he certainly was. But in saying this one must remember that his rule was very different from that of other men, in Europe and the Middle East yesterday and today,

---

[97] The replacement of Kemal by the allegedly more Turkish-sounding Kamal was of brief duration, and did not pass into common usage.

[98] *IA*, i. 798.

to whom the same term is applied. An autocrat by personal and professional bias, dominating and imperious by temperament, he yet showed a respect for decency and legality, for human and political standards, that is in astonishing contrast with the behaviour of lesser and more pretentious men. His was a dictatorship without the uneasy over-the-shoulder glance, the terror of the door-bell, the dark menace of the concentration camp. Force and repression were certainly used to establish and maintain the Republic during the period of revolutionary changes, but no longer; and after the executions of 1926 there was little danger to life and to personal liberty. Political activity against the régime was banned and newspapers were under strict control. But apart from this, talk, and even books and periodicals, were comparatively free. Critics of the régime from the humbler classes were left alone; critics among the ruling *élite* were, in accordance with earlier Ottoman practice, punished with governorships or embassies in remote places. Violence was rare, and was usually in response to violent opposition.

The subsequent rise of military régimes in other Muslim countries in the Middle East has led some observers to see in Atatürk and his Revolution the prototype of these later movements. There is, however, very little resemblance between them. Atatürk was not a revolutionary junior officer seizing power by coup d'état, but a general and a pasha, taking control by gradual, almost reluctant steps in a moment of profound national crisis. He and his associates, though imbued with new ideas, were by status and habit men of the old Ottoman ruling *élite*, with centuries of military and Imperial experience. Even after the destruction of the Empire and the banishment of the dynasty, they still had the assurance and authority to demand—and receive—obedience, not needing either to court popularity or enforce submission. And so they were able to carry through their Revolution by a kind of paternalistic guidance, without resort to the whole monstrous apparatus of demagogy and repression familiar in the European dictatorships and their imitations elsewhere.

It was as a soldier that Atatürk first rose to lead his people— as the brilliant and inspired leader who snatched the Sick Man of Europe from his death-bed and infused him with a new life and vitality. His first great achievements were in the heroic mode—in fashioning an army, a movement, and a nation from the débris of the shattered Empire and driving the invaders from the national soil.

Yet it is not in these achievements, great as they were, that the true greatness of Atatürk lies. Rather does it lie in his realization that all this was enough—and yet not enough; that the military task was completed, and another, very different one remained. In 1923, at the moment of his triumph, there were many opportunities which might have tempted a military commander to seek more glory, or a nationalist leader to arouse new passions. He renounced them all, and with a realism, restraint, and moderation unusual among heroes, warned his people against all such heady adventures. The next task was at home—for when all the invaders, military, financial, political, had gone, there still remained the problem of rebuilding the country, already backward, now further weakened by long years of war and internal struggle. It is the supreme merit of Kemal Atatürk that he—the Ottoman soldier, the victorious hero, was able to see this, and to make the immense effort of imagination and courage that it required of him. In a society that despised labour and trade, where ingenuity was an infidel trick and the military virtues the only universally accepted standard, the Gazi Pasha became a civilian President, and setting aside his uniform, appeared to his people in a top hat and evening dress. With this new image of himself Kemal Atatürk, the master of social symbolism, made it clear to his people that, for the time being, the age of martial valour in holy war had ended; the time had come for the solid, bourgeois virtues of industry, skill, and thrift, needed in the hard, unglamorous, but urgent task of developing the country and raising the standard of living of her people.

In his political ideas Kemal Atatürk was an heir to the Young Turks—more especially of the nationalist, positivist, and Westernizing wing among them. The two dominant beliefs of his life were in the Turkish nation and in progress; the future of both lay in civilization, which for him meant the modern civilization of the West, and no other. His nationalism was healthy and reasonable; there was no arrogant trampling on the rights or aspirations of other nations, no neurotic rejection of responsibility for the national past. The Turks were a great people of great achievement, who had gone astray through the evil effects of certain elements and forces among them; they must be restored to the path of progress, to find their place in the community of civilized nations. 'The Turks', he said in 1924, 'are the friends of all civilized nations. Countries vary, but civilization is one, and for a nation to progress it must take part in this single civilization.'[99]

Unlike so many reformers, Kemal Atatürk was well aware that a mere façade of modernization was worthless, and that if Turkey was to hold her own in the world of our time, fundamental changes were necessary in the whole structure of society and culture. Opinions are divided on the success and on the wisdom of some of his policies. If on the one hand there were complaints that the reforms were limited in their application to the towns and urban classes, and brought little change to the peasant mass of the population, on the other hand there were many who felt that the reforms were too violent and abrupt, and caused a rupture with the religious and cultural traditions of the nation that was harmful in its effects on the younger generation.

Whatever views one may hold on these points, this much is indisputable—that, at the darkest moment in their history, the Kemalist Revolution brought new life and hope to the Turkish people, restored their energies and self-respect, and set them firmly on the road not only to independence, but to that rarer and more precious thing that is freedom.

[99] Baydar, p. 49.

CHAPTER IX

The Republic after Kemal

Any human being who believes that the destinies of other human beings depend wholly upon him personally is a petty man, failing to grasp the most elementary acts. Every man is doomed to perish physically. The only way to stay happy while we live is to work, not for ourselves, but for those to come.

KEMAL ATATÜRK, March 1938.

The ultimate results of a social struggle can never be of the kind envisaged by those who carry it out. Some such struggles depend on an infinite and complex series of circumstances beyond the controllable range of human intellect and action. This is most true of revolutions that demand superhuman efforts and that effect hasty and radical changes in society.

MILOVAN DJILAS, 'The New Class', 1957.

ON 11 November 1938, the day after Atatürk's death, the Grand National Assembly of Turkey unanimously voted to appoint Ismet Inönü, his lifelong friend and closest collaborator, as his successor. The vital decision seems to have rested with three men: Ismet Inönü himself, Marshal Fevzi Çakmak, the Chief of Staff, and Celâl Bayar, a banker and economist who had replaced Ismet Inönü as Prime Minister in September 1937. They agreed on Ismet as President, and co-operated in ensuring a smooth transition and a stable and continuous régime. The first President of the Turkish Republic was dead, but the Republic lived, and the second President was chosen and took office, without break or interruption. On 25 January 1939 Celâl Bayar was replaced as Prime Minister by Dr. Refik Saydam, who remained in office until his death in June 1942.

The spontaneous and moving demonstrations of grief by the great mass of the people at the death of Atatürk showed clearly that, whatever conflicts and repressions there might have been in the past, he had by then succeeded in winning the respect and indeed the love of the Turkish people. The old, reactionary opposition was crushed; no new opposition, offering not a mere return to the past but a different way forward, had yet appeared— and in the meantime a new generation was growing up in the schools that had never known any régime but the Republic.

It was as well that Inönü could count on a tranquil and loyal country, for difficult and dangerous times lay ahead. When Atatürk died, the war clouds were already gathering over Europe, and there is an oral tradition that his last political testament to his people had been 'to be as ready as possible and then, come what might, to stay on England's side, because that side was certain to win in the long run'.[1]

Authentic or not, this dictum seems to have expressed the views at least of Ismet Inönü, who on 19 October 1939 signed a treaty of alliance with Great Britain and France. But by the summer of 1940 there were few in Turkish government circles who shared them. Yakup Kadri Karaosmanoğlu, then Turkish ambassador at The Hague, has described how, when he returned to Ankara, after a shattering ordeal, in May 1940, and was 'bold enough' to state his belief that England would not be defeated, 'among all our statesmen only Ismet Inönü and Refik Saydam took me seriously'. The Secretary-General of the Ministry, far from attaching any importance to his views, accused him of misleading the President with false information.[2]

The fall of France, the hostile attitude of Russia, and the extension of German power or influence over most of Europe led the Turkish government to the conclusion that nothing would be gained by provoking a German invasion and an almost certain German conquest. They therefore decided, in June 1940, not to fulfil their obligations under the treaty of alliance. Instead, they embarked on a policy of uneasy and ambiguous neutrality, in which the one firm and guiding principle was the determination not to repeat the tragic error of October 1914. Turkish opinion was, to a large extent, sympathetic to the Allies, but from 1940 that sympathy was vitiated by a widespread conviction that the Axis would win; in June 1941, when German expansion in the Balkans had brought the German armies within 100 miles of Istanbul, the Turks tried to insure themselves by signing a friendship and trade agreement with Germany, in which, however, they stipulated that Turkey would maintain her treaty obligations to Britain.

After the German attack on Russia in 1941, Turkish feelings towards the Axis began to assume a more positive form. Russia

[1] Lewis V. Thomas and R. N. Frye, *The United States and Turkey and Iran* (1951), p. 89.

[2] Karaosmanoğlu, *Zoraki Diplomat* (1955), pp. 34–35.

U

was after all their ancient hereditary enemy, against whose relentless southward advance they had been fighting a desperate rearguard defence for centuries; and the scanty reserve of goodwill built up during the period of revolutionary fraternity had been dissipated by Soviet hectoring in 1939. In attacking Russia, the Germans won the support of an important body of Turkish opinion, and added genuine sympathy to the previous calculation.

The Allies, of course, increased their pressure on Turkey to join what was now becoming the Grand Alliance. On 3 December 1941 President Roosevelt extended lease-lend aid to Turkey; in February 1943 Mr. Churchill visited Turkey and met Turkish statesmen at Adana; in December 1943 President Inönü went to Cairo to meet the British and American leaders. But Inönü still hung back, and Turkish opinion in general supported him in his policy of neutrality. One of the main considerations was mistrust of Russia, and the widespread feeling that Nazi conquest and Soviet liberation were equally to be feared. 'What we would really like', remarked a Turk during the war, 'would be for the Germans to destroy Russia and for the Allies to destroy Germany. Then we would feel safe.' This proved impossible to arrange, and by 1943 the ruling circles in Ankara began to realize that the Axis cause was in any case doomed to defeat. From this time on the Turks began to enter into ever closer economic and military relations with the West, and aided the Allied cause in a variety of ways. In August 1944 they broke off diplomatic relations with Germany, and on 23 February 1945 declared war on Germany in order to comply with the formalities of entry to the United Nations Conference in San Francisco.

The war years subjected Turkey to severe economic strains, and increased the scale and severity of government intervention in economic life. The etatist laws already provided the framework for a system of wartime controls, and a 'National Defence Law', approved on 18 January 1940, gave the government extensive emergency economic powers. The second five-year plan, launched in 1939, was nullified by the high rate of military expenditure and the shortage of raw materials, and even agricultural production was adversely affected by the maintenance of partial mobilization.[3]

Foreign trade, on the other hand, flourished. Turkish products

[3] Hershlag, *Turkey*, pp. 177 ff.

were in high demand, and were sold at strategic rather than commercial prices. This development, coupled with the high rate of government expenditure and the shortage of essential commodities, led to a considerable inflationary pressure.[4] Great fortunes were being made by the merchants, brokers, and agents in Istanbul. Partly because of tax evasion, but mostly because of the absence of any effective modern system of tax assessment and collection, these fortunes were substantially exempt from taxation or control by the government.

In these circumstances, the government decided on an emergency fiscal measure—a capital levy. Such a levy, in a country going through an economic and financial crisis, would have been both normal and justifiable, as a means of collecting revenue and as an instrument of control over the national economy. In fact, the levy was conceived and applied in a manner neither normal nor justifiable.[5]

The *Varlık Vergisi* (capital tax), as it was called, was approved by the Assembly on 11 November 1942, and came into force next day.[6]

Two groups had made the largest profits from the war; the large farmers, who had gained enormously from the rise in agricultural prices, and the merchants and middlemen of Istanbul, who had been in a position to exploit both the high value of Turkish exports and the desperate shortage of necessary imports. The farmers consisted almost entirely of Muslim Turks; the merchants were still largely, though not entirely, members of the three minority communities, the Greeks, Jews, and Armenians.

---

[4] Ibid. pp. 179–80.

[5] There are many accounts of the capital levy, the most accessible being those of L. V. Thomas and G. L. Lewis in the books already cited. For a detailed and documented account by a senior tax official see the work of Faik Ökte, cited below.

[6] Faik Ökte, the Defterdar (Director of Finance) of Istanbul, has recorded that when the details of the law were published in the press, his former Professor at the Faculty of Economics telephoned him early in the morning to ask for explanations. The conversation, as he relates it, ran as follows:

'—Faik, my boy, the text of the capital tax appeared in this morning's paper.
—Yes, Professor.
—Naturally the journalists got it wrong, they gave an incomplete text. . . .
—No, in all the newspapers I saw the text was complete. . . .
—How so, complete? No provision for objections or appeal! No indication of the rate of taxation. . . .
—That is the kind of tax it is, Professor.
—My boy, have you all gone mad!' (*Varlık Vergisi Faciası* (1951), p. 64.)

The tax law provided for a levy on property owners, owners of large farms, business men, and certain categories of taxpayers, who were paying tax on salaries or earnings. Owners of large farms could not be taxed at more than 5 per cent. of their capital; limited companies would be required to pay between 50 and 75 per cent. of their net profits for 1941. For other taxpayers, assessments would be made by special commissions, 'in accordance with their opinions'.

In this last category no rate of taxation was ever announced, no declaration of income or capital was ever required. The local tax boards made their estimates, and posted the lists of payments to be made. Their decisions were final, and not subject to appeal. Payment was required within fifteen days, failing which fines would be imposed. If payment was not made within a month the defaulters would be deported for forced labour.

It soon became apparent that the really important data determining a taxpayer's assessment were his religion and nationality. From subsequent revelations, it is known that the taxpayers were classified in two separate lists, the M list, for Muslims, and the G list, for non-Muslims (*Gayrimüslim*). Later, two other categories were added, E for foreigners (*Ecnebi*) and D for *Dönme*, members of the Sabbatayan sect of Jewish converts to Islam. *Dönmes* paid about twice as much as Muslims, non-Muslims up to ten times as much. Foreigners, on instructions from Ankara, were to be assessed at the same rate as Muslims,[7] but poor registration and inefficient administration led to the taxing of many foreigners as if they had been non-Muslim Turkish citizens, thus provoking the intervention of the foreign embassies and consulates on behalf of their nationals.

Early in January 1943 the press began to publish lists of names of defaulters, together with the amounts of their assessments, and it was announced that they would be sent to break stones for the new road at Aşkale. On 12 January the press announced relaxations for salaried persons, minors, women, the aged, and the sick. The remaining defaulters would be deported, and would have to pay the cost of their transport, food, and medical treatment if required. Tax defaulters serving with the colours would be transferred to the forced labour camps on completing their military service.

[7] Except for Jewish subjects of the Axis states, who were excluded from this privilege (Ökte, p. 81).

Although appeals were not allowed, taxpayers had a constitutional right of petition, and by January more than 10,000 petitions were received by the Revenue Department, almost all of which were rejected. Only a number of assessments, on persons already dead or businesses already bankrupt, were cancelled. Arrests and seizures of property went on daily, and the auction rooms were choked with confiscated property. The first party of deportees, numbering thirty-two, left Istanbul for Aşkale on 27 January.

The lists of names appearing in the press of defaulters and of persons arrested or deported, consisted almost entirely of non-Muslims—Greeks, Jews, and Armenians. The press, led by the pro-Axis *Cümhuriyet* and *Tasvir-i Efkâr*, expressed cordial approval, and spoke of people of 'alien blood', 'Turks only in name', who must be punished for their disloyalty and ingratitude.

In fact, it was the loyal, rather than the disloyal, who were punished. Those members of the minorities who had retained or obtained foreign protection at the time of the armistice and Allied occupation were able to get their assessments reduced to the Muslim level or something near it; those who had trusted in the new Republic and thrown their lot in with it, were subjected to victimization and punishment.[8]

Through the spring and summer the arrests, seizures, and deportations continued, almost all of non-Muslims. Many business men were ruined by assessments greater than their total possessions; others, though wealthy enough to pay, were bankrupted because no time was allowed them to find enough liquid money.[9] Most tragic was the position of the numerous poor—the artisans, wage-earners, and even the beggars, ragmen and boot-blacks, licensed occupations with lists of licence-holders in official possession. These, if non-Muslims, were in most cases taxed at figures wildly beyond their ability to pay, and then sold up for their failure to do so. Later, some remissions were granted in this category.

In June 1943 it was announced that the capital levy would be wound up by 31 July, and that persons who had not paid by that date would be deported to labour camps. The Prime Minister, in a speech to the People's Party congress on 15 June, denied indignantly that the capital levy had been used as an instrument to crush the minorities. It was true, he said, that 105 million out of the 270 millions collected so far had been paid by members of the

---

[8] cf. Ökte, pp. 123–4.   [9] Ibid. p. 149.

minorities and foreigners, but this was reasonable since they had all the real estate and sources of wealth in their hands.

By this time, the star of Germany was setting, and Western interest in the tax was becoming a source of discomfort.[10] On 21 September it was announced that the Finance Department was preparing lists of remissions and on 1 October Ahmet Emin Yalman, the editor of *Vatan*, published the first criticism of the tax to appear in the Turkish press.[11] At the end of October the Prime Minister gave an interview to the editor of a Greek-language newspaper in Istanbul, and denied that the minorities had suffered any injustice. In December 1943, just before Inönü's visit to Cairo to met Roosevelt and Churchill, the last deportees were brought back to Istanbul. On 15 March 1944—the day the Allies began their final assault on Monte Cassino—a law was passed by the Assembly releasing all defaulters still detained and cancelling all amounts still unpaid. The capital levy, in expiring, thus achieved its final ineptitude, by penalizing those who had made payment and rewarding those who had somehow managed to avoid it.

In a book written in 1947 and published in 1951, Faik Ökte, the Defterdar of Istanbul, tells with complete frankness the story of the origins, application, and end of the capital levy, in which, albeit with distaste and reluctance, he played the leading part required of him by his office. Turkey, he says, needed an extraordinary tax on capital, in the situation in which she found herself at that time. She did not need this misbegotten offspring of German racialism on Ottoman fanaticism.[12]

The receipts from the tax amounted to 314,920,940 Turkish liras—at the rate of exchange of that time, roughly £28 million. This was 74·11 per cent. of the total amount demanded.[13] In his final chapters the former Defterdar of Istanbul examines the results of the 'lawlessness and disorder'[14] involved in the enrich-

---

[10] Apart from occasional expressions of fatherly approval in Germany, the Turkish capital levy had hitherto passed without comment or criticism in the world press. The Allied conspiracy of silence seems to have been first broken in an Armenian weekly, *Hairenik*, in Boston, which on 30 June, under the title 'The Beast Breaks Loose Again', denounced the tax as a new piece of Turkish barbarism. A more balanced discussion appeared in a series of five articles in the *New York Times* from 9 to 13 Sept., which described the tax and its application in some detail, and considered the political implications of what had happened.

[11] Ökte, pp. 195–6.   [12] Ibid. pp. 38–39.   [13] Ibid. p. 197.
[14] Ibid. p. 209.

ment of the treasury by this amount. The business world of Istanbul had been shaken and dislocated.[15] The tax had actually worked to the advantage of the black market, enriching the large operators by the opportunities it afforded them and increasing the number of small operators by the ruination of legitimate businesses and the destitution of those who had lived by them.[16] The tax had failed to achieve its economic objectives, and had ended with the complete collapse of the price policy that had inspired it.

The most precious currency that we lost by this tax in the realm of finance was the confidence of the citizen in the state. . . . Industry, commerce, all economic life can only live by breathing an atmosphere of confidence; with the capital levy this atmosphere was poisoned. . . .[17]

The effect on Turkey's reputation abroad was even worse. The good reputation which the Turkish Republic had won since its establishment for financial probity and for religious tolerance was shattered. It was not easy to build up again.

For the Turkish patriot, the most unforgivable aspect of the capital levy was the degradation which it brought to the sovereignty and dignity of Turkey. By imposing unjust and discriminatory taxes on foreign citizens, Turkey invited the intervention of the powers in her internal affairs; by then rectifying those assessments under foreign pressure, the government of Atatürk's Republic had themselves brought back the most shameful and degrading features of the long-abolished Capitulations.

It is with this final comment that Faik Ökte ends his book: 'For my part, I am still astonished that for this blow struck against the honour and dignity of the state, we were not all of us, with the Prime Minister at our head, indicted before the High Council.'[18]

The capital levy was a sad affair. It has been since described and discussed by foreign observers and was probably, in the long run, more harmful to the 'honour and dignity' of the Turkish state than to its immediate victims. Its effects should not, however, be exaggerated. In a Europe dominated by Hitler's Germany, Republican Turkey's one essay in persecution was a mild and gentle affair. For the Turks, it should be remembered, Germany was an essential and central part of that Europe which they so much admired and had for more than a century been trying to emulate. They had seen how the Nazis behaved in

15 Ibid. p. 202.   16 Ibid. p. 203.   17 Ibid. p. 210.   18 Ibid. p. 213.

Germany and had also seen the statesmen of Europe accept them and fraternize with them; subsequent denunciations of Nazi tyranny lost much of their cogency in following after the outbreak of war, and seemed to be no more than acts of political warfare. To the outside observer, Europe could no more disclaim the Germans than Germany could disclaim the Nazis.

The liquidation of the capital levy was accompanied by other evidences of diminishing German influence. In May 1944 demonstrations by students in Ankara led to the investigation by the police of pan-Turanian groups, accused of holding fascist, racialist, doctrines and—what was more to the point—of plotting to overthrow the régime and the constitution and establish a government that would bring Turkey into the war on the side of Germany.[19]

The trial and condemnation of the pan-Turanians in September 1944 was an obvious attempt to placate the Soviet Union; it failed in its purpose. In spite of this and other advances by the Turkish government, the Soviets would not be placated, and on 19 March denounced the Turco-Soviet treaty of friendship and neutrality which had been signed in 1925 and was due for another renewal. This opened the way to the presentation of a series of demands for territorial concessions, bases, and a revision of the Montreux Convention, all of which Turkey steadfastly rejected.

The eclipse of Nazi Germany by defeat, the estrangement of Soviet Russia by political conflict, removed the two influences which, during the 1930's and early 1940's, had seemed for a while to be supplanting the liberal and democratic West and setting Turkey an example of totalitarian autocracy in her path of modernization. Once again, as in 1918, the democracies had triumphed over their autocratic enemies, and were setting the tone of progress and development. And, although, in the hard years that followed, many nations and governments revised their estimates of the balance of power and prospects, and adjusted their allegiances accordingly, the Turks have seen no reason to abandon the Western alignment of their foreign policy, or the Westernizing trend of their internal development.

---

[19] On these movements see Jäschke, 'Der Turanismus und die kemalistische Türkei', in R. Hartmann and H. Scheel, eds., *Beiträge zur Arabistik, Semitistik und Islamwissenshaft* (1944), pp. 468–83; R. Oğuz Türkkan, 'The Turkish Press', *MEA*, i (1950), 142–9; C. W. Hostler, 'Trends in Pan-Turanism', ibid. iii (1952), 3–13 and *Turkism and the Soviets* (1957); Karpat, pp. 264 ff.

The Coming of Democracy [20]

Perhaps the most important single fact in the democratic development of post-Kemalist Turkey is that in May 1950 a really free and fair election was held which resulted in an overwhelming victory for the opposition over the government. After twenty-seven years of almost uninterrupted rule by the Republican People's Party, most of the time without any opposition party to challenge it, a government of that party presided over a free and peaceful election which resulted in its own defeat and replacement. This momentous event, without any precedent in the history of the country and region, bears remarkable testimony to the constructive work of the Kemalist régime, and to the political maturing of the Turkish people under its aegis. In a sense, the electoral defeat of the People's Party was its greatest achievement—a second revolution, complementing and completing that earlier revolution out of which the Party itself had sprung.

Democracy did not come easily to Turkey. The idea and the desire were not new. Unlike so many Eastern countries, where liberty is a synonym for independence, Turkey had had a genuine democratic movement, concerned not only with the rights of the nation against other nations, but also with the rights of the individual within the nation. But this movement, despite its widespread intellectual influence, had had little political success. Two constitutional régimes, in 1876 and 1908, begun with high hopes, had ended in frustration and failure, and even the populist régime of Kemal Atatürk, failing in its two experiments with tolerated opposition, had ended as the personal autocracy of the head of state.

After the death of Atatürk there was some deterioration. In the hands of lesser men than himself, his authoritarian and paternalist mode of government degenerated into something

[20] Accounts of post-war political developments in Turkey will be found in a number of general books, notably those of L. V. Thomas and G. L. Lewis. The most recent and comprehensive survey is that of Karpat. For details of events, Jäschke's *Kalender* (*Die Türkei in den Jahren 1942–51*, 1955), OM, WI, and the RIIA, *Survey* continue to provide useful information. To them may be added a number of new periodicals, notably *MEJ* (from 1947), *MEA* (from 1950), and *C. Or. contemp.* (from 1944). It is in the last-named that the most comprehensive coverage will be found. Among Turkish publications, one of unique value is Tunaya's *Partiler*, essentially a collection of documents relating to party politics in Turkey, but also including much valuable interpretation and presentation.

nearer to dictatorship as the word is commonly understood. The disappearance of Atatürk's own dominating personality and the rise of a new generation influenced by the constitutional ideas of the victorious West undermined the popular acceptance of authoritarian government inherited from the past, and forced the régime to rely more and more on simple repression. The strains and stresses of the war years, the burden of mobilization, the universal threat of foreign espionage and infiltration, all reinforced the need for a strong government, and lent some colour of justification to the repressive measures adopted. These included martial law, a strict control of the press and publications, and an extension of police powers and activities.

Then, after the war, came the swift and sudden change which ended one-party rule in Turkey and set the country, so it seemed at the time, on the high road to liberal, parliamentary democracy.

The process began in 1945 when Turkey joined the United Nations, and the Charter, which had recently been approved in San Francisco, came up for ratification in the Turkish Assembly.

The time and the atmosphere seemed favourable to democracy, and on 19 May the President himself, at a sports festival in Ankara, had spoken of land distribution and democratic development: 'In our political life democratic principles will prevail on a still greater scale.'[21] A group of members of the People's Party took the opportunity to propose a number of legal reforms which would guarantee, inside Turkey, those rights and liberties to which the Turkish government was giving its theoretical approval at the United Nations. The leaders of the group were Celâl Bayar, deputy for Izmir, a banker and economist who had played a part in the War of Independence and had been Prime Minister in 1937–9; Professor Fuad Köprülü, deputy for Kars, a distinguished scholar and historian and an outstanding figure in the intellectual life of Turkey, Adnan Menderes, deputy for Aydın, a lawyer and cotton-planter, and Refik Koraltan, deputy for Içel, a lawyer with extensive experience as judge and provincial governor. All but Köprülü were prominent and experienced members of the parliamentary group of the People's Party.

The party had always allowed some measure of internal discussion and criticism, and a free vote was often taken at a closed

[21] *C. Or. contemp.*, ii (1946), p. 294.

party meeting before an issue was made public in the Assembly. On this occasion too the issue was first raised inside the party. On 17 June 1945 six by-elections were due to be held, and the government decided not to appoint official candidates. A week earlier, on 12 June, a party group meeting was held to discuss the elections, and it was on this occasion that the four rebels presented a joint memorandum proposing certain changes in the party programme and in the law. The proposal was rejected by a vote that was unanimous except for the four signatories of the memorandum.[22] But this time the minority broke with precedent and persisted in bringing their proposal before the Assembly. On 15 August, when the United Nations Charter came before the Assembly for ratification, Menderes argued that 'Turkey, by signing the Charter, had definitely engaged to practice genuine democracy'.[23]

These arguments failed to shake the government or its tame majority, and the rebels now adopted the radical innovation of turning to the public. Ahmet Emin Yalman, editor of the newspaper *Vatan*, had more than once shown himself ready to defy both authority and public prejudice; he now opened the columns of his newspaper to the rebels, who in the third week of September 1945 published signed articles criticizing the 'totalitarian' line that the government and party were following and proclaiming their own belief in democracy.[24]

A period of acute political tension followed. On 21 September a secret meeting of the party decided to expel Menderes and Köprülü, for breach of party discipline; Koraltan now wrote an article in *Vatan*, defending Menderes and Köprülü, and declaring: 'I and my three colleagues have done nothing but work for the strengthening of the foundations of national sovereignty and the principles of the party. It is not we who have forsaken these principles; it is those who decided to expel our two colleagues.'[25] The party responded to this challenge, and on 27 November, by a vote of 280 to 1, the group decided to expel Koraltan himself. In the meantime Celâl Bayar had, on 26 September, resigned his membership of the Assembly. On 3 December, in solidarity

[22] Tunaya, *Partiler*, p. 648 n. 8.

[23] Yalman, 'The Struggle for Multi-Party Government in Turkey', *MEJ*, i (1947), 53.

[24] Yalman, *Turkey in my Time* (1956), p. 223.   [25] Tunaya, *Partiler*, p. 649 n. 11.

with his three colleagues, he resigned from the Republican People's Party.[26]

Violent attacks on the seceders appeared in the press, and for a while it seemed as though the Government were contemplating strong repressive action. Then, suddenly, there was a complete change of policy. On 1 November 1945, in his speech at the opening of the new session of the Assembly, President Inönü recommended a number of important changes: in place of the two-stage elections by colleges, there was to be a single, direct election, by secret ballot; laws restricting the constitutional liberties of the citizen, especially the laws relating to the press, associations, and the power of the police, should be repealed. Turkey, he said, was not a dictatorship, but it did lack an opposition party; the laws should be amended so that those who differed from their colleagues, instead of working as a clique or faction, could declare their convictions and programmes and function openly as a party.

This is the right road for the development of our political life; and this is the more constructive way for the welfare and the political maturity of the nation. We shall strive with all our strength so that differences of political opinion do not lead to enmity between our compatriots.[27]

On 7 January 1946 the President's desire for an opposition was gratified, when the Democratic Party was registered in Ankara.[28] Its founders were the four People's Party rebels of the previous year. They were soon joined by others, and began to prepare for their constitutional role of opposing and attempting to replace the government.

Their task was not made easy for them. In his speech in November, President Inönü had said that the next general election would take place in 1947, on the completion of the current term of the Assembly. In April 1946, however, the congress of the People's Party, with the obvious purpose of catching the new party before it was ready for an electoral contest, decided to put the date of the elections forward. The general elections were to be held on 21 July 1946; municipal elections were to be held immediately. The Democrat Party decided to boycott the municipal elec-

---

[26] Tunaya, *Partiler*, p. 649 n. 12.

[27] Inönu, *Söylev*, i. 400; cf. *C. Or. contemp.*, iii (1946), 669 ff.

[28] On the slightly earlier opposition party of Nuri Demirağ, see below, p. 377.

tions, but to contest the general elections, in which they put up candidates for 273 out of 465 seats. Sixty-one were elected as well as six independents. The Democrat Party had shown itself a lusty infant. Democrat candidates had won considerable successes in the big towns, and would certainly have won many more elsewhere, had party and government officials in various parts of the country been able to resist the temptation to intimidate the voters and adjust the votes.

On 7 August a new People's Party cabinet was formed, headed by Recep Peker, who was regarded as representing the authoritarian wing of the party. He wasted little time; on 20 September amendments to the press law and penal code gave the government renewed powers of control, and an attempt was made to stop the mounting wave of criticism against abuses in the election by invoking the martial law that was still in force.[29]

The attempt failed. Turkey now had a vigorous and determined parliamentary opposition, and a lively and active independent and opposition press. Both played an important part in the progress towards democracy of the next four years. The struggle was not easy, but the democratic forces were much helped by the rise of new and more liberal elements within the People's Party itself.

Relations between government and opposition were at first bad, and mutual accusations and recriminations, in the Assembly and in the press, kept political tension at a high pitch.[30] Finally, President Inönü himself intervened, as a kind of umpire, in June 1947. He convened a series of meetings, together and separately, with the Prime Minister and the Democrat leaders, for an exchange of opinions and, more particularly, grievances. Then, on 12 July 1947, he issued a declaration describing these discussions and his own reactions to them.[31] In the multi-party state, he said, the President should be above politics, a non-partisan head of state, with equal duties to both parties. In the conversations, the government had accused the Democrats of sedition, the Democrats had accused the government, or some of its agents, of oppression. He found the first charge baseless, the second exaggerated; in any case, he had obtained assurances from both sides of good, democratic behaviour.[32]

---

[29] Yalman, *Turkey*, p. 229.   [30] Ibid. pp. 239–40.
[31] Text in Tunaya, *Partiler*, p. 688.   [32] Yalman, *Turkey*, p. 240.

The President's action did much to help the smooth functioning of parliamentary government in Turkey. It also had the immediate effect of precipitating a crisis in the ruling party, which became manifest at the summer meeting of the party parliamentary group, held on 26 August 1947. After eight hours of heated discussion, the meeting gave Recep Peker the vote of confidence that he asked for—but it was no longer unanimous. Thirty-five deputies, most of them young, voted against Peker. The press at once acclaimed them as heroes, and did not fail to point out that their number would certainly have been much greater had Peker not insisted on an open vote.[33] On 3 September six ministers resigned, and on the next day, when the Prime Minister asked the party group for authority to reconstruct the cabinet, the number of dissenters rose to 47, of abstainers to nearly 100. Recep Peker's second cabinet, faced by determined opposition inside as well as outside the party, lasted only a few days. On 9 September he resigned from office, and was succeeded by Hasan Saka, who remained in power until 16 January 1949. In his four cabinets and still more in the government of Professor Şemseddin Günaltay, who followed him, the liberal group within the People's Party occupied an important position.

Meanwhile the Democrat Party was also torn between extremist and moderate wings. After one or two minor splits and disagreements, a more serious one occurred in the summer of 1948, when a group of dissident Democrats, mostly deputies, accused the party of insufficient vigour in opposing the government, and founded a new party of their own. The National Party (*Millet Partisi*), founded on 20 July 1948, also rallied the support of some disgruntled members of the People's Party, and were able to persuade Marshal Fevzi Çakmak,[34] the former Chief of the General Staff, to give them the prestige of his name and leadership. The new party rapidly became a focus of more conservative and sometimes even anti-secularist opinion.[35]

Through this and other defections, the strength of the Democrat Party in the Assembly sank from 61 in 1946 to only 31 in 1950.[36] Nevertheless its strength and influence in the country continued to grow, the more rapidly as the restrictions on political activity

---

[33] Tunaya, *Partiler*, pp. 563–4; Yalman, *Turkey*, p. 243.
[34] See *EI*² ('Çakmak, Fevzi').   [35] Tunaya, *Partiler*, pp. 712–3 and n. 8.
[36] Ibid. p. 657.

were one by one relaxed. The Law of Associations was modified
to allow opposition groups, and on 20 February 1947 a law was
passed permitting the establishment of 'workers' and employers'
unions and regional federations'.[37]

In December 1947 martial law was at last ended, and the press
began to enjoy a freedom of expression and criticism previously
unknown. The new cabinet of Professor Şemseddin Günaltay
announced in its statement of policy on 23 January 1949: 'We
shall take the rules of the Western democracies as our model. . . .
Freedom of conscience is sacred to us . . .'. The next day the
Prime Minister declared to the Assembly: 'I shall work sincerely
to establish democracy. . . . For the future of our country, this is
the only method that I, as an historian, can be sure of. . . .
Demagogy leads to dissolution or dictatorship.'[38]

Certain restrictions, however, remained in force. The foreign
policy of the government could not in effect be criticized, but this
restriction was the less resented as there was a substantial measure
of agreement between all parties on this matter.

All forms of Communism were, after an interval of uncertainty,
banned. In 1945, profiting from the relaxation of censorship, a
number of leftist publications began to appear. The first was
the daily newspaper *Tan*, which reappeared in May after an
interval of suspension, and, under the editorship of Zekeriya
Sertel, began to express mildly pink opinions. Towards the end
of the year other, more openly pro-Soviet journals appeared,
notably the weekly *Görüşler* (Views) and the daily *Yeni Dünya*
(New World).

Pro-Russian sentiments had never had much appeal for Turks;
they were particularly odious at a time when the Soviet Government was presenting territorial and other demands to Turkey.
At the end of November the greater part of the Istanbul press,
including, after a day of hesitation, the opposition *Vatan*, launched
a campaign against the leftists. On 4 December mobs of students
attacked and destroyed the offices of *Tan* and *Yeni Dünya* as
well as a number of bookshops reputed to stock Communist
literature.[39] There was very little sympathy in Turkey for the
Communists and fellow-travellers, who were regarded as little
better than Russian agents. On the other hand, there were many

---

[37] See below, pp. 469 ff.   [38] Jäschke, *Kalender*, 23 Jan. 1949.
[39] Yalman, *Turkey*, p. 226.

who regretted that, in order to deal with them, recourse should have been made to such perversions of democracy as press demagogy and mob violence.[40]

In 1946, with the ending of one-party rule, attempts were made to form left-wing parties, none of them very successful. At least one of them was Communist inspired—the Socialist Workers' and Peasants' Party of Turkey, founded 20 June 1946 and led by a veteran Communist, of early vintage. The party was suppressed under martial law on 1 December 1946, and its leaders arrested on charges of Communist agitation. At the same time some pro-Communist papers and unions were banned.[41]

From this time on, in the face of growing Soviet hostility to Turkey, severe repression of Communist activities and ideas enjoyed general support—though at times this restriction was so interpreted as to make any serious discussion of social problems a hazardous undertaking. Occasional attempts to restrict the freedom of the press in other respects failed in the face of the new and potent force of public opinion.

Social Change

While Turkish politics were moving in the direction of a more effective parliamentary democracy, Turkish society had entered on the transition from the rooted and enclosed conformity of the traditional order to the modern community of mobile, participant citizens.[42]

The population of Turkey had been increasing steadily but not overwhelmingly under the Republic—13½ million in 1927, 16 in 1935, nearly 18 in 1940, nearly 19 in 1945, nearly 21 in 1950. At the same time, the proportion of Turks living in cities was rising significantly, as the figures in the table on page 305 show.

The increase in urbanization naturally brought with it an increase in literacy, which rose, according to official figures, from 10·6 per cent. in 1927 to 20·4 per cent. in 1935, 30·2 per cent in 1945, and 34·6 per cent. in 1950. The breakdown of the last figure shows 43·2 per cent. literacy among the under sixteens, 48·4 per cent. among men generally, and 13·4 per cent. even in

---

[40] Thomas and Frye, p. 111.

[41] Tunaya, *Partiler*, p. 704; Laqueur, *Communism*, p. 215.

[42] On the significance of this process in Turkey, see D. Lerner, *The Passing of Traditional Society* (1958).

villages—i.e. places with fewer than 5,000 inhabitants. Among males in cities the figure is as high as 72 per cent.

Proportion of the population in cities with:

	over 20,000 inhabitants	over 50,000 inhabitants *(percentage)*	over 100,000 inhabitants
1927	12·5	7·7	6·2
1935	13·0	8·0	6·4
1940	13·7	8·6	6·4
1945	14·1	9·5	7·4
1950	14·7	10·2	8·3

A literate, urban population develops new interests and habits, and is anxious to be kept informed of what goes on about them. The number and circulation of newspapers rose steadily; the number of wireless sets increased from 46,230 in 1938 to 176,262 in 1945, 240,525 in 1948, and 412,270 in 1951, mostly privately owned. In the same period the number of private letters sent was more than doubled, the number of telephones almost quintupled.[43] The novel and still more the short story flourished, theatres began to attract small audiences and cinemas larger ones, and football drew vast and passionate crowds.

The modernization of communications had begun in the nineteenth century, with the introduction of European-style coaches for the gentry of Istanbul. They were followed by coupés, victorias, omnibuses, trams, and finally cars. The increased traffic in the streets of Istanbul and the other cities soon led to further demands and reforms—paved roadways, sweeping and drainage, lighting and policing, and a modern municipal authority to supply and maintain these services.[44]

As the Turkish city was rebuilt and reorganized to cope with the new and expanding traffic that filled its streets, so the whole country was transformed by the new network of railways and roads. The replacement of the caravan by the train, of horse, ass, and camel by car, bus, and lorry, has made possible the movement

---

[43] Details in the statistical year-books (*Istatistik Yıllığı*) published by the Turkish government. The above data was assembled from the very useful tables given by Lerner, and in *Investment in Turkey*, published by the U.S. Dept. of Commerce (1956).

[44] See below, pp. 387 ff.

w

of persons, commodities, and ideas on a hitherto undreamt-of scale, and has given the Turkish people a new mobility, social and mental as well as physical, that has prepared them for integration in the modern world.[45]

The Election [46]

On 15 February 1950, after long debates, the Assembly approved a new electoral law, in a form agreed by both the People's and Democrat Parties. A little later the parties began their electoral campaigns, with equal broadcasting time, access to halls for public meetings, and full press facilities. The People's Party spoke of agrarian reform and opportunities for private enterprise, and promised more democracy; the Democrats attacked them for their slowness, and demanded greater freedom, both political and economic—the relaxation of etatism, more private enterprise, and, for the workers, the right to strike. The National Party was more concerned with a relaxation of secularism and a revival of Islam.

Both of the two main contenders, the Democrats and the now dominant liberal wing of the People's Party, promised freedom and democratic progress. But perhaps even more significant than the promises of the two parties was the fact that they were making them—that government as well as opposition were actually wooing the electorate, instead of bullying them. In this new exercise the opposition were naturally more adept.[47]

On 14 May Turkey went to the polls. Of close on 8·5 million voters, 88 per cent. cast their votes. They elected an Assembly of 408 Democrats, 69 People's Party, 1 National Party, and 9 Independents. After twenty-seven years the People's Party had allowed itself to be defeated in a genuinely free and honest election and, having been defeated, had peacefully handed over power to the victors. The question may well be asked why it did so—why the party, with its immense powers of control and repression and its long unchallenged supremacy, was ready in this way to prepare, organize, and accept its own downfall.

[45] On mobility in its various aspects see Lerner, *passim*.

[46] For contemporary appreciations of the 1950 election, see S. J. Weinberger, 'Political Upset in Turkey', *MEA*, i (1950), 135–42; B. Lewis, 'Recent Developments in Turkey', *Int. Aff.*, xxvii (1951), 320–31.

[47] Thomas and Frye, p. 108.

Many explanations have been offered. Turkish cynics—who are very cynical—say that the whole thing was due to a miscalculation. The People's Party leaders, they say, were confident of a victory in a free election and for that reason alone allowed it to be free. Had they realized what would happen, they would have taken suitable precautions.

Such an explanation seems superficial and unsatisfactory. Most observers in Turkey in the months preceding the election were convinced that in a really free poll the Democrats would sweep the country—only they could not believe, even after the new electoral law, that a free election could really take place. The People's Party leaders must have been aware of the trends of opinion in the country. Moreover, the election itself was not an isolated phenomenon, but the last of a series of steps towards democracy extending over several years.

Foreign cynics, and some Turks, attribute these changes to a desire to please the West, and especially the Americans. They point to the economic difficulties and to the isolated and exposed position of Turkey at the end of the war, and argue that most of the liberalizing reforms of earlier times had come when Turkey needed the support of the West against her northern neighbour. In 1945 Turkey, as a result of her over-prolonged neutrality, was regarded with some disfavour in the West, while Russia might still have hoped for the acquiescence if not the support of her former comrades-in-arms. Faced with the Russian demands in 1945 and 1946 for bases in the Bosporus, as well as threats to the eastern frontier, Turkish statesmen may well have felt that some dramatic gesture was necessary to rally Western opinion to their side.

Western support was in fact forthcoming. The Turkish government, with British and American encouragement, stood firm against the Russian demands. In May 1947 the announcement of the Truman doctrine brought a new assurance of American support. In August 1949 Turkey became a member of the Council of Europe.

In foreign policy at least Turkey had identified herself fully and unreservedly with the West. Did this mean that the advance towards democracy inside the country was no more than a reflection at home of a policy pursued abroad or, to put it more crudely, a piece of window-dressing designed to please and flatter Turkey's Western allies?

No doubt the desire to impress and win over the West had its place among the motives that impelled Ismet Inönü to relax the authoritarian régime in 1945—just as the great Ottoman reforms that came at the time of the Crimean War and the Congress of Berlin were not unrelated to the need of the Ottoman Empire for Western Europe's help against Russia. But it would be a grave error to conclude from this that these various stages of Turkish reform were no more than diplomatic subterfuges. The rulers of Turkey were not likely to change their form of government and surrender power to an opposition, merely to please a foreign state. And, if they did not know it from the start, they must soon have realized that the extension or restriction of democratic liberties in Turkey would have only a limited influence on a decision in Washington to help or abandon them.

The liberal and constitutional movement in Turkey has a long history, going back to the first impact of Western political ideas on Turkish intellectuals. In the period following 1945 there were many indications of a pro-Western and therefore pro-democratic trend running much deeper than the temporary alignments of international relations. At the lowest level, it expressed itself in the prevalence of chewing-gum and leopard-skin shirts on the beaches of the Bosporus and the streets of Istanbul; at the highest, in the study of the English language and of English and American literature and history, in the university, the school, and the home, and in a self-criticism that verged at times on the morbid.

Many different factors contributed to this growth of pro-Western, pro-democratic feeling. The movement no doubt owed much to the prestige that attaches to military victory, and therefore to the characteristic institutions of those that have won it. It was further helped when the United States inherited the place of Germany, in Turkish eyes, as their main bulwark, and therefore model, in resistance to the ancient Russian threat. But there was more than that. In the Kemalist Republic a new generation had grown to maturity, for whom the main objectives of the nationalist creed had already been accomplished, and nationalism alone was no longer enough. Brought up in an age of intensive Westernization, they were deeply attracted by the Western liberal tradition, and saw in democracy not just a matter of fashion or diplomacy, but the means of achieving the final integration of Turkey, on a footing of equality and mutual respect, in the free Western world.

A more extreme form of the theory of American influence is the attribution of the change to direct American intervention. There is no doubt that American pressure was exerted rather strongly in favour of private enterprise and against etatism, and the moves of the People's Party government in this direction were no doubt due in large measure to the terms of American loans and the advice of American advisers. There is, however, no evidence supporting the theory of direct American action in favour of political change. The most that can be said is that they helped to create a favourable atmosphere.

Apologists for the People's Party claim that they had always been devoted to democratic ideals, and that only the harsh conditions of the war years prevented them from achieving them earlier. As applied to the cabinets that ruled Turkey during the war years, it is difficult to take this claim seriously; but much is certainly due to what one might call the Kemalist wing of Kemal's party—the younger men who grew up under the Republic and took the ideals and promises of their founder seriously, and who began to predominate in the final phase of People's Party rule.

There were also practical reasons for the change. By 1945 the strains of the war years had given rise to really serious discontent, and President Inönü may have sought to follow the example set by Atatürk in 1924 and 1930, and open a safety-valve of licensed and limited opposition. In Democrat Party circles the argument was sometimes put forward that Inönü intended no more than this, but the opposition, once started, went far beyond the restricted role intended by the government and became strong enough to force radical changes. There is probably some truth in this explanation, though it should be remembered that this development would not have been possible without a general change in the climate of opinion in Turkey, not least in the ranks of the People's Party itself.

The Democrat victory in 1950 was more than a change of party; it was a plebiscite. All who had a grievance against the People's Party—and after twenty-seven years there were many—found and took the opportunity to register a complaint against it. After so long a period, even a party of angels would probably have been swept out of office.

It is, however, possible to distinguish, among the vast mass of supporters of the Democrat Party in 1950, certain important interests and groups that played a role in the formation of the party and its policies. One of these is the country magnates, the large and medium landowners, especially in Anatolia. Before the Republic, the landlords and rich peasants had held a dominant position in rural Anatolia, not unlike that held by their equivalents beyond the southern and eastern frontiers. In some areas, notably in the east, virtual dynasties of landowners had survived the Ottoman reforms, and still enjoyed semi-feudal privileges over vast estates. The Kemalist Revolution brought radical changes. Like Mahmud II and the statesmen of the *Tanzimat*, Atatürk was a determined centralizer, and he resumed and continued their policy of eliminating the privileges and autonomies of the great *derebey* feudal families. By his day, it was only in the east that these survived in any numbers, and even there, after the rebellions, he had made a determined effort to break up the big estates.

The resentments of these magnates were reinforced by active fear when, after lengthy debates and controversies, a land reform law[48] was passed by the Assembly and entered into effect on 11 June 1945, by an odd coincidence the day before the Four presented their proposals for reform to the People's Party group.

It was, not surprisingly, the landowners, feudal or otherwise, who most feared the new law. But, while the law added the last straw to the growing resentments of the magnates against the People's Party, it did nothing to win them the goodwill of the peasantry. The peasants, weary of years of chivvying by People's Party officials and seeing no obvious benefit in the new law, were ready to take their line from the landlords and rich peasants, and to follow them in revolting against the People's Party régime. The peasants had got to the point of voting against the government; they still did so, however, under the guidance of their own rural leadership.

The influence of the magnates was not the only power that mobilized the accumulated resentments of the peasants against the People's Party. The leaders of the Muslim religious revival that had been growing steadily in force and scope for some years also favoured a change. Between 1946 and 1950 the People's Party had adopted an increasingly tolerant attitude towards the

---

[48] See below, pp. 467 ff.

manifestations of religious revival that were appearing in Turkey, but the religious leaders had never really forgiven the party of Atatürk for the enforced secularization of the 1920's and 1930's, and when the opportunity came to turn against the People's Party they gratefully seized it. Religious leaders still commanded considerable support in the country, especially in the villages and small country towns, and among the artisans and small shop-keepers in the larger cities. By an odd paradox, the introduction of modern communications extended the influence of religious conservatism. The village woman used to wear a veil only when she visited the town. With the development of roads and bus services, many villages all over Turkey have been brought within closer range of urban influences; for most of them, however, the centres of radiation are not Istanbul, Ankara, or Izmir, but the smaller provincial towns, traditionally and still today the strong-holds of religious and social conservatism. There are many villages where the veil has appeared for the first time as a result of technical progress.

Another and quite different element in the pro-Democrat camp was the new commercial and industrial middle class that had grown up in Turkey during the previous decades. These were increasingly restive under the etatist policies of the People's Party, against which they now revolted in the name of democracy and free enterprise. In a sense, the revolt against etatism was the measure of its success, for it was the etatist impulse, supplemented by the opportunities afforded by six years of neutrality in a world war, that led to the emergence of this new Turkish middle class. For this class, the more or less benevolent paternalism of the People's Party had become an irksome anachronism. They rallied with enthusiasm to a party which promised freedom of enterprise, and an economic system more akin to the expanding capitalism of the West.

The magnates, the peasants, the new commercial class, and the old religious class were probably the most important elements among the supporters of the Democrat Party in 1950. There were others too. The non-Muslim minorities, though they too had benefited from a much more liberal policy in the post-war years, could feel little affection for the party responsible for the fiscal pogrom of 1942, and supported the Democrat Party the more readily for its sympathetic attitude to commercial interests.

Popular rumour included even the army and the bureaucracy among those who transferred their allegiance to the Democrats—the latter with a very real grievance in a scale of salaries that had become absurdly inadequate in the face of the increased cost of living. Finally, there was the undifferentiated mass of the population—all those who during the twenty-seven years of People's Party domination had inevitably developed grievances of one sort or another against the government or its various agencies, and who were the more attracted by Democrat promises since the Democrat Party was unembarrassed by any previous record of government.

In spite of the strength and variety of Democrat support, the actual victory, when it came, was a surprise to all—mainly because people, both Turks and foreigners, simply would not believe that a party which had for so long enjoyed a monopoly of power would allow itself to be defeated or, if defeated, would quietly give way to the victors.

In the event, the prophets of doom were all confounded. The election was fair, orderly, and peaceful, and the transfer of power took place with no more fuss or incident than is usual in the oldest and securest of democracies.

The atmosphere immediately after the elections was almost apocalyptic. In Ankara a preacher in the Tacüddin mosque gave thanks to God in the Friday prayer for having freed Turkey from the government of the godless People's Party. Near Bursa, some peasants began to divide up the big estates, and when asked what they were doing, replied: 'Now we have democracy.' In Istanbul, taxi-drivers cocked the Turkish equivalent of a snook at policemen and refused to obey their orders—and even the policemen themselves seemed a little uncertain as to what powers they still retained. Discoloured patches of wallpaper appeared on countless walls, where once the portrait of Inönü had rested; off-the-mark vendors sold 'Democrat Lemonade' in the streets, and an eminent Turkish historian wrote of the election as 'the greatest revolution in the history of Turkey, accomplished without bloodshed . . . and leaving no further obstacle to her progress'.

The transfer of power by a free election was certainly a bloodless revolution, comparable, in its way, with the revolutions of 1876, 1908, and 1923. But it soon became apparent that once again, it was something less than the millennium. Peasants, taxi men, and others who had shown an excess of zeal in their interpretation of democracy duly received a lesson in political science. Policemen breathed again, and swung their truncheons with something like the old verve. And the historian gradually discovered that after all a few obstacles still remained on Turkey's path of progress and freedom.

PART II

Aspects of Change

CHAPTER X
Community and Nation

The Fatherland of a Muslim is the place where the Şeriat prevails.

M. SAID HALIM PAŞA, 1917.

Nation is not a racial, ethnic, geographical, political, or voluntary group or association. Nation is a group composed of men and women who have gone through the same education, who have received the same acquisitions in language, religion, morality, and aesthetics.

ZIYA GÖKALP, 1923.

The Fatherland is the sacred country within our present political boundaries, where the Turkish nation lives with its ancient and illustrious history, and with its past glories still living in the depths of its soil.

REPUBLICAN PEOPLE'S PARTY PROGRAMME, 1935.

In the treaty of Küçük Kaynarca, of July 1774, the Sultan was forced to make two humiliating concessions. The first was the renunciation of the ancient Ottoman suzerainty over the Khan of Crimea and the Muslim Tatars of the northern Black Sea shore, who now became independent as a preliminary to their absorption by Russia nine years later; the second was the acceptance of certain rights of intervention, which became a virtual right of protection by the court of Russia over the Orthodox Christian Church in the Ottoman Empire.[1]

To compensate for this loss of suzerainty abroad and diminution of sovereignty at home, the Sultan himself asserted a new claim.

As to the practices of religion [says the treaty], the Tatars being of the same religion as the Muslims, and his Sultanian Majesty being as Supreme Mohammedan Caliph, they are to conduct themselves towards him as is prescribed in the rules of their religion, without, however, compromising their political and civil independence as has been laid down.[2]

[1] See arts. 7 and 14 of the treaty, which provided the basis for claims to rights of intervention far in excess of what is specified in the text.

[2] Art. 3. The title 'Supremo Califfo Maomettano', which appears in the Italian original text of the treaty, is increased in the French translation to 'Souverain calife de la religion mahométane'; in the Turkish version it is reduced to 'Imām al-Mu'minīn wa Khalīfat al-Muwahhidīn' (Cevdet, *Tarih*, i. 359)—a title connoting no such general claim as is asserted in the versions for foreign consumption. On this question see Becker, 'Bartholds Studien über Kalif und Sultan', *Der Islam*, vi (1916), 408 ff.; Nallino, *Raccolta di Scritti*, iii (1941), 245-6; Jäschke, in *WI*, n.s., i. 196-7.

The claim by the Ottoman Sultan to a kind of religious pontificate extending over Muslims other than his own subjects was new and unprecedented. Since the extinction of the classical Islamic Caliphate in medieval times, there had been no single, universally recognized titular head of the whole Islamic community, and each monarch had become, in effect, a Caliph in his own realms, using some of the titles and exercising some of the prerogatives of the Caliphate, but only as an adjunct to his secular sovereignty. The assertion of religious authority beyond the frontier was a radical departure—an attempt, for the first time since the fall of the Abbasids, to establish a universal Islamic leadership, and to claim it for the house of Osman. It is about this time that the legend first makes its appearance, of how the last of the Abbasid Caliphs in Cairo had transferred the Caliphate to the Ottoman Sultan Selim I in 1517.[3] In the hard times that lay ahead, the Ottoman claim to Muslim leadership was to arouse growing enthusiasm at home, and win increased acceptance abroad.

The early nineteenth century was, for the peoples of Islam, a period of defeat and humiliation, when the European powers, having already demonstrated their military and commercial superiority, moved forward to establish their direct rule. Napoleon, by his swift conquest of Egypt in 1798, had shown the way, demonstrating, at the same time, how ludicrously easy it was to conquer and administer even one of the heartlands of Islam, and how necessary it might be to do so in order to forestall a conquest by a European rival.

The lesson was quickly learnt, and the European powers swiftly staked out their claims across the whole length of the Islamic world in Asia, Europe, and Africa. In India British rule or control was extended over most of the peninsula, and by 1818 no Indian state remained that was fully independent. In South East Asia the British and Dutch swept away the last vestiges of independence, and incorporated the Malay lands firmly in the European colonial system. Nearer home, the Turks saw the southward advance of Austria and Russia bring important Muslim territories under European rule, and offer a direct threat to the security of both Turkey and Persia. In South Eastern Europe

---

[3] This legend, which first appears in d'Ohsson's *Tableau général de l'Empire ottoman*, i (1788), 269–70, was probably invented to support this new claim; cf. Becker, 'Bartholds Studien', and R. Tschudi, *Das Chalifat* (1926), p. 20.

Bessarabia was lost to Russia; Greece and Serbia to new independent Christian states. In the North, Russia, which had long since liquidated and absorbed the Tatar Khanates of the Volga and the Caspian shores, in 1783 annexed the Khanate of the Crimea, and prepared for a further advance into the Caucasus. In 1806 the Russians captured Baku, the cession of which, together with Derbend, Shirvan, and other places, was confirmed by a defeated Persia in the treaty of Gulistan of 1813. Still further Russian annexations of Persian territory were sanctioned by the treaty of Turkmanchay of 1828.

The transfer of these Turkish-speaking, Muslim lands from Persian to Russian control, together with the absorption by Russia of the Christian kingdom of Georgia, brought Russian power to the eastern as well as the western borders of the Ottoman Empire. In this new configuration, not only the possession of its remoter provinces, but the very existence of the Empire was threatened.

These dangers did not pass unperceived in Istanbul. In 1822 Akif Efendi, later *Reis-ül-Küttab*, wrote a memorandum setting forth the dangers that menaced the Empire and the three possible choices that lay before it. After examining the attitudes of the Christian nations towards Islam, and their dealings with Turkey, still the most powerful of Muslim states, Akif tried to show how the Ottoman Empire, and the Muslims generally, could preserve their independence against Europe, and more especially against the encroachments of Russia which he regarded as the major enemy. In conclusion,

the Muslims must choose between three resolutions: either, faithful to the command of God and the law of Muhammad, we must, regardless of our property and our lives, defend to the last what provinces we still retain; or we must leave them and withdraw to Anatolia; or finally—which God forbid—we shall follow the example of the peoples of Crimea, India, and Kazan and be reduced to slavery. In fine, what I have to say can be reduced to this: in the name of the faith of Muhammad and the law of Ahmed, let us proclaim the Holy War and let us not cede an inch of our territory.[4]

Akif thus saw three possible courses before the Turkey of his day—defence, as champions of Islam, of the whole Empire,

[4] Cited in V. D. Smirnow, *Manuscrits turcs de l'Institut des langues orientales* (1897), item 26. My thanks are due to Professor P. Wittek for this reference.

subjection to colonial rule, or retreat to the Anatolian heartland, from which the Turks had first crossed into Europe. During the century that followed, the Turks unsuccessfully attempted the first, successfully avoided the second, and finally, under the pressure of events more than of ideas, successfully adopted the third.

In interesting contrast with the alternative resolutions described in 1822 by Akif Efendi was the challenge to choose between three different principles of loyalty thrown down in 1904 by Akçuraoğlu Yusuf (later known as Yusuf Akçura), a young Tatar from the Russian Empire, whose family had settled in Turkey. After completing his education in France, he found the Turkey of Abdülhamid closed to him, and returned to his native village in Russia. From there he sent an article to *Türk*, a periodical published in Cairo by a group of Turkish political exiles who had found a refuge in British-occupied Egypt. Yusuf's essay, entitled *Üç tarz-ı Siyaset* (three kinds of policy) was published in the issues of May and June 1904, and then reprinted as a pamphlet. Among the many ideological discussions published by the Young Turks in exile, it struck a new and significant note—that of Turkish, as distinct from Muslim or Ottoman, nationalism.[5]

In this essay, which was later to have great influence in Turkey, Yusuf formulates and examines three possible bases of unity in the Ottoman state. The first is Ottomanism, the aspiration of the nineteenth-century liberal reformers for a common Ottoman citizenship and loyalty, irrespective of religion or origin. The second is Islam, the traditional basis of the Ottoman Empire and its Muslim predecessors, since refurbished in the pan-Islamic policies of Abdülhamid. Yusuf discusses both of these at some length and dismisses them as failures. Ottomanism is a political loyalty, which Ottoman subjects owe to the state, but there is no Ottoman nation and it is wasted effort to try and create one. A pan-Islamic policy, aiming at a union of Islamic peoples, would encounter fewer internal obstacles. It would, however, be bitterly, and in all probability successfully, resisted by the Christian powers, and the Turks would gain nothing and lose much by squandering their efforts on an irrelevant and probably unrealizable ideal. As a third possibility he suggests Turkism—'a Turkish

---

[5] Yusuf's own account of the pamphlet, its origins, and its influence will be found in his invaluable survey of the Turkist movement, 'Türkçülük', *Türk Yılı*, i (1928), 396 ff.

national policy based on the Turkish race'. For such a policy, he argued, there were fewer internal obstacles than for Ottomanism, fewer external obstacles than for pan-Islam. A Turkist policy would rally the loyalties of the dominant Turkish race within the Ottoman Empire, and reinforce it with that of the many millions of Turks, in Russia and elsewhere, beyond the Ottoman frontiers.

The differences between the choices of Akif Efendi and of Akçuraoğlu Yusuf illustrate the evolution of Turkish ideas and ideologies during the intervening years. For Akif, the question of the basis of identity and loyalty simply does not arise. The Empire is an Islamic Empire, the champion of Islam as a whole, and the struggle in which it is engaged is the ancient clash of Islam and Christendom. The choice he offers is a purely practical one— between defence, retreat, and surrender. For Yusuf, on the other hand, it is the very basis of Turkish corporate identity that has become a matter of doubt and discussion. Islam is now only one of three alternative possibilities—and even then it is no longer the simple, strong, spontaneous loyalty to the House of Islam of earlier times, but a new, subtler, and feebler thing, a political response and an emotional reaction to alien challenges and influences, known by the appropriately hybrid name of pan-Islamism. Yusuf's two other alternatives—Ottomanism and Turkism— would have been meaningless to Akif and his contemporaries. The conflict and interaction of these ideas, and of the loyalties which they evoke, have, however, dominated Turkish political thought during the past century, and exercised a profound influence on the evolution of the Turkish state and nation. It would be rash to state that the Turkish people have made their final choice among the different paths that lie before them. This much, however, can be said—that in the Turkish Republic Akif's second best, the retreat to Anatolia, has been successfully adopted, though with a theoretical justification which would have been incomprehensible to Akif, and which is derived, with some important modifications, from the Turkist ideologies of which Akçuraoğlu Yusuf's third choice is an example.

Identity and Loyalty in Islam

In a well-known passage in his *Prolegomena*, the great Arab historian Ibn Khaldūn tells us that the Caliph Umar I once said to the Arabs: 'Learn your genealogies, and be not like the

x

Nabataeans of Mesopotamia who, if asked as to their origin, reply:
"I came from such and such a village." [6]

It may be doubted whether the attribution of this dictum to
Umar is authentic, but Ibn Khaldūn's historical flair did not
betray him when he cited it as an expression of the sentiments of
the Arabs at the time of the great Islamic conquests. The Arab
conquistadores were a tribal aristocracy identified by descent and
kinship, full of contempt for the land-bound peasants who were
classified by the places they inhabited.

This identity of blood was at first reinforced, and then replaced,
by an identity of faith—by the bond of a common acceptance of
Islam, and common membership of the Islamic community. The
nucleus of the later Islamic polity was the religio-political community which the Prophet founded and led in Medina—the
Umma dūn al-nās, the community distinguished from the rest of
mankind. [7]

Such distinctions were not new; Greeks and Barbarians, Jews
and Gentiles, are obvious examples from the ancient world. The
ancient Arabs too had divided mankind into Arabs and non-Arabs,
'Arab and *'Ajam*, and this sentiment lived on into Islamic times.
The distinction was ethnic, not territorial; there is not even a word
in Arabic for Arabia, which is called the land or peninsula of the
Arabs. In time, as the Arabian Arabs merged into the cosmopolitan
Islamic Empire which they had created, the distinction *'Arab–
'Ajam* was overshadowed by the antithesis *Muslim–Kāfir*—the vital
and permanent division between believer and unbeliever, between
the Muslims and the rest. This became and remained the fundamental division of mankind among the Muslim peoples—more
important than kinship, language, country, or political allegiance.
The world was divided into the *Dār al-Islām*, the House of Islam,
and the *Dār al-Ḥarb*, the House of War, or lands under infidel
rule, and between the two there was a perpetual state of war,
interrupted only by truces, and preordained to end with the
incorporation of the whole world into the House of Islam. Besides
the *Harbî* or infidel beyond the frontier, there was also the *Zimmi*
(from Arabic *Dhimmī*), the protected non-Muslim subject of the
Muslim state, whose position was determined by the *dhimma*, or

---

[6] *Muqaddima*, ed. Quatremère, i. 237.

[7] For a recent examination of the *Umma* by a social scientist see C. A. O. van
Nieuwenhuijze, 'The Ummah; an Analytic Approach', *Studia Islamica*, x (1959), 5–22.

pact, between his community, called *millet*, and the dominant community of Islam.

The fundamental aim of Islamic policy was to incorporate the *Dār al-Ḥarb* in the *Dār al-Islām*, and to turn the *Harbî* infidels into Muslims or, if that were not possible, into *Zimmîs*. The essential classification—political, social, even economic—was Muslim, *Zimmî, Harbî.* This tripartite distinction between the believer, the subjugated unbeliever, and the hostile unbeliever was far more important than such divisions as Turks, Greeks, and Slavs in the Balkans or Turks, Persians, and Arabs in Asia. Loyalty to a place was known, but it was to a village or quarter, at most to a province, not a country; loyalty to one's kin was ancient and potent, but it was to the family or tribe, not to the nation. The ultimate loyalty, the measure by which a man distinguished between brother and stranger, was religion. For the Muslim, his fellow believer, of whatever country, race, or language, was a brother; his Christian neighbour, his own infidel ancestors, were strangers.

Among the different peoples who embraced Islam none went farther in sinking their separate identity in the Islamic community than the Turks. Though, as we shall see, some traces of a Turkish group self-awareness remained, the Turks retained but few memories of their pre-Islamic past and raised no racial barrier between Turk and non-Turk. The traditional Ottoman Turkish conception of the nature of the state and community in which they lived can clearly be seen, on two different levels, in their historiography and in their customs tariffs.

Until the early nineteenth century the Ottoman Turk regarded the society in which he lived as the culmination of two lines of development—or rather, since it is questionable how far the notion of development is present in traditional Islamic patterns of thought, of two series of historical events. The first of these began with the mission of Muhammad, the rise of Islam, and the establishment of the Caliphate; the second with the rise of the House of Osman and the Ottoman Empire. The link between the two was provided by the invasions of the Seljuk Turks and the creation of the Seljuk Sultanates, first in Persia and then in Anatolia. These events form the main theme of Ottoman historiography. The histories of the subject *millets* are treated only in so far as they affect Ottoman history. The history of the Christian neighbours and enemies of Turkey receives some slight attention;

the pre-Islamic history of the Turks and of Turkey receive none at all.[8] The classical Ottoman historians were products of an advanced and sophisticated civilization, and their writings must rank among its greatest achievements. It is the more remarkable that they should have been so totally uninterested, either in the history of their nation, before it was converted, or of their country, before it was conquered, for Islam.

The same scale of values is reflected, in a more material form, in the old Ottoman customs tariffs. In this, as in most Islamic fiscal laws, there are discriminatory rates of assessment. The Ottoman codes recognized these rates—the lowest for Muslims, the highest for *Harbîs*, and a medium rate for *Zimmîs*.[9] The believer, the hostile infidel, the subject infidel—these were the three recognized categories, and nationality, even political allegiance had no bearing on them.

After the basic loyalty to the Islamic community, the next loyalty was political—to the lawful head of the Islamic state. In the period following the Turkish and Mongol invasions of the Middle East, the dynastic principle became firmly established, and in the Ottoman Empire in particular the House of Osman, through the long centuries of its rule, came to enjoy the un-questioning and spontaneous loyalty of most of its Muslim subjects —even of many of its Christian subjects. The Sultan may not always have been loved by his subjects, but he was generally accepted as the legitimate Muslim head of a Muslim Empire, and as the heir of the great Emperors of the Muslim past.

Within the Ottoman Islamic Empire the dominant group was Turkish. Despite the early prevalence of Arabs and Persians in the higher ranks of the religious hierarchy, and the influence at times of Persian as a courtly and polite language, the ruling language of the Empire was Turkish, and the court, army, and bureacracy alike made use of it. The cosmopolitan governing *élite* of the Empire was recruited from men of many races, but the use of Turkish was a normal adjunct of membership, and Turkish was usually the language spoken by their descendants.

On the other hand there is only sporadic evidence of any sense

---

[8] See B. Lewis, 'History-writing and National Revival in Turkey', *MEA*, iv (1953), 218 ff.

[9] Numerous examples will be found in the Ottoman *Kanuns*, notably in the collection edited by Ö. L. Barkan and published in Istanbul in 1943 (index under *harbi*).

of Turkish national identity. The first Turkish converts to Islam, as has already been noted, identified themselves completely with their new faith, and seem to have forgotten their separate Turkish past with astonishing rapidity and completeness. The Mongol conquests, which established the supremacy of an unconverted steppe people, still following its old religion, in the heartlands of Islam, brought the prestige of domination to the traditions and customs of the steppe, and aroused in the Turks as well as in the Mongols a new pride and interest in their own distinctive heritage. This development is especially noticeable during the fifteenth century. Timur (d. 1405), who initiated the second great wave of Mongol conquest, was himself a Turk and not a Mongol, and by his time the Turks had come to predominate in the empires of the steppe peoples. Timur had a Turkish as well as a Persian chancery, and had his victories celebrated in Turkish chronicles which have unfortunately not survived.[10] Under his Timurid successors, the courts of Shiraz, Samarkand, and especially Herat became the centres of a Turkish cultural revival. Pre-Mongol Turkish writings were collected and studied, and a series of new translations and original works produced, which mark the beginning of a new Turkish literature. By far the most important among the authors was the great poet Ali Shīr Nevā'ī (1441–1501), who may in a sense be called the Chaucer of the Turks. The first major poet to use the Turkish vernacular, he both argued and demonstrated its fitness to serve as a literary medium, and exercised a profound influence in all the lands of Turkish speech.

The language used by Ali Shīr Nevā'ī was eastern or Chatagay Turkish, and in his day the main centres of Turkish life and culture were still in the East, and not in the remote, quasi-colonial territory of Anatolia. The Chagatay language was, however, well enough understood among the Anatolian Turks, and the writings of Nevā'ī and other eastern authors were known and appreciated. There were contacts of various kinds between the Ottoman and Timurid courts, and the prestige of the ancient centres of civilization in the east stood high among the rude pioneers of the western frontier. The first signs of a Turkish national revival in Turkey date from the reign of Murad II. During his reign the passage in the first book of the History of Rashīd al-Dīn (d. 1318), dealing with the early history of the Turkish tribes, was translated from

10 Bombaci, p. 125.

Persian into Turkish, and other works adapted or composed on Turkish antiquities. These stories were incorporated in the historical traditions of the Ottoman ruling house, which was now linked for the first time with Central Asian Turkish legends and traditions, and given a line of descent from the legendary hero Oğuz Khan.[11]

The Oğuz legend remained part of the official historiographic myth right down to the end of the Empire, but apart from this, the phase of Turkish antiquarianism and Turkish identification soon came to an end. The deflection of the Ottoman Empire away from a Turkish and back to an Islamic identity may be ascribed at least in part to three successive events. The conquest of Constantinople in 1453, rounding off the Sultanate of Rum, made the Turks more conscious of an Imperial, as distinct from a merely tribal mission. The rise of the Turkish but Shi'ite power of the Safavids in Iran cut them off from the eastern Turkish world, and flung them into bitter religious conflict with their nearest Turkish neighbours. The conquest of Syria and Egypt in 1516–17 and of Iraq in 1534 brought the ancient centres of Islamic Empire under their rule and conferred upon them the burden of an Islamic Imperial heritage and mission.

Under the double weight of the Imperial and Islamic traditions, in the twofold struggle against Christendom and heresy, the nascent Turkish sense of national identity was overlaid and effaced. In Ottoman writings up to the middle of the nineteenth century, and in many of them much later, the word 'Turkey' is not used. It was a Western term, used by Westerners to describe a country which the Turks themselves usually called 'the lands of Islam', 'the Imperial realm', 'the divinely guarded realm', or, when more local definition was required, 'the land of Rum'. The Roman name remained as common Turkish usage for the Ottoman Empire until comparatively modern times, and only gradually gave way to 'the Ottoman Dominions'. All these expressions were of course understood to include the whole of the Empire and not simply the area inhabited by the Turkish nation, the very existence of which was concealed.[12] When, in the mid-

---

[11] P. Wittek, 'De la défaite d'Ankara à la prise de Constantinople', *R. Ét. isl.* (1938), pp. 27 f. and 'Yazıjıoghlu 'Alī . . .', *BSOAS*, xiv (1952), 644 ff.

[12] Sometimes the term Rum was used to distinguish the old Ottoman provinces, i.e. Anatolia and Rumelia, from the Arab lands acquired after 1516.

nineteenth century, the Young Ottomans, under European influence, wished to speak of their country as 'Turkey', they were hard to put to it to find a Turkish equivalent for the name. At first they made use of the word Turkistan, a Persian formation meaning Turk-land. Later, probably because this term was already pre-empted for Central Aisa, they abandoned it in favour of *Türkiye*, an adaptation of the European name, which in 1923 became the official designation of the country.

The word 'Turk' was indeed used, but only to denote the nomads or peasants of Anatolia. When Koçu Bey, in 1630, complains that the corps of Janissaries has been overrun with outsiders and interlopers, he speaks of 'Turks, Gypsies, Tats, Lazes, muleteers and camel-drivers, porters, footpads, and cutpurses'.[13] Even Halet Efendi, who went to Paris in 1802, seems to have been shocked to find himself called the 'Turkish ambassador', and, when congratulating himself on having countered a hostile manœuvre, remarks that this time they had not found him the 'Turkish ambassador'—i.e. the ignorant boor—that they wanted.[14] As late as 1897 an experienced British traveller in Turkey could still remark

at the present day the name 'Turk' is rarely used, and I have heard it employed only in two ways, either as a distinguishing term of race (for example, you ask whether a village is 'Turk' or 'Turkmen'), and as a term of contempt (for example, you mutter 'Turk Kafa', where in English you would say 'Blockhead').[15]

Yet, within a century of Halet's death, the Ottoman dynasty was deposed, Islam disestablished, and a secular Republic proclaimed, on the basis of the Turkish nation and the Turkish homeland. These new conceptions and new loyalties—the nation and the fatherland—struck deep roots in Turkey, and have, by modification, became associated with some of the deepest instincts of the Muslim Turkish people. Their origin and early development must, however, be traced in the workings of European influence.

European Influence: Patriotism and Nationalism

The modern conception of patriotism originated in Western Europe, where, first in England, then in France and other countries, the state ceased to be the king, and instead became

[13] Koçu Bey, chs. 5 and 9.   [14] E. Z. Karal, *Halet*, p. 55.
[15] Sir W. M. Ramsay, *Impressions of Turkey* (1897), p. 99.

identified with the nation, the people, or the fatherland. Echoes of the Greek *polis* and the Roman *patria*, drowned at the time of the Renaissance and Reformation by the clash of Church and State and of Church and Church, were heard more clearly in the Age of Reason. The new sentiment of nation and country began among the independent Western nations, where sovereignty and nationhood were axiomatic, and where nation-states, with well-defined national territories, in fact existed before the idea of the nation-state emerged. In these countries, the patriotic lovers of liberty were concerned with asserting the rights of the individual against domination by authority, rather than of the group against domination by other groups—in other words, not so much with independence, which they already possessed, as with freedom, which they were struggling to win.

This early, Western European type of nationalism was utilitarian, practical, and liberal; it dealt with nations defined by visible and objective criteria, such as territory and sovereignty. To some extent language too was a criterion, though it cannot have been a rigid one, since in the eighteenth century both Britain and France were countries of a plurality of languages. More important was the occupation of a common territory, defined by the jurisdiction of a common sovereign authority. It may thus more appropriately be called patriotism, rather than nationalism.

It was this Western European type of patriotism that first affected the Islamic world, and gave rise to the attempt, finally unsuccessful, to focus loyalty on an Ottoman fatherland, and on a vaguely defined Ottoman nation.

The two words used in Turkish for fatherland and nation were *vatan* and *millet*, and it is instructive to examine their semantic development. *Vatan* is a Turcicized form of *waṭan*, a classical Arabic word meaning place of birth or residence. A man's *vatan* might be a country, a province, a town, or a village, according to context. In this sense a *vatan* could inspire sentiment and loyalty, and these find frequent expression in classical literature—but the word had no more political significance than the English word home.

In the course of the nineteenth century the overtones of the French word *patrie* began to affect the Islamic word *vatan*. As early as the 1790's, Ali Efendi, the Turkish ambassador to the *Directoire*, in describing French arrangements for the care of disabled soldiers, speaks of men who had suffered 'in the cause of the Republic and out of zeal for their *vatan*'.[16] This was a new notion for Ali Efendi's time, and it is likely—for he was not a perceptive man—that he or his interpreter was merely translating literally from an original he did not understand. But by 1841 Handjeri's Turkish-French dictionary includes the equation *vatan = patrie*, together with new derivatives for patriot and patriotism, and examples of their use, in Turkish and French, which are purely Western in inspiration. By the mid-century *vatan*, in the political sense of fatherland, was in common use in the Turkish press, and in 1866 there was even a newspaper called *Ayine-i Vatan* (the Mirror of the Fatherland).

The word *millet*, from the Arabic *milla* and perhaps ultimately of Aramaic origin, occurs in the Koran with the meaning of religion. It was later extended to mean religious community, especially the community of Islam. In the Ottoman Empire it came to be applied to the organized and legally recognized religious communities, such as the Greek Christians, the Armenian Christians, and the Jews, and by extension also to the different 'nations' of the Franks. Even as applied to the Frankish nations the term was at first understood as having a primarily religious sense. Thus, the English were recognized in the sixteenth century as the 'Lutheran nation', and non-English Protestants were regarded as being under their protection. In the Empire, there was a Muslim *millet*, but no Turkish or Arab or Kurdish *millets*; there were Greek and Armenian and Jewish *millets*, but as religious communities, not as ethnic nations. Until the late nineteenth century, Greeks and Slavs alike formed part of the Greek Orthodox *millet*, while on the other hand Gregorian and Catholic Armenians formed separate *millets*. It is not until a comparatively late date that one encounters the idea of national entities transcending religious distinctions. Even then the idea is still recognizably alien, with dubious rights of domicile.

Both words—*vatan* and *millet*—occur in the Rescript of the Rose Chamber of 1839, in a way which significantly reveals the confusion of ideas between the old Islamic loyalty and the new, imperfectly assimiliated patriotism. The text speaks of 'zeal for dynasty and nation (*millet*) and love of country (*vatan*)', in a

16 Ahmed Refik, ed., '. . . Ali Efendinin Sefaretnamesi', *TOEM*, (1329 A.H.), p. 1459.

context which is quite clearly intended to refer to all Ottoman subjects irrespective of religion. Yet a little farther on, the same document speaks of 'the people of Islam and other nations (*millet*)' within the Empire, as separate and distinct entities. 'Other nations' and 'foreign nations' are common expressions in Turkish administrative and journalistic usage at the time. Both clearly mean nations other than Islam; 'foreign nations' mean those not under Muslim rule, and therefore correspond to the 'House of War' of earlier days. At no time do they include non-Ottoman Muslims, who, although they may be strangers, are not foreigners in the Islamic Empire. It is not until the 1860's that we find frequent reference to an Ottoman *millet*—and here too it is far from clear whether all Ottomans are meant, or whether this is a new name for the Muslims. In the first leading article of the *Tercüman-i Ahval*, published in 1860, Şinasi discusses the interests of the fatherland (*vatan*) and remarks that while the non-Muslim subjects of the Empire had their own newspapers, there were no 'truly Ottoman' newspapers, since hitherto no member of the 'dominant *millet*' had been willing to publish one.[17] In the same spirit, an article in the *Tasvir-i Efkâr* in 1862 speaks of 'the Ottoman *millet*, the owner and master of the country'.[18]

Namık Kemal, the apostle of liberal patriotism, adopts a milder tone, but he too, in his patriotic writings, shows that he never really distinguished between what was Ottoman and what was Islamic. A good example of this is a famous leading article, on patriotism, which he published in 1868 in *Hürriyet*, one of the journals issued by the Young Ottomans in exile. In an eloquent appeal to the patriotic pride of his readers, he reminds them that their country had produced such great sovereigns as Sultan Süleyman the Magnificent and the Caliph Umar, such men of learning as Farabi, Avicenna, Ghazali, and Zamakhshari; and he saw nothing incongruous in including medieval Arab and Persian Muslims, and an ancient Arabian Caliph, in his appeal to 'Ottoman' pride. The fatherland of Namık Kemal's loyalties included the Caliphs of Medina as well as the Sultans of Constantinople among its former rulers.

[17] *Tercüman-ı Ahval*, no. 1, 21 Oct. 1860. Reprinted in Ozön, *Son Asır Türk Edebiyatı Tarihi* (1941), pp. 419–20, and in the Şinasi volume of the *Türk Klas.*, pp. 72–74.

[18] *Tasvir-i Efkâr*, 27 June 1862, reprinted in Özön, *Son Asır*, pp. 420–1; Şinasi (*Türk Kl.*), p. 74.

The Fatherland [he says in a later article] does not consist of imaginary lines drawn on a map by the sword of a conqueror or the pen of a scribe: it is a sacred idea, sprung from the union of the many lofty sentiments, such as nation, freedom, welfare, brotherhood, property, sovereignty, respect for ancestors, love of family, memory of youth....[19]

A practical problem of the time illustrated the obstacles in the way of Ottoman patriotism. In May 1855 the Ottoman government announced that the duty and privilege of military service, hitherto restricted to Muslims, would be extended to the Christian subjects of the Empire. This declaration, issued to the ambassadors of the European powers, was part of the diplomatic preparation for the peace conference at the end of the Crimean War. The promise of the Porte included the abolition of the poll-tax levied on non-Muslims, as well as the admission of the Christians to the army, where they would be allowed to rise to the rank of colonel, and to the civil service, where they could rise to the highest grade.[20]

In early times, the Ottoman Sultans had not scrupled to make use of Christian auxiliaries and even, for a short time, to include Christian fief-holders in their feudal cavalry.[21] But all this was long past and forgotten; for many centuries the Ottoman armies had been the Muslim armies of a Muslim state, and the inclusion in them of Christian soldiers would have been a self-evident absurdity. In fact, the Christian beneficiaries of this act of emancipation were even less anxious to accept the privilege of arms than were the Muslims to confer it, and the attempt to recruit Christian soldiers was soon abandoned amid general satisfaction. Instead of serving in the army, the non-Muslim subjects of the Empire were permitted to commute their duty of military service to an exemption fee, the *bedel*,[22] which happened to coincide exactly, in the method of assessment and collection, with the abolished poll-tax. In this way the liberal reformers were able to serve both their instincts and their ideals.

In Europe, the promise and its abandonment were dismissed as just another piece of Ottoman insincerity. But in fact the Ottoman government gave long and earnest consideration to the problem

---

[19] *Ibret*, 22 Mar. 1873. Reprinted in Özön, *Namık Kemal*, p. 265; cf. Rossi, in *OM*, xxiii (1943), 364–5.

[20] Engelhardt, i. 126.   [21] cf. above, p. 5.   [22] See above, p. 114.

of non-Muslim recruitment, which, besides appealing to Western and liberal opinion, offered the tempting bait of a new accession of manpower for the depleted Ottoman armies. During the Grand Vezirate of Fuad Paşa a special commission discussed the matter. Cevdet Paşa, in his deposition to the commission, laid his finger on the essential difficulty. In times of special stress and urgency, he asked, when a commander wishes to urge his men to supreme endurance and self-sacrifice, on what basis is he to appeal to them? For Muslims, the most effective appeals are those of religion—holy war, martyrdom in battle, the struggle for the true faith against the infidel. These are the appeals to which they have been accustomed since childhood, and it is to them that they respond most readily. The loyalty, courage, and endurance of Muslim soldiers are due largely to their religious sentiments and devotion.

But in time of need, how could the Colonel of a mixed battalion stir the zeal of his soldiers? In Europe, indeed, patriotism has taken the place of religious devotion, but this happened at the end of their feudal period; their children hear the word fatherland (*vatan*) while they are still small, and so years later the call of patriotism has become effective with their soldiers. But among us, if we say the word 'fatherland' all that will come to the minds of the soldiers is their village squares. If we were to adopt the word 'fatherland' now, and if, in the course of time, it were to establish itself in men's minds and acquire the power that it has in Europe, even then it would not be as potent as religious zeal, nor could it take its place. Even that would take a long time, and in the meantime our armies would be left without spirit.[23]

Namık Kemal was not unaware of the difficulties and contradictions involved in the Ottoman fatherland. Other nations, he said, loved their fatherlands, but none of them could feel wholly confident and secure about their future. Every country had its own dangers and difficulties. The English feared Irish separatism and the Russian approach to India (which apparently formed part of the English *vatan*), the French strove to reconcile order and liberty, the Germans and Italians were anxious for their newly won unity, the Russians for their vast conquests. 'As for us, we imagine that the differences of race and religion among our countrymen might bring total dissolution to our country.'[24]

---

[23] Cevdet, 'Maruzat', *TOEM*, (1341 A.H.), p. 273; cf. his *Tarih*, vi. 18.
[24] *Ibret*, 22 Mar. 1873, reprinted in Özön, *Namık Kemal*, pp. 267–8.

Against this foreboding Namık Kemal offered his readers what proved to be specious reassurances. Diversity was not necessarily a weakness; with a wise policy it might even be a factor of progress. In any case, the various races and religions were so thoroughly mixed that, with one exception, there was no province of the Empire which could form a separate government or transfer to another state—for where could these people hope to find such freedom and tolerance as in the Ottoman Empire? The exception was the Arab lands. In them there lived a population of many millions, speaking a separate language and feeling themselves to belong to a separate race. But the Arabs were bound to the Empire by Islamic brotherhood and allegiance to the Caliphate, and their separation was not to be feared.[25]

Once again the real bond is Islam. The Christians would not leave because it would not be practicable for them to do so; the Arabs would stay because of Islamic brotherhood and loyalty. In a poem celebrating the 'Ottoman Fatherland', Namık Kemal proudly reminds his readers that it was in their country that Christ was born and ascended to heaven, that the light of God came down to Moses, that Adam found a substitute for Paradise, that Noah's Ark came to rest, that 'from the song of David and the moan of Socrates, religion and reason became keepsakes for one another'—that is, the Biblical and Hellenistic heritages merged in Islam—and he concludes

> Go, fatherland, swathe yourself in black in the Ka'ba,
> Stretch out an arm to the garden of the Prophet.[26]

It is in the last couplet that the poet's real loyalty finds expression. There was no Ottoman nation, and, as Akçuraoğlu Yusuf later remarked, it was wasted effort to try and create one. The Ottoman fatherland held many nations, which had once been held together, even the non-Muslims among them, by a common allegiance to the dynastic sovereign. The Ottoman liberals, and after them the Ottoman constitutionalists, tried to replace that allegiance by a new Ottoman patriotism, which would group all the many peoples of the Empire in a single political loyalty and identity. 'There is a new Ottoman nation . . .', said Ahmed Midhat, 'and Ottomanism consists in recognizing, as a basic political allegiance, the quality of subject of the Imperial

[25] Ibid. [26] *Vatan-i Osmani*, cited by Kaplan, p. 113.

Sovereign.'[27] The same principle appears in the programme of the Committee of Union and Progress, and formed the basic policy of the Young Turk government in 1908. But the cause was hopeless. The old dynastic allegiance was indeed being undermined by the new ideas of nationality coming from Europe, and affecting, in the first instance, the Christian peoples of the Empire. But when the national idea conquered them, they began to think of themselves, not as Ottomans, but as Greeks, Serbs, Bulgars, and Armenians. Against these heady visions the pallid doctrine of Ottomanism, so dubiously supported even by the Turks themselves, had little chance of success. The struggle of the Christian peoples for national independence and the Turkish reaction against it—armed insurrection and armed repression—created a new bitterness between Muslims and Christians. The Bulgarian rising of 1876, the Armenian revolutionary movement of the 1890's, the Cretan insurrection of 1896–7, the activities of the revolutionary committees, the famous *komitadjis*, in the Balkans, all helped to create in the Turks a profound mistrust of their Christian compatriots and of the European great powers looming behind them; at the same time the repressions and massacres with which the Turks responded reinforced the determination of the Christian peoples in the Empire to seek their salvation, not in citizenship, but in separation. In the end, the nationalist ideas that were destroying the Empire would reach even its Imperial masters. But in the meantime an older claim on their loyalty was again asserted.

Pan-Islamism [28]

When Namık Kemal felt the dawn of doubt as to the loyalty of the Arabs to the Ottoman Empire, he reassured himself with thoughts of Islamic brotherhood and allegiance to the Caliphate— to that throne of which the Arabian Umar, as well as the Turkish Süleyman, had been occupants.

During the second half of the nineteenth century new humiliations made the Muslims of the world more ready to turn to the Turkish Sultan for protection and leadership. In India the

[27] Rossi, in *OM*, xxiii. 367.

[28] The literature on pan-Islamism is extensive, and of unequal value. For useful brief introductions to the Ottoman variety see Rossi, pp. 366 ff.; and anon., 'Le panislamisme et le panturquisme', *RMM*, xxiii (1913), 179–220.

suppression of the last vestiges of the Mughal Empire, after the Mutiny of 1857–8, left the Muslims of that country without a focus for their loyalty, a Muslim sovereign to name in their prayers. In Central Asia the Russians conquered Samarkand in 1868, and reduced the Amirate of Bokhara to the status of a 'native state' in the Russian Empire. In Africa in 1881–2 the British occupied Egypt and the French Tunisia; in 1891 the Germans declared a Protectorate over Dar es-Salaam.

Already in the early 1870's, Namık Kemal was aware of a Western threat, both intellectual and imperial, to the Islamic world, and urged that the Ottomans take the leadership in defending Islam against it. His pan-Islamism was, however, cultural rather than political—'the way of uniting the people of Islam must be sought, not in political aims or doctrinal disputes, but in the presence of preachers, in the pages of books'.[29] His pan-Islamism was linked with his desire for modernization. Since the Ottomans were the nearest of the Muslims to Europe, they were the most advanced on the path of modernization, and were thus the natural leaders of Islam on this path. The Muslims would certainly unite one day in progress. But at the same time

Since the Caliphate is here, and since . . . in the suitability of the place and the readiness of the people in nearness to Europe, the present home of civilization, in wealth and in knowledge, this country is the most advanced of all the Muslim lands, this union of which we speak will surely have its centre here. . . . When that happens, the light of knowledge will radiate from this centre to Asia and Africa. Facing the balance of Europe, a new balance of the East will come into being, and in that way the scales of justice will come into the world of men. . . .[30]

Namık Kemal speaks of the union of Islam as being a general objective in his day. The Crimean War, the Indian Mutiny, the conquests of Britain, France, and Russia in Muslim lands, all helped to foster these ideas. Towards 1870 an organization was formed in Central Asia, to resist Russian and British advances. Agents were sent to the Middle East, and contact made with the Sultan. Nothing came of these efforts, which were forgotten during the wars of 1877–8 and the interlude of liberal constitutional

[29] *Ibret*, 13 June 1872; reprinted in Özön, *Namık Kemal*, pp. 77–78.
[30] Ibid. reprinted in Özön, *Namık Kemal*, p. 33.

government. But pan-Islamism was not dead, and the third article of the 1876 constitution formally claims the 'high Islamic Caliphate' for the house of Osman. Under Abdülhamid a form of pan-Islamism became official policy—though with a very different content from Kemal's preaching of freedom and progress.[31] There was a wide range of pan-Islamic ideologies, from the Ottoman official version to the more radical teachings of the redoubtable Jamāl al-Dīn al-Afghānī (1839–97), the apostle of the Islamic reaction against the West. For most of their followers, the causes of the decline of Islam were to be sought, not in any internal weaknesses or defects, but in the aggressive imperialism of Christian Europe, which sought to enslave the Muslims and destroy Islam. The danger was twofold; the establishment of foreign political, military, and economic supremacy in the Muslim lands, and the undermining, by foreign intellectual influences, of the basic beliefs and values of Islam. The task was to drive out the foreign invaders, abolish foreign concessions and immunities, restore the true Islamic faith—and, some added, to reunite all the Muslims in a single state, under its lawful sovereign, the Caliph.

Such a task was obviously beyond the capacities of the Ottoman Empire, but the espousal of such a programme offered many advantages to Abdülhamid. Inside the Empire, the appeal to Muslim loyalty could win support for his efforts to repress the liberals, nationalists, reformers, and other opponents of his autocratic power. Outside the Empire, he might hope to rally an important body of Muslim opinion to his support and, by creating difficulties for the Imperial powers in their Muslim territories, forestall possible action against Turkey.

His policy was for a while remarkably successful. The Sultan's emissaries were at work in Algeria and in Egypt, in India and even in Japan, stirring up Muslim opinion, gaining new support for the Ottoman Sultanate, and taking full advantage of the new media of communication at their disposal. The measure of their success may be seen in the widespread concern aroused all over the

[31] O. Depont and K. Coppolani, (*Les Confréries religieuses musulmanes* (1897), pp. 257 ff.) attribute a major role in pan-Islamic propaganda to the dervish orders, some of whose leaders, resident in Istanbul, they regard as the Sultan's principal agents in this field. This interpretation, which has been followed by several subsequent writers (e.g. Nallino, in his article 'Panislamismo' in the *Enciclopedia Italiana*) is decisively disproved by Snouck-Hurgronje, 'Les Confréries religieuses, la Mecque et le Panislamisme', *Verspreide Geschriften*, iii. 189 ff.

Islamic world by the Greco-Turkish war of 1897—a local affair
that would have passed unnoticed in earlier times. Ottoman
victories were celebrated in many lands, and were followed by
stirrings or outbreaks among the Muslims in India and the East
Indies, Turkestan, Madagascar, and Algeria. Even after the
deposition of Abdülhamid, the Young Turks continued to enjoy
the support of the Muslim world in their struggles against their
Balkan enemies, and pan-Islamic solidarity was a matter of grave
—indeed exaggerated—concern to the Allies in the First World
War.[32] The last flickers of pan-Islamic sentiment can be seen in
the pathetic intervention of the Indian Muslim leaders on the
question of the Caliphate in 1923.[33]

Turkism [34]

In 1897, in a mood of passionate loyalty engendered by the
brief Greco-Turkish war, a young poet called Mehmed Emin
published a volume of verse entitled *Türkçe Şiirler* (Poems in
Turkish). Abandoning the formal language and quantitative
prosody of the Ottoman court poets, Mehmed Emin wrote in
simple popular Turkish and in the stressed verse used in folk
poetry. Still more remarkable, he adopted a word which, in
Turkish usage, had connoted a boorish, ignorant peasant or
nomad, and proudly proclaimed himself a Turk—

> I am a Turk, my faith and my race are mighty

and in another place—

> We are Turks, with this blood and with this name we live.[35]

Mehmed Emin still defined his loyalty first by faith, and was
indeed a deeply religious man; but with this new word a new
concept of identity had found its way into the collective self-
awareness of the Turkish-speaking Ottoman Muslims.

[32] On the pan-Islamic activities and propaganda of the Young Turks see Y. H.
Bayur, *Türk Ink. Tar.*, ii/4, pp. 88 ff., 314 ff., 374 ff.

[33] See above, p. 258.

[34] On the Turkist movement, the classic account is that of Akçuraoğlu Yusuf in
Türk Yılı, i (1928), 290–455. See also U. Heyd, *Foundations of Turkish Nationalism*
(1950); Gökalp, *Turkish Nationalism and Western Civilization* (tr. and ed. by Niyazi
Berkes, 1959); Karpat; Rossi, in *OM*, xxiii. 361 ff.

[35] Reprinted in the Mehmet Emin volume in *Türk Klas.*, p. 18; Akyüz, *Antoloji*,
p. 20, &c. See Rossi, p. 371.

Y

Ottomanism had proved a failure. Islamic loyalty still dominated the sentiments of the great mass of Turks, as it had done for centuries past, but its modern political avatar, pan-Islamism, had won only limited successes, and held, moreover, a diminishing appeal for the Western-educated, westward-looking younger intellectuals.

The Western European concept of the territorial and political nation had proved difficult of application to the Ottoman Empire, and was basically irrelevant to its historic situation and present needs. There was, however, another kind of national sentiment in Europe, that was to have far greater impact on the people of the Ottoman Empire. In central Europe, where there were no well-defined and long-established territorial nation-states such as England and France, the visible and external criteria of nationhood—land and state—were insufficient. In the continental Empires, there were Germans, Czechs, Poles, and Hungarians, but no Germany, no Czech-land, no Poland, and only a shadow of Hungary. None of these nations could be defined in terms of sovereign states; none could even be defined, with any precision, by their territorial limits. In place of the patriotism of Western Europe, a different sentiment arose—nationalism, romantic and subjective in its criteria of identity, all too often illiberal and chauvinistic in its expression.

This kind of national sentiment corresponded much more closely to the ethnic confusion of the Ottoman Empire, with its intermingled populations grouped by such intangible criteria as faith and kinship. Nationalism—loyalty to the group—evoked a ready response; patriotism—loyalty to one's country—for long remained alien and unintelligible.[36]

Among the peoples of the Ottoman Empire the last to be affected by the national idea were, not unnaturally, the masters

---

[36] English 'nationality' and French 'nationalité' indicate the country and state of which one is a citizen or subject. German uses 'Staatsangehörigkeit'—state-belonging —in this sense, and employs 'Nationalität' in an ethnic and not a legal sense. The same appears to be true of the East European languages—e.g. in Stalin's writings on the 'nationality problem' and in the Soviet visa form. In this case Turkish follows German, and not, as is usual in loanwords and neologisms, French usage. Turkish official forms usually contain two spaces, one for *tabiiyet*, which corresponds in meaning with the German 'Staatsangehörigkeit', the other for *milliyet*, an abstract form from *millet*. All citizens of the Turkish Republic are of Turkish *tabiiyet*; their *milliyet*, however, may be Greek, Armenian, Jewish, or, for the majority, Muslim and Turkish interchangeably. To this day Muslim is the more usual way of answering this question.

of the Empire themselves. It was only slowly, and under foreign influence, that the Turks at last began to recover a sense of their separate national identity as Turks, as a Turkish nation distinct from—though included in—the Ottoman state and the Islamic religion.

One of the most important sources of these ideas was the new European science of Turcology. From the eighteenth century onwards a series of Orientalists, working from Chinese and Islamic sources, had studied the history and languages of the eastern and pre-Islamic Turks. As a result of their work, a new picture emerged of the role of the Turkish peoples in the history of Asia and Europe, and new light was thrown on the hitherto obscure history of the Turks before they entered Islam. In time this new knowledge of a forgotten and rejected chapter in their history reached the Turks themselves, and helped to accomplish a great change in the way they conceived their corporate identity, their relations with other groups past and present, and their place in the two fundamental visions of the human predicament, the historical and the philosophic.[37]

One channel by which these new ideas reached the Turks was the student missions; by the mid-century these were going to European universities and academies in increasing numbers, and were inevitably affected by the ideas current there. Another was the group of Hungarian and Polish exiles who settled in Turkey after the unsuccessful revolutions of 1848, bringing with them the romantic nationalism of central Europe. Several of these, converted to Islam and permanently established in Turkey, played a role of some importance in the introduction of new ideas in Turkey. Such for example was the Pole Hayreddin, who contributed many articles to the newspapers *Terakki* and *Basiret*, and played some part in the founding of the Galatasaray school.[38] Another was Mustafa Celâleddin Paşa, *né* Constantine Bozęcki, author of a book, in French, entitled *Les Turcs anciens et modernes* and published in Istanbul in 1869; in this he argued that the Turks were ethnically akin to the peoples of Europe, and belonged to what he called the 'Touro-Aryan' race—the Turanian subsection of the Aryan race. The purpose of these theories was to demonstrate that the Turks were Europeans, and to minimize the differences dividing them from their European subjects. The historical

---

[37] B. Lewis, in *MEA*, iv. 218 ff.   [38] Süngü, in *Bell*, no. 78 (1943), 328.

section of the book includes a survey of ancient Turkish history based on the writings of a number of European Turcologists, and emphasizes the great role of the Turkish peoples in human history.[39]

Of Western Turcological writings two books in particular—neither of them of any great scholarly value—seem to have had a considerable influence. One was the *Grammar of the Turkish Language*, with a long historical introduction on the Turkish peoples, published in London in 1832 by Arthur Lumley Davids. A French translation appeared in 1836 and attracted Turkish attention. Its grammatical portions helped to inspire the *Kavaid-i Osmaniye* of Fuad and Cevdet Paşas, published in 1851, the first modern Turkish grammar to appear in Turkey. More important in the present context, its introduction served as the basis of a defence of the Turks—not, as would have been normal at the time, of the Muslims or Ottomans—written by Ali Suavi for the first issue of his fortnightly *Ulum*, published in Paris in 1869.[40]

Another author who influenced the growth of Turkish consciousness among the Turks was Léon Cahun, a French teacher and writer who became friendly with the Young Ottomans during their stay in France in the 1860's, and wrote extensively on Turkish subjects. His best-known book was the *Introduction à l'histoire de l'Asie*, published in 1896, containing a semi-scientific, semi-romantic account of the history of Asia in which great stress is laid on the role of the Turkish nomads of the Central Asian steppe. Cahun's book was published in a Turkish translation in 1899, and many Turkish writers testified to its formative influence.

Of far greater importance as a scholar than either of these was the Hungarian Arminius Vambéry (1832–1913), who during his residence in Turkey came into contact with many Turkish intellectuals, and retained their friendship and attention for years

---

[39] Akçuraoğlu Yusuf, pp. 394 ff.; Rossi, in *OM*, xxiii. 362. His son, Maj.-Gen. Enver Paşa, was a member of the Ottoman General Staff. Ömer Naili Paşa, a Hungarian refugee who became a senior Ottoman offier, is named as an influential and effective supporter of the Young Ottomans (Ebüzziya Tevfik, in *Yeni Tasvir-i Efkâr*, issue of 21 June 1909; cf. Kuntay, *Namık Kemal*, i. 359); another Hungarian, Daniel Silaki (*sic*), is mentioned among the distributors of Young Ottoman pamphlets in Istanbul (Kuntay, *Namık Kemal*, i. 281). It is interesting to note that the *émigré* Turkish Communist poet Nazım Hikmet has adopted Polish nationality and the surname Bozęcki.

[40] Tanpınar, pp. 220 ff. On Davids' influence see further Köprülü, *Millî Edebiyat*, pp. 45–46, and Heyd, *Foundations*, p. 105.

after. Turcology was especially cultivated in Hungary, where it derived encouragement from the theory, formerly held, of a common origin of the Magyars and the Turks, and from the Hungarian desire for Turkish support against the common danger of pan-Slavism.[41]

As early as 1839 Hungarian scholars used the word Turan, an ancient Iranian name for the country to the north-east of Persia, to describe the Turkish lands of Central and South East Asia, and applied the term Turanian to a group of peoples and languages comprising Turkish and Mongol as well as Finnish, Hungarian, and others. As a linguistic and ethnological classification this has long since been abandoned. As a political idea Turanianism and pan-Turanianism have retained some vigour.

In political circles in Turkey the impact of Turkish nationalist ideas was for long negligible. True, we do find Fuad Paşa, in a conversation with Stratford Canning, remarking that the Empire rested on four foundations, not one of which could be dispensed with: 'The Islamic religion (*millet*), the Turkish state (*devlet*), the Ottoman Sultans, and the capital in Istanbul.'[42] In this, however, Fuad Paşa was probably expressing no more than the sense of cultural identity of the Turkish-speaking ruling group within the Empire, perhaps in a form influenced by European usage. He was certainly not putting forward any idea of Turkish racial or ethnic identity and dominance.

For the first signs of a Turkish national consciousness among the Ottoman Muslims we must turn to the intellectual life of the nineteenth century, and especially to the writers on history and language. Ahmed Vefik Paşa (1823–91), scholar and statesman, the translator of Molière and Speaker of the first Ottoman parliament, is credited with being the first to stress that the Turks and their language were not merely Ottoman, but were the westernmost branch of a great and ancient family stretching across Asia to the Pacific. Süleyman Paşa (d. 1892) was the author of a universal history, published in 1876, which included a section on the pre-Islamic Turks—the first in modern Turkish historiography—based chiefly on Davids and other European writers. Şemseddin Sami Fraşeri (1850–1904) was an Albanian whose career illustrates the way in which the Balkan peoples, now

[41] Lewis, in *MEA*, iv. 218 ff.; Heyd, *Foundations*, pp. 104 ff.
[42] Cevdet, *Tezakir*, p. 85.

accessible to Western influences, served as carriers for new ideas. Though a philologist rather than an historian, Sami Fraşeri, by his lexicographic and encyclopaedic work, did much to help the growth of the new feeling of Turkish self-awareness. Perhaps the most important was Necib Asım (1861–1935), the first real Turco-logist in Turkey. He was much influenced by Cahun, whose words he translated into Turkish, and also by the Turcological dis-coveries and publications in Europe, especially in Hungary, with which he had close personal connexions.

Towards the end of the nineteenth and the beginning of the twentieth century, the movement towards Turkism received a political impetus from another source, the Russian Turks—Muslim Tatars and Turks from the Volga, Central Asia, Azerbayjan, and Crimea, numbers of whom were coming to live in the Ottoman Empire. These exiles from Russia were often of a high standard of education; some of them had been through Russian high schools and universities. They were acquainted with the very considerable achievements of Russian Turcology; they had encountered—and reacted against—the pan-Slav movement and *mystique*; they were affected by the populist and revolutionary tendencies current among the intelligentsia of the Russian Empire, to which they belonged. At the same time they were familiar with the new political and social ideas current among some circles in the Ottoman Empire.

The Ottoman reaction to Balkan separatism, the Tatar revolt against Russian pan-Slavism, the response of Turkish and Tatar intellectuals to the new ideas and examples set by European nationalisms, the nourishment of Turkish pride by Turcological discovery—all these, at a time of Ottoman defeat and Muslim abasement, combined to encourage the growth of Turkism, of the new political movement based, not on a dynasty, a faith, or a state, but on a people—the Turkish people, in its vast territories extending from Europe to the Pacific.[43]

Although the terms Turan and pan-Turanianism remained in occasional use, the movement was in effect pan-Turkish, for the Muslim Turkish peoples, in Turkey and Central Asia, showed little interest in their putative Christian or pagan brothers in Hungary or Mongolia. Tatar intellectuals in Russia, led by the Crimean Gaspıralı Ismail or Ismail Gasprinski (1841–1914), began a new

[43] See V. Minorsky, 'Turan', in *EI¹*.

kind of pan-Turkish movement, at first mainly cultural, then more and more political. Pan-Turkist ideas were also disseminated among the Turks in Turkey by *émigrés* from the Russian Empire, such as Akçuraoğlu Yusuf (1876–1939), Ağaoğlu Ahmed (1869–1939), and Hüseyinzade Ali (1864–1941).

Pan-Turkist ideas found little support among the Young Turk groups in exile, and such occasional expressions of them as Akçuraoğlu Yusuf's article, cited above, were either disregarded or refuted. The Young Turks were dedicated to the idea of the union—or association—of the Ottoman Empire, and Ottomanism, rather than Turkism, remained their official credo after their victory in 1908. But the march of events was leading in another direction. The loss of one province after another in Europe was solving the problem of the Christian subjects by ending their subjection, and left an empire not only dominated by Muslims, but also predominantly inhabited by Muslims. The defection of the Muslim Albanians, and the stirrings of dissent among the Muslim Arabs, both encouraged and were encouraged by the growing insistence on the Turkishness of what remained. On the one hand, there was a sharpening impression, both at home and abroad, that Ottomanism, in administrative practice, meant enforced Turkification; on the other, there was a mounting wave of pan-Turkish cultural and to a lesser extent, political activities, with a lively periodical literature and a network of Turkist clubs.

The first of these was the *Türk Derneği*, the Turkish Society, founded in Istanbul on 24 December 1908. With this society, the declared purpose of which was to study 'the past and present achievements, activities, and circumstances of all the peoples called Turk', the name 'Turk' emerged from the obscurity in which it had lain hidden, and the Turkist movement acquired its first platform in Turkey.[44]

The objectives of the *Türk Derneği* were scholarly and cultural—'to study and make known the ancient remains, history, languages, literatures, ethnography and ethnology, social conditions and present civilizations of the Turks, and the ancient and modern geography of the Turkish lands'. As well as a number of well-known Turkists, its members included Ottoman non-Muslims and foreign Orientalists; its president was the heir-apparent, Prince Yusuf Izzeddin. In 1911 the *Türk Derneği* began to publish a

[44] Akçuraoğlu Yusuf, pp. 435 ff.

monthly journal of the same name, of which only seven issues appeared.

The disappearance of the monthly *Türk Derneği* was followed very shortly by the appearance of a new journal, the *Türk Yurdu* (Turkish Homeland), which rapidly became the organ of a more systematic and political form of Turkism. Its founders were the poet Mehmed Emin, the author Ahmed Hikmet, Dr. Akil Muhtar, Ağaoğlu Ahmed, Hüseyinzade Ali, and Akçuraoğlu Yusuf. The three last-named were all Russian Turks; Akçuraoğlu Yusuf was the editor of the journal. In September 1912, when Ahmed Hikmet was sent to take up a consular appointment in Vienna, his place on the *Türk Yurdu* was taken by Ziya Gökalp (1876–1924), who was rapidly becoming the outstanding theoretician of the Turkist movement.[45] Under this editorial board, the *Türk Yurdu* became an important and influential organ, and a platform on which the major theoretical issues of cultural and political Turkism were discussed and elaborated.

Closely associated with the *Türk Yurdu* was the *Türk Ocağı*, (Turkish Hearth), a kind of club founded in 1912. Its aims were 'to advance the national education and raise the scientific, social, and economic level of the Turks, who are the foremost of the peoples of Islam, and to strive for the betterment of the Turkish race and language'. This it would do by opening clubs called Turkish Hearths, organizing courses, lectures, and debates, publishing books and pamphlets, and opening schools. The society would confine itself to national and social ends, and would take no part in politics, nor associate itself with any political party. The *Türk Yurdu* became its principal organ.[46]

The Turkish Hearths increased rapidly in number, not only in Istanbul but also in many provincial centres. Many prominent literary figures joined the movement, and contributed both to its journal and to the activities of its branches. In these centres, incidentally, mixed audiences met for the first time, and women were able to make their first appearance on a public platform, both as speakers and as performers in amateur theatricals.[47]

---

[45] On Ziya Gökalp see Heyd, *Foundations*, where further literature is cited. A selection of his writings, in English translation, was published by Niyazi Berkes. On the whole, Gökalp's influence seems to have been exercised more through personal relations than through his published works.

[46] Akçuraoğlu Yusuf, pp. 439 ff.; Rossi, pp. 377 ff.

[47] Edib, *Turkey Faces West*, pp. 116–17.

Even in Salonika, the Rumelian capital of the Union and Progress movement, a Turkist trend soon appeared, and found expression in the literary review *Genç Kalemler* (Young Pens), founded in 1911. One of its regular contributors was Ziya Gökalp, who in his poem 'Turan', published in 1911, produced this much-quoted verse formulation of pan-Turanianism.

> The country of the Turks is not Turkey, nor yet Turkistan,
> Their country is a vast and eternal land: Turan![48]

For the Turkish exiles and immigrants from the Russian Empire, pan-Turanianism or pan-Turkism was indeed a political programme, which in its maximalist form implied the political unification of all the Turkish-speaking peoples, in Turkey, Russia, Persia, Afghanistan, and China, in a single state. The main obstacle to this, the power of Russia, would be overcome with the help of the Western states.

Among the Turks of Turkey this programme won only limited support. Their interest in the movement was social, cultural, and literary—a greater awareness of their separate identity as Turks, a new feeling of kinship with their rediscovered ancestors and their remote cousins, a new interest in Turkish language, folklore, and tradition. On the question of a closer political association with these cousins, Ottoman Turkish opinion was at first more cautious. The outbreak of war in 1914, with Turkey fighting Russia as the ally of two mighty military empires, aroused wider and more extensive hopes, and in 1914 Ziya Gökalp opened his poem *Kızıl Destan* (Red epic) with the couplet:

> The land of the enemy shall be devastated,
> Turkey shall be enlarged and become Turan.[49]

After a rebuff caused by the defeats of the Ottoman armies, these hopes flared up again after 1917, when the Russian Revolution and the collapse of the Russian Empire seemed to offer a tempting opportunity to liberate and unite the Turkish peoples and thus achieve the pan-Turkish dream. It was partly under the inspiration of such ideas that Enver Paşa embarked on his ill-fated schemes, the invasion of Trans-Caucasia in 1918, and his subsequent adventures in Central Asia.

[48] *OM* (1924), p. 576; Heyd, *Foundations*, p. 126; Rossi, p. 378.

[49] Heyd, *Foundations*, p. 43. See also G. Jäschke, 'Der Turanismus der Jungtürken', *WI*, xxiii (1941), 1–54.

The distinctions between the three brands—Islamism, Ottomanism, Turkism—are not always easy to see. The Ottomanists
revealed that, despite their professions, they were not prepared to
concede real equality to non-Muslims; the Turkists made it clear
that their greater Turkish family was limited to those professing
Islam, and excluded the rest. To this extent, both groups were
Islamists, and the Ottomanist leaders were indeed ready to make
use both of pan-Islamism and pan-Turkism when they suited
their ends.

Ottomanism was manifestly dying; the question was whether
Islam or Turkism would inherit its place, as the basis of cohesion
and loyalty of the Turkish people. Ottomanism had been a loyalty
to an Empire and a dynasty—but the Empire was breaking up,
and the dynasty going into exile. Islam and Turkism had this in
common, that they were both non-territorial; there was no
country and no government in existence defined by either of
them. The Muslim Turks of Turkey might classify themselves as
Muslims—by faith and law; or as Turks—by language and real
or imagined descent; they had not yet thought of defining themselves as the people of a country—of Turkey.

Patriotism

It was this new idea—of a territorial nation-state based on the
Turkish nation *in Turkey*—that makes its first appearance in the
early days of the Kemalist Revolution. The National Pact of
1919–20, containing the basic demands of the nationalists in
Anatolia, speaks of areas 'inhabited by an Ottoman Muslim
majority, united in religion, in race and in aim', in which full and
undivided sovereignty is required.

The Pact still speaks of 'Ottoman Muslims' and not of Turks,
and the word Turk appears nowhere in the document. But
Mustafa Kemal soon made it clear that he was fighting for the
people of Turkey, and not for any vaguer, larger entity beyond
the national frontiers, whether defined by religion or by race. In
a speech delivered on 1 December 1921, he explicitly rejected
these movements as useless and dangerous:

Gentlemen! Every one of our compatriots and coreligionists may
nourish a high ideal in his mind; he is free to do so, and no one will
interfere. But the government of the Grand National Assembly of
Turkey has a firm, positive, material policy, and that, gentlemen, is

directed to the preservation of life and independence . . . within defined national frontiers. The Grand National Assembly and government of Turkey, in the name of the nation they represent, are very modest, very far from fantasies, and completely realistic. . . .

Gentlemen, we are not men who run after great fantasies and present a fraudulent appearance of doing things which in fact we cannot do. Gentlemen, by looking as though we were doing great and fantastic things, without actually doing them, we have brought the hatred, rancour, and malice of the whole world on this country and this people. We did not serve pan-Islamism. We said that we had and we would, but we didn't, and our enemies said: 'Let us kill them at once before they do!' We did not serve pan-Turanianism. We said that we could and we would, and again they said: 'Let us kill them!' There you have the whole problem. . . . Rather than run after ideas which we did not and could not realise and thus increase the number of our enemies and the pressure upon us, let us return to our natural, legitimate limits. And let us know our limits. Gentlemen, we are a nation desiring life and independence. For that and that alone may we give our lives.[50]

The Ottoman Empire was dead. For centuries the Turkish people had squandered their energies and their blood in the useless struggle to conquer and defend alien lands and peoples. Now that Empire was gone, and for the Turks too its passing was a liberation from an intolerable burden. For their Muslim and Turkish brothers elsewhere the people of Turkey had the greatest sympathy and the warmest of feelings—but no more. Their destiny and their responsibility lay in their native land, which it was their duty to free, to defend, and to rebuild. From this task they must not be distracted by vast and visionary schemes of Islamic or Turanian unity, which were either outdated or premature.

The growth of cultural nationalism since 1908 had accustomed the new generation of Turks to the idea of Turkishness—of identity and loyalty based on the Turkish nation. The Kemalist Republic brought a new idea—that of Turkey—the land of the Turks. So new was this idea, that the Turkish language had even lacked a name for it. The Young Ottomans had used the Persian form Turkistan; Mehmed Emin had spoken of *Türkeli*—Turkland, and only during the Young Turk period had the name *Türkiye* come into common usage. It was first adopted officially by the Kemalist state in Anatolia, to mean the remaining central core of

[50] *Söylev*, i. 193, 195–6.

the Ottoman Empire inhabited by Turks. It was used as the name of the country in the law of 1921, and in the republican constitution of 1924. In the forceful phrase of Peyami Safa, 'Pan-Islamism sailed away from Istanbul with the Allied fleets and fled with Vahideddin; Ottomanism was lynched at Izmid with Ali Kemal.'[51]

This new idea of the territorial state of Turkey, the fatherland of a nation called the Turks, was by no means easy to inculcate in a people so long accustomed to religious and dynastic loyalties. The frontiers of the new state were themselves new and unfamiliar, entirely devoid of the emotional impact made by the beloved outlines of their country on generations of schoolboys in the West; even the name of the country, *Türkiye*, was new in conception and alien in form, so much so that the Turkish authorities hesitated for a while between variant spellings of it.[52]

The Religious Minorities

A good example of the confusion of concepts and loyalties prevailing at this time can be seen in the Greco-Turkish exchange of populations, arranged after the treaty of Lausanne. Greece and Turkey had ended their conflict, and a separate agreement between them provided for the permanent settlement of minority problems by a compulsory exchange of populations. Between 1923 and 1930 about a million and a quarter Greeks were sent from Turkey to Greece, and a rather smaller number of Turks from Greece to Turkey.

At first sight this exchange seems a clear indication of the prevalence on both sides of nationalistic and patriotic ideas, and of the desire to give greater unity and cohesion to the nation and the fatherland. Yet on closer examination of what actually took place, it begins to appear that other ideas and other loyalties were still at work. The Greeks of Karaman who were 'repatriated' to Greece were Greek Christians by religion—yet most of them knew no Greek. Their language was Turkish—which they wrote in the Greek script—and the inscriptions in their abandoned churches and cemeteries in Karaman still testify to their linguistic Turkishness. In the same way, many of the repatriated Turks from Greece

[51] Safa, p. 87; cf. Rossi, in *OM*, xxiii. 381. Ali Kemal (1867–1922) was Minister of the Interior in Damad Ferid Paşa's cabinet, and a relentless enemy of the nationalists. In November 1922 he was arrested in Pera and sent to Ankara for trial, but was seized and lynched by a mob in Izmid.

[52] *WI*, n.s., ii (1953), 279; iii (1954), 278–9; iv (1955), 61.

knew little or no Turkish, but spoke Greek—and wrote it in the Turco-Arabic script. What took place was not an exchange of Greeks and Turks, but rather an exchange of Greek Orthodox Christians and Ottoman Muslims. A Western observer, accustomed to a different system of social and national classification, might even conclude that this was no repatriation at all, but two deportations into exile—of Christian Turks to Greece, and of Muslim Greeks to Turkey.

In general, the status of the religious minorities in Turkey is a good indication of the progress—and setbacks—of these new ideas. Toleration is of course a relative matter. According to the principles professed by modern democracies, toleration means the absence of discrimination. In that sense, the old Ottoman Empire was not tolerant, since non-Muslims were not the civic and social equals of the followers of the dominant faith, but were subject to a number of legal disabilities. But complete toleration is new and insecure even in the most enlightened modern democracies, and there have been appalling lapses from it. It would hardly be reasonable to look for it in the old Ottoman Empire. If we define toleration as the absence, not of discrimination, but of persecution, then the Ottoman record until the late nineteenth century is excellent. The well-known preference of the fifteenth-century Greeks for Muslim rather than Frankish rule was not without its reasons. The confrontation of Islam and Christendom in the fifteenth and sixteenth centuries has sometimes been compared with the cold war of the mid-twentieth. In making the comparison, we should remember that the movement of refugees then was from West to East.

With the visible decline of Ottoman power and the rise of European influence in the nineteenth century, there was a catastrophic change for the worse in the position of the Ottoman non-Muslims. The material relationship between Muslim and Christian had changed beyond recognition. Even the theoretical basis of association was gone. The old, mutually accepted relationship between Muslims and *Zimmîs*, conferring a definite and agreed status and rights on the latter, had been undermined and destroyed by new ideas and new ambitions. Liberal principles required the Turks to give the subject peoples full equality of rights in the state; national principles entitled these peoples to rebel against it, and set up independent states of their own;

Christian and Imperial principles enabled the powers of Europe to intervene on their behalf, supporting their claims both to citizenship and to secession. In these circumstances, suspicion, fear, hatred—and sometimes, we may add, the high example of Western intolerance—transformed the Turkish attitude to the subject peoples. Turkish weakness and uncertainty, in the face of foreign invasion and internal rebellion, often led to terrible oppression and brutality.

Most tragic was the case of the Armenians, who at the beginning of the nineteenth century were still known as the *Millet-i Sadıka*, the loyal community, and were described by a well-informed French visitor as the minority group most loyal to the Ottoman Empire and most trusted by the Turks. The change began with the Russian conquest of the Caucasus in the first quarter of the nineteenth century, and the creation of a Russian Armenia on the eastern border of Turkey, where the Armenian Church was established and recognized and where Armenian governors and generals ruled provinces and commanded armies. A stir of hope passed through Turkish Armenia, where, combining with the new national and liberal ideas emanating from the West, it gave rise to an ardent and active Armenian nationalist movement, seeking to restore an independent Armenia.

For the Turks, the Armenian movement was the deadliest of all threats. From the conquered lands of the Serbs, Bulgars, Albanians, and Greeks, they could, however reluctantly, withdraw, abandoning distant provinces and bringing the Imperial frontier nearer home. But the Armenians, stretching across Turkey-in-Asia from the Caucasian frontier to the Mediterranean coast, lay in the very heart of the Turkish homeland—and to renounce these lands would have meant not the truncation, but the dissolution of the Turkish state. Turkish and Armenian villages, inextricably mixed, had for centuries lived in neighbourly association. Now a desperate struggle between them began—a struggle between two nations for the possession of a single homeland, that ended with the terrible holocaust of 1916, when a million and half Armenians perished.

In the Turkish Republic, the constitution and the law accorded complete equality to all citizens. Yet even on the official side, in the structure and policies of the state, there were signs that, despite secularism and nationalism, the older idea that Muslim equals Turk and non-Muslim equals non-Turk persisted. In some respects the participation of non-Muslims in the public life of Turkey actually decreased after the establishment of the Republic, although their legal status on paper was higher than ever before. Certain forms of discrimination continued—for example, non-Muslims were called up for military service but did not bear arms and were not commissioned, while the number of non-Muslims in the civil service dwindled rapidly. All this can be largely but not wholly explained by their ignorance of Turkish and their self-isolation from the social and cultural world of the Turks. The cosmopolitan Islamic Empire had assigned a definite place and function to the non-Muslim minorities; the nationalist Republic could offer little to those who either would not or could not join the dominant group. While on the one hand Turkish-speaking Orthodox Christians from Anatolia were classed as Greeks and sent to Greece, the children of Muslim Bosniaks or Albanians, Kurds or Arabs settled in Istanbul were accepted as Turks. Significantly, religion still appeared on identity cards and other official documents, and the designation Turk was in common usage restricted to Muslims; the rest were known as Turkish citizens, but never as Turks.

Feelings towards the non-Muslims varied. The exacerbated hatreds of the last years of the Empire reached their climax after the 1918 Armistice, when many Ottoman Christians made no secret of their delight in the Allied occupation. Thereafter, as the memories of the occupation and of the war receded into the past, relations between Muslims and non-Muslims improved. The latter, despite successive improvements in their status, remained separate and distinct, extruded from the body of the nation. The fundamental weakness of their position was once again revealed in the episode of the capital levy in 1942–3.[53]

The Anatolian Fatherland

However strange the idea, however great the difficulties, a Turkish national state was in fact coming into being. The Balkans, for long the centre of gravity of the Ottoman Empire, were lost. The Arab countries, the heartlands of Islam, had gone their several ways. Anatolia, after the final bloody struggle against the Armenians and the Greeks, had been held as a Turkish land, and even the capital was now transferred from cosmopolitan, Levantine,

[53] See above, pp. 291 ff.

Imperial Constantinople to an Anatolian hilltown with a Seljuk citadel.

The idea of a Turkish nation had made rapid headway among the Turkish educated classes. It had, however, brought with it a new danger. The loss of the Empire was recent, and still rankled with many, to whom the idea of a comparatively small nation-state seemed unsatisfying and unattractive. In pan-Turkist circles and especially among the Tatar exiles, the idea was current that a new Imperial destiny awaited the Turks, whose task it was, not to revive the polyglot and multi-national Ottoman Empire, but to create a new pan-Turkish Empire of the Turkish and Tatar peoples from the Aegean to the China Sea.

To all such projects and ambitions Mustafa Kemal was firmly opposed. The Turks had a long and hard task to perform in Turkey. Their Turkish brothers elsewhere might enjoy their sympathetic interest and friendship; they must, however, work out their own political fate, and not try to distract the Turkish Republic from the work in hand to remote and dangerous adventures.

What was needed was patriotism rather than nationalism— loyalty to the objective, legally defined, sovereign Republic of Turkey, rather than to an ill-defined and variously interpreted entity like the nation.

The term *vatan*, fatherland, had had a chequered history in modern Turkey. In the mid-nineteenth century, according to Cevdet Paşa, it would have meant, to a Turkish soldier, no more than the village square; by the late nineteenth century, to Namık Kemal, it suggested the whole Ottoman Empire, including— perhaps especially—the Holy Cities of Arabia. For the pan-Turkist Ziya Gökalp in 1911, it was neither Turkey nor Turkistan but the vast land of Turan. Yet as late as August 1917, the Grand Vezir Mehmed Said Halim Paşa could still firmly assert that 'the fatherland of a Muslim is the place where the *Şeriat* prevails'.[54]

It was against this variegated background of traditions and ideas that Kemal sought to inculcate the new idea of an Anatolian Turkish fatherland. His aim was to destroy what remained of the Islamic and Ottoman feelings of loyalty, to counter the distractions of pan-Islamic and pan-Turkist appeals, and to forge a new

[54] Quoted in Inal, *Sadrıazamlar*, p. 1892.

loyalty, of the Turkish nation to its homeland. His chosen instrument was history. The Ottoman Historical Society had been wound up. A new Turkish Historical Society was founded in 1930, to serve as the medium of state policy for the imposition of certain historical theories. Its tasks included the drafting of new historical syllabuses and textbooks, on patriotic lines, for use in schools and universities.

In 1932 a Turkish historical congress was convened in Ankara, which was inspired by Mustafa Kemal and attended by professors and teachers of history from all over Turkey, as well as by scholars and delegates from abroad.

The theory propounded by Kemal and his disciples was, briefly, that the Turks were a white, Aryan people, originating in Central Asia, the cradle of all human civilization. Owing to the progressive desiccation of this area, the Turks had migrated in waves to various parts of Asia and Africa, carrying the arts of civilization with them. Chinese, Indian, and Middle Eastern civilizations had all been founded in this way, the pioneers in the last named being the Sumerians and Hittites, who were both Turkic peoples. Anatolia had thus been a Turkish land since antiquity. This mixture of truth, half-truth, and error was proclaimed as official doctrine, and teams of researchers set to work to 'prove' its various propositions.[55]

It would be a grave error to deride all this as the whim of an autocrat. Kemal was too great a man to organize an elaborate campaign of this sort out of mere caprice, or out of a simple desire for national self-glorification. One of the reasons for the campaign was the need to provide some comfort for Turkish national self-respect, which had been sadly undermined during the last century or two. First, there was the demoralizing effect of a long period of almost uninterrupted defeat and withdrawal by the Imperial Ottoman forces. Then there was the inevitable reaction to Western prejudice. It is difficult not to sympathize with the frustration and discouragement of the young Turk, eager for enlightenment, who applied himself to the study of Western languages, to find that in most of them his name was an insult. In

[55] Lewis, in *MEA*, iv. 224 ff. The 'historical thesis' is extensively discussed in the earlier publications of the *Türk Tarih Kurumu* (Turkish Historical Society), and in most of the general books about Turkey. For a rather forlorn recent statement of the former official purpose, see Ahmet Cevat Emre, *Atatürk'ün Inkılab Hedefi ve Tarih Tezi* (1956).

z

the English dictionary the Turk shares with the Jew[56] and the Welshman the distinction of having given his name to a term of abuse. The mixture of prejudice, ignorance, and cynicism that disfigures most European writings about the Turks can have given him no very high opinion of the European ideal of disinterested historical inquiry and the search for truth. His opinion will not have been raised by the readiness with which some European institutions and scholars, for political reasons, lent their encouragement to the Turkish official thesis. Once upon a time the Turk had been accustomed to despise his neighbours and his enemies from the comfortable altitude of superior religion and Imperial authority. Empire was gone, and the growth of secularism was depriving him even of the consolations of religion.

Though the encouragement of Turkish pride and self-respect was no doubt an essential part of Kemal's purpose, it was probably not his primary objective. This was to teach the Turks that Anatolia—Turkey—was their true homeland, the centre of their nationhood from time immemorial, and thus to hasten the growth of that ancient, intimate relationship, at once mystical and practical, between nation and country that is the basis of patriotism in the sovereign nation-states of the West.

During the years that followed, the wilder historical theories were quietly abandoned and decently buried, but the patriotic loyalty which they had served to encourage grew steadily. In the schools and universities of the Republic a new generation grew up for whom the Empire was a burden now happily cast off, and the now familiar rectangle of the Turkish Republic the focus of their loyalties and aspirations.

The widening gulf between Turkey and the eastern Islamic world; the gathering momentum of Westernization and modernization; the rise of a new secular-educated generation brought up to accept the Turkish Republic as the final fruition of land and people—all these fostered a deepening consciousness of territorial identity; the embattled neutrality of Turkey amid the swirling currents and buffeting storms of a Second World War made it at once more vivid and more concrete.

While the larger loyalties of the Muslim Turks were being

---

[56] This companionship in obloquy, which has parallels elsewhere in Europe, may in part account for the prominence of Jews among European Turcologists and Turcophiles, such as Davids, Cahun, Vambéry, and, of a different kind, Disraeli.

transferred and modified in the as yet unresolved equation of Islam, Turkism, and Turkey, their lesser loyalties were still given, much as before, to the smaller, more local groupings of kin and craft, tribe and brotherhood. These even found a new function with the coming of contested elections. The best hope for the future lay in the sometimes painful emergence, out of all the groups, of the individual—better informed and more self-reliant, with a growing awareness of his place, his rights, and his duties in a free modern society.

CHAPTER XI

State and Government

O you who believe, obey God, obey the Prophet, and obey those among you who hold authority.

KORAN, iv. 62.

He who applies and administers a decision is always more powerful than he who makes it.

MUSTAFA KEMAL, 1921.

CENTRAL GOVERNMENT

Constitution [1]

DURING the nineteenth century the Turkish reformers tried, by legislative enactment, to give Turkey the form and structure of a European state. European laws and judiciary, European ministries and administrative procedures were copied with more or less fidelity, usually from French originals, and promulgated by Imperial decree. The culmination of this process saw the Ottoman constitution of 1876, the supreme achievement of the liberal reformers, which was to turn the Ottoman Empire into a parliamentary democracy, and the Ottoman Sultan into a constitutional monarch. The original, this time, was not French but Belgian, the Belgian constitution of 1831 combining the advantages of being liberal, monarchical, and written in French.

But the Ottoman Empire was not Belgium. The Belgian constitution worked well enough in Belgium, where it was the result of centuries of Belgian history, and where the Belgian parliament was the apex of a pyramid of responsible elected assemblies with its base in the Belgian parish and borough councils. The same constitution, adapted into Turkish, was inevitably irrelevant, unrelated to Turkish conditions, and ultimately unworkable.

This constitution was not formally abrogated, but with the

---

[1] On the development of the Ottoman and Turkish constitutions see *EI*² ('Dustūr' by B. Lewis), and *IA* ('Kanun-i Esasi' by Hüseyin Nail Kubalı). Discussions of constitutional developments will be found in Jäschke, in *WI*, v. 5–56; Pritsch, 'Die türkische Verfassung vom 20 April 1924', *MSOS*, xxvi–xxvii/2 (1924), 164–251 and Jäschke, 'Auf dem Wege zur türkischen Republik', *WI*, n.s., v (1958), 206–18. See further above, pp. 156 ff., 250 ff., and 260.

closing of parliament by Abdülhamid on 14 February 1878 it was in fact tacitly suspended for thirty years. It was restored on 1 August 1908, when soon after the Young Turk Revolution a *Hatt-i Humayun* from the Sultan to the Grand Vezir Said Paşa declared the constitution to be fully effective and in force again, and supplemented it with a number of further provisions, extending the personal liberty of the subject and guaranteeing its inviolability. The Rescript prohibited arrest and search except by lawful procedures, abolished all special and exceptional courts, introduced for the first time the principle of freedom of travel, and guaranteed the security of the mails and the freedom of the press. A striking omission from this festival of freedom was that the notorious article 113 of the 1876 constitution, reserving to the Sultan the exclusive right to deport persons dangerous to the state, was for the moment left unchanged. It was abolished in the following year.[2]

The Rescript of August 1908, restoring the constitution, thus in fact made important additions to it. After the opening of parliament on 17 December 1908 further proposals for constitutional changes were made and debated. The need for revision was generally agreed on, and a constitutional commission was formed, to prepare draft proposals. Amid the burst of legislative activity of the first Young Turk parliament, there was no time for a detailed and systematic revision of the whole text of the constitution. Instead, the drafting commission produced a series of *ad hoc* amendments, modifying some articles and remaking or replacing others. The Bill became law on 21 August 1909.

These amendments, though piecemeal, amounted to a major constitutional change, the purpose of which is clear. The Committee of Union and Progress dominated both houses of parliament; the palace, even after the deposition of Abdülhamid, was still feared as the possible source of a reactionary coup. The amendments therefore aimed at strengthening parliament and weakening the throne. Both the Sultan and the Grand Vezir, whom the Sultan nominated, were reduced in stature and authority. The sovereignty of parliament was triumphantly affirmed.

The resulting weakness of the executive was found inconvenient

---

[2] On these and the following constitutional changes, see Jäschke, in *WI*, v. 20 ff.; texts in Gözübüyük and Kili (trans. in Kraelitz-Greifenhorst).

to the Young Turks themselves, and the constitutional struggles of the next ten years were caused by their efforts, sometimes fiercely resisted, to restore the executive power. The new Sultan, Mehmed V, proved himself a harmless and loyal collaborator, and the Unionists soon began to feel safe enough in their control of the palace and the Grand Vezirate to want them strong rather than weak. Towards the end of 1911 they submitted proposals to parliament to this effect. These were bitterly opposed by the opposition, on the grounds, it was made clear, that they would strengthen, not the Sultan, but the Committee of Union and Progress. In the parliamentary and constitutional crisis that followed, parliament was dissolved. After the elections of April 1912, the Unionists were securely in power, and on 18 May tabled more than 100 draft laws, including a proposal to amend several articles of the constitution. These amendments, increasing the Sultan's authority over parliament, became law on 28 May 1914. Subsequent amendments, in January 1915 and March 1916, still further increased the powers of the Sultan, who was now able to convene, prorogue, prolong, and dismiss parliament almost at his discretion.

The final amendment to the old constitution came in April 1918. The parliament inaugurated in May 1914 had reached its legal term, and new elections were due. These were clearly not possible at the time, and an amendment to the constitution authorized the prolongation of parliament, by emergency enactment, in time of war.

On 21 December 1918 the new Sultan, Mehmed VI, dismissed parliament and ruled through the Grand Vezir. New elections began in December 1919—the sixth and last general election in the Ottoman Empire. The Chamber assembled on 12 January 1920, prorogued itself on 18 March and was dissolved by the Sultan on 11 April. The last Ottoman parliament had ended its final session. Twelve days later the Grand National Assembly of Turkey held its opening session in Ankara.

Mustafa Kemal and the nationalists in Anatolia were at first very careful to maintain legal continuity. They made war against the foreign invader and occupier; not against the lawful sovereign or his government, to whom they were careful to show due respect. Kemal first came to Anatolia with an appointment from the Sultan. When he was deprived of this, some new status was necessary; he found it through the Association for the Defence of the Rights of Eastern Anatolia, with its headquarters in Erzurum. On 24 August 1919 Mustafa Kemal, 'former inspector of the Third Army, officer, retired', together with a group of similarly 'retired' associates, addressed a formal message to the vilayet of Ezurum, asking for legal recognition of the 'Representative Committee' of this association, 'in accordance with the Law of Associations'.[3]

This legally recognized 'Representative Committee' provided the link from the old to a new legality. When it seemed clear that the last legal parliament in Istanbul were no longer free agents, Kemal and his associates proceeded to hold elections to an emergency assembly to meet in Ankara. Even in this revolutionary action, Kemal still sought for continuity; his order to all vilayets, independent sanjaks, and officers commanding army corps begins by referring to the dissolution of parliament under foreign pressure, and the consequent inability of the deputies to perform their duties. For this reason, the national interest required the immediate convening of an assembly in Ankara, 'which will be furnished with extraordinary powers and will permit members of the chamber that has been dissolved to come to Ankara to take part in it'. Only then does Kemal 'in the name of the Representative Committee', go on to order elections, to be conducted by colleges of electors.[4]

When the assembly met, Mustafa Kemal was elected as its President; significantly, the vice-president was Celâleddin Arif, the last President of the Chamber of Deputies. On the third day, 25 April, the Assembly resolved on the creation of its executive arm. After a lengthy discussion, two commissions, an executive commission and a drafting commission, were elected, the second to draft proposals for a permanent executive, the first to act in the meantime. On 1 May 1920 the draft was submitted. After a heated debate it was passed and at once became effective. In accordance with its terms, a first 'Committee of Executive Delegates', of

[3] *Nutuk*, i. 67; *Documents*, no. 41; cf. *Speech*, p. 59. See also Jäschke, 'Die ersten Verfassungsentwürfe der Ankara-Türkei', *Mitt. Aus.-Hoch. Univ. Berlin*, xlii/2 (1939), 58.

[4] *Nutuk*, i. 420 ff.; *Speech*, pp. 364 ff.; cf. Jäschke, p. 59. On the formation and development of the Grand National Assembly see further the two important studies of Tunaya, 'Osmanlı Imparatorluğundan Türkiye Büyük Millet Meclisi Hükumeti Rejimine Giriş', in *Prof. Muammer Raşit Sevig'e Armağan* (1956); and 'Türkiye Büyük Meclisi Hükumeti'nin Kuruluşu ve Siyasi Karakteri' (offprint, Ist., n.d.).

eleven men, was elected. The Assembly had acquired a government.[5]

On 22 April, the day before the Assembly opened, Mustafa Kemal sent out a circular to the army and provincial administration, informing them that from the following day 'the National Assembly will be the lawful authority to which all civil and military authorities and the entire nation must turn'.[6]

The Assembly itself was less certain of its status and functions. It was a mixed body, including some 125 civil servants, 13 municipal officials, 53 soldiers (10 of them pashas), 53 men of religion (including 14 muftis), and 5 tribal chiefs. The remaining 120 odd members were engaged in commerce, farming, in the professions—including 40 merchants, 32 farmers, 20 lawyers, 1 journalist, 2 engineers, and a single artisan—a master gunsmith. No less than 92 of its members had belonged to the last Chamber of Deputies.[7]

Many of the members remained firmly attached to the Sultan-Caliph, and insisted that all their actions had a provisional and emergency character. The Assembly argued from the start that it could not be made to recognize a provisional head of government or to form a regency, and voted, perhaps a little ambiguously, that the Sultan-Caliph, when he had been liberated from his present constraint, would resume his functions within the framework determined by the laws which the Assembly would adopt.[8] Meanwhile, the liberation of the Sultan-Caliph from enemy hands was a prime objective of the Assembly and the conservatives went so far as to say that 'we find ourselves in the necessity of creating a government without a head'.[9] In fact, avoiding the term government, they approved the creation of a 'committee of executive delegates' to fulfil the same purpose.

The Assembly, which thus shied away even from the idea of forming an interim government, was far from desiring to frame a constitution. But the strong hand of its leader, and the relentless pressure of events, drove it irresistibly in that direction.

Mustafa Kemal thought from the start in terms of a constituent assembly. The bitter struggle fought against the Assembly by the Sultan's Government and by its irregular forces

[5] Tunaya, 'Karakter', pp. 6–11.

[6] *Nutuk*, i. 432; *Speech*, p. 375.   [7] Tunaya, 'Karakter', p. 5.

[8] Jäschke, in *Mitt. Aus.-Hoch. Univ. Berlin*, xlii/2, p. 60; *Hist.*, pp. 52–53.

[9] Tunaya, 'Karakter', p. 7.

in Anatolia, even more than the occupation of parts of Anatolia by foreign armies, drove more and more of the deputies to follow his lead.

There were several paths which the drafters of a new Turkish constitution might take. The arguments of the Westernizers and the Islamists, brought into the open after 1908, were familiar. The Western forms of parliamentary democracy, though for the moment tarnished by Western hostility to Turkey, were well known, and moreover, bore the laurels of victory over their authoritarian opponents. In the East, a new system of government was arising out of the chaos of the Russian Revolution. In September 1920 a 'Congress of Eastern Peoples' assembled in Baku, to proclaim the message of revolutionary Communism to the peoples of Asia. Enver Paşa appeared in Moscow and elsewhere, and a Communist movement, known as the Green Army, for a whole played a certain role in Anatolian affairs.

Turkish material interests at that moment lay with the Soviets against the West, and a friendly agreement between Kemal and the Bolsheviks was indeed signed in March 1921. But Kemal had no intention of making Turkey a Communist state, and managed with remarkable skill to avoid the closer embraces of his new and redoubtable neighbour.[10]

As early as August 1920 the Assembly was debating constitutional proposals, and devoting its attention to such problems of Western political thought as the separation of powers—a matter of great concern also to the Young Turk parliaments. Then, on 20 January 1921, the Grand National Assembly passed the 'Law of Fundamental Organizations'—in fact the provisional constitution of the new Turkey. The law, after declaring the sovereignty of the nation, went on to state that

the executive power and the legislative authority are vested and expressed in the Grand National Assembly, which is the only real representation of the people.

The state of Turkey is administered by the Grand National Assembly and its Government bears the name of the 'Government of the Grand National Assembly'. . . .

---

[10] On the early relations between the Kemalists and the Bolsheviks, see Laqueur, *Communism*, pp. 205 ff. This account can now be amplified in the light of the memoirs of Gen. Cebesoy, the first Kemalist envoy to Moscow (*Memoirs*, ii); cf. Jäschke, in *WI*, n.s., v. 44 ff.

The remaining articles dealt with the holding of elections and the conduct of government business.[11]

The sovereignty of the people . . . the state of Turkey . . . these were new and revolutionary ideas, and their appearance in a constitutional enactment marks the first decisive step in the legal processes that transformed Turkey from an Islamic universal empire into a secular national state.

The transitional phase, which began with the formation of the Grand National Assembly, was completed with the proclamation of the Republic and the promulgation of the new constitution.[12]

The idea of a Republic in Muslim territory was strange, but not wholly new.[13] In the welter of theorizing on government and the state in the last years of the Ottoman Empire republican ideas did not appear, and it is indeed doubtful whether it would have been possible to express them.[14] But since 1918 republics had sprung up in several places. In the summer of 1918, after the dissolution of the ill-starred Transcaucasian Federation, the Turkish-speaking Muslims of Russian Azerbayjan proclaimed a republic—the first Muslim republic in modern times. Their example was followed by the Bashkir, Kirghiz, and other Turkic peoples of the former Russian Empire, who preferred to give this form to their short-lived freedom. Though all these republics were conquered and reconstituted by the Communists, the name and form of republican autonomy remained, and to many at that time bore great promise.

The republican idea soon began to appear outside Russia. As early as November 1918, the North African leader Suleymān al-Bārūnī made an unsuccessful attempt to establish an Arab republic in Tripoli. In Syria too republican ideas were current in some circles, and the institutions set up by the French mandatory authorities in Syria and Lebanon clearly tended towards republics, even though these were not formally proclaimed until after the Turks had set the example.

The world situation obviously favoured the republican cause.

[11] Jäschke, in *Mitt. Aus.-Hoch. Univ. Berlin*, xlii/2, and idem. in *WI*, n.s., v. 206–18. Text in Gözübüyük and Kili, pp. 85 ff.

[12] Debates in Gözübüyük and Zekai Sezgin, *1924 Anayasası hakkındaki Meclis Görüşmeleri* (1957).

[13] cf. B. Lewis, 'The Concept of an Islamic Republic', *WI*, n.s., iv (1955), 1–9, and *EI*² *s.v.* 'Ḏjumhūriyya'.

[14] cf. the remarks of Atatürk, quoted by Emre, p. 5.

The great autocratic monarchies on both sides in the World War—
Germany, Austria, Russia—had collapsed in ruin. France and
America gave the example of old republics with power, wealth,
and victory; Germany and Russia of new republics struggling to
rise from ruin and defeat to something better. Britain, which
might have provided the example of a monarchy both democratic
and successful, was temporarily obscured from Turkish view by a
bitter political conflict. The Turkish Assembly had already agreed
that sovereignty belonged to the people. They could also see that
success belonged to the republicans.

The proclamation of a Republic in Turkey was by no means
unresisted. It has, however, never been seriously challenged; and
with one major and several minor amendments, the constitution
remained in force until 1960.

The Head of State

At first sight, the most striking change that took place as a
result of the Kemalist Revolution was in the headship of the state.
In place of the dynastic, divinely sanctioned Sultan-Caliph, there
was a secular, elected, chief executive; in place of a bearded,
braided emperor, a clean-shaven, dinner-jacketed President.

But the change was more gradual and less abrupt than might
appear. The tendency in the Turkish state throughout the nineteenth century had been towards increased personal despotism.
The old Ottoman Sultans had been, within the limits of the
Islamic law and the social system of the Empire, autocratic rulers.
The Sultans of the seventeenth and eighteenth centuries, however,
had lost most of their effective power to the vezirs and courtiers in
the capital and to the pashas and notables in the provinces, and
had little more effective power than a feudal king in medieval
Europe. Under Selim III and his successors, and especially under
Mahmud II and Abdülaziz, the personal ascendancy of the
sovereign was restored—and not only restored, but carried to new
heights unknown in earlier times. This was no longer the old
Islamic autocracy, but a vastly strengthened personal despotism,
freed from the limiting intermediate powers that had been swept
away by the reformers, and sustained by such modern devices as
the telegraph, the railway, and the gendarmerie.

This growth of personal rule was observed, resisted, and from
time to time interrupted—though not for long. The constitutional

interlude of 1876–8 ended in the reinforced personal rule of Abdülhamid; the constitutional millennium of 1908 expired in the dictatorship of the Young Turk triumvirate, of Enver, Talât, and Cemal Paşas.

This time it was no longer the Sultan who ruled, but a small group of ministers acting in his name. From a shadow Sultan to no Sultan proved, in the event, not too difficult a transition. Cemal and Enver were both soldiers; so too were Mustafa Kemal and Ismet. The incantatory flourish of constitution, parliament, party, and election does not hide the basic fact that the Republic was established by a professional soldier leading a victorious army and maintaining himself, in the early stages at least, by a combination of personal and military power.[15]

During Kemal's last years there seems to have been an estrangement between him and his old comrade-in-arms Ismet Paşa, and Ismet had been replaced as Prime Minister by Celâl Bayar, a banker and a civilian. But when Kemal died in 1938, it was the soldier Ismet who succeeded him as President—and a persistent rumour has it that it was the army that determined the final choice.

Yet the régime, though military in its origin and for a long time authoritarian in character, was never a mere military dictatorship. Perhaps because his personal autocracy could be grafted on to a living tradition, Kemal could dispense with the trappings of militarism, and tried to create a new republican and civilian legality. Both he and Ismet renounced military titles and uniforms; the constitution clearly subordinated the military to the civilian power, and the army withdrew into a silent loyalty. With the victory of the Democrat Party in the general elections of 1950, a civilian President and a civilian Prime Minister took over the government of Turkey.

Between 1923 and 1950 the Turkish Republic had only two Presidents. Kemal's re-elections by the Assembly were no more than a matter of form. In fact he enjoyed life tenure, with powers as great as those of any Sultan, appointing and dismissing Prime Ministers and other ministers at will. Ismet Inönü inherited the same powers and for a while, during the difficult and dangerous years of the Second World War, even reinforced them. But in the period after 1945 there was a significant shift in authority.

[15] See Rustow, in *Wld. Polit.*, xi (1959), 513–52, and espec. 545–6.

Democracy had won new laurels of victory—and the Assembly of the post-war years was more active and more demanding than its predecessors. The appearance, for the first time in many years, of a group of opposition members radically altered the situation, transferring the centre of internal political activity from the ante-room of the presidential palace to the lobbies of the Assembly. Ismet himself, by encouraging or permitting the growth of real parliamentary democracy in these years, and by attempting to place the presidential office above the political mêlée, helped the process.

In May 1950 the people, having owned sovereignty since 1923, exercised it for the first time. They elected an Assembly—the Assembly elected a President—the President appointed a Prime Minister. Both were civilians, of civilian background. The President remained the head of the state; the play of politics and personality would determine whether he would also remain the effective head of the government, or whether he would leave this task to the Prime Minister and himself withdraw into a largely formal primacy.

Ministers and Ministries

In the old Ottoman Empire the Sultan had been the sole repository and source of power in the state. He had appointed the Grand Vezir and other vezirs, the chief Finance Officer (*Defterdar*), the army and navy commanders, and other high officers of state. From early times, a state council, known as the Imperial Divan (*Divan-i Humayun*), assembled every morning in the Topkapı Palace, in the room known as the Dome Chamber (*Kubbe-altı*). It was presided over by the Grand Vezir. Those who attended were the 'Dome Vezirs'—so-called because of their participation in this assembly, the Kaziaskers of Rumelia and Anatolia, the Kadi of Istanbul, the *Nişancı* (chief officer of chancery), the Defterdar, the Agas of the Janissaries and of the Cavalry Corps, and, when he was in the city, the Kapudan Paşa of the fleet. It thus included the heads of the Chancery, the exchequer, the judiciary, and the armed forces, each of whom had his own personal staff and establishment.

During the seventeenth century this system was abandoned. The withdrawal of the Sultan Mehmed IV from Istanbul to Edirne and the energetic Grand Vezirate of the Köprülüs initiated a change in practice. In 1654 the Grand Vezir acquired an official residence and office, which came to be known as *Paşa Kapısı*, the Pasha's Gate or, more commonly, as *Bab-i Ali*, the Sublime Porte. This henceforth became the effective centre of the Ottoman Government, and the Grand Vezir its effective head. The *Divan-i Humayun* still met occasionally in the palace, but for purely ceremonial matters, while the real business of government was conducted elsewhere. There seems to have been no regular system of ministerial meetings, but in case of necessity the civil, military, and religious chiefs met at the Sublime Porte under the presidency of the Grand Vezir. If he were on campaign, they might meet in the palace of the *Şeyh-ül-Islâm* or the acting Vezir.

A new order began with the reforms of Mahmud II, who first tried to introduce the European system of ministries.[16] His first ministries were not really experiments in Westernization, but moves in an internal struggle, to bring the religious hierarchy under closer state supervision. It was not until some years later, in 1836–8, that the Sultan took the first steps towards the creation of ministries in the Western style, by giving Western titles to some of the officers of the Sublime Porte, and then even to the Grand Vezir himself.[17]

The change of style from Grand Vezir to Prime Minister was of short duration, lasting only for fourteen and a half months, after which the old title was restored. A second attempt to introduce the European title was made during the first constitutional interlude, then dropped after less than four months, then restored in the following year by Abdülhamid, then dropped again, after about three and a half years, in 1882. Thereafter the title Grand Vezir remained in official use until the end of the Empire.

These changes in the style of the chief minister were of no great importance, and the Turkish historian Abdurrahman Şeref is probably right in dismissing them as mere make-believe. The process, however, of extending the activities of government to new areas suggested by European example, and of creating new departments of the central government to deal with them, continued. In 1839 a Ministry of Works was set up, with the task of improving trade, agriculture, and economic life generally. In 1870 police matters, already withdrawn from the department of

---

[16] See above, pp. 94 ff.

[17] Şeref, *Tarih-i Devlet-i Os.*, ii. 470–5 (Interior) and 507 (Foreign Affairs), and *Tar. Mus.*, pp. 264 ff. (on the title of Prime Minister).

the Serasker (Commander-in-Chief), were handed over to a separate Ministry of Police; while the Seraskerate itself was evolving into a closer likeness of a Ministry of War. In 1879–80 this name was in fact briefly introduced and then dropped; it was reintroduced after the revolution of 1908.

Two other innovations greatly reduced the authority of the ulema. In 1857 a Ministry of Education took over and extended the former personal interest of the sovereign in schools and colleges, and transferred this important field from religious to secular control. In 1879 a Ministry of Justice assumed the direction of the new courts and judiciary set up by the reformers, and thus again reduced the area of religious jurisdiction.[18]

With these the main departments of state of the Empire were established. Subsequent additions were the Ministry of the Navy, the Ministry of Trade and Agriculture, separated from the Ministry of Works; the Ministry of Post, Telegraphs, and Telephones; and, by a decree of 30 July 1918, a Ministry of Food.

The advent of the Republic brought important changes. The ministries were of course all moved to Ankara, the new capital, where they were in time housed in separate buildings. Some of them, as the Ministries of Foreign and of Internal Affairs, for the first time became physically separate entities. But for all of them the departure from the old Imperial city, and from the overshadowing pressure of such ancient centres as the palace and the Sublime Porte, opened the way to a new phase of development in republican, secular Ankara.

The new régime created several new ministries, once again reflecting the extension of the area of government activity, notably in social and economic matters. A Ministry of Health and Social Welfare dates back to the days of the first Ankara government. A Ministry of Labour was established in January 1946, and has developed rapidly since then.[19]

The Civil Service

During the nineteenth century the term *mülkiye*, roughly 'civilian', came into general use, to designate the civil service,

---

[18] For a useful general survey of the ministries in the first half of the nineteenth century, see Şeref, *Tarih-i Devlet-i Os.*, ii, 464 ff.

[19] A. Gorvine and L. L. Barber, *Organization and Functions of Turkish Ministries* (1957).

both central and provincial, as distinct from the other two branches of the government, the military (*askeriye*) and the religious (*ilmiye*). The Department of Internal Affairs, established by Mahmud II in 1836, was originally called *mülkiye*, and although this name was changed to *dahiliye* (internal) in the following year, the term *mülkiye* remained in general use for the non-military, non-ecclesiastical servants of the state.

The recruitment and maintenance of a civilian bureaucracy for the new and reconstructed ministries and departments presented various problems. Between 1833 and 1846 a series of ordinances laid down the tables of rank, precedence, titles, and honours for the new service, and incidentally established a new precedent by according them to offices instead of to officers.[20] But there were more practical problems to settle in the creation of a modern civil service.

One of the central problems was that of recruitment. The new system of secular schools set up by Mahmud II and his successors provided more recruits, but they were still sadly inadequate. In about 1872, in a memorandum to the Grand Vezir, Cevdet Paşa remarked:

If we are still deficient as regards judicial officials, we are even more deficient as regards executive officials, and are growing daily more so. It is an urgent necessity to expand the *mülkiye* school in accordance with the time and situation, to rearrange the programme of studies correspondingly, to employ its graduates progressively in important posts, and thus to train competent administrative officials. Our immediate obligation is to take care to choose and employ those who are already fairly experienced and thus put the state administration on the right path. If we give up finding jobs for men, and instead make it our policy to find men for jobs, then it is certain that within a short time officials capable of administering the country will emerge. . . .[21]

This doctrine, and Cevdet's immediately following argument, that these officials should be paid regular and adequate salaries, proved too revolutionary and too difficult. Recruitment in fact continued to be by patronage and apprenticeship. A young man in his early or middle teens joined a department on the recommendation of some well-connected relative. He served for a while as a kind of apprentice, making himself generally useful, and

---

20 *IA* ('Bala', by Cavid Baysun), and sources quoted there.
21 'Vakanüvis Cevdet Paşa'nın Evrakı', *TOEM*, no. 44 (1333 A.H.), p. 103.

receiving no salary. Eventually he might hope to be assigned a rank and rate of pay, and thus enter on the ladder of officialdom. His further promotions depended only partly on his merits; partly also on seniority, and above all on favour.

Pay was low and irregular, but employment in the government service was still eagerly sought after. No other civil career offered equal prestige, or even equal security of tenure. Successive reforms, concerned more with the safety of the official than with his efficiency, made him almost immune from dismissal.

Under the Republic the position of the civil servant was changed several times by new laws, the basic one being that of March 1926.[22] These laws laid down regular conditions of service, an establishment, and a scale of salaries which has been honoured. Recruitment was partly by competition, partly by nomination, the latter right being granted to various central and provincial public authorities, for certain kinds of post only. The number of candidates accepted was often determined by considerations other than the number of known vacancies to be filled. Pay, though now regular, remained low, and its purchasing power was diminished by successive inflations. The high degree of centralization, both in the country as a whole and in each individual ministry, left but little room for independent initiative.

If the civil servant was helpless under the authority of his official superiors, he remained a great power in his relations with the common people. The role of the civil servant in Anglo-Saxon democracy is perhaps best expressed by the term civil servant. The Turkish official, at least in departments exercising some authority over the public, was no civil servant. The Turkish term is *memur*—literally, one who is commanded, and the word, of course, expresses his relationship to the authority that employs him. For the mass of the people, however, he was not a servant but a master, or at least a shepherd, and was still accepted by the masses as such. Social attitudes rarely keep pace with changes of régime, and it was no easy matter to eradicate the vestiges of the centuries-old tradition whereby the official and the policeman wielded and shared in the autocratic authority of the Sultan.

---

[22] Başgil, p. 64. On the value to the young Republic of the trained reserves of manpower inherited from a much larger Empire, see the penetrating observations of D. A. Rustow, 'Foreign Policy of the Turkish Republic', in R. C. Macridis, ed., *Foreign Policy in World Politics* (1958), p. 315.

The fact that this authority was often benevolent and paternal, and those who wielded it conscientious and well intentioned, mitigated but did not resolve the difficulty. Political conceptions and practices changed greatly in Turkey, and the constitution recognized the people as the source of sovereignty, but the lower ranks of the hierarchy were less easy to persuade to part with their little brief authority—the more dear to them since it had ceased to carry with it any important economic privilege. The miserably inadequate salaries that most Turkish officials received did not improve their tempers. The processes of Westernization during the last century had made things worse rather than better. The need to conform to a Western social and sartorial standard added further financial burdens to the hard-pressed Turkish official, and the models offered by Western officialdom in Turkey and abroad were not always of the best. In Anatolia official arrogance was still modified by the innate courtesy of the old Turkish tradition. In Istanbul Westernization all too often resulted only in superimposing the morose fussiness of the French *fonctionnaire* on the alternating indolence and insolence of the Ottoman bureaucrat. A real change clearly required a re-education of both the official and the citizen. Among the most encouraging development of recent years are the many signs that this process has already begun.

The Cabinet

One of the more significant governmental reforms of Mahmud II was the establishment of the Privy Council—*Meclis-i Hass*. This body was in part a revival of the former *Divan-i Humayun*, in part an imitation of the Western Council of Ministers. It met twice weekly at the Sublime Porte, under the presidency of the Grand Vezir, and discussed current problems. Unlike the former Divan, it made no appointments, and dispensed no judicial decisions. Unlike a cabinet, it had no corporate existence or responsibility, and its members were all appointed directly by the Sultan. Even though the various ministers and high officials were in theory responsible to the Grand Vezir, in fact they were the Sultan's servants, individually nominated and dismissed by him.

At first the Privy Council was merely one of a number of such bodies, often eclipsed by others, such as the Councils of Justice, of Reform, and of Military Affairs, that dealt with more definite and tangible tasks. The gradual modernization of the administration, however, gave increasing importance to the central committee of ministers, which, under a Grand Vezir strong enough to impose his will on both his colleagues and the Sultan, could be a useful instrument of government. The efforts of Fuad Paşa, for example, to hold the Council together against the interventions of Sultan Abdülaziz, recapitulate the Western evolution towards cabinet government.[23]

The constitution of 1876 recognizes the existence of a Council of Ministers, presided over by the Grand Vezir, and assigns to it 'all important state matters, both external and internal'. There is, however, no approach to collective responsibility. The Grand Vezir and the *Şeyh-ül-Islâm* are appointed by the Sultan at his discretion; the other ministers are nominated by Imperial *irade* and all are individually responsible for their activities.

The Rescript restoring the constitution in 1908 made an important change, giving the Grand Vezir the right to appoint all the ministers other than the Ministers of War and of the Navy who, like the *Şeyh-ül-Islâm*, were to be appointed by the Sultan. This led to the fall of the Grand Vezir Said Paşa, and a few days later his successor, Kâmil Paşa, secured a new Rescript reserving the nomination of all ministers, other than the *Şeyh-ül-Islâm*, to the Grand Vezir.

The change was taken a step farther with the constitutional reforms of 1909. These laid down clearly that the Grand Vezir was responsible for choosing and forming the cabinet. They also laid down, for the first time, the collective responsibility of the ministers for the general policy of the government. The relationship between the cabinet, the sovereign, and parliament, with such questions as dismissal, resignation, and prorogation, remained the subject of bitter constitutional struggles right through the Young Turk period.[24]

As early as November 1921 Mustafa Kemal asked the Grand National Assembly in Ankara to pass a law on ministerial responsibility, but without result. In July 1922 the Assembly reserved to itself the right directly to elect the ministers and the Prime Minister, and in April 1923 finally passed the Law of Ministerial

---

[23] Karal, *Osmanlı Tarihi*, vii. 142 ff.

[24] Şeref, *Tar. Mus.*, pp. 348 ff.; Kraelitz-Greifenhorst, pp. 3 ff.; Jäschke, in *WI*, v. 20 ff.

Responsibility.[25] This was confirmed in article 46 of the republican constitution, which reproduces the revised text of 1909.

Parliaments and Parties[26]

Turkey has had three periods of parliamentary government, the first constitutional period, from 1876 to 1878, the second constitutional period from 1908 to 1920, and the third period, which may be dated from the convening of the Grand National Assembly in Ankara in 1920.

The constitution of 1876 provided for a two-chamber legislature; an elected Chamber of Deputies, and a Senate nominated by the Sultan, its members not to exceed one-third of the number of deputies. The procedure was laid down in an *irade* of 28 October 1876, on a basis of restricted franchise and indirect elections.[27] The elections of 1876 and 1877 were both held under this system. An electoral law, the preparation of which was required by the constitution, was actually drafted and discussed in 1877, but it did not become law until after the revolution of 1908. The remaining elections of the Ottoman Empire were held in accordance with its provisions.[28] These improved and extended the framework of the *irade* of 1876, but retained the restricted franchise and the system of electoral colleges.

The Grand National Assembly of Ankara consisted of a single chamber, and the Kemalist governments never attempted to reintroduce a second, whether nominated or elected. In other respects the republican régime showed itself to be conservative in electoral matters. The old electoral law remained in force, with its system of indirect or two-stage elections. It was not until 1946 that the system of direct election was accepted; it was fully applied in the general election of May 1950. Progress was more rapid in the extension of the franchise. As early as April 1924 the limitation of the franchise to tax-payers was abolished, together with some other restrictions. In 1934 the more radical step was taken of extending the vote to women, and henceforth all Turkish citizens, men and women, aged 22 and over, were entitled to vote.

[25] Jäschke, *Kalender*; Gözübüyük and Kili, pp. 88, 92; *Nutuk*, ii. 663.

[26] The best available discussion of electoral systems and procedures in Turkey are those of Tunaya in his *Partiler* and his article in English, 'Elections in Turkish History', *MEA* (1954), 116–20. (cf. Tunaya and Reşit Ülker, *Mufassal Fihristli Özetli Milletvekilleri Seçimi Kanunu ve Ilgili Mevzuat*, 1954, for the texts of the electoral laws).

[27] Aristarchi, v. 306.   [28] Trans. in Kraelitz-Greifenhorst, pp. 65 ff.

A reform of far-reaching importance, going beyond the mere form and procedure of the elections, was brought by the new electoral law of 15 February 1950. This law, passed with the approval of both the government and opposition parties, made a number of changes, including the secret ballot and public counting of votes; by far the most significant was the transfer of the supervision and control of the elections, both centrally and locally, from the executive to the judiciary. This measure, by making the judge instead of the Vali the supreme electoral authority in each constituency, was one of the main guarantees of the free and fair general election of May 1950.[29]

In the Turkish electoral system the constituency was the vilayet, or province, which returned a certain number of members according to its population. The first constitution specified one member for 50,000 inhabitants; in 1923 the number was reduced to 20,000, then in 1934 raised again to 40,000. This last figure remained in force. The vilayets are of unequal size; thus Istanbul has a million and a half inhabitants, while Hakkâri has only some 50,000. In each vilayet the parties nominated candidates, to the number of seats assigned to that vilayet, and the voter had to indicate his choice. This in effect has meant, in most of the vilayets, voting by lists.

Between 1876 and 1950 fourteen general elections were held, two in the first period, four in the second, and the rest in the third. None were held between 1877 and 1908. Of these fourteen elections, only five—those of 1908, 1912, 1919, 1946, and 1950—were contested by more than one party. Of these five, only one —that of 1950—resulted in an opposition victory and a transfer of power.[30]

The first beginnings of political parties in Turkey may be traced in the mid-nineteenth century, and already indicate the several different lines of development known to European party politics. The 'Society of Zealots', responsible for the Kuleli Incident of 1859, was a clique of conspirators, aiming at the violent overthrow of the régime by assassination.[31] The 'New Ottoman Society' of 1865 was a band of liberal patriots and idealists, aiming

[29] Details in Tunaya and Ülker.

[30] Besides the People's Party, a number of independent candidates stood in the election of 1931.

[31] See above, p. 148.

at education, persuasion, and influence.[32] At the same time Fuad Paşa, in his unsuccessful attempt to induce the pashas to act in concert against the Sultan's influence, was groping towards another and quite different kind of political party organization.

During the first constitutional period no parties emerged to contest the elections of 1876 and 1877, or to form groups in the parliaments of that time. It was not until the despotism of Abdülhamid was well established that a number of illegal, opposition groups were formed, with the common object of overthrowing it.

By far the most important of them was the Committee of Union and Progress, which dominated the parliaments of the second constitutional period. In the general election of 1908, only one other party, the Liberals (*Ahrar*), offered candidates, in Istanbul only. All of them were defeated. After the election, however, a number of deputies, chiefly Christians, began to form a parliamentary opposition group favourable to the liberals; several other new parties were formed, and also found supporters among disgruntled deputies.

None of these were, however, strong enough to offer any real threat to the monopoly of power of the Committee of Union and Progress. The only serious challenge came from the Liberal Union, which won a brief victory in the famous by-election of December 1911. It did not long enjoy it, and in 1913 the Committee, back in power,[33] established a virtual dictatorship. The opposition parties were suppressed, and some of their leaders exiled. The elections of May 1914 were held with one party only participating; the Committee remained the only party until the armistice in 1918.

The general elections of 1919 were contested by a large number of groups, new and old. Yet the only discernible victors were two groups that did not officially participate—the Committee of Union and Progress, which no longer existed, having dissolved itself at its last party congress on 14–19 October 1918, and the nationalists who had already appeared in Anatolia.[34]

Of the many parties formed in Istanbul in the course of the year 1919, the most important was the Liberal Union, formally reconstituted, after a period of quiescence, in January of that year. Though it would be an exaggeration to describe it as the party in

[32] See above, p. 149.   [33] See above, p. 220.   [34] Tunaya, *Partiler*, p. 402.

power, the Liberal Union and its leaders did play a role of some importance in the series of ministries that ruled in Istanbul between the end of the war and the end of the Empire. It failed however, to win any extensive following in the last Ottoman parliament.

The People's Party, created by Mustafa Kemal as the political instrument of his struggle for the reform of Turkey, was the direct successor of the Association for the Rights of Anatolia and Rumelia, which served during the phase of armed struggle for liberation. An inaugural general meeting was held in August 1923 and in November of the same year the new party took over the organization and assets of the now superseded Associations. A year later, in November 1924, the name of the party was changed to Republican People's Party.

Opposition groups were present in the Ankara régime almost from the beginning. In the summer of 1922 a splinter group was formed in the Association for the Defence of Rights, with the declared objective of resisting any personal despotism. The group approved the sovereignty of the Assembly, but opposed the autocracy of an individual—in other words, of Mustafa Kemal. It presented no candidates in the 1923 elections and thereafter played no further part in politics.[35]

On two occasions Mustafa Kemal experimented with a tolerated opposition—the Progressive Republican Party in 1924–5, and the Free Republican Party in 1930.[36] These experiments ended with the suppression of the opposition parties, and the reinforcement of the Gazi's control over the party in power, even to the point of personally nominating the candidates for parliament. After the party congress of 1935, the virtual coalescence of party and state was formalized; at the centre, the Minister of the Interior and the Secretary-General of the party were the same person; in the provinces, the Vali was chairman of the provincial party organization.[37]

The party congress of 1939, after the Gazi's death, decided to separate the party somewhat from the state, and to experiment with another kind of opposition. Party and government appointments were dissociated, and an 'independent group' constituted among the People's Party deputies in the *Meclis*, with instructions

[35] Ibid. pp. 537–8. [36] See above, pp. 260–1 and 274–5.
[37] Tunaya, *Partiler*, pp. 570 ff.

to function as a parliamentary opposition. The group was abolished by the party congress of 1946.[38]

Apart from two brief episodes, the RPP was in undisputed control from 1923 to 1945, when other parties were again permitted. Since, during that period, the party in power was under no obligation to seize, to win, or even to defend its control of the state against political opposition, it had no need of those techniques, electoral or conspiratorial, which in varying circumstances are so important in party political life. The RPP was not so much a means of gaining and holding power, as an instrument for exercising it. Diverging from a pattern common in the Middle East and elsewhere, it was more than a clique of notables in the capital with allies in the provincial cities, grouped by personality rather than programme; it possessed a nation-wide constituency organization, and was dedicated to a consistent and realistic programme of work. Fulfilling many important functions, both educational and executive, it became in effect part of the apparatus of republican government. In every rural centre of Turkey there was a local RPP branch, whose officials were the agents of the Kemalist Revolution. It was they who guided the peasantry, by means varying from persuasion to compulsion according to circumstances, and in doing so took over many of the social and economic powers formerly wielded by the rural magnates. An outstanding example of the educational and social work of the party was the network of 'People's Houses' and 'People's Rooms' (*Halkevi* and *Halkodası*). These had their origins in the Turkish Hearths (*Türk Ocağı*), founded in 1912.[39] They were revived in 1924, and in 1927 held a congress in Ankara. By a resolution of the party conference of 1931, the RPP decided to take over and expand their activities, and to set up 'People's Houses' in towns all over Turkey. In 1940 these were supplemented by 'People's Rooms' in small towns and villages, and by 1950, when the RPP fell from power, there were over 4,000 such rooms, as well as nearly 500 houses. The purpose of these houses was avowedly to inculcate in the people of Turkey the principles of the Revolution, especially republicanism, nationalism, and laicism. This they did through lectures, classes, and meetings, libraries and publications, dramatic, sporting, and other activities, concerts and exhibitions, and social assistance and guidance of various kinds.

[38] Tunaya, *Partiler*, pp. 573 ff.; Karpat, p. 396.   [39] See above, p. 344.

All these activities conform fairly closely, in form perhaps more than in content, to what became the pattern of the role of the party in the one-party state in Europe at that time—the Fascist Party in Italy, the Communist Party in Russia, the Nazi Party in Germany. In one respect, however, the Republican People's Party of Turkey differs most strikingly from its compeers elsewhere; for no other party of dictatorship prepared, organized and accepted its own peaceful supersession. Twice before—unsuccessfully—the RPP had experimented with a tolerated opposition. In 1945 it tried for a third time—and successfully procured its own defeat.

In 1945 and 1946 the Law of Associations and the penal code were amended to facilitate the formation and the operation of political parties besides the RPP. Political propaganda and activity became free, save only for two restrictions, on Communism and on clericalism—or, more precisely, anti-laicism. The advocacy of Communism or of the restoration of the Sultan-Caliph were contrary to the fundamental principles of the Republic, and could not be tolerated. Within these principles, the rights of opposition and criticism were conceded and recognized.

The first new party to appear and end the long monopoly of the RPP was the so-called National Recovery Party (*Millî Kalkınma Partisi*) founded on 18 July 1945, with an authorization from the Vali of Istanbul.[40] Its founders were Nuri Demirağ, a firm supporter of free enterprise and a sharp critic of the policy of etatism; Hüseyin Avni Ulaş, a member of the 'Second (opposition) Group' in the Association for the Defence of Rights in 1923; and Cevat Rifat Atılhan, who afterwards left and became associated with a number of extreme right-wing organizations.

This party, with its rather mixed leadership and programme, attracted little support; it did, however, establish precedents for organization and opposition, and was soon followed by many others. Between 1945 and 1950 no less than twenty-seven parties came into existence, some with such resounding names as the Social Justice Party, the Workers' and Peasants' Party, the For the Fatherland Only Party, the Cleansing and Defending Party, the Defence of Islam Party, the Idealist Party, the Pure Democrats Party, the Free Democrats Party, the Land, Property, and Free Enterprise Party, as well as a variety of toilers and workers, socialists and liberals.

[40] Tunaya, *Partiler*, pp. 639 ff.

Of all these parties, however, only two were of any real political importance; the Democrat Party,[41] founded on 7 January 1946, and the National Party,[42] founded on 20 July 1948. In 1950, under the new electoral law, the Democrats won 407 out of 487 seats, and thus became the government of Turkey—the first in Turkish history to have won power by purely constitutional and parliamentary means. It remained to be seen whether they would exercise it by the same means.

Provincial Government

The Ottoman Empire in its classical form has been described, by a kind of loose analogy with medieval Europe, as a military feudalism. The basic unit of provincial government was the sanjak. Its governor, the Sanjak-Bey, was a military officer; he was paid by the grant of a fief, and his primary duty was to superintend and, in time of war, to mobilize the feudal cavalrymen holding fiefs in his province. A group of sanjaks formed an eyalet governed by a Beylerbey, or governor-general. The Beylerbey, whose term of office was usually brief, enjoyed a large measure of military and financial autonomy.

During the seventeenth and eighteenth centuries the decentralization of the Empire advanced rapidly. With the relative decline in importance of the feudal levies and the increase in the numbers and cost of the paid regulars, the concern of the central government in the provinces became more financial and less military. The surviving *timars* were sharply reduced by Selim III, and finally abolished by Mahmud II in 1831.

Meanwhile, however, the leasing of crown revenues to tax-farmers had led to the emergence of a new kind of feudalism, based on money rather than service. Coupled with the growth of the autonomies of the *ayan* and the *derebeys* during the eighteenth century, it led to the almost complete loss of control over the provinces. The imposition on Mahmud II, by a conference of provincial notables, of a charter of provincial autonomy in 1808 marked the culmination of this process of feudal decentralization.

But Mahmud II, who gave formal recognition to the rights of the provincial notables, was determined to end them. After the conclusion of the war with Russia in 1812, he turned his attention

---

[41] Tunaya, *Partiler*, pp. 648 ff.; Karpat, pp. 408 ff.
[42] Ibid. pp. 712 ff.; Karpat, pp. 431 ff.

to what he regarded as his first major task—the restoration or establishment of the authority of the central government in the provinces. By a series of military campaigns and police actions, he was able to overcome the rebellious pashas and the local notables, destroying the institutions as well as the autonomies of provincial government. The New Order created by Mahmud and continued by his successors was at once more centralized and more autocratic. [43]

In one respect Mahmud's campaigns left the old order unchanged. Although the provinces were brought under the direct control of the central government—which in the circumstances of the time meant the personal control of the Sultan—there was still no financial or fiscal centralization. Provincial revenues were still farmed out by *iltizam*, and the tax-farmer, though bereft of his political privileges, still interposed himself between the taxpayer and the treasury.

A fatal custom still exists [says the Rescript of the Rose Chamber of 1839] although it can only have disastrous consequences; it is that of venal concessions, known under the name of 'Iltizam'. Under that name the civil and financial administration of a locality is delivered over to the passions of a single man; that is to say, sometimes to the iron grasp of the most violent and avaricious passions, for if that contractor is not a good man he will only look to his own advantage.

The Rescript goes on to abolish *iltizam*, and to decree that all Ottomans shall be subject only to fixed and direct taxation, 'according to their means'. A few months later, in December 1839, the government decreed that, with effect from 1 March 1840, governors of provinces, cities, &c., would be paid fixed salaries, that promotions to senior appointments would be made on merit alone, and that provincial governors would collect only the fixed legal taxes, through newly appointed civilian tax officials. [44]

It was one thing to decree the millennium, quite another to apply it. The first effect of the abolition of the sale of offices was a shortage of money; the new financial administration, however well-intentioned, was inexperienced and inept; the new paper currency depreciated rapidly, and before long almost all classes of society felt their interests to be endangered by these alien and ineffective reforms.

[43] See above, pp. 76 and 88 ff.   [44] Bailey, pp. 198 ff.; Temperley, pp. 236 ff.

In the wave of reaction following the dismissal of Reşid Paşa in 1841, the provincial reforms were abandoned, and the old fiscal system restored. In February 1842 the civilian tax collectors in the provinces were removed, and the collection of taxes returned to the military governors and their contractors, with the assistance of councils of local notables.[45]

These councils, established by Reşid Paşa, were modelled on the French *Conseils Départementaux*, with the difference that they were permanently in session, and interfered actively in the administrative and judicial affairs of the province. Inevitably, they became centres of bitter local partisan strife, and the executive power, caught between a remote and inactive central authority and a lively and obstructive local council, was reduced to complete ineffectiveness. Eventually some of the evils of premature centralization and democracy were removed. A ferman of 28 November 1852 restored the powers of the governor, making him once more the effective authority in his province. At the same time the legal powers of the police and army, weakened to the point when they could barely maintain order, were reaffirmed and extended.[46]

The compromise between the old and new orders was less than satisfactory, and it was natural that in the new phase of reform that followed the Crimean War attention should once again be given to the problems of provincial administration. The interest of the European godfathers of the reform was directed particularly to the Balkan provinces of the Empire, and in 1859–60 a proposal for an international commission of inspection in the European provinces was averted only by the Grand Vezir, Kıbrıslı Mehmed Paşa, going on one himself.[47]

Discontent and rebellion among the Balkan Christians had become an accepted feature of life in the Empire, but the spread of the disorder to the staunchly Muslim province of Syria in 1860–1—and the resulting foreign intervention—were a danger signal that could not be ignored. Fuad Paşa himself, then Minister of Foreign Affairs, went to Syria to investigate, and severely punished the culprits.[48] In his notes on the troubles, Fuad Paşa

[45] Engelhardt, ii. 50.   [46] Ibid. i. 105–110; Karal, *Tarih*, vi. 31–32.

[47] Rasim, *Osmanlı Tarihi*, iv. 2095, ff.; Karal, *Tarih*, vii. 152.

[48] Rasim, iv. 2083 ff.; cf. W. Miller, *The Ottoman Empire and its Successors, 1801–1922* (1923), p. 302.

lays great stress on the maladministration from which the provinces of the Empire were suffering. In a country as large as the Ottoman Empire, it was difficult to find an adequate number of officials with the desired qualities. Many officials had in fact misused governmental powers, and for this reason the tendency had been to reduce their competence and strengthen the control of the central government. This had brought some benefits, but at the same time it had reduced the status and authority of provincial officials and, in the eyes of a populace accustomed to being governed by quite other means, made them appear as contemptible nonentities. In a country made up of many races and religions, this feebleness and disrepute into which the provincial administration had fallen led to grave dangers.[49]

The problem of provincial government continued to exercise Fuad Paşa and his circle. Inspectors were sent to the provinces, including such well-known figures as the historian and jurist Cevdet and the scholar and statesman Ahmed Vefik. A special commission, presided over by Cevdet, was formed to examine the inspection reports, and make recommendations.

In 1864 Fuad Paşa, who had meanwhile again become Grand Vezir, had his solution ready—the new Law of Vilayets. His idea, according to the evidence of Cevdet, was to group the provinces into larger units, and place them under the control of carefully chosen able and experienced men. These would be given greatly extended discretion, and would need to refer to Istanbul only in the most important matters. This would have the further advantage of freeing the ministers from ordinary routine, and allowing them to concentrate on high affairs of state.[50]

On this basis a provincial code was drafted and promulgated in 1864. The old eyalets were replaced by substantially larger vilayets, twenty-seven in number, and each governed by a Vali with extensive powers. Within the vilayet a chain of authority was established. The vilayet was divided into sanjaks—the old, feudal name, but with quite a new meaning; the sanjak into kazas, the kaza into *nahiyes* and villages. Under the authority of the Vali, the sanjak was administered by a *mutasarrıf*, the kaza by a Kaymakam,

[49] Rasim, loc. cit; Karal, *Tarih*, vi. 31.

[50] 'Maruzat', in *TOEM*, no. 87 (1341 A.H.), 269–70; cf. Karal, *Tarih*, vi. 153 and Mardin, *Ahmet Cevdet Paşa*, pp. 53 ff.

the *nahiye* by a *müdür*, the village or quarter by an elected *muhtar* (headman). At vilayet, sanjak, and kaza levels there was to be an administrative council, formed by the Governor, the chief judge, the chief finance officer, and the chief secretary, together with four representatives of the population, two Muslim and two non-Muslim, and the religious heads of the Muslim and non-Muslim communities. The representative members were to be chosen by a complicated and restricted franchise. The council was to meet under the presidency of the governor. To avoid a return to the anarchy of the Rose-Chamber experiment, the council was forbidden to interfere in judicial matters.

The Vali's administration was divided into civil, financial, police, political, and legal affairs. For each of these he had subordinate officials placed under his orders, though the finance officer, continuing a traditional Ottoman and Islamic practice, was responsible for his accounts directly to the Ministry of Finance. The Vali was also responsible for recruiting and appointing his staff. Apart from the councils, an annual general provincial assembly was to be convened, with four delegates elected by each sanjak, again two Muslim and two non-Muslim. These assemblies met for a few years, before they were abolished, together with the rest of the apparatus of representative government, by Abdül-hamid.[51]

This law, with its hierarchy of Valis, *mutasarrıfs*, kaymakams and *müdürs*, administering vilayets, sanjaks, kazas, and *nahiyes*, is clearly based on the French system of provincial administration, through the *départements*, *arrondissements*, cantons, and communes. Though Fuad Paşa's law gave the Ottoman Vali considerably more discretion than was enjoyed by the French *Préfet* on whom he was modelled, the general tendency of the law was towards centralization and uniformity. It was more especially on the latter ground that it was criticized by Cevdet Paşa, an advocate, in general, of conservative gradualism. The provinces of the Empire, he said, differed greatly from one another, both in their geographical and their ethnographical circumstances, and could not all be treated in the same way. In each region an administrative reform should be undertaken, taking account of local conditions

---

[51] Engelhardt, i. 193–8; Temperley, p. 237; Karal, *Tarih*, vii. 153; Sax, pp. 372 ff.; Ismail Hakkı Göreli, *Il Idaresi* (1952), p. 6. Text in *Düstur*, i. 4 ff.; trans. in Young, i. 29 ff. and Aristarchi, iii. 1 ff.

and of the historical background. Cevdet saw this as a process requiring much knowledge, skill, and time.[52]

Cevdet did offer general principles and observations. The classical Ottoman Empire had not been a centralized state. The *Tanzimat* reformers had attempted to introduce a centralized administration, but grave difficulties had arisen. Since then they had chopped and changed between centralized and decentralized government, with the result that all was confusion and anarchy. The first necessity was to decide on the general principle of government, and then to determine the duties and responsibilities of officials of all three groups, administrative, judicial, and military. Finally, officials should be regularly and adequately paid.

The servants of the state should be superior to the mass of the people in ability and competence. But if there is no recompense, outstanding persons among the population will have no inclination to the service of the state, and will choose other professions, leaving only mediocrities to carry on the business of the state. These, lacking all prestige in the eyes of the people, will be quite unable to administer men who are in fact their superiors.[53]

Order and consistency, recruitment and pay, the competence, integrity, and prestige of the service—Cevdet had put his finger on some of the main difficulties of applying a uniform, centralized administration in regions as diverse and as mixed as the Ottoman provinces. On the other hand, however, there were new factors favouring centralization, two of particular importance. One was the improvement in communications—the introduction of the telegraph at the time of the Crimean War, and the rapid extension of roads and railways from about 1862 onwards.[54] The other was the loss of several of the predominantly Christian Balkan provinces; this, by leaving the Empire more homogeneous, made it easier to devise and apply a national provincial system.

The law of 1864 was of course not immediately and universally applied. Nor was there any intention of doing so. In accordance with a common practice of the Ottoman reformers, Fuad Paşa began with a pilot project—the model and experimental vilayet of the Danube. This new vilayet, chosen for obvious political

---

[52] Karal, *Tarih*, vii. 153.   [53] Cevdet in *TOEM*, no. 43 (1333 A.H.), 103.

[54] Karal, *Tarih*, vii. 267–73; cf. above, pp. 180 ff.

reasons, was entrusted to one of the ablest administrators in the Ottoman service—the famous Midhat Paşa.

Midhat's term of office as Vali of the Danube province showed that, given the necessary goodwill and ability, the new system could work very well. Within two years he had restored order, introduced the new hierarchy, provided agricultural credits, extended roads, bridges, and waterways, started industries, opened schools and orphanages, founded a newspaper, and increased the revenues of the province from 26,000 to 300,000 purses.[55]

Midhat's success in reviving the Sick Man of Europe was not to the taste of the expectant heirs; in 1868, as a result of Russian and Serbian intervention at the Porte, he was recalled, and in 1869 posted as Vali of Baghdad. There, in a remote and backward Asian province of the Empire, he was able to repeat his achievements, and bring order and progress to the people of Iraq.

With these successes to guide them, the Ottomans gradually extended the new system to the whole Empire, at the same time introducing such legislative modifications to the provincial code as seemed desirable. In 1870 a revised general provincial code delimited the functions and authority of provincial officials from the Vali down to the village *muhtar*.[56]

The constitution of 1876 contained a whole section relating to the provinces. This affirmed the principle of decentralization and the separation of powers in provincial administration, and declared that a special law would regulate the election of members of provincial administrative councils and general assemblies and the powers and duties of the Vali, these last to include public works, and the improvement of agriculture, industry, commerce, communications, and education.

The question of provincial administration received earnest attention from the short-lived Ottoman parliament of March 1877, and a new vilayet law, of 101 articles, was actually debated and passed by the lower house. It had, however, not yet reached the Senate when parliament was closed, and the debate, the law, and the constitution itself were shelved indefinitely. Instead, a new law was published, in 1880, by a mixed commission of Ottoman and

---

[55] Midhat, *Life*, pp. 38 ff.; Karal, *Tarih*, vii. 154–5.
[56] *Düstur*, i. 625; Young, i. 47; Göreli, p. 7.

foreign officials. Its purpose appears to have been to answer the clauses in the treaty of Berlin relating to Ottoman administration, and to satisfy the powers that their requirements had been met. Significantly, this law is not included in the Ottoman corpus of laws. The basic Ottoman provincial law remained that of 1864, with minor subsequent amendments.[57]

The revolution of 1908 and the restoration of the constitution raised once again the question of the application of article 108, prescribing decentralization and the separation of functions in provincial government. After long investigations and deliberations by two successive special commissions, a draft law was submitted to parliament in 1910. The parliamentary consideration of this bill was protracted and difficult; inevitably, it was affected by the strains of the Tripolitanian and Balkan wars, and by the growing tendency towards a more centralized, more authoritarian régime. The law finally accepted, on 26 March 1913, has remained the basis of Turkish provincial administration ever since. To meet the requirements of clause 108 of the constitution, the jurists of that time evolved the theory of the dual character of vilayet government. The vilayet administration was conceived as having two aspects; one general, as components of the national apparatus of government, the other special or local, as decentralized administrative entities, with a recognized legal personality. By thus admitting the Western conception of corporate legal persons into the legal and administrative structure of the country, the legislators of 1913 were taking an important step away from Islamic and towards European legal principles. The aim of the law was to give the Vali the necessary powers and discretion to maintain order, carry out public works, and conduct local affairs effectively, while at the same time preserving the national authority of the Ministry of the Interior.[58]

An important change in nomenclature was made by the 'Fundamental Law' of 20 January 1921, passed by the Grand National Assembly in Ankara. This divided the country into vilayets, the vilayets into kazas, and the kazas into *nahiyes*. The old title of sanjak was dropped, but in fact it was the older, large-scale vilayet that ceased to exist, since the old sanjaks now become vilayets, directly dependent on the central government.

The situation created by the law of 1913 was not changed by

[57] Engelhardt, ii. 250–5.   [58] Göreli, p. 17.

the proclamation of the Republic, nor by the republican constitution of 20 April 1924, which reaffirmed the principle of decentralization and separation of functions in provincial government. It was confirmed by the vilayet law of 18 April 1929, which remains in force.[59] This law confirms the dual character of the vilayet, as a territorial and administrative subdivision of the national government, with a Vali appointed from the capital, and at the same time as a unit of local government, with a recognized legal personality. In the latter capacity it has its own budget, its own legislative and executive branches, and can own property.

In the theory of Turkish law the vilayet and its subdivisions thus provide the local government of the country. In fact the control of the Ministry of the Interior in provincial affairs is very strict. The Vali, Kaymakam, and others are all ministry-appointed permanent officials. The vilayet budget is provided from the centre; it may be supplemented by loans, but not by local taxation, which the vilayet council has no power to impose. The council, an elected body, meets normally for forty days in the year, under the presidency of the Vali. If he disapproves its decisions, he may refer them to the Council of State in Ankara for a final verdict. The council's duties are to audit the expenditure of the previous year, and to pass the current budget, which has been prepared by the Vali and submitted to the vilayet permanent commission. The budgets must be finally ratified by the cabinet in Ankara and the President of the Republic. The vilayet council may also discuss and lay down policy on public works, agriculture, education, and social services. When it is not in session its functions are discharged by a four-man permanent commission.

The kaza is not a legal person, and has no elected assembly. Its administrator, the Kaymakam, is a subordinate of the Vali, but is a central government official appointed from Ankara. The *nahiye*, the smallest sub-unit of the vilayet, is administered by the *müdür*, also a central government officer, but on a different ladder of promotion from the Kaymakam and Vali. He presides over a *nahiye* council, consisting of the local officials and technicians, together with one elected representative from each village or municipality. Finally, there is the village, established as a legal entity for the first time by the village law of 18 March 1924. The

[59] Ibid.; Başgil, p. 49; Jäschke, *Kalender*, under date; idem, 'Die grösseren Verwaltungsbezirke der Türkei seit 1918', *MSOS*, xxxviii (1935), 81–104.

villagers elect a *muhtar* and council of elders, in which the school-teacher and the imam are *ex officio* members. Although the *muhtar* is an elected official who represents the villagers, he is also in effect, and usually in the first instance, an administrative officer, representing the central government in the village and carrying out whatever instructions reach him through the chain of command. Much the same is true of the *muhtar* in the *mahalle*, or quarter of a town. He too is subject to the authority of the vilayet for many purposes. For others, however, the *mahalle* is part of the municipality, a quite separate organization with a very different background and history.[60]

Municipal Government[61]

Although classical Islam was in many respects an essentially urban civilization, the classical Islamic system of law and government takes very little account of the city. Islamic law does not recognize corporate persons, and Islamic history shows no recognized, privileged cities, with corporate status and rights. Just as there was no state but only a ruler and his agents, no court but only a judge and his helpers, so there was no city but only a conglomeration of families, quarters, and guilds, each with their own chiefs and leaders.

The *Şeriat* contains no municipal code, and the town never became a legal or political entity—neither as a fief, nor as a commune. Those charged with its government were not municipal officers, nor yet feudatories; still less were they civil servants in the modern sense. For the most part they were royal officers, with revocable, delegated powers from the sovereign; or else members of the religious class, charged with certain duties of prevention and enforcement, where the provisions of the Holy Law were concerned.

In Ottoman Istanbul police duties, fire-fighting, and public order generally were entrusted to certain military officers with regiments designated for these tasks. The supervision of the markets was the duty of the *muhtesib*, a member of the ulema class whose task it was to enforce the rules relating to prices and quality

[60] On Turkish provincial government see further *Kaza ve Vilayet Idaresi üzerinde bir Araştırma* (Ank., 1957); A. Gorvine, *An Outline of Turkish Provincial and Local Government* (1956).

[61] For a survey of Turkish municipal institutions see *EI²* ('Baladiyya', by B. Lewis). Details and documents in Nuri, *Mec. Um. Bel.*

of merchandise offered for sale, and in general to act as a censor of morals and to maintain public decency and morality. The function of the *muhtesib*, a post going back to medieval Islamic times, is called *ihtisab*. A third official was the *Şehr-emini*, or City Commissioner. This office, which appears in Istanbul soon after the Ottoman conquest, was probably modelled on a Byzantine original, since there seems to be no trace of it in earlier Ottoman towns. The City Commissioner was not merely a royal officer but, more specifically, a palace functionary. His chief tasks were the financial supervision of the palace, the provision of food, clothing, and other palace needs, the maintenance and repair of the palace and of other royal and governmental buildings in the city, and similar duties. The office ranked high on the ladder of promotion of the finance branch of the bureaucracy. It was abolished in 1831.

The first approaches towards modern municipal government was made by Sultan Mahmud II, in the period after the destruction of the Janissaries. As with so many of his reforms, the purpose seems to have been to centralize and thus better to control certain functions previously performed by quasi-independent bodies—in this case the ulema. In 1827 an inspectorate of *ihtisab* was set up, which centralized certain duties, connected with market controls, inspection of weights and measures, &c., hitherto performed by the *muhtesib*. In 1829, with the same general aim of centralizing control and reducing the powers of the ulema, the system of *muhtars* was introduced in the quarters of Istanbul. Until that time there had been headmen in villages, whose duties, as far as the government was concerned, were chiefly fiscal. In towns, where no agricultural taxes were to be assessed and collected, there were no headmen, and the duties of keeping registers of the male population, recording movements, transfers, &c., were the responsibility of the Kadis and their deputies; in the quarters of the town they fell to the local imams. Under the new law these duties were transferred to the *muhtars*, of whom two, a first and a second, were to be appointed in every town quarter. The Imperial Historiographer Lûtfi says that the purpose of this measure was to end the laxness and incompetence of the imams.[62] A little later, the *muhtar* was reinforced by a committee of elders of from three to five persons. In time, this system was extended to other cities.

A new phase began in 1854, when two important changes were

[62] Lûtfi, ii. 173.

initiated. The first of these was the revival of the title of *Şehr-emini*, City Commissioner, in abeyance since 1831. Though the name was the same, the new office had nothing to do with the old; it was rather an adaptation of the French *préfecture de la ville*, and was chiefly concerned with the supervision of markets, the control of prices, &c.—the chief functions of the former *ihtisab*. The Inspectorate, established in 1827, was abolished, and its duties transferred to the Prefect, who was to be assisted by a city council drawn from the guilds and merchants.

This change in nomenclature seems to have had little practical effect, and complaints began to be made about official neglect of municipal problems. A few months later a decision was taken by the High Council of Reform to establish a municipal commission. The leading spirit in the commission was Antoine Aléon, a member of a rich French banking family that had settled in Turkey at the time of the French Revolution. The other members were drawn chiefly from the local Greek, Armenian, and Jewish communities. There were, however, some Muslim Turks, including the Chief Physician Mehmed Salih Efendi, one of the first graduates of Sultan Mahmud's medical school. The commission was instructed to report on European municipal organization, rules, and procedures, and to make recommendations to the Sublime Porte.

A number of factors had combined to induce the Ottoman government to take these steps. European financial and commercial interests in the capital had been growing steadily, and a new quarter was developing in Galata and Pera, with buildings, blocks of flats, shops, and hotels in European style. An important change was the vast increase in the number of horse-drawn carriages of various kinds. At the beginning of the nineteenth century there were few such carriages in Istanbul, since their use in the city was limited to a small number of privileged persons, such as the *Şeyh-ül-Islâm* and the Grand Vezir. A somewhat larger number were allowed to ride on horseback in the city, and the rest, even including many officers and officials, had to walk. During the early nineteenth century these old rules were disregarded, and, says Cevdet Paşa, 'even some of the non-Muslim subjects, without authorization, could be seen in public places on caparisoned horses'.[63] Such unauthorized horse-riding by infidels,

63 Cevdet, ix. 185–6.

'being unseemly in the eyes of the people', was banned, but the numbers of carts and carriages, both the local varieties and imported coaches from Europe, increased rapidly.[64]

All this created a demand, which was put forward by the European residents, with the support of the Europeanized elements among the local population, for proper roads and pavements, street-cleaning and street-lighting, sewers and water-pipes. The presence in Istanbul of large allied contingents from the West during the Crimean War gave a new impetus and a new urgency to these demands, and, in the new phase of reform that began in 1854, some attention was given to the problems of municipal organization and services in the capital. Even the liberal reformers took notice of these questions, and the poet and publicist Ibrahim Şinasi contributed an article to the *Tasvir-i Efkâr* on the lighting and cleaning of the streets of Istanbul.[65]

The records of the proceedings of the High Council of Reform on these matters reflect clearly the various preoccupations of the Ottoman government. The creation of a city prefecture, under the recently created Ministry of Commerce, was in part an attempt to meet a new need by installing the relevant European apparatus. There was also the usual desire to impress Western observers. Ill-wishers, says a document in the Council's records, had accused the Imperial government of doing nothing and caring nothing for the adornment and improvement of the capital, and were saying that nothing would come of the proposed system of municipal districts. It was therefore necessary to show practical zeal.[66]

The Commission sat for four years, and then presented a report to the High Council of Reform, recommending a number of municipal services and improvements. The Commission also recommended the imposition of a special tax for municipal purposes, the organization of separate municipal finances, and the appointment of itself to apply municipal laws and regulations.

The High Council of Reform decided to accept these recommendations, but to limit their application, for the time being, to an experimental municipality, to be established in the European

---

[64] See M. Rodinson, 'Araba', *J. As.*, ccxlv (1957), 273–80.

[65] Reprinted in Ebüzziya, *Nümûne*, pp. 227–35.

[66] Quoted in Ergin, *Türkiyede Şehirciliğin Tarihî Inkişafı* (1936), p. 125.

quarter of Galata and Pera. This district, though the first to be organized, was officially named the sixth district, possibly, as a Turkish historian has suggested, because the sixth *arrondissement* of Paris was believed to be the most advanced of that city. The reasons for this decision are set forth in a protocol of 9 October 1857. Municipal services and improvements were badly needed, and should be provided; the cost should not fall on the state treasury, but should be met by a special levy from the townspeople who would benefit. It would be impracticable to apply the new system to the whole of Istanbul at once, and it was therefore decided to make a start with the sixth district, consisting of Pera and Galata, where there were numerous fine buildings. The district contained a large number of foreign establishments and a preponderance of foreign residents who were acquainted with the practice of other countries and would be willing to accept the expense of municipal institutions. When the merits of these institutions had been demonstrated by this example, a suitable occasion would be found to apply them generally.

The constitution and functions of the municipality of the sixth district, also known as the model district, were laid down in an Imperial *irade* of 7 July 1858. The municipal council was to consist of a chairman and twelve members, all appointed by Imperial *irade*, the chairman indefinitely, the others for three years. All were to be unpaid. The council would appoint a number of permanent officials, including a civil engineer and an architect, who would receive salaries. The municipality would have the right to assess, impose, and collect rates and taxes, to raise loans within limits laid down, and in certain circumstances to expropriate property. The chairman was to submit his budget to the council for discussion and inspection, and then to the Sublime Porte for ratification, without which it would not be valid.

These measures, while accepting and providing for the discharge of certain new responsibilities as to the town, hardly represent an approach to the European conception of municipal institutions. For one thing the reform was limited to a single urban district with a predominantly European population; more fundamental, there was still no recognition of the city as a corporate person, for such an idea remained alien to Islamic conceptions of law and government; nor was there any suggestion of election or representation. What was created was a new kind of administrative agency, appointed by and responsible to the sovereign power, with specified and limited tasks and with a measure of budgetary autonomy. Such special commissions were by no means new in Ottoman administration. The novelty lay in the kind of function entrusted to it.

The 'model commission' worked well, and in 1868 a code of municipal regulations was issued, which was to extend the system to the rest of Istanbul. Each of the districts of the city was to have a municipal committee, and to send its chairman and three delegates to a general municipal assembly for all Istanbul. This assembly, together with a Council of Prefecture, of six persons, appointed and paid by the Imperial government, was to function under the Prefect of the city, who was to remain a government official.

The provisions of this code seem to have remained a dead letter until 1876–7 when, under the impetus of the constitutional movement, new municipal codes were issued for the capital and for provincial towns. The Istanbul code of 1876 was a rearrangement of that of 1868, and proved as ineffectual. Finally, in 1878, a new and more realistic version was published, which in time was put into operation. This divided the city into ten municipal districts. The elaborate apparatus of councils and committees provided by the earlier codes was abolished. What was left was an appointed Council of Prefecture, to assist the Prefect, and a government-appointed director for each of the ten districts. This system, ensuring the full and effective control of the sovereign power, remained in force until the revolution of 1908.

In the provinces the policies of the reformers followed much the same line. Such earlier authorities as the *ayan* had been abolished. The *muhtar* system, inaugurated by Mahmud II, was introduced into the quarters of most of the larger towns, and the vilayet law of 1864 laid down regulations for their election. In the vilayet law of 1870, provision was made for the establishment of municipal councils in provincial cities, along the same general lines as in the code for Istanbul. There is no evidence that anything was done about this. Some attempt, however, seems to have been made to implement parts of the provincial municipal code of 1877, according to which each town was to have an elected municipal council, consisting of six to twelve members, according to population, with the district doctor, engineer, and veterinary surgeon as *ex-officio* advisory members. One of the councillors was to be mayor, not by election but by government appointment; the budget and estimates were to be approved by a municipal assembly, meeting twice yearly for this purpose, and in turn responsible to the General Council of the province.

After the revolution of 1908 a new attempt was made to introduce democratic municipal institutions. The law of 1876, with some amendments, was restored, and a serious attempt made to put it into effect. The experiment was not very successful. The personnel of the district committees, though enthusiastic, were inexperienced, and there was little co-operation between districts for common purposes. In 1912 a new law finally abolished the system. In its place a single Istanbul prefecture was established with nine district branch offices each directed by a government official. The Prefect was assisted by a general assembly of 54 members, to which 6 delegates were elected from each of the 9 districts. As in earlier electoral systems, the franchise was restricted by property and income.

In this as in so many other respects, the new régime was returning to a more centralized system of government, though without abandoning all the forms of democracy. In spite of many difficulties the Young Turk régimes did in fact make some progress in improving the amenities of Istanbul, notably in drainage, garbage disposal, and fire prevention.

This system remained in force in the early years of the Republic. The first municipal measure of the republican government was a law of 16 February 1924 setting up a prefecture in Ankara, with a 'General Assembly' of twenty-four members. The constitution followed broadly that established in Istanbul in 1912, but with some changes, the general effect of which was to restrict the autonomy of the municipality in financial and security matters and place it more strictly under the control of the Ministry of the Interior.

On 3 April 1930 a new law of municipalities was passed. The names *Şehr-emini* and *Şehr-emanet*—prefect and prefecture—were abolished, and replaced by *belediye* and *belediye reisi*, usually translated municipality and mayor. Under Sultan Abdülhamid, the offices of prefect and governor (Vali) of Istanbul had in fact been exercised by the same person. This arrangement, which secured complete governmental control over the municipal business of the capital, was criticized by the Sultan's liberal opponents, and in 1909 the new régime formally separated the prefecture from the governorship. The law of 1930 provided a compromise; in Istanbul, though not elsewhere, the office of mayor would be combined with that of Vali, and the incumbent nominated by the Ministry of the Interior. The vilayet and municipality administrations, however, would be separate, and the municipal councillors elected as elsewhere. This arrangement continues in force; it is interesting that whereas in Turkish documents the incumbent is usually called Vali, in foreign languages he is normally described as mayor. This Janus-like posture of the head of Turkey's largest city has remained a subject of controversy. In the general election of 1950 the separation of the two offices and the creation of an elective mayoralty formed part of the Democrat Party programme.

The law recognizes municipalities, like villages, as having corporate legal identity and legally defined boundaries, and thus takes municipal government in Turkey across one of the most important barriers separating Islamic from Western legal concepts. It provides a set of rules governing the election and functioning of municipal bodies, and with some modifications has remained in force to the present day.

CHAPTER XII

Religion and Culture

Just as physical bodies have length, width, and depth, so the social consciousness also has three dimensions—nationality, religion, and modernity. I propose to test the validity of this observation first with regard to language, which is the best mirror of social consciousness.

ZIYA GÖKALP, 1913.

The Turkish nation is ready and resolved to advance, unhalting and undaunted, on the path of civilization.

MUSTAFA KEMAL, 1924.

IN April 1921, in occupied Istanbul, a religious service was held in honour of the fallen in the war of independence in Anatolia. Yakup Kadri Karaosmanoğlu, the distinguished Turkish author, was present, and has described in striking terms the thoughts and feelings that moved him. As he listened to the recitation of the *Mevlûd*, the ode in honour of the Prophet's birthday that serves in Turkey as a requiem, the realization came to him that his life during the past ten years, in pursuit of modernism and secular nationalism, had been a nightmare from which he was now awakening. The ideals which he and his contemporaries had followed were false and harmful; here was the truth. The true home of his people was not 'the national club, the cultural lecture, the political meeting', but the mosque and congregation, 'the house, home, and fatherland' of this nation. Only the simple, ignorant people had understood this and had preserved the true values which the intellectuals, with their apeing of the West, had forgotten.

Yesterday for the first time the common people, whom we had always despised as ignorant and idle, taught the intellectuals of this country some divine truths. One of these is that the heart is superior to the mind. Another is that apart from sincerity and devotion and simple faith there is no way of salvation. The third is that there must be no separation between the nation and the religious community.[1]

---

[1] Printed in Ergin, *Muallim Cevdet'in Hayatı, Eserleri ve Kütüphanesi* (1937), pp. 324–7; cf. Rossi, 'La cultura araba presso i Turchi', in *Caratteri e Modi della cultura araba* (1943), p. 236.

These words, written in April 1921, make strange reading in the light of the secularist policies adopted by the victors after the completion of those victories that had so deeply stirred Yakup Kadri's religious loyalty. That a man of his generation and of his education should, in the moment of profound national crisis, have rallied instinctively to Islam is striking enough; but it was more than a momentary or individual reaction. The independence movement itself, in its earlier phases, was strongly religious in character. Its aims were to rescue 'Islamic lands' and 'Islamic populations' from foreign—i.e. Christian—rule and its declarations were addressed to 'Muslim compatriots'.[2] One-fifth of the numbers of the first Grand National Assembly belonged to the class of professional men of religion, and some of them, both from the ulema and the brotherhoods, played an important part in the Kemalist movement.

Secularism and Laicism

On 5 April 1920 Damad Ferid Paşa formed his fourth cabinet, determined to destroy the nationalists in Anatolia, and on 11 April the *Şeyh-ül-Islâm* Dürrizade Abdullah issued his famous *fetva* against them.[3] The Caliph and the *Şeyh-ül-Islâm* both seemed to have gone over to the side of the invaders and occupiers, and in the bitter civil struggle that followed between the nationalists and the so-called 'army of the Caliphate', Turkish secularism for the first time became a serious political force.[4]

Though militant laicism was new, traces of what might be called anti-clericalism can be found in earlier periods of Ottoman history. The ancient chronicles, for example, reflect the resentments of the frontiersmen at being subjected to the hierarchy and restraints of Islamic orthodoxy; popular poetry, legend, and anecdote reflect the occasional doubts of the faithful as to the complete integrity and disinterestedness of their spiritual guides.

During the Young Turk period, secularist and positivist ideas enjoyed a certain vogue. Comte and Haeckel as well as Voltaire and Rousseau found their translators and admirers, with effects that sometimes went beyond the intellectual circle—as for example the Young Turk officers who made a point of honour of drinking cognac and eating ham. More important than the

---

[2] D. A. Rustow, 'Politics and Islam in Turkey . . .' in Frye, p. 71 n. 1.

[3] See above, p. 246.   [4] cf. Rustow, loc. cit; Jäschke, in *WI*, xviii. 54–69.

out-and-out positivists were those who preached the separation of religion and the state—the forerunners of the laicism of the Republic. The most notable was the ideologist of Turkism, Ziya Gökalp. It was perhaps unfortunate that, to render the unfamiliar French term *laïque*, he should have used the word *lā-dīnī*, which could mean irreligious. In the opinion of a well-qualified Turkish observer, the resulting confusion between laicism and irreligion 'did much to lead the Muslim clergy, with the Shaykh al-Islam at their head, into a hostile attitude'.[5]

Besides these modernist tendencies, there was also something of a religious revival in the Young Turk period, which found expression in a number of influential magazines and books; both the intellectual and the political life of the second constitutional era were profoundly affected by the debates and conflicts between the different groups of modernists and religious conservatives.[6] The strength and aims of some of the latter can be seen in their repeated attempts, from the Volkan group onwards, to stir up Muslim fanaticism against the modest reforms of the Young Turk governments.

Through all these changes, the religious hierarchy in Turkey remained immensely strong. Despite the efforts of liberals, Ottomanists, and nationalists, the religious basis of the state had been reaffirmed by the assertion, in the late nineteenth and early twentieth centuries, of an Ottoman Caliphate; the religious loyalty of the people had been sharpened and intensified by the long series of foreign and civil wars, all of them against Christian adversaries. The First World War, with its German-made *jihad* and its British-made revolt in Arabia, blurred the simple lines of religious identity and conflict, but the Kemalist struggle to defend Anatolia against the ancient and familiar Greek Christian enemy brought a new intensity of religious identification and loyalty.

The defection of the Caliph and the *Şeyh-ül-Islâm* in the midst of the struggle were bitter blows, only partially atoned for by the counter-*fetva* of the Mufti of Ankara. Even after this the nationalists still tried to avoid a break; only twelve days after the *fetva* of

[5] Abdulhak Adnan-Adıvar, 'Interaction of Islamic and Western Thought in Turkey', in T. Cuyler Young, ed., *Near Eastern Culture and Society* (1951), pp. 125–6.

[6] For a survey of these ideological movements see Tunaya, ' "Islamcılık" Cereyanı.' cf. above, pp. 229 ff.

Dürrizade the Grand National Assembly began its proceedings with public prayers and reaffirmed its loyalty to the Sultan. As late as February 1921 a pan-Islamic conference met in Sivas, for the obvious purpose of rallying world Muslim opinion to the nationalist cause.[7]

The bitter hostility of the supreme religious authorities in Istanbul, and the military and terrorist action of 'the army of the Caliphate' whom they launched against the nationalists, made the reconciliation impossible. Even so, Kemal attempted a compromise by retaining the Caliphate, under the Republic, after the Sultanate had been abolished.[8] But this compromise, utterly alien to the spirit of Islam, accorded neither with the traditions of the past nor with the needs of the moment, and was abandoned after a few months.

Within four years, in a series of swift and sweeping changes, Kemal repealed the Holy Law and disestablished Islam. The stages are well known—the restriction and then prohibition of religious education, the adoption of European civil and penal codes, the nationalization of pious foundations, the reduction and eventual elimination of the power of the ulema, the transformation of social and cultural symbols and practices, such as dress and headgear, the calendar and the alphabet. The coping-stone of the edifice of legal secularism was laid in April 1928, when Islam was removed from the constitution.[9]

But the frontal assault on the *Şeriat* and the hierarchy of its exponents was only one aspect of the religious conflict. There was another, less publicized by Western writers, but vitally important— the struggle with the dervish brotherhoods, known as *tarikat*, from an Arabic word meaning way or path.

The Tarikats [10]

Turkish Islam had always functioned on two levels; the formal, legal, dogmatic religion of the state, the schools and the hierarchy;

---

[7] Rustow 'Politics and Islam', pp. 75 ff.; Jäschke, in *WI*, xviii. 63 ff. (where translations of the two *fetvas* are given).

[8] See above, pp. 252 ff.

[9] For a detailed account of these changes, see Toynbee, in RIIA, *Survey, 1925*, i. 25–81; cf. the monthly surveys in *OM*, and above, pp. 256 ff.

[10] The Muslim *tarikats* have still received very little attention from Western scholarship. The only comprehensive study is still that of Depont and Coppolani, mainly concerned with North Africa and of course rather out of date. For Turkey it may be

and the popular, mystical, intuitive faith of the masses, which found its chief expression in the great dervish orders.

The interior of an Islamic mosque is simple and austere. There is no altar and no sanctuary, for Islam has no sacraments and no ordained priesthood. The imam—the authorized representative of orthodoxy—has neither priestly nor pastoral function; he is a leader in prayer, and a guide in religious law. Public prayer is a disciplined, communal act of submission to the One, remote, and immaterial God. It admits of no saints and no mediators, no drama and no mystery. Like Judaism and, with a few exceptions, Christianity, orthodox Islam has rejected dancing from among the devotional arts; unlike them, it has rejected music and poetry too, and confines its liturgy to the recitation of a few simple formulas of piety.

From early times the orthodox faith—austere in its worship, abstract in its teachings, remote and conformist in its politics—failed to satisfy the religious and social cravings of important sections of the population. In medieval times they had often found satisfaction in various Shi'ite sects, stigmatized by the ulema as heretical; since the Mongol invasions they had turned rather to the brotherhoods which, though frequently accused of heterodox leanings and regarded with suspicion by the hierarchy, had remained within the broad framework of Sunni orthodoxy.

To these brotherhoods, and their dervish leaders, the common people turned for help and guidance where orthodox Islam was lacking or deficient. To supplement the austere ritual of the mosque, there was the ecstatic prayer meeting in the dervish convent, aided by music, song, and dance. To compensate for the academic aloofness of the ulema, there was the warm, personal influence of the dervish, the friend, pastor, and guide; to bridge the orthodox gulf between man and God, there were saints and intercessors and holy men, and the hope of a mystical union with the Godhead.

supplemented by J. P. Brown, *The Dervishes* (1868; re-edited by H. A. Rose, 1927); Ubicini, letter 5; Hasluck, and, among more recent scholarly studies, H. J. Kissling, 'The Sociological and Educational Role of the Dervish Orders in the Ottoman Empire', in Von Grunebaum, ed., *Studies in Islamic Cultural History* (1954), pp. 23–35; Snouck-Hurgronje, iii. 149–206 (important corrections to Depont and Coppolani on the role of the *tarikats* under Abdülhamid); on the role of the *tarikats* in the Young Turk period, Hartmann, iii. 14 ff. 69, 92 ff., 191 ff., 221 ff., &c., and *RMM*, xxii (1913), 171–2. In general, Jäschke, in *WI*, n.s., i. 58 ff.

All the dervish orders were to some extent unorthodox and their teachings and practices were the subject of repeated criticisms and denunciations by the custodians of the law. This did not prevent the brotherhoods from retaining and extending their influence over the Muslim masses, who found in the dervishes their real religious guides. While the ulema were becoming a wealthy, hereditary caste, the dervishes remained part of the people, with immense influence and prestige among them. Often, in earlier times, we find the dervishes as instigators of religio-social revolts— for piety against legalism, for sanctity against learning, for the masses against the ruling political and religious order. At other times we find them penetrating into the apparatus of government, and wielding a powerful though hidden influence on the actions of ministers and Sultans.

The different orders were by no means always in accord. Often there were bitter rivalries between them, aggravated by the personal antagonisms of their leaders, and the state did not, at times, disdain to pit them against one another.[11] These differences were sometimes doctrinal as well as personal and sectarian. Some orders stood comparatively close to orthodoxy, such as the Kadiris, the Halvetis, and the Nakşbendis—though the quietism and docility of the first contrasted strongly with the driving political ambitions of the second and the aggressive fanaticism of the third. Others, like the widespread Bektaşi and Mevlevi orders, were lax and latitudinarian, suspected of Shi'ite tendencies, and of pandering to the Christian and pagan beliefs and practices that had lingered on among the common people. Both had extensive followings in Turkey; both came to play a great role in the Ottoman Sultanate. The Bektaşis had their main support among village populations, especially in European Turkey. The origins of the order have been sought in Central Asia and even in Turco-Mongol Shamanism; later, in Anatolia and Europe, the Bektaşis absorbed a good deal of popular Christianity, and played an important role as a link between the Turks and their Christian subjects, for whom they offered a gentler transition to Islam. They were closely associated with the corps of Janissaries, serving as chaplains for its newly Islamized recruits. The Mevlevis were a more urban order, flourishing especially in the provincial towns of Anatolia, but with important branches in Rumelia also, notably

---

[11] Kissling, p. 31.

in Salonika. They too obtained a position of influence in the state, thus counter-balancing the Bektaşis and their Janissary acolytes. The head of the Mevlevi order was a well-known and highly respected figure; from 1648 he officiated at the ceremony of girding the sword of Osman, on the accession of a new Sultan.[12]

By the eighteenth century the brotherhoods had established themselves in almost every town and village in Turkey. Through their close links with the guilds and corporations, they were able to dominate the professional and social, as well as the religious life of the artisan and much of the merchant classes. Though primarily popular movements, they had their adherents and lay brothers in all walks of society, reaching even into the higher ranks of the governing *élite*. During the seventeenth and eighteenth centuries they even managed to penetrate the orthodox institution itself, and, by impressing a more personal and more ethical stamp on orthodox thought and education, helped to bring the two levels of Islam closer to one another.

In the revulsion against European conquest in the nineteenth century, the brotherhoods played an active role. Most of these actions were outside Turkey—the Nakşbendis in the Russian Caucasus, the Senusis in North Africa, the Khatmiyya in the Sudan, for example; their struggle against modernism and Western rule was bound to have repercussions in Turkey, however, and in the late nineteenth and early twentieth centuries several of the more activist orders seem to have created or revived branches in Turkey. Notable among these was the Ticani order, a Berber offshoot of the Halvetiyya, which spread to Turkey at a comparatively recent date.[13]

Little is heard of the brotherhoods during the period of *Tanzimat*, when, after some initial resistance,[14] they seem to have remained indifferent to the political arguments and changes of the time.

[12] For a brief general account of the Bektaşi order see *EI*[2], ('Bektāshiyya', by R. Tschudi); for a more detailed study, J. K. Birge, *The Bektashi Order of Dervishes* (1937); on their political role, E. E. Ramsaur, 'The Bektashi Dervishes and the Young Turks', *Moslem Wld*. (1942), pp. 7–14. On the Mevlevis, see *EI*[1] ('Mawlawiyya', by D. S. Margoliouth), and Gölpınarlı, *Mevlânâ'dan sonra Mevlevîlik* (1953).

[13] For their earlier history see *EI*[1] ('Tidjaniyya', by D. S. Margoliouth); for comments on their more recent activities in Turkey, see E. Marmorstein, 'Religious Opposition to Nationalism in the Middle East', *Int. Aff.*, xxviii (1952), 344–59.

[14] The Bektaşi were for a time banned, after the destruction of the Janissaries; see above, p. 78.

They return to prominence during the reign of Abdülhamid II, when several of their leaders, profiting from the religiosity of the Sultan, obtained positions of influence and dignity in his entourage. It is interesting, however, that the dervish leaders closest to the Sultan were Arabs, such as the Syrian Abu'l-Huda and the Hejazi Sayyid Ahmad As'ad, leaders of the Rifa'i order, or the Medinese Muhammad Zafir, leader of the Shadhiliyya, to which the Sultan himself is said to have belonged.[15]

The role of the brotherhoods in Sultan Abdülhamid's pan-Islamic policy has been greatly exaggerated. The more purely Turkish orders, the Bektaşis and Mevlevis, remained coldly indifferent, while even the Shadhili and Rifa'i orders seem to have used their twin vantage points, in Istanbul and in Arabia, more for mutual rivalries and recriminations than for a common pan-Islamic endeavour.[16]

Several of the orders, with their religious and political opposition to authority, seem to have sympathized with the Young Turk conspirators against Abdülhamid; the widespread and quasi-Masonic organization of the orders made them useful allies. The Bektaşis, in particular, seem to have had close links with the Young Turks, several of whose leaders, including Talât Paşa, Rıza Tevfik, and the *Şeyh-ül-Islâm* Musa Kâzım Efendi were members of the brotherhood. Other orders, too, notably the antinomian Melamis, claim to have played an active role in the revolutionary movement.[17]

After the revolution of 1908 the brotherhoods attracted the attention of several of the rival political parties and factions. Their usefulness was obvious. They had wide distribution and profound influence; the high regard and affection in which they were held by the mass of the people contrasted both with the tarnished glories of the old political order and the untried innovations of the new. Young Turks and Old Turks tried to make the brotherhoods and convents the vehicles of their propaganda. In thus confusing popular religion and party politics, they established a practice which was followed to the end of the Empire, and which has not yet been extirpated in the Republic.

The political role of the brotherhoods during the second

---

[15] Snouck-Hurgronje, pp. 191–7.   [16] Ibid. pp. 149 ff.

[17] See Hartmann for the best information on the brotherhoods in this period. The various *tarikats* are listed in the index.

constitutional period is not easy to determine with any accuracy. Some, like the Nakşbendi order, seem to have been systematically opposed to any derogation from the rule of the Caliphate and the Holy Law; others, like the Bektaşis, seem to have rejoiced in the overthrow of the personal tyranny of Abdülhamid, and to have offered sympathy and even help to the Young Turks. In the main, however, the dervishes seem to have allowed themselves to be used as tools in a political game which they did not understand. Even the headship of some of the orders was affected. In 1908 Abdülhalim Çelebi, the hereditary chief of the Mevlevi dervishes, was deposed by the Young Turks and replaced by Veled Çelebi, a man of letters and a patriot, who contributed many articles in the press, and who formed and led a Mevlevi volunteer brigade during the First World War. In 1918 he was deposed by the Sultan's government, and replaced by his predecessor Abdülhalim, who, however, represented Konya in the first National Assembly. Veled Çelebi served in the Assembly in 1923, and played a role of some importance.[18]

In general the brotherhoods seem to have rallied to the support of the nationalists in Anatolia. The first Grand National Assembly included ten of their leading *şeyhs*, drawn from the Mevlevi, Bektaşi, and even the Nakşbendi order.[19] Their role there was an active one, and Kemal himself seems, at one time, to have sought an alliance with the Bektaşis. But relations with the dervishes, as with the ulema, were affected by the breach with Istanbul, and some of the brotherhoods gave active and effective support to the army of the Caliphate.

The great secularizing reforms of 1924 were directed against the ulema, not the dervishes; but it soon became apparent that it was from the dervishes, not the ulema, that the most dangerous resistance to laicism would come. The ulema, long accustomed to wielding the authority of the state, were unpractised in opposing it. The dervishes were used to independence and opposition; they still enjoyed the confidence and loyalty of the common people and, unlike the ulema, were untarnished by collaboration with the invader. In some areas, notably in the Kurdish provinces, veritable dervish dynasties had emerged, replacing the vanished *derebeys* and autonomous princes as the exponents of local particularism. The rebellion of 1925 has been described as a Kurdish nationalist or

[18] Gölpınarlı, *Mevlevîlik*, pp. 273 ff. [19] Tunaya, 'Karakter', p. 5.

secessionist movement, but in view of its dervish leadership and its declared objectives, it seems not unreasonable to accept the government's description of it as a religious reaction against the secularizing reforms. The two characters are in any case difficult to distinguish. On 29 June 1925 the 'independence tribunal' in Diyarbakır passed sentence of death on the leaders of the rebellion. The same judgement ordered the closing of all the dervish convents in Kurdistan.[20]

After this warning, Kemal prepared for a more comprehensive attack on the brotherhoods and on the way of life that they represented. In August 1925 he went on a visit to Kastamonu and Inebolu. It was on this occasion that he and the officials accompanying him first wore Panama hats, and that, in a series of speeches, he launched the great attack on the fez, the gown, the *shalvar*, and the rest of the traditional garments of Turkish Muslims. His attack, however, was not limited to the symbols of the old way of life. In a speech delivered in Kastamonu on 30 August he spoke of the dervish convents, retreats, and brotherhoods, of their so-called saints and holy men, of the tombs to which the ignorant and superstitious went to seek for help and guidance.

. . . the aim of the revolutions which we have been and are now accomplishing is to bring the people of the Turkish Republic into a state of society entirely modern and completely civilized in spirit and form. This is the central pillar of our Revolution, and it is necessary utterly to defeat those mentalities incapable of accepting this truth. Hitherto there have been many of this mentality, rusting and deadening the mind of the nation. In any case, the superstitions dwelling in people's minds will be completely driven out, for as long as they are not expelled, it will not be possible to bring the light of truth into men's minds.

Kemal then gave some examples of these superstitions, and went on to speak of the saints and their tombs, and more generally, of the brotherhoods and their convents:

To seek help from the dead is a disgrace to a civilized community. . . . What can be the objects of the existing brotherhoods (*tarikat*) other than to secure the well-being, in worldly and moral life, of those who follow them? I flatly refuse to believe that today, in the luminous presence of science, knowledge, and civilization in all its aspects, there exist, in

[20] See above, pp. 260 ff.

the civilized community of Turkey, men so primitive as to seek their material and moral well-being from the guidance of one or another *şeyh*. Gentlemen, you and the whole nation must know, and know well, that the Republic of Turkey cannot be the land of *şeyhs*, dervishes, disciples, and lay brothers. The straightest, truest Way (*tarikat*) is the way of civilization. To be a man, it is enough to do what civilization requires. The heads of the brotherhoods will understand this truth that I have uttered in all its clarity, and will of their own accord at once close their convents, and accept the fact that their disciples have at last come of age.[21]

The blow against the brotherhoods was not long delayed. On 1 September Kemal returned to Ankara, and on the following day, after a meeting of the cabinet, he announced a series of new decrees. By these decrees, confirmed by laws passed in November in the Assembly, the brotherhoods were dissolved and banned, their assets impounded, their convents and sanctuaries closed, their prayer meetings and ceremonies prohibited. Henceforth, Turkey was to be free from

şeyhs, dervishes, disciples, *dede, seyyid, çelebi, baba, emir, nakib, halife*, fortune-tellers, magicians, witch-doctors, writers of amulets for the recovery of lost property or the fulfilment of wishes, as well as the services, dues, and costumes pertaining to these titles and qualities. . . .[22]

These measures, accompanied by the ban on the fez and turban, aroused widespread resistance—far more than had the deposition of the Caliph and the repeal of the *Şeriat*. In the words of the official history:

The closing of the convents and monasteries, the abolition of the religious orders had naturally displeased the many fanatical *şeyhs* and dervishes, who, living in idleness in these homes of laziness, exploited the religious sentiments of the credulous people and put all their interests in the reaction. In several regions they tried to raise the people against the achievements of the Revolution and against the republican régime. But they were swiftly punished, and the nation adopted and rapidly assimilated these reforms.[23]

Significantly, the powers of the independence tribunals were renewed by the Assembly in February and again in May 1926; their work, supported by the military and even the naval forces of the Republic, was swift and efficient.

[21] *Söylev*, ii. 217 ff.; cf. *Hist.*, pp. 233–4, and Imece, pp. 59 ff.
[22] Jäschke, in *WI*, n.s., i. 61–62.   [23] *Hist.*, pp. 235–6.

By a curious oversight, article 75 of the constitution, guarantee-ing freedom of 'religion, doctrine, *tarikat*, or philosophic belief', had remained in force, even while the *tarikats* were dissolved and suppressed. This inconsistency was remedied by an amendment of 5 January 1937, rewording the article and omitting the reference to *tarikat*. The Minister of the Interior of the time made the purpose clear. The dervish brotherhoods were an evil legacy from the past, distracting the Turks from the true 'way', that of nation-alism, resting on the true knowledge, that of the positive sciences. This was the way of the greatest benefit for the material and moral life of the Turks.[24]

Religious Reform

The basis of Kemalist religious policy was laicism, not irreligion; its purpose was not to destroy Islam, but to disestablish it—to end the power of religion and its exponents in political, social, and cultural affairs, and limit it to matters of belief and worship. In thus reducing Islam to the role of religion in a modern, Western, nation-state, the Kemalists also made some attempt to give their religion a more modern and more national form.

The principle of the separation of religion from politics appears already in the Law against High Treason, passed by the Grand National Assembly on 29 April 1920 in response to the anti-nationalist *fetva* of Dürrizade, and containing provisions against the misuse of religion for political purpose. The principle was reaffirmed in the Criminal Code of 1926, which lays down penal-ties for those

who, by misuse of religion, religious sentiments, or things that are religiously considered as holy, in any way incite the people to action prejudicial to the security of the state, or form associations for this purpose. . . . Political associations on the basis of religion or religious sentiments may not be formed (Art. 163).

The same code prescribes punishments for religious leaders and preachers who, in the course of their functions, bring the admin-istration, laws, or executive actions of the government into dis-repute, or incite to disobedience (art. 241 and 242) or who conduct religious celebrations and processions outside recognized places of worship (art. 529).[25]

It was one thing to exclude the professional exponents of Islam

[24] Jäschke, in *WI*, n.s., i. 63.   [25] Ibid. pp. 54–55.

from the workings of a modern, national state. It was quite another to modernize and nationalize Islam itself. But the attempt was made. For the *tarikats* there could be no mercy. Their popular support, their radical traditions, their Masonic organization, all made them too little amenable to state control, too dangerous for experiment. The ulema, on the other hand, with their hierarchy, their schools, and their habits of intellectual and administrative discipline, seemed to offer a more favourable field for an experiment in Erastian Islam.

The reorganization of the hierarchy was initiated with the law of 1924, abolishing the office of *Şeyh-ül-Islâm* and the Ministry of Religious Affairs and pious foundations which, in the Ankara government, had taken over most of the functions of the *Şeyh-ül-Islâm's* department. In their place two separate offices were established, a Presidency for Religious Affairs (*Diyanet Işleri Reisliği*) and a Directorate-General of Pious Foundations (*Evkâf Umum Müdürlüğü*). The head of Religious Affairs was nominated by the Prime Minister, to whose department he and his office were attached. These duties were the administration of mosques, convents, &c., the appointment and dismissal of imams, preachers, muezzins, and other mosque functionaries, and the supervision of the muftis generally. The Directorate of Pious Foundations, not directly subordinated to any ministry, was responsible for the administration of the *evkâf* that had been taken over by the state, and for the maintenance of religious buildings and installations. From 1931 it also took over the payment of religious functionaries, leaving the Presidency of Religious Affairs with little more than the appointment of preachers, the censoring of their sermons, and the giving of an occasional ruling on a point of Holy Law.[26]

The bureaucratization of the ulema, begun by Mahmud II, had reached its logical conclusion. Islam had been made a department of state; the ulema had become minor civil servants. General education had already been taken out of the hands of the ulema. There remained the question of religious education, which the state now prepared to take over.

By the laws of 1924 the *medreses*—the old theological seminaries —were closed. The state did, however, make some attempt to provide for the further training of religious personnel. At the lower level, the Ministry of Education established some training

26 Jäschke, in *WI*, n.s., i. 96 ff.; Rustow, 'Politics and Islam', pp. 82–83.

schools for imams and preachers; at the higher level, the old Süleymaniye *Medrese* was reconstituted as a faculty of divinity in the University of Istanbul—also, therefore, under the ultimate control of the Minister of Education of the Republic in Ankara.

This new faculty of divinity was intended to serve as the centre of a new, modernized, and scientific form of religious instruction, more appropriate to a secular, Westernized republic. In 1928 the faculty appointed a committee to examine the problem of reform and modernization in the Islamic religion, and to make proposals through the University to the Ministry of Education. The chairman of the committee was Professor Mehmed Fuad Köprülü; its members included the professors of psychology and logic as well as a number of theologians.

Its report, published in June 1928, begins with a clear assertion that religion is a social institution; like other social institutions it must meet the needs of social life and keep pace with change and development. 'Therefore, in the Turkish democracy, religion should also manifest the vitality and progress which it needs.'

It is almost impossible [the report goes on] with the modern views of society, to expect such a reform, however much the ground may be ready for it, from the working of mystic and irrational elements. Religious life, like moral and economic life, must be reformed on scientific lines, that it may be in harmony with other institutions. . . .

The recommendations of the committee, for the achievement of this purpose, was grouped under four headings. The first, 'the form of worship', speaks of the need for clean and orderly mosques, with pews and cloakrooms. 'People must be urged to enter into them with clean shoes.' The second, on 'the language of worship', insists that this must be Turkish, and that all prayers and sermons should not be in Arabic but in the national language. The third, on 'the character of worship', seeks to make worship beautiful, inspiring, and spiritual. For this the mosque needs trained musicians and also musical instruments. 'The need is urgent for modern and sacred instrumental music.' The fourth, and last, deals with 'the thought side of worship'. Printed, set sermons must be replaced by real religious guidance, which only preachers with the necessary philosophic training would be competent to give.[27]

[27] Cited in Lutfy Levonian, *The Turkish Press* (1932), pp. 174 ff.

It was possible to turn the Ottoman Sultanate into a national republic, with a president, ministries, and parliament. It was not possible to turn the mosque into a Muslim church, with pews, organ, and an imam-precentor. In all but one respect, the recommendations of the committee were a dead letter, and even the faculty of divinity itself proved to be premature. The teachers, themselves of the *medrese* tradition, did not take kindly to the task assigned to them, and the atmosphere of the time was not conducive to its realization. The abolition, in 1929, of Arabic and Persian as subjects of instruction in the secondary schools reduced both the numbers and the competence of the students. After some abortive attempts at reform, the faculty was finally suppressed in 1933, and replaced in due course by an Institute of Oriental Studies attached to the faculty of arts. During the nine years that the faculty of divinity existed, the number of its students dropped from 284 to 20. In the same period there was a parallel decline in the schools for imams and preachers, and the last two such schools were closed in 1932. Except for the comparatively unimportant schools for Koran-readers, formal religious education disappeared in Turkey, and the attempt to form a new class of modern religious guides was completely abandoned.

Only one of the recommendations of the 1928 committee had any practical consequences—that of the Turkicization of worship. Attempts were made to translate the Koran and the Traditions of the Prophet into Turkish, and in 1932 the Assembly voted a sum of TL4,000 for the preparation and publication of such a translation. It was not completed. An attempt to translate the mosque service into Turkish was abandoned in the face of opposition. In one respect, however, the government held firm. Even if Arabic were still to be used inside the mosque, it could not be tolerated in public places. Years before, Ziya Gökalp, the theoretician of Turkish nationalism, had demanded that the call to prayer, from the minarets of Turkish mosques, should be uttered in the Turkish language.[28]

> A land where the call to prayer from the mosque is recited in Turkish
> Where the peasant understands the meaning of the prayer in his worship,
> A land where in the schools the Koran is read in Turkish,
> Where, big and little, everyone knows the command of God—
> This, O son of the Turks, is your fatherland.[29]

[28] Heyd, *Foundations*, pp. 102–3.   [29] *Yeni Hayat*, 1918.

On 30 January 1932 the cry 'God is great' resounded from the minarets of Santa Sophia, for the first time, in Turkish, and shortly afterwards a version of the call, in 'pure' Turkish, was prepared by the Linguistic Society and published by the Presidency of Religious Affairs. A Turkish melody was ordered from the Conservatory in Ankara.[30] Muezzins all over Turkey were instructed in the new version, and an order issued early in 1933 made it an offence to give the call to prayer in Arabic. 'It seems that this one act of government interference in the ritual caused more widespread popular resentment than any of the other secularist measures.'[31]

Survival and Rebirth [32]

During the 1930's the pressure of secularization in Turkey became very strong indeed. Although the régime never adopted an avowedly anti-Islamic policy, its desire to end the power of organized Islam and break its hold on the minds and hearts of the Turkish people was clear. The prohibition of religious education, the transfer of mosques to secular purposes, reinforced the lesson of the legal and social reforms. In the rapidly growing new capital, no new mosques were built. Most striking, and most symbolic, was the fate of the great basilica of Santa Sophia in Istanbul. Sultan Mehmed the Conqueror, in the moment of triumph over Byzantium, had made it a mosque; the Republic made it a museum.[33]

In spite of all this, there is much evidence that the secularization of Turkey was never quite as complete as was sometimes believed. In the first place, there were many indications of the persistence, beneath the surface, of popular religion in the form of the cult of dervish *şeyhs*, especially in Anatolia. As late as 1930

---

[30] Jäschke, in *WI*, n.s., i. 74–75.   [31] Rustow, 'Politics and Islam', p. 84.

[32] Religious revival in Turkey in recent years has attracted the attention of many writers. Besides the writings of Jäschke and Rustow already cited, mention may be made of the following: Heyd, 'Islam in Modern Turkey', *R.C.As.J.*, xxxiv (1947), 299–308; B. Lewis, 'Islamic Revival in Turkey', *Int. Aff.*, xxviii (1952), 38–48; Thomas, 'Recent Developments in Turkish Islam', *MEJ*, vi (1952), 22–40; H. A. Reed, 'Revival of Islam in Secular Turkey', ibid. viii (1954), 267–82; A. L. Tibawi, 'Islam and Secularism in Turkey Today', *Quart. R.* (1956), pp. 325–37; Paul Stirling, 'Religious Change in Republican Turkey', *MEJ*, xii (1958), 395–408; W. Cantwell Smith, *Islam in Modern History* (1957), pp. 161–205. For a discussion of religion and politics by a Turkish scholar, see Karpat, pp. 271 ff.

[33] Rustow 'Politics and Islam', p. 84.

a striking incident occurred in Menemen, near Izmir. A young Kemalist officer called Kubilay heard a local dervish leader addressing the populace and attacking the régime. When he remonstrated, he was seized by the mob, held down, and slowly beheaded, amid the acclamation of the *şeyh* and his supporters. The guilty were punished, and a monument was erected to the memory of Kubilay, at which a ceremony of commemoration was held every year until 1951.

After the death of Atatürk there were rumours of a religious restoration, but apart from the return of Muslim chaplains to the army in May 1940 nothing very much happened. The first open sign of religious opposition to the secularist policy of the state appeared in 1940. In the previous year the Turkish Ministry of Education decided to publish a Turkish edition of the *Encyclopaedia of Islam*, the great co-operative work published in Leiden by an international team of European Orientalists. The Turkish edition was not to be a mere translation. Many articles which were out of date were to be revised or rewritten by Turkish scholars, and many new articles added, but the whole was intended to be in the same spirit of scientific scholarship as had informed the Leiden publication. A group of religious-minded Turks, led by Eşref Edib, who had been editor of the Muslim periodical *Sebil-ür-Reşad* in the Young Turk era, protested energetically against this project. They said that the so-called *Encyclopaedia of Islam* was not really an encyclopaedia of Islam but against Islam, and that it was the work of Christian missionaries, aimed partly at assisting missionaries in their endeavours and partly at undermining the basis of the Muslim faith. They criticized the Ministry of Education for sponsoring this allegedly anti-Islamic project, first in letters and articles in the press and then in a periodical which they published themselves. In 1941 they began the publication of a rival encyclopaedia of their own, entitled *Türk Islâm Ansiklopedisi* (Turkish Encyclopaedia of Islam), on the same pattern as the official one, but with all the contributions written from what they believed to be a strictly Muslim point of view. Each fascicule of their encyclopaedia was accompanied by a magazine supplement containing violent and often scurrilous criticisms of the current fascicules of the other encyclopaedia which were meanwhile issuing from the Ministry.

The new post-war democracy of Turkey gave a very much

greater degree of freedom of expression to all trends of opinion, including of course the religious leaders, who now proclaimed more and more openly their hostility to secularism and their demands for an Islamic restoration.

The first issue that was publicly debated was that of religious education. The debate began with private discussions and moderately phrased articles in the press, and then, on 24 December 1946, a full-dress debate was held on the subject in the Assembly in Ankara. Several members of the Government Party spoke in favour of restoring religious education, and although the Prime Minister firmly refused to accede to their request, the mere fact that the debate was held at all was widely regarded, in the rather authoritarian Turkey of that time, as portending a coming change of policy. A long controversy followed in the press, parliament, and elsewhere. Should religious education be tolerated? Should it be compulsory or optional in schools? Should it be controlled by the Ministry of Education or by the Presidency of Religious Affairs, which, after years of quiescence, was now burgeoning into new life? These questions were eventually settled by a compromise. At the beginning of 1949 religious education was reintroduced to Turkish schools. It consisted of two hours' instruction on Saturday afternoons, and was only to be taken by children whose parents specifically asked for it. The overwhelming majority did. The textbook was prepared by a joint committee of representatives of the Ministry of Education and the Presidency of Religious Affairs, and presents a modernized version of Islam which Muslims in, say, Mecca or even Damascus would probably have some difficulty in recognizing.

The next step came in October 1950, when it was decided to make religious education compulsory—or rather, when parents were required to opt out instead of in, as previously. This applied only to the fourth and fifth classes of the primary schools. For the rest of the school years religious instruction remained optional.

These changes, together with the growing interest in religious matters and the increase in public worship, raised the question of religious higher education. For many years there had been no higher religious instruction, and the religious revival therefore revealed an acute shortage of people competent to teach religion, even in schools, and to undertake the various religious functions in mosques. This lack of men with a serious religious education gave scope to fanatics and illiterates in the religious revival, often with unfortunate results. It was no doubt for this reason, at least in part, that the government decided to restore the faculty of divinity, which opened its gates to students in October 1949. Several features of the new faculty strike the outside observer. Unlike its predecessor, it was not in Istanbul, the old religious centre, with its great mosques, libraries, and traditions, but in Ankara, the new city, the heart of republican Turkey and the seat of the government. Unlike the old *medreses*, it was a part of the University, and therefore ultimately under the control of the Ministry of Education. The first chairs to be established included Islamic Art and History of Religions.[34]

After the war there were a number of signs of increasing religious activity, and one of the most striking was the growing self-assertiveness of religious functionaries. For a long time they had been very quiet and did not dare to raise their voices, certainly not in the towns, and hardly even in country places. Now they began to be much more in evidence. The wearing of religious garb outside mosques was still forbidden, but the beret, which presents obvious advantages for Muslim worship, became the social equivalent of the former turban of the religious hierarchy. For a time even the beret was banned in Turkey, precisely because it had assumed that character, but soon old gentlemen with beards and berets were to be seen in many places, voicing their views and demands with growing vigour. The survivors of the ulema had become more ambitious. Some of them openly demanded control of religious education, and they began, in a tentative way, to intervene in politics. In about 1950 they started a demand for the return of the *evkâf* to the Presidency of Religious Affairs, and if that is granted—it has not been yet—it will of course give them a great increase in power and influence.

Mosque attendance rose considerably. Many of the mosques were now equipped with amplifiers; inscribed Arabic texts appeared on the walls in cafés, shops, taxis, and in the markets, and were offered for sale in the streets. Religious books and pamphlets were written and published on an ever-increasing scale. Besides a great number of pamphlets of popular piety, there were

---

[34] Reed, 'The Faculty of Divinity in Ankara', *Muslim Wld.*, xlvi (1956), 295–312, and xlvii (1957), 22–35.

books on Islam, biographies of the Prophet and other figures, works on Islamic history, theology, and mysticism, translations of and commentaries on the Koran.

Quite a considerable number of Turks began to make the pilgrimage to Mecca. In 1950 there were nearly 9,000, in spite of the fact that the government gave no allocation of foreign currency for the purpose. Three of the major Istanbul dailies sent special correspondents to cover the pilgimage, and the popular press in general gave increased attention to religious matters.

Far more significant were the many signs of a revival of the *tarikats*, which had continued to exist secretly right through the republican era. It was natural enough that the dervish brother-hoods should be encouraged by the growing official tolerance of Islam to reassert themselves, but apparently the government was not prepared to extend the same indulgence to popular, mystical Islam as to orthodoxy. This government mistrust of the *tarikats* was not new. Even the sultans, in earlier times, had looked askance at some of the orders because of the suspicion of heterodoxy and dissidence attached to them, and of the dangerous, pent-up energies which they could release. During the war years there were occasional arrests of dervish *şeyhs*. A major episode began in April 1950 when a *şeyh* of the Ticani order, called Kemal Pilâvoğlu, was arrested and brought to trial in Ankara. The trial awoke very great interest; thousands of the *şeyh's* followers thronged the streets outside the court house, came into the court-room and interrupted the trial by shouting and demonstrating. Eventually, for the remainder of the proceedings, the court house had to be guarded by a cordon of 200 policemen. The *şeyh* claimed to have 40,000 followers. Later there were a number of similar proceedings against other orders—Nakşbendis in May 1950, Mevlevis in June, Kadiris in March 1951.[35]

A considerable religious press grew up in Turkey during and after the war, and by 1950 there were many periodicals devoted wholly or mainly to religious matters and to the propagation of religious ideas. These may be divided into three main categories. The most widely read were the popular journals, mainly weekly magazines, addressed primarily to artisans and peasants, to be read aloud where necessary. They presented a form of simple piety

---

[35] Rustow, 'Politics and Islam', pp. 97 ff.; Jäschke, *Kalender*, 1942–51, index 'Derwischorden'.

which probably very well reflected the mind of the people to whom they were addressed. A second group has been well described as 'Boulevard Fascism with religious colouring matter'. The outstanding example was *Büyük Doğu* (Great Orient), a rather scurrilous periodical, appearing at irregular intervals and edited by the poet Necib Fazıl Kısakürek. *Büyük Doğu* was clericalist, nationalist, and monarchist, and appeared to be a Turkish *calque* on the *Action Française*, with the House of Osman in place of the 'forty kings who in a thousand years made France'. The third and most interesting group consists of those journals with some intellectual pretensions. The most important were the *Türk Islâm Ansiklopedisi*, *Selâmet*, and *Sebil-ür-Reşad*. The last purported to be a revival of the journal of the same name published under the Young Turks. Most of the contributors were survivors from that period, and were incidentally also responsible for many of the religious books which were appearing. These journals appeared to enjoy the support of the Presidency of Religious Affairs.

The content of these journals was somewhat disappointing. The religious journals of the Young Turk period maintained a very high standard, and were written by men thoroughly conversant with Islam, its literature, its doctrines, its traditions. But most of these men were dead, and the few survivors showed all too plainly the scars of thirty years of frustration and isolation. In the absence of any religious higher education, no successors could appear to replace them. The journals were for the most part clericalist rather than religious in any real sense. They were xenophobe, usually anti-Western, often anti-Christian, treating most of what they discussed in a rather crude and violent political manner. Articles on India, for example, which occasionally appeared, consisted of communal pamphleteering, and showed no awareness of the very important religious problems and trends in modern Indian and Pakistani Islam. Much of their content consisted of apologetics, with the familiar distortion of true Islamic values by restating them in terms of the dominant Western concepts: the historical romanticism in the presentation of the recent and remoter Islamic past; the inferiority complex that induces learned Muslims to seize on chance remarks by one or other Westerner in praise of Islam and inflate their importance beyond all reason. This romantic approach to history is found in other Muslim countries, where Muslim thinkers strive unnecessarily to justify their own civilization in Western terms. It has some novel variants in Turkey, as, for example, in the parallel attempts to show that the Ottoman ulema were really good Kemalists and Republicans and that Kemal himself was a good and faithful Muslim.

Only occasionally does one find a serious attempt to face the problems of Islam in the modern world and the role of Islam in a modern state. Here the ideas derive mainly from two sources— the Indian and Egyptian reformers of the nineteenth century. Ahmed Hamdi Akseki, the late chief of the Presidency of Religious Affairs, and Ömer Rıza Doğrul, one of the most active religious journalists, were both good Arabic and English scholars, and translated books from both sources.

It is still not easy to assess the political role of this religious revival in modern Turkey. With the restoration of freedom of opinion Islam necessarily became a political issue again, and the fear of giving the advantage of religious support to the other side led both of the major parties to give at least toleration, often encouragement, to this movement. At the same time both the Republican and Democrat Parties seemed anxious to keep it within bounds. No interference was tolerated in matters which the government regarded as vital. The *tarikats* were still held in check, the *evkâf* were not restored. Despite the demands of some extremists, such changes as the return to the Arabic alphabet or the repeal of the social legislation of the Republic were not under serious consideration. At the same time it was clear that the strength of the religious revival was such, that in a democratic Turkey no party could dare to ignore it, or even perhaps to oppose it. If the revival continued to grow in strength and momentum, it was not impossible that even these reforms might be endangered.

What elements supported the religious revival? From 1924 religion was not an open political factor in Turkey, and its real strength and basis of support are not very well known. The younger intellectuals—those educated in the schools and universities of the Republic—seemed, with some exceptions, to be very little affected and to regard it with feelings ranging from irritation to contempt. The main opposition to it was in the universities. But their dislike of the current form and leadership of clerical reaction should not mislead us into thinking that they had done with Islam itself. Islam is too deeply rooted an element in the Turkish national identity to be lightly cast aside, and a form of faith more suited to nationalist intellectuals may yet awake a wide response.

Officials, as a class, are extremely sensitive to changes in the direction of the wind. In the civil service, in the army, and even in parliament piety became fashionable, and while by no means all favoured the full programme of the reactionaries, many felt that both for moral and for political reasons some restoration of Islamic belief and practice was necessary for the health of the Turkish people. The peasantry were still as religious as they had always been. For them there was no question of a revival—the only difference was that they could now express their religious sentiments more openly.

Perhaps one of the strongest elements supporting the revival was the class known in Turkey as the *esnaf*—the artisans and small shopkeepers in the towns. These were generally very fanatical, and, like the peasants, many of them were connected with one or another of the *tarikats*. Finally, the merchant class was interested in any additional form of insurance against Communism, and had a tradition of pious observance, at least in the provinces.

How far the religious revival was in fact an insurance against Communism was a subject of some discussion. The accusation is often made, in secularist quarters, that the revival, at least on the level of popular, dervish religion, was inspired by Communist agitators. The Anatolian brotherhoods have in the past been no strangers to a form of primitive religious communism which clever propagandists might exploit for political ends. Developments in other Muslim countries show that Communism is not averse to collaborating with movements of mass fanaticism where these appear to offer the best chance of undermining the existing order. How far this was happening in Turkey is anyone's guess—though on the whole the ancient and deep-rooted Turkish mistrust of Russian expansionism makes Turkey a singularly barren soil for Communist seeds.

The leaders of the religious revival were mainly men of the older generation, survivors from the Young Turk period. They seem to have recruited very few young men to their number, and many secularist intellectuals claimed that there was no real religious revival at all, but simply a reassertion by certain people

DI

of sentiments which for a long time they had to keep hidden and could now proclaim openly. The movement, they said, would die with the generation which sponsored it, and was only of transitory significance.

This point of view is difficult to accept. Islam has profound roots among the Turkish people. From its foundation until its fall the Ottoman Empire was a state dedicated to the advancement or defence of the power and faith of Islam. Turkish thought, life, and letters were permeated through and through by the inherited traditions of the classical Muslim cultures, which, though transmuted into something new and distinctive, remained basically and unshakeably Islamic.[36]

After a century of Westernization, Turkey has undergone immense changes—greater than any outside observer had thought possible. But the deepest Islamic roots of Turkish life and culture are still alive, and the ultimate identity of Turk and Muslim in Turkey is still unchallenged. The resurgence of Islam after a long interval responds to a profound national need. The occasional outbursts of the *tarikats*, far more than the limited restoration of official Islam, show how powerful are the forces stirring beneath the surface.

The path that the revival will take is still not clear. If simple reaction has its way, much of the work of the last century will be undone, and Turkey will slip back into the darkness from which she so painfully emerged. But that is not the only way, nor the most probable. In Turkey, as in other Muslim countries, there are those who talk hopefully of achieving 'a synthesis of the best elements of West and East'. This is a vain hope—the clash of civilizations in history does not usually culminate in a marriage of selected best elements, but rather in a promiscuous cohabitation of good, bad, and indifferent alike. But a true revival of a religious faith on the level of modern thought and life is within the bounds of possibility. The Turkish people, by the exercise of their practical common sense and powers of improvisation, may yet find a workable compromise between Islam and modernism that will enable them, without conflict, to follow both their fathers' path to freedom and progress and their grandfathers' path to God.

[36] See the thoughtful observations of H. A. Reed, 'The Religious Life of Modern Turkish Muslims', in Frye, pp. 108–48.

Script and Language [37]

According to a doctrine introduced to Turkey from Persia at the end of the fourteenth century, and adopted by the Bektaşi order of dervishes, the image of God is the face of man, the mark of man is language, and language is expressed in the twenty-eight letters of the Arabic script, which thus contain all the mysteries of God, man, and eternity.

Orthodox Muslims would not go as far as the *hurufiya*, as the followers of these teachings are called, in their reverence for the Arabic script. They would, however, attach special sanctity to the language and writing in which the Koran was revealed. For the believer, the text of the Koran—including the script in which it is written—is uncreated, eternal, and divine. In the mosque, where representational painting or sculpture would be regarded as blasphemy verging on idolatry, their place is taken by calligraphy. The interior decoration of the mosque is based on the extensive use of Arabic writing—the names of God, the Prophet, and the early Caliphs, the Muslim creed, and verses or even whole chapters from the Koran. Many different styles of writing are used, and in the hands of the great masters the art of calligraphy achieved an intricate and recondite beauty, the mainsprings of which are not easy of access for one brought up in the Western tradition. For Muslims, the Koranic text is literally divine; to write or read it is in itself an act of worship. These decorative texts are the hymns and fugues and icons of Muslim devotion—a key to the understanding both of Muslim piety and of Muslim aesthetics.

In many societies there is a close link between religion and writing—nowhere more clearly than in the Ottoman world. The language of the South Slavs is written in Latin letters by the Catholic Croats, in Cyrillic by the orthodox Serbs. In Syria the

[37] The best comprehensive study of this subject is Uriel Heyd's monograph, *Language Reform in Modern Turkey*. Among the numerous writings on the reforms in the Turkish language and script, the following may be mentioned: J. Deny, 'La Réforme actuelle de la langue turque', *En Terre d'Islam*, x, n.s. (1935), 223–47; Rossi, 'La Questione dell' alfabeto per le lingue turche', *OM*, vii (1927), 295–310; id., 'La Riforma linguistica in Turchia', *OM*, xv (1935), 45–57; id., 'Un Decennio di Riforma linguistica in Turchia, 1932–42', *OM*, xxii (1942), 466–77; id., 'Venticinque anni di rivoluzione dell' alfabeto e venti di riforma linguistica in Turchia', *OM*, xxxiii (1953), 378–84; H. W. Duda, 'Die Gesundung der türkischen Sprachreform', *Der Islam*, xxvi (1942), 77–100. For a history of the phases of linguistic reform and simplification see Agâh Sırrı Levend, *Türk Dilinde Gelişme ve Sadeleşme Safhaları* (1949).

common Arabic language has been written in Arabic script by Muslims, in Syriac script by Christians, in Hebrew script by Jews. Greek-speaking Muslims in Crete wrote Greek in Arabic letters, while Turkish-speaking Christians in Anatolia wrote Turkish in Greek or Armenian letters, according to their Church. Not language, but script was the visible and outward sign distinguishing Muslim from unbeliever.

Turkish had not always been written in the Arabic script. The oldest known Turkish writings—the seventh-century Orkhon inscriptions—are in a runic script, and during the eighth and ninth centuries the Uygur alphabet, of north Semitic origin, came to be extensively used in Central Asia. With their conversion to Islam, however, the Turks, like all other Muslim peoples from West Africa to Indonesia, adopted the Arabic writing. By the beginning of the present century they had been using it for close on a millennium, and all other kinds of writing had been long since forgotten.

The Arabic alphabet, though admirably suited to Arabic, is peculiarly inappropriate to the Turkish language. Although Turkish contains many loanwords borrowed from Arabic and Persian, its basic structure remains very different from both, with a range of forms and sounds that the Arabic script is unable to convey. Arabic writing is in itself by no means easy to learn; in Ottoman Turkish its difficulties were augmented by a gap between spelling and pronunciation wider even than in English.

The difficulty of Ottoman Turkish was not limited to the script in which it was written. The language itself had become heavy and artificial, borrowing not only words but also expressions and even whole phrases from Persian and Arabic. In its best days Ottoman Turkish had been a magnificent instrument of expression, a worthy medium of an Imperial civilization; but in later times, and in the hands of inferior manipulators, it had become heavy, inelastic, and incredibly tortuous. For official use, a complex and intricate chancery style was evolved, full of allusion and artifice, and by the eighteenth and early nineteenth centuries Ottoman prose in general had degenerated into mere bombast—vast expanses of contorted syntax and swollen verbiage where the thin rivulet of meaning was lost in the trackless wilderness of words.

As long as writing was a privileged mystery, the perquisite

of the governing and religious *élites*, these difficulties did not greatly matter—on the contrary, they helped to restrict access and increase prestige. But the impact of Westernization and modernization in the nineteenth century raised new problems, to which liberal and national ideologies offered new answers. The Ottoman script and language were found inadequate as a medium of modern education and as a vehicle of modern knowledge and ideas; the new, secular urban middle class of officials, officers, lawyers, journalists, publicists, and politicians became increasingly impatient of the delays and restraints which their language imposed on them.

The first to raise the question of a reform in the script seems to have been Mehmed Münif Paşa (1828–1910), a Turkish publicist and public servant who was especially active in the translation and dissemination of Western scientific and scholarly literature. In May 1862, in a speech to the recently-founded 'Ottoman Scientific Society', he raised the question of a reform in the alphabet, as a necessary preliminary to the advancement and dissemination of science. Ottoman orthography was hard to teach, hard to learn; worse still, it was inaccurate and ambiguous, and could easily mislead instead of informing a reader. It was unsuited to the printing press, 'the most powerful instrument for the spreading of knowledge'; compared with the Western alphabet it was expensive and inefficient, needing two or three times as many characters. To meet these difficulties Münif Paşa proposed a reformed Arabic typography.[38]

Fourteen months later another proposal for typographical reform was made by Ahundzade Feth Ali, an Azerbayjani Turk who was Oriental Dragoman to the Russian governor of the Caucasus. Feth Ali came to Istanbul and presented to the Sultan a scheme for a revised alphabet to replace the ordinary Arabic letters used by Muslim peoples. His proposal was referred by the Grand Vezirate to the Ottoman Scientific Society for consideration. The Society, in its report, conceded the reality of the problem, but could not recommend the acceptance of Feth Ali's proposals as a solution.[39]

[38] Levend, pp. 167 ff.; Fevziye Abdullah Tansel, 'Arap Harflerinin Islâhı ve Değiştirilmesi hakkında ilk Teşebbüsler ve Neticeleri, 1862–84', *Bell.*, no. 66 (1953), 224 ff. On Münif Paşa see further Tanpınar, pp. 150 ff.; Mordtmann, i. 173 ff., and below, p. 431.

[39] Levend, pp. 169 ff.; Tansel, p. 226.

In 1869 the question became a matter of public controversy. An article in the newspaper *Hürriyet*, published by the Young Ottoman exiles in London, bitterly criticized the teaching of children in Turkish schools. While Armenian, Greek, or Jewish children at their parish schools learnt to read newspapers and letters within six months and to write letters within a year, Muslim children studied for many years without being able to read a newspaper, and even their teachers were usually unable to write a decent letter. The fault, said the author of the article, was not in the children, who were not lacking in natural intelligence, but in the whole system of education.

This article provoked an interesting reaction from Malkom Khan, Persian ambassador to the Sublime Porte. In a letter written in Persian to the editors of *Hürriyet*, he agrees that the system of Muslim education is bad, but lays the main blame on the Arabic script, the continued use of which makes adequate education impossible, and prevents the Muslims from attaining the level of European civilization. In the inadequacy of the Arabic alphabet, Malkom Khan saw the root cause of all the weakness, the poverty, insecurity, despotism, and inequity of the lands of Islam.

In a reply to Malkom Khan, published in *Hürriyet*, Namık Kemal concedes that the cause of Turkey's ills is lack of knowledge, but cannot agree that all can be blamed on the inadequacy of the alphabet. After all, he points out, English writing is as erratic and ambiguous as Turkish, yet in England and America illiteracy is very rare. The Spaniards, on the other hand, who enjoy a phonetic script, are far below the English or American level of education. In any case, Kemal says, the practical difficulties of changing the script would be insuperable.

In a letter written in 1878, Namık Kemal even gives some consideration to the possibility of writing Turkish in Latin letters. Among his objections to the adoption of the Latin alphabet are the difficulty of rendering Arabic letters in them, the awkwardness of writing from left to right ('for us, it would be like wearing trousers too narrow to bend at the knee'), and the irrelevance of alphabetic reform to the major educational problems. Some reform was indeed needed, as a practical measure, but it should take the form of modification of the Arabic letters, not of their abandonment.[40]

[40] Levend, pp. 170 ff.; Tansel, pp. 227–49.

The question of a reform of the Arabic script continued to be raised from time to time, especially in relation to typography. During the First World War another aspect of the problem appeared—the difficulties of military communication, in a medium so subject to ambiguity and error. Enver Paşa, the Minister of War, even went so far as to devise a modified Arabic script, to be used by Turkish officers in sending handwritten messages. Like other attempts at reform, it had little effect, and the end of the Ottoman Empire found the Arabic script still in a position of unchallenged supremacy.[41]

While the movement of alphabetical reform thus got off to a series of false starts, attempts at linguistic and stylistic simplification achieved more positive results. Already in the fifteenth century there had been a literary movement in favour of 'simple Turkish' (*Türkî-i basit*), to stem the flow of Persian and Arabic words and phrases into Turkish usage.[42] The movement had little effect, and the flow swelled into a flood tide.

A new phase began in the nineteenth century. One of the first reformers was the *Reis-ül-Küttab*, Akif Paşa.[43] A conservative in politics, totally ignorant of European languages and literatures, he nevertheless inaugurated a literary revolution. Abandoning the involved and ponderous 'bureaucratic style' (*usûl-i kalem*) that had become usual in Ottoman government offices, he attempted to write a simpler style, more natural and more direct. This example was followed and bettered by others, and in the writings of a mid-nineteenth-century author like Cevdet Paşa we find a model of clear and elegant Ottoman prose.

Even in this form, however, the written language remained remote from the speech of the people, and largely unintelligible to the man in the street. Many officials, moreover, were unaffected by the new style, and continued to write their orders and memoranda in the obscure and verbose chancery style of the past. A more militant attack on the old style was initiated in 1868 by Ziya Paşa, this time with a political slant, both nationalist and democratic. In a famous article called 'Poetry and Composition' (*Şiir ve inşa*), written during his exile in London, Ziya attacks the classical Ottoman court literature as artificial and alien, a medley of imitations of Arabic and Persian originals. In its place, Turkish

[41] Levend, pp. 355 ff.   [42] See above, p. 9.

[43] On Akif, see Gibb, *Ottoman Poetry*, iv. 327 ff.; Tanpınar, pp. 60 ff.; above, p. 319.

writers should turn for inspiration to the neglected but authentic Turkish folk literature, where they would find the true genius and the real language of their people. The same obscure and artificial language was still used in government offices. This made for oppression and tyranny. An essential safeguard of the rights of the subject is that he should be able to understand the language of laws and administrative orders. Thus he would be able at once to recognize and denounce any violation of his rights.

At the present day, if the officially proclaimed orders and regulations are read aloud in the presence of the populace, is any useful purpose served? Are these documents produced only for those who are proficient in the art of writing, or are they to enable the common people to understand the orders of the government? The government has issued commercial regulations for everybody; there are orders and regulations concerning tithes and taxes and the like—but let the common people in Anatolia or Rumelia be asked about them, and it will be seen that the wretches have no idea. That is why even now, in our country, the people do not know what the *Tanzimat* are or what reforms the new order has accomplished, and in most places therefore remain in the power of self-appointed local notables and tyrannical governors and officials, and are maltreated in the old, bad ways of before the *Tanzimat*, without being able to tell anyone their trouble. In France and England, on the other hand, if an official even partially violates an existing law the common people at once bring a claim against him, because the laws are written in a language which the people understand and are duly conveyed to everybody.[44]

Ziya Paşa's arguments found many supporters, more especially in his appeal for a more national language. Grammars and dictionaries began to appear, one of which, published in 1874, significantly referred to the language as Turkish instead of, as previously, Ottoman. A number of Persian and Arabic words which had never gone into common use were dropped from the dictionaries, while common Turkish words and expressions, previously debarred, were now admitted to dictionaries and works of literature. Persian and Arabic words in Turkish were now used according to Turkish grammar and not, as previously, according to the grammatical rules of their languages of origin. Correct Ottoman usage thus no longer rested on three sets of rules of

[44] Text in Ebüzziya, *Nümune*, pp. 271 ff. (reprinted in the new script in Levend, pp. 134 ff.).

accidence and syntax. Most striking of all, some of the exponents of the new nationalism began to point to the affinities between Ottoman Turkish and the Turkic languages in the East, and to suggest that it was from them, rather than from Arabic or Persian, that new terms should be borrowed.[45]

In general, the linguistic and stylistic reformers of the nineteenth century found it easier to formulate theories than to apply them. Ziya Paşa's essay, cited above, is a good example of the artificial and Persianized style which he condemns, and there were but few authors who managed to write the simple, popular Turkish which they held up as an ideal. Still more words of alien origin came into the language, as nineteenth-century writers turned to Arabic and Persian, in much the same way as Europe turned to Latin and Greek, as a reserve store of roots from which new terms could be formed.

Already during the nineteenth century the first Turkish newspapers played an important role in the creation of a new, simpler Turkish prose style. After the revolution of 1908 the role of the press was vastly increased. The rulers of the revolutionary state were anxious to be understood—by Turks and non-Turks, at home and abroad. Above all, they were anxious to convey their message to the simple Turkish soldiery, on whom their power rested, and for whose allegiance there were dangerous competing interests.

The decade of Young Turk rule gave a great impetus to the development of simpler Turkish. The repeated struggles for power—whether electoral, demagogic, or military—needed swift and effective use of the new mass media of information. The series of wars in which the new régime was involved made a different but no less cogent demand for simple and accurate communication. The printing press and the telegraph both played a great part in the simplification of Turkish. The writers who, from 1911, produced the Salonika literary journal *Genç Kalemler* (Young Pens), drew up rules for a purified but not purist style. Even the bureaucracy played its part, using the new, simplified style in its orders and regulations. By the end of the Ottoman Empire, the high Ottoman mandarin style was already dead. Its place had been taken by a flexible, living idiom, based on the spoken language of the educated classes of

[45] Heyd, *Lang. Ref.*, p. 13.

the capital. It still contained, however, an immense vocabulary of Persian and Arabic words; though greatly simplified, it was still far from the vernacular of the common people.

The idea of romanization appeared very early in the history of the Kemalist state. It was discussed at the economic congress in Izmir in 1923, when a proposal for the adoption of the Latin alphabet was put forward and discussed. It was defeated, on 2 March 1923. An attempt to raise the matter in the Grand National Assembly the following year met with a similar lack of success.

Meanwhile definite action had been taken among the Turkish-speaking peoples east of the Turkish border. Already in 1921–2 experiments were made with a Latin alphabet in Azerbayjan and the North Caucasus, and in July 1922 it was reported that a memorandum on romanization from the Government of Azerbayjan had been received in Ankara. On 1 May 1925 a decree of the supreme Soviet of Azerbayjan established the Latin alphabet as the official script of the Azeri Turkish language. In the spring of 1926 a congress of Turcologists assembled in Baku, under Soviet auspices. One of its decisions was to introduce the Latin in place of the Arabic script in the Turkic languages of the Soviet Union, and in the following years a number of varying Latin scripts were introduced in Central Asia.[46]

One aim of this Soviet policy of romanization was to reduce the influence of Islam; another was no doubt to cut off contact between the Turks of the Soviet Union and those of Turkey, who were still using the Arabic script. The contrary consideration —that of maintaining contact between the different Turkic peoples—induced some Turkish nationalists to favour the adoption of the Latin script in Turkey. When, eventually, this was done, the Russians countered again by abolishing the Latin script and introducing the Cyrillic, thus reopening the gap between the Soviet Turks and Turkey.

This, however, was still in the future. In 1925–8 Azerbayjani exiles in Turkey were particularly active in urging the romanization of Turkish, by which they hoped to save their homeland from complete isolation. The idea of romanization fitted well with the policies of Kemal, though for different reasons. The Latin alphabet appealed to him less as a link with the Azerbayjan Republic than

---

[46] J. Castagné, 'La Latinisation de l'alphabet turk dans les républiques turko-tatares de l'U.R.S.S.', *R. Ét. islam.*, i (1927), 321–53.

as a barrier against the Ottoman Empire. By learning a new script and forgetting the old, so it seemed, the past could be buried and forgotten, and a new generation be brought up, open only to such ideas as were expressed in the new, romanized Turkish.

The new script was officially adopted in November 1928, and the old Arabic script outlawed from the New Year. The erection of this great barrier against the past obviously created a new and unprecedented opportunity for linguistic reform, and from the first there seems to have been a clear intention of exploiting it.[47]

It was not, however, until 1932 that the first practical steps were taken. On 12 July of that year, on a directive from Mustafa Kemal, the Turkish Linguistic Society was founded;[48] its task was 'to bring out the genuine beauty and richness of the Turkish language and to elevate it to the high rank it deserves among world languages'.[49] The work was planned like a military operation, and a series of committees appointed to organize and direct the assault on the various sectors—linguistics, etymology, grammar, terminology, lexicography, and the like.

Within two months the Society was ready to launch a general offensive. In September 1932 the first Turkish Language Congress assembled in the Dolmabahçe palace, in the presence of Mustafa Kemal himself. The proceedings of the Congress were widely publicized, and in the months that followed a number of decrees and directives gave governmental aid and sanction to its decisions. Apart from its scholarly work of collection, research, and publication, the Society's main task was the simplification and purification of the Turkish language. The idea was not new, but the scope, scale, and manner of the reform were very new indeed; for none of the earlier pioneers had ever conceived a reform as radical as that which the Society, with government support, undertook.[50]

The first task was the completion of a process already begun by earlier literary reformers—the reduction and eventual elimination of the Arabic and Persian grammatical and syntactical forms, many of which still remained embedded in Turkish literary usage. This was followed by a far more radical step—the assault

[47] Heyd, *Lang. Ref.*, pp. 24–25.

[48] cf. above, p. 353, on the parallel Historical Society.

[49] Statutes of the Society, art. 2; cited by Heyd, pp. 25–26.

[50] Heyd, *Lang. Ref.*, pp. 26 ff.

on the Arabic and Persian vocabulary itself. For more than 1,000 years the Turks had been a Muslim people, sharing in the common Islamic civilization of the Middle East. Arabic and Persian had been their classical languages, and had made a contribution to their vocabulary comparable in scale and content with the Greek, Latin, and Romance elements in English. The earlier language reformers had been content to remove foreign constructions, and foreign words that were rare, learned, or archaic. The radicals of the Linguistic Society were opposed to Arabic and Persian words as such, even those that formed an essential part of the basic vocabulary of everyday spoken Turkish. On the one hand, the Society prepared and published an index of alien words, condemned to deportation; on the other search parties collected and examined purely Turkish words, from dialects, from other Turkic languages, and from ancient texts, to serve as replacements. When no suitable words could be discovered, resuscitated, or imported, new ones were invented.

This planned exchange of lexical populations reached its height during the years 1933–4, when it coincided with a general movement of secularization and Westernization. It is significant that the hue and cry after alien words affected only Arabic and Persian—the Islamic, Oriental languages. Words of European origin, equally alien, were exempt, and a number of new ones were even imported, to fill the gaps left by the departed.

Some pruning of the exuberant verbiage of late Ottoman style was certainly necessary; the use of whole phrases and idioms from Arabic and Persian could obviously not continue in a language which was to be no longer the plaything of chancery scribes and palace littérateurs, but the medium of communication of a literate, modern, and advancing nation. Reform was needed—but not all would agree on the wisdom and success of the reforms accomplished. The attempt of the reformers to strip away the accretions of 1,000 years of cultural growth seemed at times to bring impoverishment rather than purity, while the arbitrary reassignments of words and meanings often led to confusion and chaos.[51]

In 1935, therefore, a new directive was issued. The invention

---

[51] A parallel movement in English might have imposed folkwain for omnibus, revived ayenbite and inwit for remorse and conscience, and renamed Parliament the Witenagemot.

and imposition of new words was halted, and a number of familiar and indispensable Arabic and Persian words were granted reprieve and naturalization. To provide a theoretical justification for this retreat, the doctrine was promulgated that 'a number of words which are used in our language and which until now were thought to have been taken from foreign languages had originally passed from Turkish into those languages'.[52] In other words, where it proved impracticable to provide a Turkish substitute for a foreign word, a Turkish etymology would serve instead.

This kind of theorizing, and some other dubious doctrines that were launched in aid of it,[53] never won much support outside the inner circle of the Linguistic Society, and were allowed after a time to fade into decent oblivion. The reform, however, despite occasional setbacks, continued, and achieved a final symbolic triumph when the Turkish constitution itself was translated into 'pure' Turkish and promulgated in January 1945.[54]

It was the last victory of the purists. No longer sustained by the firm hand of Mustafa Kemal, they faced a rising tide of criticism from teachers, writers, journalists, and scholars, who protested against what they regarded as an impoverishment and debasement of the language. Even the objective of simplicity, they said, had been forgotten, and a new, artificial official language created that was as remote and obscure to the ordinary Turk as the high Ottoman chancery style had been to his forefathers.[55]

In December 1949 the Linguistic Society, at its sixth congress, adopted a markedly more moderate position, and tried to give itself a less political and more scholarly character. In its subsequent work, though it has not entirely abandoned the idea of purity, it has been much more concerned with simplicity.[56] Finally, in December 1952, by an overwhelming majority, the National Assembly decided to withdraw the 'pure Turkish' constitution and repromulgate the text of 1924.

[52] Translated and quoted in Heyd, *Lang. Ref.*, p. 33.

[53] On the Sun-language theory (*Güneş-Dil teorisi*), proving that all civilization came from the Turks and all languages from Turkish, see Heyd, *Lang. Ref.*, pp. 33–34. Authorized expositions, in French and Turkish, will be found in the journal of the society, *Türk Dili, Belleten*, for 1937 and 1938.

[54] For an analysis of the new text, see M. Colombe, 'Le Nouveau texte de la constitution turque', *C. Or. contemp.*, iv (1946), 771–808.

[55] Heyd, *Lang. Ref.*, pp. 44 ff.   [56] Ibid. pp. 84 ff.

The idea was mooted at the time of preparing yet a third version of the constitution which, avoiding both the archaism of the 1924 text and the artificiality of the 1945 version, would really be written in the living language of the country. Perhaps wisely, it was decided that parliament was not the place for linguistic discussions, nor the constitution the appropriate text for stylistic experiments.[57]

A comparison between the text of the 1924 constitution and the current language of Turkish literary, journalistic, and official usage will reveal how much the reform really accomplished. To the Turk of the present day, this thirty-five-year-old document, with its numerous Arabic and Persian words and constructions, bears an archaic, almost a medieval aspect. Though certainly more intelligible than the 'pure Turkish' version of 1945, it contains many expressions that are now obsolete, and must be explained to the Turkish schoolboy or student of the new generation. Even the famous speech of Mustafa Kemal, delivered in October 1927, has become a difficult and archaic text, requiring notes and explanations for the children of the new Turkey. The written language of today is unmistakably different from that which was used before the reform, and books a bare half-century old, even when transcribed into the new script, are as difficult for a Turkish schoolboy as Chaucer or even Langland for his English contemporary.

The main and really significant change has been to bring the written language closer to the spoken. In all countries there is a gap between the languages of speech and of writing, which differ from one another in texture, in style, and to some extent in grammar and vocabulary. In Ottoman Turkey they were two different languages, and an illiterate man could not hope to understand a normal written text even if it were read aloud to him.

In the new Turkey this gap has been closed. The language of books, newspapers, and government documents is the same as the spoken language—or at least, no more different from it than is normal in the countries of the West. Of the linguistic and cultural effect of this change in their language, only the Turks themselves can judge. The educational and social effects of the transformation will be obvious to all.

[57] Heyd, *Lang. Ref.*, p. 51.

Scholarship and Science

All these changes in the manner and form of expression were, in the last analysis, secondary to the greater and infinitely more difficult process of changing the ideas expressed. Modern civilization rested very largely on its scientific achievement. How were European science and the European scientific method to be adapted and adopted in Turkey?

The main instrument was of course to be education, and from the start the Turkish reformers, modernizers, and Westernizers have given a central place to education in their projects of reform. As far back as the mid-nineteenth century the first attempts were made to create an academy and a scientific society, for the encouragement of scholarship and science in the Ottoman Empire.

The *Encümen-i Daniş* (Society of Knowledge) was first suggested at the Council of Education in 1845, and was formally authorized by an Imperial *irade* in 1851. Obviously modelled on the Académie Française, it consisted of forty Turkish members and a number of corresponding members including such European Orientalists as Hammer, Bianchi, and Redhouse. Its programme included the encouragement of letters and sciences, and the advancement of the Turkish language. It was publicly inaugurated with a speech by Mustafa Reşid Paşa, indicating the part the Academy was to play in the renovation of the country. Its work was, however, impeded by the political instability of the time, and it petered out in 1862 without having accomplished more than the sponsorship of a few books.[58]

The *Cemiyet-i Ilmiye-i Osmaniye* (Ottoman Scientific Society), modelled on the Royal Society of England, was founded in 1860 by Münif Paşa, a graduate of the Translation Chamber, and was very much his personal creation and medium. Its most important achievement was the publication of the *Mecmua-i Fünûn*, journal of sciences, which was the first scientific periodical in Turkish. Including articles on history, geology, geography, and philosophy, as well as the natural sciences, it gave to its readers a clear and vivid picture of Western achievements in these fields, introduced them to the language and manner of modern science, and played a role in nineteenth-century Turkey analogous to that of the

[58] B. Lewis, 'Andjuman' in *EI²*.

Grande Encyclopédie in eighteenth-century France. It ceased publication during the cholera epidemic of 1865, and after a brief resumption some years later was closed down by Sultan Abdül-hamid in 1882.[59]

The further development of scholarship in Turkey was considerable. With encouragement and support from successive governments, Turkish universities and learned societies have sponsored a truly impressive output of research and publication, notably in history, archaeology, language and literature, the general aim of which is to recover and illuminate the Turkish past. Great progress has also been made in the social sciences. Not all the work is of equal value, and some, notably in the 1930's, was directed to political rather than scholarly ends. Turkish scholars have, however, shown a growing regard for the standards and an increasing familiarity with the methods of critical scholarship, and in so doing have acquired a significance that is more than purely local.[60]

The adoption of European science, requiring entirely new attitudes as well as techniques, proved far more difficult. The first steps in the introduction of Western science into Turkish education were taken in the eighteenth century; by the beginning of the twentieth century scientific subjects were a normal part of the school curriculum, and have since found an important place in the universities. Yet the output of trained scientists is still pitifully inadequate to the needs of a modern state, and the volume of research well below the Western level. It was easy enough to teach the new knowledge, with a scientific instead of a religious authority behind it. It was quite another matter to inculcate and develop the scientific mentality, without which no real scientific progress is possible. A Turkish psychologist, in a recent appraisal of the progress of Westernization, sees in this the cardinal failure of the whole movement, and warns his countrymen, especially the intellectuals, of the consequences of their inability to master this fundamental element of the modern civilization of the West. Some have held that Western civilization derives from Greek, Latin, and

---

[59] Tanpınar, pp. 151–4; Cevad, *Maarif*, pp. 69 ff.; Berkes, in Frye, pp. 63–64; Adnan-Adıvar, in Young, p. 124. Adnan notes that 'since the principal collaborators of the *Majmū'-i-Funūn* had studied in England, most of their essays were inspired by Anglo-Saxon works'. On Münif Paşa see above, p. 421.

[60] On the historians, cf. B. Lewis, in *MEA*, iv. 218–27; Kerim K. Key, *An Outline of Modern Turkish Historiography* (1954).

Christian sources, and that therefore the Turks, who do not share its classical and Christian heritage, cannot hope to become full participants in it. To them he replies that modern Western civilization is, in essence, not so much classical and Christian, as scientific. Therein lies the cause of past failures, and the hope of future success, in the Westernization of Turkey.[61]

Literature and the Arts [62]

The starting-point of the new Turkish literature under European influence is, by convention, the year 1859, when Ibrahim Şinasi published a lithographed booklet containing 100 or so verse translations from Racine, La Fontaine, Lamartine, Gilbert, and Fénélon.[63] In the same year Münif Paşa, founder of the Scientific Society, published a group of dialogues translated from Fontenelle, Fénélon, and Voltaire,[64] introducing to his readers some strange and exotic notions on 'patriotism, social ethics, and female education', as well as other topics.[65]

Thereafter the translation movement developed rapidly. One result, of far-reaching effect, was the introduction of two entirely new genres—the drama and the novel. These translations and adaptations helped to familiarize Turkish readers and spectators with some aspects of European manners and customs otherwise entirely alien to them, and thus remotely to anticipate the acceptance of these customs by themselves. The number of readers and playgoers was no doubt very small—but so too was the number of those who made Turkey's successive revolutions.

The Westernization of Turkish literature—the genres, the forms, the themes, the prosody, and the style—proceeded rapidly. At first the new literature was largely derivative and imitative, chiefly of French models. But by the time of the Young Turk régime a new and original literature was emerging, in which the Western models are familiar and, so to speak, naturalized. Nor

---

[61] Turhan, *Garblılaşmanın Neresindeyiz* (1959). See also the same author's study of cultural change, *Kültür Değişmeleri*.

[62] On Turkish literature in the nineteenth and twentieth centuries, see the standard works already cited by Bombaci and Tanpınar, and the very useful Turkish manual by Özön, *Son Asır Türk Edebiyatı Tarihi*. Useful shorter accounts will be found in *EI*[1] ('Turks, literature' by M. F. Köprülü), and Key, 'Trends in Modern Turkish Literature', *Muslim Wld.*, xlvii (1957), 318–28.

[63] *Tercüme-i Manzume* (Ist., 1276 A.H.). On Şinasi see above, p. 133.

[64] *Muhaverat-i Hikemiye* (Ist., 1276–7 A.H.).   [65] Tanpınar, p. 152.

is that all. With the cultural radiation of the Turkist movement, Turkish writers achieved a new revival from within, drawing sustenance from old cultural roots deep in Turkish life. The cult of the medieval bard Yunus Emre, the revival of the Turkish syllabic verse of folk-poetry in place of the now almost abandoned Perso-Arabic prosody, the influence of folklore and folk literature on modern writing, are all reflections of the same tendency to look beyond the formal heritage of Ottoman court civilization to the long-neglected riches of Turkish popular life and art that lay beneath it. Nor has even the Ottoman past been wholly abandoned. The passing of years and the mellowing of memories have permitted a more impartial assessment of the values of the old culture, and in the work of some modern writers we find the interesting phenomenon of a consciously evocative neo-classicism, playing on the glories and legends of a past that has become remote and exotic to the Turks themselves. There could be no better proof of the magnitude of the change that had taken place.

The phases of Westernization in literature are closely paralleled in Turkish architecture, where we can observe the first Italianate influence in the so-called Turkish baroque of the eighteenth century, the mixture of styles in the nineteenth, to the point of introducing Corinthian columns and capitals into the design of the minaret, and the neo-classical and modernistic styles of the twentieth.[66]

The revival of Turkish folk tradition, though of considerable cultural influence, is of course of far less significance in modern Turkish literature than the massive and dominating influence of the West. This is still more so in Turkish art and music, where modern painters and composers, trained in the West, have broken away from the classical Islamic art and music of the Ottoman Empire, and have also sought inspiration in the folk arts of Anatolia.

The beginnings of modern Turkish art were formal and official. A museum was opened in 1868, a museum school in 1874, a School of Fine Arts in 1881. In the words of a modern observer,

the school based itself firmly, and unfortunately, on the usual western academic canons common to all Écoles des Beaux Arts; it ignored

---

[66] For examples, see plates 1–3. See further, Behcet Unsal, *Turkish Islamic Architecture* (1959), espec. pp. 28, 48, 56 and 68. A school of architecture was opened in 1894 (Ergin, *Maarıf*, iii. 839).

Turkish traditions of decorative art, of colour, pattern, line and arabesque, and turned to representational and academic art, which was European and foreign.[67]

Within this tradition some quite competent work was done, and the way opened to a fuller development in the twentieth century. Most of this was still Parisian painting in Turkey rather than Turkish painting, and it is only very recently that Turkish painters have begun to feel their way to an authentic idiom of their own. In this they are certainly helped by the growth of a non-representational art in Europe, that is more intelligible in terms of their own ancient traditions of calligraphy and design.

In 1926 a statue of Kemal by a Viennese sculptor was unveiled at Seraglio Point in Istanbul. It was followed by two others in Ankara, and then by many more all over Turkey. The significance of this public defiance of one of the most deep-rooted of Islamic prejudices was social and political rather than artistic; it did, however, prepare the way for the acceptance of this new art, where the complete absence of any inherited tradition—except perhaps for the newly discovered Hittite remains—posed problems quite different from the problems of synthesis confronting the writer, architect, painter, or musician.

As with so much else, the beginnings of Western music in Turkey were military. After the destruction of the Janissaries in 1826, the Sultan wished to find a substitute for the famous Janissary *Mehter* of reed-pipes, trumpets, cymbals, and kettle-drums. In 1831 Giuseppe Donizetti, brother of the more famous Gaetano, was invited to Istanbul to organize a band, and taught in the Imperial School of Music established by the Sultan.[68]

The first Turkish musical student in Europe was Saffet, a flautist, who went to France in 1886. A small number of others followed, and in 1923 a municipal Conservatory of Music was founded in Istanbul. The Republic went still further, founding and endowing a state conservatory in Ankara, a National Opera, two symphony orchestras, and a number of smaller schools and groups.

[67] J. Steegman, 'Turkish Painting', *The Studio*, May 1946, p. 130; cf. the comments of Georges Duhamel in *La Turquie nouvelle* (Paris, 1954), pp. 90 ff. On the history of the school see Ergin, *Maarif*, iii. 919 ff.

[68] Ergin, *Maarif*, ii. 311–15; Lûtfi, vii. 61 (on Donizetti's promotion to the rank of Miralay). According to a source quoted by Ergin, he later became a pasha. On a performance of Rossini by a 'military band' of 'royal pages', see Slade, i. 135.

In spite of all this, and of a series of distinguished visitors and advisers from Liszt to Hindemith and Bartok, the acclimatization of Western music in Turkey has made but slow progress. A few talented Turkish composers and performers have won high reputations abroad, but the response to Western music, even among the Westernized intelligentsia, is limited in the extreme. As science after scholarship, so also does music limp after literature in the Turkish movement of Westernization—for music, like science, is part of the inner citadel of Western culture, one of the final secrets to which the aspiring newcomer must penetrate.

CHAPTER XIII

Élite and Class

First, let it be known to his Imperial Majesty that the origin of the good order of kingship and community and the cause of the stability of the foundations of the faith and the dynasty are a firm grasp of the strong cord of the Muhammadan law. For the rest, let the Imperial attention and favour be given to the men of religion, who with care and knowledge attend to the affairs of the subjects entrusted to the Emperor by God, and to the soldiers who give up their lives in the Holy War. Let him show favour to the worthy men of every class, and contempt for the unworthy.

MEMORANDUM OF KOÇU BEY.

All Turks are equal before the law and are without exception obliged to observe it. Every kind of group, class, family and individual privilege is abolished and prohibited.

TURKISH CONSTITUTION, 1924; Article 69.

IN 1784, when the French ambassador Choiseul-Gouffier was urging military reform on the Turkish government of the time, he remarked in a letter home: 'This is not like France, where the King alone is master of decision. In Turkey, on the contrary, to get something done one has to convince the jurists of the ulema and both the present and previous occupants of positions of power.'[1]

Choiseul-Gouffier was not alone in this judgement. In 1803 a Muslim visitor from India, Mirza Abu Talib Khan, remarked of the Turks:

I learned that their Emperors have not the power of shedding blood unjustly, nor can they follow the bend of their inclinations or passions with impunity. On all affairs of consequence they are obliged to consult their nobles, who are kept in proper subjection by the hope of promotion or the fear of punishment. . . .[2]

Adolphus Slade, discussing the reforms of Mahmud II, accuses him of 'the entire subversion of the liberties of his subjects', and, realizing that 'liberties of the subject' might seem to his readers

[1] Léonce Pingaud, *Choiseul-Gouffier* (Paris, 1887), p. 82 (cited by Karal in *Tanzimat*, p. 23).

[2] *The Travels of Mirza Abu Taleb Khan . . . written by himself in the Persian language*, trans. by C. Stewart (London, 1814), iii. 60.

an odd expression to apply to Turkey, he goes on to explain how the Sultan, though despotic in name, had in fact been limited by many checks and restraints, which served to protect the people against tyranny.[3]

All this is in marked contrast with the familiar picture of the Turkish state, drawn by the majority of European travellers and political theorists from the Renaissance onwards, as the very model and prototype of autocratic and arbitary power. Thus, for example, Choiseul-Gouffier's comparison between the freedom of the French king and the restraints imposed on the Turkish Sultan is in specific contradiction with an earlier comparison between the two monarchies, made by no less a connoisseur of political power than Niccolò Machiavelli:

> The examples of these two different Governments now in our dayes, are, the Turk and the King of France. The Turks whole Monarchy is govern'd by one Lord, and the rest are all his Vassalls; and deviding his whole kingdom into divers Sangiacques or Governments, he sends severall thither: and those hee chops and changes, as hee pleases. But the King of France is seated in the midst of a multitude of Lords, who of old have been acknowledg'd for such by their subjects, and being belov'd by them, injoy their preheminencies; nor can the King take their States from them without danger.[4]

In the two and a half centuries between Machiavelli and Choiseul-Gouffier, many great and important changes had taken place. The evolution of the French monarchy is familiar enough— the ending of feudal independence, the reduction of the vassals to courtiers, the centralization of authority, the growth of royal despotism. The transformation of the Ottoman monarchy in the same period is far less known. Yet the history of the Ottoman Empire in this period was no cycle of Cathay; it was a time of great changes, in society and state—changes very different from the familiar pattern of European development, but equally relevant to the understanding of what followed.

The Breakdown of the Old Order

In the first half of the sixteenth century the classical Ottoman system was at the height of its power and efficiency, and it is small wonder that contemporary European observers saw in it the

---

[3] Slade, i. 214 ff.   [4] *The Prince*, trs. by E. Dacres (1640), ch. 4.

pattern and exemplar of a ruthless, centralized absolutism. If some, loyal to the entrenched privileges of the European estates, saw in the Sultanate the terrible example of arbitrary and capricious power, there were others who looked forward to the new European age of enlightened royal despotism in the nation-state, and saw in Turkey the model of the disciplined, efficiently governed centralized monarchy.

By an irony of history, at the very time when Machiavelli and other European political thinkers were contrasting the weakness of the French king with the might of the Turkish Sultan, processes were beginning in both countries which in time would reverse the roles of the two monarchs. In France the magnates would become courtiers, the autonomous regions administrative districts, and the king grow in power and authority over all his subjects and all his realm until he could truly say 'L'État c'est moi'. In the Islamic Empires the same Arabic word Sulṭān had denoted both the state and the sovereign; but there the courtiers became magnates, the provinces principalities, the slaves of the Imperial household its masters, and 'the lord of the world' the puppet of his wives, his eunuchs, and his slaves.

When Süleyman the Magnificent was invested with the sword of Osman in 1520, he became master of a perfect machine of absolutist government, over an empire stretching from Hungary to the borders of Persia, from the Black Sea to the Indian Ocean. True, he was subject to the unalterable provisions of the Holy Law, but the Holy Law itself conceded him almost absolute power, and the hierarchy of its exponents were the firm prop of his authority among the people. The government and the army—the men who ruled and the men who fought—were his personal slaves; privileged and immune as against the mass of the people, but totally without rights as against the will of their sovereign. The regular replacement of the old cadres by new intakes of slaves of humble origin forestalled the growth of a hereditary aristocracy at the centres of power, while at the same time the feudal gentry, bound to the Sultan by their revocable, functional fiefs, were nevertheless secure enough in their holdings to have an interest in the prosperity of agriculture and the well-being of the countryside.

The religious institution, as it has been called, enjoyed un-disturbed control of law, justice, religion, and education. Its head was the *Şeyh-ül-Islâm*, the Chief Mufti of the capital, presiding over a great hierarchy of kadis and muftis, with territorial jurisdictions like Christian justices and bishops. Its members, the ulema, were exempt from taxation, and unlike their colleagues of the slave establishment could transmit their possessions, and in effect their status, from generation to generation, thus forming perhaps the only secure hereditary possessing class in the Ottoman Empire.

The Ottoman historians date the decline of the Empire from the death of Süleyman the Magnificent, and it is indeed in the second half of the sixteenth century that the first signs of breakdown in the Ottoman institutional structure begin to appear.

One of these, to which the memorialists frequently allude, was the decay of the sipahi class.[5] As the feudal cavalry decayed, the standing army increased rapidly, and so too did the cost of maintaining it. This was no doubt one of the main reasons for the seizure of vacant fiefs. To secure a quick and easy cash return, the Sultan did not administer the revenues of these lands directly, but farmed them out on various kinds of leases and concessions. These were all of a monetary and not a military nature. Some were tax-farms, others were usufructuary assignments. At first they were for a brief term; later the practice spread of granting the tax-farmer a life interest which, by abuse, became heritable and alienable. The system spread rapidly all over the Empire. Not only crown lands were affected. Many fiefs were granted, as appanages, to dignitaries or favourites at court, who exploited them in the same way, and eventually many even of the sipahis farmed out the revenues of their *timars*.

The economic and social power derived from the permanent local control of tax-farms and leases produced a new propertied, influential class in the provinces, which soon began to play a prominent part in local affairs. This class interposed itself between the government and the peasantry, and intercepted much of the revenue. In theory they only held possession as lessees or tax-farmers, but as the government, through growing weakness, lost control of the provinces, these new landowners were able to increase both the extent of their holdings and the security of their tenure. In the seventeenth and eighteenth centuries they even began to usurp some of the functions of government.

[5] On the sipahi and the *timar*, see above, pp. 30 ff. and 89.

The Ayan *and* Derebeys[6]

The term *ayan* had been in use since early times in the general sense of provincial or local notables, usually merchants. It now came to denote a definite social group or class of old and new landlords, exercising important political functions. At first these were resisted as a usurpation, but amid the financial and administrative strains of the eighteenth century the central government found it expedient to delegate more and more of the conduct of provincial affairs, notably the running of the provincial towns, to the *ayan*, who began to resemble a freeholding landed gentry. They elected their own leaders and representatives, who were recognized rather than appointed by the government. In 1786 the government, fearing their growing power, tried to oust them from town government and to appoint its own city provosts, but after five years it was compelled to abolish the provosts and restore the rule of the *ayan* and their system of election.

By this time the *ayan* had become more than a provincial gentry and magistracy. In some areas, especially in Rumelia, some of the *ayan* maintained their own private armies, levied taxes, and dispensed justice, and at times there is no clear distinction between them and the *derebeys*, some of whom at least seem to have emerged from their ranks.

In Anatolia the *derebeys* had become a kind of feudal vassal-princes ruling over autonomous, hereditary principalities. In time of war they served, with their own contingents, in the Ottoman armies, which to a large extent came to consist of such quasi-feudal levies. Though given formal titles as collectors and intendants by the Sultan, they were in effect independent within their own territories. By the beginning of the nineteenth century almost the whole of Anatolia was in the hands of the various *derebey* families—only two eyalets, Karaman and Anadolu, remaining under the direct administration of the Porte.[7]

When Bayrakdar Mustafa Paşa, one of the *ayan* of Ruschuk, became Grand Vezir and master of the Empire in 1808, the *ayan* had triumphed in the capital itself. It is significant that soon

---

[6] Uzunçarşılı, *Alemdar Mustafa Paşa*, pp. 2 ff., and 'Ayan', in *IA*; Miller, *Mustafa Pasha*, pp. 363–5; *EI*² ('Ayan', by H. Bowen); Gibb and Bowen, index. cf. above, p. 38.

[7] 'Derebey' in *EI*², and above, p. 378.

after his seizure of power he exacted a 'deed of agreement' from the Sultan recognizing and confirming the status and rights of the *ayan* in the Empire, and submitted it for ratification and signature to a conference consisting largely of *ayan* and *derebeys*, invited to the capital. Thus at the dawn of the nineteenth century the Sultan was brought to Runnymede, to sign a charter that gave formal recognition to feudal rights and autonomies in the Ottoman Empire. They were to be of short duration. Sultan Mahmud, like King John, had the will to suppress his baronage and gentry. The nineteenth century also supplied him with the means.[8]

Agrarian Change [9]

Selim had already made the first, unsuccessful attempts to curb the feudal autonomies of the magnates and restore the long-forgotten authority of the sovereign power. Mahmud, by a series of effective military and police actions in Europe and Asia, completed the process.

The suppression of these quasi-feudal autonomies did not, however, halt the important agrarian changes that had been taking place. Sultan Mahmud deprived the *ayan* of their armies and their courts; he left them in full, indeed in increased control of their lands.

It was not the *ayan*, but the sipahis who were deprived of their lands. In 1831 the *timars*, still comprising a considerable part of the agricultural land of Turkey, were taken over by the state.[10] They were not, however, administered directly by state agents, but were farmed out, in ways not unlike the leases on crown lands in earlier times, to tax-farmers and lessees of various kinds, who, coalescing with the survivors of earlier groups, begin to form a new landlord class in the Turkish countryside.

In the classical Ottoman land system *mülk*—freehold—was comparatively rare, and was to be found chiefly in towns or their immediate neighbourhood. It consisted normally of building land, together with some orchards, vineyards, and vegetable

---

[8] See above, pp. 73 ff.

[9] The economic history of Turkey in the nineteenth century is still to be written. In the meantime, the best guides on agrarian matters will be found in Barkan's study of the *Tanzimat* land laws, in *Tanzimat*, pp. 321–421, and Inalcık's 'Tanzimat Nedir?' in *Tarih Araştırmaları 1940–1941*, pp. 237–62. For briefer accounts in English see Inalcık, in *Muslim Wld.*, xlv (1955), 221–8, and Karpat, pp. 77 ff.

[10] See above, pp. 88 ff.

gardens in or near the town. Most farm land was *miri*—domain land—and was either granted as a *timar* to a sipahi or leased to a tax-farmer. During the period of Ottoman decline the latter became increasingly common, and the holders of such leases began to acquire, in fact though not in law, the rights and powers of freeholders.

This happened in several ways. The Sultans had always had the right to grant *miri* land as *mülk*, and occasionally did so to favoured or meritorious persons. Such estates became full legal freehold, alienable and heritable according to the Şeriat laws governing freehold property. Such grants, which involved the formal renunciation of the taxes due from *miri* but not *mülk* lands, were, not unnaturally, few and exceptional.

Another method was by forceful usurpation. In times and places where the authority of the Sultan was weak and remote, powerful individuals sometimes succeeded in seizing *miri* lands by force, exercising *mülk* rights over them, and obtaining subsequent recognition.

During the early nineteenth century the growth of freehold estates was maintained from two main sources. One was the sale of *miri* lands, as freehold, by the government, in order to meet deficits in the treasury. The other was the sale, by auction, of a special kind of lease conferring very extensive rights and powers on the purchaser.

It was by this kind of sale that many of the impounded *timar* estates passed into the hands of a new possessing class. Under Mahmud and his successors, such sales seem to have been very frequent. The purchaser, who was given a deed called *tapu temessükü*, had, in theory, no legal right to freehold ownership, but only a lease of revenues. In fact, however, his rights were steadily extended and confirmed, and the trend of most of the agrarian laws of the *Tanzimat* period was to transform these leases into something barely distinguishable from freehold. Changes in the rules concerning transfers and registration increased the value of the *tapu temessükü*, which became a veritable title-deed, while the laws were successively modified to allow inheritance by sons, daughters, and other relatives.

These leases were often of some size. The Land Law of 1858 prohibits the acquisition of a whole populated village as an estate by an individual. This would seem to indicate an awareness, by the statesmen of the *Tanzimat*, of the growth of large estates, and a desire to restrict it. This ruling seems, however, to have had little practical effect. The commercial and financial developments of the time, including the expansion of Turkish agricultural exports, brought a flow of ready money, and created a class of persons with sufficient cash to bid for leases, buy estates, and lend money on land. The new laws gave them legal powers to enforce contracts of debt and sale; the new police protected them from the hazards which formerly attended such enforcements.[11]

In this way, in the course of the nineteenth century, a new freehold landlord class came into existence, controlling much of the countryside of the Empire. In the Balkan provinces this gave rise to bitter social struggles, which continued after those countries had won their independence. In western and central Anatolia it produced the familiar figures of the Ağa, the rich peasant or landlord, dominating and often owning the village, and of his still more powerful protector, the merchant landowner residing in the town.

The position of the peasant was much worsened by these changes. As the *tapu*-holder became a freeholder, the peasant became a hired labourer or share-cropping tenant with no rights at all—so that his emancipation from feudalism left him rather worse off than before. As well as government taxes, he had to pay part of his crop as rent, and sometimes render personal service in addition. Turkish folk-literature in the nineteenth and fiction in the twentieth century reveal a bitter struggle between the impoverished and unhappy peasant and the landlords who dominate and exploit him. His only champion is the bandit— *eşkıya*—the runaway peasant who takes to the hills and fights against the oppressors and the government forces that maintain them.[12] There are many tales of such Anatolian Robin Hoods; their prototype is the famous Köroğlu, whose Sheriff of Nottingham was the *derebey* of Bolu.[13]

In some of the eastern versions, Köroğlu is not a countryman

[11] See especially Inalcık, 'Tanzimat Nedir', pp. 244 ff. The whole course of development shows remarkable resemblances to what was happening in Khedivial Egypt, British India, and elsewhere in Asia and Africa.

[12] Information on the *eşkıya* will be found chiefly in the numerous locally produced works on local history. A notable example is the series of books by M. Çağatay Uluçay on the history of Manisa, including two volumes on brigandage and popular movements in Saruhan (*Saruhan'da Eşkıyalık ve Halk Hareketleri*, Manisa-Istanbul, i. 1944, ii. 1955).

[13] On Köroğlu, see *EI*[1] and *IA* s.v.

but a nomad. It is no accident, for the nomadic tribesmen had found their lives dislocated and disrupted by the social and economic changes of the time. The outstanding example is Çukurova, the plain of Cilicia, now a rich agricultural area with important industrial developments. In the nineteenth century it was a thinly populated and pestilential marshland, vaguely claimed by the chiefs of the nomadic Turkoman tribes of the surrounding mountains. In 1840, after a period of Egyptian occupation, it was returned to Turkey, and became part of the vilayet of Aleppo. The Egyptian administration had made some attempt to foster the cultivation of cotton, but with little effect, and the land remained empty.

A new phase began in 1866, when the Sultan's government embarked on a new programme of pacification and settlement. A military force, known as the 'Improvement Division'—*Fırka-i Islâhiye*—landed at Iskenderun, and advanced into the inner Taurus and Amanus mountains. These mountains, and the plain north and east of Adana which they dominated, were partly ruled by *derebey* families such as the Kozanoğlu of Kozan, the Menemencioğlu and the Kökülüoğlu, partly controlled by Turkoman tribes and bands of brigands. The aim of the expedition was to subjugate the independent *derebeys* and tribal chiefs, destroy the power of the bands and nomads, and thus prepare the way for agricultural settlement.

The pacification once completed, colonists were needed—and the displaced tribesmen were most unwilling to settle on the land. Three thousand families of Nogay Tatars, who had migrated from Russia after the Crimean War, were settled on both banks of the Ceyhan river above Misis, and Egyptian fellahin were imported to work on the new cotton plantations; they were later followed by Muslim repatriates from Crete, from Salonika, from the Balkans, and from North Africa, as these lands were successively lost to the Empire. Tribal rebellions were put down, and a period of social and often violent unrest culminated in the acquisition by private owners of almost the whole of what had become a flourishing area of intense cultivation.[14]

[14] The chief source for these events is Cevdet Paşa, 'Maruzat', *TTEM*, no. 14/91 (1926), 117 ff. See further Hamit Sadi Selen, 'Türkiyede bir iç iskân örneği', in *Iskân ve Şehircilik Haftası Konferansları* (Ank., 1955), pp. 91–97, and, for later developments and recollections, W. Eberhard, 'Nomads and Farmers in South-eastern Turkey; Problems of Settlement', *Oriens*, vi (1953), 32–49.

European Activities [15]

One of the factors leading to the settlement of the Cilician plain was the increased Western demand for cotton. In general, Turkey was becoming more involved in the economic patterns of development of the West. Until the Crimean War, the Ottoman government, despite the increasing burden of public expenditure needed for the new armies and administrative services, had managed to avoid incurring foreign debts. In 1854, the costs of waging modern war and the opportunities offered by a Western alliance combined to induce the Ottoman government to seek a loan on the money markets of London and Paris. On 4 August 1854 the Sultan issued a ferman authorizing the borrowing of £3 million. The interest rate was 6 per cent., the amortization 1 per cent., the issue price £80. Underwriters' commissions reduced the amount actually received still further, to about half the nominal amount, and the Ottoman government was obliged, within less than a year, to seek a further loan, this time of £5 million.[16] This new loan, for war purposes, was guaranteed by the British and French governments, with the result that the Ottomans were able to obtain more favourable terms. Rothschilds of London floated the loan at $2\frac{5}{8}$ premium and 4 per cent. interest.

The Anglo-French guarantee, while ensuring better terms, also brought the first infringements of Turkish financial independence. The guarantors had specified that the loan was to be used for war purposes; they also claimed the right to appoint a commissioner each, to supervise the employment of the funds and verify the treasury accounts. The work of the commissioners seems to have been effectively frustrated by the Ottoman officials with whom they dealt, but an important principle had been established.[17]

The war ended, but the demand for money grew and became more imperious. A first peacetime loan in 1858 to cover the withdrawal of the depreciated *Kaime*[18] brought only temporary relief, and soon the need to service earlier loans, coupled with the reckless extravagance of Sultan Abdülaziz, led to a mounting series of new

---

[15] On the loans and their effects there is a vast literature: see especially du Velay; D. C. Blaisdell, *European Financial Control of the Ottoman Empire* (1929). For a Turkish viewpoint see Refii Şükrü Suvla's article 'Tanzimat Devrinde Istikrazlar', in *Tanzimat*, pp. 263–88.

[16] Blaisdell, pp. 28 ff.   [17] du Velay, p. 143; Blaisdell, p. 28.

[18] See above, p. 109.

loans, following one another at almost annual intervals. The inevitable end came on 6 October 1875, when the Sublime Porte announced its intention of paying in cash only half of the interest and amortization on the loans; the other half would be covered by the issue, during the following five years, of 5 per cent. bonds, which would be delivered to the bondholders.

In a time of mounting troubles, even this was impossible to maintain. In 1876 further payments were missed or deferred, and finally, on 20 December 1881, corresponding to 28 Muharrem 1299, the Ottoman Government issued the document known as the Muharrem Decree.[19] This decree, based on an agreement negotiated with representatives of the European bondholders, set up a 'Council of the Public Debt', which was henceforth to ensure the service of the Ottoman Public Debt. The Debt, by now amounting to nearly £200 million, was to be met from certain state revenues reserved for the purpose. The Council, directly controlled by and responsible to the foreign creditors, was to take full charge of them. The effect was to give Turkey a second and independent exchequer, controlling a large part of the national revenue. By 1911 the Council had a staff of 8,931 persons, as against 5,472 in the Imperial Ministry of Finance.[20]

The penetration of European finance was inevitably accompanied by extensive economic penetration in other fields also. Foreign capital began to play an important part in the development of the country, notably in communications and services, but also in agriculture and in the nascent Ottoman industries. Tobacco, for example, which provided employment for important numbers, was constituted a monopoly in 1884 and granted to a Franco-Austrian company. By 1914 the Company had made a profit of 30 million Turkish gold pounds, of which 23 million were paid in tax to the Council of the Public Debt. Railways, tramways, and ports, gas, electricity, and water, were all operated by foreign concessionaire companies, as were also most of the few mines and factories.[21] By a law of 1867 foreigners obtained the right to own land.

These economic developments produced two important social consequences. One was the decline and ruination of native hand industries, which were quite unable to compete with the cheap,

---

[19] du Velay, pp. 463 ff.; Blaisdell, pp. 90 ff. [20] Conker and Witmeur, p. 46.
[21] Ibid. pp. 47 ff.

imported European goods. This process had begun as far back as the sixteenth century. In the nineteenth century it reached critical proportions, and caused severe unemployment and growing distress, notably in Anatolia.[22]

At the same time a new native middle class was coming into being, as buyers, agents, importers, distributors, and generally as the financial and commercial representatives of the foreign interests—in a word, as what are known in the Far East as compradors. The dangerous feature was that this new class consisted predominantly of non-Muslims. The Turk still preferred the three professions of religion, government, and war, and left commerce, with its degrading infidel associations, to the Christians and Jews. They accepted it, and some, notably among the Greeks and Armenians, grew rich and powerful.

The Christian Middle Class

There had been such Christian merchant classes in Turkey before, as for example in the sixteenth century, when the Greek Michael Cantacuzenos held court as a merchant prince in Ottoman Istanbul. In the sixteenth century the Turks had relied very heavily, in commerce, diplomacy, and many fiscal matters, on the Jews—the only community possessing the necessary aptitudes yet free from suspicion of treasonable sympathies with the Christian powers. The Jewish community declined together with the Ottoman Empire, and during the seventeenth and eighteenth centuries the Jews, ousted almost everywhere by Greeks and Armenians, became relatively insignificant. During the eighteenth century the Greek and Armenian communities, as a consequence of the decline of Ottoman power, became stronger and more cohesive, and profited both commercially and culturally from their contacts with the greater Christian world.[23] Many of them obtained *berats*—certificates—from the European embassies and consulates, which assured them important commercial and fiscal privileges. Originally intended to protect locally recruited interpreters and consular agents, these *berats* were granted or sold to growing numbers of local merchants, who were thus able to acquire a privileged and protected status. During the period of

[22] Karpat, pp. 81 ff.

[23] Gibb and Bowen, i/2, pp. 233 ff.; cf. A. H. Hourani, 'The Changing Face of the Fertile Crescent in the XVIIIth Century', *Studia Islamica*, viii (1957), 103 ff.

Western strength and Ottoman decline, the Capitulations, originally granted with almost contemptuous condescension to small
groups of visiting foreign merchants, had been transformed into
a system of extra-territorial privilege and immunity. By the sale
of *berats* it was extended by abuse to many local merchants, who
thus acquired a considerable advantage over their Ottoman
fellow subjects.

The Turkish authorities attempted to curb the traffic in *berats*,
and at the end of the eighteenth century Selim III tried to compete
with the European consuls by himself selling *berats* to Christian
and Jewish merchants. In return for a fee of 1,500 piastres, these
berats conferred the right to trade with Europe, together with
important legal, fiscal, and commercial privileges and exemptions.
These grants, enabling Ottoman non-Muslims to compete on
more or less equal terms with foreign or foreign-protected
merchants, created a new privileged class, known as the *Avrupa
Tüccarı*, the Europe merchants. In this class, the Greeks, thanks to
their maritime skills and opportunities, were able to win a position
of pre-eminence. It was reinforced by the advantages which they
derived from the use of the neutral Ottoman flag during most of
the years of the revolutionary and Napoleonic wars.

In the early nineteenth century the *berat* system was extended
to Muslim merchants, who for a slightly smaller fee, of 1,200
piastres, could obtain a *berat* of membership of the Muslim guild
of the *Hayriye Tüccarı*, the 'merchants of benefaction'. The response
was, however, meagre, and the merchant class remained predominantly non-Muslim.[24]

By the mid-century these terms and institutions had fallen into
desuetude. The Christian merchants remained, however, and
began to play a new and important role in the penetration of
European commerce and investment. What distinguished them
from such classes in earlier times was that, in addition to enjoying
the patronage and protection of the European great powers, many
of them now cherished national aspirations of their own that were
ultimately incompatible with Ottoman loyalty. At the same time
they—or rather their European patrons on their behalf—were
putting forth comprehensive demands for civic and fiscal rights
which effectively undermined the previously accepted principle
of Muslim political primacy in the Empire.

[24] See B. Lewis, 'Berātlı', in *EI²*.

The Muslim Reaction

The rise of a new Christian middle class, prosperous, self-assertive, and potentially disloyal, coincided ominously with the ruination of the Muslim Turkish craftsmen and small merchants. The contrast between the two led to a sharpening of religious and national tensions, and to a rising wave of hostility directed both against the foreigner and the Ottoman Christian. As early as the 1860's, Namık Kemal and his Young Ottoman companions had complained of the growing subservience of the Ottoman Empire to European economic interests, and had commented on both the laxness of Turkish statesmen and the thrust of the comprador class. In the main, however, the Muslim Turkish intelligentsia continued to find its outlet and careers in the service of the state, and its theoretical interests in the problems of the state, religion, and nation. Fundamentally unconcerned with the affairs of merchants, craftsmen, and peasants, it was content to leave both economic activity and economic criticism to others.

Industry [25]

One problem, however, did retain some attention—that of industrialization. The general decay of Ottoman industry dates from the early nineteenth century, when Turkey, along with many other countries, underwent the shattering impact of the expanding industrial capitalism of Europe, and a flood of cheap manufactured goods flowed into the Turkish market. The most important imports were textiles, and the old-established Turkish cotton and silk manufactures suffered accordingly. Other imports included ironware, knives, clocks, paper, and manufactured sugar, and once again the Turkish local industries failed to compete. [26]

The process begun in the first half of the nineteenth century was completed in the second half. Apart from a few necessary local craftsmen such as cobblers, tailors, and the like, the manufacturing arts disappeared almost completely, and Turkey became an exporter of raw materials and importer of manufactured goods. The altered demand for clothing and household accessories resulting from social Westernization on the one hand, and the

[25] On Ottoman industries in the *Tanzimat* period, see Ömer Celâl Sarç, 'Tanzimat ve Sanayiimiz', *Tanzimat*, pp. 423–40; on the later period Conker and Witmeur.

[26] Sarç, pp. 425–6.

restriction imposed on Turkish fiscal policies by the Capitulations on the other, no doubt helped to bring this about, but the main cause must be sought in the basic inability of a weak, pre-modern economy like that of Turkey to resist the competitive impact of modern capitalist industry.[27]

The value of industry as a source of wealth and power was soon realized in the Middle East. Such early observers as Halet Efendi and Sadık Rifat Paşa[28] comment on it, and such rulers as Abdülmecid in Turkey and Muhammad Ali Paşa in Egypt tried to build factories and establish industries by decree. But industrialization was not a magic talisman that could be used, in a single flourish, to conjure up the gorgeous and fabulous treasures of the West. Perhaps the best example is Sultan Abdülmecid, a ruler of goodwill and progressive intentions, who during his reign encouraged or directly initiated the establishment of more than 150 factories. Only three of them have survived to the present day.[29] The state factories were ill conceived, inefficient, often irrelevant to the country's needs, and were only able to sustain a parasitic life on constant government subsidies. Most of them were closed or abandoned, sometimes after only a few months work. Such private industry as came into being was for the most part foreign controlled and foreign operated. It was inevitably limited, since industrial development, with all the immense difficulties arising from the lack of suitable personnel, could not compete in attractiveness with the quick, cheap, and easy export of the raw materials in which the country abounded.

The rather crude mercantilism of the statesmen of the *Tanzimat* was in any case hopelessly irrelevant, both to the bustling nineteenth century and to the fatalistic Turkish population. In the hands of a government too weak to enforce its policies, too poor to apply them, it could end only where it did, in failure, breakdown, and impoverishment.[30]

The Young Turks: Land Laws

Even by the early twentieth century the Young Turk revolutionaries, in their discussions and arguments both before and after

---

[27] Ibid. pp. 427–34.   [28] See above, pp. 127 ff.

[29] Turhan, *Garblılaşmanın Neresindeyiz?*, p. 41; cf. Sarç, p. 435. In the same way Slade, in 1832, discussing Selim III, speaks of 'the manufactories (now in ruins) he established' (i. 211).

[30] See the penetrating observations of Sarç, pp. 439–40.

the Revolution, devote comparatively little attention to economic matters. Their most important enterprise in this field was the reform of the land law, which had undergone no serious change since the law of 1858 and amendment of 1867.[31] A group of 'temporary' laws, passed in February 1910, brought important changes in the land law, especially on the questions of corporate ownership, mortgage, and inheritance. Further modifications were enacted in March 1911 and February 1913, the last providing for a regular system of delimitation and registration of real property, and estimation of values and revenues. As late as the war years, a further reform removed the last traces of the notorious *iltizam* system. These laws did indeed simplify the complex and often anomalous situation left by the *Tanzimat* reforms. They were, however, also responsible for some hardship among the small peasants. The basis of the new law of inheritance was the German civil code, but certain rules which in the German code applied only to real estate in towns were in the Turkish law extended— probably by inadvertence—to farmlands and forests. This led to excessive subdivision, to frequent dispossessions, and to grave dislocation and distress.[32]

Economic Nationalism

During the last years of the Empire, the growing nationalism of the Young Turks led them to initiate some economic and social changes which were to reach a fuller development under the Republic. During the reign of Abdülhamid, the economic penetration of the Empire by Europe, especially by Germany, had proceeded rapidly. It continued after the Revolution of 1908, but the Young Turks were becoming conscious of it, if only as a political problem—the infringement of Turkish sovereignty. The 'Turkish Hearths'[33] were particularly active in calling for greater national economic activity, as a prior condition for economic emancipation. A few rather desultory steps were taken to stimulate local enterprise. An attempt in 1913–14 to abolish the economic Capitulations[34] came to nothing, but a 'society for national

---

[31] See above, pp. 116 and 224.

[32] Mardin, 'Development of the Shari'a under the Ottoman Empire', in Khadduri and Liebesny, pp. 287 ff. See also Nord; Louis Steeg, 'Land Tenure', in Mears, pp. 238–64.

[33] See above, p. 344.   [34] Karpat, p. 83.

consumption' was founded in July 1913, and launched a campaign to encourage the consumption of home-produced in place of imported goods.[35] The same year a law was passed to encourage industry, and a first industrial census, for the years 1913–15, was completed in 1915.[36]

Another instrument of this policy was a consumers' co-operative movement, started in Istanbul. As far back as 1860 Midhat Paşa, while governor of the Danube province, had established the first agricultural credit co-operatives. These, however, had no successors, and a genuine co-operative movement did not appear in Turkey until after the 1908 revolution. The producers' co-operatives never really got past the stage of making laws and preparing plans, but from 1909 onwards consumers' co-operatives appear in several districts in the capital, where their growth was encouraged by the shortages and difficulties of the war years. They disappeared when the war ended, perhaps because of the political direction and exploitation to which they had been subjected.[37]

A first prerequisite to any national economic development was a genuinely national bank, for all the existing banks, including the Imperial Ottoman Bank, were more or less under foreign control. After some discussion, a party congress of the Committee of Union and Progress in 1916 decided on the establishment of a National Credit Bank. The bank was opened in January 1917; its capital was 4 million Ottoman pounds, half paid-up, and an issue of 400,000 £10 shares was expressly limited to Ottoman subjects. The guiding spirit seems to have been Cavid Bey, the Finance Minister; with him on the provisional board of directors were Hüseyin Cahid [Yalçın] and a number of prominent merchants.[38]

Under the auspices of the bank, other enterprises were begun, notably two insurance companies. The founding of companies by private enterprise with local capital was given wide publicity,

---

[35] Y. H. Bayur, *Türk Ink. Tar.*, ii/4, pp. 494-6.

[36] Hallûk Cillov, 'Les Recensements industriels en Turquie', *R. Fac. Sci. Éc. Univ. Ist.*, xiii (1951–2), 163 ff. Conker and Witmeur, pp. 55 ff.

[37] Orhan Tuna, 'Küçük San'atlar ve kooperatifçilik Meseleleri', *Istanbul Üniversitesi Çanakkale Haftası 1952* (1953), pp. 100–2. There is also a more detailed study on Turkish co-operatives by Z. Fahri Fındıkoğlu.

[38] Tunaya, *Partiler*, pp. 204–5; Karpat, p. 83. The National Credit Bank (*Itibar-i Millî*) was merged in 1927 with the Bank of Affairs (*İş Bankası*) which had been established in 1924.

and factories were opened with impressive ceremonies.[39] At the same time foreign companies were required by law to have a certain number of Ottoman subjects on their boards of directors. A boycott of Greek-owned shops, ostensibly in reprisal for Greek ill-treatment of Turks in Macedonia, was also no doubt intended to increase the Turkish, as distinct from merely Ottoman participation in the advantages of commerce.[40]

These efforts to foster Turkish commerce and industry, made in the final phase of Ottoman decline, could achieve little, and in any case came to an end with the defeat of the Empire and the flight of the Young Turk leaders. They did, however, indicate some of the lines of economic policy and development which, at a later and more favourable time, the Turkish Republic was to follow.

Social Change: the New Élite

It is not possible to identify, with certainty, any important changes in the economic basis of social prestige and political power in Hamidian Turkey. It is, however, possible—and for an Islamic society like the Ottoman Empire this is far more important —to distinguish certain new social and professional elements, and to observe their emergence among the governing and cultivated *élites* of the country. These new elements came from a wider variety of social backgrounds than their predecessors. This social diversification of the educated *élite*, and perhaps even more the sheer increase in its numbers, gradually ended the cosy intimacy of earlier struggles. The Young Ottomans and the first constitutionalists had, with few exceptions, all been members of the inner circle of prestige and power, on the same social level and often personally acquainted with the men of the régimes they were opposing, and therefore always able to reach some sort of personal accommodation with them before things became really serious. Even in the first decades of the Hamidian period this remained true, when the Sultan found it worth while to send a pasha to Europe to tempt the exiles home with promises of pardon and promotion.[41] But as the literate *élite* became larger and more diverse, the personal bond was weakened, the struggle for power became sharper and fiercer, and the penalties for failure more

[39] Tunaya, pp. 204–5.   [40] Bayur, *Türk Ink. Tar.*, ii/4, pp. 493–4, Karpat, p. 84.
[41] See above, p. 196.

terrible and more final. Ironically, it was the Young Turks themselves, and not the old-fashioned Sultan, who inaugurated the large-scale execution of political opponents. By that time, the governing *élite* of the Empire had expanded beyond the dimensions of a family circle, and the change was reflected in the sharper conflicts and harsher tone of political life.

Among these new elements in the educated *élite* four are of special importance—officers and civil servants, lawyers and journalists. Men of these four professions played a role out of all proportion to their numbers in the preparation and establishment of the new Turkey.

Journalism and the law were entirely new professions in Turkey. Under the traditional order the only publicly recognized system of law and judicature was the *Şeriat*, the Holy Law of Islam. Its authorized exponents—muftis and kadis, jurisconsults and judges, were men of religion, identified by education, status, and function with the theologians and preachers, and forming, with them, the great Islamic hierarchic institution under the supreme authority of the *Şeyh-ül-Islâm* in Istanbul. But the establishment of new, secular codes, and of new, secular tribunals to administer them, also created a demand for new secular lawyers—judges, to perform a task for which the old kadis showed themselves ill equipped, and also advocates, to exercise a profession and develop a skill not previously known in the Islamic world. Secular lawyers were at first few in numbers and importance; the training schools of Abdülhamid increased them in both respects, and helped to prepare them for the new role they were to play in the structure of a modern state.

Like advocacy, journalism too was a new profession, without precedents and therefore without social traditions or connexions. The first journalists, in the *Tanzimat* period, had been part-time amateurs, men of letters, officials, or politicians, dabbling with a new medium the full potentialities of which they failed to appreciate. To some extent this is still true of the Hamidian period, when many journalists combined their activities with government appointments, teaching, or other professions. There was, however, a clear and rapid development of professional journalism—of a class of men skilled in the collection, presentation, and discussion of news and earning their principal livelihood through the press. The growth of literacy—according to Ahmed Emin the rate was tripled in the last quarter of the nineteenth century—and the increased desire for news and other information made newspaper publishing a profitable enterprise, and gave the journalist a new standing and influence.

In some of the Arab successor states of the Ottoman Empire the radical advocates and journalists were able, for a while, to play a decisive role in political life. In the Turkish Revolution the role of the lawyers and journalists, though important, was subordinate to that of two other elements in the new *élite*—the officers and the civil servants.

The army and the bureaucracy were of course no new professions in Turkey; on the contrary, they had, together with the men of religion, formed the three pillars on which the traditional political and social order had rested. But unlike the men of religion, they had undergone a tremendous transformation. For more than a century the Ottoman state had lavished its best efforts on military and administrative reform—to create the modern army which alone could resist the European enemy, and the modern state on which, as time had shown, that army must depend. New methods and equipment, new schools and curricula, had produced a new kind of officer and official—open to Western influences and ideas, aware of the diminished status of their country, and adding to their ancient loyalty a new, radical patriotism inspired by European example. After all the changes and reforms, the military and bureaucratic classes, broadly recruited but self-perpetuating, retained a deep conviction of their privileges and responsibilities in the defence and government of the Empire—of a status and authority to which the rest of the population still gave automatic and spontaneous recognition. As late as 1920 the first Grand National Assembly of the Kemalist revolution, meeting in Ankara, included among its members 138 officials, 53 soldiers, and 53 men of religion—nearly two-thirds of the total.[42]

The Revolutionaries: Kemalist Populism

It is thus very difficult to isolate and identify any clear economic factors or forces in the earlier phases of the Turkish revolutionary struggle. The contenders for power were different groups or factions within the governing *élite*—all of them dependent on the

[42] See above, p. 246; cf. the comments of D. A. Rustow in Macridis, pp. 315–16.

state for a livelihood, and regarding the public service as a natural and proper career for men of their kind.

The Young Turks had, however, brought one important change —the broadening of the popular basis of political interest and participation. The army had always drawn its recruits from a wider circle than the religious hierarchy, with its entrenched dynasties of rank and wealth, or the bureaucracy, with its inevitable bias in favour of the capital and its insistence on traditional, formal education. The poor and the provincial, the low-born and the uneducated, all had their chance in the armed forces, and in the course of the nineteenth century the expanding, modernized army offered the most promising career open to talent.[43]

The Young Turk Revolution, and the emergence of the officer corps as the dominating factor in political affairs, thus broadened the range of political activity and concern far beyond the small circle of the palace and the Sublime Porte, within which they had previously remained. The events of the following years encouraged and accelerated this change. The series of elections, both general and local; the increase in literacy and the swift expansion of the press; above all, the growing practice of contenders for political power to appeal for public support by meetings and rallies and even local party branches, helped to create a new attitude to politics among many Turks who had previously regarded such matters as outside their competence and irrelevant to their lives.[44]

As well as political participation, the Young Turks also provided the first schooling in direct action. In 1913 they launched a simultaneous campaign of irredentist agitation and guerrilla activity in the vain hope of recovering the lost province of Western Thrace. It would seem that in the autumn of 1918, foreseeing the military defeat of the Empire, they began to make preparation for a resistance movement in Anatolia.[45]

In these circumstances, it is not surprising that some observers at the time, both Western and Turkish, should have regarded the new nationalist movement in Anatolia as a disguised reappearance of the discredited Committee of Union and Progress. In a sense, they were not entirely wrong. It soon became apparent, however, that something new and different was afoot—and there was some anxiety as to what it might be.

Ahmed Izzet Paşa, the Grand Vezir of the Armistice, tells in a

[43] Rustow, in *Wld. Polit.*, xi. 515.   [44] Ibid. p. 541.   [45] Ibid. p. 541–2.

letter how in the winter of 1920–1, when the return to the Greek throne of King Constantine had cooled the philhellene ardour of the Allied governments, they began to consider the possibility of an accommodation with the nationalists, and to make anxious inquiries about them. A number of British officers came to see him and, believing him to be in secret communication with the men in Anatolia, made searching inquiries into his political opinions and, especially, wanted to know whether the Anatolians were completely tied up with the Bolsheviks. Izzet Paşa replied that

this group consists in the main of military commanders and their staffs, of country notables and landowners, and of intellectuals; it is therefore inconceivable that they should have any inclination to Communist theories. However, if the Western powers insist on applying unjustified pressure, it is not unlikely that they will throw themselves into the arms of Russia.[46]

Izzet Paşa, on his own statement, was choosing his words carefully; in doing so, he was giving a first formulation of what was, elsewhere, to become a classical political ploy. At the same time, his characterization of the nationalist movement was remarkably accurate, and his description of their attitude to Communism amply borne out by subsequent events.

There was, however, a time, in the early days of the movement, when Kemal himself gave voice to radical social and economic views. Speaking in Ankara on 1 December 1921, he had said:

If we must define our government sociologically, we would call it 'people's government'. . . . We are toiling people, poor people, who work to save their lives and independence. Let us know what we are! We are people who work and who must work to be saved and to live. For this every one of us has the right and the authority, but only by working do we acquire that right. There is no room, and no right, in our society for men who want to lie on their backs and live without working. Populism is a social principle that seeks to rest the social order on its work and its law. Gentlemen! We are men who follow a principle that entitles us, in order to preserve this right and to safeguard our independence, to struggle as a whole nation against the imperialism that seeks to crush and the capitalism that seeks to swallow our very nationhood . . . that is the basis on which our government rests, a clear sociological basis. . . . But what can we do if we don't resemble democracy, we don't resemble socialism, we don't resemble anything?

[46] Quoted by Inal, p. 1996; cf. Rustow, in *Wld. Polit.*, xi. 542.

Gentlemen, we should be proud of defying comparison! Because, gentlemen, we resemble ourselves![47]

Kemal's populism, which later found its way into the programme of the Republican People's Party and even into the Turkish constitution, was far from being an empty word. Besides its well-known political and cultural implications, it also connoted certain economic and, still more, social ideas, which found expression in several measures of the republican government. With the signing of the peace treaty with the West and the progress of Westernization, it had, however, lost its outspoken anti-capitalist quality, and had been more concerned with such matters as the ending of surviving feudal privileges in the remoter areas of rural Anatolia.

On 17 February 1923 Mustafa Kemal inaugurated an economic congress in Izmir. In a speech of welcome to the assembled delegates, he spoke to them of the urgent need to seek and find the means of rapid economic development, and thus heal the economy of the nation from the wounds left by the neglect and incompetence of centuries:

Comrades, you come directly from the classes of the masses who really constitute our nation, and are chosen by them. You thus know at first hand the condition and the needs of our country and nation, the hopes and sorrows of our people. The words that you will utter, the measures that you will prescribe, may be considered as directly spoken by the people . . . the voice of the people is the voice of God.

Kemal then went on to discuss at length the futility of purely military power, the squandered blood and effort of the great Turkish Empires of the past:

My friends, those who conquer by the sword are doomed to be overcome by those who conquer with the plough, and finally to give place to them. That is what happened to the Ottoman Empire. . . . The arm that wields the sword grows weary and in the end puts it back in the scabbard, where perhaps it is doomed to rust and moulder; but the arm that holds the plough grows daily stronger, and in growing stronger becomes yet more the master and owner of the soil. . . .

In a word, national sovereignty must rest on economic sovereignty, without which political and military victories, however great, are empty and transitory. Likewise, without economic

[47] *Söylev*, i. 190–1. The last phrase has become a favourite text for quotation.

effort, the greatest and most sacred national objectives would be no more than paper enactments and empty fancies. The economic servitude of the public debts, the Capitulations, the concessions, must give way to a free and expanding national economy.

To achieve all this, great changes would be needed—the mechanization of agriculture, the development of industry, the improvement of communications: 'We must turn our country into a network of railways and motor roads . . . for while the West and the world use cars and trains, we cannot compete against them with donkeys and ox-carts on natural tracks.'

In this task, the whole nation would have to work together. The Turkish people were not divided into classes with conflicting interests. On the contrary, their existence and efforts were mutually necessary.

At this moment, my listeners are farmers, artisans, merchants and workers. Any of these can become the antagonist of another. But who can deny that the farmer needs the artisan, the artisan the farmer, the farmer the merchant, and all of them need one another and the worker.[48]

The congress continued its deliberations until 4 March. Although some of its discussions were devoted to such matters as the introduction of the Latin script, the congress did consider a number of economic problems, and at its final session passed an economic pact (*misak-i iktisadî*), which was to be the economic counterpart of the National Pact passed in both Ankara and Istanbul.[49]

The four groups mentioned in Kemal's speech—traders, farmers, artisans, and workers—were all represented at the congress, and met in separate groups. But the explicit rejection of class-war ideologies by Kemal in his opening speech set the keynote for the congress, and indeed for the social and economic ideologies of the Kemalist state, for a number of years.

This by no means meant the abandonment of the social radicalism—or populism—of the early days of the movement. On the contrary, during the 1920's two further measures of great importance were adopted, both in the field of agrarian reform.

---

[48] Text of Kemal's speech in *Söylev*, ii. 99 ff.; cf. *Hist.*, pp. 270 ff. and 312.

[49] On the economic pact see *OM*, ii (1923), 593, 671, and the published proceedings, *Zabıtlar*; on the National Pact cf. above, p. 243.

The first of these was the abolition, by a law of 17 February 1925, of the tithes (*Öşür*). This tax, with its roots going back to the medieval Islamic fiscal system, had become a serious abuse, irregular in its incidence and often greatly exceeding the legal tenth. A law of 1840[50] had standardized the tithes at the rate of one-tenth, which was later reduced to one-twelfth. The tax was calculated on the gross product, and was not subject to any allowances. Providing a large part of the revenues of the state, it had constituted a heavy burden on the peasantry.

With the abolition of the tax, the state monopolies—tobacco, matches, alcohol, &c.—now came to be a major source of state revenue, and the main burden of supporting the state was thus transferred from the small peasants to the landlords and towns-people who were the monopoly's principal customers. The republican government, by this measure, thus brought a major change in the material situation of the village population, and no doubt helped to assure their loyalty, or at least their quiescence, during the upheavals that followed.

The other major reform undertaken by the Republic was in landownership. The introduction of the Swiss code in 1926 had unified and modernized the system of land tenure, thus legally terminating such traces of feudalism as remained in the country. Legal termination was, however, insufficient, and a number of great landowners, notably in the south and the east, still enjoyed the status almost of *derebeys* in the provinces. Even in the more advanced parts of the country, the large landowner in the town, with his ally or dependant the rich peasant in the village, still wielded enormous powers over the peasantry.

These powers the Kemalist régime sought—with only limited success—to reduce or eliminate. One method was land distribution—the granting of lands by the state to landless peasants and new immigrants. Land distribution laws were passed in 1927 and 1929, but progress was very slow, and between 1923 and 1934 only 711,000 hectares were distributed.[51] The most important dis-tributions were in the eastern provinces, where, in addition to its social policies, the government was anxious to break the power of the feudal and tribal chiefs that had led the rebellion of 1925.

[50] Barkan, in *Tanzimat*, pp. 354 ff.; Inalcık, in *Muslim Wld.*, xlv. 226.
[51] Barkan, 'La Loi sur la distribution des terres', *R. Fac. Sci. Éc. Univ. Ist.* (1944–5), pp. 44 ff.

In some parts, especially in the Aegean provinces and in Karaman, a new class of landowners, with medium-size estates, was formed when the lands formerly held by Greeks were given, after the exchange of populations, to Muslim immigrants and to veterans of the war of independence. These last, with their close connexions with the new régime, often took over the prestige and authority formerly exercised by the local agas and landlords.[52]

There was another change, even more damaging to the privileges of these landowners. All over the country local branches of the People's Party were set up, with an active and well-defined role. In Kemal's Turkey the local party officials were the agents of the Kemalist revolution, giving 'advice' to the peasantry on a wide variety of subjects; in so doing they took over many of the powers formerly held by the magnates.[53]

The radicalism of the Kemalist régime in agrarian matters was not matched in its dealings with the urban working class. The Turkish working-class movement reached an important landmark in its development when it was able to participate, as a separate group, in the Izmir economic congress. During the period of the war of independence several attempts were made to form socialist and trade union groups, and, since their activities were directed chiefly against foreign enterprises, they were able to win a certain place in the national movement. Communist influences, however, appeared in several of these groups, and in the period after 1923, when Turkish policy was moving away from Russia and towards the West, the attitude of the state towards these movements became less tolerant. A labour code on liberal principles, which had been drawn up, was rejected, and a number of restrictions imposed. The emergency Law for the Maintenance of Order of March 1925 put an end to socialist and trade unionist activities.[54]

---

[52] A vivid fictionalized picture of these changes in an Aegean village will be found in Kemal Bilbaşar's story *Pembe Kurt* (Pink Wolf; Ist., 1953). See also above, p. 444.

[53] See above, p. 376.

[54] On the Turkish labour and trade union movements see Lütfü Erişçi, *Türkiyede Işçi Sınıfının Tarihi* (1951); Kemal Sülker, *Türkiyede Sendikacılık* (1955); Tunaya, *Partiler*, pp. 463 ff.; Laqueur, *Communism*, pp. 205 ff. (on Communist movements). Some Russian and other publications are listed by R. P. Kornienko in his review of Erişçi's book in *Sovietskoye Vostokovedenie*, iii (1957), 198–203. On the emergency law see above, pp. 269 ff.

Etatism [55]

The world crisis of 1929 opened a new phase in the economic and social development of the Turkish Republic. The pressure of economic necessity impelled the Turkish state to undertake more and more extensive economic activities, and led it, in 1931, to adopt etatism as a central plank in its programme; at the same time, the rise of dictatorship and of dictatorial movements in several of the European states discredited political as well as economic liberalism, and made it easier for the Turkish state to acquire and exercise the new political powers that went with its new economic responsibilities.

The new policy does not seem to have been inspired by any new ideological trends, or to have been directly due to any external theoretical influences. The crisis had, however, brought a certain revival of anti-Western and anti-capitalist feeling in Turkey; the new economic co-operation with Russia brought some renewal of the comradeship of the early years of the Republic. It was in these circumstances that a new ideological trend appeared in Turkey, known by the name of *Kadro*, the periodical that was its organ. *Kadro* was published between 1932 and 1934; its leading figures were Yakup Kadri Karaosmanoğlu, a distinguished Turkish novelist and, later, diplomat,[56] and a number of other writers and intellectuals. The policy of the *Kadro* group, which at first enjoyed some measure of official support, has been described as 'a superficial combination of Marxism, nationalism, and corporatism'.[57] Turkey, according to their analysis, had no accumulated capital and therefore no class struggle; it was the duty of the state to accumulate and utilize capital, and thus forestall the emergence of a class struggle. In this new economic state, a cadre—*kadro*—of qualified and competent leaders would direct the state economy in the interests of the masses who would follow and accept their leadership. The Turkish Revolution was part of a world-wide struggle for liberation from capitalism and imperialism; the Turkish state was concerned primarily with the creation of an advanced technology and developed economy, with itself as both supreme arbiter and active director of all economic and social matters.

[55] See above, pp. 280 ff.   [56] On Yakup Kadri, see above, pp. 289 and 395.
[57] Karpat, p. 70. Dr. Karpat's examination of the *Kadro* group has found the main basis of what is said here.

This blend of ideas from Rome, Constantinople, and Moscow was not of long duration. The frank discussion of economic and social problems, and the markedly radical character of some of the analyses and solutions propounded, led to the polite suppression of the journal and the exile of its editor as ambassador to Albania. The *Kadro* group was, however, the only one to undertake such analyses in Turkey in many years, and its influence on Turkish intellectuals has remained considerable.[58]

The acceptance of Russian models and the presence of Russian experts no doubt had their effect, irrespective of the wishes of the Turkish leaders, in extending state control and discouraging private industry. But apart from all this, the doctrine that 'the state must take charge' was, in a country like Turkey, an easy and familiar one, well in accord with the inherited traditions and habits of both the rulers and the ruled. To the Kemalist régime, authoritarian, bureaucratic, and paternalistic, the idea of state direction and control in economic life came as a natural and obvious extension of the powers, prerogatives, and functions of the governing *élite*. If economic development were really necessary, it would be undertaken by those who were responsible, in this as in all else, for the safety and well-being of the nation. It was far too important to be left to infidel business men and ignorant peasants.

Etatism thus meant, in effect, the intervention of the state as a pioneer and director of industrial activity, in the interests of national development and security, in a country where private enterprise was either suspect or ineffective. Some development had already been undertaken in the first ten years of the Republic, notably in the extension of the railways and the organization of the tobacco, match, and alcohol monopolies. The first Turkish five-year plan, applied from 1934 to 1939, attempted a massive advance.

'The main lines of the programme', says the Turkish official report, 'and the extent of the projected industries, were determined

---

[58] Karpat, pp. 70–73. Yakup Kadri's account of the end of *Kadro* appears in his autobiographical work *Zoraki Diplomat* (The Unwilling Diplomat), pp. 22 ff. The journal, he says, was published with the consent of the People's Party, and its sole purpose was to clarify and explain the Party's principles. A rag-tag and bobtail of opportunists and bureaucrats could not run a revolutionary movement; a revolutionary party could not be constructed without cadres. They also wanted to demonstrate that the economic system called etatism was not the same as monopolism, and should not serve as a means of loading private and sectional interests on the back of the people. On *Kadro* see further the group of articles in *Forum* (Ankara), Oct.–Dec. 1958.

solely by the desire to enable the country to meet its requirements . . .'[59] Certainly they were not determined by normal
economic consideration, and economists have found it easy to list
the errors and failures of the etatist industrialization, responsibility for which must be shared between the Turkish planners
and their foreign expert advisers.[60]

Nevertheless, with all their defects, the plans did bring an
important increase in Turkey's industrial output, which between
1927 and 1939 rose from 0·14 per cent. to 0·23 per cent. of the
world total. Only Russia and Japan reported more rapid industrial development.[61] Though productivity remained poor and
urbanization slow, capital accumulation and investment advanced, bringing progress also in private industry, and there is
some evidence of a rise in the standard of living, albeit a slow and
limited one.[62] Perhaps more important than the economic
achievements were the social changes which, unintended and
probably undesired, followed in their wake. The economic
activities of the Turkish government may have been incompetent
and misdirected; they did, however, create new openings and new
careers, and initiate the process which in time gave Turkey something she had never had before—a Turkish middle class of
business men, managers, and technicians. The social and political
consequences of the emergence of this new element were to
transform Turkey in the next generation.

The War Years

During the gradual economic recovery of the 1930's, there was
a slow but significant accumulation of capital in private possession.
The many opportunities offered by Turkish neutrality during the
war years gave a new impetus to this movement. The Turkish
tax system, despite an overhaul in 1934, was still based on gross
earnings, and was not supported by any modern apparatus of
assessment, control, and collection. Bearing heavily on earners of
fixed wages and salaries, it allowed both the merchants and the
farmers to retain and accumulate their wartime riches, almost
unscathed by direct taxation.[63]

[59] *Turkey on the Way of Industrialization* (Ank., 1937), p. 38.
[60] See above, pp. 281–2.   [61] Hershlag, in *Kyklos*, p. 332.   [62] Ibid. p. 339.
[63] Karpat, pp. 92–93; cf. Nasuhi Bursal, *Die Einkommenssteuerreform in der Türkei* (1953).

Two emergency fiscal measures were introduced during the war, with the purpose of taxing the wartime profits of the merchants and farmers, and thus helping to relieve the strain on the public treasury. The first was the capital levy of November 1942,[64] which fell primarily on the commercial classes in the towns. For the agricultural population another form of taxation was introduced whereby the state compulsorily acquired a proportion of the crop at fixed prices. At first limited to wheat, rice, butter, and some other foodstuffs, the levy was later extended to almost all agricultural products. ·

The incidence of the two levies was very uneven. From the farmers, the state bought between a quarter and a half of their grain, paying from two to three times the pre-war price. It left them free to sell the remainder at free market prices, which at times rose to twenty times the pre-war level. The capital levy, which soon turned out to have other purposes beside the purely fiscal, was eventually abandoned. In the event it proved to have done little damage to the position of the non-Muslim capitalist class as a whole; it had of course done none to the new Turkish Muslim capitalist class that had been coming into being.

The Democratic Opposition, 1945–50

The end of the war found Turkey with a new class of rich men, confident and ambitious; on the one hand they faced a mass of wage-earners and peasants who were distressed and discontented; on the other, a government of bureaucrats and soldiers who, by their wartime policies, had shown a dangerous incomprehension of business needs, a disrespect for the rights of property, and an economic paternalism that was both irksome and ineffective.[65]

There had, of course, been middle-class elements in Turkey before, but they were not Turkish and not Muslim. Separated from the dominant majority by both religion and language, the Greek, Armenian, and Jewish merchants and entrepreneurs of the Ottoman Empire had never been able to rise to the social and political role played by the new middle classes elsewhere. However great their economic power, it was to a large extent

[64] See above, pp. 291 ff.

[65] Note, for example, the sharp criticism of etatism at the economic congress held 22–27 Nov. 1948 (Jäschke, *Kalender*). cf. Karpat, pp. 92–93.

neutralized by the Ottoman system of communal organization, which effectively prevented them from exercising much influence on Turkish society or the Turkish state. If anything, they acted as a kind of buffer or shock-absorber, receiving the impulses that came from the West through commercial and financial contact, but not transmitting them to the Turkish, Muslim heart of the Ottoman state and society.

The appearance of a genuinely Turkish middle class, which was an essential part of the Turkish nation, was, therefore a development of the first importance. These new Turkish business men and managers were self-confident, self-reliant, and ambitious; they were becoming very resentful of the controls and restrictions imposed upon them by what they had begun to regard as the dead hand of officialdom. The civil servant was falling from the dizzy eminence that he once occupied in the Turkish social hierarchy. No longer was a civil service appointment the ultimate dream of every Turk with a secondary school education, nor a young bureaucrat the most sought-after bridegroom for a Turkish father with marriageable daughters. The appearance of a new and flourishing commercial class was radically changing the political balance of forces in the country, and affecting even her traditional social ethos.

The rise of this class was still hardly represented in the structure of government. Among the 453 deputies elected to the Assembly in 1943, 127 were public servants of various kinds, 67 members of the armed forces, 89 lawyers, and 59 teachers. Only 49 were merchants, 45 farmers, 15 bankers, and 3 industrialists.[66]

Land Reform

The new middle classes were already sharply critical of the government. They were soon joined by the landowners and country magnates. During the summer of 1945 the People's Party, returning to its populist origins, introduced a Land Reform Bill. On 14 May, after considerable preliminary argument, the Bill was submitted to the Assembly; on 11 June, after long parliamentary debates, it was passed and became law.

There had been earlier land reform laws under the Republic, but their scope had been limited and their effect, in application, still more so. The law of 1945 looked different. The objects of the

[66] *Vatan*, 11 Mar. 1943.

law, as stated in the first paragraph, were to provide land and means for peasants with none or too little, and to ensure the full and effective use of the arable lands of the country. The method was to grant land to such peasants, together with twenty-year, interest-free loans for development, and other material help. The land was to come from unused state lands and pious endowments, municipal and other publicly owned land, reclaimed land, land of unknown ownership, and land expropriated from private individuals. For the last-named category, all landed property in excess of 500 *dönüm* (123·5 acres) would be nationalized. Compensation would be paid on a sliding scale; the greater the area held, the lower the rate. It would be paid in instalments, over twenty years, in 4 per cent. treasury bonds. The law also laid down that the new holdings acquired under its provisions must not be split among heirs. It was estimated that about a third of the rural population, some 5 million persons, would benefit under the law, which, if fully applied, would effect a major revolution, transforming Turkey into a country of independent peasant smallholders.

The law was bitterly criticized; discussion in both the press and the Assembly was conducted with a vigour and acrimony unknown for many years. It was attacked from both left and right— by the left as Nazi, by the right as Communistic. Its defenders denied that it had anything to do with ideologies of left or right. It was a purely practical measure, carefully prepared, designed to bring a long overdue reform to Turkey's medieval countryside, and to free the peasants from thraldom to feudal landowners.[67]

The application of the law, delayed by political considerations, was excruciatingly slow, and in 1950, after further prolonged discussions, the nationalization limit was raised from 500 to 5,000 *dönüms*. The distribution began in 1947 with state lands and pious foundations, and by 1950 only a few score thousand *dönüms* had been distributed.

Workers and Peasants

The working class is a relatively new phenomenon in Turkey. In the nineteenth century there were barely a few thousand who could be properly so described, employed on the railways, the

[67] *Akşam*, 18 May 1945. On the Turkish land reform, which has been rather neglected by Western writers on Turkey, see Inalcık, in *Muslim Wld.*, xlv. 227–8; Barkan, in *R. Fac. Sci. Éc. Univ. Ist.* (1944–5), pp. 44–132 and his *Çiftçiyi Topraklandırma Kanunu* (1946); Karpat, pp. 99 ff.

water works, and other public utilities, the state arsenal and ordnance factories, the coal mines at Ereğli, and a few factories for matches, carpets, cloth, and the like. A large proportion of the workers were women, girls, and children. Thus in 1897, 121 out of 201 workers employed at the Istanbul match factory were women; about half of the 1,000 workers at the cloth-mill at Bakırköy were children.[68]

The first organized group seems to have been a 'society in favour of workmen' (*Ameleperver Cemiyeti*), founded in 1871, which may possibly have had some part in the strike at the naval arsenal at Kasımpaşa in 1872. This strike, the first in Turkey, was a joint effort of some 600 Muslim and Christian workmen, whose wages were several months in arrears. The workers struck after petitions and requests to the Sultan, the Grand Vezir, and the Ministry of the Navy had failed to produce results. On the principle of no pay, no work, they downed tools; they were paid a few days later.[69]

The illegal opposition movement of the 1890's also produced its labour wing, with the founding, in 1895, of the secret 'Ottoman Labour Society' (*Osmanlı Amele Cemiyeti*) among the workers at the ordnance factories at Tophane. The society lasted about a year, ending when its leaders were arrested and deported.[70]

The Young Turk Revolution of July 1908 unleashed a wave of strikes, of which nearly thirty occurred during the months of August and September. They were halted by a 'Provisional Law of Stoppage of Work' of 25 September, which showed clearly that the Committee of Union and Progress did not look with favour on the labour movement. The mutiny of April 1909, and the proclamation of martial law that followed it, provided the opportunity for further repressive measures, which severely limited the activities of the new labour unions and associations that were springing up.[71]

In the summer of 1909 the 'stoppage of work' law, despite charges that it served foreign economic interests, was passed by the parliament. A new 'Law of Associations', of the same year, also regulated labour organizations. Trade unions were permitted, except in 'enterprises that carry out public services' (Art. 8), a loose

---

[68] Sülker, pp. 7–9.   [69] Ibid. pp. 11–12; Erişçi, p. 8.

[70] Sülker, pp. 11–12; Erişçi, p. 8.

[71] Sülker, pp. 13 ff.; Erişçi, pp. 8 ff. According to Sülker (p. 16), the anti-strike law was demanded by German capitalists, and drafted by Count Ostrorog, Counsellor to the Ministry of Justice.

expression which covered the great majority of the working class.

This law, though permitting trade unions in private enterprises not providing public services, deprived the labour and union movement of the participation of those sections which had been most active and advanced, and in fact inhibited the growth of real trade unionism for nearly forty years. During the period of the armistice and the war of independence there was some revival of activity in Istanbul, within a patriotic rather than a class framework, and the workers succeeded in obtaining separate representation at the Izmir economic congress in 1923.[72]

In the following years, however, economic pressure and authoritarian example led to an increasingly severe attitude towards labour, culminating in the draft labour law of 1932. This law, prepared under the aegis of the newly established Ministry of Economics, was passed by the Assembly in July 1936. The new law, which had been prepared with the help of German (not Nazi) advisers, dealt with conditions of employment and work, and provided for compulsory labour inspection and compulsory arbitration committees for disputes.[73] As far back as 1931 the People's Party, in its programme, had denounced the attempt to arouse class consciousness. The revised Law of Associations of July 1938 formally prohibited organizations on a class basis.[74]

During the war years the Turkish government, like many others, imposed extensive controls and assumed power of direction of labour. From 1945, however, as part of the general movement of political and economic liberalization, a new status was accorded to labour. On 7 January 1945 a Ministry of Labour was established; in 1946 a new Law of Associations repealed the ban on class organizations and a number of trade unions promptly appeared. Soon some of them were accused of Communist tendencies and disruptive activities, and were prosecuted under the martial law that was still in force. The position of the unions was finally regularized by the 'Workers' and Employers' Unions and Regional Federations Law' of 20 February 1947, drafted with the help of two British expert advisers. It still remains in

[72] See above, pp. 459–60.

[73] On the labour laws see Ferit H. Saymen, *Türk İş Hukuku* (1954); Cahit Talas, *La Législation du Travail en Turquie* (1948); and, more generally the International Labour Office report on *Labour Problems in Turkey* (1950).

[74] Art. 9: 'Associations on the basis or in the name of family, community, race, sex, or class may not be founded'; cf. Sülker, p. 33.

force. This law still withheld the right to strike, but in other respects allowed the free formation of both unions and confederations. The number of unions rose to 73 in 1940, 77 in 1949, 88 in 1950, 137 in 1951, and 239 in 1952. An all-Turkish federation of unions was formed in Izmir in 1952, with an estimated membership of 150,000 workers.[75]

The peasants still had no distinctive organization of their own, and the various attempts to found a peasants' party, after both the First and Second World Wars, evoked little response.[76] The peasants were, however, increasing rapidly—and consciously—in status and political importance. The Republic had always paid lip-service to the Anatolian peasant, praising him as the backbone of the country—but deciding what was best for him, and sending government and party officials to enforce it. The peasant, accustomed for centuries, perhaps for millennia, to submit to the authority of the landlord and the state, had passively accepted this role.

The first major development in the Turkish countryside was the establishment of the Village Institutes. These, set up by a law of 1940, were to provide a five-year course of practical education for village boys and girls at public expense, and then send them back to their villages as schoolteachers and, more generally, as guides to more modern husbandry and hygiene. By their eighth anniversary, on 17 April 1948, there were twenty institutes with 15,000 pupils. A twenty-first was opened in Van in November of the same year.[77]

The Institutes were much criticized; they were at different times accused of inefficiency, of leftism, and of People's Party politics, and were eventually subjected to changes which modified their character very considerably. The awakening of the village, however, was no longer left to a few enthusiasts. In the 35,000 villages of Anatolia, the peasants of Turkey were at last stirring. Two fortunate harvests put the peasant on his feet economically; the return to party politics and free elections brought politicians to court his favour—and thus to enable him to demand something in return.

The really massive change in the Turkish countryside came

[75] Erişçi and Sülker, *passim*; also Tuna, 'The Organization of the Turkish Confederation of Trade Unions', *R. Fac. Sci. Écon. Univ. Ist.* (1953), pp. 109–19.

[76] On these parties see Tunaya, *Partiler, passim*.

[77] Jäschke, *Kalender*, 17 Apr. and 18 Nov. 1948. On the village institutes see further Karpat, pp. 377–80; Mahmut Makal, *A Village in Anatolia* (1954). This latter work is a most remarkable human document from a graduate of one of these institutes.

after the war, with the new wave of economic development. Within a few years many thousands of tractors entered Turkey, transforming Turkish agriculture, revolutionizing the village society that lives by it, and even battering their way into the new Turkish literature that mirrors these changes. The tractor is not only a source of wealth; it also confers prestige and status on its owner, gives a sense of power and nobility to its driver, and serves the village community in a thousand unsuspected ways.

There were many other material improvements, bringing greater comfort to the villagers, and a closer degree of participation in the life of the national community. In the neighbourhood of the towns, bus services, piped water, electricity, daily newspapers, and access to urban amenities heralded the dawn of a new age; even in remoter places, a local road, a daily bus, and a few battery-operated wireless sets brought new contacts with the outside world, a new awareness of membership of the larger community, and the beginning of a new process of far-reaching social change.

The peasant, at first mistrustful, then with growing confidence, has responded to this situation. With means, comforts, and amenities undreamt of in an earlier age, he has become more confident and more independent. In recent years, he has begun to show an awareness of his political power and of his human dignity that is probably without precedent in the past history of the country and that has few parallels among her neighbours. The problems of the Turkish peasant are far from solved—social and religious, economic and technological questions of profound importance remain to be faced and overcome. But the Turkish peasantry, numbering over 70 per cent. of the population of the country, have emerged from their ancient submission, to participate in public affairs of their country, to speak their word on the formation and exercise of government. Kemalism had brought the revolution to the towns and townspeople of Turkey, but had barely touched the villages. A second, silent revolution was now reaching the deeper layers of the nation, and starting a new transformation.[78]

---

[78] On the change in the peasantry see the illuminating essay of H. A. Reed, 'A New Force at Work in Democratic Turkey', *MEJ*, vii (1953), 33–44; also Paul Stirling, 'Social Ranking in a Turkish Village', *Brit. J. Sociol.* iv (1953), 31–44; and Lerner, pp. 19 ff. and 111 ff.

CHAPTER XIV

Conclusions:
The Turkish Revolution

The success that we have won until today has done no more than open a road for us, towards progress and civilization. It has not yet brought us to progress and civilization. The duty that falls on us and on our grandsons is to advance, unhesitatingly, on this road.

KEMAL ATATÜRK.

A ruined land on the edge of a precipice . . . bloody battles with various enemies . . . years of struggle and then, respected at home and abroad, a new country, a new society, a new state, and, to achieve these, ceaseless revolutions—this, in a word, is the Turkish general revolution.

KEMAL ATATÜRK.

Those who have grasped the purpose of the Revolution will always be able to safeguard it.

KEMAL ATATÜRK.

THE Turkish Revolution began, in the formal sense, with the forcible overthrow of an old political order and the establishment of a new one in 1908. In another sense, however, it has been going on for nearly two centuries. It began when a series of defeats at the hands of once-despised enemies forced the Turks, for the sake of survival, to adopt European weapons, to invite European advisers, and thus, however reluctantly, to admit all the new ideas and institutions that underlie the modern state and army. The first reforms were the work of autocratic rulers, who sought only to train and equip better armies. The high cost of military modernization led to severer taxation and harsher rule. Reformers and rebels were not always the same people in the Turkish transformation, and often they were in conflict with one another. Some of the most active reformers were men of autocratic disposition and habit, wielding an accepted authority, and indeed giving it a new strength and pervasiveness. The overcoming of conservative resistance involved the abrogation or enfeeblement of the traditional checks on the sovereign power, which was further reinforced by modern instruments of control.

These changes, and the resulting growth of despotism, did not pass unchallenged, the more so in an age when Europe, the model and example of enlightenment, offered a wide choice of secular ideologies of revolt. Liberal, patriotic, and even revolutionary ideas infected the Turkish students and cadets, diplomats and military attachés, who came to explore the secrets of the mysterious Occident; in time these ideas found their way to Turkey, where they gave a new impetus and a new direction to the young officers and officials, and led to the successive constitutional and popular movements of 1876, 1908, and 1920.

The basic change in Turkey—from an Islamic Empire to a national Turkish state, from a medieval theocracy to a constitutional republic, from a bureaucratic feudalism to a modern capitalist economy—was accomplished over a long period, by successive waves of reformers and radicals.

Some have seen in the Turkish Revolution no more than a series of reluctant and tardy responses to external stimuli and influences—to military defeat and diplomatic pressure, to the loss of provinces to foreign rule and the penetration of the home-land by foreign culture and commerce. Certainly the sources of inspiration of both reformers and radicals came from foreign ideologies and the successive phases of both the Turkish reform and Revolution were opened by military and diplomatic events —though here, it may be noted, the most powerful stimuli were not those of the remote great powers of Europe, but of the former subject peoples, whose swift rise and progress inflicted a sharper lesson and a deeper humiliation. It was the Greek rising and the successes of Muhammad Ali that finally provoked Mahmud to rid himself of the useless Janissaries and experiment with some-thing new; it was the Greeks again, landing at Izmir in 1919, who goaded the defeated and dispirited Turks to make a fresh and final effort to save and renew themselves. It would, however, be a gross over-simplification to attribute the whole Turkish movement, as some have done, to these European pressures and influences. Europe may have provided both the starting gun and the winning-post in the Turkish race against history; she did not provide the motive force.

It is natural to seek for parallels between the Young Turk and Kemalist Revolutions and the great European revolutions, in England, France, and Russia, and indeed points of resemblances are not lacking. In the Turkish *ancien régime* as in the others we can see such familiar pre-revolutionary features as financial stringency coupled with commercial expansion, administrative reform with governmental inefficiency, a questioning of fundamental allegiances among the rulers and intellectuals and a progressive withdrawal of consent on the part of important sections of the governed. In the Turkish Revolution we can see the characteristic succession of hope, terror, and dictatorship, in the transition from the constitutional millennium of 1908 to the repressions of the Young Turk triumvirate, and finally an authoritarian Republic in which Atatürk seems to take his place beside Bonaparte and Cromwell—even to the point of encountering and overcoming a Turkish La Vendée in the mountains of Kurdistan, and an Oxford among the ulema.

Yet, on closer examination, these resemblances seem to be superficial rather than fundamental. Although, as early as 1693, William Penn had proposed to include Turkish delegates in his proposed Diet of Europe, Ottoman Turkey was not a European country but an Islamic empire, drawing its inspiration from another faith, and shaped by another set of historical events and circumstances. True, Islam and Christendom had many elements in common, derived from the Hellenistic, Hebraic, and Middle Eastern heritage which both had shared—and perhaps these elements of unity made easier the ultimate transition of the Turks to a European civilization. But the great events and movements of European history had broken against the religious and military barriers that separated Islam from Christendom, leaving Turkey unaffected, even unaware. The struggle of Church and State, the Renaissance, the Reformation and Counter-Reformation, the scientific awakening, humanism, liberalism, rationalism, the Enlightenment—all the great European adventures and conflicts of ideas passed unnoticed and unreflected in a society to which they were profoundly alien and irrelevant. The same is true of the great social, economic, and political changes. The rise and fall of the baronage, the emergence of the communes, the rebirth of trade, the rise of the new middle class, the struggles of money and land, of city-state, nation-state, and Empire—all the swift yet complex evolution of European life and society, have no parallel in the Islamic and Middle Eastern civilization of the Ottomans. The growth and change and clash that preceded and shaped the

Turkish Revolution were thus radically different from those of the English, French, and even, though perhaps to a lesser extent, the Russian Revolutions.

The realization of these differences has led some observers to see in the Turkish transformation the prototype of the nationalist revolutions—of the struggle of the countries of the Middle East and Asia to throw off Western domination. Here too resemblances are not lacking. Though Turkey, unlike the Arab lands, Central Asia, India, and Indonesia, never fell under direct European rule, she nevertheless experienced many of the same processes as they did. The economic and diplomatic ascendancy of the Western powers in Turkey provided the setting—the well-intentioned reforming efforts of the Turkish régimes did the rest. The results were strikingly similar to those in the colonial empires: the old industries were destroyed by the competition of cheap manufactured imports; the old communal agrarian order was dislocated by the misguided introduction and rigid application of European legal concepts, which transformed tax-farmers into freeholders and added to the immemorial sufferings of the Oriental peasantry such new European afflictions as distraint and eviction; above all, an old and accepted system of social, economic, and political functions and responsibilities was disrupted and destroyed, leaving a void that was hard to fill. In Turkey, which remained an independent state, hasty and energetic reformers carried through their reforms with a ruthlessness and a precipitancy in striking contrast with the cautious conservatism of most Imperial authorities. In the event, they seem to have destroyed better than they built. While their Westernizing innovations often proved superficial and impermanent, their destruction of the old system of social bonds and obligations was final. Even the compensating advantages of the Imperial peace brought by the colonial régimes—security, unity, material advancement, efficient and conscientious government, the formation of a trained modern civil service—were lacking in Turkey, which encountered only the commercial and diplomatic pressures of Western power. This was an imperialism of interference without responsibility, which would neither create nor permit stable and orderly government.

It is perhaps by this point—the retention by the Turks of the final responsibility for their affairs—that we can explain some of the significant differences between the Turkish and other eastern revolutions. During the nineteenth and early twentieth centuries, the experience of Turkey in Westernization was in general shared with a number of other countries. Since 1918 there have been striking divergences. In Turkey the stream has been broadened and deepened—elsewhere it has been stopped, deflected, or reversed. In the Turkish, as in other modern revolutions, nationalism has been a tremendous force. It has, however, operated in a notably different way. Turkey is not a new state, where political thinking is still dominated by the problem of foreign rule and the fight to end it. Turkish leaders have accepted as well as asserted their responsibility for the affairs of their country, and have shown a cool realism and practical sense derived from long experience of government. They have been able to assess situations and define objectives—to make decisions related to facts, and to abide by them.

Another significant difference between the Turkish and some other nationalist leaders was the different vision of history that determined their attitudes to the conflicting power blocks and ideologies of the modern world. For the Turks, as for the others, imperialism was the great enemy. But for the Turks the really important part of the imperialist phenomenon was not the maritime expansion, since the sixteenth century, of Western Europe, which had affected them only indirectly; it was the overland expansion, during the same period, of Eastern Europe, which had brought the old Turkish lands north and east of the Black Sea and the Caspian under Russian rule, and forced the Ottoman Empire to fight a long series of bitter wars, in a rearguard defence against the Russian advance to the Mediterranean. Thus, while other nationalists looked to Russia for sympathy and support against the West, Turkey looked to the West for help against Russia, and continued, even after many of the others had turned away, to see in the West and in the Western way of life the best hope for the future. The Turkish nationalist struggle in its final phase—that of 1919–23—was directed against Western and not Russian encroachments, but it was followed by a more radical and determined effort of Westernization than ever before.

The attempt has been made, using methods derived from European history, to explain the successive phases of the Turkish Revolution as a struggle between economically defined classes for control of the state, or as an upsurge of a popular movement, seeking freedom from tyranny. Though a love of freedom and a conflict of classes can both at times be discerned, neither provides a fully adequate approach to the facts of modern Turkish history. Though important class changes followed the actions of the revolutionary régimes, they do not seem to have caused them, or to have determined the functioning of the state, which lived and acted as a vital, dominating power in itself. Far more important than the ruling class—if indeed such a thing can be identified— was the ruling *élite*; the small, associated groups of men who, in conjunction with the sovereign authority itself, effectively controlled the day-to-day working of the apparatus of power. There were several of these administrative, religious, and military *élite* groups, defined not primarily by economic class, but by training, function, and method of recruitment. Their formation, rivalries, and vicissitudes are vital to the understanding of the Turkish Revolution, for in a sense the Kemalist Republic was the culmination of a long process, whereby the Turkish governing *élite* transformed itself, the state, and finally the country. Not the least important aspect of this change was the broadening and diversification of the *élite* itself, which came to draw, for its recruitment, on ever wider circles of the population, and thus involved more and more of the Turkish nation in an active interest and even participation in the conduct of public affairs. This process was accelerated by economic development, the spread of education, the development of mass media of communication, and the emergence of new social classes disinclined to acquiesce in the paternalistic government of the old ruling groups. In this way the *élite*, no doubt unconsciously, helped to prepare its own eventual supersession by a more democratic form of government resting on a new social and economic order.

Among the Turks, the two terms most frequently used to denote their revolution are nationalism and Westernization—and the two are not, as in other parts of the world, in contradiction with one another. Besides its international aspect, already noted, the Turkish nationalist Revolution has an important internal aspect. At one time, in Turkey, it was fashionable to speak of the Revolution as a rising of the Turks against the Ottomans, as the liberation of the last of the subject peoples of the Ottoman Empire. This interpretation, though at first sight it may seem a little fanciful, contains an important element of truth. The loss of most of the Rumelian provinces, the transfer of the capital to Ankara, the successful struggle of Turkish Anatolia, all make the change from the Ottoman Empire to the Turkish Republic more than one of nomenclature. Anatolia, the Turkish heartland, had always taken second place to Rumelia, the home of most of the cosmopolitan ruling class of the Empire—even the Young Turk Revolution, in its successive phases, had rested on Macedonia and Thrace, and Kemal himself was born in Salonika. But the shift in the centre of gravity and the cult of Anatolianism made Anatolia the real as well as the sentimental centre of the nation, and gave to the Anatolians an opportunity that they had not had before. The great Rumelian bureaucratic, religious, and military families are dwindling and losing their importance. The Anatolian country boys—*Memleket çocukları*—and still more the Anatolian country lords and gentry are inheriting their places, and making Turkey a Turkish state in fact as well as in name.

For many Turks, the great transformation which has taken place in their country is to be defined, not merely in terms of economy or society or government, but of civilization. The essential change attempted by the Turks in their Revolution was one of Westernization—another step in the westward march of the Turkish people that began 1,000 years ago, when they renounced China and turned to Islam. Now, renouncing a large part though not the whole of their Islamic heritage, they have turned to Europe, and made a sustained and determined effort to adopt and apply the European way of life in government, society, and culture. Opinions differ as to the measure of success achieved in this attempt; there can, however, be no doubt that in large and important areas of the public life of Turkey the Westernizing revolution is accomplished and irreversible.

In this transformation, the replacement of old, Islamic conceptions of identity, authority, and loyalty by new conceptions of European origin was of fundamental importance. In the theocratically conceived polity of Islam, God was to be twice replaced: as the source of sovereignty, by the people; as the object of worship, by the nation. It is no doubt due to our common human frailty that, in the first flush of enthusiasm, the second was easier to accomplish than the first.

There was a time when the causes of both faith and freedom seemed in grave danger in the Turkish Republic. Since then, there has been a marked improvement in the prospects of both. The rigid secularism of the past, which, in the words of one observer, was turning Turkey into a 'positivistic mausoleum', has been relaxed, some would say to the point of danger of a clerical counter-revolution.

The cause of freedom, too, has made important if hard-won advances. Since the apocalyptic days which followed the first free election in May 1950, there have been many disappointments, and few can doubt that the Turkish experiment in democracy has been going through grave difficulties. Just as in the times of trial which followed the Young Turk Revolution of 1908, so now also there are some who are ready to write off Turkish democracy as a failure and its exponents as fools or frauds. But for one who was present in Turkey in those days, it is difficult to believe that the great hopes of that time were wholly in vain, or that they have been wholly abandoned. Amid all the difficulties and setbacks, there is still much that gives encouragement for the future. The social changes that preceded and accompanied the rise of demo- cracy have continued, and given greater strength and numbers to the new groups and elements whose interests and aspirations are with freedom; it is these groups which have made free institutions work, and are best able to preserve them. Finally—and perhaps most important of all—there is the personal quality that has been shown by so many Turks of different allegiances and from different walks of life—a quality of calm self-reliance, of responsi- bility, above all of civic courage. Without these, no attempt at democracy, however well-intentioned, can succeed. Against them, the ancient habits of autocracy and acquiescence cannot indefinitely survive.

SELECT BIBLIOGRAPHY

I. WORKS IN TURKISH

Abdullah, Fevziye. Mizancı Mehmed Murad Bey. *Tar. Derg.*, no. 3–4 (1950–1), 67–11. [*See also* Tansel.]

Adıvar, Halide Edib. *Türkiye'de Şark, Garp ve Amerikan Tesirleri*. Ist., 1946.

Adnan-Adıvar, Abdülhak. *Osmanlı Türklerinde Ilim*. Ist., 1943.

Aksüt, Ali Kemali. *Sultan Aziz'in Mısır ve Avrupa Seyahati*. Ist., 1944.

Akyüz, Kenan. *Tevfik Fikret*. Ank., 1947.

—— ed. *Batı Tesirinde Türk Şiiri Antolojisi*. Ank., 1953.

Ali, Kılıç. *Istiklâl Mahkemesi Hatıraları*. Ist., 1955.

—— *Kılıç Ali Hatıralarını Anlatıyor*. Ist., 1955.

Amca, Hasan. *Doğmayan Hürriyet*. Ist., 1958.

Arıburnu, Kemal. *Millî Mücadele ve Inkılâplarla Ilgili Kanunlar . . . I.* Ank., 1957.

Arif, Mehmed. *Anadolu Inkılâbı*. Ist., 1923.

Arif, Mehmed. Humbaracı-başı Ahmed Paşa Bonneval. *TOEM*, pts. 18–20. (1328 A.H.).

Asım, Ahmed. *Asım Tarihi*. 2 vols. Ist., n.d.

Ata, Tayyarzade. *Tarih-i Ata*. 5 vols. Ist., 1291–3 A.H.

Atatürk, Kemal. *Atatürk'ün Söylev ve Demeçleri* (Collected Speeches). 3 vols. Ist., 1945–52.

—— *Nutuk*. 2 vols. Ank., 1950–2.

—— *Atatürk'ün Askerliğe dair Eserleri*. Ank., 1959.

Atay, Falih Rıfkı. *Başveren Inkılâpçı*. Ist., n.d.

—— *Niçin Kurtulmamak*. Ist., 1953.

Barkan, Ömer Lûtfi. *Çiftçiyi Topraklandırma Kanunu*. Ist., 1946.

—— Türk Toprak Hukuku Tarihinde Tanzimat ve 1274 (1858) Tarihi Arazi Kanunnamesi, in *Tanzimat*, 321–421.

Baydar, Mustafa. *Atatürk Diyor ki*. Ist., 1957.

Baykal, Bekir Sıtkı. 93 Meşrutiyeti. *Bell.*, no. 21–22 (1942), 45–83.

Baysun, Cavid. Mustafa Reşit Paşa, in *Tanzimat*, pp. 723–46.

Bayur, Hilmi Kâmil. *Sadrazam Kâmil Paşa Siyasî Hayatı*. Ank., 1954.

Bayur, Hikmet. *Türk Inkılâbı Tarihi*. i, ii, pts. 1–4, iii, pt. 1. Ist., 1940–53.

—— Ikinci Meşrutiyet Devri üzerinde bazı Düşünceler. *Bell.*, no. 90 (1959), 267–85.

Birand, Kâmiran. *Aydınlanma Devri Devlet Felsefesinin Tanzimatta Tesirleri*. Ank., 1955.

Bıyıklıoğlu, Tevfik. *Trakya'da Millî Mücadele*. 2 vols. Ank., 1955–6.

—— *Atatürk Anadolu'da, 1919–21*, i. Ank., 1959.

Cebesoy, Gen. Ali Fuat. *Millî Mücadele Hatıraları*. Ist., 1953.

Cebesoy, Gen. Ali Fuat. *Moskova Hatıraları.* Ist., 1955.
—— . . . *Siyasî Hatıraları.* Ist., 1957.
Cemal Paşa. *Hatırat, 1913–22.* Ist., 1922.
—— *Hatıralar.* Ist., 1959.
Cemalüddin Efendi. *Hâtırât-i Siyasiye.* Ist., 1336/1917.
Cevad, Mahmud. *Maarif-i Umumiye Nezareti Tarihçe-i Teşkilât ve Icraatı.* Ist., 1339 A.H.
Cevdet Paşa, Ahmed. *Tarih-i Cevdet.* 12 vols. Ist., 1301–9 A.H.
—— *Maruzat. TTEM,* 14th year (1340 A.H.), 15th year (1341 A.H.), 16th year (1926).
—— *Tezakir,* i, ed. Cavid Baysun. Ank., 1953.
Danişmend, Ismail Hami. *Izahlı Osmanlı Tarihi Kronolojisi,* iv. Ist., 1955.
Daver, Bülent. *Türkiye Cümhuriyetinde Lâyiklik.* Ank., 1955.
Dursunoğlu, Cevat. *Millî Mücadelede Erzurum.* Ank., 1946.
Duru, Kâzım Nami. *Ittihat ve Terakki Hatıralarım.* Ist., 1957.
Durusoy, M. O. and Gökman, M. M., *Atatürk ve Devrimleri Biblio-yoğrafyası.* Ank., 1957.
Emre, Ahmet Cevat. *Atatürk'ün Inkılab Hedefi ve Tarih Tezi.* Ist., 1956.
Ergin, Osman [*see also* Nuri, Osman]. *Türkiyede Şehirciliğin Tarihî Inkişafı.* Ist., 1936.
—— *Muallim Cevdet'in Hayatı, Eserleri ve Kütüphanesi.* Ist., 1937.
—— *Türkiye Maarif Tarihi.* 5 vols. Ist., 1939–43.
Erişçi, Lütfü. *Türkiyede Işçi Sınıfının Tarihi.* Ist., 1951.
Esad, Mehmed. *Üss-i Zafer.* Ist., 1243/1827.
Esad, Mehmed. *Mirât-i Mühendishane.* Ist., 1312 A.H.
Esmer, Ahmet Şükrü. *Siyasî Tarih, 1919–39.* Ank., 1953.
Fuat, Ali. Ricali Tanzimattan Rifat Paşa. *TTEM,* n.s. (1930), 1–11. [*See also* Türkgeldi.]
Gerçek, Selim Nüzhet. *Türk Gazeteciliği, 1831–1931.* Ist., 1931.
—— *Türk Matbaacılığı,* i: *Müteferrika Matbaası.* Ist., 1939.
Gökalp, Ziya. *Türkleşmek, Islâmlaşmak, Muasırlaşmak.* Ist., 1918.
Gökbilgin, M. Tayyib. *Millî Mücadele Başlarken.* Ank., 1959.
Gölpınarlı, Abdülbâki. *Mevlânâ'dan sonra Mevlevîlik.* Ist., 1953.
Göreli, Ismail Hakkı. *Il Idaresi.* Ank., 1952.
Gövsa, Ibrahim Alâettin. *Türk Meşhurları Ansiklopedisi.* Ist., n.d.
Gözübüyük, A. Ş. and S. Kili. *Türk Anayasa Metinleri.* Ank., 1957.
Gözübüyük, A. Ş. and Sezgin, Zekai. *1924 Anayasası Hakkındaki Meclis Görüşmeleri.* Ank., 1957.
Halim Paşa, Prince Mehmed Said. *Buhranlarımız.* Ist., 1330–8 A.H.
Iğdemir, Uluğ. *Kuleli Vakası hakkında bir Araştırma.* Ank., 1937.
Imece, Mustafa S. *Atatürk'ün Şapka Devriminde Kastamonu ve Inebolu Seyahatları.* Ank., 1959.

Inal, Mahmud Kemal. *Osmanlı Devrinde Son Sadrıazamlar.* 14 pts. Ist., 1940–53.

Inalcık, Halil. Tanzimat Nedir, *in Tarih Araştırmaları.* Ank., 1941, pp. 237–63.

Iskit, Server R. *Türkiyede Neşriyat Hareketleri Tarihine bir Bakış.* Ist., 1939.

—— *Türkiyede Matbuat Rejimleri.* Ist., 1939.

Islâm Ansiklopedisi. Istanbul, 1941–

[Inönü], Ismet Paşa. *Inönü'nün Söylev ve Demeçleri.* Ist., 1946.

Kâmil Paşa. *Tarih-i Siyasî-i Devlet-i Aliye-i Osmaniye.* 3 vols. Ist., 1327 A.H.

Kaplan, Mehmed. *Namık Kemal; Hayatı ve Eserleri.* Ist., 1948.

Karabekir, Kâzım. *Istiklâl Harbimizin Esasları.* Ist., 1951.

Karal, Enver Ziya. Yunan Adalarının Fransızlar tarafından Işgalı ve Osmanlı-Rus Münasebâtı, 1797–8. *Tar. Semineri Derg.,* i (1937), 100–25.

—— *Fransa-Mısır ve Osmanlı Imparatorluğu, 1797–1802.* Ist., 1940.

—— *Halet Efendinin Paris Büyük Elçiliği, 1802–6.* Ist., 1940.

—— Osmanlı Tarihine dair Vesikalar. *Bell,* no. 14–15 (1940), 175–89.

—— Nizam-i Cedide dair Layihalar. *Tar. Ves.,* i (1942), 414–25; ii (1942–3), 104–11, 342–51, 424–32.

—— *Osmanlı Imparatorluğunda ilk nüfus Sayımı.* Ank., 1943.

—— *Selim III'ün Hat-ti Hümayunları; Nizam-i Cedit.* Ank., 1946.

—— *Osmanlı Tarihi,* v-vii. Ank., 1947–56.

Karaosmanoğlu, Yakup Kadri. *Vatan Yolunda; Millî Mücadele Hâtıraları.* Ist., 1958.

—— *Zoraki Diplomat.* Ist., 1955.

Kaynar, Reşat. *Mustafa Reşit Paşa ve Tanzimat.* Ank., 1954.

Kemal, Namık. *Vatan yahut Silistre,* ed. M. N. Özön. Ist., 1943.

Köprülü, M. Fuad. Vakıf Müessesesinin Hukukî mâhiyeti ve Tarihî Tekâmülü. *Vak. Derg.,* ii (1942), 1–35.

Kuntay, Mithat Cemal. *Namık Kemal.* 3 vols. Ist., 1944–56.

—— *Sarıklı Ihtilâlcı Ali Suavi.* Ist., 1946.

Kuran, Ahmed Bedevi. *Osmanlı Imparatorluğunda Inkılâp Hareketleri ve Millî Mücadele.* Ist., 1956.

Levend, A. S. *Türk Dilinde Gelişme ve Sadeleşme Safhaları.* Ank., 1949.

Lûtfi, Ahmed. *Tarih-i Lûtfi.* 8 vols. Ist., 1290–1328 A.H.

Mardin, Ebul'ulâ. *Medenî Hukuk Cephesinden Ahmet Cevdet Paşa.* Ist., 1946.

Midhat, Ahmed. *Üss-i Inkılâb.* Ist., 1294/1877.

Midhat, Ali Haydar. *Hâtıralarım, 1872–1946.* Ist., 1946.

Nadi, Yunus. *Ihtilâl ve Inkılâb-i Osmani.* Ist., 1325 A.H.

Niyazi, Ahmed. *Hâtırât-i Niyazi.* Ist., 1326 A.H.

Nuri, Osman. *Abdülhamid-i Sani ve Devr-i Saltanatı.* 3 vols. Ist., 1327/1909.

Nuri, Osman. *Mecelle-i Umur-i Belediye*, i. Ist., 1922.

Nuri Paşa, Mustafa. *Netaic ül-Vukuat.* 4 vols. Ist., 1294–1327 A.H.

Ökte, Faik. *Varlık Vergisi Faciası.* Ist., 1951.

Öz, Tahsin. Fransa Kıralı Louis XVI ci'nin Selim III'e Namesi. *Tar. Ves.*, i/3 (1941), 198–202.

—— ed. Selim III ün Sırkatibi tarafından tutulan Ruzname. *Tar. Ves.*, iii (May 1949), 183–99.

Özön, Mustafa N. *Namık Kemal ve Ibret Gazetesi.* Ist., 1938.

—— *Son Asır Türk Edebiyatı Tarihi.* Ist., 1941.

Rasim, Ahmed. *Osmanlı Tarihi.* 4 vols. Ist., 1326–30 A.H.

—— *Istibdaddan Hakimiyet-i Milliyeye.* 2 vols. Ist., 1923–5.

Rauf, Leskovikli Mehmed. *Ittihad ve Terakki Cemiyeti ne idi?* Ist., 1327 A.H.

Rifat Paşa, Sadık. *Müntehabât-i Asar.* Ist., n.d.

Safa, Peyami. *Türk Inkılabına Bakışlar.* Ist., n.d.

Said Paşa. *Said Paşanın Hâtırâtı.* 3 vols. Ist., 1328 A.H.

Şanizade, Mehmed Ataullah. *Tarih.* 4 vols. Ist., 1290–1 A.H.

Sarç, Ömer Celâl. Tanzimat ve Sanayiimiz, *in Tanzimat*, pp. 423–40.

Saymen, Ferit H. *Türk Iş Hukuku.* Ist., 1954.

Şehsuvaroğlu, Haluk Y. *Sultan Aziz. Hayatı Hal'ı Ölümü.* Ist., 1949.

Şeref, Abdurrahman. *Tarih-i Devlet-i Osmaniye.* 2 vols. Ist., 1309 A.H.

—— *Tarih Musahabeleri.* Ist., 1340 A.H.

Siyasal Bilgiler Fakültesi. *Kaza ve Vilâyet Idaresi üzerinde bir Araştırma.* Ank., 1957.

Sülker, Kemal. *Türkiyede Sendikacılık.* Ist., 1955.

Süngü, Ihsan. Galatasaray Lisesi'nin Kuruluşu. *Bell.*, no. 28 (1943), 315–47.

—— Tanzimat ve Yeni Osmanlılar, *in Tanzimat*, pp. 777–857.

Süreyya, Mehmed. *Sicill-i Osmani.* 4 vols. Ist., 1308–15 A.H.

Suvla, Refii Şükrü. Tanzimat Devrinde Istikrazlar, *in Tanzimat*, pp. 263–88.

Talât Paşa. *Talât Paşa'nın Hatıraları*, ed. H. C. Yalçın. Ist., 1946.

Tanpınar, Ahmet Hamdi. *XIX Asır Türk Edebiyatı Tarihi.* 2nd ed. Ist., 1956.

Tansel, Fevziye Abdullah. Arap Harflerinin Islâhı ve Değiştirilmesi hakkında ilk Teşebbüsler ve Neticeleri, 1862–84. *Bell.*, no. 66 (1953), 224–49.

Tarihi Muhakeme, i. Ist., 1919.

Tevfik, Ebüzziya. *Nümûne-i Edebiyat-i Osmaniye.* 3rd ed. Ist. 1306 A.H. (Ist ed. 1296/1878).

—— Yeni Osmanlılar. *Yeni Tasvir-i Efkâr.* 1909.

Toğan, A. Zeki Velidi. *Bugünkü Türkili (Türkistan) ve yakın Tarihi.* 2 vols. Ist., 1942–7.

Tuna, Orhan. Küçük San'atlar ve Kooperatifçilik Meseleleri. *Ist. Üniv. Çanakkale Haftası 1952.* Ist., 1953.

Tunaya, Tarık. Amme Hukukumuz bakımından ikinci Meşrutiyetin Siyasî Tefekküründe 'Garpçılık' Cereyanı. *Ist. Univ. Huk. Fak. Mec.*, xiv (1948), 586–630.

—— *Türkiyede Siyasî Partiler, 1859–1952.* Ist., 1952.

—— Türkiye Büyük Meclisi Hükumeti'nin Kuruluşu ve Siyasî Karakteri. Ist., n.d.

—— Amme Hukukumuz Bakımından, ikinci Meşrutiyetin Siyasî Tefekküründe 'Islamcılık' Cereyanı. *Ist. Univ. Huk. Fak. Mec.*, xix (1954).

—— Osmanlı Imparatorluğundan Türkiye Büyük Millet Meclisi Hükumeti Rejimine Geçiş', in *Prof. Muammer Raşit Seviğ'e Armağan.* Ist., 1956.

—— Türkiyenin Siyasî Gelişme Seyri içinde Ikinci 'Jön Türk' Hareketinin Fikrî Esasları, in *Prof. Tahir Taner'e Armağan.* Ist., 1956.

—— and Reşit Ülker. *Mufassal Fihristli Özetli Milletvekilleri Seçimi Kanunu ve Ilgili Mevzuat.* Ist., 1954.

Turan, Osman. Türkler ve Islamiyet, *Ank. Univ. Dil ve Tar.-Coğ. Fak. Derg.*, v (1945–6), 457–85.

Turhan, Mümtaz. *Kültür Değişmeleri.* Ist., 1951.

—— *Garblılaşmanın Neresindeyiz.* 2nd ed. Ist., 1959.

Türk Devrim Tarihi Enstitüsü Yayımları. *Cümhurbaşkanları, Başbakanlar ve Millî Eğitim Bakanlarının Millî Eğitimle ilgili Söylev ve Demeçleri,* i. Ank., 1946.

Turkey, Min. of Evkaf. *Evkâf-i Humayun Nezaretinin Tarihçe-i Teşkilâtı.* Ist., 1335 A.H.

—— Min. of Ed. *Tanzimat,* i. Ist., 1940.

Türkgeldi, Âli. *Mondros ve Mudanya Mütarekelerinin Tarihi.* Ank., 1948.

Türkgeldi, Ali Fuad. *Görüp Işittiklerim.* 2nd ed. Ank., 1951.

Ülgener, F. *Iktisadî Inhitat Tarihimizin Ahlâk ve Zihniyet Meseleleri.* Ist., 1951.

Uluçay, M. Çağatay. *Saruhan'da Eşkıyalık ve Halk Hareketleri.* 2 vols. Manisa-Istanbul, 1944–5.

Unat, Faik Reşit. Ahmet III Devrine ait bir Islâhat Takriri. *Tar. Ves.,* i (1941), 107–21.

—— Atatürk'ün Askerlikten Istifası. *Tar. Ves.,* n.s., i (1955), 3–8.

Us, Hakkı Tarık. *Meclis-i Meb'usân, 1293–1877.* 2 vols. Ist., 1940.

Uşaklıgil, Halid Ziya. *Saray ve Ötesi.* 3 vols. Ist., 1940–1.

Uzunçarşılı, Ismail Hakkı. Sadrazam Halil Hamit Paşa. *Türkiyat Mecmuası,* v (1936), 213–67.

—— Selim III'ün Veliaht iken Fransa Kralı Lüi XVI ile Muhabereleri. *Bell.,* no. 5–6 (1938), 191–246.

—— *Alemdar Mustafa Paşa.* Ist., 1942.

—— Ali Suâvi ve Çırağan Vak'ası. *Bell.,* no. 29 (1944), 71–118.

Uzunçarşılı, Ismail Hakkı. V Murad'i Tekrar Padişah Yapmak Isteyen K. Skaliyeri-Aziz Bey Komitesi. *Bell.*, no. 30 (1944), 245–328.

—— Çerkes Hasan Vak'ası. *Bell.*, no. 33 (1945), 89–133.

—— Beşinci Sultan Murad'ın Tedâvîsine ve Ölümüne ait Rapor ve Mektuplar 1876–1905. *Bell.*, no. 38 (1946), 317–67.

—— *Midhat ve Rüştü Paşaların Tevkiflerine dair Vesikalar.* Ank., 1946.

—— *Osmanlı Devletinin Merkez ve Bahriye Teşkilâtı.* Ank., 1948.

—— Ondokuzuncu Asır Başlarına kadar Türk-Ingiliz Münasebatına dair Vesikalar. *Bell.*, no. 51 (1949), 573–650.

—— *Midhat Paşa ve Taif Mahkûmları.* Ank., 1950.

—— Asâkir-i Mansure'ye Fes Giydirilmesi hakkında Sadr-i Âzam Takriri ve II Mahmud'un Hatt-i Humayunu. *Bell.*, no. 70 (1954), 223–30.

—— 1908 Yılında Ikinci Meşrutiyetin ne Surette Ilân Edildiğine dair Vesikalar. *Bell.*, no. 67 (1956), 103–74.

Yusuf, Akçuraoğlu. *Üç Tarz-i Siyaset.* Ist., 1327 A.H.

—— Türkcülük. *Türk Yılı*, i (1928), 289–455.

2. WORKS IN OTHER LANGUAGES

Adnan, A. *La Science chez les Turcs ottomans.* Paris, 1939.

Adnan-Adivar, Abdulhak. Interaction of Islamic and Western Thought in Turkey, *in* T. Cuyler Young, ed., *Near Eastern Culture and Society.* Princeton, 1951, 119–29.

Allen, Henry E. *The Turkish Transformation: a study in social and religious development.* Chicago, 1935.

Alp, Tekin [Moise Cohen]. *Le Kemalisme.* Paris, 1937.

Aristarchi, G. *Législation ottomane.* 7 vols. Istanbul, 1873–88.

[Atatürk, K.] *A Speech Delivered by Ghazi Mustapha Kemal, President of the Turkish Republic, October 1927.* Leipzig, 1929.

Babinger, F. *Stambuler Buchwesen im 18 Jahrhundert.* Leipzig, 1919.

—— *Die Geschichtsschreiber der Osmanen und ihre Werke.* Leipzig, 1927.

Bailey, Frank Edgar. *British Policy and the Turkish Reform Movement.* Cambridge, Mass., 1942.

Barkan, Ömer Lutfi. La Loi sur la Distribution des Terres aux agriculteurs et les problèmes essentielles d'une réforme agraire en Turquie. *R. Fac. Sci. Éc. Univ. Ist.* (1944–5), 44–132.

Başgil, Ali Fuad and others. *La Turquie.* Paris, 1939. (No. VII in H. Levy-Ullmann and B. Mirkine-Guetzevitch, eds., *La Vie juridique des peuples.*)

Becker, C. H. *Islamstudien.* 2 vols. Leipzig, 1932.

Belin, [F.A.]. Étude sur la propriété foncière en pays musulman et specialement en Turquie. (*J. As.*, 1862). Reprint Paris, 1862.

Belin, [F.A.]. Essai sur l'histoire économique de la Turquie. (*J. As.*, 1885.) Reprint Paris, 1885.

Berkes, Niyazi. Historical Background of Turkish Secularism, *in* R. N. Frye, ed. *Islam and the West*. The Hague, 1957, pp. 41–68.

Birge, John K. *A Guide to Turkish Area Study*. Washington, 1949.

Blaisdell, D. C. *European Financial Control in the Ottoman Empire*. New York, 1929.

Bombaci, Alessio. *Storia della letteratura turca*. Milan, 1956.

Boppe, A. La France et le 'militaire turc' au XVIIIᵉ siècle. *Feuilles d'Histoire* (1912), 386–402 and 490–501.

Bursal, Nasuhi. *Die Einkommenssteurreform in der Türkei*. Wintherthur, 1953.

Canard, M. Coiffure européenne et Islam. *Annales de l'Institut d'Études Orientales* (Algiers), viii (1949–50), 200–29.

Cahun, Léon. *Introduction à l'Histoire de l'Asie, Turcs et Mongols des Origines à 1405*. Paris, 1896.

Castagné, J. La Latinisation de l'alphabet turk dans les républiques turko-tartares de l'U.R.S.S. *R. Ét. islam.*, i (1927), 321–53.

Caussin de Perceval, A. P. *Précis historique de la Destruction du Corps des Janissaires par le Sultan Mahmoud en 1826*. Paris, 1833.

Cillov, Halluk. Les Recensements industriels en Turquie. *R. Fac. Sci. Écon. Univ. Ist.*, xiii (1951–2), 162–77.

Colombe, M. Le Nouveau texte de la constitution turque. *C. Or. contemp.* iv (1946), 771–808.

—— Une Lettre d'un prince égyptien du XIXᵉ siècle au Sultan ottoman Abd al-Aziz. *Orient*, v (1958), 23–38.

Conker, O. and E. Witmeur. *Redressement économique et industrialisation de la nouvelle Turquie*. Paris, 1937.

Davison, R. H. Turkish Attitudes concerning Christian-Muslim Equality in the Nineteenth Century. *American Historical Review*, lix (1953–4), 844–64.

—— 'European Archives as a source for later Ottoman history', *in Report on Current Research on the Middle East 1958*. Washington, 1959, pp. 38–41.

—— 'The Question of Fuad Paşa's "Political Testament" '. *Belletin*, no. 89 (1959), 119–36.

Deny, Jean. L'adoption du Calendrier Grégorien en Turquie. *RMM*, xliii (1921), 46–53.

—— Les 'Souvenirs' du Gâzi Moustafa Kemal Pacha. *R. Ét. islam.*, i (1927), 117–222.

—— and R. Marchand. *Petit Manuel de la Turquie nouvelle*. Paris, 1933.

—— La Réforme actuelle de la langue turque. *En Terre d'Islam*, n.s., x (1935), 223–47.

Depont, O. and K. Coppolani. *Les Confréries religieuses musulmanes.* Algiers, 1897.

Djemal Pasha, Ahmed. *Memories of a Turkish Statesman, 1913–1919.* London–New York, 1922.

Doctrines et programmes des partis politiques ottomans. *RMM*, xxii (1913), 151–64.

Duda, H. W. Die Gesundung der türkischen Sprachreform. *Der Islam*, xxvi (1942), 77–100.

—— *Vom Kalifat zur Republik.* Vienna, 1948.

Duhamel, Georges. *La Turquie nouvelle.* Paris, 1954.

Dwight, D. W. *Constantinople; Settings and Traits.* New York–London, 1926.

Eberhard, W. Nomads and Farmers in South-Eastern Turkey: Problems of Settlement. *Oriens*, vi (1953), 32–49.

Edib, Halide [Adıvar]. *Memoirs.* London, 1926.

—— *The Turkish Ordeal; being the Further Memoirs of Halide Edib.* London, 1928.

—— *Turkey Faces West.* New Haven, 1930.

—— *Conflict of East and West in Turkey.* 2nd ed. Lahore, 1935.

Elliot, Sir Henry. *Some Revolutions and Other Diplomatic Experiences.* London, 1922.

Emin, Ahmed. *The Development of Modern Turkey as measured by its Press.* New York, 1914.

—— *Turkey in the World War.* New Haven, 1930. [*See also* Yalman.]

Encyclopaedia of Islam. 1st ed. 4 vols and Suppl. Leiden, 1913–38. 2nd ed. 1954–

Engelhardt, Ed. *La Turquie et le Tanzimat.* 2 vols. Paris, 1882–4.

Fesch, Paul. *Constantinople aux derniers jours d'Abdul-Hamid.* Paris, 1907.

Fischer, A. *Aus der religiösen Reformbewegung in der Türkei.* Leipzig, 1922.

Franco, M. *Essai sur l'histoire des Israélites de l'Empire Ottoman.* Paris, 1897.

Frye, R. N., ed. *Islam and the West.* The Hague, 1957.

Gibb, E. J. W. *A History of Ottoman Poetry.* 6 vols. London, 1900–9,

Gibb, H. A. R. and Harold Bowen. *Islamic Society and the West*, i: *Islamic Society in the Eighteenth Century*, pt. 1. London, 1950. Pt. 2. London, 1957.

Gökalp, Ziya, trans. and ed. Niyazi Berkes. *Turkish Nationalism and Western Civilization.* London, 1959.

Gooch, G. P. and Temperley, Harold. *British Documents on the Origins of the War 1898–1914*, v. London, 1928; ix/i, London, 1933.

Gorvine, A. and L. L. Barber. *Organization and Functions of Turkish Ministries.* Ank., 1957.

Gorvine, A. *An Outline of Turkish Provincial and Local Government.* Ank., 1956.

Graves, P. *Briton and Turk.* London, 1941.

Grunebaum, G. E. von, ed. *Unity and Variety in Muslim Civilization.* Chicago, 1955.

Hammer-Purgstall, J. von. *Geschichte des Osmanischen Reiches.* 10 vols. Pest, 1827–35. 2nd ed. 4 vols. Pest, 1835–40.

Hartmann, M. *Der islamische Orient,* iii: *Unpolitische Briefe aus der Türkei.* Leipzig, 1910.

Hershlag, Z. Y. Turkey: Achievements and Failures in the Policy of Economic Development during the Inter-War Period 1919–39. *Kyklos* (1954), 323–50.

—— *Turkey; an Economy in Transition.* The Hague [1960].

Heyd, U. Islam in Modern Turkey. *R. C. As. J.*, xxxiv (1947), 299–308.

—— *Foundations of Turkish Nationalism.* London, 1950.

—— *Language Reform in Modern Turkey.* Jerusalem, 1954.

Hostler, C. W. Trends in Pan-Turanism. *MEA*, iii (1952), 3–13.

—— *Turkism and the Soviets.* New York, 1957.

Hüber, R. *Die Bagdadbahn.* Berlin, 1943.

Hurewitz, J. C. *Diplomacy in the Near and Middle East: a Documentary Record.* 2 vols. Princeton, N.J., 1956.

Imhoff, Gen. Die Entstehung und der Zweck des Comités für Einheit und Fortschritt. *WI*, i (1913), 167–77.

Inalcık, Halil. Land Problems in Turkish History. *Muslim World*, xlv (1955), 221–28.

International Bank for Reconstruction and Development. *The Economy of Turkey.* Baltimore, 1951.

International Labour Office. *Labour Problems in Turkey.* Geneva, 1950.

Jäschke, G. Die Entwicklung des osmanischen Verfassungsstaates von den Anfängen bis zur Gegenwart. *WI*, v (1918), 5–56.

—— and Pritsch, E. Die Türkei seit dem Weltkriege. Geschichtskalender 1918–1928. *WI*, x (1927–9), 1–154.

—— Die Türkei seit dem Weltkriege. ii: Türkischer Geschichtskalender für 1929 mit neuem Nachtrag zu 1918–1928. iii: Für 1930. iv: Für 1931–1932. *WI*, xii (1930–1), 1–50, 137–66; xv (1933), 1–33.

—— Der Freiheitskampf des türkischen Volkes. *WI*, xiv (1932), 6–21.

—— Zur Geschichte des türkischen Nationalpakts. *MSOS*, xxxvi/2 (1933), 101–16.

—— Der Weg zur russisch-türkischen Freundschaft. *WI*, xvi (1934), 23–28.

—— Die grösseren Verwaltungsbezirke der Türkei seit 1918. *MSOS*, xxxviii (1935), 81–104.

—— Die Türkei in den Jahren 1933 und 1934. Geschichtskalender. *MSOS*, xxxviii (1935), 105–42.

—— Nationalismus und Religion im türkischen Befreiungskriege. *WI*, xviii (1936), 54–69.

—— Kommunismus und Islam im türkischen Befreiungskriege. *WI*, xx (1938), 110–17.

—— Die ersten Verfassungsentwürfe der Ankara-Türkei. *Mitt. Aus. Hoch. der Univ. Berlin*, xlii/2 (1939), 57–80.

—— Vom Osmanischen Reich zur Türkischen Republik. Zur Geschichte eines Namenswechsels. *WI*, xxi (1939), 85–93.

—— Der Turanismus der Jungtürken. Zur osmanischen Aussenpolitik im Weltkriege. *WI*, xxiii (1941), 1–54.

—— *Die Türkei in den Jahren 1935–1941*. Leipzig, 1943.

—— Der Turanismus und die kemalistische Türkei, *in* R. Hartmann and H. Scheel, eds. *Beiträge zur Arabistik, Semitistik und Islamwissenschaft*. Leipzig, 1944, pp. 468–73.

—— Zur Krisis des Islams in der Türkei. *Beitr. z. Arabistik, Semitistik und Islamwis.*, 1944, pp. 514–30.

—— Das osmanische Scheinkalifat von 1922. *WI*, n.s., i (1951), 195–217, 218–28.

—— Der Islam in der neuen Türkei. *WI*, n.s., i (1951).

—— Ankara wird Hauptstadt der neuen Türkei. *WI*, n.s., iii (1954), 262–7.

—— *Die Türkei in den Jahren 1942–1951*. Wiesbaden, 1955.

—— Beiträge zur Geschichte des Kampfes der Türkei um ihre Unabhängigkeit, *WI*, n.s., v (1957), 1–64.

—— Auf dem Wege zur türkischen Republik. *WI*, n.s., v (1958), 206–18.

—— Das Ende des osmanischen Sultanats. *Studien zur Auslandskunde, Vorderasien*, I/i, 113–36.

Jonquière, A. de la. *Histoire de l'Empire Ottoman*. 2 vols. 3rd ed. Paris, 1914.

Jorga, N. *Geschichte des osmanischen Reiches*. 5 vols. Gotha, 1908–13.

Juchereau de Saint-Denys, A. de. *Révolutions de Constantinople en 1807 et 1808*. 2 vols. Paris, 1819.

Karpat, K. H. *Turkey's Politics; the Transition to a Multi-Party System*. Princeton, 1959.

[Kay, J. E. de]. *Sketches of Turkey in 1831 and 1832*. New York, 1833.

Kemal, Ismail. *The Memoirs of Ismail Kemal Bey*, ed. by Sommerville Story. London, 1920.

Key, Kerim K. *An Outline of Modern Turkish Historiography*. Ist., 1954.

—— The Origins of Turkish Political Parties. *World Affairs Interpreter*, xxvi (1955), 49–60.

—— *Namık Kemal: Patriotic Poet of Turkey. An Inquiry into the Sources for a Study of Namık Kemal*. Washington, 1955.

—— *Origins of the Young Turk Movement, 1839–1908.* Washington, 1955.

—— Trends in Turkish Historiography, *in Report on Current Research on the Middle East 1957.* Washington, 1958, pp. 39–46.

—— Trends in Modern Turkish Literature. *Muslim World,* xlvii (1957), 318–28.

Khadduri, M. and Liebesny, H. J., eds. *Law in the Middle East.* Washington, 1955.

Kraelitz-Greifenhorst, F. von. *Die Verfassungsgesetze des osmanischen Reiches.* Vienna, 1919.

Lagarde, L. Note sur les journaux français de Constantinople à l'époque révolutionnaire. *J. As.,* ccxxxvi (1948), 271–6.

—— Note sur les journaux français de Smyrne à l'époque de Mahmoud II. *J. As.* (1950), 103–44.

Laqueur, W. Z. *Communism and Nationalism in the Middle East.* London–New York, 1956.

—— *The Soviet Union and the Middle East.* London–New York, 1959.

Lerner, D. *The Passing of Traditional Society.* Glencoe, 1958.

Levonian, Lutfy. *The Turkish Press; Selections from the Turkish Press showing Events and Opinions, 1925–32.* Athens, 1932.

Lewis, Bernard. History-writing and National Revival in Turkey. *MEA,* iv (1953), 218–27.

—— The Impact of the French Revolution on Turkey. *Journal of World History,* i (1953), 105–25.

—— The Concept of an Islamic Republic. *WI,* n.s., iv (1955), 1–9.

—— Democracy in Turkey. *MEA,* x (1959), 55–72.

Lewis, Geoffrey L. *Turkey.* London, 1955.

Marcère, E. de. *Une Ambassade à Constantinople; La Politique orientale de la Révolution française.* 2 vols. Paris, 1927.

Makal, Mahmut. *A Village in Anatolia.* London, 1954.

Mardin, Ebul'ulâ. Development of the Shari'a under the Ottoman Empire, *in* M. Khadduri and H. J. Liebesny. *Law in the Middle East.* Washington, 1955, i, 287–91.

Marmorstein, E. Religious Opposition to Nationalism in the Middle East. *Int. Aff.,* xxviii (1952), 344–59.

McCullagh, F. *The Fall of Abd-ul-Hamid.* London, 1910.

Mears, E. G. and others. *Modern Turkey.* New York, 1924.

Midhat, Ali Haydar. *The Life of Midhat Pasha.* London, 1903.

Miller, A. F. *Mustafa Pasha Bayraktar.* Moscow, 1947.

Miller, W. *The Ottoman Empire and its Successors.* Cambridge, 1923.

Moltke, Helmut von. *Briefe über Zustände und Begebenheiten in der Türkei aus den Jahren 1835 bis 1839.* 5th ed. Berlin, 1891.

Morawitz, Charles. *Les Finances de Turquie.* Paris, 1902.

[Mordtmann, A. D.]. *Stambul und das moderne Türkenthum.* 2 vols. Leipzig, 1877.

Muhiddin, Ahmed. *Die Kulturbewegung im modernen Türkentum.* Leipzig, 1921.

Mustafa, Seid. *Diatribe de l'ingénieur sur l'état actuel de l'art militaire, du génie et des sciences à Constantinople.* 1st ed. Scutari, 1803. 2nd ed. Paris, 1910.

Nallino, C. A. La Fine del così detto califfato ottomano. *OM*, iv (1924), 137–53 (reprinted in *Raccolta di Scritti*, iii. Rome, 1941, pp. 260–83).

Nord, E. *Die Reform des türkischen Liegenschaftsrechts.* Leipzig, 1914.

Odysseus [Sir Charles Eliot]. *Turkey in Europe.* London, 1900.

d'Ohsson, Mouradgea. *Tableau général de l'Empire ottoman.* 7 vols. Paris, 1788–1824.

Orga, Irfan. *Phoenix Ascendant.* London, 1958.

Ostroróg, Count Léon. *The Angora Reform.* London, 1927.

Østrup, J. *Det Nye Tyrki.* Copenhagen, 1931.

Padel, W. and Steeg, L. *La Législation foncière ottomane.* Paris, 1904.

Parker, J. and C. Smith. *Modern Turkey.* London, 1940.

Pears, Sir E. *Forty Years in Constantinople.* London, 1916.

—— *Life of Abdul Hamid.* London, 1917.

Petrosian, Yu. A. *'Novye Osmani' i Borba za Konstitutsiyu 1876 g. v Turtsii.* Moscow, 1958.

Pritsch, E. Die türkische Verfassung vom 20 April 1924. *MSOS*, xxvi–xxvii/2 (1924), 164–251.

Ramsaur, E. E. The Bektashi Dervishes and the Young Turks. *Moslem World* (1942), 7–14.

—— *The Young Turks; Prelude to the Revolution of 1908.* Princeton, 1957.

Ramsay, Sir W. M. *Impressions of Turkey.* London [1897].

—— *The Revolution in Constantinople and Turkey.* London, 1909.

Reed, H. A. The Religious Life of Modern Turkish Muslims, *in* R. N. Frye, ed. *Islam and the West.* The Hague, 1937, pp. 108–48.

—— A New Force at Work in Democratic Turkey. *MEJ*, vii (1953), 33–44.

—— Revival of Islam in Secular Turkey. *MEJ*, viii (1954), 267–82.

—— The Faculty of Divinity in Ankara. *Muslim World*, xlvi (1956), 295–312 and xlvii (1957), 22–35.

—— Turkey's new Imam-Hatib Schools. *WI*, n.s., iv (1955), 150–63.

Rodinson, M. Araba. *J. As.*, ccxlv (1957), 273–80.

Rosen, G. *Geschichte der Türkei vom Siege der Reform im Jahre 1826 bis zum Pariser Traktat vom Jahre 1856.* 2 vols. Berlin–Leipzig, 1866–7.

Rossi, E. La Questione dell'alfabeto per le lingue turche. *OM*, vii (1927), 295–310.

—— Il decennale della Repubblica di Turchia (29 ottobre 1923–29 ottobre 1933). *OM*, xiii (1933), 541–57.

Rossi, E. La Riforma linguistica in Turchia. *OM*, xv (1935), 45-57.

—— Un Decennio di Riforma linguistica in Turchia, 1932-42. *OM*, xxii (1942), 466-77.

—— Dall' Impero ottomano alla Repubblica di Turchia; Origine e sviluppi del nazionalismo turco sotto l'aspetto politico-culturale. *OM*, xxiii (1943), 359-88.

—— Venticinque anni di rivoluzione dell'alfabeto e venti di riforma linguistica in Turchia. *OM*, xxxiii (1953), 378-84.

Rummel, F. von. *Die Türkei auf dem Weg nach Europa.* Munich, 1952.

Rustow, D. A. The Army and the Founding of the Turkish Republic. *World Politics*, xi (1949), 513-52.

—— *Politics and Westernization in the Near East.* Princeton, 1956.

—— Politics and Islam in Turkey 1920-1935, *in* R. N. Frye, ed., *Islam and the West.* The Hague, 1957, pp. 69-107.

—— Foreign Policy of the Turkish Republic, *in* Macridis, R. C., ed., *Foreign Policy in World Politics.* Englewood Cliffs, N.J., 1958, pp. 295-322.

Sarç, Ömer Celâl. Economic Policy of the New Turkey. *MEJ*, ii (1948), 430-46.

Sarrou, A. *La Jeune Turquie et la Révolution.* Paris–Nancy, 1912.

Sax, C. von. *Geschichte des Machtverfalls der Türkei.* 2nd ed. Vienna, 1913.

Schacht, J. *Esquisse d'une histoire du droit musulman.* Paris, 1952.

Schlechta-Wssehrd, O. M. von. Die osmanischen Geschichtsschreiber der neuren Zeit. *Denkschriften der phil. hist. Classe der Kaiserl. Ak. der Wissenschaften*, viii (1856), 1-47.

Senior, N. W. *Journal Kept in Turkey and Greece in the Autumn of 1857 and the Beginning of 1858.* London, 1859.

Slade, A. *Record of Travels in Turkey, Greece &c. . . . in the Years 1829, 1830, and 1831.* 2 vols. London, 1832 (2nd ed. 1854).

Smith, E. D. *Origins of the Kemalist Movement.* Washington, 1959.

Smith, W. C. *Islam in Modern History.* Princeton, 1957.

Snouck-Hurgronje, C. *Verspreide Geschriften*, iii. Bonn-Leipzig-Hague, 1923.

Societé pour l'Étude de l'histoire turque. *Histoire de la République turque.* Ist., 1935.

Stamatiadis, Epaminondas I. Βιογραφίαι τῶν Ἑλλήνων Μεγάλων Διερμηνέων τοῦ Ὀθωμανικοῦ Κράτους. Athens, 1865.

Steegman, J. Turkish Painting. *The Studio*, May 1946, pp. 129-35.

Stirling, Paul. Social Ranking in a Turkish Village. *British Journal of Sociology*, iv (1953), 31-44.

—— Religious Change in Republican Turkey. *MEJ*, xii (1958). 395-408.

Taeschner, Fr. Die geographische Literatur der Osmanen. *ZDMG*, n.s. 2, lxxvii (1923), 31–80.

—— and G. Jäschke. *Aus der Geschichte des islamischen Orients.* Tübingen, 1949.

[Taghizade, S. H.] Les Courants politiques dans la Turquie. *RMM*, xxi (1912). 158–221.

—— Le Panislamisme et le Panturquisme. *RMM*, xxii (1913), 179–220.

—— Les Rapports du mouvement politique et du mouvement social dans l'Empire ottoman. *RMM*, xxii (1913), 165–78.

Talas, Cahit. *La Législation du travail en Turquie.* Geneva, 1948.

Temperley, H. W. V. British Policy towards Parliamentary Rule and Constitutionalism in Turkey (1830–1914). *Cambridge Historical Journal*, iv (1932–34), 156–91.

—— *England and the Near East.* London, 1936.

Thomas, L. V. Recent Developments in Turkish Islam. *MEJ*, vi (1952), 22–40.

—— and R. N. Frye. *The United States and Turkey and Iran.* Cambridge, Mass., 1951.

Thornburg, M. W. and others. *Turkey, an Economic Appraisal.* New York, 1949.

Tibawi, A. L. Islam and Secularism in Turkey Today. *Quarterly Review* (1956), 325–7.

Toderini, G. *Letteratura turchesca.* 3 vols. Venice, 1787.

Tott, Baron F. de. *Mémoires.* 4 vols. Maestricht, 1785.

Toynbee, A. J. The Islamic World since the Peace Settlement. *Survey of International Affairs, 1925*, i.

—— and Kirkwood, K. P. *Turkey.* London, 1926.

Tschudi, R. *Das Chalifat.* Tübingen, 1926.

Tuna, Orhan. The Organization of the Turkish Confederation of Trade Unions. *R. Fac. Sci. Éc. Univ. Ist.*, (1953), 109–19.

Tunaya, T. Z. Elections in Turkish History. *MEA*, v (1954),116–20.

Türkkan, R. Oğuz. The Turkish Press. *MEA*, i (1950), 142–9.

Ubicini, A. *Lettres sur la Turquie.* 2 vols. Paris, 1853—4.

Unsal, Behcet. *Turkish Islamic Architecture.* London, 1959.

U.S. Dept. of Commerce. *Investment in Turkey.* Washington, 1956.

Velay, A. du. *Essai sur l'histoire financière de la Turquie.* Paris, 1903.

Washburn, G. *Fifty Years in Constantinople.* Boston-New York, 1909.

Webster, D. E. *The Turkey of Ataturk. Social Process in the Turkish Reformation.* Philadelphia, 1939.

Weinberger, S. J. Political Upset in Turkey. *MEA*, i (1950), 135–42.

White, Charles. *Three Years in Constantinople.* 3 vols. London, 1846.

Wittek, P. Türkentum und Islam, I. *Archiv für Sozialwissenschaft und Sozialpolitik*, lix (1928), 489–525.

—— Le Rôle des tribus turques dans l'empire ottoman. *Mélanges Georges Smets*. Brussels, 1952, pp. 554–76.

Yalman, Ahmed Emin. *Turkey in my Time*. Norman, 1956.

Young, G. *Corps de droit ottoman*. 7 vols. Oxford, 1905–6.

Young, T. C. ed. *Near Eastern Culture and Society*. Princeton, 1951.

Ziemke, K. *Die neue Turkei, Politische Entwicklung 1914–1929*. Berlin-Leipzig, 1930.

Zinkeisen, J. W. *Geschichte des osmanischen Reiches in Europa*. 8 vols. Hamburg-Gotha, 1840–63.

Index

(*Note:* Until the general adoption of surnames in 1934, Turkish usage with regard to personal names differed considerably from that of the West.[1] For ease of reference, Turkish persons listed in this index have been placed under their last names where these are given—i.e. the surname for those who lived to adopt one—but under the last component of the personal name for those who did not. Titles which, in Turkish usage, follow the name—Ağa, Bey, Çelebi, Efendi, Hanım, Paşa—are not taken into account.)

1 See above, p. 283.

Printed in Great Britain by
The Camelot Press Ltd., London and Southampton

Maps

THE OTTOMAN EMPIRE
IN 1792

AUSTRIAN E

BOSNIA

MONTE NEGRO

To Venice

MOROCCO

Mediterrane

Algiers

ALGIERS

Tunis

TUNIS

TRIPOLI

Tripoli

AUSTRIA-HUNGARY

BESSARABIA
To Russia 1812

RUMANIA
Independ. 1878

BOSNIA
Aust. Occup.
1878

Belgrade

SERBIA
Trib. 1815-17
Ind. 1878

Plevna

BULGARIA
Trib. 1878; Indep. 1908

H

N
To Serbia
1878

Sofia

E. RUMELIA
To Bulg. 1885.

M
To
M 1878

ALBANIA

MACEDONIA

Edirne

Istanbul

THE BALKAN
PENINSULA IN 1878

To Greece
1881

Ottoman Boundary 1792

Ottoman Empire 1878

Vassal States 1878

GREECE
Ind.
1829

Samos
Trib. 1832

H   Herzegovina
M   Montenegro
N   Novibazar

0   100   200

Scale of Miles

1775→

MOLDAVIA
Jassy
grade
WALLACHIA
DIN
Silistre
MELI
Ruschuk
Edirne
Istanbul
Bursa
Izmir
DEREBEYS
ETE
CRETE

RUSSIA

1792
I. 1774
1774
CRIMEA

Black Sea

Caspian
Sea

Ankara
DEREBEYS
NOMAD
TRIBES
Konya
Adana

Trabzon

GEORGIA

Erzurum
Kayseri

KURDISTAN

Mosul

PERSIA

BAGHDAD

Aleppo

CYPRUS

n Sea

Beyrut
Akka
Alexandria

SYRIA
Damascus
Jerusalem

Baghdad

EGYPT
Cairo

WAHHABIS

Aswan

Red

HIJAZ

Medina

Mecca

Jidda

Sea

Suakin

Massawa

Approximate limits
of the Empire

North African States
under Ottoman suzerainty

Areas under autonomous
and tribal rulers

Lands lost, 1774-1792

0   200   400

Scale of Miles

E. G. MORTON

THE OTTOMAN EMPIRE IN 1908

- – – Nominal Boundary
- Dependent States
- Territory occupied or protected by foreign powers
- Lands lost since 1792

0   100   500
Scale of Miles

MOROCCO

ALGERIA
(French)

Tunis

TUNIS
(Fr. 1881)

Mediterranean

Tripoli

Ghadames

TRIPOLI
(Ottoman direct rule from 1835)

BAR

FEZZAN
(Ottoman 1842)

Ghat

AUSTRIA
BOSNIA

MONTENEGRO

Re

AUSTRIA – HUNGARY

RUMANIA

BOSNIA
(Austrian annexation 1908)

SERBIA

MONTENEGRO

BULGARIA

To Rum 1913

To Bulgaria 1885

To Bulgaria 1913

ALBANIA
Indep. 1913

To Serbia 1913

To Bulgaria 1913

Edirne

Istanbul

To Greece 1913

To Greece 1913

GREECE

To Italy 1912

THE BALKAN
PENINSULA IN 1913

Turkish Losses since 1878

0   200
Scale of Miles

RUMANIA

Plevna
BULGARIA
Sofia
astir
Seroz
Edirne
Istanbul

Bursa

Izmir
Aydin

ECE

Konya
Adana

tonomous 1898)
Sea

Cyprus
(Brit. Prot)
1878

RUSSIA

Black Sea

Ankara

Sivas
Kayseri

Nizib

Aleppo

Beyrut
Damascus

Jerusalem

Trabzon
Erzurum

Kars

Caspian
Sea

PERSIA

Baghdad

Alexandria
Cairo
Suez
Canal

EGYPT
(British Occupation
1882)

HIJAZ

Red Sea

Medina

Jidda
Mecca

Suakin

Massawa

ASIR

YEMEN

San'a

Aden

Basra
KUWAIT
(Brit. Prot
1901)

AL HASA

QATAR

E. G. MORTON

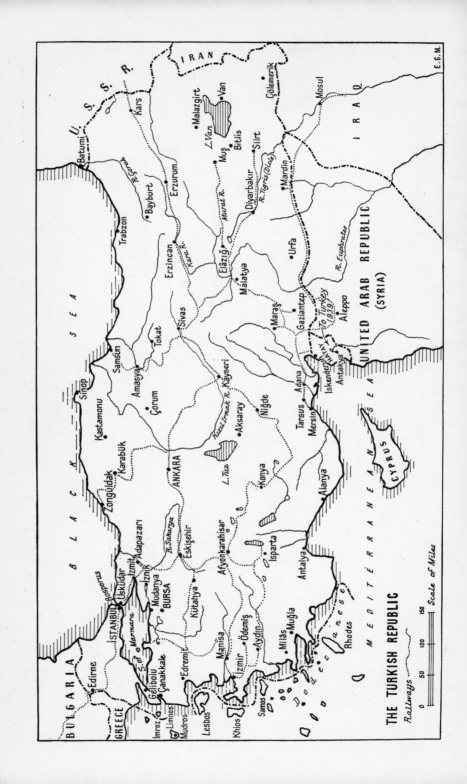

THE TURKISH REPUBLIC

Railways ....

Scale of Miles

0   50   100   150

The Massage Center

Healing Arts Associates
8 Carpenter St., Norwich, VT 05055
call for an appointment: 802-649-1149
www.themassagecenternorwich.com

WORLD
Medicine

The East West Guide to
Healing Your Body

WORLD
Medicine

The East West Guide to
Healing Your Body

TOM MONTE
and The Editors of *EastWest Natural Health*

Jeremy P. Tarcher/Perigee

Jeremy P. Tarcher/Perigee Books
are published by
The Putnam Publishing Group
200 Madison Avenue
New York, NY 10016

Requests for such permissions should be addressed to:
    Jeremy P. Tarcher, Inc.
    5858 Wilshire Blvd., Suite 200
    Los Angeles, CA 90036

Published simultaneously in Canada

Library of Congress Cataloging-in-Publication Data

Monte, Tom.
    World Medicine: The East West guide to healing your body / by Tom Monte
and the editors of Natural Health.
        p.   cm.
    Includes bibliographical references.
    ISBN 0-87477-733-X (paper); ISBN 0-87477-755-0 (case)
    1. Alternative medicine.   2. Medicine.   3. Healing.   I. Natural Health.
II. Title.
R733.M65   1993   92-43052 CIP
615.5 ' 3—dc20

Illustration Credits:

Page 23: Illustration by Polly Jordan. Page 24: Copyright © 1990 by Terry
Oleson, Ph.D. Page 32: Illustration copyright © 1984, Dr. Vasant Lad.
Reprinted with permission of Lotus Light, Box 1008, Silver Lake, Wisconsin,
53170. Page 40: Courtesy of Health and Homeopathy Publishing, publisher
of *The Family Guide to Homeopathy* by Alan Horvilleur, M.D. Pages 134–35:
Reprinted with permission from *The Yellow Emperor's Classic of Internal
Medicine,* translated by Ilza Veith, copyright © 1947, 1975 Ilza Veith. Page 179:
Copyright © 1987, Organica Press. Reprinted with permission. Page 295:
Illustration copyright © 1988, Windpfered Verlag. Reprinted from *The Chakra-
Handbook* with permission of Lotus Light, Box 1008, Silver Lake, Wisconsin,
53170. Page 325: From *The Principles of Light and Color* by Edwin Bobbitt,
copyright © 1992 Sun Publishing Company. This book is available from Sun
Publishing Company.

Anatomical drawings are by Nancy Kriebel, medical illustrator.

Design by Susan Shankin

Cover illustration of venous system © M. Kulyk, Science Source/Photo
Researchers

Printed in the United States of America
1   2   3   4   5   6   7   8   9   10

This book is printed on acid-free paper.

To the memory of Rob Allanson,
teacher and friend

CONTENTS

ILLUSTRATIONS

ACKNOWLEDGMENTS

IT IS IMPOSSIBLE for me to acknowledge all of the friends who supported me in the writing of this book. Nevertheless, I wish to express my heartfelt thanks to the following people, whose assistance was essential to making this book a reality.

To Leonard Jacobs, who has helped me in countless ways throughout my professional life.

To the teachers, healers, and visionaries—many of whom are represented in the pages of this book—who have empowered lay people with the knowledge and the tools to heal themselves. Especially to Michio and Aveline Kushi, Nathan and Ilene Pritikin, who taught me new ways of seeing health and how it could be enhanced.

To Robert Allanson and William Tims, who in the early 1980s wrote a series of articles for *East/West Journal* that revealed the first synthesis of an East-West view of the body.

To editors Mark Mayell and Connie Zweig, at *Natural Health* magazine and Jeremy P. Tarcher, Inc., respectively, who kept me on track during the writing of this book.

To my wife, Toby, and my three children, who each day give me the inspiration and support to do this work.

THE MAGIC AND MYSTERY OF THE HUMAN BODY

*T*HE HUMAN BODY is a realm of wonder and dread. Inside each of us is a greater magic than anything contrived by human imagination. The workings of the body can barely be comprehended, much less matched, by human invention. The heart beats 100,000 times a day, 2.5 billion times in the average lifetime. The eyes perceive ten million gradations of light. The nose can differentiate among thousands of odors and fragrances. The brain takes in billions of bits of information, organizes them, and offers a staggering array of responses. Who can consider the turbulence of human emotions, the insight and comprehension of a single mind, or the purity of a child's love without standing back in awe that so much magic can be contained in so finite a package?

No artist yet has managed to fully capture the mystery reflected in the eyes, the grace and strength in the hands, or the allure in the legs. The body is the realm in which art and utility become one.

Yet, it isn't only with wonder that one approaches the human form, but with trepidation, too. You need only to listen to your heart beat, or consider all those electrical impulses flashing across your rippled brain, to awaken to the terrible fragility of life. In-

In modern Western society biomedicine not only has provided a basis for the scientific study of disease, it also has become our own culturally specific perspective about disease, that is, our folk model.

GEORGE ENGEL

deed a child can listen to a conch and say he hears the ocean roar, but when an adult places his ear to another human chest, he listens to the sounds of life and death, and the whisper of immortality. It is the presence of this ultimate reality that takes the body beyond the limits of science and into the worlds of ethics, culture, religion, and spirit.

The body is many worlds in one. Consequently, if you ask an anatomist, a psychologist, an artist, and a priest for their views on the body, you will likely receive four distinct answers, all of them correct. Travel to other cultures and ask the same question of Middle Eastern, Chinese, and Native American healers, and each will give you a vastly differing description of the human form. Each of these accounts also will be correct. In fact, no single view of the body offers a definitive understanding.

The people of each culture are tempted to believe that they possess the only "true" way of seeing the body and life itself. At best, this is a quaint human trait. At worst, it is a form of blind arrogance. There is no ultimate view of the body, any more than there is an ultimate language. There are, in fact, many ways of understanding the great mystery that resides in the human form. Each approach has its strengths and weaknesses, its insights and limitations.

We live at a time when people crave information about the human body. We yearn for greater self-sufficiency when it comes to our health and health care. Many of us would like to heal ourselves of illness or prevent disease, using methods that have fewer toxic side effects than many of today's modern pharmaceuticals. So we are turning increasingly to the tools of the ancient past, and combining them with the techniques and understanding of modern science.

Today, people are transcending their cultural borders to understand the views of other traditions, other peoples. In medicine we are building bridges between East and West, ancient and modern, spirit and matter. One of the challenges that confronts us in our bridge-building is crossing the chasm that exists between worldviews. The ancients—both of East and West—saw the world as a unified whole in which all phenomena are intimately connected. We moderns see life as a series of disconnected parts, most of which have nothing to do with each other.

Today, we are struggling to reconcile these two fundamental

philosophies, especially in the field of healing. We want to understand our individual organs and functions, but also to see how each relates to the whole body, mind, and spirit. We search for knowledge to better understand ourselves, our bodies, and thereby live more fully satisfying lives.

Your Body: Friend or Foe?

One of the shortcomings of the modern approach to health care is the belief that we are victims of either our body's planned obsolescence or of germs—tiny agents that are invisible, pernicious, and arbitrarily infectious. We "catch" a cold, or we "come down" with the flu, as if the illness descends mysteriously from above. Other clichés reveal our thinking: "He was never sick a day in his life and then suddenly he got this!" In other words, our friend was going along fine, minding his own business, when bingo—his body broke down. He was an innocent victim of some mysterious illness.

Our methods of treatment reveal even more deeply this ingrained set of attitudes. Most treatments are designed to suppress symptoms or kill the invader. How often do we stop to think that perhaps those symptoms are really the body's way of telling us that something in our behavior is causing an underlying disease, or that the common cold may have a beneficial effect on our health? How many of us believe that the body has the power to heal itself?

To understand your body's language and to learn from your illnesses, you must learn to see the body as a friend with its own operating system, its own healing powers, and its own laws for maintaining health. Too often people think of the body as an enemy, failing us when we least expected it, or when we needed it most.

This book explores the vastly different ways of looking at your body and your health. We're going to show you that there are many ways to understand your body—ways you hadn't thought of before, but that make a difference in how you see yourself, how you treat your body, and how well it works. We hope to place you on better terms with your body, to help you recognize your body as a friend.

That is not as difficult as you might think. It requires nothing

The mechanistic view of the human organism has encouraged an engineering approach to health in which illness is reduced to mechanical trouble and medical therapy to technical manipulation.

Fritjof Capra

Western scientific medicine is largely concerned with objective, nonpersonal, physiochemical explanations of disease as well as its technical control. In contrast, many traditional systems of healing are centered on the phenomenon of illness, namely, the personal and social experience of disease . . . Where Western scientific medicine focuses on curing the disease, traditional medicine aims primarily at healing the illness—that is, managing the individual and social response to disease.

DAVID S. SOBEL

more than what you would give to any friend: attention, understanding, intelligence, and love. And why not? Your body is the best gift that's ever been given to you. It is also one of the greatest paradoxes you will face in life. On one hand, it is an infinite mystery. On the other, it is so simple and self-revealing that even a child can understand how it works, and what can be done to support its health and well-being. Throughout the pages of this book, we'll be confronting that paradox—the mystery and the simplicity of the human form. We'll introduce you to many of the wonders of your body. We'll also show you many of the simple steps you can take to keep yourself well, or to overcome illness when it appears.

We're going on a journey through a remarkable kingdom, a place in which miracles and magic are everyday occurrences. In no other place in this world are more wondrous things happening than inside each of us.

Let's begin our journey with an ordinary tour: a walk in the park. Our park is both beautiful and commonplace. Expanses of green grass; groves of trees here and there; a lake. Sunlight tints the leaves on the trees and the grass below your feet with a hint of golden color. The park is filled with people: a Little League baseball game is going full tilt over there; periodically, a runner lopes by at your elbow; an elderly couple strolls arm-in-arm over there, while a pair of young lovers sit at a park bench to your right. Ahead, a father and son attempt to get their kite up into the air, while under a stately oak to your left is a young mother entertaining her infant daughter with a rattle. At another bench is a young man nursing a cold, passing a tissue frequently to his nose. Finally, on the other side of the park, in the pools of sunlight and shadow, an elderly Chinese man performs a solitary, slow-moving dance called tai chi.

At the baseball game, a boy of about thirteen, fully decked out in baseball regalia, approaches the plate. Baseball chatter chirps from the onlookers in the bleacher seats, from the players in the field, and from those sitting on the bench. The batter takes his stance in the batter's box, raises the bat above his right shoulder, and fixes his gaze upon the pitcher. The pitcher takes in the measure of the batter and settles into his stance. He turns his gaze to the catcher who signals the pitch to throw. The wind kicks up some dust from the mound as the umpire—dressed like a benign

Darth Vadar—crouches behind the catcher and awaits the pitch. The duel is engaged. The pitch is on the way. The batter has less than a second to assess the pitch and accurately direct his bat to strike the ball.

The act of hitting a speeding baseball with a bat is one of the most difficult challenges in sport, but the accomplishment seems even greater when you realize what the body must do almost instantaneously to accomplish that feat.

The baseball is visible to the batter because it reflects waves of energy, known as electromagnetic radiation or light. Those light waves, traveling at 186,000 miles per second, reach the batter's eye before the ball reaches the plate. The eyes instantly focus on the waves of light by precisely adjusting various parts of the eye: the cornea, which is the clear, convex window at the front of the eye; the pupil, the opening right before the lens; and the lens itself. All of these adjustments are performed in concert by muscles within the eye that respond to orders from the brain. The brain will tell the various parts of the eye to contract or expand, depending upon whether or not it is receiving a clear image.

Once the light enters the eye, it strikes the retina, a membrane of nerves the size of postage stamp that sits at the back of each eye. The retina binds the light to certain chemicals within the nerves, sparking an electrical impulse that travels from the retina to the brain, via the optic nerve. The visual cortices are located in the back of the brain, in both the left and right hemispheres. The brain receives multiple images because the left and right eyes perceive the light from slightly different vantage points. Also, the image is upside down, thanks to the fact that the light is refracted, or bent, within the eye. The brain puts these images together instantly and, voilà!, here comes the baseball.

It's a fastball, about belt-high and, yes, it's in the strike zone. The batter assesses the pitch and decides to swing. He's got a fraction of a second left to bring the bat around and hit the ball. No problem. He can do it.

Electrical nerve impulses start to flash from the visual cortices to other parts of the brain. First, the signals speed to the most primitive parts, the cerebellum and the pons, both located at the top of the spinal cord, at the base of the brain. Here are located computer-like programs that coordinate muscles and bones to move in graceful harmony. These programs have been established

5

during the many hours the boy has spent practicing his swing. Next, electrical impulses fly to the motor section of the cerebral cortex, located within a thin layer of gray cells that covers the entire surface of the brain. The motor cortex is located at the very top of the brain, in a band that stretches across the left and right hemispheres. The cerebral cortex is the most advanced part of the brain. It refines the programmed movements of the cerebellum and pons to make them more finely tuned to the behavior of this particular pitch. From the motor cortex, nerve impulses—the actual orders—are sent to the spinal cord and then to the respective parts of the body, such as the shoulders, arms, hands, hips, legs, and feet. Each signal provides specific orders to each part of the body, which must perform its act in concert with the whole. No one knows exactly how this is accomplished, but it is.

Our young friend's eyes follow the ball as it rockets toward him. Suddenly, the bat is in motion. His body is centered at the waist, head down, shoulders and arms flowing through the pitch. Crack! The young player is all elbows and knees as he hurries to first base. Heads in the bleachers and on the field turn in unison to follow the ball as it arcs gracefully to the gap in left-center field. The batter rounds first base and slides into second, disappearing in a cloud of dust. Safe. He can't suppress a big smile. He's elated that he hit the ball, as is half the crowd, but even he doesn't realize what magic he just performed.

Making Sense of the Magic

Magic was humanity's earliest explanation for how the body worked. Long before systematized approaches to health and the body were organized some 6,000 years ago, humanity's ancestors used potions, amulets, rings, and charms to rid the body of harmful demons and spirits that brought illness and suffering. The eyes, especially, were seen as sites of power and magic. Warrior tribesmen of New Zealand ate the eyes of tribal chiefs because they believed the deity lived within them. The eyes of animals were routinely used medicinally to treat eye problems. One ancient Egyptian potion for blindness was made up of the water from hogs' eyes, honey, and lead, all of which was injected into the eyes of the blind. (The success rate of this treatment has understandably gone unrecorded.) Shamans used the fierce "powers" in the eyes to frighten demons, which were believed to be the source of illness. To this day, many traditional peoples still believe that shamans have the ability to cure and harm people with the powers in their eyes.

Humankind's understanding of the body began to emerge from the mists of superstition some 5,000 years ago, when the body began to be studied extensively in China, India, Greece, and Egypt. Despite their differences in language and metaphors, all of these early cultures approached the body from the same basic worldview. These traditional peoples saw life as an integrated whole, a unity. The body was approached as a unified system in which the physical, mental, and spiritual aspects of life were one. Moreover, each life was united with the life of the universe itself. It is one life, which all things share.

In China, this ultimate unity was seen as the creator of two archetypal forces, called yin and yang. These two forces manifest in everything in the material universe and make the relative world possible. Like poles of a magnet, yin and yang attract each other and thus produce movement and energy. In China, that universal life energy is called chi, or qi.

The idea of a universal life force was common among virtually all traditional peoples. In India it is called prana, in Japan ki, and in ancient Greece, pneuma.

In a number of ancient societies the healers performed crude surgeries, did autopsies, and investigated the structure and function of organs and tissues. But their investigations were often guided by a simple question: What causes this mass of flesh to function? What gives an organ life? Their answer was that in addition to the corporeal body, there is a more fundamental entity, which is this underlying energy that is life itself. This life energy infuses the entire human being, causing the body to have vitality, movement, and function. The life force also gives the body the power to heal wounds, to overcome disease, and succeed in the face of difficulty and challenge.

Death is seen as the moment the life force leaves the flesh. Without the life force, none of the bodily functions continue. The flesh is revealed as merely a matrix of earthly substances that immediately decay and return to the earth.

The idea of a life force points to a major difference between

Modern medicine is already in its twilight years. It is about forty or fifty years old, and by now there's been a chance for the ill effects to catch up with the originally heralded benefits. The breakthroughs have turned out to be breakdowns, and most of the shiny metal has turned out to be tarnished.

ROBERT MENDELSOHN

7

these early traditional societies and modern ones dominated by the tools and techniques of scientific medicine, and especially between East and West. In traditional systems, such as the Chinese and Greek, the body is seen as having the ability to cure itself of illness. The physician serves only to assist the body's own healing powers. Conversely, modern medicine uses drugs and surgery to overcome disease. Antibiotics, for example, kill a pathogen, while surgery removes organs and their related problems altogether. Rather than encourage the body's healing powers, the modern medical doctor uses medicine to deal directly with the illness.

In the Chinese system, the life force flows through the body in specific channels, or meridians. These channels of energy unite the entire body into an organized whole, much like integrated circuitry unites an electrical unit. But the channels of energy also make certain organs and senses particularly intimate and mutually dependent upon each other.

Opposing Worldviews in Everyday Life

Let's return to the park and see how the ancient and modern systems approach the same problem from differing angles. Just ahead of us a boy and his father are flying a kite. The kite is up in the air and waving gently in the wind. Occasionally, a gust blows the kite toward some trees to the left. As father and son follow the kite with their eyes, the father admonishes the boy to keep the kite away from the trees. We notice that the boy is wearing thick glasses; he's nearsighted, which means he has trouble focusing on objects at a distance. He's probably having a hard time seeing the kite clearly and judging its proximity to the trees.

The Chinese say that the health of the eyes is directly dependent on the condition of the liver. The liver, say the Chinese, rules the eyes by nourishing them with qi. The liver is regarded as the root of vision, in that it continually sends qi to the eyes. An unhealthy liver will be unable to provide the eyes with adequate life force, causing degeneration in the muscles and parts of the eye, thus affecting clarity of vision. Almost all eye problems, including lack of visual acuity, glaucoma, and cataracts, are related to liver imbalances, say the Chinese. This relationship is evidenced when jaundice and other liver disorders cause the eyes to yellow.

It's more important to know what kind of patient has a disease than what kind of disease a patient has.

HIPPOCRATES

The system works in both directions. Eye strain can cause liver disturbances.

In a traditional medicine such as the Chinese system, the body is seen in ever-widening relationships. The workings of any single organ is seen within the context of the whole. Thus, an eye problem will be approached as a symptom of an underlying imbalance in the body, particularly in the liver. A Chinese healer will address an eye problem by treating the eyes and the liver, and whatever might affect these organs. This would include an examination of the person's environment, food choices, relationships, emotional life, and working patterns. All of these areas would be looked at for their effects on the flow of qi within the body. The concentric circles ripple outward, until the healer and the patient have arrived at a specific set of causes. The healer will then prescribe an array of herbs, dietary recommendations, perhaps massage or acupuncture, and exercises to reestablish harmony within the body. The Chinese healer is working to strengthen the underlying life force, though he or she may also provide some symptomatic relief as well. Once the life force is reestablished, the body's own healing mechanisms have the ability to overcome any illness or disorder, including many forms of eye impairments.

In the West, the body is seen as a biochemical machine in which the parts are separate and distinct. It is understood in ever-smaller units—that is, as tissues, organs, cells, molecules, and atoms. For this reason, Western science is often referred to as reductionist, meaning it is searching for the single underlying unit that makes up the body or, in the case of disease, a single pathogen or physical impairment that gives rise to symptoms.

A Western physician, therefore, sees an eye problem as confined largely to the eye and its related parts. Treatment consists of eyeglasses to compensate for weak vision, or drugs or surgery to correct the malfunctioning eye.

The understanding of a life force has larger applications—it even applies to a baseball player's swing. An athlete's performance, or any action, for that matter, is not merely an act of biochemistry, but an attunement with this all-pervasive life force, which is the underlying power of the universe. The player who is attuned to the universe in this way cannot help but be perfect in the moment. But in order to achieve that perfect unity between the body and the life force, the mind must be "empty."

The human organism is much larger than we imagine, for as a living entity it is inseparable from a "personal ecology," its working balances with the world. The body is also a much more porous entity than we see, through which millions of microorganisms and foreign molecules circulate. These cohabitors and invaders are held in check by the body's homeostatic, immunological, and detoxification systems and by the benign flora of the gut and other ecological forces.

JOSEPH D. BEASLEY

9

Biological explanations for what happens when you hit a baseball are not only useless, say modern practitioners of traditional Chinese medicine, but serve to get in the way of your ability to attune yourself to the power of the universe. Explanations are the work of the "mind," the concept-forming aspect of your identity. The mind fragments and interprets experience. It tells you which parts of experience are important and which parts are unimportant. But the perfect swing lies in a state in which you are empty of "mind," empty of labels or concepts, and free to apply your skill unfettered to the task at hand. You don't think about the act. You simply do it, and thereby come into harmony with the underlying life force that is creating the moment itself. By being attuned to the underlying power or truth, the batter and ball become one.

In his introduction to Eugene Herrigal's book, *Zen in the Art of Archery,* Daisetz T. Suzuki explains this principle as it applies to archery: "In the case of archery, the hitter and the hit are no longer two opposing objects, but are one reality. The archer ceases to be conscious of himself as the one who is engaged in hitting the bull's-eye which confronts him. The state of unconsciousness is realized only when, completely empty and rid of the self, he becomes one with the perfecting of his technical skill, though there is in it something of a quite different order which cannot be attained by any progressive study of the art." Suzuki goes on to explain that when the archer eliminates self-consciousness or mind, he or she comes into "contact with the ultimate reality."

From this perspective, hitting a speeding baseball has little to do with the ball itself, but with coming into right relationship with the underlying truth—the ultimate reality—that guides the movements of the ball, the pitcher, the batter, and the bat.

Coming into relationship with that reality depends in part on one's own sensitivity and spiritual development. As Herrigel says about archery: "The Japanese does not understand [archery as] a sport but, strange as this may sound at first, a religious ritual. And consequently, by the 'art' of archery he does not mean the ability of the sportsman, which can be controlled, more or less, by bodily exercises, but an ability whose origin is to be sought in spiritual exercises and whose aim consists in hitting a spiritual goal, so that fundamentally the marksman aims at himself and may even succeed in hitting himself." Thus, the game becomes a means of self-development.

Just as archery is regarded as a spiritual exercise in the Orient, so too is self-defense. The man performing that slow dance under the trees in the park is actually meditating. Tai chi, an ancient martial art, is a way of experiencing the central current of life, often called Tao, that flows all around and through us. He moves as if he is gracefully pushing masses of air to slow-moving music. Every action is a study in balance: a forward push is rounded off and turned into retreat; retreat stimulates advancement. He is attempting to align himself with the yin and yang of qi, trying to experience the power that drives the universe. By moving in harmony with that subtle yet all-powerful force, he not only experiences the source of health, but also learns to draw it toward him and influence it. He is thus protected from negative influences, and he himself becomes a force for regeneration and health wherever he goes.

Even from the standpoint of Western science, the notion of an underlying energy that animates the body is not so far-fetched. In fact, the body itself is an electrical unit. Every organ and, indeed, the entire nervous system works on the basis of electrical currents. The heart is an electrical pump. It beats by virtue of electrical impulses generated within the heart muscle by two nodes, one at the top of the heart and the other in the wall that separates the two sides of the heart. The electrical charges fired by these nodes flow through fibrous bands that permeate the heart muscle and stimulate the familiar expansion and contraction of the heart. Indeed, that expansion and contraction is created by two oppositely charged ions which together cause electrons to flow along these bands of muscle fibers. As we will see in the last chapter, the concept of an underlying life force composed of electromagnetic energy is now being seriously explored by Western scientists, and receiving surprising support.

We appear to be individual bodies, but this individuality is also a constant state of equilibrium between a true personal authenticity and a continuous participation with the collective energy of all humanity and all existence.

RICHARD MOSS

PART ONE

Six Systems of Healing

VARIOUS TRADITIONAL PEOPLES around the world have long included among their medicinal practices such therapies as diet and herbs, compresses and poultices, massage techniques and acupuncture, purgatives and sweats. They have been particularly well developed in four major medical systems: Chinese, Ayur-Veda of India, Greek medicine, and homeopathy.

But beyond the efficacy of specific herbs or techniques lies a more fundamental understanding of health. Health is typically defined in traditional medical systems as a state of balance and wholeness. These systems are based on the belief that humans are unified with—even the product of—the vast forces that maintain the cosmos. Illness is caused when one or more of these forces within a person is imbalanced. Medicine is the means of restoring balance.

For the Chinese, health is achieved by creating harmony between the opposing powers of yin and yang. When the organs maintain a balanced condition, when they do not become too contracted or too expanded, the life force or qi flows smoothly throughout the body. Each organ receives optimal life force; it is capable of warding off illness and efficiently eliminating waste. When one or more organs, however, becomes excessively contracted or expanded, qi flow becomes blocked. Once the life force is diminished, the organ becomes sluggish, inefficient, and stagnant—a perfect host for disease.

Organs, blood vessels, or tissues can become excessively contracted by any number of influences, including stress, emotional turmoil, excessive amounts of animal foods and salt, excessive work and not enough play, injury, or lack of exercise. Organs can become overly expanded through emotional imbalance, dietary influences such as excessive sugar or alcohol, drugs, the absence of work and an excess of inactivity, and lack of exercise. Health is established by restoring balance to one's lifestyle, and thus to the organs or system of the body. This, in turn, causes the life force to flow freely and optimally once again. Once the life force flows optimally throughout the body, the organs themselves can throw off the underlying causes of disease. They are capable of healing themselves. In such a system, the illness is itself a symptom of a diminished life force.

Balance is the means to health and long life, say the Chinese, Greeks, and Indians. By eliminating extremes in behavior, life can be enjoyed fully, without excessive burdens.

The oldest medical book in the world is *The Yellow Emperor's Classic of Internal Medicine,* the basis of Chinese medicine. It describes the balance of yin and yang this way: The sages of old used "temperance in eating and drinking. Their hours of rising and retiring were regular and not disorderly and wild. By these means the ancients kept their bodies united with their souls, so as to fulfill their allotted span completely, measuring unto a hundred years before they passed away.

"Nowadays people are not like this; they use wine as a beverage and they adopt recklessness as usual behavior. They enter the chamber [of love] in an intoxicated condition; their passions exhaust their vital forces; their cravings dissipate their true [essence]; they do not know how to find contentment within themselves; they are not skilled in the control of their spirits. They devote their attention to the amusement of their minds, thus cutting themselves off from the joys of long [life]."

Protection of the life force through moderation was the key to health and long life. Hippocrates, the Greek physician known today as the father of medicine, had a similar view. He taught that health is achieved by balancing four humors, or fluids, within the body. As long as these fluids remained in harmony among each other, an individual experienced good health. When they became imbalanced, one suffered illness.

In both the Greek and the Chinese systems, imbalances are often corrected by the body by merely "discharging" the stagnation or excesses stored within. Hippocrates referred to this discharge as catharsis (derived from the Greek *katharsis* or *katharmos*), which means the purging or cleansing of the system, especially the bowels. The common cold could, for example, serve to eliminate toxins and excesses that are the basis for disease.

NATURE CURES, PHYSICIANS ASSIST

To a conventional medical doctor, the runny nose, sneezing, cough, and watery eyes of a typical cold are seen as merely irritating symptoms that should preferably be eliminated as quickly as possible. Medication is designed to do just that. But from the point of view of most traditional medicines, the common cold, with its sneezing, runny nose, and frequent urination, is a highly efficient way of eliminating accumulated toxins and waste.

Hippocrates said that although health is the natural state of humans, disease is also a natural process that follows an organic pattern. During that illness there are key points at which the physician can intercede and assist the patient in restoring health. Hippocrates called these points of "crisis" or "opportune moments" at which balance and the forces of health can be restored. Hippocrates also implied that disease seems to serve some kind of evolutionary or maturing process. According to Philip Wheelwright,

University of California scholar and author of *The Presocratics,* illness can serve to create what Hippocrates called a new "blended maturity" among the elements within.

Like the Chinese, Hippocrates developed an extensive array of foods, herbs, and physical therapies (such as poultices and compresses) to restore balance to the body. "Proper food and drink, calmness of mind and body, suitable exercise, and the like, are among the chief ways in which the bodily conditions can be made as favorable as possible to the speedy and firm completion of the cycle through illness and back again to health," writes Wheelwright.

Today, scientists are demonstrating the effectiveness of such methods, especially herbs. Said John Hopkins University researcher Erwin Ackerknecht: "It is amazing what an enormous number of effective drugs is known to the primitives. From twenty-five to fifty percent of their pharmacopoeia is often found to be objectively active." This should not be as amazing as it sounds. The World Health Organization has identified 121 modern drugs made totally from plant compounds. Ackerknecht points out that our modern knowledge of a vast array of drugs comes chiefly from traditional peoples. University researchers are now studying the powerful healing properties found in herbal remedies from the natives of the Brazilian rain forest and other traditional cultures.

How did traditional people discover their methods? The easy answer is trial and error, but you will not get that response when you ask a Chinese sage or a Native American medicine man how they arrived at their information.

"From ancient times the communication with Heaven has been the very foundation of life," said the Yellow Emperor. "This foundation exists between yin and yang and between heaven and earth. Therefore the sages preserved the natural spirit and were in harmony with the breath of Heaven and were thus in direct communication with Heaven."

In *Planet Medicine,* Richard Grossinger quotes a Native American who explains how members of his tribe came to understand nature and its healing arts: "We know what the animals do, what are the needs of the beaver, the bear, the salmon, and other creatures, because long ago men married them and acquired this knowledge from their animal wives. Today the priests say we lie, but we know better."

The Cherokee Indians say that animals invented disease to reduce the human population. But the plant kingdom discovered the animals' plot and called a council meeting at which the plants decided to provide healing remedies to humanity when stricken by illness. All plants were to have some healing properties, no matter how common or seemingly useless they might appear to be.

To traditional peoples, the world was alive with powers, life forces, and spirits. Mountains, rivers, trees, and boulders all possessed personality and even soul. Their oneness of nature was not an abstract concept, but a deep and personal relationship in which people talked to the four winds, the sun, the stars, and the moon. These were minor deities, the emissaries of the Great Spirit.

The healer mediated between the human world and the world of the transcendent powers. Healers, therefore, served as both physician and priest. Shamans the world over called upon the powers of healing implicit in the universe to rid the sick of evil or noxious spirits. There were no conceptual boundaries between mind and body and soul. Whatever was in the spirit became manifest in the body, and vice versa. The perception of life was not linear, but circular. Thus, treatment included the physical and the spiritual—food, herbs, and physical therapy, along with ritual, jewels and crystals, and prayer.

Today, scientists know that such methods work. The powers of the mind have just begun to be explored, but studies are showing that the invisible realm of thoughts, emotions, and belief systems dramatically influences health in positive and negative ways. Studies have shown that belief in recovery can be as powerful as any medication.

At Mount Sinai School of Medicine in New York, Dr. Steven J. Schliefer and his coworkers have found that highly emotional states, such as bereavement, have a deadening effect on the immune system. One type of immune cells, the lymphocytes, often fail to respond in the presence of a pathogen in people who have recently suffered the loss of a loved one. Men who suffer the loss of a spouse have a 40 percent higher mortality rate within their own age groups than those who do not experience such loss. Dying of a broken heart might just as well be expressed as a broken immune system. If these people pass through the bereavement period, their immune systems rebound.

But even subtle changes in mood and behavior affect internal chemistry. The power of laughter to heal is now well documented, but science is showing that even a smile can change both mood and internal chemistry. Dr. Robert Zajonc, a psychologist at the University of Michigan, has found that certain facial muscles have the ability to raise and lower the temperature of the blood flowing to the brain. Such changes can affect brain chemistry, particularly the function of the hypothalamus gland, located in the brain. Other research has shown that changes in the hypothalamus, in turn, alter the function of the immune, endocrine, cardiovascular, and respiratory systems.

Thus, a new form of shamanism is emerging called psychoneuroimmunology, or the study of how the mind affects the body. Clearly, the boundaries between body, mind, and spirit—once thought to be inviolate—are giving way.

Today, a new set of views is taking hold, a belief system that looks much like our ancient traditions, but is supported and transformed by our modern sciences. The sciences of medicine and physics are building bridges, too. When the physicist looks deeply into the world of the atom and its even tinier realms, he or she is discovering a unity that the ancients would have agreed with, and understood. The words of eminent physicist David Bohm are strangely reminiscent of the Yellow Emperor or Lao Tsu: "Ultimately, the entire universe (with all its 'particles,' including those constituting human beings, their laboratories, observing instruments, etc.) has to be understood as a single undivided whole, in which analysis into separately and independently existent parts has no fundamental status."

Though they differ in language and metaphor, most traditional medical systems are based on these principles of health as a state of balance or wholeness, governed by a universal life force, with illness resulting from imbalances within the body that block the life force from flowing optimally and freely within the body. Also, the symptoms of disease are seen as the body's effort at self-healing. Let's now have a closer look at each healing system, including the conventional modern medical one, to understand their respective metaphors and see beyond them.

CHAPTER 1

CHINESE MEDICINE

𝓝O OTHER MEDICAL SYSTEM deserves the title "traditional" more than Chinese medicine. Modern Western medicine, which we often refer to as "traditional," is only two centuries old. Chinese medicine, on the other hand, is at least 3,000 years old, and is still being used to treat tens of millions of people in China and other places around the world. From the view of a traditional Chinese healer, modern medicine is the "experimental" system because people have relatively little experience with it, and certainly the "alternative" because it is far from the precepts upon which the Chinese system is built.

Chinese medicine is based on the view that humanity is part of a larger creation, a greater body, that is the universe itself. Each of us is subject to the same laws that govern the stars, the planets, the trees, and the soil. In this way, Chinese medicine is essentially "macroscopic," in that its understanding of health begins with an understanding of nature, and the laws that govern it. To follow the laws of nature is to be blessed with good health, long life, and good fortune, say the Chinese. Ultimately, this path leads to a revelation about one's own life and the life of the universe itself.

To investigate the workings of the body is, for the Chinese, to

Nature, time, and patience are the three great physicians.

CHINESE PROVERB

explore the nature and origin of the universe. All the forces that created and shaped the universe are present in the human being, and consequently rule our health and destiny. Health care is, therefore, a spiritual pursuit in which the healer serves as both physician and priest.

Chinese medicine is based on *The Yellow Emperor's Classic of Internal Medicine,* written at least 2,500 years ago. The *Yellow Emperor's Classic* formed the basis of Chinese medicine and the foundation for most of Asian medicine, including the systems adopted by Japan, Korea, the Philippines, and other Asian countries. (The exception is India, which may have been influenced by the Chinese, but developed its own system, called Ayur-Veda.) Indeed, virtually all of the Oriental health systems flourishing in the West today—including acupuncture, shiatsu, acupressure massage, macrobiotics, Do-In, and sotai—are based upon Chinese medicine.

The first law that Chinese medicine is based upon is the law of yin and yang. According to the Chinese, all life and the entire material universe originated from a single unified source, called Tao, which is an integrated and undifferentiated whole that is present in everything. Tao created two opposing forces—yin and yang, which are archetypal opposites that combine to create everything in the relative world. The chart below lists their respective characteristics.

	YIN	YANG
Cosmic Bodies	earth	heavenly realms
	moon	sun
Temperament	passive	aggressive
	mentally active	physically active
	following	leading
	asleep	awake
Time of day	night	day
Season	fall and winter	spring and summer
Magnetic pole	negative	positive
Temperature	cold	hot
Density	contracted to solid	expanded and hollow

Speed	slow	fast
Relative moisture	moist to saturated	dry
Body location	feet lower extremities	head upper extremities
Organs	dense, internal organs: kidneys, lungs, heart, liver, bones	hollow, surface organs: intestines, spleen, gall bladder, skin
Height	low	high
Distance	near	far
Sides	left	right
Light	darkness	light
Sexual characteristics	female	male
Constitution	female	male

Yin and Yang, the two principles in nature, and the four seasons are the beginning and the end of everything and they are also the cause of life and death. Those who disobey the laws of the universe will give rise to calamities and visitations, while those who follow the laws of the universe will remain free from dangerous illness, for they are the ones who have obtained Tao, the Right Way.

THE YELLOW EMPEROR

Yin and yang are relative terms. Individual women and men can be more or less yin or yang. Some women are far more yang than some men. Each gender has an inherent or archetypal nature, according to the Chinese. Men are constitutionally more yang, women constitutionally more yin.

Yin and yang are each incomplete without the other. By combining, they create all phenomena. Thus, everything is composed of a unique mix of both. Take the moon, for example. The moon is yin in comparison with the sun. However, the moon possesses both yin and yang characteristics, because it has both a dark side (yin) and a light side (yang).

Individuals, too, have both yin and yang aspects. Certain characteristics within the same person can reflect both yin and yang. A passive person (yin) can be stubborn (yang), for example, or a chaotic person (yin) can be domineering (yang).

As the chart shows, Chinese divided the body into yin and yang parts. Certain organs are considered yin, some others more yang. The attraction of yin and yang creates movement and energy, an energy known in China as qi, or the life force. Qi energy is all around us and infusing us. The life force permeates the entire universe; it is an infinite resource available to all.

THE BODY'S ENERGY CHANNELS

Qi flows through the body in precise and orderly patterns called meridians. They can be understood as deep rivers of energy running through the body. There are fourteen meridians, twelve of which are associated with organs in the body, while two have the responsibility of unifying various systems.

Each meridian runs vertically, bringing qi to specific parts of the body. No part is left unnourished of qi, unless a meridian becomes blocked or stagnant. This causes an imbalance in the flow of life force. Such imbalances can be compared to placing a big rock in a river: behind the rock, the water becomes excessive and powerful; in the lee of the rock, the water is diminished.

This imbalance—one side yang, the other yin—causes an imbalance among organs. Certain organs can become excessive or hyperactive (yang), while others can become deficient and hypoactive (yin). There can be excessive swelling or expansion (yang), or too much contraction (yin).

Without adequate life force, tissues and organs become stagnant. They can no longer eliminate waste from cells. As waste products accumulate, the blood-cleansing organs become stressed. Eventually, their capacity to clean the blood is exceeded. Accumulation of toxins (such as fat, cholesterol, ammonia, uric acid, triglycerides, and carbon dioxide) creates an environment for disease to manifest.

The Chinese, Greeks, and Indians believed that the symptoms of disease are actually the body's efforts to cure itself. Fever, runny nose, diarrhea, frequent urination, sweating, and other "symptoms" are actually the body's way of throwing off the underlying conditions that cause disease.

The underlying accumulation of toxins weakens the immune system sufficiently to allow a virus to take hold within the system. But more specifically, the accumulation of toxins diminishes the life force, which is the foundation of health. The continued diminution of the life force results in death.

In Chinese medicine, all health care is designed to balance qi. Treatment is meant to bring harmony between deficiency and excess, between yin and yang.

Virtually all behavior can affect the flow of qi in the body. Too much rest or complacency can make one loose and weak (yin),

As the twentieth century draws to a close, China faces a historic choice. How will it preserve the riches of its traditional medicine while embracing the specific technologies and interventions of Western medicine? For our part, we in the West are now looking more carefully, and less condescendingly, at alternative practices of medicine and mind-body interactions. We are using scientific technologies to investigate nonspecific therapies and placebo effects.

HERBERT BENSON

which can be balanced and healed by greater amounts of work and activity (yang). People who work excessively and experience too much stress, on the other hand, need relaxation to restore equilibrium and health to life.

The Chinese categorized virtually every activity, food, and herb according to the yin and yang spectrum. Because these are relative values, a single object or activity can be more yang than some things, more yin than others. For example, exercise is considered more yang than writing, but both would be considered yang activities compared to watching television, eating, or sleeping, each of which is progressively more yin.

The Chinese used the effects of foods, herbs, and other therapeutic techniques to restore balance and harmony to the body. If a person's condition is too contracted, for example, expansive foods and activities restore balance; if the condition is too expanded, contracting foods and activities create balance.

The preeminent form of therapy in Chinese medicine, of course, is acupuncture. Acupuncture is the one part of Chinese medicine that nearly all Westerners have heard of or seen, though few Westerners understand its purpose.

Since qi energy is an infinite resource permeating the entire environment, it can be directed into the body to restore health. An acupuncturist uses needles as antennae to direct qi to organs or functions of the body. However, the needles also can be used to drain qi where it is excessive; to warm parts of the body that are cool or stagnant; to decrease or increase moisture; and to reduce excessive heat. The acupuncturist does this by selecting specific points along specific meridian lines and then applying various needling techniques to bring about the desired results. There are as many as 2,000 points, but traditional acupuncturists use somewhere between 150 and 200 points.

Diagnosis of health and illness is done by using several techniques, including physiognomy, or relating facial and body features to internal organs; examining the tongue, iris, and sclera of the eye; and palpating the pulse.

Pulse diagnosis was raised to a high art in China. The pulse is sensed by placing three fingers with varying amounts of pressure on the radial artery at the wrist. With pulse diagnosis, the Chinese physician is said to read six organs on each wrist, or a total of twelve organs and meridians. According to a number of acupunc-

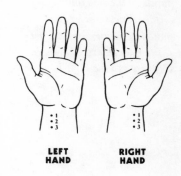

Acupoints on the Wrist

LEFT HAND **RIGHT HAND**

Three points on each wrist correspond with certain organs. The left wrist reveals the condition of (1) heart and small intestine; (2) liver and gall bladder; and (3) kidney and bladder. The pulses of the right hand reveal the condition of (1) lungs and large intestine; (2) spleen and stomach; and (3) heart governor and triple heater.

23

How the Ear Reveals the Body

The Chinese first recognized some four millennia ago that manipulating acupuncture points on the ears could relieve certain illnesses. Ear acupuncture treatments have been further developed by both the Chinese and the French.

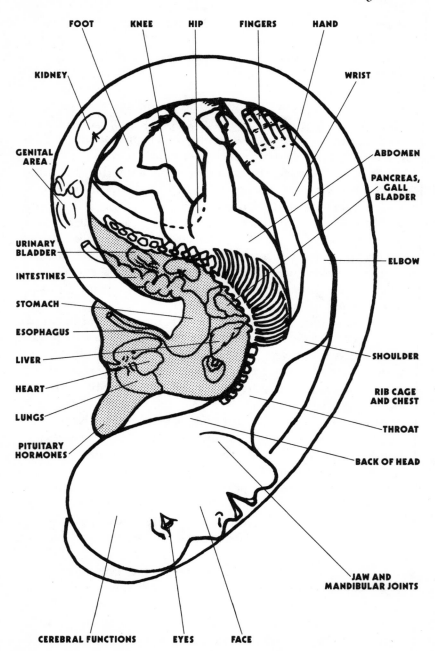

FOOT KNEE HIP FINGERS HAND

KIDNEY

WRIST

GENITAL AREA

ABDOMEN

PANCREAS, GALL BLADDER

URINARY BLADDER

ELBOW

INTESTINES

STOMACH

ESOPHAGUS

SHOULDER

LIVER

HEART

RIB CAGE AND CHEST

LUNGS

THROAT

PITUITARY HORMONES

BACK OF HEAD

JAW AND MANDIBULAR JOINTS

CEREBRAL FUNCTIONS EYES FACE

ture practitioners, it takes years to master the art of reading the pulse.

Beyond the law of yin and yang is the most all-encompassing tool in traditional medicine: The Five Element Theory, the basis of Chinese medicine and the central tool for diagnosis and treatment.

THE FIVE ELEMENT THEORY

Nowhere in the Chinese philosophy is the relationship between the macrocosm and the microcosm more precisely detailed than in the Five Element Theory. This links the seasons of the year, aspects of nature, and the body's organs, as well as specific foods, herbs, and treatments that will cure disease. It is also used for agricultural planning, healing, psychology, maintaining harmony in relationships, and even divination. This incredible tool single-handedly demonstrates the Chinese talent for seeing the unity within apparent diversity.

For our purposes, we'll examine the Five Elements from the perspective of understanding the body and healing. According to the theory, all change occurs in five distinct stages. Each of these stages can be associated with a particular time of the year; a particular element in nature; and a pair of organs within the body. Energy moves within the body in the same pattern that it does in nature, say the Chinese—the seasonal cycles. In the Chinese system, however, there are five seasons: fall, winter, spring, summer, and late summer, the latter proceeding from mid-July to mid-September. The five stages of change, their related seasons, aspects of nature, and related organs are as follows:

Summer is associated with fire and the heart and small intestine. These organs and season are, therefore, referred to as the Fire Element.

Late summer, proceeding from July to mid-September, is a time between the intensity of summer and the decline of fall. It is regarded as a stable time of the year and, hence, associated with the earth. The Earth Element is also associated with the stomach and spleen. (Many modern interpretations of the Five Elements also link the pancreas with the Earth Element.)

Fall is associated with metal and the lungs and large intestine. This is the Metal Element.

The differences between traditional Chinese and Western medicine have to do with the ways in which diseases are perceived, diagnosed, and treated. It remains to be seen how the two systems compare in terms of efficacy. But the systems need not be mutually exclusive. There is no reason why physicians cannot combine the finest elements of both schools. A Chinese proverb says, "The methods used by one man may be faulty; the methods used by two men will be better."

DAVID EISENBERG

Winter is associated with the kidneys and bladder and the winter months, from December 21 to March 21. It is known as the Water Element.

Spring is associated with the liver and gall bladder and the tree or wood. It is known as the Wood Element.

If you plot these five stages on a circle, as we have below, you will see that each stage leads to the next. Each stage of element nourishes those related organs within the element, and then passes qi on to the next stage. For example, the Fire Element provides qi to the heart and small intestine and then passes qi onto the Earth Element, the stomach, spleen, and pancreas. For this reason, Fire is called the mother of the Earth Element, because it provides life force to the Earth organs. This is called the nourishing or creative cycle.

At the heart of traditional Chinese medicine is the Five Elements Theory, which healers use both to diagnose and treat illness. The Five Elements—Fire, Wood, Water, Metal, and Earth—link the seasons of the year, aspects of nature, the body's organs, and specific foods, herbs, and treatments. It is also used for agricultural planning, healing, psychology, maintaining harmony in relationships, and even divination. This incredible tool typifies the Chinese talent for seeing the unity within apparent diversity.

The Five Elements

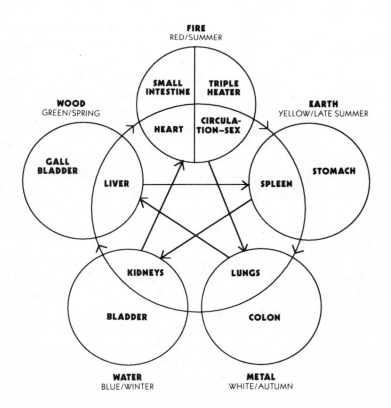

FIRE
RED/SUMMER

WOOD
GREEN/SPRING

EARTH
YELLOW/LATE SUMMER

SMALL INTESTINE TRIPLE HEATER

HEART CIRCULA-TION-SEX

GALL BLADDER

LIVER SPLEEN

STOMACH

KIDNEYS LUNGS

BLADDER COLON

WATER
BLUE/WINTER

METAL
WHITE/AUTUMN

Wood nourishes Fire. Thus, the liver and gall bladder nourish the heart and small intestine with qi.

Fire nourishes Earth. The heart and small intestine nourish the spleen and stomach (and pancreas) with qi.

Earth nourishes Metal. The spleen and stomach provide qi to the lungs and large intestine.

Metal nourishes Water. The large intestine and lungs provide qi to the bladder and kidneys.

Water nourishes Wood. Kidneys and bladder pass qi on to the liver and gall bladder.

There is more than just nourishment in life, however. There are also limitations. Organs must be governed, too. Thus, there is also a controlling cycle. To illustrate this need, consider that a river is powerful because of the quantity of its water and the presence of its banks, which direct the flow of water by providing limits. Without such limits, the water overflows its banks and floods, thus destroying the river and the surrounding geography. As long as there are limits imposed on the water, the river has power to move obstacles out of the way, eliminate waste, or even drive a turbine to generate hydroelectric power. The water itself would be considered the nourishing power of the river, while the banks would be considered the controlling influence.

It is the same in the body. Organs must be nourished and governed. In this way, they have sufficient power and energy to eliminate waste and maintain harmony. The controlling cycle is as follows:

Fire controls Metal. Thus, the heart and small intestine control or limit energy within the lungs and large intestine.

Earth controls Water. The stomach, spleen, and pancreas limit or control the energy flowing within the kidneys and bladder.

Metal controls Wood. The lungs and large intestine control or limit the energy flowing in the liver and gall bladder.

Water controls Fire. The kidneys and bladder control the energy within the heart and small intestine.

Wood controls Earth. The liver and gall bladder control the energy flowing in the stomach, spleen, and pancreas.

The analysis goes even further. Each element and organ group is nourished by specific foods and herbs, while other foods and herbs control this specific organ group. Just as each organ grouping is associated with a season, so it is also associated with a particular time of day or night. The liver, for example, is most active between the hours of 1 A.M. and 3 A.M.; the heart is most active between 11 A.M. and 1 A.M.; the kidneys are most active between 3 P.M. and 5 P.M.

Traditional Oriental healers use this information to diagnose and treat. If every element is working optimally, there are no symptoms and there is optimal health. If, on the other hand, one or more of the organs is blocking energy, the organ system which is nourished by it will suffer. Consequently, those who damage their liver often suffer from heart or small intestine troubles, while those who damage their spleen, stomach, and pancreas also suffer from diseases of the large intestine and lungs.

Chinese medicine embodies a remarkable union of technical competence and spiritual force. Because it is also a successful method of alleviating suffering, Chinese medicine may succeed in bringing popular attention to the unifying concepts of the East more quickly and completely than any other manifestation of Oriental thought.

LEON HAMMER

Looking at the body according to the Five Elements, one can easily see the harmony within our systems, and come to know the importance of each organ to the body as a whole. For example, typically we would say that digestion is performed by the stomach and intestines, but according to the Five Elements, digestion is absolutely dependent on the healthy functioning of the spleen.

Biologically, we know that the spleen filters the blood of broken and dead cells and infuses the blood with immune cells, such as lymphocytes and other white cells. In Western medicine, the spleen is not considered essential to life and is often surgically removed in the case of certain cancers and other disorders.

However, Oriental medicine regards the spleen as one of the supremely important organs and essential to the orderly functioning of life. Spleen energy—that is, qi emanating from the spleen—governs the movement of food through digestion. Spleen energy helps to transport the food through the intestinal tract. As it does this, it also assists the small intestine in turning the essence of food—that is, the essential nutrients—into blood and qi energy. The spleen sends qi to the lungs and large intestine. In this way, it nourishes these two organs with life force, making possible both breathing and elimination of waste.

To understand how the controlling cycle influences the body, let's look at the relationship between the Water and Fire Elements.

Very often, people eat too much salt, which causes kidney disorders. Kidney and bladder (the Water Element) control the heart and small intestine function (Fire Element). Consequently, kidney disorders, especially those arising from excess salt intake, cause illnesses of the Fire Element, such as heart disease and high blood pressure. If we wish to treat this condition, we must treat the controlling element, which in this case is the Water Element. By sharply reducing salt, oils, and fats and by increasing mild aerobic exercise (Fire Element), we strengthen both the Water and Fire Elements and their corresponding organ systems.

Chinese medicine is such an extremely complex and sophisticated healing system that any summary must ultimately do it an injustice. In addition to its two fundamental principles—the law of yin and yang and the Five Elements—is an array of other diagnostic and medicinal tools that are themselves refinements upon this foundation. Illnesses arise out of imbalances within the body that are characterized as "too dry," or "too moist." An organ can contain excessive "heat," or "fire." It can be "cool," or "damp." The body can also contain too much "wind," meaning that there is excessive movement or instability in organs or systems that should be still. These refinements upon yin and yang and the Five Elements are applied to every condition, so that constipation, for example, does not arise merely from stagnation, but from too much "cold," perhaps, or excess "dryness."

Every imbalance, however, ultimately arises from a person's way of life, which is to say, a person's relationship with the universe itself. Thus, the Chinese healer restores balance by combining appropriate herbs, diet, and medicinal practices, along with changes in the patient's personal way of living.

CHAPTER 2

AYURVEDIC MEDICINE

All diseases of the body can be destroyed at the root by regulating the Prana; this is the secret knowledge of healing.

SWAMI VISHNU-
DEVANANDA

LEGEND SAYS THAT the system known as Ayur-Veda, or the knowledge of long life, was given to one of the Hindu rishis, or "seers," by the god Indra. When that may have happened, no one knows, but scholars do know that the Ayurvedic system goes back at least to the fifth century B.C. and is based on the Vedas, the oldest known philosophical and spiritual writings.

Like the Chinese and Greek systems, Ayur-Veda sees health within a universal context. Human life, say the Hindus, is an extension of the life of the creator, or what the Vedas refer to as "cosmic consciousness." Health is based upon one's relationship with cosmic consciousness. The healer serves to reestablish harmony between the individual and the life of the universe by balancing universal forces within each person. These forces are both complementary and unique: they complete each other and yet maintain their own identities and natures.

As with most traditional health systems, Ayurvedic medicine is also based upon a creation myth. From a single, unified and cosmic consciousness two forces emerged, one male, the other female, called Shiva and Shakti, respectively. These two forces combined to create multiple levels of being that include cosmic intelligence, ego and physical forms, including humankind.

Cosmic consciousness is also manifest as a life force, which the Hindus call "prana." This life force is the animating power of life. It not only provides vitality and endurance to each living being, but is also the basis of healing. The life force manifests in physical form as the Five Elements, which are bound together by three forces, called the Three Doshas. Let's consider the Five Elements first.

Ayur-Veda teaches that the body is composed of the Five Great Elements: Earth, Water, Fire, Air, and Ether. These elements are not seen in the purely material sense, but are metaphorical categories that describe functions and aspects of the human body. For example, the breakdown and absorption of food during digestion can be seen as a Fire function. The human digestive tract is the body's crucible, its oven, in which food is "prepared" for assimilation and utilization by the body. The Earth Element stands for all the mineral substances that make up the body, including those that combine to create bone, cartilage, and contribute to muscle formation (such as calcium). Earth is also associated with the body's solid waste. Water, of course, would represent all the liquid substances of the body, including blood, mucus, lymph, hormones, semen, fat, urine, and other fluids. It is also associated with the kidneys and genitals. Air is the substance that animates the body and gives it the ability to move, and thus is linked to the nervous system. Ether, the most subtle and abstract of the Five Elements, is the principle of form and idea from which the body draws its archetypal design; it thereby holds the body together.

Since the elements are seen as interdependent functions, they are often present in the same activity. For example, while Earth is responsible for bones, the activity of walking, which involves both bone and muscle, includes Earth and Fire—Fire, because this element is responsible for the expenditure of energy.

Each of these Five Elements is responsible for the creation of individual senses and their ongoing functions. Fire is associated with the eyes and seeing; Air with touch and the skin; Water with taste and the tongue; Earth with smell and the nose; and Ether with hearing and the ear.

If you take a scalpel and start to dissect the human body, you will get past the level of organs, tissues, cells, molecules, atoms, and elementary particles, only to end up with a handful of nothing. All physical matter is basically a bundle of energy waves vibrating in the void. Yet is this void really a nothingness, or is it the very womb of reality?

DEEPAK CHOPRA

31

The Seats of Vata, Pitta, and Kapha

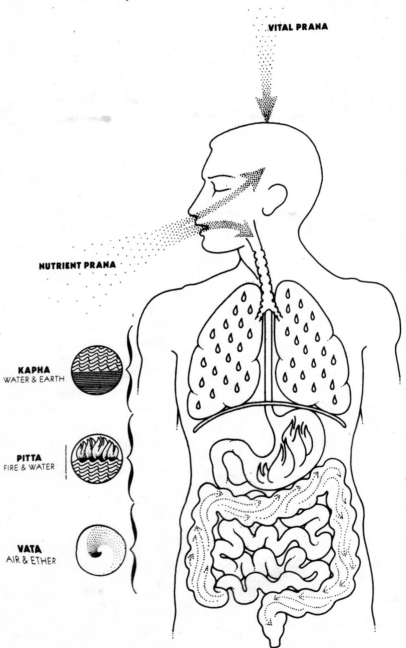

VITAL PRANA

Like the Chinese and Greeks, the traditional healers of India developed a healing system based on an underlying life energy. The system is called Ayur-Veda, and the life energy prana. Prana activates the body and mind, and is manifested in the human body according to the five basic elements (Ether, Air, Fire, Water, and Earth) and the three basic principles or doshas (vata, pitta, and kapha).

NUTRIENT PRANA

KAPHA
WATER & EARTH

PITTA
FIRE & WATER

VATA
AIR & ETHER

The Three Doshas

Having achieved form and substance, the body maintains harmony and health by balancing the three forces within it—the three doshas or vata, pitta, and kapha. Vata and kapha are seen as opposites, while pitta is the mediating force between the two extremes. The three doshas act on the Five Elements. They are the moving forces behind the substances and functions represented by the Five Elements. When the three doshas are balanced, the body functions harmoniously. When there is an imbalance among the doshas, illness results.

Vata represents the force of kinetic energy within the body. It ceaselessly stimulates motion, including the function of the nervous system, muscles, heart, blood flow, and thoughts. It is the vata activity in the brain that stimulates thought; the vata activity in the heart that stimulates beating; in the muscles that creates movement; in the nervous system that sparks electrical impulses and communication. Vata is associated with the Air Element.

Kapha is the source of potential energy. It is responsible for stability, groundedness, holding, and physical strength. Kapha causes tissues to be moist and lubricated. It is, therefore, associated with the lymph and with mucus. It is closely linked with the elements Earth and Water.

Pitta is most closely associated with Fire. It causes the burning of energy and the creation of heat within the body. It governs digestion, assimilation, and the metabolic processes of cells. It is linked with all the fiery aspects of life—hunger, curiosity, and thirst. Pitta mediates between kinetic energy (vata) and potential energy (kapha). Just as a fire burns and endures by transforming potential energy into kinetic, so pitta utilizes the two opposite forces to bring movement and endurance to bodily function.

If left to itself, vata would burn itself up; it would consume life in an intense blaze of ceaseless activity. Kapha, on the other hand, would decline into indolence and inactivity. Pitta must mediate between the two; but if either kapha or vata is excessive, pitta also will suffer, because both movement and rest must be equally available in order for pitta to function properly.

As we have seen, each of the three doshas may be present in the same organ, depending on whether it is currently active or at rest. However, individual organs are more closely aligned with

The Buddhists admonish us not to confuse the finger with that to which it points. Not only have we forgotten that the finger is pointing, or toward what it is pointing, but we believe that our reality can be resolved and understood by dissecting the finger, by breaking it down to its atoms and molecules as though somehow that is the ultimate reality and that's going to answer those questions for us. It's not that it's wrong, it's just incomplete.

KENNETH PELLETIER

33

specific doshas. Below are the three doshas and their corresponding organs:

Vata

Bones, including bone marrow
Brain, especially motor activity
Colon, when active
Heart
Lungs, specifically in the act of breathing
Nervous system

Pitta

Blood
Brain, in the synthesis of stored information, memory, and
   learning
Eyes, when awake
Hormones, in their active phase, as when stimulating an activity
Liver
Small intestine, especially during digestion and assimilation
Spleen

Kapha

Brain, especially in its capacity to store information
Joints
Lymph
Mouth
Stomach
Chest cavities

The three doshas give rise to and stimulate physical functions, and also create individual states of consciousness. In general, a balance between the doshas will create a high state of aliveness in which intellect and emotions are balanced; activity is governed by awareness of one's limitations; desire is balanced with understanding and forgiveness. Imbalance among the doshas, especially when one of them is excessive, will create distortions within the personality.

At its best, kapha represents emotional stability, "centeredness," and forgiveness. A kapha-type person recognizes his or her

The Theory of Tridoshas is one of the grandest and noblest contributions of ancient India to world culture. Although it has been known and practiced in India for over 3,000 years, its tenets are unknown or little known in the different parts of the civilized world. In the various medical systems of the world, for understanding diseases—and the diseased— the Tridosha doctrine is unique and supreme. Its practical value in diagnosis and treatment is without a parallel. It should be studied, grasped and applied in all medical systems without exception.

B. BHATTACHARYA

place in the larger configuration and can draw nourishment from work, relationships, and environment. He or she has a natural understanding of limits and boundaries.

When kapha is imbalanced, there is a tendency toward acquisitiveness, accumulation, and greed. The person has an inability to forgive, a possessiveness toward relationships and resources, and a desire to receive more than one has worked for.

Vata provides natural grace in movement and healthy motor function. The person with a balanced vata understands the needs of the body and its natural urges. He or she has a healthy ability to move on to the new and the untried, to let go of outdated relationships and behaviors.

When vata is imbalanced, a person has a hunger for sensory experiences, especially sex. He or she also has a heightened fear, anxiety, and skepticism toward others and may be controlled by nervous energy. He or she may be unable to feel "grounded" or emotionally stable and often gets exhausted.

Pitta provides a yearning for knowledge, for new experience, and understanding. Pitta causes one to see the broad picture, to understand divergent needs and to harmonize people's seemingly conflicting desires. Pitta types have a willingness to delve into details, to break down resistances, to work hard, and play hard. However, when pitta is imbalanced, a person feels great physical hunger, digestive problems, and thirst. There is a lack of gratitude for what is given, because it never seems enough, and much anger as a result of unfilled expectations. Pitta people may feel considerable hatred and jealousy.

The human body is the universe in miniature. That which cannot be found in the body is not to be found in the universe. Hence the philosopher's formula, that the universe within reflects the universe without. It follows, therefore, that if our knowledge of our own body could be perfect, we would know the universe.

MAHATMA GANDHI

CONSTITUTIONAL BODY TYPES

The doshas manifest in unique combinations in each person, thus giving rise to individual body types that lean toward one dosha or another. Some people have a body type that was more influenced by vata prenatally, while another will have more pitta characteristics. Each dosha creates tendencies within each of us, but because no one is perfectly balanced, one or two of the doshas will have dominated during the shaping of the constitution and the personality.

These imbalances will provide unique strengths and weaknesses, and thus create tendencies toward specific kinds of disorders and illnesses. Below is an overview of the three dosha types. No one is entirely a vata, pitta, or kapha person. People tend to be combinations of these three archetypal constitutions. But each of us has leanings toward one or the other. Ayurvedic physicians maintain that the three doshas combine to create eight basic constitutional types, which represent most people.

Those who have the kapha body type are stocky and often heavy-set, but frequently are surprisingly agile and athletic. If they overeat or avoid exercise, they can easily become overweight. They tend to be slow-moving, slow to excite or rile, and emotionally stable. They sleep like babies, are generally jolly, and can accumulate much wealth. Their approach to life is steady and slow. They like the status quo. They do not have a strong physical hunger for food or drink; rather, they derive emotional satisfaction from what they consume.

Kapha people have a tendency toward illnesses afflicting the kapha-related organs, especially the lungs, lymph, and stomach. Because of their weight and the kapha tendency to reduce movement and circulation, they also can suffer from heart disease. Peter Ustinov, former Secretary of State George Schultz, and George Simenon's famous detective, Maigret, are good examples of the kapha body type.

The pitta body type is often athletic, muscular, extremely active, and ruddy-skinned. Those who have this kind of body are intense people, hard-working and smart. They have excellent digestion, lots of energy, and usually do most things quickly. They tend to have fiery natures, be inspirational to others, and are leadership-oriented. Pitta people have excellent appetites; they hunger for food, experience, and learning. They can be easily irritated and impatient. They are often highly focused and directed in life. Once they desire something or lock onto a goal, they can be very committed and determined. However, this tendency gives pitta people the capacity for obsession and fanaticism. They must learn to lighten up. They can lose perspective, becoming jealous and violent. Vladimir I. Lenin and Margaret Thatcher are examples of pitta people.

Pitta body types are prone to illnesses affecting the pitta organs, especially the liver and gall bladder, blood, small intes-

How does Ayurveda achieve [its] noble aim and difficult task? Not by discovering and then destroying the various germs or bacilli, worms and viruses, but by the simple device of raising the individual resistance of the body and providing active immunity by vigorous discipline—not only on the physical and mental levels, but also at the spiritual and supra-mental levels.

R. K. GARDE

tine, and spleen. They can easily suffer from ulcers, as well. They should beware of cancer and stroke.

Since vata is continually moving, those with a vata body type are prone to dryness—dry skin, dry hair, and a humorless outlook on life. Vata people are small-boned, thin, and narrow-chested. They do not have a lot of flesh and are often so thin that their ribs and hips protrude. They are often nervous people and unable to sit still. Others sense that they are being consumed by something. They have little interest in food or drink, and often eat on the run. This leads to constipation, a chronic problem with vata types. They can be very cerebral, intellectual, and smart, though their thinking tends toward abstraction rather than concrete or practical ideas. The vata type is susceptible to illness of the vata organs, as well as arthritis, lower back problems, and lung disorders. Don Knotts (Barney Fife) and Woody Allen are examples of vata people.

The three doshas affect how the life force, prana, flows through the body, whether it is balanced, excessive, or deficient in certain organs. Ayur-Veda also maintains that this life force flows through the body in a definite pattern of meridians, or rivers of energy. These meridians correspond roughly to the Chinese system of acupuncture. And like the Chinese, the Ayurvedic physician uses the pulse and physiognomy to diagnose the patient. For foods, herbs, and treatments related to each dosha and element, see the specific chapter for each organ.

GREEK MEDICINE

HIPPOCRATES WAS A TOWERING and even revolutionary figure of his day. Born on the Greek island of Cos in 460 B.C., he founded the first school of medicine dedicated to the scientific understanding of health and the body. He refused to consider health and illness as a gift or punishment visited upon humanity by the gods. Instead, he regarded each as the consequence of "natural" and "orderly" processes that could be understood and, in the case of illness, treated.

There is debate over whether Hippocrates wrote any of the materials attributed to him. What most scholars believe is that Hippocrates wrote some of the texts penned under his name, and that many of the rest were transcribed from his lectures. In any case, much of his general understanding and many of his methods have been preserved. Ironically, the man who today is called "the father of medicine" has little influence over modern medical thinking. He is more apt to be cited as an inspiration by practitioners of alternative medicine, many of whom regard his fundamental precepts as still valid.

For Hippocrates, all living things move toward specific and knowable goals. Each living thing plays a part in a more grand cycle, which is essentially healthy and constructive. When illness manifests, the body's natural tendencies are to heal itself and restore the individual to its larger social purpose.

Health is the natural state of humanity, Hippocrates believed. Illness is also natural, however, and is governed by natural laws that are understandable. As such, illness follows a specific pattern. The physician's job is to intervene in that process at precise moments to assist the body in healing. The healing process thus consists of a triad: physician, patient, and the conditions surrounding the patient. All three must participate in the recovery process. "It is not enough for the physician to do his duty," Hippocrates said. "He must also receive cooperation from the patient, from the attendants, and from the external circumstances."

Like the early pioneers of Eastern medical systems, Hippocrates understood health and illness as relative states of balance. Elements exist within the body that must be balanced for health to exist. Illness, therefore, is a state of imbalance.

In one of the fragments of his writings, entitled *The Nature of Man,* Hippocrates described the basic constitution of human beings, and the fundamental elements that must be balanced to reestablish health.

"The human body contains blood, phlegm, yellow bile, and black bile," Hippocrates wrote. "These constitute the nature of the body, and through them a man suffers pain or enjoys health. A man enjoys the most perfect health when these elements are duly proportioned to one another in power, bulk, and manner of compounding, so that they are mingled as excellently as possible. Pain is felt when one of these elements is either deficient or excessive, or when it is isolated in the body without being compounded with the others."

According to Philip Wheelwright, Greek scholar and author of *The Presocratics,* the "excessive element is an intruder and a usurper: it must be either expelled or sent back to its proper place in the bodily complex." The body accomplishes this feat through the disease process itself, which is seen as the corrective action taken by the body to heal itself. The physician assists this process, says Wheelwright, through the use of "proper food and drink, calmness of mind and body, suitable exercise, and the like," which assists the "completion of the cycle through illness and back again to health."

Wherever the art of medicine is loved, there also is love of humanity.

HIPPOCRATES

39

Hippocrates

The great Greek physician Hippocrates (c. 460–377 B.C.) is a pioneering figure in medicine who termed healing "the noblest of all the arts." His ideas on the balance of health and illness, and the role of the healer in the healing process, are still studied by alternative practitioners.

Though scientific in his approach, Hippocrates had no hesitation in calling medicine an art. "The healing art is the noblest of all the arts," he said. As such, the physician must study each patient individually and adapt to the conditions of the illness.

"Nature was at work before any teaching began, and it is the part of wisdom to make adjustments to the situation that nature has provided," he told his students. Specifically, Hippocrates maintained that the physician must intercede at only the right moment in the process of healing. Once the moment has been reached, the physician must act quickly. "Time is that in which there are opportune moments, and an 'opportune moment' is that in which there is not much time." Hippocrates called these moments *kairos,* the root for "crisis." It was during such "healing crises" that the body reached a moment of truth in which restoration of health or death hung in the balance. At this moment, *pepsis* or the forces of healing could be assisted and illness overcome.

"The wise physician will know when to try to aid and accelerate the peptic process and when to let it alone," says Wheelwright. The doctor "must watch for the 'opportune moment' when the situation is exactly right for the exercise of his art."

Hippocrates maintained that the whole process could have beneficial effects. Illness could serve to create a new order among the four humors, as well as eliminate poisons and wash away impurities within the system. The Greek word that was used was *katharsis,* meaning to purify, especially the digestion. Once this purification was complete, one could achieve a new state of being, "a blended maturity" as Hippocrates called it.

Like his Asian counterparts, Hippocrates encouraged his students and fellow physicians to be humble and to recognize the true source of healing. "The healing art involves a weaving of a knowledge of the gods into the texture of the physician's mind . . . For it is not by individual cleverness that a physician is effective. Although he has his hands on many aspects of an ailment, it may still happen that the cure comes about quite spontaneously. Of course, whatever contributions the healing art is able to make should be accepted from it. But the path of wisdom in the art lies in making final acknowledgment to Those Very Ones."

Ancient Hippocratic medicine is no longer practiced as such, but its influence formed the basis of a medical tradition that flowed from Galen to Parascelsus to Avicenna, and thus to many traditional healers practicing today. Among modern healers, Hippocratic principles are most clearly in evidence in the system known as naturopathy.

We are bound to our bodies like an oyster is to its shell.

PLATO

41

HOMEOPATHY

LATE IN THE EIGHTEENTH CENTURY, the German physician Samuel Hahnemann became discouraged by the prevailing practice of medicine, which in his day used such techniques as bloodletting and blistering to treat illness. Doctors of the time also employed a number of substances, such as mercury, now recognized to be extremely toxic. Hahnemann found that these methods were not only ineffective, but made the patient sicker and often caused death.

A deeply spiritual man, Hahnemann believed that physicians were meant to assist the body's natural healing mechanisms, rather than administer chemicals that would override those mechanisms. His lifelong dream was to discover "if God had not indeed given some law, whereby the diseases of mankind would be cured."

Disenchanted, Hahnemann decided to drop the practice of medicine and earn his living by translating. He was translating medical texts when he came upon one by William Cullen, a Scottish physician. Cullen maintained that cinchona bark cured fever by virtue of its astringent and bitter qualities. Hahnemann was incredulous and decided to test the hypothesis on himself. He took a dose of the cinchona, which contains quinine, a well-known medicine for fever and malaria. Instead of producing astringency, the cinchona caused fever and the symptoms of malaria in the healthy Hahnemann. He repeated the same experiment using other medicines, with similar results.

Based on these experiments, Hahnemann stated, "A substance that produces a certain set of symptoms in a healthy person has the power to cure a sick person manifesting those same symptoms." He thus articulated the first of several principles of what would be the new medicine of homeopathy. He called the principle the Law of Similars, which in essence states that like cures like. The name homeopathy joined the Greek words *homoios,* which means like, and *pathos,* for pathology or sickness.

The Law of Similars revealed to Hahnemann how the body reacts to disease. He maintained that the presence of an illness stimulates the body's defense system to eliminate the illness. That defensive reaction produces symptoms, which are part of the body's effort at eliminating the underlying disease. The symptoms are not the illness, said Hahnemann, but part of the curative process.

Hahnemann maintained that the effective medicines actually produce a condition similar to the illness itself, which arouses the body's defense system against the underlying disease. In effect, the medicine makes it easy for the body to recognize the underlying disease and mobilize its defenses against the illness. The outward manifestations of this effort are symptoms. A cough, for example, is the body's attempt at expectorating the pathogen; fever is hostile to the underlying pathogen; mucus attempts to isolate it and allow it to be driven from the body as a runny nose, sneezing, and watery eyes. This was, of course, an ancient understanding of symptoms, as was his belief that the body was animated by an underlying life force, which Hahnemann called the "vital force."

Strictly speaking, the Law of Similars was not by itself a new principle either. It was known among Ayurvedic physicians two thousand years earlier, and was central to the medical approaches of Hippocrates and Paracelsus, the sixteenth-century philosopher, alchemist, and physician. Still, it was in direct opposition to the prevailing medical approach of the West, which Hahnemann termed "allopathy." Allopathic healers basically prescribe drugs

The first holocaust may well have been the execution of several million women who were accused of being witches because they practiced herbal medicine.

HENRY EDWARD
ALTENBERG

43

The material organism, without the vital force, is capable of no sensation, no function, no self-preservation; it derives all sensation and performs all functions of life solely by means of the immaterial being (the vital force) which animates the material organism in health and disease.

SAMUEL HAHNEMANN

to create the opposite effect of a symptom in the body. Allopaths treat swelling, for example, by administering drugs that will directly reduce swelling. Symptoms are suppressed, which Hahnemann contended causes the disease to go deeper into the body. This leads to a more serious condition, which is harder to cure.

Hahnemann wanted to reduce the severity of the symptoms caused by medicine, and thus decided to reduce the size of the dosage. Remarkably, he found that the smaller dose was even more effective against the underlying illness. Further experimentation led Hahnemann to his next principle, which he called the Law of Potentization or the Law of Infinitesimals. This states that the smaller the dose of medicine, the greater its potency or its effect on the body's vital force. Thus, a microdose of the medication actually strengthens the vital force against the illness. Hahnemann developed a method to dilute medicines down to infinitesimal doses by diluting the quantities and then shaking them (which homeopaths call succussion). This process is done successively until, for some dosages, only molecular amounts of the original medicine remain.

CONTROVERSY AND CRITICISM

Homeopathy has drawn its most hostile criticism on the basis of its Law of Infinitesimals, because orthodox physicians have maintained that there isn't enough of the medicine left after dilution to have any effect on an illness. Homeopaths point out, first, that the body manufactures only 50–100 millionths of a gram of thyroid hormone each day—an infinitesimal amount, which, if absent, will prevent healthy metabolism. Essential trace minerals and certain vitamins also are absorbed and utilized by the body in infinitesimal quantities, yet their presence or absence determines health or illness. Yet, homeopaths also agree that the complete reason why infinitesimal amounts work is not yet fully understood.

Hahnemann's mystical bent led him to believe that dilution and succussion actually reduced the material substance to its spiritual essence, which, in his mind, accounted for the medicine's enhanced power. Like the Native American, Greek, Oriental, and Ayurvedic physicians before him, Hahnemann maintained that the underlying reality of the physical world is essentially spiritual. But unlike many modern spiritual teachers, who view such matters as abstract, Hahnemann insisted that this underlying spiritual power was physically present in the form of energy. Later, other homeopathic physicians offered similar, if more scientific, suggestions.

In 1954, Dr. William E. Boyd of Glasgow stated, "The power of the solution does not depend solely on the degree of dilution but on the special progressive method of its preparation; the energy latent in the drug is apparently liberated and increased by a forceful shaking of the liquid at each stage of the process." Other homeopathic physicians have maintained that the shaking and dilution of medicines have the same effect as rubbing a material substance until it becomes magnetized. According to homeopath Dr. F. K. Bellokossy of Denver, Colorado, "We thus produce electrical fields around every particle of the powered drug; and the more we triturate [grind], the stronger electrical fields we produce, and the more potentized becomes the triturated material."

Thus, homeopathy embraces yet another fundamental principle of ancient or traditional medicine: the presence of an underlying spiritual energy that is the governing foundation of the material world. Like its predecessors, homeopathy is at least in part spiritual medicine.

Homeopathy has been used safely since 1810, when Hahnemann first published his findings. Since then, millions of people have relied exclusively on homeopathy for the treatment of virtually all types of illnesses. In addition to these clinical experiences, numerous scientific studies have been done to test the homeopathic hypothesis, with a number of them favorably supporting the practice.

Probably the most controversial episode in the scientific testing of homeopathy took place in 1989, when a group of researchers led by French physician Jacques Benveniste reported findings that confirmed the efficacy of homeopathic medicines. After the study was published in *Nature*, the prestigious British science journal, it was attacked worldwide. *Nature* even took the unusual step of sending a team of debunkers, consisting of a magician, a journalist, and an expert on fraud (none was an immunologist familiar with the underlying medical science), to Benveniste's lab to replicate—and presumably repudiate—the original study.

Homeopathy is essentially not only many-sided but all-sided. She investigates the action of all substances, whether articles of diet, beverages, condiments, drugs or poison. She investigates their action on the healthy, the sick, animals and plants. She gives a new interpretation to that ancient, oft-quoted saying of Paul, Prove all things—*a new meaning, a new application that acts universally.*

CONSTANTINE HERING

45

After spending two days in his laboratory, not surprisingly they claimed that they could not reproduce his results and termed the original study's findings a "delusion." Undaunted, in the winter of 1991, Benveniste reported another series of experiments that once again validated the homeopathic thesis. His work was published in the journal of the French Academy of Sciences.

Commenting on the case, Dana Ullman, president of the Foundation for Homeopathic Education and Research in Berkeley, California, said, "The serious threat that the microdose phenomena and homeopathy poses to science and medicine is clear and evident [from] the strong antagonism that the initial research created. The fact that the critics ignored and continue to ignore the numerous other studies [that] support the action of the microdose is further evidence of this denial and ultimately of an unscientific attitude."

CHAPTER 5

NATUROPATHY

NATUROPATHY TRACES ITS ORIGINS in the U.S. to a German-born healer named Benedict Lust, who, in 1902, launched a newspaper called *The Naturopath and Herald of Health*. Lust had procured the name "naturopathy" from its originator, John H. Scheel, who ran a hospital in New York State. In his newspaper's opening editorial, Lust wrote that "'Naturopathy' is a hybrid word. It is purposely so. No single tongue could distinguish a system whose origin, scope and purpose is universal—broad as the world, deep as love, high as heaven. . . . We believe in strong, pure, beautiful bodies . . . thrilling perpetually with the glorious power of radiating health. . . . We plead for the renouncing of poisons from coffee, white flour, glucose, lard, tobacco, liquor and the other inevitable resources of perverted appetite."

Lust drew his evangelical zeal from having cured himself of tuberculosis by using the water cure of Father Sebastian Kneipp, an Austrian priest who prescribed hot and cold baths to treat disease. In 1892, Kneipp sent Lust to the U.S. as a missionary for the water cure. Once he arrived, Lust obtained doctorates in both osteopathy and medicine, and eventually opened his own school of massage, chiropractic, and naturopathy in New York.

Naturopathy, as Lust defined it, is the use of nontoxic healing

The art of medicine consists of amusing the patient while nature cures the disease.

VOLTAIRE

47

In Tibetan medicine, physicians and pharmacologists are not separate persons. A doctor must know all aspects of medicine. Therefore, especially during the summer, students accompany physicians to the mountains to study herbs and plants, taking particular notice of their potencies, faults, and advantageous qualities. Then during the winter, they learn how to manufacture medicines. Thereby, they learn all aspects of medical practice.

YESHI DONDEN

methods derived from the best traditional healing systems from around the world. In that sense, naturopathy did not originate with Lust, or with any single person, but has its roots in Greek, Oriental, and European medical traditions. With these systems, it shares a belief in an underlying life force, but not an explicit allegiance to a specific unifying principle such as yin and yang or the Five Elements. In his 1919 book *Philosophy of Natural Therapeutics,* Henry Lindlahr, among the pioneers of naturopathy, wrote that "every living cell in an organized body is endowed with an instinct of self-preservation which is sustained by an inherent force named *the vital force of life.*" Sounding very much like a Hippocratic or Chinese physician, Lindlahr went on to say that "every acute disease is the result of a healing effort of nature."

Today, naturopaths employ a diversity of natural therapies, including acupuncture, homeopathy, botanical remedies, chiropractic, therapeutic massage, diet and nutrition, fasting, colonics, hydrotherapy, and compresses. Naturopathic physicians who have attended an accredited four-year program (there are currently two in the U.S.) are trained in most of the same scientific disciplines taught in conventional medical schools. Consequently, a naturopath also will occasionally employ medical tests, such as blood and urine analysis, for diagnosis. Moreover, most naturopaths acknowledge that modern medicine, including drugs and surgery, has a place in crisis intervention, though they remain committed to using nontoxic and noninvasive methods.

Dr. Ross Trattler, naturopath and author of *Better Health Through Natural Healing,* summarizes the basic disease process and its causes as follows:

- Accumulation of toxic material within the body due to poor circulation, poor elimination, and lack of exercise.
- Unhealthful diet that is rich in harmful ingredients (fat, cholesterol, sugar, artificial ingredients, and excess protein) and low in essential vitamins, minerals, and fiber.
- Improper posture and body structure, including spinal misalignment, poor muscle tone, and blood and lymph stagnation.
- Destructive emotions, including fear, stress, resentment, hatred, self-pity, all of which have a debilitating effect on internal organs and the immune system.

- Suppressive drugs, such as antibiotics and vaccinations, which some studies have found depress the immune system.
- Excessive alcohol, coffee, and tobacco.
- Environmental agents in the soil, air, water, and workplace.
- Parasites, virus, and infection.
- Genetic factors that create specific weaknesses, which allow accumulated toxins and these other factors to manifest as disease.

Like the Chinese and Greek systems, naturopaths regard illness as the body's effort at self-cleansing. Sneezing, coughing, fever, sweating, diarrhea, frequent urination, and rest are all methods used by the body to eliminate the underlying conditions that promote illness. Pain is seen as a message from the body that something is wrong. Such conditions as inflammation are the body's method of localizing problems to allow the rest of the system to function unimpeded. Naturopaths say that the body will place toxins at specific places in an effort either to eliminate the poisons, or to keep them from getting to organs that are vital to life. If not appropriately dealt with early, these accumulated toxins can eventually become tumors and cancer.

HEALING WITH HERBS

Naturopaths regard the underlying life force as the source of the body's ability to heal itself. Medicine is intended to assist this life force. Among the most frequently used remedies in natural medicine, and the oldest, are herbs. The medicinal effects of herbs are categorized by their effect on the body. For instance, some of the most common properties of herbs are:

- *Alterative:* heals and purifies the blood, without creating side effects.
- *Anodyne:* relieves pain.
- *Astringent:* causes contraction and stops discharge.
- *Antiemetic:* stops vomiting.
- *Antiseptic:* stops decay and putrefaction.
- *Antispasmodic:* relieves and prevents spasms.
- *Demulcent:* relieves inflammation.
- *Diuretic:* increases the secretion and flow of urine.
- *Emetic:* induces vomiting.

The naturopathic physicians of modern times do not discard a method simply because it is old; neither do they immediately embrace a technique because it is new, popular, and heavily advertised. The methods of naturopathic medicine have been rigidly tested upon the anvil of time and experience.

JOSEPH BOUCHER

49

- *Emmenagogue:* promotes menstruation.
- *Emolient:* softens and soothes inflamed tissue.
- *Febrifuge:* reduces or eliminates fever.
- *Laxative:* stimulates bowel elimination.
- *Nervine:* soothes nervous system and treats nervous disorders.
- *Sedative:* promotes relaxation and sleep.
- *Tonic:* invigorates and strengthens whole body.

Herbal and dietary healing are the basis of most traditional medicines, from Asia to the Americas. The practice of using herbs and food as medicine may go back as far as 60,000 years. Yet naturopathy, like chiropractic, homeopathy, and Chinese medicine, has come under repeated attack by medical doctors who maintain that such practices are quackery. Still, scientists have been turning herbal properties into drugs for most of this century, and dietary therapy is now reaching the mainstream.

The overall diet recommended by most naturopaths is similar to what's recommended today by the U.S. Surgeon General and what China's Yellow Emperor recommended thousands of years ago: whole grains, fresh vegetables, beans, fish, and fruit, and little animal fat. Naturopaths also frequently prescribe vitamin and mineral supplements, especially to boost the immune system.

Naturopathy is a method of curing disease by releasing inner vitality and allowing the body to heal itself. The methods that the naturopath uses should be looked on only as useful tools that help release this vital healing power. In and of themselves, they are not intrinsically healing.

ROSS TRATTLER

CHAPTER 6

CONVENTIONAL MODERN MEDICINE

ODERN MEDICINE, the dominant form of health care in the world today, is poised between two trends: an increasing reliance upon technology and highly sophisticated scientific procedures for both diagnosis and treatment of illness, and a growing awareness of the importance of disease prevention and the central role of self-care and more holistic practices. Will these two seemingly opposite trends merge in the next twenty years to create a new form of medicine, which will ultimately combine the modern and the ancient, the technological and the philosophical? A closer look at the historical antecedents of modern medicine may help to answer this important question.

First, a note about terminology. Conventional, orthodox, or modern medicine is also known as allopathy. *Allo,* from the Greek for "other," and *pathos,* for "suffering, disease," combine to refer to the use of treatments that cause the opposite effect as that created by the disease. So, if an illness causes inflammation, allopathic healers prescribe remedies that directly reduce swelling. The term was coined by Dr. Samuel Hahnemann, the creator of homeopathy, the system of using minute doses of substances that induce the same effect in the body as the symptom of the disease.

The whole imposing edifice of modern medicine, for all its breathtaking successes is, like the celebrated Tower of Pisa, slightly off balance.

PRINCE CHARLES

51

The mainstream of medicine cannot be identified with any one medical system; rather the mainstream is formed by all the tributaries. Is it even right to assume that there should be a mainstream at all? Perhaps we need to keep the natural rivers running freely, rather than dammed and confined.

TED KAPTCHUK

Modern medicine as such is a relatively recent development. While it claims Hippocrates as "the father of medicine," that claim is rooted in only one aspect of Hippocrates' method. He was the first physician to bring scientific and analytical reasoning to health care. In the process, he set medicine apart from religion or myth. Hippocrates' method of questioning and observing the patient closely to recognize the underlying illness and its cause remains among the most important methods of diagnosis. On the other hand, few of his ideas on the stages of disease, or his healing methods—diet, herbs, and a wide variety of natural remedies—are respected or used by orthodox medical doctors today.

Despite its claim on the Greek physician, modern medicine didn't really emerge until the early sixteenth century when Andreas Vesalius, a Flemish physician, did some of the earliest experiments in anatomy. About 100 years later, in 1628, William Harvey, the great English physician, first described the circulation of blood and the functioning of the heart. In 1660, Dutch naturalist Antonj van Leeuwenhoek created the first high-powered microscope, capable of magnifying objects 300 times, which provided an essential tool for inquiry into the inner workings of the body.

Around the same time, the French philosopher René Descartes' work crystallized the concept of mechanism and dualism, effectively creating the model of the body as machine, separate and distinct from mind. Less than a century later, Isaac Newton provided the mathematical and scientific underpinnings to these concepts, which became the dominant worldview of the West for the next 300 years.

These advances formed the foundation for the pivotal medical discoveries of the nineteenth century. The most significant was by French scientist Louis Pasteur who, during the 1860s, proved that microscopic organisms, such as viruses and bacteria, could cause disease. German bacteriologist Robert Koch advanced the theory still further, positing four conditions that must be satisfied to establish the causative organism of a specific disease; these conditions became known as "Koch's Rule."

In 1895, German scientist Wilhelm Roentgen discovered X rays and led the way to the development of a practical X-ray machine. By passing X rays, highly charged waves of energy, through the body and then onto a sensitive photographic plate, scientists found that they could create an accurate image of parts of the body's interior.

The Medicine of Science and Technology

X-ray diagnosis and advances in microscopes awakened scientists to the power of new technologies to provide information. Scientific medicine was increasingly looking at the body at the cellular level for the answers to health questions. This coincided with the dominant need of its day, namely, to find solutions for the leading causes of death. During the eighteenth and nineteenth centuries in the Western industrialized nations, these causes were primarily pneumonia and influenza. By contrast, heart disease and cancer were less of a concern. The discovery of bacterial and viral agents as the cause of some infectious illnesses appeared to be one step short of finding the fountain of youth.

Pasteur's work still stands as among the greatest achievements in medicine. His germ theory as the origin of disease gained overriding acceptance in the West in the early twentieth century. Since almost all illness was thought to originate from microscopic organisms, scientists began to search for the means to kill these tiny creatures. The tools that seemed to offer the most promise were synthetic drugs.

It is sometimes argued that modern pharmacology is merely a more sophisticated version of the ancient practice of herbology, but in fact the two disciplines bear only superficial resemblance to each other. Traditional herbology holds that everything about a medicinal plant is "active": its shape, which is created by specific natural or energetic forces; its taste, which will often indicate the part of the body the plant will influence; its stage of maturity; the place it was grown; the time of year and method by which it was harvested; and, finally, the plant's "spiritual origin" and mythological significance. In this sense, medicinal plants are seen to have "powers" that extend beyond the action of any single chemical constituent. They have not only material substance, but what might be termed energetic or spiritual properties.

In contrast, the practice of modern pharmacology is based on the development of concentrated, purified chemical substances that target one aspect of the disease process. In 1805, scientists

The problem here is that the practice of the art of medicine has now developed into what is called "the delivery of health-care." Health-care is a commodity and falls under, as it were, the laws of "Caesar." Caring for the sick is not and cannot be entirely a commodity for it requires of man faculties that are aspects of the movement toward inner consciousness, a movement that obeys other laws than the laws of rationalistic, societal order. It requires a nonegoistic attention and a nonegoistic intellect. The practice of medicine, therefore, places the physician between the two worlds, and it does so far more obviously and inescapably than any other profession in our culture.

Jacob Needleman

isolated and extracted morphine from opium and thus gave medicine its first "pure" painkiller. This began the practice of extracting what chemists thought were the active ingredients in plants. In 1935, the antibacterial agents called sulfonamides were formed. These were followed by penicillin, streptomycin, and tetracycline in the 1940s (penicillin was originally discovered in 1928, but not produced as medication until a decade and a half later). Today, the pharmaceutical industry uses genetic engineering to develop some new drugs. In such cases, there is no real link with plants, except to derive some genetic material to combine with new compounds.

Since the 1940s, new drugs followed by the thousands. The original antibiotics proved miraculous against infectious disease, and medical scientists bathed in the glory of their success. Scientists believed that a chemical cause and pharmaceutical cure for every illness would soon be found.

Looking back, however, it's clear that the eradication of many infectious diseases cannot be attributed entirely to the development of antibiotics. Improvements in sanitation and personal hygiene, which in the West took place more or less concurrently with the arrival of antibiotics, played an important role in the eradication of infectious diseases. Still, the effectiveness of these drugs convinced doctors and scientists of the power of chemistry, and set medicine on an irrevocable course that dominates Western society today.

Along with the development of the modern pharmaceutical industry came a slew of new discoveries and new machines. They quickly formed the cornerstone of medical diagnosis. Among these were the recognition in 1901 of three distinct blood groups, and the increasing understanding of blood constituents and analysis; the creation in 1906 of the electrocardiograph (EKG), used to record the electrical impulses of the heart; and the invention in 1932 of the electron microscope, capable of magnifying images to a power of five million. At the same time, lower-dose X-ray machines were developed, making X rays safer; more sensitive photographic technology provided clearer pictures; and radioactive dye was combined with X-ray technology to provide more accurate images of human organs.

Still later, scientists developed such high-tech procedures as computerized axial tomography (CAT) scanning and magnetic

The realities of medical economics encourage doctors to do less and less listening to, thinking about, sympathizing with and counseling of patients—what doctors call "cognitive services." Instead, the doctor is encouraged to act, to employ procedures.

DAVID HILFIKER

resonance imaging (MRI) to produce three-dimensional pictures of the interior parts of the body. Blood and urine analysis became highly sophisticated, with doctors relying heavily upon such tests for diagnosis. It is not uncommon for one doctor to send another the patient's records, and for the second doctor to confirm or offer a diagnosis without even seeing the patient. This has led critics of modern medicine to contend that tests and machines so dominate the healing profession that the *art* of healing is in danger of being lost entirely.

Concurrent with this remarkable growth in pharmacology and technology, surgery passed through a similar evolution. Surgery goes back more than 6,000 years, at least to the ancient Egyptians and Peruvians. But the principles of modern surgery originated with such innovators as Frenchman Ambroise Paré, who in 1542 bound a wound by securing strips of cloth to the skin and then joining the strips with stitches. Ether was first used as an effective anesthesia in 1842, "laughing gas" (nitrous oxide) in 1845, and chloroform in 1847.

History played a role in shaping the course of medicine during World War II, when wound treatment provided surgeons with an understanding of how the body's immune system could be suppressed to accept skin grafts, foreign implants, and transplanted organs. With this new knowledge, the first coronary bypass was performed in 1951 by Canadian Arthur Vineberg in Montreal, and the first heart transplant in 1967 by South African surgeon Dr. Christiaan Barnard.

Consistent with other branches of medicine, surgery now focuses on ever-smaller parts of the body, using microscopes and tiny instruments. It is also becoming even more technologically advanced, using such new high-tech tools as lasers and minute cameras to perform operations from within the body itself.

One of the things the average doctor doesn't have time to do is catch up with the things he didn't learn in school, and one of the things he didn't learn in school is the nature of human society, its purpose, its history, and its needs . . . If medicine is necessarily a mystery to the average man, nearly everything else is necessarily a mystery to the average doctor.

MILTON MAYER

THE BIRTH OF A NEW MEDICINE

Today, modern Western medicine stands as a monolith on the world stage. Few other spheres of human endeavor have developed so rapidly and in so singular a fashion. In the U.S., it employs millions of people and accounts for a huge share of the country's gross national product. In terms of its sheer influence

I see surgery as a passing fancy . . . It's a rather stupid way to treat disease. A surgical operation is nothing more than an artificial disease that is superimposed on the previously existing disease in the hope that the amalgamation of the two will redound to the benefit of the patient. It is usually a vain hope.

RICHARD SELZER

over the daily life of most people, the health care industry is perhaps unrivaled.

Ironically, modern medicine is now in the throes of a revolution, in part because the disease patterns of the Western world have changed. Today, the leading causes of death in the U.S. are no longer infectious diseases but degenerative ones, such as illnesses of the heart and arteries, cancer, and diabetes. Studies have determined that these illnesses are caused primarily by lifestyle factors, such as dietary habits, stress, and patterns of thinking, feeling, and behaving.

In other words, the leading killer diseases no longer fit into the germ theory paradigm. Modern medicine's failure to cure these illnesses, which don't really fit its worldview, and its enormous drain on many Western societies' economies, have revealed the system to be highly inflexible to the prevailing needs of modern life. The medical industry remains strongly wedded to crisis intervention, and its overreliance on extremely expensive tests, procedures, and technologies today threatens to bankrupt entire nations. At the same time, many common drugs and surgical procedures have undergone insufficient testing, or cause terrible side effects, raising doubts over the efficacy of some of medicine's methods and the veracity of its claims. Finally, because the industry in the U.S. has long served as its own watchdog, it has failed to deal adequately with such problems as overpricing and overuse.

Though most of orthodox medicine adheres stubbornly to its technological and pharmaceutical methods, a new and powerful trend is underfoot, which emphasizes the prevention of illness and the use of simpler, noninvasive methods of healing. Better diet, more active lifestyle, and healthier interpersonal relationships are the core constituents of this route to health.

Pasteur saw the future. He recognized that, although we all breathe in many pathogens, only a few of us become ill. He apparently recognized this fact as significant. On his deathbed, the great scientist is said to have told friends that his archrival, Claude Bernard, was correct in maintaining that the body withstands disease or embraces it by virtue of its overall health. "Bernard is right," Pasteur confided. "Microbes are nothing, the soil is everything."

PART TWO

The Organs

IT IS ONE THING to talk abstractly about universal forces and humanity's relationship with the cosmos, and quite another to confront the realities of specific organs, their functions, and the illnesses that afflict them. Yet, it is in this very realm that the differences between East and West are both stark and marvelous. Here, the West focuses on specific material objects. It looks at the stomach and sees muscle, mucous lining, and fibrous tissues. On the other hand, the East sees function, behavioral patterns, and metaphor. One objectifies; the other characterizes.

To best describe the body's organs, we'll combine these complementary approaches, exploring physical anatomy and personal

The Major Organs of the Body

The internal organs are layered in the body. This frontal illustration simplifies the overall anatomy by showing one kidney and the gall bladder, normally behind the liver, and the pancreas, normally behind the stomach.

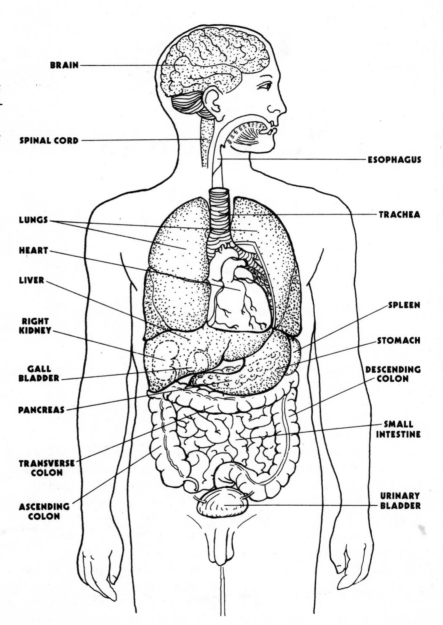

BRAIN

SPINAL CORD

ESOPHAGUS

TRACHEA

LUNGS

HEART

LIVER

SPLEEN

RIGHT KIDNEY

STOMACH

DESCENDING COLON

GALL BLADDER

PANCREAS

SMALL INTESTINE

TRANSVERSE COLON

ASCENDING COLON

URINARY BLADDER

and cultural experience. We'll consider historical reports and modern research. Throughout, we'll be referring to Eastern and ancient approaches as "traditional," meaning that they have been handed down through many centuries within specific cultures. This is, of course, somewhat of a simplification (Chinese medicine, for instance, is composed of a number of distinct healing traditions), but a useful one. Though "traditional medicine" is sometimes used to refer to modern Western medicine, we prefer the terms allopathic, conventional, or orthodox medicine.

Let's begin our cross-cultural exploration into the complex and wondrous realm of the organs with a look at how food and drink become mind and body.

CHAPTER 7

THE STOMACH

ᵂITH A NAME that comes from the Latin *alere,* to nourish, the alimentary canal is the route that food takes in its journey through the body. It is composed of the mouth, teeth, tongue, pharynx, esophagus, stomach, small intestine, and large intestine.

The mouth, which contains thirty-two teeth and the tongue, also contains salivary glands that secrete saliva. Saliva is an alkaline liquid composed of about 99 percent water, plus some minerals, cells, and inorganic salts. It also contains the enzyme amylase, which assists in the digestion of carbohydrates. The average person produces about three pints of saliva per day.

Saliva serves many important functions, including moistening and lubricating the mouth and food, dissolving food particles to facilitate taste and swallowing, beginning digestion of carbohydrates, cleansing the mouth, and neutralizing many poisons, bacteria, and foreign agents.

The pharynx is a passageway that connects the back of the mouth and nasal passages to the esophagus. Like the esophagus, it is a muscular tube that is lined with a mucous membrane and allows both air and food to pass. At the lower portion of the phar-

To eat is human; to digest, divine.

CHARLES TOWNSEND
COPELAND

The Digestive System

The digestive system includes the entire path that food and nutrients take on their journey through the body, from the mouth and esophagus to the large and small intestines.

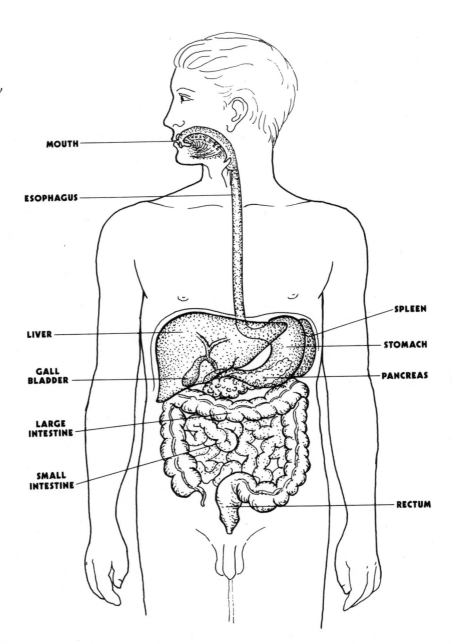

MOUTH

ESOPHAGUS

LIVER

GALL BLADDER

LARGE INTESTINE

SMALL INTESTINE

SPLEEN

STOMACH

PANCREAS

RECTUM

ynx lies the larynx, the organ responsible for voice production. The larynx serves as a passageway for air from the pharynx to the trachea, or windpipe. Below the larynx is the laryngopharynx, which connects to the esophagus and permits food to pass to the stomach.

The muscles within the esophagus expand and contract, creating a peristaltic action that forces food downward to the stomach. Interestingly, gravity plays only a small part in getting food from the mouth to the stomach, as evidenced by the fact that you can drink while standing on your head.

A WINDOW ON THE STOMACH

One of the great contributions to medical knowledge of the digestive tract was made involuntarily, courtesy of an obscure French-Canadian man named Alexis St. Martin. On June 6, 1822, he was accidentally shot when a nearby musket fell and discharged both shot and wadding into his left side. The shot blew a large hole into St. Martin's stomach and lung, both of which protruded through his rib cage. Fortunately, U.S. Army surgeon Dr. William Beaumont was on the scene. Beaumont stuffed St. Martin's stomach and lung back inside the hole and proceeded to do what he could to stop the bleeding. It was touch and go for several weeks; Beaumont had to feed St. Martin through a tube inserted into his anus.

Miraculously, St. Martin made a full recovery, except that the hole in his stomach and side remained open. This presented a rather unusual problem. As long as the hole was bandaged inside the chest wall, well against the stomach, St. Martin could eat without incident. But when the bandage was removed, his food and drink escaped—and an observer could actually look right into St. Martin's stomach and see its internal workings.

Eventually, Beaumont realized the significance of St. Martin's hole and proceeded to conduct experiments to study how the stomach worked. To do this, Beaumont would put small amounts of food inside silk sacks and insert them into St. Martin's stomach for an hour or so to find out what exactly the stomach was up to when it contained food. Among his discoveries was the first positive identification of hydrochloric acid as a main constituent of stomach fluids. He also found that when a person gets angry (as

St. Martin often did when Beaumont's experiments grew tiresome), the stomach moves around a bit and becomes flushed with blood. Beaumont experimented extensively on St. Martin's gastric juices, sometimes even tasting them. He recorded his findings in *Experiments and Observations on Gastric Juice and the Physiology of Digestion* (1833).

A wanderer by nature, St. Martin moved around the country quite a bit, perhaps in the vain hope of shaking the indominable Dr. Beaumont. Alas, the good doctor followed Alexis everywhere, testing the miraculous stomach whenever possible, but often lamenting that St. Martin was a "difficult and uncooperative" subject. Their collaboration was an odd but historically important relationship. Medical historian Douglas Guthrie noted that Beaumont managed to carry off "a fine piece of research in the face of unusual difficulties." History has even given St. Martin's orifice Beaumont's name: researchers refer to it as "Beaumont's window." Today, we don't need Beaumont's window to know what the stomach looks like and what it does.

The stomach is located below the diaphragm, slightly to the left of the sternum. It is a hollow organ, shaped like a balloon or a boxing glove, with the fat end connected to the esophagus at the top, and the constricted end connected to the duodenum (the first part of the small intestine) at the bottom. The purpose of the stomach is to store food, to secrete digestive juices and churn the food into a creamy mass, to begin the digestion of proteins, and, finally, to gradually secrete the liquid mixture in slow increments into the duodenum.

The stomach's capacity is about three pints. Its ability to store food makes it possible for you to do something other than eat every twenty minutes, which is what you'd have to do to support your nutrient and energy requirements if you had no stomach. (It is actually possible to survive without a stomach.) The stomach wall is composed of longitudinal and circular muscles that enable the stomach to churn food and turn it into a thick liquid. The stomach is also lined with special glandular cells that secrete gastric juices. The muscles and glands are supplied by blood vessels and nerves. At the bottom of the stomach, where it opens into the duodenum, a powerful muscle, called a pyloric sphincter, forms a ring that opens and closes, acting as a gateway between the stomach and the small intestine.

As you've no doubt experienced, gastric juices may be released into the stomach as soon as you see or smell food. Once you eat, the stomach releases pepsin, an enzyme that breaks down proteins to make them accessible to the small intestine, and hydrochloric acid, which kills bacteria on the food and assists the pepsin. An enzyme called intrinsic factor is also released to assist in the preparation of vitamin B12, which usually accompanies protein foods, so that the vitamin can be absorbed later by the small intestine. Finally, special glands secrete mucus to form a protective lining that prevents the stomach from digesting itself or being consumed by the acid.

Within the animal kingdom, stomach sizes vary according to the kinds of diets that animals consume. Carnivores tend to have larger stomachs than herbivores, relative to the rest of their digestive tracts. The stomachs of dogs and cats, for example, make up between 60 and 70 percent of their digestive tracts, while the stomach of a horse, an herbivore, consists of only 8 percent of its digestive system. This is why you see herbivores continually grazing, while carnivores are able to avoid eating for longer periods of time.

In humans, the stomach's role in digestion depends on the kinds of foods we consume and their relative composition of carbohydrates (used by the body for immediate and enduring energy needs), fat (a secondary energy supply, stored in tissues, and used when carbohydrate reserves have been exhausted), proteins (groups of amino acids used for cell replacement and repair), and vitamins and minerals (both essential to the proper function of cells). Of these, only protein is digested by the stomach.

The mouth and small intestine digest carbohydrates. The enzymes in saliva begin to break down the carbohydrates and prepare them for further digestion and, finally, absorption into the small intestine. Thus, in order to be digested properly, carbohydrate foods must be chewed thoroughly. Chewing ensures that the carbohydrates are mixed with sufficient quantities of saliva and its enzymes. Carbohydrate-laden foods that contain little protein do not require much action by the stomach and tend to move quickly on to the small intestine. (This is why many people find that they're hungry an hour after eating Chinese food, for instance.)

Fats and oils (which are liquid fats) are digested and absorbed exclusively in the small intestine. It is a slow process that begins immediately after the fats are released into the small intestine, which forces other foods still in the stomach to wait in line to be released into the small intestine. There they are broken down by the action of bile salts from the liver. They are then turned into fatty acids and glycerol (fatty acids in an alcohol base) by a pancreatic enzyme called lipase.

Of course, fat-rich foods are often rich in protein, too, which also must be acted upon by the stomach in order to be digested. Consequently, a fat- and protein-rich meal can take as much as six hours to evacuate the stomach. The energy requirements for such an undertaking are considerable, which explains why you often want to sleep after a heavy meal.

Fat slows digestion, but a variety of foods stimulate the stomach's activity, particularly its secretion of acid. Refined grains, coffee, tea, tobacco, sugar, alcohol, spices, and fried foods increase acid production by the stomach. Many drugs, such as aspirin and steroids, also increase stomach acids. So does stress. The foods may also stimulate the organ itself, causing greater churning action and speeding the digestive process. People who have coffee, brandy, cigarettes, or cigars after a heavy meal are taking advantage of these substances' ability to stimulate stomach activity.

Vitamins and minerals are so small that they do not need to be acted upon extensively to be prepared for absorption, which takes place in the small intestine.

WHEN DIGESTION GOES WRONG

The most frequent and minor stomach disorders are, of course, indigestion, heartburn, and gas. These disorders are caused by overeating, eating too quickly, eating foods that are rich in fat or spices, or stress. Generally, all of these conditions arise from excess stomach acid. Doctors recommend an over-the-counter antacid medication, but these drugs have side effects and can disguise symptoms that may become an ulcer.

The most common form of stomach disorder is a peptic ulcer, which is a wound in the stomach wall, usually about a half inch to an inch in diameter. About 60 percent of stomach ulcers are formed in the duodenum, with the remaining occurring somewhere in the lower part of the stomach. Ulcers can also occur in the esophagus, with rare occurrences in lower parts of the small intestine.

The typical symptom is a gnawing pain in the abdomen, especially when the stomach is empty, leading many people to complain about ulcer symptoms at night. A related problem is gastritis, which is the inflammation of the mucous membrane of the stomach, usually caused by aspirin or alcohol, infection, excessive bile acids, or stress. Gastritis may cause the same symptoms as an ulcer, though it is usually less severe.

From the perspective of conventional medical doctors, the cause of stomach ulcers is excessive stomach acid coupled with a decrease in the production of protective mucus. Most doctors acknowledge that diet plays a role in the onset of both of these factors, particularly the excessive consumption of alcohol, cigarettes, spicy foods, and aspirin, all of which increase stomach acids. Conventional treatment includes the reduction or elimination of such substances, along with the use of drugs, such as antacids, which neutralize stomach acid, and/or pharmaceuticals designed to reduce acid production, such as cimetidine, ranitidine, or famotidine.

If drugs are ineffective, surgery is often required. Surgeons may perform a vagotomy, which involves cutting the fibers of the vegas nerve that control acid production, or they may do a partial gastrectomy, which is the surgical removal of part of the stomach.

Another common stomach disease is cancer. Malignancies of the stomach kill about 15,000 Americans annually. Studies consistently show that diet is the leading cause of stomach cancer, especially diets rich in salted, smoked, and pickled foods. The Japanese, who consume large amounts of such foods, suffer the highest rate of stomach cancer in the world. Orthodox medical treatment may include the complete removal of the stomach.

THE STOMACH AS ENERGY SYSTEM

From the traditional Chinese perspective, organs have both physiological and psychological functions. Those functions are associated with particular aspects of nature, where those characteristics are demonstrated. For example, the stomach and spleen are asso-

You can only cure retail but you can prevent wholesale.

BROCK CHISHOLM

ciated with the Earth Element. According to this understanding, the stomach receives food and separates the gross matter, or nutrients, from the qi, or life force. It sends nutrients downward to the small intestine to be further digested and absorbed. Qi is sent to the spleen, which disperses it to a number of other organs, including the large intestine and the lungs.

The stomach is seen as the source of emotional stability or centeredness, having the characteristics of solidity associated with the earth. This is further reflected by the fact that the stomach is located in the center of the body, and is therefore seen as a kind of psychological center, a balancing point, around which our lives revolve. A strong stomach gives a person the sense of being emotionally balanced ("grounded") in the midst of changing conditions. A weak stomach makes a person nervous and anxiety-prone.

The stomach, which is the receiver or accepter of food, is further seen as a metaphor for humanity's ability to embrace and accept life. In this sense, food is a metaphor for human experience. Those who can eat and digest a wide variety of foods have a great capacity to enjoy life and adapt to many different kinds of experiences. Those whose tastes are highly restricted or picky tend to live more narrowly and censor much of what life offers. In the same way, those who have chronic stomach problems tend to be cautious about what they can and cannot eat or do; they are understandably afraid of what might upset their stomachs. On the other hand, those who can eat everything tend to be sense-oriented and to want new experiences.

The Chinese maintain, however, that the law of paradox is always at work. Those who have strong stomachs are prone to overindulge in food and drink. They are, therefore, vulnerable to illness and death due to food-related causes. Those with weak stomachs, if they are wise, have an incentive to take good care of themselves, limit their eating, and thus enjoy long life. In the former case, a person's strength becomes his or her weakness; in the latter case, a person's weakness becomes his or her strength. Traditional systems emphasize moderation as the key to wisdom, health and longevity, no matter how strong an individual's stomach is.

The Earth Element organs are associated with the emotions of "sympathy." A strong stomach will be revealed in a person as compassion and understanding for other people. Such a person will not be weak, however. He or she sees the larger issues involved in situations, and therefore has balance and perspective.

A weak stomach, on the other hand, can give rise to one of two extremes: excessive sympathy, or a lack of compassion and understanding, which shows itself in extreme selfishness or boorishness. In either case, people with weak stomachs tend to see themselves as victims to a far greater extent than those with stronger stomachs. So, a person with a weak stomach may demonstrate excessive self-pity, self-preoccupation, or hypochondriasis, for example. Such people have little care or understanding for others, simply because they are preoccupied with what may affect their health adversely. So, they lack compassion.

The spleen is sometimes referred to as the mother of the large intestine because it provides life energy to the organ. Consequently, foods, behavior, and emotions that upset the stomach and spleen will have a direct effect on large intestine function. When the spleen is upset or imbalanced, its ability to send qi to the large intestine will be impaired. If the stomach and spleen become excited, it will send excess qi to the large intestine, causing diarrhea. If the spleen and stomach become deficient, it will send an inadequate amount of qi to the large intestine, causing constipation.

The movement of life energy by the stomach and spleen are seen as taking opposite directions. The stomach rules the descending movement—that is, to the small intestine—while the spleen controls the ascending movement. Because the stomach and spleen function interdependently, any stomach disorder is seen as a spleen imbalance as well. Vomiting is a classic example. Vomiting occurs when the stomach becomes too contracted at the duodenum, while the spleen becomes expanded and excited. This represents a set of extremes. The stomach does not allow energy and food to pass downward into the small intestine. Meanwhile, the spleen's excited condition forces energy and food upward. This condition is brought about by excesses in eating or stress or poor habits. For example, foods that are overly contractive, such as meat, hard cheeses, salt, or eggs, cause the stomach to become contracted and the duodenum to close. Extremely expansive foods, such as spices, sweets, or alcohol, excite and expand the spleen. So, a night of pepperoni pizza and wine is usually followed by heartburn and/or a quick trip to the bathroom.

The digestion of fats after a meal can be seen as a purely biochemical process involving only the breakdown of the fat particles (chylomicra) by the appropriate enzymes. But observations made on a teacher of anatomy in his forties revealed that the mere prospect of having to lecture to medical students slowed down the rate at which chylomicra disappeared from his bloodstream. The digestion of fat particles is retarded by almost any disturbance in the life routines. Thus, mental processes can affect the course of physiological processes as seemingly simple as the digestion of food.

RENÉ DUBOS

In general, traditional Chinese healers see heartburn, belching, and stomachaches as stomach and spleen disorders. For the Chinese, the life force moves in orderly and specific cycles, as with the seasons or the course of a day. Each organ-group is associated with a particular time of the year. The stomach is associated with late summer, roughly mid-July to mid-September. At this time of the year, the stomach and spleen receive the most qi. This can be a time of healing for these organs, or a time in which symptoms arise if underlying problems exist in the Earth Element organs.

Each day, with its alternating periods of light and dark, is a microcosm of larger cycles taking place during the course of the year. The Chinese maintain that the stomach is most active between 7 A.M. and 9 A.M., generally the breakfast hours. Then the stomach receives the most abundant amount of qi that it will receive during the day.

The Chinese also associate each organ with a particular sense, such as taste, smell, or hearing. When the organ functions optimally, the corresponding sense will be acute. Also, each organ is stimulated more by one particular taste than by another. Not surprisingly, the sensation associated with the stomach is taste, and the flavor that stimulates it most is the sweet flavor. Thus, moderate use of sweet-tasting foods can heal the Earth Element, while overconsumption can weaken the Earth Element organs.

The stomach and spleen rule the imagination or the world of ideas. People with sparkling or creative ideas are said to have strong stomachs.

Singing is thought to have a strengthening and medicinal effect on the Earth Element organs. The combination of harmonious vibration (song) and deep, rhythmic breathing soothes and calms the Earth Element. People who sing well are said to have strong stomachs, and a traditional Chinese healer may encourage those with weak stomachs to sing more.

RESTORING HARMONY TO YOUR EARTH STOMACH

The above information is used by Chinese healers to diagnose and treat the stomach. If, for example, a patient suffers symptoms during the early morning hours, the stomach is suspected of being involved in the illness. Also, excessive sympathy, a lack of compassion, a generalized inability to taste food, excessive nervousness, or anxiety (the Woody Allen type) all suggest a stomach imbalance.

That imbalance is the result of a diminution or an excess of qi. The organ is either hypoactive or hyperactive. Either type of imbalance can be caused by an excess of certain foods or certain conditions in life. For example, there can be too much sugar in your diet, or too much stress in your life. The restoration of qi and balance to the organs begins by harmonizing or moderating the various conditions in one's life. Moderate eating, sleeping, working, and playing, along with the use of foods that heal the stomach, will restore balance and health.

Excess consumption of the following foods is frequently at the root of a stomach imbalance, according to Chinese healers, who'll usually encourage the person to reduce or abstain from the foods so that the stomach can heal itself.

- Spices, including foods such as hot green or red peppers.
- Salt, including foods such as pickles.
- Refined grains, such as white bread and other white flour products.
- Alcohol, especially sweet wines, which are said to injure the stomach and spleen.
- Sweets, especially refined sweets, such as white sugar.
- Artificial ingredients, such as food colors, preservatives, and flavors.

The Chinese also warn against eating too much animal food, such as red meat, dairy products, and eggs, because of the high protein content, which requires greater effort on the part of the stomach to digest, and the fact that they are typically rich in fat, which further stresses digestion. They also point out that frequent use of most drugs, ranging from caffeine in coffee, nicotine in tobacco, and alcohol in beer and wine, to prescription pharmaceuticals and recreational drugs, have an adverse effect on stomach function.

Lifestyle issues related to stomach disorders include:

- Excess stress.
- Chronic anxiety or nervous tension.

- Exclusivity, haughtiness, or arrogance.
- The refusal to engage in life's ups and downs (which may be a cover for a general fear of life, nervousness, and tension).
- Irregular hours, such as retiring late to bed, or rising late in the morning.
- Poor or chaotic eating habits, such as eating on the run, failing to chew food properly, eating right before bed (which requires the stomach to be active while the rest of the body gets to rest), and mixing foods together on the same plate and then eating foods at once.

HEALING THE STOMACH

In general, foods that grow in late summer and early fall are said to be healing to the Earth Element, including the stomach, because these foods are the product of the same forces that produce and nourish the stomach. In other words, the qi in the following foods enhances stomach qi:

- Grains: millet, sweet corn, and kudzu.
- Vegetables: collard greens, all types of squash, and rutabaga.
- Chickpeas.
- Fruits: apple, raisins, orange, sweet cherry, figs, and honeydew melon.
- Fish: salmon, tuna, and swordfish.
- Sweeteners: barley malt and rice syrup.
- Shiitake mushrooms.

For stomach problems, including indigestion, here are three Japanese folk remedies: a quarter-teaspoon or so of umeboshi plum, to alkalize the stomach; a cup of hot bancha tea with two drops of shoyu; and boiled and puréed squash, carrot, and onion, drunk at room temperature.

Some stomach-healing recommendations from the naturopathic realm include:

- Carrot, celery, and cabbage juice, especially when symptoms arise; drink two to four times per day.

- Cabbage juice, especially when symptoms arise; drink two to four times per day, unless already taking carrot, celery, and cabbage juice.
- Herbal teas with comfrey, licorice, goldenseal, or aloe vera juice; one cup two times per day.
- Whole grains, boiled and well chewed.
- Squash, broccoli, collard greens, carrots, or other foods rich in vitamin A.
- Vitamins: A and B complex.
- Minerals: zinc and iron.

Now good digestion wait on appetite.
And health on both!

WILLIAM SHAKESPEARE

No other organ is so intimate with food as the stomach. It's commonly recognized that various kinds of foods cause the stomach to suffer, but you may not realize that food also can heal the stomach. The approaches described above have been used for centuries to do just that.

Homeopathic remedies for indigestion:

CHAMOMILLA: When an attack of indigestion follows a fit of anger and irritability. Stomach distended with gas, abdomen cramping, bitter mouth, flushed cheeks, aversion to warm drinks.

NUX VOMICA: For the hard-driving type who indulges in too much food, coffee, liquor, tobacco. Heartburn, belching, bloating after eating. May be constipated.

PULSATILLA: Wake up feeling like you have stones in your stomach. Peevish. Dry mouth, bad taste, not thirsty. Pain one-half hour after eating, aversion to fatty foods and snug clothing.

Homeopathic remedies for nausea and vomiting:

ARSENICUM: Nausea, vomiting, diarrhea due to spoiled food. Burning pain after eating relieved by warm drinks.

IPECAC: Nausea, gripping pains in the intestines. Nausea from moving objects or reading in a car.

NUX VOMICA: "Wants to and can't." Could refer to vomiting, moving bowels, or urinating. Patient is awake after 3 A.M. and falls asleep toward morning. Wakes feeling wretched.

73

Herbs for the stomach:

GINGER: Relieves indigestion, nausea, vomiting.

BASIL: Treats stomach cramps.

CATNIP: Treats upset stomach.

CHAPTER 8

THE SPLEEN

HE SPLEEN HAS baffled people for centuries. In his 1876 book *Doctors and Patients,* Dr. John Timbs recalled the lament of a Scottish physician who one day confessed, "I wish more people would die of diseases in the spleen, that men might know what purpose the spleen is intended to answer."

In the absence of knowledge came myth. In the literature of both East and West, the spleen ranks second only to the heart as the organ cited as a major source of human feelings. Unfortunately, early anatomists and etymologists must have seen the spleen as the shadow of the heart, for they have ascribed to it a host of unpleasant characteristics. The *American Heritage Dictionary* notes the obsolete and archaic definitions of the word *spleen* as the seat of mirth, caprice, melancholy, and ill-temper. To be spleenful, says the dictionary, is to be "ill-humored, peevish, and irritable." To "vent one's spleen" connotes the unlovely act of spouting venom at one's neighbor.

Shakespeare attempted to lift the spleen out of its murky depths by acknowledging its finer side. In the first act of *A Midsummer Night's Dream,* he intoned that in the spleen are felt the paradoxes of love, its quickly passing joys and its lingering sorrows:

The body is not only more mysterious than we know, it is more mysterious than we can know.

ANONYMOUS

Making it momentary as a sound,
Swift as a shadow, short as any dream,
Brief as the lightning in the collied night,
That, in a spleen, unfolds both heaven and the earth . . .

In the Talmud, Jewish scholars note that the spleen produces laughter. When the spleen is ill, states one scholar, a person is given to foolish laughter, but when one "extirpates the splenic tumor, laughter ceases and such people always have a serious demeanor."

The Oriental and Occidental always have seen things from opposing points of view, and no organ demonstrates this better than the spleen. If the Biblical axiom that "the last shall be first" applies to any organ of the body, then, according to the Chinese, it applies best to the spleen. To the Chinese mind, which has always elevated the lowly and celebrated the hidden, the spleen is responsible for an array of important functions, not the least of which is to act as a receiver of ideas. The spleen, say the Chinese, picks up the refined vibrations, the very thoughts, of the universe.

Western medical science knows a lot more about the spleen than it once did, but the organ is still shrouded in mystery. To an orthodox medical doctor, the spleen has a limited array of functions. Like the appendix and the tonsils, the spleen is largely considered expendable and not essential to life. When the spleen is removed, other organs, principally the liver and the lymphatic system, are said to take up its responsibilities. According to the American Medical Association, the removal of the spleen "has no known ill effects."

In a number of traditional medical systems, however, the spleen is invested with great worth. The spleen is seen as the ruler of everything from joy and laughter (by the Hebrew and Greek systems), to balancing potential and kinetic energy (Ayurvedic), to "transformation and transportation" within the body and spirit (Chinese).

FORM AND FUNCTION

The spleen is located on the left side of the abdomen. It is fist-sized and weighs approximately seven ounces. It is a spongy, dark red organ, composed of fibrous tissue that gives it the capacity to expand and contract, and it thus can contain a variable amount of blood. Between its fibrous bands are tissues called splenic pulp.

This pulpy material produces lymphocytes and phagocytes, two types of immune cells that are essential to immune function.

The organ is surrounded by smooth muscle. During exercise, or when stimulated by nerves or hormones, the organ can contract, sending more blood into the system. In the center of the spleen is an indentation, called a hilius, where the organ receives oxygen-rich blood via the splenic artery. The splenic vein runs out of the hilius, transporting blood filled with carbon dioxide out of the organ and back to the heart.

The spleen filters the blood of broken and worn-out red blood cells and bacteria. These cells are destroyed by phagocytes and lymphocytes. Hemoglobin and iron are recovered from the worn-out cells and stored in the spleen, to be used in the formation of other cells and bilirubin, the pigmentation in bile. The spleen also stores blood and can control the amount of blood available to the body by its capacity to expand and contract.

During fetal life, the spleen creates red blood cells. Shortly after birth, however, this role is passed on to the bone marrow.

Medical doctors are beginning to recognize an important immune function for the spleen. The immune cells that it produces create specialized antibodies designed for specific antigens or illnesses. The spleen introduces these immune cells into the bloodstream as blood passes through the organ, and thus increases the number of immune cells in the body. People who have their spleens removed have weaker immune systems, and are more vulnerable to infections and disease.

The spleen can become enlarged due to a variety of illnesses, including malaria, infectious mononucleosis, tuberculosis, typhoid fever, hemolytic anemia, and some forms of cancer, including leukemia, Hodgkin's disease, and lymphomas. The spleen also can be ruptured when it receives a severe blow, as from a fall or an auto accident, which can cause severe bleeding and death. In such cases, doctors will often surgically remove the spleen and tie off the splenic artery.

TRANSFORMING THE QI FROM FOOD

Traditional Chinese healers maintain that the spleen is a primary organ of digestion. They say that it transforms the foods' nutrients into qi, governs the orderly flow of blood throughout the body, nourishes the four limbs with qi, and helps the body discern the five tastes (bitter, sweet, pungent, salty, and sour). Also, the spleen is responsible for the capacity to perceive creative ideas and enjoy understanding of others.

According to the Five Elements Theory, the spleen is joined by the stomach to form the Earth Element. The spleen nourishes the lungs and large intestine (the Metal Element). The stomach and spleen are nourished themselves by the small intestine and heart (the Fire Element). From this schematic, it becomes clear that the spleen is linked to the entire digestive system. While the stomach deals with foods' mass, the spleen absorbs and distributes the energy or vibration that comes from the digestive process (the actual movements of the stomach and small intestine) and the quality of energy that emerges from the food itself. Chinese healers say that spices, for example, have a particular energy all their own that affects digestion. That energy is considerable, especially when you consider that their mass is small and therefore should not present the problems to digestion that they do. Those problems emerge from the chemical nature of the spices, and the energy they release during metabolism. That energetic influence greatly affects the workings of the spleen.

The spleen distributes this qi to the small and large intestine. The quality of that energy, whether it is smooth and fluid or unstable and chaotic, will determine how well or how poorly you digest your food. Thus, Chinese healers see digestive problems, such as belching, flatulence, and a rumbling stomach, as related to the health of the spleen. So, too, are heartburn, acid indigestion, and nausea. These symptoms often indicate an excess of energy that the spleen cannot distribute in an orderly fashion. When the spleen passes excessive or chaotic energy on to the large intestine, diarrhea or spastic colon may result.

If the spleen is chronically weak or deficient, it may not be able to absorb and distribute the qi that emanates from many foods, especially spices, sugar, and wine, which the Chinese maintain are especially injurious to the spleen. Usually this kind of spleen deficiency causes intermittent or chronic constipation. In this case, the spleen is simply unable to pass sufficient qi onto the large intestine. When the intestine receives inadequate life force, it is unable to do its job.

Traditional Chinese medical theory recognizes that a healthy spleen maintains appropriate blood levels throughout the body, and also ensures that the blood remains in its normal patterns. Violations of these patterns, such as internal bleeding or excessive or deficient menstrual bleeding, are said to be related to a spleen imbalance. While obviously other organs are also involved in such cases, traditional healers contend that the spleen also must be treated if healing is to result.

In the case of the menstrual cycle, the spleen assists in maintaining its rhythm and duration. The spleen supports the process of accumulation and release of blood within the uterus. Spleen imbalances may play a role in excessively long, short, or irregular periods. Symptoms of premenstrual syndrome (PMS) are often related to spleen disharmonies.

The taste that has the strongest influence on the spleen is sweet. Mildly sweet taste tonifies and strengthens the spleen, while intense sweetness stimulates but injures it. With other Earth Element organs, the spleen helps maintain blood sugar levels. Excess consumption of sugar results in hypoglycemia or low blood sugar. Low blood sugar occurs when highly refined sugar is eaten regularly, causing blood sugar levels to increase rapidly. The pancreas secretes insulin to make the sugar available to the body as fuel in the form of glucose. The fuel is quickly burned, causing a rapid drop in available blood sugar. The resulting low blood sugar levels cause a variety of symptoms, including hunger, lethargy, fatigue, irritability, and depression.

When blood sugar levels drop, the body requires refueling. It craves carbohydrates, the principal source of energy in the food supply. If a person answers that craving, however, by eating refined or simple carbohydrates instead of complex carbohydrates (such as from whole grains, beans, and vegetables), the rollercoaster ride of elevating and rapidly declining blood sugar levels continues. Meanwhile, the spleen and pancreas become weaker. To effectively treat low blood sugar, you should try to strengthen the Earth Element by avoiding refined sugar. (See below for ways to cope with sugar cravings).

Because the spleen has difficulty dealing with acidic foods, saliva acts as a balancing agent for the spleen. In general, saliva, which is slightly alkaline, and alkaline foods are tonifying and strengthening to the spleen. Thus, the Chinese maintain that saliva is intimately connected with the spleen. The condition of the

Although analytical approaches to the body and its intake and surroundings have provided much useful information, such fragmented investigations have also obscured dynamic interrelationships which have an important bearing in medicine.

THERON RANDOLPH

79

spleen may affect how much an individual salivates. Often, when a person suffers from indigestion, the salivary glands secrete more saliva, which in turns has a medicinal effect on the spleen. Those with chronically dry mouths, on the other hand, may suffer from deficient spleens. Chewing and salivating make food more accessible to the digestion, but also to the taste buds and ability to smell. The Chinese maintain that the spleen governs the capacity to taste and smell, in part through its intimate connection with saliva.

Ayurvedic healers also see the spleen as a centering force and a place in which balance and harmony are made between opposites. The spleen is most influenced by the pitta dosha, which balances the kinetic energy of vata and the potential energy of kapha. Interestingly, the foods that Ayurvedic healers recommend as healing to the spleen coincide a great deal with the Chinese system. For example, Ayur-Veda recommends both sweet and bitter-tasting vegetables. In the Chinese system, sweet-tasting vegetables directly support the Earth Element, while bitter-tasting vegetables support the Fire Element (heart and small intestine), which in turn nourishes the Earth Element (spleen).

DELICACY AND STABILITY

As an Earth Element organ, the spleen is seen as a source of inner stability and centeredness. Paradoxically, the spleen is perhaps the most delicate of the internal organs. In a sense, it is the weak link in the body's inner chain. Therefore, when the spleen is healthy and firm, when the weakest link is strong, the whole body is healthier, more balanced, and secure.

The emotion associated with the spleen is understanding and sympathy. Spleen imbalances often result in one of two emotional extremes. Those with excited or excessive spleen conditions are prone to excessive sympathy. These people often have a saccharine sweetness about them, and may cry so easily as to constantly embarrass themselves. Such people show such abundant empathy that it seems to know no limits. They lack a certain balance or centeredness associated with a strong spleen.

Those with deficient spleens, on the other hand, may have an utter lack of compassion. They are so direct and rude as to have all the diplomacy of a loaded gun. Their brusqueness is so brutal that it indicates an almost total inability to understand or empathize with another human being.

Using the Five Elements again, we can see that understanding (Earth) controls the emotion associated with the Water Element, fear. Therefore, a strong and healthy spleen will give a person understanding and perspective when frightening events occur. However, if the spleen is weak, fear may dominate, because the controlling influence of the spleen is weak.

Often, a person experiences a combination of weak spleen energy with excessive kidney energy, causing chronic anxiety and fear. People who are perpetually anxious can be drawn to sugar to help stimulate spleen energy, but the effect of the sugar is to further weaken the spleen, once its stimulating effects have worn off.

Chinese healers say that the spleen likes dry weather rather than damp, humid, or rainy days. Those with weak spleens are particularly influenced by the weather. They detest damp, foggy, or rainy weather, which often causes them to be depressed, especially if the bad weather is extended. Conversely, sunny days have a greater than average effect on restoring hope and security to those with weak spleens. In the same vein, the Chinese say that the spleen rules skin pigmentation.

Interestingly, recent scientific research into Seasonal Affective Disorder, or SAD, has revealed that brain levels of the hormone serotonin are diminished in the absence of strong sunlight. Controlled studies have demonstrated that sunlight has an antidepressant effect on people with SAD. Researchers have noticed that such people, when deprived of sunlight, crave sweets and feel better after they have eaten sweet foods. All of this tends to confirm the Chinese perspective on the spleen's relationship to mood, weather, and the sweet taste.

The season that influences the spleen most is late summer, August and September. The time of day that the spleen is most active is 9 A.M. to 11 A.M. It is during these months and hours that the spleen can do its greatest healing, provided that the conditions are right. The spleen wants and needs a sweet taste, but excessive sweetness can injure the spleen. Paradoxically, very small amounts of salt in cooking, such as in soups and stews, helps to alkalize the food and calm and strengthen the spleen. Like too much sugar, however, too much salt harms the spleen.

Health is not so much the absence of dis-ease as it is the presence of an optimal healing process.

M. Scott Peck

Chewing food well and thoroughly mixing it with saliva is a direct way of strengthening the spleen. The following foods strengthen the spleen, when eaten in moderate amounts:

• The grains millet, sweet corn, barley, oats, rice, and wheat.
• Squash, especially acorn, butternut, buttercup, hubbard, hokkaido pumpkin, spaghetti, or pumpkin.
• Vegetables, including asparagus, squash, broccoli, brussels sprouts, cabbage, cucumber, cauliflower, celery, green beans, and leafy greens such as collards.
• The roots parsnips, sweet potato, yams, and rutabaga.
• Chickpeas.
• Shiitake and button mushrooms.
• Sweet fruits, such as apples, oranges, raisins, grapes, melons, figs, pears, plums, prunes, and cherries, and cooked fruit and compotes.
• White fish and shrimp.

Here is a sweet drink that is especially balancing to the spleen. Chop into small pieces one squash, two carrots, two parsnips, and one onion. Boil until the entire mash becomes liquid. Keep adding water to ensure that the vegetables are fully dissolved or leave only a residue of fiber at the bottom of the pot. Drink two or three times daily for hypoglycemia, sugar cravings, and spleen imbalances.

A small bowl of miso soup every day, made with wakame seaweed, also works well to establish a healthy spleen. Use about one-quarter teaspoon of miso per cup of soup, and one tablespoon-sized shard of wakame per cup.

For indigestion, gas, and upset stomach, try sucking on an umeboshi plum, a Japanese pickled plum, available in most health food or natural food stores.

For constipation, boil brown rice with carrots, onions, and grated ginger root. Cook with a pinch of sea salt until rice is soft, usually about forty-five minutes to an hour, and chew well.

There are also some lifestyle considerations for problems concerning spleen and digestion:

• Chew every mouthful thirty-five to fifty times each.
• Avoid extremely hot or cold beverages. Excessively cold beverages especially can shock the system. Also avoid drink-

ing during meals. Liquids dilute stomach juices, preventing complete digestion.

- Avoid eating while emotionally upset or under stress. Stress impairs digestion and can lead to stomach upset, constipation, or diarrhea.
- Always sit while eating, rather than standing.
- Avoid overeating and eating too frequently. Excess food burdens organs and makes all forms of indigestion, constipation, and diarrhea more likely.
- Avoid eating large amounts of highly acidic foods, including tomatoes, eggplant, citrus fruit, and spices.

While the spleen is seen as unessential in the West, it is seen as a master organ in the East. The body's ability to ward off illness depends greatly upon the health of the spleen. Because the spleen plays an important role in the immune system, the health of the spleen is central to the body's ability to deal with infection and allergic reactions.

Herbs for the spleen:

MANDARIN ORANGE PEEL: Used to treat indigestion. Especially tonic for the spleen.

SAFFLOWER: Good for delayed menses, stagnated blood, poor circulation, blood clots, lower abdominal pain caused by blood congestion.

SAFFRON: One of the finest blood vitalizers known. Stimulates circulation and regulates spleen.

CEANOTHUS (red root): Used for enlarged spleen, lymphatic congestion, despondency, melancholy.

CHAPTER 9

THE INTESTINES

If we don't take care of the body, where will we live?

ANONYMOUS

ACCORDING TO AN EGYPTIAN LEGEND, Thoth, the god of medicine and science, descended upon the Nile in the form of an ibis, a sacred bird with a long beak. Before him was a group of priest-physicians. Thoth proceeded to fill his beak with water and then inject it into his anus. The doctors got the message, and began administering enemas to patients, including the Pharaoh himself. In fact, the physician who gave the Pharaoh enemas came to be known as "Guardian of the Royal Bowel Movement." Humanity has been administering enemas ever since, as well as trying a host of other treatments to achieve that long-sought state of intestinal health.

Concern for intestinal disorders was among the reasons that surgery was created in the West. The Western world's first secular school was a medical college established in Salerno, Italy, in 900 A.D. Both men and women taught and practiced medicine at this rarefied and prestigious institution. Scholars presented the methods of Hippocrates, Galen, and Avicenna, the revered Arabian physician, combining them with a limited range of surgical procedures, including operations to remove obstructions from the intestines. Early accounts of a renowned Salerno surgeon, Roger Frugardi, note that "Roger could cut well . . . [and] could clot bleeding with mummy powder, or finely cut hair of the hare . . . Torn intestines were sewn together over an elderwood tube, or an animal's trachea."

Louis XIV of France was among the first patients to undergo bowel surgery. Louis was a glutton and had frequent enemas, sometimes in the presence of visitors to the throne. Eventually Louis developed a growth in his rectum. He contacted Dr. Charles Francois Felix to have it surgically removed. The doctor set the date of Louis's operation six months in advance so that he could practice his technique on folks of lower status. This was highly advisable, as Louis was known to be harsh with bad doctors. Fortunately, for both king and doctor, the surgery was successful.

During the Victorian era, intestinal health became the rage in England, France, and the U.S., prompting the creation of spas that emphasized colonics and enemas. This spurred nineteenth-century humorist Henry Wheeler Shaw to note, "A reliable set of bowels is worth more to a man than any quantity of brains."

Today, intestinal distress continues to plague humanity. Constipation is the most common digestive problem in America, and laxatives are a major industry. Forty million Americans purchase them annually, 8 million of them chronically, spending more than $250 million in the process. Ronald Reagan and Tip O'Neill are two well-known Americans with advanced intestinal disease. Reagan had polyps, fingerlike tumors that grow in the large intestine. O'Neill had colon cancer, a disease that strikes 110,000 Americans each year and kills over 50,000 annually.

In the Third World, 4.5 million children under the age of five die each year of diarrhea. About 200,000 American children are hospitalized annually for the illness, which is easily treatable. Yet, more than 5,500 American children died from diarrhea between the years 1973–1983.

Asian and African cultures that subsist on traditional, high-fiber diets show little trace of intestinal disease, including cancer. Numerous recent studies confirm that intestinal health is almost assured by eating the right foods.

THE NUTRIENT ABSORBER

The small intestine runs from the stomach to the large intestine, coiling throughout the lower abdomen. It is approximately 1.5

A complete bacteriological analysis of one tiny sample of human feces could take a year or more to accomplish, which is an indication of the complexity of this vast ecosystem that lies within us all.

LEON CHAITOW

inches in diameter and twenty-two feet long. But because it's contracted upon itself, much like an accordion, its length within the body is a little more than six feet.

The small intestine is divided into three sections. The duodenum is a short, curved tube, about ten inches long, that is attached to the stomach and receives both the bile and pancreatic ducts. It extends to the jejunum, which is about nine feet long and coils upward to the left. The jejunum attaches to the ileum, which is about twelve feet long, and coils downward to the right.

The ileum joins the large intestine at a bulblike structure called the cecum. Within the cecum is the ileocecal valve, which is a barrier created by a pair of lips within the intestinal canal that prevents food from flowing back into the small intestine once it reaches the colon.

The tube itself is composed of four layers. The innermost lining is a mucous membrane permeated with many villi, fingerlike projections that absorb nutrients. These villi are covered with millions of fronds, even tinier mounds that absorb nutrients and increase the surface area of the organ. In total, the surface area of the small intestine is roughly 100 square feet. The cells that make up the mucous membrane are shortlived. Every two to four days the entire lining is replaced. This kind of volatility makes the cells highly vulnerable to radiation, whether from X rays or radioactive particles.

The second layer is called the submucosa, and is extensively crisscrossed with blood vessels. These vessels take up the nutrients absorbed by the villi and bring the nutrient-rich blood to the liver, its first stop on its journey throughout the body.

The third layer is the muscular coat composed of longitudinal and circular muscles that create peristalsis, which moves the food particles along the intestinal canal. Finally, the entire organ is surrounded by connective tissue, which protects and supports it.

The small intestine contains trillions of bacteria, though the initial stages of the organ, the duodenum and parts of the jejunum, are essentially sterile due to the acid secretions from the stomach. Still, some bacteria do get past the stomach and, once inside the intestines and beyond the acid environment, they begin to multiply.

The types of bacteria within the intestines vary among individuals according to such factors as diet and use of antibiotics and other medications, many of which destroy intestinal bacteria. Bacteria in the intestines play a positive role by assisting in the breakdown of food and digestion, making nutrients more accessible to the bloodstream.

Among the more common species of bacteria that reside in both the small and large intestine are *E. coli,* candida albicans or yeast, and lactobacteria, of which lactobacillus is a widely known strain. Harmful bacteria, such as *E. coli* and candida albicans, secrete toxins that, if produced in sufficient quantities, can cause disease. Lactobacteria, on the other hand, are helpful to the body. They produce some vitamins, such as vitamin K, and digestive enzymes, which assist in the breakdown of foods.

Studies have shown that diets rich in animal foods, especially red meat, increase the population of harmful bacteria, and the amount of their disease-producing secretions, in the large and small intestine.

The purpose of the small intestine is to digest and absorb nutrients. Though carbohydrate digestion is begun in the mouth and the stomach digests some proteins, the vast majority of digestion and virtually all absorption are carried out in the small intestine. Here, enzymes are released to help break down foods and make them more available to the tiny villi. The small intestine also secretes mucus, which binds the food matter, called chyme, and makes it less abrasive to the organ surface.

Intestinal transit time (the time elapsed between consumption of food and elimination) depends to a great extent on the overall health of the intestines and the kinds of foods consumed. Fiber-rich foods move quickly through the organ, but heavier, fat-rich foods take far more time. On the average, food spends about four to six hours in the stomach, another five to six hours in the small intestine, and another fifteen to twenty-four hours in the large intestine before it is finally eliminated from the body.

The most common intestinal diseases are those of the large intestine. The small intestine is rarely affected by tumors, for example, and cancer of the small intestine is uncommon, at least as a point of origin. (Malignancies that originate elsewhere in the body can spread to the organ, however.)

The most common form of bacterial or viral infection is Crohn's disease, which most often affects the small intestine. The ileum is its most common site, but the disease can manifest as a series of patches throughout the small and large intestine. Crohn's disease is accompanied by a range of symptoms, including inflammation of the intestinal lining, diarrhea, fever, weight loss, anemia, loss of appetite, weakness, and fatigue. Most of these symptoms are created because the inflammation of the intestinal wall prevents efficient absorption of nutrients. In addition, ulcers can form in the intestinal wall, sometimes causing bleeding. A fistula, or a tear in the lining of the intestines, can occur, causing bleeding and infection. This is often treated by surgery. Swelling of the intestinal lining can create an obstruction and thus prevent food from passing. This, too, is treated with surgery.

According to the American Medical Association, the cause of Crohn's disease is unknown. In the U.S., Crohn's disease affects only three to six people per 100,000 population, though it has been increasing during the past thirty years.

Treatment includes anti-inflammatory drugs and other drugs, such as corticosteroids, used to control the body's use of nutrients. Those who suffer from tears in the intestinal lining may need to be hospitalized and given blood transfusions. There is no medical cure for Crohn's disease; for many, the illness becomes chronic, with periods of dormancy and flare-ups.

FIRE AND JOY

Traditional Chinese healers view the small intestine as a yang, expanded organ. In the Five Element system, its partner is the heart, a contracted organ. Both form the Fire Element. Its season is summer, during which time the small intestine receives its optimal amount of qi. Thus it is during the summer months that healers have the best opportunity to heal the small intestine of many maladies, if the patient stays in harmony with the season by not eating foods that are too fatty, heavy, or well cooked, and by not suffering excessive heat.

"The injuries caused by the heat of summer cause intermittent fever in the fall," says the Yellow Emperor, meaning that harm done to the small intestine and heart in the summer will manifest as an illness in the fall.

In the same way, the small intestine receives its optimal amounts of life force during the hours of 1 P.M. to 3 P.M. This, of course, is the typical siesta time in warm climates, the period after the large meal when energy is diverted to the stomach and small intestine.

The emotion associated with a balanced Fire Element is joy. Laughter is healing to the heart and small intestine. Imbalances tend to show up as lack of joy and even depression when the Fire Element is deficient, and hysteria when it is excessive. People who are manic-depressive often suffer from some kind of Fire imbalance.

The tastes that nourish the Fire Element are bitter and slightly burnt. The Fire Element's color is red and its direction is the south, which means that Fire is strongest nearer the equator.

The Fire Element is nourished by the Wood Element (liver and gall bladder), and in turn nourishes the Earth Element (stomach and spleen). When the liver is blocked, due to cirrhosis, for example, the small intestine and heart will suffer, and heart disease is likely. Such people tend to eat more fiery foods (spices, tomatoes, slightly burned steak) to compensate for the deficient qi being sent to the Fire organs from the liver. These people will have fiery red faces, due to the expanded capillaries in the skin, and equally fiery dispositions.

Fire is controlled by the Water Element (the kidneys and bladder). Indeed, as we will see in the discussion of the heart, the kidneys are implicated in many heart conditions. The Fire Element controls the Metal Element (lungs and large intestine).

The Chinese maintain that the stomach and spleen work in coordination with the small intestine. The stomach passes the food's raw material, its nutrients, to the small intestine, while the spleen passes the pure qi, or life force, to the small intestine.

There is a kind of reciprocal relationship among the small intestine, stomach, and spleen. Imbalances in the small intestine will prevent the smooth transfer of life energy from the spleen to the small intestine. Small intestine disturbances will also prevent the organ from accepting chyme from the stomach. In this way, small intestine imbalances upset both stomach and spleen functions. In the same way, imbalances in the stomach and spleen upset the small intestine.

Which, then, is the superior or ruling organ in digestion? The Chinese say the spleen.

On the Five Element schematic, the spleen provides qi to the large intestine (the Earth Element nourishes the Metal Element) and small intestine. Therefore, all digestive problems are seen as related to spleen imbalances.

It's important to keep in mind that small intestine problems are directly related to stomach and spleen imbalances. Therefore, treatment of the small intestine includes the care and treatment of these organs, as well.

Like all traditional healing systems, Chinese medicine is based on the fundamental principle that the body can heal itself, if given the right conditions. Those conditions are arrived at, first, by eliminating the poisons that are causing the illness in the first place; second, by employing acupuncture, foods, and herbs that support the optimal flow of qi to the organ; third, by maintaining daily activities that support healing; fourth, by addressing the underlying psychological and spiritual issues that may be involved in the cause of disease.

All traditional medicine treats illnesses in this way, including those of the small intestine.

Foods that are considered healing to the small intestine include the following:

- *Grain:* Corn on the cob, whole corn, and glutinous millet.
- *Seeds:* Sunflower and sesame seeds (both in small amounts).
- *Vegetables:* Brussels sprouts, asparagus, endive, okra, scallion, dandelion, and chicory.
- *Fruit:* Apricots, raspberries, strawberries, and raisins.
- *Beans:* Red lentils.
- *Medicinal soups:* Miso or tamari broths, with small amounts of wakame seaweed (about one tablespoon-size shard of seaweed per cup of soup), and vegetables. Miso and tamari create alkaline broths that sooth and tonify the small intestine, stomach, and spleen. They contain digestive bacteria and enzymes that assist digestion. For indigestion, chronic stomach and small intestine problems, a light miso soup (one-quarter teaspoon of miso per cup of soup) in the morning will help to alleviate stomach and digestive problems.
- *Animal foods:* Shrimp.
- *Fibrous foods:* To cleanse and strengthen the small intestine, be sure that the diet is composed chiefly of whole grains,

fresh vegetables, and fruits. These foods are rich in fiber and assist in cleansing the small intestine of fat deposits and undigested waste.

Strengthen the spleen by including Earth Element foods in the diet. (See chapter on spleen.)

Avoid the following foods until small intestine symptoms disappear:

- Red meat and all fatty animal foods. Fat requires greater quantities of bile acids (see section on the large intestine, below), which create and exacerbate ulcers and any inflammation.
- Spices, especially hot spices, which irritate the intestinal lining and cause greater acid reactions in the stomach. Hot spices are fire foods, but clearly too much fire to create a balanced condition in the small intestine and heart.
- Highly acidic foods, such as peppers, eggplants, and tomatoes, until symptoms abate.

(See large intestine and spleen for related illnesses of the digestive system.)

Lifestyle considerations for improving small intestine function: Chew every mouthful of food at least thirty-five times each. Chewing breaks down food and makes it easier on the stomach and small intestine to digest food. Saliva assists in the digestion of carbohydrates. Saliva also makes the food more alkaline, which creates less gas. (Gas is experienced in the stomach and intestine, of course, but it is caused by spleen imbalances, according to the Chinese.)

Walk daily, weather permitting. Walking increases oxygen intake and circulation, which improves small intestine function. Aerobic exercise is good for the Fire Element; it strengthens and helps to cleanse organs of waste.

Laughing is healing to the small intestine—to say nothing of the rest of our lives. Laughter concentrates life force in the small intestine region. As an experiment, focus on your solar plexus region the next time you laugh. You'll notice that laughter is concentrated in this part of the body—especially a really good "belly laugh." Laugh, and your small intestine laughs with you.

THE SEAT OF PITTA

Of the three doshas (vata, pitta, and kapha), the one most closely related to the small intestine is the pitta dosha. Pitta mediates between the state of kinetic energy (vata) and potential energy (kapha). Vata is associated with the nervous system, the realm of activity and movement. Kapha is associated with physical stability and the lubrication of the body. Pitta is associated with digestion and metabolism—the fire within.

The small intestine is said to be the "seat of pitta," meaning that, like the Chinese system, Ayur-Veda closely associates the small intestine with the Fire Element. It is here that the raw materials of life (nutrition) are converted and made accessible to the body. The small intestine is the crucible of the body. Small intestine problems, therefore, reveal a weakness in the pitta dosha.

The following foods and tastes will balance and strengthen pitta energy:

- *Grains:* Barley, oats, rice (including basmati rice), and wheat.
- *Vegetables:* Asparagus, broccoli, brussels sprouts, cauliflower, celery, daikon, green beans, leafy greens, lettuce, mushrooms, okra, peas, parsley, sprouts.
- *Beans:* Lentils, chickpeas, mung beans, tofu.
- *Fruit:* Apples, apricots, pears, avocado, melons, oranges, plums, prunes, raisins.
- *Animal foods:* Shrimp and small amounts of chicken, without the fat.
- *Tastes:* Avoid excesses of sour, salty, pungent, and hot spices. Eat small amounts of sweet, bitter, and astringent foods.

Naturopaths recommend a whole-food diet to deal with digestive problems. Whole grains, fresh vegetables, beans, and fruit are emphasized as part of the healing regimen. Also among the most frequently recommended foods are kelp and other seaweeds. Foods rich in the following vitamins are recommended for digestive problems:

- *Beta carotene, or the vegetable source of vitamin A:* Squash, collard greens, broccoli, carrots, and brussels sprouts.

- *B Vitamins:* Whole grains, leafy greens, sea vegetables, peas, and beans.
- *Vitamin B12:* Present in all animal foods, including fish. Include white fish as part of your regular diet (at least once per week). Cod, haddock, flounder, sole, and halibut are among the fish lowest in fat and richest in nutrition, including B12.
- *Vitamin C:* Present in broccoli, sauerkraut, sprouted beans, cabbage, squash, tart fruits such as strawberries, and citrus fruit.
- *Vitamin E:* In whole grains, especially wheat, wheat germ, and dried beans.

(If a person has been on a particularly unhealthy diet for many years, supplementation of these vitamins may be necessary for a short period. See a naturopath for specific recommendations.)

Herbs that aid digestion include: Chamomile tea (soothes and heals), dandelion tea (cleanses blood of toxins), ginger root tea (stimulates digestion and circulation), goldenseal (tea or infusion; heals and cleans blood), and slippery elm (tea or infusion; heals and cleans blood). One or two of these teas can be used, alternating them every two days.

For ulcers, drink chamomile tea, three times per day.

Like so many other parts or of the body, the small intestine is an organ we typically take for granted, at least until it causes us trouble. Yet, its health is among the easiest to maintain. So, the next time you're having a shrimp dinner, or a little chamomile tea, think of your small intestine, with gratitude.

THE LARGE INTESTINE

The large intestine is about six feet long, and two inches wide. It is shaped like an inverted horseshoe, and frames the many coils of the small intestine. There are no villi within the large intestine wall, only small pores that absorb mostly water.

The organ is made up of four sections: an ascending colon, which joins with the small intestine at the cecum, a bulblike structure within which the ileocecal valve is located; the transverse colon, which travels latterly just below the diaphragm; the descending colon, which is the downward leg of the organ that brings waste material to the pelvic portion, called the sigmoid colon. The sigmoid colon is an "S" shaped tube that, after the last bend in the "S," continues as the rectum, the anal canal, and its opening, the anus. The rectum is lined with a set of thick vertical muscles that narrow to an inner sphincter muscle and, at the anus, an outer sphincter.

At the cecum—where the small and large intestine join—is a small wormlike structure, about three and a half inches long, known as the appendix. According to the American Medical Association, the appendix "has no known function." (Traditional medical systems maintain that there are no unnecessary parts of the body, and that even the appendix serves an important function.) In appearance, the appendix is a miniature intestine. Its interior is basically a replica of the colon, with a concentration of lymph glands within the mucous membrane.

Living inside the large intestine are many trillions of bacteria (the organ is more heavily populated than the small intestine). As with the small intestine, the colon is filled with a variety of healthful and harmful bacteria (described above in the section on the small intestine). As we will show, the health of the large intestine and the effect of its bacteria are greatly influenced by diet.

These bacteria help convert nutrients into essential vitamins, including vitamin K, which are then absorbed by the intestine. They also create gas (methane, hydrogen, and carbon dioxide), through the putrefaction and fermentation of foods.

The primary purpose of the large intestine is to absorb water from the liquid waste of the small intestine, thereby making the waste solid, and efficiently eliminating it from the body. The organ also absorbs some vitamins and minerals not taken up by the small intestine.

L.A. Belly and Other Intestinal Problems

Otherwise known as gastroenteritis, swelling of the stomach and/or intestine is usually caused by viral or bacterial infection. Foreign bacteria can find their way into the intestine via poorly prepared or unclean food, or the consumption of water that contains unfamiliar bacteria (Americans traveling in Mexico often contract diarrhea, commonly called "Montezuma's Revenge";

Mexicans traveling the U.S. sometimes get "L.A. Belly," the same disease with a different name). These bacterial infections usually pass within a few days or a week. Typhoid and cholera are among the serious forms of bacterial infections, and are considered life-threatening.

Single-celled animals such as protozoa, giardia, and amoebas also can cause inflammation of the small and large intestine. Larger parasites, such as tapeworms or pinworms, can give rise to these symptoms, too.

Ulcerative colitis usually affects the descending colon and/or rectum. Like Crohn's disease (see small intestine), colitis causes swelling and ulcers to form in the intestinal wall. Blood and mucus emanating from the ulcers are often discharged in the stools. Other symptoms include abdominal pain, diarrhea, and occasionally fever.

Colitis is most prevalent among young adults. Though the illness may arise from the presence of bacteria, virus, or amoebas, the cause is still unknown, according to the AMA.

Treatment includes antibiotics to deal with infection; corticosteroid drugs to control nutrient absorption; and special diets that include multiple vitamin and mineral supplements. The diets are designed to restrict foods that promote gas and intestinal irritation. The foods commonly avoided are cabbage, beans, spices, milk, alcohol, and drinks that are either excessively cold or hot.

Antibiotics taken for more than two weeks can worsen the symptoms of colitis. Antibiotics upset the bacterial balance within the intestines by killing healthy bacteria and promoting harmful growth. This, of course, can exacerbate the symptoms.

Complications resulting from the illness (such as internal bleeding and fistula) may require surgery. If infection is the cause, the symptoms of colitis usually pass without treatment.

Diverticula are small sacs, or protrusions, in the lining of the intestines. Pressure from within the intestine causes these sacs to form. Often, undigested food gets caught in the sacs and remains there to putrefy and foster the growth of harmful bacteria. The formation of these sacs within the intestine causes that part of the colon to weaken, thus preventing healthy peristalsis and efficient bowel elimination.

Diverticulosis is the presence of diverticula in the intestines. Diverticulitis is a complication of diverticula in which inflammation occurs within the sacs; occasionally, a hole forms in the lining, as well. Symptoms of diverticulosis include bloating, pain, and alternating diarrhea and constipation. There can be bleeding if ulcers or holes form within the intestinal wall.

Both of these conditions are rare in developing countries and those where the diet consists mainly of whole grains, vegetables, and fruits. Fiber is one of the primary means of treatment for the illness, as well as antispasmodic drugs, and bed rest.

Irritable bowel syndrome is the name given to alternating bouts of diarrhea and constipation, often accompanied by diverticula, intestinal bloating, discomfort, and gas.

One of the three common forms of cancer in the Western world (besides breast and prostate cancer), colon cancer is unquestionably caused by a high-fat diet, and specifically the consumption of red meat. In December 1990, *The New England Journal of Medicine* reported the results of the largest study ever conducted on the relationship between diet and colon cancer. For six years, researchers followed 88,751 women between the ages of thirty-four and fifty-nine, recording their dietary habits and health patterns. The results showed that as fat intake and red meat consumption rose, so too did the rates of colon cancer. Those eating the most animal fat were twice as likely to develop colon cancer as those eating the least.

These findings were consistent with an enormous body of evidence that has been showing for decades that dietary fat causes colon cancer. The National Research Council of the National Academy of Sciences said in 1982 that fat—especially saturated fat found in animal foods—has a "causal" relationship with cancer, especially colon cancer. In 1979, the U.S. Surgeon General urged Americans to reduce their overall fat intake to reduce their risk of cancer and heart disease. The Surgeon General recommended specifically that Americans reduce their consumption of red meat.

Dr. Walter Willet, a researcher at the Brigham and Women's Hospital in Boston who directed the most recent study, stated, "If you step back and look at the data, the optimum amount of red meat you eat should be zero."

Scientists believe that fat causes cancer in a number of ways. Increased fat intake causes the liver to produce more bile acids in order to break down the fat in the intestinal tract. These acids act upon carcinogens, already present in the bowel, making them more virulent.

At the same time, fat within the colon increases the population of anaerobic bacteria that secrete estrogens. These estrogens, scientists have found, promote the growth of tumors. So, too, do high blood levels of cholesterol.

These factors—dietary fat and cholesterol, bile acids, estrogens from bacteria, and carcinogens derived from food and other environmental sources—combine to deform the DNA of cells and cause unrestricted growth, or cancer.

While there are dietary constituents that promote tumor growth, there are also foods that prevent intestinal disease. Low fat and cholesterol diets have been shown to reduce the size and the number of tumors in the bowel. Diets high in fiber have been shown to prevent all forms of intestinal problems, especially cancer. Studies dating back to the mid-1970s performed by Drs. Denis Burkitt and Hugh Trowell demonstrated that people living on high-fiber diets have low rates of intestinal disease, including cancer.

As shown in the chapter on the stomach, fat slows digestion and intestinal transit time. Fiber speeds up intestinal transit time and thus diminishes the likelihood of carcinogens remaining in the bowel to promote the growth of tumors.

Former director of the National Cancer Institute Dr. Gio Gori has reported that Japanese who remain in Japan and subsist on their traditional diet show low rates of cancer. However, when they come to the West and adopt the American high-fat diet, their cancer rates—including colon cancer—increase to those of Americans.

Finally, vegetables rich in vitamins A, E, and C—the so-called antioxidants—have been shown to enhance immune function (see chapter on the immune system) and prevent serious disease, including cancer.

THE RIGHT WAY OF LIVING

The Chinese view the large intestine as a yang, or expanded organ. It is regarded as one of the "six bowels"—the others being the stomach, small intestine, bladder, gall bladder, and an organ

The person who is afraid to alter his living habits, and especially his eating and drinking habits, because he is afraid that other persons may regard him as queer, eccentric, or fanatic forgets that the ownership of his body, the responsibility for its well-being, belongs to him, not them.

PAUL BRUNTON

of qi, known as the "Triple Heater." The triple heater is composed of three spheres of life energy that supply qi to the upper, middle, and lower parts of the thorax, coordinating the internal organs, according to the Chinese.

The large intestine is joined by the lungs as a paired set. Together, they form the Metal Element. The Metal Element is associated with dryness (the function of the large intestine is to draw water from food) and the color white.

The large intestine and lungs receive their optimal amounts of healing energy during the autumn months. During the day, the large intestine receives the most qi between the hours of 5 A.M. and 7 A.M. These are ideal months and times to take appropriate measures to heal the large intestine. Conversely, problems associated with the large intestine and lungs tend to manifest during the fall and in the early morning hours.

The food that has the greatest healing effect on the large intestine, according to Chinese medicine, is rice. Orientals revere rice as the "gift of the gods"; it was and still is their central food. Rice, more than any other grain, said the Chinese, strengthens and heals the large intestine.

Today, science understands that fiber from whole grains, vegetables, and fruit promotes intestinal health above all other foods. (See foods that heal the large intestine, below.) Fiber is undigestible vegetable matter. It speeds intestinal transit time; cleanses the colon of accumulated fat and stored-up waste; and treats diverticulosis.

The large intestine meridian begins at the tip of the index finger (large intestine point #1) and proceeds along the top of the hand, up the inner ridge of the arm, to the back of the shoulder, up the neck, and around the mouth. Ted Kaptchuk writes in *The Web That Has No Weaver* that the large intestine meridian has a branch that goes to the lungs and the large intestine, as well.

Problems associated with the shoulders, neck, and around the mouth are all related to disorders of digestion, according to Chinese medicine. So, too, are sinus problems, especially sinus congestion. The Chinese maintain that the large intestine is responsible for moving energy and waste downward and out of the body. When this downward movement is impeded, energy becomes backed up, especially in the upper respiratory tract and sinus areas. Treating sinus problems, therefore, includes treating the large intestine. Once the large intestine becomes unblocked, energy from the lungs and sinuses will flow downward and out once again.

In the same way, clear thinking is also associated with healthy elimination. Anyone who has been constipated knows that one of the first side effects of "irregularity" is a sluggish or "constipated" mind.

Human intestines, which are essentially a single system, some twenty-eight feet in length, perform their duties by moving crude matter (food) a great distance. They do this by virtue of their ability to expand and contract, their peristaltic action. In order for the power and dynamism of this expansion and contraction to endure, there must be considerable energy. As any engineer will tell you, all energy is made possible by the existence of a polarity between opposites, like the north and south poles of a magnet, or the positive and negative ions of an electrical charge.

The Chinese maintain that the long, expansive intestinal system must be balanced by a short or contracted organ in order to maintain a dynamic balance. Hence, the appendix. Unlike modern medicine, the Chinese do not view the appendix as an unnecessary appendage. There are no unnecessary organs; everything exists for a reason. The appendix serves as the intestinal tract's opposite pole, in the same way that the south pole of a magnet serves the north. Together, they create the dynamism that makes movement and function possible.

Removal of the appendix will, therefore, weaken the overall digestive tract. Those who have had the appendix removed should eat foods that provide optimal nutrition and are easy to digest and eliminate.

The Yellow Emperor said that the "lower intestines are like the officials who propagate the right way of living and they generate evolution and change." What he meant was that there is little ambiguity about the colon: we know very well when it is healthy or ill. To live according to the limits and peculiarities of the large intestine is to follow the "right way," because health is sustained in a large measure by our ability to eliminate poisons from the body. To change our behavior when intestinal health changes is to live in harmony with "evolution and change," meaning that to follow the dictates of our intestines ensures health and longevity, say the Chinese.

Evolution often means letting go of the past. The large intestine serves this purpose in the body: it receives the unwanted aspects of food from the small intestine and eliminates what is unneeded. The act of digestion and elimination can be seen as a metaphor for our ability to absorb what is useful from our experiences (a small intestine function) and eliminate what is unnecessary, harmful, or holds us back (a large intestine function).

People with disorders of the large intestine tend to live in the past. They hold onto things that should have been let go of a long time ago. For this reason, their lives are often burdened by sadness and grief. Taking care of the large intestine, say the Chinese, is the first step toward forgiveness and letting go of the past.

It's no coincidence, therefore, that the emotion associated with the large intestine is grief. People with weak intestines often have a weeping tone in their voice; they tend to speak with a hint of sadness. Since the mind and body are one, our psychological efforts at letting go of the past enhance the function of the large intestine.

The entire intestinal tract is regarded as the "roots" of the body. They are lengthy and absorbing. They draw nourishment from the earth in the form of food. When the roots are strong, we can draw the nourishment we need from life. If we are poorly nourished by life, Chinese healing begins by strengthening the intestines.

Our roots also stabilize us against the vicissitudes of life. The old axiom of a person having "guts," or courage, comes from this perception: the roots within the body give us a strong foundation in the face of danger.

FOODS TO KEEP YOUR INTESTINES HAPPY

The following foods and herbs are used in Chinese medicine to strengthen and treat the large intestine.

- *Grain:* Brown rice, sweet rice, mochi (pounded sweet rice).
- *Vegetables:* potato, sweet potato; cabbage, Chinese cabbage, celery, watercress, turnip greens, mustard greens; all roots, including daikon, carrot, lotus root, ginger, turnip, taro root potato.
- *Beans:* navy, soybeans, great northern, tofu, and tempeh.
- *Fish:* Cod, haddock, herring, flounder, halibut, scrod, carp.

- *Fruit:* Pears, peaches, loquat.
- *Herbs:* Garlic, dill, fresh grated ginger, horseradish, nutmeg, Job's tears, cinnamon, basil, fennel, bay leaf, black pepper, coriander, rice bran, cayenne, thyme, licorice.

There are dietary considerations for specific illnesses. Irritable bowel syndrome and diverticulosis can be caused by extremes in lifestyle, diet, and stress. Irregular hours, chaotic behavior, and chaotic relationships all lead to spastic bowel behavior.

When foods that have a contractive effect on the body, such as red meat and other animal foods, are combined with those that are extremely expansive, such as spices, sugar, and alcohol, spastic colon and diverticula are often the result. Individually, these foods represent extremes in qi. The body will try to balance these extreme influences, usually with little success.

The initial effects are indigestion, gas, heartburn, and alternating bouts of diarrhea and constipation. The forceful expansion and contraction will cause alternating tightness and inflation of the intestinal tract.

Finally, the absence of fiber in the diet causes accumulation of waste, especially undigested animal protein, fat, and sinew.

For constipation:

- Boil brown rice with carrots, onions, and grated ginger root. Cook with a pinch of sea salt until rice is soft, usually about forty-five minutes to an hour. Chew well.
- Ginger tea. Grate a tablespoon of fresh ginger in the bottom of a tea cup; pour hot water or kukicha (bancha) tea over grated ginger. Add one or two drops of tamari or shoyu to tea. Drink hot.
- Kuzu and apple juice drink. Kuzu, also known as kudzu, is a hardy root and an excellent herb for the intestines. Boil apple juice. Use two and a half tablespoons of kuzu per cup of juice. Dissolve kuzu in cup of cold water before adding to juice. Stir kuzu into juice, while simmering juice. Liquid will gradually thicken into a gelatin. Turn off flame and allow to cool.

For diarrhea:

- Kuzu and umeboshi plum drink. Dissolve five tablespoons kuzu in two cups of cold water; add an umeboshi plum and bring to a boil. Stir water while simmering until liquid thickens. Eat while hot.

- Pressure-cooked white rice, with a pinch of sea salt; white rice can be mixed with brown rice and pressure-cooked, as well.
- White potato, boiled.

Note: Constipation and diarrhea should subside quickly on a whole-foods diet. If either of these conditions persist, seek appropriate health-care advice. Persistent diarrhea during infancy is a dangerous condition; parents should seek appropriate medical advice immediately. See chapters on the spleen and small intestine for additional information on digestive disorders.

Foods to avoid: Red meat, fried foods, dairy products, especially hard cheeses and milk. If constipated, avoid eggs and all refined foods.

Naturopath Ross Trattler points out that the most common causes of intestinal disorders are diets rich in refined foods and deficient in fiber; excesses of meat, milk products, fried foods, coffee, tea, alcohol, and acid-producing foods; overeating; inactivity; stress; and long-term laxative use. He also includes pregnancy, anemia, and appendectomy among other causes of chronic constipation. Among Trattler's recommendations for constipation are:

- Stew figs and prunes in a small amount of apple juice for fifteen to twenty minutes. Eat and drink broth at night, at least two hours before sleeping, and as the first meal in the morning. This is a very effective treatment that can be used on an ongoing basis for chronic constipation.
- *Herbs:* Cascara sagrada, a natural herbal laxative. Cascara should only be used in conjunction with general improvement in diet and lifestyle. Bowels can become dependent upon any laxatives, including cascara. Small doses of cascara are recommended (fifteen to twenty drops in water).
- Chamomile tea.
- Garlic, either raw or in cooking, in small amounts.
- Aloe vera juice.
- Slippery elm, either as infusion or tea.
- Licorice root tea.
- Psyllium seed.

- Flax seed.
- Hot and cold sitz baths.
- *Avoid the following foods while constipated:* all refined grains, coffee, tea, sugar, spices, alcohol.
- *Lifestyle:* daily exercise. Walking, sit-ups to strengthen abdomen, leg lifts, while lying on your back, to strengthen abdomen.

For diarrhea, Trattler recommends the following:

- Green apples with no skin.
- Banana.
- Barley water (boil barley, making broth very watery).
- Carrot and cabbage juice.
- Toasted white bread (Trattler recommends this for one to two days; use only highly refined bread).

Ayurvedic tradition views the large intestine as the province of the vata dosha, meaning that it is most influenced by the kinetic force within the body. The vata dosha controls bodily movements. When it is depleted or deficient, digestion becomes lethargic and constipation results. When vata is excessive, we are more likely to suffer from diarrhea or ulcers. When efficient elimination is prevented, skin problems arise, according to Ayurvedic medicine. Since the skin is a major organ of elimination, it naturally attempts to compensate for the inability of the intestines to fully eliminate waste and toxins. However, this often results in rashes, blemishes, or acne. Repressed emotions disturb vata and create intestinal imbalances.

Ayur-Veda teaches that we must cultivate detachment from our emotions. During meditation, emotions must be allowed to rise to the surface, be witnessed and experienced fully, and then released. Repression only leads to ill health.

Foods that balance and support the vata dosha are as follows:

- *Grains:* rice, wheat, and oats.
- *Vegetables:* cucumber, cooked vegetables, including leafy greens, okra, onion, potato, radishes, squash, asparagus, beets, carrots.
- *Fruit:* apricots, avocado, berries, cherries, grapefruit, grapes, lemons, melons, oranges, peaches, plums.

- *Herbs:* senna leaf tea, dandelion root, psyllium seed, prunes, bran, flaxseed husk, castor oil, raisins, mango juice, grape juice.
- If suffering from intestinal disorders, avoid raw vegetables, eggplant, white potato, peppers, tomatoes.

A homeopathic remedy for constipation is pulsatilla, especially for women and pregnant women with morning sickness. For those who are addicted to laxatives, take nux vomica a few hours before bed for several days, but not as a permanent substitute for the laxatives. Sulphur is good for those who experience pain while defecating, and byronia for those with hard, dry stools and for children who are constipated, or for those whose constipation is the result of the anticipation of an upcoming professional or social event.

Like the ancients, we are still struggling to achieve intestinal health. It is as important as ever. Fortunately, there is an abundance of information today that we can turn to for help. For the vast majority of those who suffer from intestinal disorders, a cure can be as close as your next meal.

Homeopathic remedies for gas:

CARBO VEGETABLIS: For belching and gas, no matter what you eat.

CHINA: Midsection feels distended. Stomach feels full of gas.

LYCODIUM: Fullness before you finish eating or after a light meal. Belt feels too tight. Rumbling gas.

Homeopathic remedies for hemorrhoids:

ARNICA: Useful for hemorrhoids that develop after childbirth.

SULPHUR: Itching and burning around anus, made worse by bathing.

COLLINSONIA: Feels like there are sticks in rectum. Usually constipated.

NUX VOMICA: Itching that feels better from cool bathing.

CHAPTER 10

THE GALL BLADDER

THE GALL BLADDER is a pear-shaped organ, about three inches long, and found at the back of the liver, on the right side of the body. It serves as a reservoir for bile, produced by the liver to emulsify fats. Bile flows from the liver to the gall bladder via a small tube, called the cystic duct, which is a branch of the common duct.

The gall bladder is composed of four layers of tissue: an inner lining of mucous membrane; a layer of smooth muscle; a layer of connective tissue; and a covering layer of tissue, called serosa. When food passes from the stomach into the small intestine, hormones stimulate the gall bladder to expel bile into the first stage of small intestine, called the duodenum. Bile breaks down the fats, permitting them to be absorbed by the small intestine.

Bile is a mixture of bile acid (also called bile salts) and cholesterol. The cholesterol acts as a buffering agent, preventing the bile acids from eating away at the gall bladder and small intestine.

To wish to be healthy is a part of being healthy.

SENECA

ILLNESSES AFFECTING THE GALL BLADDER

By far, the most common illness affecting the gall bladder is gall stones. Sixteen million Americans suffer from gall stones, twelve million of whom are women. No one is certain why this disparity between the sexes exists, but it may be due to the dropoff of estrogen levels in postmenopausal women, which is associated with higher cholesterol levels and greater incidence of heart disease.

Each year, 500,000 gall bladder surgeries are performed. The operation is called a cholecystectomy. Gall stones are composed almost entirely of cholesterol.

People who consume high-fat and high-cholesterol diets have higher rates of gall stones than those who consume low-fat and low-cholesterol diets.

Common symptoms of gall stones include pain and tenderness on the right side of the body. Occasionally, the pain can be sharp and severe, causing people to think they are experiencing a heart attack or an appendicitis. Sometimes, stones can be found in the cystic or common ducts, which can cause serious complications. The most common form of treatment is the surgical removal of the gall bladder.

AN UPRIGHT OFFICIAL

"The gall bladder occupies the position of an important and upright official who excels through his decisions and judgment," explained the Yellow Emperor, meaning that the gall bladder plays an important role in our decision-making function. This assertion springs from the Five Element Theory, which states that the liver and gall bladder are responsible for controlling and balancing anger.

All emotions are grounded in various parts of the body. A person with a healthy liver and gall bladder will have a balanced temperament, but one whose liver and gall bladder are troubled will likely suffer outbursts of anger and ill-temper. This, of course, will lead to rash decisions. When the liver and gall bladder are balanced and healthy, decisions are made from emotional equilibrium, a characteristic of a healthy Wood Element. However, when decisions are difficult to make, many Oriental healers will

God heals and the doctor takes the fee.

BENJAMIN FRANKLIN

urge people to eat simply, avoid extremes in emotions, and meditate, so that harmony can be restored throughout the body, and the gall bladder function can assist in making a correct decision.

The gall bladder is the recipient of bile from the liver, which in Chinese medicine is viewed as taking the liver's excess. If the liver becomes excessive and produces too much bile, the gall bladder will suffer, since its capacity to store bile is limited.

The gall bladder is most vulnerable to dietary fat and cholesterol, which are the major causes of gall stones. People who subsist on diets low in fat and cholesterol have a lower incidence of gall stones, as compared to those of Western nations, where fat and cholesterol consumption is higher. Since the liver and gall bladder comprise the Wood Element, the gall bladder is strengthened by the same foods (wheat and leafy greens), tastes (sour), and emotions (avoidance of anger) as those mentioned in the chapter on the liver.

The gall bladder meridian begins at the temples, zigzags along the sides of the head, behind each ear, and then runs down the neck and shoulders. From there, it travels along the sides of the body, and down the outside of each leg. The meridian continues to the fourth toe, next to the little toe. As a diagnostic point, traditional healers will examine the fourth toe to see if a bunion protrudes from it. The presence of such a bunion usually indicates some kind of gall bladder imbalance. (Other factors are examined to corroborate that assessment and make it more detailed.)

Many headaches are caused by liver and gall bladder imbalances. Any disturbance in the liver also will upset the gall bladder, which in turn will create an imbalance of qi along the gall bladder meridian. Such imbalances often will manifest in the form of headaches, since the gall bladder meridian begins at the temples and covers both sides of the head. Sometimes these kinds of headaches are referred to simply as gall bladder headaches. Many people who suffer such headaches will see yellow blotches before their eyes, indicating a disturbance in the bile. They are prevalent in the springtime, when the liver and gall bladder are receiving an increase in qi, and when underlying symptoms may manifest.

Perhaps the clearest and most persuasive insight into our modern epidemic of gall bladder problems was made by Nathan Pritikin, the late scientist and creator of the Pritikin Program for Diet and Exercise. Pritikin pointed out that bile, which is composed of bile salts, cholesterol, and lecithin, is kept in solution by a delicate harmony of these three constituents. The most important is the bile salts-to-cholesterol ratio. The bile salts are acid. Without this acid, the cholesterol would form crystals and stones. So, there must be sufficient bile acids to keep the cholesterol from forming stones in the gall bladder. When the cholesterol in the bile becomes too concentrated, it saturates the bile acids and begins to form crystals and then stones.

In a healthy gall bladder, the cholesterol content is around 350 mg. Most Americans who eat a standard high-fat diet have gall bladder cholesterol levels in excess of 650 mg. This quantity of cholesterol cannot be kept in solution by the available quantity of bile acids, which allows the cholesterol to form stones.

Pritikin maintained that the surest way to cure gall stones is to lower the body's overall cholesterol level. This will reduce the cholesterol in the gall bladder, and thus create a healthy bile-to-cholesterol ratio. Once this ratio is reestablished, the bile acids can dissolve the cholesterol crystals and stones, and restore health to the gall bladder. This can be done, he said, as long as there are no stones in the cystic duct, the canal leading from the gall bladder to the common bile duct. Once stones are in the cystic duct, they can seal off the gall bladder and cause serious problems, for which surgery may be necessary. Ultrasound and X-ray tests can confirm if gall stones exist and where they are located.

Naturopaths and other traditional health counselors can offer dietary programs that include a gall bladder flush. The flush is one of several kinds of drinks that include olive oil and herbs, which together cause the gall bladder to pass the stones into the small intestine and then eliminate them through the feces. This can be a dangerous procedure; the stones can get caught in the cystic duct if they are too large. Before attempting such a flush, people should know the size of the stones and get a variety of opinions.

Some common therapeutic agents for the gall bladder (and liver, too) according to Dr. Ross Trattler:

- Apple juice.
- Beet extract tablets.
- Beet tops and juice.
- Dandelion tea and greens.
- Grapefruit juice.

Herbs for the gall bladder:

CELANDINE: Reduces inflammation of bile ducts.

FRINGE TREE: Increases bile flow.

OREGON GRAPE ROOT and YELLOW DOCK: Stimulate bile.

Six to eight glasses of water a day will help prevent gall stones.

CHAPTER 11

THE LIVER

Indeed, the liver is so crucial biologically that it can be called the balance of the wheel of life.

HAKIM G. M. CHISHTI

$\mathcal{P}$OISONING ALWAYS HAS been among the favored methods of assassination, largely because it is efficient, silent, and neat. However, there have been cases when the intended victim refused to succumb, no matter how powerful the poison, or the quantity consumed. Among the more famous of these stubborn victims was the Russian mystic, Rasputin.

During the early part of this century, Rasputin exercised great influence over the ruling Russian family, Nicholas II and his wife Alexandra. His power was particularly strong with the czarina, Alexandra, who regarded him as a spiritual master and the savior of the Russian people. Through Alexandra, Rasputin influenced national policy, disposed of ministers who opposed his power, and appointed people who supported him. By 1916, people were saying he ruled Russia by day and seduced the ladies of the court by night. Some historians credit Rasputin with bringing down the ruling Romanov family, having thoroughly corrupted their morals with his theory that if one wants to be close to God, it is necessary to become the greatest sinner imaginable. To this end Rasputin put considerable effort, especially indulging his passion for the fairer sex. When it became clear that his hold on Alexandra was ironclad, a powerful Russian elite—who disagreed with the direction of their country—decided that Rasputin had to go.

The plot was simple enough: On December 16, 1916, Rasputin was invited to the house of an associate, where he would be fed cakes and wine laced with abundant quantities of potassium cyanide. The conspirators made certain that the dosages of cyanide in a single cake or one glass of wine were sufficient to kill a large elephant.

A short while after arriving at the house, Rasputin was eating and drinking copiously. Apparently, he had taken a liking to the cakes and wine and was presently wondering aloud what time the women—whom the host had promised—would arrive. In a nearby room, a group of conspirators waited for Rasputin to die, but just the opposite happened. The only apparent effect from the food and drink on Rasputin was his unhappiness with the absence of female company.

Frightened by Rasputin's mysterious powers over the poison, the host excused himself from his guest's company and hurried into the nearby room to beg advice from his fellow murderers. Feed him more poison, was their answer. The host complied. But alas, even greater quantities of the cyanide were impotent against Rasputin.

Fed up with the slow way, the murderers produced a gun and shot Rasputin at point-blank range. Now they were certain he was dead, and even began to relax over his body when suddenly Rasputin got up, staggered to the door, and ran out of the house. The central figure in the plot, a V. M. Purishkevich, who recorded the entire event in his diary (published under the title *The Murder of Rasputin*), ran after him, shooting wildly at Rasputin, who miraculously gained speed as he ran.

Eventually, Purishkevich managed to put two bullets in Rasputin, one in his back and another in his head. Now, the men were sure he was dead. But, driven by fear of Rasputin's mysterious powers, one of them began to hit Rasputin on the head with a heavy object. The group was horrified when the mystic opened his eyes and let out a moan. "He's still alive!" they shouted. Shaken but determined, the murderers took Rasputin to a nearby canal and threw his body through a hole in the ice and into the frozen waters. He disappeared and was finally dead. Among the questions that perplexed the killers afterwards: How did Rasputin survive such quantities of poison, to say nothing of three bullets? Each man answered it in his own way, but one thing is certain: Rasputin had a very strong liver.

THE BODY'S LABORATORY

Even the human brain cannot match the liver for its varied and essential functions. The liver is a veritable laboratory, testing and identifying chemicals that enter the system, neutralizing poisons, and creating essential blood, metabolic, and immune constituents.

The liver creates bile, which aids in the digestion of fats, and also serves as the medium by which the organ eliminates waste. In addition, the liver creates a variety of essential elements for the blood, including: albumin, which regulates water exchange between blood and tissues; complement, an immune constituent that protects against infection; coagulant, which produces blood clotting; globulin, which combines with iron to carry oxygen in the blood; and cholesterol, a protein that carries fats throughout the body.

There are two types of cholesterol created by the liver, and each type determines where fat in the bloodstream goes. LDL cholesterol (low density lipoproteins) brings lipids, or fats, to tissues and the walls of blood vessels. When there is too much LDL, atherosclerosis (the formation of cholesterol plaques) occurs within the walls of blood vessels, thus blocking the flow of blood. HDL cholesterol (high density lipoproteins) removes fats and cholesterol from the body, and thus lowers overall blood cholesterol.

The liver creates more than 1,000 different enzymes necessary for digestion and nutrient assimilation. It also creates and regulates some of the body's hormones.

The liver absorbs glucose, or blood sugar, and stores it in the form of glycogen. When the body needs energy or heat, the liver converts the glycogen back into glucose, and releases it into the bloodstream. It assists in the breakdown and metabolism of fats.

It also breaks down proteins into their component parts—amino acids—and then reassembles them into proteins appropriate for your body. The liver helps break down old red blood cells, as well.

Finally, the liver detoxifies the blood by removing drugs and other poisons, and then altering their chemical structure to render them harmless. Even drugs you might consider helpful, such as aspirin or antibiotics, are regarded by the liver as poisonous substances that must be eliminated from the organism. For this reason, physicians give prescribed dosages of drugs, in part to overcome the liver's diligence against all but the most healthful foods and substances.

Once a poison has been rendered harmless, the liver releases it as a water-soluble compound in the bile. From there, it travels to the gall bladder and small intestine. Much of the feces is composed of bile.

Needless to say, you cannot live without a liver.

YOUR BODY'S BLOOD RESERVOIR

The liver is the body's largest internal organ. In adults, it weighs anywhere from two and a half to four pounds. It is cone-shaped, extending from the left side of the sternum just below the left nipple to the right side of the body, filling much of the upper right abdominal cavity. It is composed of two lobes, a smaller left lobe, and a larger right; these are further divided into smaller sections.

The body's largest internal organ and reservoir of blood, the liver is a remarkable chemical laboratory that plays a major role in digesting foods, eliminating wastes, preventing infection, and producing essential blood elements.

The Liver

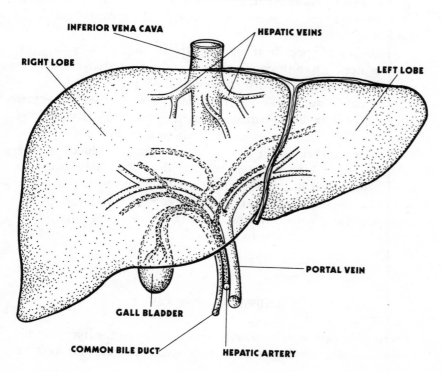

INFERIOR VENA CAVA   HEPATIC VEINS

RIGHT LOBE

LEFT LOBE

PORTAL VEIN

GALL BLADDER

COMMON BILE DUCT

HEPATIC ARTERY

The liver has a remarkable blood supply: it receives oxygenated blood from one vessel, called the hepatic artery, and nutrient-rich blood from another, called the hepatic portal vein. Blood flows through to the liver from the spleen and small intestine. Once it arrives, it passes through the organ via a network of tiny vessels called the "portal tracts," where the blood provides oxygen and nutrition to cells. Here it is purified of poisons, and receives essential blood constituents created by the liver. Eventually, the blood exits the organ via the hepatic vein, found at the back of the liver.

The liver is a great reservoir of blood. About one-quarter of the heart's entire output is held within the liver when the body is at rest. Because the body contains up to five quarts of blood, about one and a quarter quarts are passing through the organ at any moment. Much of that blood is dispersed when you exercise.

The structural unit of the liver is called a lobule, a cylindrically-shaped cell. These lobules arrange themselves in long chainlike structures. Although the liver performs an incredible array of tasks—more than 500 functions already have been counted—they are all done, apparently, by the same type of cell, the lobule.

This lack of specialization may explain, in part, why the liver is so resilient: up to three-quarters of it can be destroyed, yet the organ will continue to perform its tasks. Moreover, the liver can restore itself—much like a salamander can restore its tail—even after half of it has been damaged, if appropriate corrective actions are taken. (See illnesses associated with the liver, below.)

Bile is secreted by the liver through a series of ducts, or tiny tubular canals. Like many tributaries that ultimately join two rivers, these liver ducts link up eventually with two larger tubes, called the hepatic ducts, at the base of the liver. From there, the two form a single, or common, hepatic duct, which brings bile to the gall bladder and then to the duodenum, the first stage of the small intestine.

ILLNESSES OF THE LIVER

There are a variety of serious illnesses affecting the liver, but the most prevalent are hepatitis, cirrhosis, and cancer. Hepatitis, or inflammation of the liver, is caused mostly by the hepatitis virus or cirrhosis. There are two forms of viral hepatitis, designated as A or B. Hepatitis A, sometimes called infectious hepatitis, is spread by consuming infected food or water. Hepatitis B results from blood transfusions, sexual contact with an infected person, or through the use of contaminated intravenous needles. Type B is usually more serious than A; it is often chronic, sometimes lasting years. This, of course, increases the chances of serious liver damage and cirrhosis.

Sometimes medical tests fail to reveal the presence of either hepatitis A or B in people who nonetheless have all the symptoms of hepatitis. Doctors have labeled such forms of hepatitis as non-A and non-B. This form of the illness is often the result of infected blood transfusions, alcohol, or contact with a toxic chemical substance in the environment.

Other causes (besides cirrhosis, which is described below) are drugs and chemical poisons. Some very common chemicals, such as those found in dry-cleaning agents, can cause hepatitis, particularly if there is an underlying liver problem.

Symptoms of hepatitis are usually flulike: fever, nausea, vomiting, sweating, loss of appetite, and pain or tenderness in the upper abdomen; aching muscles; joint pain; and malaise. Sometimes hepatitis can cause jaundice, with its characteristic yellowing of the skin and eyes. This occurs because of the buildup of bile within the system.

There is no known cure for hepatitis and no effective treatment in the arsenal of orthodox medicine. Rest, nutritious diet, and the removal of the causative toxic agent (alcohol, drugs, or some other chemical toxin) are the only reliable therapies. Hepatitis can result in serious liver damage and even death. Yet, most people overcome the illness within several months.

Cirrhosis is the destruction of the liver due to the accumulation of fatty acids that cut off blood flow to the liver cells. The primary cause of cirrhosis is alcohol abuse, though drugs, chemical toxins, and birth defects can cause the disease as well.

The reason fatty acids accumulate in people who consume alcohol is that the liver selects the alcohol as its primary source of fuel. Fatty acids, which would ordinarily be the liver's chosen fuel, are therefore neglected and allowed to build up within the tissues. As fatty acids accumulate, blood supply is cut off and cells

Half of what we have taught you is wrong. Unfortunately, we do not know which half.

DEAN BURWELL

115

If I were informed tomorrow that I was in direct communication with my liver, and could now take over, I would become deeply depressed. I'd sooner be told, forty thousand feet over Denver, that the 747 jet in which I had a coach seat was now mine to operate as I pleased; at least I would have the hope of bailing out, if I could find a parachute and discover quickly how to open a door. Nothing would save me and my liver if I were in charge. For I am, to face the facts squarely, considerably less intelligent than my liver.

Lewis Thomas

die. This causes scar tissue to form, which eventually deforms the liver's normal structure, and reduces its functional size.

The first stage of the illness is called "fatty liver," because of the accumulation of fat within the organ. There may be no symptoms associated with fatty liver or even cirrhosis—that is, until the illness progresses to the acute phase. At this point a variety of dangerous side effects may manifest: high blood pressure (resulting from the destruction of veins leading to the liver); accumulation of fluids in the abdomen, caused by the liver's inability to create albumin; the vomiting of blood, due to the increase in blood pressure and the consequent rupture of veins in the esophagus; and hepatitis. Cirrhosis can be fatal on its own. It also can result in cancer of the liver.

According to the American Medical Association, men who consume an average of four 80-proof ounces of alcohol a day—the equivalent of two double shots of whiskey or four glasses of wine—have a substantial chance of contracting cirrhosis of the liver. Women require only half that amount—the equivalent alcohol intake of about two glasses of wine per day—to suffer from cirrhosis. Abstinence from alcohol can lead to a full recovery, with all or most of the liver function returning to normal.

Malignant tumors can begin in the liver or originate at some other location within the body and migrate to the liver through the blood and lymph. In the U.S., cancers originating at the liver are less common than those occurring there as a secondary site. Usually, cancers that have spread to the liver have originated in the stomach, pancreas, or intestines. Enlargement of the liver is usually the result of leukemias and lymphomas—cancers affecting the white blood cell or the lymph system, respectively.

The Body's Commanding General

The liver attempts to eliminate all the poisons that infiltrate the bloodstream. These include fat, alcohol, drugs (both pharmaceutical and recreational), and artificial colors, flavors, and preservatives. In addition, there is an equally unprecedented array of pollutants in the environment that are ingested through the air we breathe and the water we drink, which ideally should be eliminated by the liver.

Virtually all traditional medicines—that is, Chinese, Ayur-

Veda, Greek, and naturopathy—see the liver as having a limited capacity to eliminate poisons from the body. If the toxins from the diet and environment exceed the liver's blood-cleansing limits, the poisons will accumulate within the liver, the blood, and the body at large, creating a toxic internal environment that will add to a decline in liver health and function.

Other blood-cleansing organs, especially the kidneys, will be called upon to rid the body of these foreign substances. If the toxins continue to be ingested, these organs, too, will be exceeded in their capacity to cleanse the blood. Meanwhile, the immune system will be forced to maintain an ongoing war against these harmful substances.

The net effect is an overworked and exhausted immune system, an equally exhausted set of blood-cleansing organs, and an ever-increasing level of toxicity within the body. In short, a breeding ground for disease. Such a toxic condition makes the liver vulnerable to a wide assortment of illnesses, some of which modern medicine does not normally associate with the liver. Among the disorders that arise from liver disease are headaches, chronic fatigue, allergies, fatty liver, anemia, skin problems, toxemia, hepatitis, and immune deficiency. Eventually, even liver cancer can manifest.

These problems cannot occur in a healthy liver, which is simply too strong and too regenerative to be overcome by viruses or small quantities of pollution. Traditional medicine therefore treats the liver by first eliminating, as much as possible, the toxins entering the body, starting with changes in diet and exercise patterns. As we have already seen, the liver has miraculous regenerative powers and can restore health once the offending problems are eliminated. An assortment of additional remedies is offered, depending on the system employed. Let's have a closer look.

The liver is associated with the gall bladder, its paired organ, and the Wood Element. Its season is the spring, when the liver enjoys an increase in qi. This heightened state of life energy can bring about greater healing, if appropriate measures are taken, or it can cause manifestation of underlying symptoms.

Metaphorically, the liver's general condition should be similar to that of spring: light, open, and flowing with energy (as opposed to winter, which is contracted and holding back). The liver suffers most when it becomes hard and stagnant.

The liver is associated with the color green, derived from its "tree nature," and the wind. The Chinese maintain that the "wind creates wood," perhaps in part because the wind spreads seeds. In any case, too much exposure to the wind can injure the liver; the wind is said to enter the body through the neck or throat, and it is here that one should be especially protective in the winter and early spring.

The Chinese regard the liver as the commanding general of the body, coordinating an army of functions that, together, form the human organism. When the body runs smoothly and in a co-ordinated way, the general is clear, well-ordered, and in command. But if the body is chronically ill, pained, or arthritic, the general suffers. The Chinese ascribe many vital functions to the liver, which are:

- Producing bile and contributing to healthy digestion.
- Detoxifying the blood.
- Providing blood and qi to the muscles, tendons, ligaments, and nails.
- Providing blood and qi to the eyes.
- Influencing the ability to sleep deeply.
- Maintaining stable emotions, especially the emotion of anger.

According to the Five Elements, the Water Element (kidneys and bladder) nourishes Wood (the liver and gall bladder) with qi, while Wood nourishes Fire (the heart and small intestine) with life force. At the same time, the liver controls the stomach and spleen (Wood controls Earth by grasping it and holding on).

Clearly, the liver does support the small intestine function by producing bile, which helps to emulsify fats in the duodenum. It also produces more than 1,000 enzymes, which are essential to good digestion and healthy metabolism. Also, because it receives blood from the spleen, the liver controls the spleen to some extent, since the degree of the organ's receptivity could influence how the spleen functions.

Like Western medical doctors, the Chinese view the liver as a reservoir of blood. The liver ensures that adequate blood and qi are sent to the muscles, tendons, and joints. Muscles, joints, and tendons that are supple and strong reflect a healthy liver. Conversely, tendons, muscles, and ligaments that are tight, stiff, or weak reflect a deficient liver, meaning that the organ is unable to distribute adequate blood, oxygen, and qi to these areas of the body. Even injuries to tendons—such as those suffered by many professional athletes—are regarded as symptomatic of an overworked or burdened liver.

The liver is said to open into the eyes, meaning that the liver nourishes the eyes with qi (so that they can "see the mystery of Heaven and discover Tao among mankind," said the Yellow Emperor). So, most eye problems have their origin in the liver.

The maintenance of healthy vision depends upon the health of the muscle tissue within the eye itself, and the integrity of the shape of the eye. (See chapter on sight.) The shape of the eye determines where the image is focused within the interior of the eye. In myopia, for example, the light of the image is focused at a point in front of the retina—not directly upon it. The retina is the light-sensitive membrane in back of the eye. Since the retina does not receive the full and clear impact of the light, the image appears to us as blurred.

The liver not only sends qi to the eyes, it also governs the health of all the body's muscles, including the muscles within the eyes. As the liver becomes congested, its ability to send qi to the eyes is diminished, causing the weakening of the eye's muscles and its ability to maintain its original shape. Diminished qi also reduces the eyes' ability to efficiently eliminate waste, thus increasing the likelihood of floaters (cholesterol crystals and cellular waste products) inside the eye and lens.

As the flow of waste from the eye slows, pressure within the eye increases, as well, like a pinched hose or a river that is backed up. This can result in glaucoma, among the most common eye disorders today. Just as the liver influences the health of the eye, the reverse is also true: eye strain or overwork causes the liver to become tired.

Each day, the liver is said to receive optimal amounts of qi between the hours of 1 A.M. and 3 A.M. The gall bladder receives optimal amounts of qi during the hours of 11 P.M. and 1 A.M. These, of course, are prime sleeping hours. During this time, the liver is able to heal itself, as long as we are resting and the organ is not forced to deal with external stimuli. People who party late at night are damaging their livers, probably in more ways than one.

Insomnia usually affects us between the hours of 11 P.M. and 3 A.M., when the liver and gall bladder are being infused with additional qi. If the liver is congested or unhealthy, the increased qi will not flow smoothly through the organ. Instead, the liver will become unsettled, active, and even chaotic. This will give rise to an underlying discomfort, a sense of internal conflict, and excessive thinking that attempts to work through such conflicts. Hence, insomnia.

According to the principles of acupuncture, the liver meridian originates at a point on the rib cage, directly above the liver on the right, and over the spleen on the left. It travels downward along the groin and inside of the leg, over the inner part of the knee, down the calf, over the foot, and to the big toe of each foot.

When the liver becomes congested, qi becomes obstructed along the meridian, causing a diminution of the qi flowing to the sex organs and knees. This reduction of qi along the liver meridian is the main cause of hydrocele in men, or the swelling of one or both of the testicles. Rest and care of the liver (see below) are usually enough to clear up the problem in a few days.

Wherever qi flow is inadequate, problems arise. When qi is insufficient to the knees, tendons and ligaments can deteriorate and become vulnerable to injury. When qi is diminished to the toes, ingrown toenails, bumps, or an often painful turning of the toe can occur.

As the commanding general, the liver maintains both physical and emotional balance of the body. Vertigo is most often a liver disorder, according to the Chinese, and treatment of the liver restores balance.

THE SEAT OF THE SOUL

The liver maintains overall emotional stability, but imbalances reveal themselves as excesses of anger. People who abuse their livers, either through alcohol or junk food, are prone to chronic anger, which also injures the liver. As liver health is restored, anger diminishes.

The liver's role as the body's detoxifier extends metaphorically to our general capacity to maintain a clean and orderly environment. People whose desks or rooms tend to be messy usually suffer from a liver imbalance—perhaps the liver is too "cluttered," too. In the same way, clear and well-ordered thinking tends to reflect a strong and healthy liver.

The relative flexibility of the body—especially the tendons, muscles, and joints—is viewed as a metaphor for the flexibility of one's thinking. Those with strong livers have flexible connective tissues, which is reflected in flexible minds.

Such a philosophy forms the basis for both Indian yoga and Chinese exercises derived from acupuncture. The Chinese maintain that the liver is associated with tears, particularly repressed or unspent tears. When the liver begins to heal itself, anger and grief—which have been stored away within the tissues of the organ—tend to be released in the form of old tears, say the Chinese sages.

Since the liver is associated with the Wood Element, the organ is associated with the metaphor of a tree. A tree reaches upward toward the heavens, and is thus considered highly spiritual, inspirational, and exciting. The liver's natural tendency, therefore, is to restore the spirit, to lift it above the poisoned events of the day into a more pure and rarefied understanding of life. For these and other reasons, many traditional cultures maintain that the liver is the "seat of the soul."

Causes of Liver Disorders

According to Oriental medicine, the source of most liver problems is stagnation of blood and qi, brought about primarily by excessive amounts of fat, sugar (which converts in the liver to fat), alcohol, and a variety of common poisons in the food system and environment.

If the diet is composed primarily of junk foods—specifically fat, sugar, refined grains, and artificial ingredients (but no alcohol)—the liver will likely become overly contracted and deficient (yin). The organ can become tight, congested, and lethargic. Inadequate amounts of blood and qi pass from the organ to those areas that depend upon the liver for nourishment. Gradually, overall liver function will decline.

According to Chinese physiognomy, the face of a person with this type of deficient liver will be pale, drawn, and tight, with dark furrows and indentations. Such a person tends to be stiff in the joints. He or she will likely have very exact ways of doing things and a tendency toward perfectionism and intolerance. This person will likely be impatient, angry, and prone to chronic headaches.

Wherever you see two or a dozen people of ordinary bulk talking together, you know they are talking about their livers. When you first arrive here your new acquaintances seem sad and hard to talk to, but pretty soon you get the lay of the land and the hand of things, and after that you haven't any more trouble. You look into the dreary dull eye and softly say: "Well, how's your liver?" You will see that dim eye flash up with a grateful flame, and you will see that jaw begin to work, and you will recognize that nothing is required of you from this but to listen as long as you remain conscious.

Mark Twain

The most common liver problems, however, result from a diet rich in animal foods and alcohol, which combine to make the liver expanded, overactive, and inflamed (yang). This condition reveals itself on a person's face as a reddish complexion, often with the capillaries exposed at the surface. Such people tend to be fiery, and given to extremes of emotion, from anger to jolliness.

Both forms of liver imbalance can give rise to serious illness, but the inflamed liver is more prone to hepatitis, cirrhosis, and cancer.

HEALING THE LIVER

The first step in healing the liver is to eliminate excesses of fat, cholesterol, refined foods, artificial ingredients, drugs, sugar, and alcohol. Ideally, the diet should be composed of mostly low-fat fish, whole grains, vegetables, beans, and fruit. It should contain only small to moderate amounts of vegetable oils.

According to Chinese medicine, the grain that has the most healing effect on the liver is whole wheat.

Sour foods, such as lemon, grapefruit, and sauerkraut, have a medicinal effect, as well. However, the sourness of the food must be balanced. Too much sourness causes astringency, preventing the liver from releasing toxins. A balanced sourness will act as a catalyst to stimulate the liver to produce bile and release stored waste.

The beans that stimulate healing in the liver are limas, green lentils, and split peas.

Many leafy greens have an energetic nature similar to that of a tree—that is, they reach upward and outward toward the heavens. Using the law of like-cures-like, such vegetables have a medicinal effect on the liver, in that they stimulate the organ to open and circulate blood and oxygen. Vegetables that are especially helpful are broccoli, parsley, collards, and a variety of lettuces. Dark lettuces, such as romaine, are richer in nutrients, especially calcium, than iceberg lettuce, and are therefore preferable.

Carrots and carrot juice are among the most effective and widely used liver tonics in all of traditional medicine, including Chinese. They are rich in minerals and beta carotene, an antioxidant that can help prevent free radical formation and the decay of tissues within the organ. Carrots and carrot juice strengthen liver function and promote healing. Seaweeds are commonly recommended because they are rich in minerals, A and B vitamins, all of which are immune-enhancing. All kinds of squash are suggested for their rich concentrations of beta carotene, the vegetable source of vitamin A. Beta carotene is one of the most powerful immune-enhancing nutrients, as well as an antioxidant.

In general, foods should be lightly cooked. Grains should be boiled or pressure-cooked. Fruits can be eaten raw or lightly cooked (as in compotes). But all refined sweeteners should be avoided.

Regular amounts of fermented foods, such as miso, sauerkraut, and pickles, should be added to the diet to promote healthful digestion, assimilation, and elimination. But fermented foods often contain sodium, which should be minimized. So, only small amounts of fermented foods should be used per serving, but can be eaten daily.

Healing fruits include green apple, sour cherry, sour oranges, and lime.

In order to ensure maximum circulation within the organ, blood cholesterol and fat content should be kept low. Therefore, no animal-derived oils are recommended, and only small amounts of vegetable oils should be used by those attempting to restore the liver. Sesame, corn, and olive oils are the most healthful. Olive oil tends to relax the liver and stimulate release of bile and toxins. Research indicates that olive oil is an antioxidant, as well. Oil should be limited to two or three times per week until health is restored.

As with all traditional medicine, only small amounts are necessary to effect healing. Also, too much of a good thing turns into its opposite: poison.

These foods will have a healing effect on the entire Wood Element, meaning that the gall bladder also will be healed by following this same program. (See gall bladder.)

Using the Five Elements, people with liver disease should increase foods associated with the Water, Wood, and Fire Elements, while decreasing Metal foods. Water (kidney and bladder) nourishes liver function. Fire (heart and small intestine) has more than likely been diminished due to the decrease in liver qi, which would ordinarily nourish the Fire Element. Metal foods control the Wood Element, and therefore should be reduced, but not entirely eliminated.

Naturopaths recognize the same disease process within the

liver as that outlined above. The most common healing foods suggested by naturopaths are as follows:

- *Protein:* Low-fat protein foods should be eaten daily to include: fish, a few times per week; tofu, an excellent source of protein and calcium; a wide assortment of beans, rich sources of protein and fiber; and wheat germ, rich in protein and vitamin E, an antioxidant and a medicinal food for the liver.
- *Vegetables:* The diet should include a wide variety of leafy greens, rich in many minerals (such as calcium), vitamin A, and fiber; beets, with tops, rich in iron and fiber; spirulina, a sea vegetable, rich in minerals, B vitamins, and an antioxidant; and garlic, which is antifungal, antibacterial, and an immune–enhancing herb.
- *Fermented foods:* Miso, rich in B vitamins, healthful bacteria, and protein; sauerkraut, rich in bacteria.
- *Supplements:* Vitamin A, an antioxidant and one of the most powerful immune-enhancing vitamins available; B vitamins, immune–enhancing and essential for rebuilding tissue; folic acid, for immune response; and vitamin E, immune-enhancing and an antioxidant.

Herbs that have been used throughout the ages for liver disorders include the following:

- *Dandelion tea:* Perhaps the most commonly used herb for liver disorders since Galen. Dandelion directly neutralizes acids and stimulates the liver to cleanse the blood and eliminate waste via the bile. It also stimulates and strengthens immune response. Dandelion stems, twigs, or leaves can be boiled for ten minutes in water to make a tea. Allow herbs and water to steep for another ten or fifteen minutes and then drink two to three times per day. Use one tablespoon of twigs per cup of water.
- *Dandelion and burdock root tea:* Use twigs and stems from both herbs, boiled and steeped. Burdock is another blood purifier. It directly supports and stimulates the kidneys to cleanse the blood and eliminate waste from those organs. Make one tablespoon of each per cup of water.
- *Garlic:* Use two to four cloves of garlic in cooking daily, until symptoms abate.

Even as the wise physician takes full advantage of the armamentarium available to him, he never misses the opportunity to educate the patient to the truth that drugs aren't always necessary and that the human body is its own best drugstore for most symptoms.

NORMAN COUSINS

• *Other Herbs:* Celandine (as drops in water or as a tea), Culler's root (as tea), goldenseal (as drops in water, or as a tea).

In *The Way of Herbs,* Michael Tierra recommends the following liver tonic, which has been traditionally used to rebuild the organ, restore function, and assist in the "recovery from hepatitis, liver sclerosis and toxicity from a bad diet."

Oregon grape root—1 part
Wild yam root—1 part
Dandelion root, raw—1 part
Licorice—¼ part (demulcent)

Simmer the herbs in distilled water for forty minutes, using three ounces of herbs in one quart of water. Refrigerate. Take two tablespoons, three to four times per day, between meals.

CHAPTER 12

THE KIDNEYS

Life without healthy kidneys is the pits. If you have any doubts about the value of the effort you should devote to preserving the good health of your kidneys, take a trip to your local hospital's dialysis unit and see how those unfortunate patients look and how they are obliged to live.

JOHN A. MCDOUGALL

IN ORIENTAL ART—whether Indian, Chinese, or Japanese—you will see the Buddha depicted with a beautifully serene face and abnormally large ears. The message in the Buddha's face is obvious: it is the picture of bliss—gentle, yet full of vitality and compassion. This, says the artist, is the ultimate human face, the hope and the goal of humanity.

But what are we to make of those huge ears? The ears are like a pair of wings on each side of the Buddha's head. The lobes dangle around his shoulders like heavy pendulums. These are the ears of an elephant on a human being!

The answer lies hidden in the ancient Oriental art of physiognomy, the practice of reading a person's character and health in the face and body structure. Every characteristic on a person's face has meaning to the trained diagnostician, and the ears bear special significance.

To the practiced eye, they reveal, first and foremost, the constitutional or inherited strength of the kidneys. A trained physiognomist also can determine genetic strength of the circulatory, nervous, and digestive systems by examining the curves within the ear. But it is the kidneys with which the ears are most associated.

In the Orient, the kidneys are among the most revered organs because, it is said, the kidneys distribute qi throughout the body and parcel out the gifts of ancestry in the form of individual talents and life's opportunities. Whatever an individual's innate talents may be, they are believed to be housed in the kidneys, awaiting the right moment to be manifested in life. In this way, the kidneys are said to be instrumental in directing the course of a person's life, the maturation and realization of destiny. So, to care for the kidneys is to care for your very soul.

Which brings us back to Oriental art and the Buddha's ears. The Buddha's elephant ears reveal the lofty spiritual development he had attained even before he began his life. They also suggest that he had very strong kidneys.

FILTERING AND BEYOND

The urinary tract is composed of two kidneys, a bladder, two ureters, and a urethra. Each of the two ureters connects a kidney to the bladder. The urethra allows urine to pass out of the body. In the case of men, the urethra serves as a conduit for semen, as well.

We tend to think of the kidneys as the body's filter system, and indeed, that is among their important tasks. But the kidneys also identify everything that is in the blood, and then decide what to do with it. They recognize and separate waste materials from the essential elements in the blood; determine how much of a specific substance the body needs; retain that amount; and then let the rest go. And that is just the beginning.

The primary waste products that the kidneys filter are those resulting from protein metabolism, such as nitrogen, urea, and ammonia. The kidneys also eliminate excess hormones, vitamins, minerals, and foreign substances, such as food additives and drugs.

They regulate electrolyte balance, retaining more or less of the blood's supply of sodium, potassium, hydrogen, magnesium, calcium, bicarbonate, phosphate, and chloride. The quantities of these elements that are retained by the kidneys depend on the body's overall needs.

They also convert vitamin D into a usable state, a hormone. They maintain the body's acid–alkaline balance, too, by altering the acidity or alkalinity of the urine.

Blood pressure is controlled by the kidneys, as well. Depending upon the body's current blood pressure, the organs will secrete varying amounts of the enzyme renin, which converts in the blood to angiotensin. Angiotensin causes blood vessels to constrict, and thereby increase pressure. It also alerts the kidneys to retain more sodium and excrete more potassium. Sodium increases the volume of water within the body—including that within the blood—and thereby increases blood pressure.

The kidneys also produce another hormone, erythropoietin, which stimulates the body to produce more red blood cells.

When excess water is consumed, the kidneys release it; when the body needs more water they retain it. In short, the kidneys are constantly monitoring the body's overall needs, and adjusting fluid and mineral balances to meet those needs.

Remarkably, the method the kidneys use to filter the blood is not as simple as you might think. The kidneys remove the blood's constituents, separate the essential ingredients from the waste, and then reassimilate the essential parts back into the blood. The process is analogous to emptying an entire room and then putting back only what is needed.

Once it is thoroughly filtered and cleansed, the blood is collected in a holding area, called the medulla, and then allowed to continue on its journey throughout the body. The kidneys perform this task with a miraculous efficiency. About two and a half pints of blood pass through the kidneys every minute, or about 450 gallons per day.

Although we possess two kidneys, only one is necessary for life.

ANATOMY

Each kidney is about four to five inches long and weighs approximately six ounces. They stand parallel to the spine, well above the waist (not in the small of the back, as is usually believed), just behind the twelfth rib. The right kidney is below the liver, the left below the spleen; the left kidney is slightly higher than the right.

They are oval-shaped, with a slight indentation on the inside (or spinal side). Here, blood vessels, lymph glands, and nerves enter the organs. This indentation, called a hilius, is also the place from which the ureter emerges—a thin tube that allows urine to pass from the kidneys to the bladder.

Each kidney is embedded in a mass of fat, called perirenal fat, which helps support them and acts as a shock absorber. Each is kept in place by sheets of connective tissue. The kidneys touch the diaphragm and therefore move while you breathe, that is, with the expansion and contraction of the diaphragm. A tough fibrous tissue surrounds the kidneys, further protecting them from shock.

Inside, the actual filtering unit of the kidneys is called a nephron, which consists of two primary parts: The first is called a glomerulus (glomeruli is the plural), and the second a tubule. The

The Kidneys and Bladder

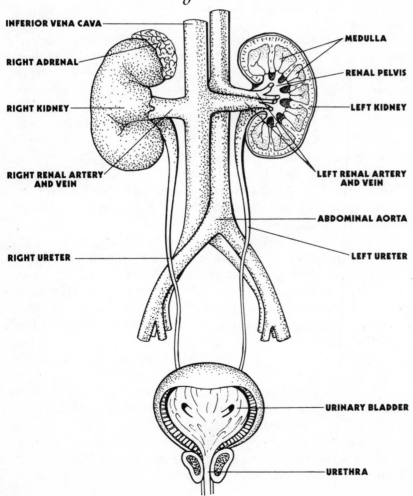

INFERIOR VENA CAVA

RIGHT ADRENAL

RIGHT KIDNEY

RIGHT RENAL ARTERY
AND VEIN

RIGHT URETER

MEDULLA

RENAL PELVIS

LEFT KIDNEY

LEFT RENAL ARTERY
AND VEIN

ABDOMINAL AORTA

LEFT URETER

URINARY BLADDER

URETHRA

The two kidneys, the urinary bladder, two ureters, and the urethra make up the urinary tract, filtering liquid nutrients and passing the waste out of the body.

129

glomerulus is a bulblike structure. The tubule is a long, wavy tentacle. The tubule surrounds the bulblike glomerulus and extends beyond it. Together they look like an octopus with a single long and wavy arm.

Capillaries form a complex net that intersects at various places with the tubule, allowing blood to flow back into the capillary system after it's been cleansed in the tubule.

During youth, there are more than 1 million nephrons in each kidney, but that number decreases with age. By the time you are, say, seventy, each kidney contains fewer than 250,000 nephrons, or about a quarter of its original filtering capacity. Aging, dietary poisons, and stress—with its consequent wear and tear—destroy nephrons.

The arteries that provide blood to the kidneys flow directly from the aorta, the primary artery of the body carrying oxygenated blood directly from the heart. From there it flows into the kidney's capillary system that leads to the glomeruli, where the first stage of filtration takes place.

Once inside a glomerulus, the blood is cleansed of its larger waste products. Then it passes onto the next stage of filtration, the long and looping tubules, which removes virtually everything from the blood, and decides what to put back in, and what to eliminate as urine. Most of what is reinstated to the blood is water (about 99 percent of it), amino acids, glucose, minerals, and vitamins.

Urine is composed mostly of water (about 95 percent) and about 5 percent solids, including urea (a by-product of protein metabolism, which makes up about 20 percent of solids); a variety of minerals, including chloride, sodium, potassium, phosphate, and sulfate; creatine, a naturally-occurring chemical; and a very small amount of uric acid. The presence of glucose (blood sugar) or protein in the urine indicates some form of disease. (See kidney-related illnesses, below. Also, see the chapter on the bladder.)

Once the blood is cleansed, it is temporarily held in the medulla, and then allowed to pass to the renal vein, which is the exit vessel leading to other parts of the body.

Meanwhile, the urine is sent from the tubules to the renal pelvis, which is a collecting point for urine. The renal pelvis empties into the ureter and then to the bladder.

The kidneys are vulnerable to a wide variety of disorders, including cancer, cysts, stones, impairment of the blood supply, infection, and autoimmune disorders. The kidneys also are affected when a person suffers from diabetes mellitus. Finally, the kidneys are highly vulnerable to stress, which, if chronic, can cause kidney damage and even death.

The most common form of kidney cancer is renal cell carcinoma, which affects people over the age of forty. Among the common symptoms are blood in the urine, swelling in the abdomen, fever, and weight loss. Another cancer is transitional cell carcinoma, which develops in the renal pelvis; it is most common among smokers and people who have taken painkillers for many years.

About half of the population over fifty has noncancerous fluid-filled cysts within the kidneys. Usually, these do not present any symptoms, and there is no medically known cause. Medical treatment includes draining the cysts or surgically removing them.

Kidney stones, also known as calculi, are caused by a precipitation of substances found in urine. About 70 percent of the stones found in the kidney or ureter—the most common sites—are made of calcium oxalate and/or phosphate. These are salts derived from calcium and oxalic acids.

Scientists do not know the cause of such stones, but believe that they may be due to a diet rich in oxalic acid. Foods such as spinach, rhubarb, sesame seeds, and coffee contain high amounts of oxalic acid. Scientists also speculate that such stones may be due to dehydration because they are most common in the summer months, when people tend to sweat more, lose more water, and have more concentrated urine.

Sometimes stones contain calcium, which is often a symptom of metabolic disorders and hyperparathyroidism, an illness affecting the parathyroid gland (see endocrine system). A small percentage of stones occur from chronic kidney infections; these are usually composed of calcium, magnesium, ammonium phosphate, and other minerals.

In poorer countries, where the diet is low in protein and phosphate, bladder stones are common. In developed countries, bladder stones are largely the result of urinary tract infections or an enlarged prostate gland, which prevents adequate elimination of urine. If a stone blocks the flow of urine, a severe infection can result and can cause kidney damage.

Stones are diagnosed by X rays, ultrasound, blood and urine analysis. The latter two tests may show infection; sometimes urine will reveal red blood cells—perhaps the result of some tissue damage done by the stones—or tiny crystals, which may indicate the presence of stones.

The passage of stones can be painful. Treatment includes bed rest, pain relievers, and increased liquid intake in order to encourage the stone to pass through the urinary tract. Since the majority of stones are less than one-fifth of an inch in diameter, they are usually passed easily. Larger stones may require surgery, however.

Once a stone enters the ureter or bladder, it can sometimes be removed by the insertion of a crushing device and a viewing tube. Other methods include the use of shock-wave treatments, which can disintegrate stones in the kidneys.

There are two kinds of stress: eustress, which is considered a healthful and enthusiastic response to a challenge, and distress, which is a response characterized by fear, mounting dread, and the anticipation of defeat or disaster. Distress causes a wide variety of physiological changes in the body. Among the most significant are changes in respiration; elevation of blood pressure and blood cholesterol levels; and hormonal imbalance, including the elevation of cortisol and epinephrine (adrenaline), all of which combine to have detrimental and sometimes destructive effects on the heart and kidneys. As blood pressure and cholesterol levels increase, the likelihood of glomeruli and tubule damage rises significantly. Also hormonal imbalance requires the kidneys to work harder and faster, thus putting added stress on these organs.

Doctors recommend a variety of medical therapies for stress, including high blood pressure medication; drugs to lower cholesterol; diets lower in fat and cholesterol; and relaxation techniques.

Often, depression sets in following extended stressful periods, in which case antidepressive medication and/or psychotherapy may be prescribed.

More than 90,000 people each year undergo kidney transplant surgery in which a donated kidney is used to replace a failed kidney. And more than 50,000 Americans have their blood filtered by artificial kidney machines each day.

He is the best physician who is the most ingenious inspirer of hope.

SAMUEL TAYLOR
COLERIDGE

132

The Site of the Will

According to practitioners of traditional Chinese medicine, the kidneys and bladder are the paired organs that make up the Water Element and govern the body's fluid content.

The kidneys are associated with the winter months, December 21 through March 21. Though they receive optimal amounts of healing energy during this season, they are injured by too much cold. The idea is that life energy descends into the earth during winter, but bursts forth in the spring. Qi does the same thing within the human body: it descends into the lower organs during winter—the kidneys, bladder, and sex organs—but rises into the liver and eventually into the heart during spring and summer.

As in all traditional medicine, balance is the key, even for those things that have potential healing and strengthening properties. Cold weather, which is contracting, directs the energy down into the kidneys, but too much cold can injure them.

As contracted organs (they are referred to in the Yellow Emperor's Classic as "lesser yin"), the kidneys can easily become too contracted and tense, thus preventing adequate blood, qi, and fluids from flowing.

"Those who disobey the laws of Winter will suffer an injury to the kidneys," stated the Yellow Emperor. "For them Spring will bring impotence, and they will produce little." In other words, they will not be able to expand and flower in the spring.

The Yellow Emperor used the word "impotence" both literally and figuratively, for the kidneys govern the sex organs and the body's overall sexual energy. The Yellow Emperor warns that too much sexual intercourse will harm the kidneys, weaken the sex drive, and reduce the overall vitality of the body. All types of sexual dysfunction originate from kidney/bladder imbalances. Deficient kidney energy can cause a variety of sex-related disorders—from premature ejaculation to infertility and sterility. Excessive kidney energy, on the other hand, can cause excessive sex drive and obsession with sex.

While qi flows through the body, the kidneys are said to be the source of the body's overall vitality. Weakness, lethargy, and lack of endurance comes from deficient kidney energy.

The emotion most associated with the kidneys and bladder is

Traditional Chinese Meridians

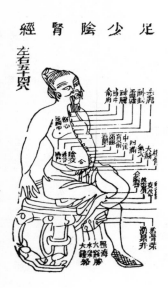

fear. People with weak kidneys will experience more fear than those with strong kidneys. Also, fear damages the kidneys and can ultimately destroy their ability to function.

The Chinese maintain that the kidneys are the site of the human will. Our ability to focus on a goal and see it through, come what may, is derived from the strength of our kidneys. If the kidneys are weak, the will is weak. Conversely, a person with strong kidneys will feel an intuitive connection with certain goals that will help him or her persevere through difficulties to see the goal's realization.

"The kidneys are like the officials who do energetic work and they excel through their ability," said the Yellow Emperor.

A person's drive to succeed is said to emanate from the kidneys. People who wish to strengthen their ambition, drive, and will are encouraged to heal their kidneys.

The kidneys draw in the breath deeply into the body. They are called the root of the breath. Interestingly, studies have shown that people who are shallow breathers are more prone to nervous tension, anxiety, and fear. Those who breathe deeply tend to be more relaxed. A Chinese healer would concur, pointing out that weak kidneys would make a person more anxiety-prone and less able to draw breath deeply into the body. Conversely, those who wish to strengthen their kidneys are advised to make a habit of deep breathing, which effectively draws qi into the kidneys, bladder, and sex organs.

Oriental healers maintain that many respiratory problems, including asthma, begin with kidney imbalance. When the kidneys are unable to draw the breath deeply into the lungs, or exhale deeply, stagnation within the lungs increases and eventually gives rise to illness.

The kidneys also rule and nourish the bones, keeping them vital, flexible, and resilient. Weak, brittle, or broken bones are, at their root, a kidney imbalance, usually resulting from deficient kidney energy or qi.

The taste associated with the kidneys and bladder is salty flavor, and the kidneys crave it. Light to moderate amounts of salt stimulate and strengthen the kidneys and bladder. Too much salt, however, can injure the kidneys, causing them to become too contracted and leading to high blood pressure.

The Yellow Emperor also warns that too much salt will cause

despondency. The Chinese maintain that excessively salty diets—or contracted life conditions—can lead to chronic depression.

Kidney energy opens into the ears, said the Yellow Emperor, meaning that kidney qi nourishes the hearing mechanism. All hearing problems, including ear infections (common in children) and hearing loss, originate from kidney imbalances (see the section on healing the kidneys, below). When kidney energy is deficient, blood and qi will be inadequate to maintain the health and vitality of the hearing mechanism. Kidney imbalance, either excess or deficient qi, can also cause ringing in the ears.

The kidneys rule the body hair. Strong, luxurious hair is a sign of strong kidneys. Conversely, split ends, broken hair, and baldness are signs of weak and (usually) deficient kidney energy. Since the kidneys rule the sex organs, unhealthy hair, especially split ends, is a sign of weak or degenerating sex organs.

Baldness occurs when the kidneys are unable to maintain proper water balance within the body. Each hair is rooted in a follicle that contains oil and water. The kidneys control the amount of water present in tissues throughout the body. When excessive amounts of water infiltrate the scalp, the hair follicles swell, allowing the hair to uproot and fall out. Hence, baldness. Hair care begins with treating the kidneys well, say the Chinese.

The kidney meridian runs upward from a point at the bottom of the foot, in the soft tissue below the ball; from there, it runs along the arch of the foot; up inside the calf and thigh; across the groin; over the stomach and the middle of the chest; to the clavicle bone. (All acupuncture meridians run in pairs, on opposite sides of the body, and are mirror images of each other.)

People with overworked and tired kidneys often suffer from weak or heavy legs. The weakness is usually perceived most acutely in the thighs.

Kidneys provide qi to the lower back area. Lower back problems, therefore, are related to kidney and bladder issues (see chapter on the bladder).

The kidneys and liver are the body's main blood-cleansing organs. When the kidneys are overworked, due to high levels of toxicity in the diet or environment, their capacity to filter the blood can be exceeded. When this occurs, the body attempts to eliminate excess waste through the skin in the form of rashes,

Antique Chinese drawings from Ling Shu Su Wen Chieh Yao, *a medical text compiled during the Ch'ing dynasty (1644–1912), show, left, the twenty-nine points of the kidney "vessel" or meridian and, right, the nine points of the heart meridian.*

135

pimples, and acne. As toxicity lowers to a level that the kidneys can handle, such rashes and blemishes disappear.

The kidneys receive optimal amounts of qi energy between 5 P.M. and 7 P.M. The bladder receives its peak qi from 3 P.M. to 5 P.M. Weakness or fatigue at these hours can indicate a kidney imbalance.

The Gift of the Ancestors

The kidneys are said to contain the gift of the ancestors, meaning that from the kidneys your life and spiritual path unfold. The kidneys possess the talents, abilities, and special gifts with which you entered the world. Your unique purpose is locked within the spiritual qi of these organs, awaiting the right moment to manifest. In this way, the kidneys are said to be responsible for maturation.

Interestingly, this corresponds with many Western and Eastern spiritual traditions, which have maintained that the true gift of heaven comes not from above, but from below. In Kundalini yoga, for example, the divine and primary energy flows upward from the base of the spine (from the area of the kidneys) to the brain, where the person receives self-knowledge, or illumination. The Gnostic traditions are founded upon a similar understanding that spiritual awakenings emerge from deep within, rather than from outside the self.

Our ability to focus on a goal and see it through to its completion determines, to a great extent, the degree of success we experience in life. Completion is not only the foundation of success, but the basis for healthy psychological and spiritual development. The kidneys play a vital role in this process, and therefore were revered among Orientals throughout the East.

Healing the Kidneys

Generally speaking, there are three essential kidney conditions: overly contracted and excessive; overly expanded and deficient; and balanced.

Foods that cause the contraction of the kidneys are salt and fatty foods, especially hard fats from red meat and hard cheese.

Eggs also cause the kidneys to contract and become excessive. So, too, does chronic fear or stress. Such foods and life conditions cause the capillaries, glomeruli, and tubules to contract. This prevents adequate blood, oxygen, and qi from flowing through the organs and causes accumulation of toxins and the degeneration of tissues. Stagnation and accumulation can lead to urinary tract infections, which, in the case of the kidneys, can be very dangerous.

Before such problems arise, however, a variety of less severe symptoms emerge. These include excessive sex drive, restless sleep, and grinding of teeth while asleep. Children often grind their teeth at night as a result of excessive kidney energy, which manifests during the day as frustration. Contracted kidneys also give rise to poor blood circulation, and cold hands and feet.

Eventually, these conditions will turn into their opposite: they will exhaust the kidneys and create deficient kidney energy. This is particularly true of stress, which, if not dealt with properly, can lead to chronic fatigue, despondency, and depression. In short, the loss of will.

Weak or expanded kidneys are the cause of another set of problems: excessive fear, anxiety, and depression; weak sex drive or no sex drive at all; poor circulation, including cold hands and feet; lack of will, ambition, or drive; inability to complete things and a general lack of direction. Deficient kidney energy can cause ringing in the ears, ear infections, and bedwetting in children.

Adequate water intake is important to healthy kidneys. There is no rule that can be followed by everyone for appropriate daily liquid intake. In general, we should drink when thirsty. However, we also should be aware of the body's need for clean, pure water, which is commonly forgotten by most of us today. The body's reaction to the first few sips of water is subtle, but revealing. Often, the body responds with such enthusiasm for pure water that we are suddenly awakened to its need, which we may have been unaware of before. This reveals the necessity of being conscious of our own physical needs, for which there is no hard rule that can substitute. We should consciously drink small amounts of clean water daily; the amount is up to you. Let your body guide you by its reaction to the water, and the frequency of urination, to determine how much water you need.

In Chinese medicine, beans are the most effective healing food for the kidneys. Beans strengthen and support kidney function and promote healing. Common beans include: aduki, black beans, chickpeas, green and red lentils, navy beans, mung beans, limas, and split peas.

Small amounts of salt tonify the kidneys, but too much salt can cause kidney damage. Use only a pinch of salt in cooking—usually the tip of a teaspoon (less than one-eighth teaspoon) is necessary to cook two to three cups of grain. Also, avoid adding salt at the table. Salt is essential in cooking grain because it opens the grain and makes it digestible.

The grain that promotes kidney function and healing most is barley.

Small amounts of salted fermented foods, such as pickles, miso, tamari, shoyu, and sauerkraut, enhance kidney function and promote healing. But these foods can also cause the kidneys to contract and stagnate if used excessively. (About one-quarter teaspoon of miso is all that is necessary for a single serving of miso soup.) Tamari and shoyu should be used only in cooking, not added to foods at the table.

For excessively contracted kidneys, watermelon and watermelon tea promote urination and elimination of waste. Watermelon relaxes the kidneys. Watermelon tea can be made by grinding dried watermelon seeds, boiling them in water, and steeping them.

Other fruits that are helpful to the kidneys include grapes (to promote urination), blackberries, blueberries, and cranberries.

According to traditional medicine, kidney stones form for several reasons:

- Overly contracted kidneys, due primarily to excess salt, fat, and cholesterol.
- Insufficient amounts of liquid intake, especially pure water.
- Excessive intake of foods rich in oxalic acid, particularly spinach, rhubarb, Swiss chard, beet tops, chocolate, and coffee.
- Refined flour and sugar, low in B vitamins, calcium, and other minerals, but rich in fat.
- Chronic stress.
- Chronic overwork, which can cause kidney fatigue and exhaustion, preventing adequate elimination of toxins.

To heal the kidneys, Oriental medicine advocates a diet low in fat and cholesterol, with only small or moderate amounts of salt.

The diet should include regular amounts of barley (two to three times per week); daily portions of beans; small amounts of sea vegetables; a variety of vegetables daily; fish; fruit; and pure water. In addition, the following foods, drinks, and preparations are recommended for kidney and bladder problems.

- *Daikon root:* This long, white radish is reputed to melt fat deposits and stones and help to eliminate stagnation from tissues throughout the body. There are two daikon drinks that serve different functions.

  To encourage urination and elimination, grate two to three tablespoons of fresh daikon into a cheesecloth sack; squeeze the sack so that daikon juice falls into a cup. Pour boiled water into the cup; add one to two drops of shoyu or tamari. Drink twice a day. Another drink is prepared as follows: Grate one to two tablespoons of daikon radish into a cup; pour hot water into the cup; add two drops of tamari or shoyu. Drink once or twice a day. This drink is reputed to dissolve blockages and stones in kidneys.
- *Burdock root:* A hardy, medicinal food, revered by Chinese, European, and American healers for many centuries. Considered one of the strongest blood purifiers in the entire herb kingdom, burdock is used for a wide variety of disorders, but is generally recognized as one of the best herbs for breaking down and eliminating waste products from metabolism. In Chinese medicine, it is regarded as a strengthening herb for the entire urinary tract and sex organs. Pressure-cook sliced burdock for fifteen minutes with sliced carrots and kombu seaweed in about one and a half inches of water.
- *Burdock tea:* Detoxifies the blood; stimulates and tonifies kidneys and bladder; and eliminates waste and stagnation within kidneys. Boil one to two tablespoons of stems, twigs, and leaves in one cup of water; steep for ten minutes and drink two to three times per day.
- *Basil:* This herb can be used in cooking and boiled in water to make a tea; it strengthens the kidneys.

In *The Way of Herbs,* Michael Tierra recommends the following herbal remedy for kidney stones.

Gravel root—2 parts
Parsley root—2 parts
Marshmallow root—2 parts
Lobelia—½ part
Ginger root—½ part

"Simmer two ounces [of these herbs] per quart of water for about an hour until the liquid is reduced by half," writes Tierra. "Add an equal volume of vegetable glycerin [about two ounces] to preserve."

In addition to the above-mentioned recommendations, naturopaths also suggest the following herbs and supplements for kidney and bladder disorders, including stones.

- *Vitamins:* A; B complex; B6; C and E.
- *Minerals:* Magnesium.
- *Herbs:* Bearberry tea, to ease passage of stones; chamomile tea, to dissolve stones; yarrow tea, also to dissolve stones; hydrangea decoction (bark of herb boiled for an hour in water), reputed to dissolve stones; nettle, leaves and roots infusion (add nettle leaves to water that's already been boiled and then allow it to steep for about twenty minutes; tightly cover pot top while steeping). Nettle, one of the most revered herbs in Europe and the Middle East, contains a variety of minerals and vitamins, all of which combine to strengthen immune function. Nettle is reputed to dissolve stones and eliminate blockages.

CHAPTER 13

THE BLADDER

*T*HE BLADDER HOLDS URINE, the liquid waste of the body, and releases it when it's full. Most people's bladders can hold up to a pint of urine, which is produced in the kidneys and flows downward through two tubes, called ureters. The average person urinates from three to eight times per day. Greater frequency can suggest any one of several possible problems, including excessive intake of fluids, urinary infection, or diabetes.

Up to the age of three to four, children have no control over their bladders. When a child's bladder is full, nerves within the walls of the bladder send a signal to the spinal cord, which relays a message back to urinate. Maturity brings with it development of the nervous system, which allows the brain to intercede in this process. When the bladder signals that it is full, the brain can tell the bladder to wait. Hence, the familiar sense of discomfort, without an untimely elimination.

The bladder is a muscular, spherically shaped sac, located in the lower part of the body directly behind the pubic bone, within the pelvis. The bladder is lined with a mucous membrane and has walls composed of three layers of tough muscle. These muscles give the bladder its ability to expand as it is filled and contract dur-

Human beings seem less capable of being healthy the more they believe they have to be healthy.

ALFRED J. ZIEGLER

ing elimination. At the back wall of the bladder are the entrances of the two ureters from the kidneys. Each ureter opening is covered with valvelike folds of skin, which prevent urine from flowing back into the ureters.

The bladder narrows at the bottom. There, at its base, is the entrance to the urethra, the tube from which the urine flows outside the body. There are circular sphincter muscles located inside and outside the area where the urethra joins the bladder. In men, the urethra passes through the prostate, which sits directly below the bladder. The prostate produces seminal fluid, which is expelled during ejaculation. Inside the prostate, the urethra has two ducts that open to the prostate, allowing semen to flow from the prostate, down along the urethra and out the penis. During urination, of course, these ducts are closed. The urethra is approximately eight to nine inches long in men, and about an inch and a half long in women.

As the bladder fills with urine, the walls expand and send nerves impulses to the brain, via the spinal cord, alerting you to the need to urinate. If you give the okay, nervous impulses from the brain order the smooth muscles surrounding the urethra to relax, allowing it to open. Next, the external sphincter is ordered to relax. Then the internal sphincter gets the same message, while the muscles within the bladder walls are ordered to contract. The bladder will continue to contract until all the urine has been expelled. It is common to hold the breath when urinating, while at the same time pushing down with the diaphragm and contracting the abdomen muscles. This puts more pressure on the bladder to eliminate.

The bladder and urethra are held in place by a group of muscles called the pelvic floor that extend from the pubis to the tail bone. The pelvic floor includes the sphincter muscles of the anus. In women, these muscles also control the vagina and support the developing fetus during pregnancy.

ILLNESSES OF THE BLADDER

The most common illnesses affecting the bladder are urinary tract infections, incontinence, and stones. In men, bladder problems also arise with disorders of the prostate. Urinary tract illnesses can involve any of the urinary organs, including the kidneys, ureters, bladder, or urethra, but most often affect the bladder (an infection called cystitis) or the urethra (called urethritis). Bacteria, which are normally present in small quantities in both the urethra and the bladder, can increase and cause infections.

Women tend to suffer urinary tract infections far more frequently than men because their urethras are shorter than mens'. The shorter urethra makes it easier for bacteria to travel up into the bladder and multiply. Also, it is easier for bacteria to pass from the intestines to the urethra in women because of the close proximity of the anus.

There are numerous other causes of urinary tract infections. In general, anything that prevents full elimination of urine from the bladder and urethra will increase the likelihood of bacterial buildup and infection. Common causes include injury to the urethra or bladder, causing inflammation, which can impair full elimination of urine; swelling of the urethra from sexual intercourse (most common in women); kidney or urethra stones; pregnancy; irritants present in bubble baths, douches, feminine sprays, or diaphragms; vaginitis; congenital abnormalities of the urethra or some other part of the urinary tract; prostate enlargement or inflammation; psychological stress; and the use of a catheter during medical tests or surgery. If the infection spreads to the kidneys, serious illness can result.

Symptoms of urinary tract infection include frequent urination, with only small amounts of urine being expelled; burning or stinging pain during urination; fever; and discomfort in the lower abdomen. Occasionally, there are chills or a foul smell to the urine.

One of the few dietary treatments that doctors will recommend is to encourage patients with urinary tract infections to drink cranberry juice, which makes the urine more acidic and thus less supportive of bacteria. Doctors also may tell patients to consume large quantities of liquids. This causes frequent urination, which will help flush bacteria from the urinary tract. Of course, frequently doctors also will prescribe antibiotics to kill bacteria and stop infection.

There are several types of incontinence, but the most common is stress incontinence, suffered mostly by women past their childbearing years. Stress incontinence occurs when small amounts of urine are released while coughing, laughing, or lifting a heavy object. Other forms of incontinence include urge in-

In the final analysis, the survival and health of the individual and [the] species may depend not so much on further developments in technology as on the collective application of common sense.

S. BRYAN FURNASS

continence, in which the need to urinate is accompanied by the inability to withhold urine, or when changes in sitting positions trigger a sudden release; and total incontinence, which is the complete inability to prevent elimination. Women far outnumber men in incidence of incontinence.

There are a variety of causes of incontinence, including nervous system disorders, such as multiple sclerosis; injury to the nervous system, brain, bladder, or pelvis; urinary infection; stones; and anger, stress, or anxiety. By far, the most common cause is weakened sphincter and pelvic floor muscles, which occurs in many women after pregnancy and childbirth. During pregnancy, the growing baby puts pressure on the pelvic floor muscles. If prenatal and postnatal exercises are not performed, these muscles can become stretched and weakened, causing the pelvic floor to sag. This allows the bladder and urethra to reposition themselves inappropriately, preventing adequate control of the bladder. Being overweight can further weaken the pelvic floor and contribute to incontinence. After menopause, hormonal changes can cause these and other muscles to degenerate, thus further exacerbating the problem and causing incontinence in older women.

Dr. Arnold Kegel, a professor of obstetrics and gynecology at UCLA, created a set of exercises for preventing and treating incontinence. They're now widely taught at childbirth classes and have helped millions of women to regain control of the muscles that control urination. Here are the basic steps:

1. Practice controlling the bladder by slowing urine flow and then stopping it. When you are able to stop the flow, hold it one or two seconds. Do this six or eight times as you urinate. You may have to do this exercise numerous times before you are able to stop the flow entirely, but eventually you will be able to control the flow without leakage. Practice relaxing and contracting the pelvic floor muscles, as well.

2. Practice relaxing and contracting the same muscles used in exercise 1 throughout the day. Hold the contraction for several seconds and then relax. Do this exercise anywhere from fifty to 100 times per day, and repeat exercise 1 when urinating.

3. Contract the pelvic floor during love-making.

In general, exercises that strengthen the abdomen will help to restore strength and control to the pelvic floor, as well.

FEAR, STRESS, AND CONTRACTION

Like the kidneys, the bladder is associated with the winter months in Chinese medicine. It is said to store the overflow of the kidneys, meaning that it stores the urine. The bladder responds to the same Water Element foods and herbs as those mentioned for the kidneys, including beans, barley, and a mild salty flavor. In the same way, the bladder is easily affected by fear and stress. Thus, maintaining calm and centeredness in difficult situations strengthens bladder function.

In general, bladder problems arise from an excess of contraction. In men, the prostate can become inflamed or contracted, causing the contraction of the urethra, which prevents full elimination of the bladder. Too much salt can cause bladder and kidney problems in both sexes, and thus prevent adequate elimination of urine.

The bladder meridian is long and complex, beginning at the inside corner of the eye and running down along the spine and the back of the leg to the foot. Since it provides qi to the spinal column, back problems are said to be related to the health of the bladder and its meridians. When the kidneys and bladder are strong, the spinal column is also strong and healthy. Back problems emerge, however, when bladder and kidney function are troubled. Given that stress powerfully affects the Water Element organs, Chinese healers say that no one should be surprised that back problems are so prevalent in modern society.

The placement of the bladder meridian is interesting because it is exposed and stretched somewhat whenever you sit down on the toilet, thus positioning the body so that the downward motion of qi will enhance the act of elimination. All rashes, blemishes, or skin eruptions along the bladder meridian are associated with the inefficient elimination of waste from the kidneys and bladder.

Urine can be a useful diagnostic tool to help determine whether you are drinking too much fluid or eating too much salt. Ideally, urine should be pale yellow in color, with only a mild

Health is the normal and harmonious vibration of the elements and forces composing the human entity on the physical, mental and moral (emotional) planes of being, in conformity with the constructive principle (great law of life) in nature.

HENRY LINDLAHR

odor. In general, the more liquid and expansive foods one consumes (such as fruits, sugar, and alcohol), the more clear the urine will be. Conversely, the more salt, fat, and animal foods you consume, the darker the urine will be. The kidneys must work harder to eliminate these waste products from the blood. Because they are emerging in sufficient quantities to color the urine, they suggest a greater possibility of kidney and bladder stone formation. For this reason, people with dark urine should drastically reduce salt and animal foods.

Healing the bladder calls for increasing Water Element foods, such as those good for the kidneys, as well as Metal and Wood. Especially helpful to the bladder are aduki beans, burdock, barley, and buckwheat. Consume only pure water or mild teas. Aromatic teas are highly expansive and tend to require more effort from the kidneys to eliminate. Also increase mineral-rich foods, such as leafy green vegetables, carrots, and other roots. Particularly helpful are small amounts of sea vegetables (one to two tablespoon servings per day) such as kelp, nori, wakame, and arame. Useful fruits include watermelon, blueberry, blackberry, cranberry, and grapes (all in moderation).

Kidney and bladder infections are caused by a decrease in circulation and elimination, often due to a diet rich in fat, sugar, and cholesterol. To heal bladder infections, avoid fatty foods and those rich in cholesterol, sugar, and artificial ingredients. Increase foods rich in beta carotene, such as carrots, broccoli, squash, and collard greens. Also increase foods rich in vitamin E, such as whole grains (especially whole wheat), and vitamin C, such as tangerines and broccoli. Increase foods rich in minerals, especially zinc (grains and seafoods). Mineral-rich foods include all leafy greens, sea vegetables, grains, and fish.

The following teas can help to strengthen the bladder and immune system to ward off infection:

Boil one to two tablespoons of burdock stems, twigs, and leaves in two cups of water and drink two or three times per day.

Boil one to two tablespoons of echinacea twigs in two cups of water and drink two times per day. Or take fifteen to thirty drops of echinacea in water or kukicha tea, two times daily until infection is eliminated. Echinacea is among the most powerful natural antibiotics in the plant kingdom.

CHAPTER 14

THE HEART

ℜo ORGAN HAS been the focus of more emotion, mythology, and technological wizardry than the human heart. We have given it credit for our greatest achievements, and blamed it for our darkest deeds. No other organ has been invested with so much meaning. It has been said that the heart is the inspiration for poetry, sacrifice, war, and peace. It is the source of love and hate, good and evil, courage and cowardice. The heart is the king of the body, the most human of all our parts.

It has always been so. The Bible asserts that the heart is the seat of the psyche, the place in which our true nature exists. "For God sees not as man sees, for man looks at the outward appearance, but the Lord looks at the heart" (1 Samuel 16:7).

It is the source of feeling, tenderness, and love. A broken heart is perhaps the saddest of all human experiences, with the possible exception of death. In fact, the former often precedes the latter. Wrote one rabbi in the Talmud: "I can tolerate any illness, any pain, but not heart pain . . ."

Even today, we consider the heart the place of truth. "He spoke from his heart," we often report when someone says something sincere and honest. The list goes on: an open heart, a deceit-

With what words will you describe this heart, so as not to fill a book . . . ?

LEONARDO DA VINCI

147

ful heart, a cruel heart, a tender heart, my heart is heavy, I love you with all my heart. These are just a few of the common expressions used to describe something deep and true about human experience. Words are clues to the psyche. Clearly, the heart has come to symbolize the truest part of our being.

The physical workings of the heart have been studied since antiquity, beginning with the ancient Egyptians, whom the early Christians believed had discovered all the secrets of anatomy. In fact, none of the earlier anatomists, including Aristotle, Galen, Avicenna, and Hippocrates, fully understood the workings of the heart. All of them maintained that the heart had only two chambers, and no one understood how blood got from the right chamber to the left. Galen said that it passed through tiny holes in the septum, the muscular barrier that separates the two sides of the heart.

In the sixteenth century, Michael Servetus, a philosopher and anatomist, wrote *The Seven Books of Mistaken Conception of the Trinity,* in which he correctly described how blood travels from the right side of the heart to the lungs, and then from the lungs to the left side of the heart. Unfortunately, his book included certain heretical statements about the unity of God and the oneness of creation. Thinking he might be able to influence Christian doctrine, Servetus sealed his own fate by sending the treatise to John Calvin, the religious zealot who, after reading the work, had Servetus tracked down, arrested, and then sentenced to death.

Upon hearing the court order him to be burned at the stake, Servetus did not plead for his life, but for the life of his convictions. "I fear that through excess of suffering I may prove faithless to myself and belie the convictions of my life," he told Calvin and the court. "If I have erred, it was in ignorance; I am so constituted mentally and morally to desire the glory of God."

Calvin tried to have every copy of Servetus's book burned with him, but three or four survived, one of which is in the National Library of Paris. Servetus's death, which occurred on October 27, 1553, put science back another seventy-five years, for it would not be until 1628 that the truth would surface again, this time in England, thanks to one of the giants of medical history.

That year William Harvey, a British doctor, published a book entitled *On the Motion of the Heart and Blood,* in which he accurately described the workings of the heart and circulation of the blood. Harvey's book revealed some of the difficulties of uncovering coronary circulation, which he studied by vivisection, and why the heart remained a mystery so long. "I found the task [of studying the heart] so truly arduous," wrote Harvey, "so full of difficulties, that I was almost tempted to think . . . that the motion of the heart was only to be comprehended by God. For I could neither rightly perceive at first when the systole and when the diastole took place, nor when and where dilation and contraction occurred, by reason of the rapidity of the motion, which in many animals is accomplished in the twinkling of an eye, coming and going like a flash of lightning; so that the systole presented itself to me now from this point, now from that; the diastole the same; and then everything reversed . . ."

No one was sure why the blood went to the lungs in the first place. Galen had said that the blood derived "air" and "natural spirits" from the lungs, which was as far as anyone had come to explaining oxygen. It wasn't until the seventeenth century that oxygen was discovered (it was called "dephlogisticated air") and not until the eighteenth century that it was named oxygen by French chemist and doctor Antonie Laurent Lavoisier.

And then there was the question of the heart's sounds. The actual beating of the heart appeared to physicians as a mysterious and indecipherable language. No one knew what to make of that familiar "lubb, dubb" until 1816, when Rene Theophile Laennec, a French physician, made a serendipitous discovery while examining an overweight woman who was suffering from tuberculosis. Modesty prevented him from placing his ear against the woman's breast, so Laennec rolled up a piece of paper and placed it near the woman's heart. "I was surprised and gratified," he later wrote, "to find that I could thereby perceive the action of the heart in a manner much more clear and distinct than I had ever been able to do by the immediate application of the ear."

Laennec, of course, had invented the stethoscope, albeit a paper one. He then produced a series of more elaborate wooden tubes, and began to study the sounds of the heart and their meaning. His masterwork, *Del'Auscultation,* which appeared in 1819, described the diagnostic meaning of various heart sounds, as well as the percussive sounds heard when a physician taps on a patient's back.

Laennec, who suffered from tuberculosis and eventually died

The Heart

A fist-sized double-pump that's also cited as the seat of the soul, the heart is truly a marvel of marvels that is still only partially understood after decades of close scientific study.

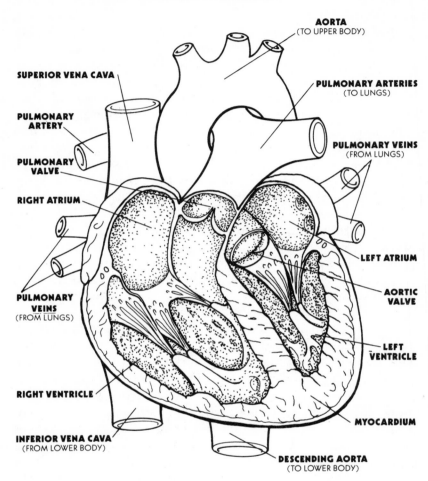

AORTA
(TO UPPER BODY)

SUPERIOR VENA CAVA

PULMONARY ARTERIES
(TO LUNGS)

PULMONARY ARTERY

PULMONARY VEINS
(FROM LUNGS)

PULMONARY VALVE

RIGHT ATRIUM

LEFT ATRIUM

AORTIC VALVE

PULMONARY VEINS
(FROM LUNGS)

LEFT VENTRICLE

RIGHT VENTRICLE

MYOCARDIUM

INFERIOR VENA CAVA
(FROM LOWER BODY)

DESCENDING AORTA
(TO LOWER BODY)

from the disease, gave the world its first heart instrument, as well as the word "stethoscope," which he derived from the Greek words *stethos,* meaning chest, and *scope,* to examine. Today electrocardiograms measure the electrical impulses coming from the heart (see anatomy and physiology of the heart, below); angiography, in which a radioactive dye is inserted into the coronary arteries and the heart itself, determines the extent to which the vessels are closed by cholesterol plaque; heart valves can be replaced; machines can take over the functions of the heart and lungs, pumping and oxygenating blood during surgery; and hearts can be transplanted from one person to another. All of this attention testifies to the value we place on this essential organ.

Meanwhile, research goes on. The Jarvik 7 mechanical heart, which was first used in humans in 1985, is a steel and plastic device that has proven a failure as a replacement for the real thing, though it has been used to keep people alive for short periods while they await a donor heart. Heart transplantation was first attempted in humans in 1967 by South African physician Dr. Christiaan Barnard. The early patients died shortly after the operations, but in 1984, a team of Stanford University physicians, led by Dr. Norman Shumway, showed that more than half of those who received heart transplants could survive up to a year.

There are a number of problems that have prevented heart transplants from becoming more widely used. The first, of course, is the tremendous difficulty of providing live hearts. Another is that the human body's immune system recognizes the new heart as a foreign object and attacks it, thus preventing the organ from surviving inside the body. Scientists point out that many cardiac patients are in need of a donated heart because coronary heart disease, the leading cause of death in the Western world, has destroyed their own. That illness is often caused by a high-fat and cholesterol diet, the typical regimen consumed in the West. In other words, it is entirely preventable by adopting the low-fat and low-cholesterol diet traditionally consumed by humans.

This brings us full circle, historically speaking. We know a lot more about the heart than the ancients did, but they probably took better care of their hearts than we do today. Indeed, many of the ancient ways of eating and living are proving to be the best medicine the heart can get.

Not One But Two Pumps

The heart beats between sixty and eighty times per minute in most of us, or about 100,000 times a day. Assuming that you are in good health and will live to be sixty-five or seventy, your heart will beat some 2.5 billion times during the course of your life.

While your body is at rest, your heart pumps about a sixth of a pint of blood per beat, or about twelve pints per minute. While exercising, it will race at about 200 beats per minute and pump a

In the midst of this machine we call a body, nothing is more orderly and reliable than the heart. Its complex workings have challenged brilliant medical minds for four hundred years. But like every other part of the body, the heart is just empty space when you get down to it. The "real" heart is not this tough bundle of twitching muscles that beats 3 billion times before it expires but the organizing power that pulls it together, that creates a thing out of nothingness.

DEEPAK CHOPRA

half pint per beat, or 100 pints per minute. Your entire blood supply passes through your heart every sixty seconds. The left and right sides of the heart pump blood in two different directions. During the average day, each side pumps approximately 2,000 gallons, or 50 million gallons in a lifetime.

To say that the heart is a marvel of marvels would be to describe this wondrous organ in understatement. No other part of the body is more appreciated by us all. Yet, our appreciation is meager in comparison to wonders performed by this miraculous organ.

The heart is about the size of a man's fist. It is shaped like an inverted cone, at the top of which is a network of blood vessels that allows blood to flow to and from the heart. It is located in the center of the chest, just behind the sternum, and tilts slightly to the left.

Most of us think of the heart as a pump, but in fact it is two pumps, a left and a right, that work in a precisely coordinated fashion. Each pump sends blood to different parts of the body. Yet, both must act in complete harmony in order for us to go on living.

Another common misconception about the heart is that it has only two phases—diastole (expansion) and systole (contraction). In fact, the heart has three phases: The first is diastole—the moment it relaxes and allows blood to enter the upper chambers, or both atria; the second is atrial systole, when both upper chambers contract, sending blood into the lower chambers, or ventricles; and the third is ventricle systole, when the lower chambers contract, sending blood to its respective destinations.

Blood enters the right atrium through the superior vena cava, a large vessel that brings blood from all over the body, and a smaller vessel called the coronary sinus, which brings blood back to the heart from the heart muscle itself. The blood that enters the right atrium is filled with carbon dioxide, having already exchanged its oxygen for carbon dioxide with cells throughout the body.

After the blood enters the right ventricle, it is pumped to the lungs via the pulmonary artery. Once in the lungs, the blood surrenders its carbon dioxide load and receives a new infusion of oxygen. We breathe out that carbon dioxide and inhale more oxygen.

Thanks to the heart's relentless beat—which forces blood to

move continuously through the body—the blood passes out of the lungs and onward to the left side of the heart, where it enters the left atrium during expansion phase (diastole), and the left ventricle during atrial systole.

From here, it is pumped into the aorta, the main highway for oxygenated blood leaving the heart. Now it is on its way to your cells.

Pumping blood through the lungs is easier than pumping it through the body's general circulation because there is more resistance in the circulatory system than there is through the lungs. Consequently, the left side of the heart is stronger and more heavily muscled than the right.

Despite the fact that the left and right sides of the heart have distinctly different tasks—one requiring greater effort than the other—the two must work in complete coordination, filling and contracting simultaneously, otherwise there would be chaos and death.

The beating of the heart is life itself. How it manages this miraculous feat is only partly understood. As far as science can ascertain, there are four main factors responsible for the heart beat: the first is the heart's unique cells which, by design, contract and expand; the second is electrical stimulation; the third is the body's nervous system; and the fourth is chemical or hormonal. Other factors, such as body heat, play a role, but these four are the primary influences.

The nature of the cardiac muscle is to expand and contract, and it is inherent in its smallest part, the cells themselves. This is true in humans and in many animals: if you remove the heart of a frog or a turtle and keep it in a saline solution, it will continue to beat, despite the fact that it is no longer connected to the body. In a human fetus, the heart begins to contract and expand before it is connected to the nervous system. Even heart cells, when grown in test-tube cultures, will carry on their own primordial dance, contracting and expanding rhythmically to a music only they can hear.

Indeed, the heart is the ultimate dancer. Unlike other muscles within the body—which can go into sustained contraction, causing cramps or spasms—the heart muscle does not go out of rhythm, unless it is changed by electric shock, trauma, or lack of oxygen.

The heart is an electrical pump, or as we said earlier, two electrical pumps working together. Electrical impulses are conducted by a series of muscle fibers. These impulses are initiated by the Sinoatrial node (SA), which sits above the right atrium, near the entrance of the superior vena cava. The SA node, which is also called the pacemaker, fires a charge that flows through the atria and down to the septum. There, another node, called the Atrioventrical node (AV), fires a second charge, which passes through a bundle of fibers (called the bundle of His) that branch through the two ventricles, thus causing them to contract.

The impulses occur with precise timing. The SA node causes the atria to contract, thus sending blood to the ventricles. At the moment the atria contract, the ventricles must be relaxed and open to receive the blood. Thus, there must be a time lapse between the firing of the SA node and the AV node, to allow ventricles to pause and remain open. Once the ventricles are filled, the AV node sends an impulse to the ventricles to contract and expel blood.

Heart rate is also controlled by a part of the nervous system called the cardiac center, located in the lower part of the brain (called the medulla oblongata). For the most part, heart rate is automatic, as described above, but nerve impulses will decrease or increase the heart rate, depending on whether we are resting or in a state of excitation.

When resting, the cardiac center will send a signal over the vagus nerve to inhibit the heart beat, thus slowing it down. When we are about to exercise, and then during exercise, the cardiac center will prevent vagus-inhibition, and instead signal acceleration of the heart beat. This occurs because muscles throughout the body need more blood and oxygen to function during exercise.

The nervous system also will increase heart rate when we are afraid (the so-called flight or fight reaction), angry, sexually aroused, or experiencing some other highly charged emotional state.

The final method of controlling heart beat is hormonal or chemical. When emotionally or physically excited, the adrenal glands will pump out norepinephrine and epinephrine, increasing heart speed; the thyroid will secrete thyroxine, which speeds metabolism and heart rate; and the nervous system will release norepinephrine. When the state of excitement has passed, the cardiac center stimulates the vagus nerve to slow down the heart rate. The nervous system will secrete acetylcholine, which inhibits the speed of the beat.

EMOTIONS AND THE HEART

One of the great ironies of heart research is that modern science is proving just how closely connected the emotions are to the health and function of the heart. An emerging science, called psycho-neuroimmunology, demonstrates that emotional states dramatically change heart rate and function, the health of our arteries, and our immune response.

The heart is the root of life.

THE YELLOW EMPEROR

Science is proving that the Biblical axiom, "A merry heart doeth good like a medicine," is more than folk wisdom. Laughter and joy are among the most powerful means of preventing heart attacks and other serious illnesses. The heart is particularly susceptible to stress and depression. Stress elevates cholesterol level, which causes atherosclerosis, a disease in which cholesterol plaque builds within the arteries—especially the coronary arteries—and blocks blood flow to the heart. Stress also changes hormonal balance, increasing norepinephrine and other hormones that increase heart rate, causing the heart muscle to require greater amounts of oxygen. By increasing cholesterol plaque, which blocks blood flow and oxygen to the heart, and creating greater demands for oxygen, stress can lead to heart attack. In short, our emotions affect our hearts directly and dramatically.

But the reverse is also true. Studies have shown that people who undergo coronary bypass surgery experience a marked decline in memory, ability to reason, and emotional life. Depression and mood changes are common among those who undergo bypass surgery, even more than a year after the surgery has been performed, according to a team of European and American scientists led by Dr. Allan Willner, of Jewish Medical Center at Long Island, New York. Scientists are baffled by this phenomenon, but theorize that perhaps some changes in brain chemistry take place during or after heart surgery.

When we consider the heart's remarkable ability to react to differing degrees of stress; the fact that the left and right sides of the heart must perform entirely different chores, requiring different degrees of torque behind the blood; and that the whole job is performed over a lifetime, we can only marvel at this organ.

Heartaches and Pain

There are a variety of illnesses that afflict the heart, but most of them manifest in a relatively small number of people. Among the less common forms of heart disease are the following:

- Birth defect, in which a structural abnormality occurs during gestation; this is usually dealt with by surgery.
- Endocarditis, or infection of the heart, afflicting some drug addicts and a minority of those who have had rheumatic fever.
- Cardiomyopathy, in which the heart muscle becomes increasingly weak, due to infection, alcohol abuse, chemical toxicity, autoimmune disorders, or a deficiency of minerals and vitamins, especially B1.
- Alcohol abuse, which can cause the heart muscle to swell and result in heart failure.
- Obesity, which can give rise to a number of heart-related illnesses, including high blood pressure, diabetes, and atherosclerosis.

Most of these are treated by removing the toxic agent, such as alcohol or chemical poisons, or by antibiotics.

Serious as these illnesses are, they are not the most common form of heart disease. That distinction is reserved for one illness above all the rest: atherosclerosis. Approximately 60 million Americans suffer from cardiovascular disease, or illnesses of the heart and arteries. These illnesses include heart attack, stroke, and high blood pressure. The underlying cause of most cardiovascular disease is atherosclerosis, a disease in which cholesterol plaque clogs the arteries leading to the heart and other organs. If the plaque becomes large enough, it can prevent adequate amounts of blood and oxygen from getting to tissues, including the heart and brain, and thereby cause a heart attack or stroke, either of which can be fatal.

Atherosclerosis is responsible for approximately 800,000 deaths per year in the U.S., and is the leading cause of death in the Western world. Bypass surgery is among the most common surgical procedures performed in the United States. More than 350,000 heart bypasses are conducted each year.

Cholesterol is a waxy substance, classified as a lipid, which is used by the body to make hormones and various cell components.

It is also a constituent of bile. All cells make cholesterol, but the liver produces most of it. The body makes cholesterol from fat and/or cholesterol that comes from your diet.

We often hear about two kinds of cholesterol: LDL, for low-density lipoprotein; and HDL, for high-density lipoprotein. Actually, LDL and HDL are not cholesterol, but proteins that carry cholesterol to different places in the body. LDL brings cholesterol to the walls of arteries, where it forms cholesterol plaque. This plaque resembles a boil growing inside the blood vessel. It is often capped by a hard, fibrous surface. Eventually, the boil can become so large as to block the flow of blood to organs, such as the heart or brain. When part of the heart does not receive adequate blood and oxygen, it suffocates and dies, an event typically referred to as a heart attack. When a part of the brain is deprived of oxygen, brain tissue dies, causing a stroke.

HDL brings cholesterol into the large intestines and out of the body. Consequently, HDL is often referred to as "good cholesterol," because it reduces the amount of cholesterol in your body.

Atherosclerosis is a leading cause of high blood pressure, or hypertension, as well. As plaque builds within the walls of blood vessels, the passageway for blood is narrowed, thus causing pressure to build within the circulatory system. Also, cholesterol plaque accumulates inside the kidneys, specifically in the glomeruli and tubules, causing blood flow within the kidneys to be reduced. This causes more pressure to build within the circulation. High blood pressure is a leading risk factor in heart attack and stroke.

Atherosclerosis in the coronary arteries of the heart is also the most common cause of angina pectoris and arrythmia, or irregular heartbeat. Angina is the characteristic pain that usually appears in the center of the chest and sometimes streaks down the left arm. It is caused when insufficient oxygen gets to the heart. Cool evenings, cold weather, or excessive demands placed upon the heart, such as too much exercise or stress, cause the heart to beat more rapidly. This increases the heart's need for oxygen. Since the coronary arteries are blocked from atherosclerosis, the oxygen demand cannot be met, resulting in pain. If the demand continues to increase, the person can suffer a heart attack.

Arrythmia is caused when the electrical system of the heart is disturbed. Cholesterol plaque inside the coronary arteries prevents adequate oxygen from getting to parts of the heart. This can damage conductive fibers within the heart muscle, thus preventing the electrical impulses from spreading evenly throughout the heart, which causes an irregular heartbeat.

The amount of cholesterol found in the blood is measured in milligrams per deciliter of blood, or as mg/dl. The average American's blood cholesterol level is approximately 220 mg/dl. Numerous scientific studies have shown that cholesterol levels above 160 mg/dl. are atherogenic, meaning that they are causing atherosclerosis in the body's major arteries, including the heart and brain. A cholesterol level below 160 mg/dl. causes the elimination or discharge of plaque from the arteries, and the reversal of atherosclerosis.

The U.S. Surgeon General has repeatedly advised Americans to reduce the level of fat and cholesterol in their diets to prevent the most common forms of cardiovascular disease.

BUILDING THE HEART MUSCLE

People with coronary heart disease should not engage in competitive sports. Competition causes us to forget our limits and increases the likelihood of overstressing the heart. The best exercise for people with heart disease is walking. Walk for twenty minutes at a mild pace, increasing the pace as your stamina increases. Rest and then continue. Do not get too far from home or from public places. Work your way up to a brisk pace over time. Walking is the safest of all exercises and can be done by everyone (except those suffering from physical handicap). For those whose hearts are in better shape, bicycle riding, tennis, or some other sports pursuit can be enjoyed. People should see their doctors before engaging in any regular exercise program.

Exercise raises HDL cholesterol, thus lowering blood cholesterol. It also stimulates the body to grow new blood vessels, which increases blood flow throughout the body, especially to the heart.

THE FIERY HEART

According to traditional Chinese medicine, the heart is joined with the small intestine to form the Fire Element. It is associated

[Although there are] vague descriptions of chest pains in the medical literature of the ancient Egyptians and Greeks [it was not until 1912 that] a classification of coronary obstructions was published in the United States . . . A condition that only the most erudite specialists could have identified as recently as 1930 is so common now that it can be diagnosed by the average person.

JEAN MAYER

with the summer months—June 21 to mid-August—and the hours of 11 A.M. to 1 P.M. During these months and hours the heart receives its optimal amounts of qi. These are also the periods in which underlying problems associated with the heart tend to surface. Fatigue at midday suggests heart trouble, according to Chinese medicine. And many people suffer heart attacks during the summer months.

Too much heat in summer injures the heart, just as too much cold in winter injures the kidneys and bladder. Moderate warmth of summer is healing.

Naturally, the heart is associated with the arteries, blood vessels, blood, and the pulse. The pulse is among the important tools of diagnosis used in Chinese medicine. (See chapter on Chinese medicine.)

The heart pumps blood throughout the body. In this way, it brings what is essential to every part of the body. It accomplishes this service through its capacity to expand and contract. The heart is, therefore, the clearest expression of yin and yang in the body. The heart functions, say the Chinese, because it follows the Tao. It is in harmony with yin and yang and therefore everything within the body—the microcosmic universe—receives what is needed and is enriched.

In the Five Element system, the heart is controlled by the kidneys (Fire controls Water). This is easily understood by the fact that if blood flows smoothly through the kidneys, blood pressure is normal and balanced. Healthy kidneys serve as a mild form of resistance to the flow of the blood, causing appropriate blood pressure to exist throughout the system.

But if the kidneys are too contracted, blood pressure increases and the heart is unduly stressed. As blood pressure increases, so, too, does resistance within the circulation, causing ever-increasing stress upon the heart. As any physician will tell you, hypertension is a leading risk factor in heart attack and stroke. Since salt is a kidney contractor in Chinese medicine, its intake must be closely monitored. Salt should be used minimally in cooking and never used as a condiment on foods. Processed foods that contain salt should be avoided.

Conversely, if the kidney energy is weak or expanded, there will be low blood pressure and thus the heart will have to work

*As to diseases, make a habit of
two things: to help or at least
to do no harm.*

HIPPOCRATES

harder to pump blood. Low blood pressure—though not as severe a problem as high—can be unhealthy, as well.

The heart is also associated with the sweat, especially the kind of sweat created by nervous tension. Sweaty palms, for example, are a symptom of an overworked and excited heart.

The heart controls the tongue and speech. All speech problems, such as stuttering or poor enunciation, are heart related. Stuttering is said to be caused by weak heart qi, perhaps caused by excessive kidney qi. The kidneys may be overactive from too much salt and liquids; this can cause the kidneys to restrict heart energy and thus prevent adequate life force from flowing from the heart to the tongue. Without an adequate supply of heart qi, the tongue is hesitant, redundant, and has trouble shaping words.

Murmurs, palpitations, excessively high or low blood pressure will all affect the way a person speaks. The Chinese treat speech problems by balancing and harmonizing heart energy.

The tongue is also one of the most direct ways of diagnosing the heart. If the tongue is deeply red to purple, heart qi is excessive; the heart is overworked and struggling for greater amounts of oxygen. There is probably suffering from atherosclerosis. Such a person will be driven, overly aggressive, and prone to violent outbursts of temper. If the tongue is pale or whitish pink, heart qi is deficient. The heart is weak and lethargic. The person may be suffering from anemia. (A coated or whitish tongue indicates digestive problems, especially stagnation throughout the intestinal tract. The body is attempting to eliminate waste in any way it can, including through the mouth, as indicated by the excess coating on the tongue.)

The grains that provide the greatest qi to the heart are corn and millet. The tastes that nourish the heart most are bitter and slightly burnt tastes.

The heart is associated with joy. Interestingly, joy is not considered an emotion so much as a state of inner tranquility. For the Chinese, joy rises from within when we do what we love. At that moment, we are attuned to our essential nature, our true inner being. Joy is, therefore, a kind of compass, a guide, to the nature of the soul.

From this state comes such well-known phrases as "follow your heart" and "follow your bliss," the latter made familiar by mythologist Joseph Campbell to describe the true path of the soul.

When heart qi is excessive, the emotional reaction tends to be hysteria. The heart and the breath are the most obvious rhythms of our bodies. Both are largely involuntary (though the breath easily comes under voluntary control), and both are a reflection of our current state of being. A person with an easily excited heart tends to react emotionally to changes in his or her environment. He or she quickly loses perspective, seeing life as extremes of success and crisis.

The heart is associated with laughter in Chinese medicine. Laughter lightens the heart, and also heals it, just as singing is said to be therapeutic to the spleen.

The color associated with the heart is red. An excessively red complexion, especially when capillaries are visible at the surface of the skin, indicates a swollen and overworked heart. Red-colored clothing—a red tie, for example, or a red dress—can stimulate heart energy and all its associated characteristics in one's life. It connotes passion, initiative, leadership, aggression.

The Yellow Emperor states that the heart controls the spirit, the part of us that fights for what we believe in. In both East and West, the heart has long been associated with courage. "He showed real heart" or "She has the heart of a lion" are common phrases used to describe people who persevere in the face of great adversity. "Weak-hearted" or "the faint of heart" suggests a weak spirit or a fearful person.

Using the Five Elements again, we can see that joy is restricted or limited by fear, the emotion associated with the Water Element. The more we are ruled by fear, the less chance we have of following our true inner natures. So, fear keeps us from experiencing joy.

Fear or stress (another word for fear) causes heart disease. Fear changes heart rate and respiration, elevates cholesterol level, and creates hormonal imbalances. Fear can destroy the heart. For those with heart disease, it is essential to limit stress or fear, either by removing oneself from stressful situations, or acting more courageously, or both. At the same time, more emphasis should be placed upon doing what one truly enjoys. By encouraging joy, laughter, and spontaneity—all of which are the opposites of fear—we encourage heart qi and thus strengthen the heart. The heart is associated with beginning a great adventure—"taking heart"—and setting out on our journey.

So, it is important to begin things that we have been postponing for one reason or another. Begin, initiate, show courage—these are the characteristics of a strong and healthy heart.

Avoid foods rich in fat and cholesterol, especially red meat, whole dairy products, eggs, and poultry. Also, consumption of oils should be reduced, especially oils that are composed of saturated fats, such as palm kernel, coconut, and peanut oils.

It is also important to limit or avoid alcohol, which weakens the heart muscle.

Foods such as coffee, chocolate, colas (which contain caffeine), hard liquors, beer, and wine all stimulate the heart. Continuous use of the more extreme of these foods, such as liquors, coffee, chocolate, and wine, tend to have a weakening effect on the heart in the long run, however. This, say the Chinese, conforms with the law of yin and yang. Those things that excite and overly stimulate the organ (or the entire body) leave it exhausted in the end. Moderation is the key.

The following foods are used in Chinese medicine to strengthen the heart.

- *Grain:* corn, including whole corn and corn on the cob; glutinous millet; amaranth.
- *Vegetables:* asparagus, brussels sprouts, chives, dandelion, endive, scallions.
- *Beans:* azuki, red lentils, mung beans.
- *Fruit:* apricot, raspberry, persimmon, strawberry, watermelon.
- *Fish:* shrimp, in small to moderate amounts.
- *Herbs:* In general, herbs and spices should be mild. All fiery herbs overly stimulate the heart and thus tax the organ. Herbs that are beneficial to the heart include cinnamon (warms and improves circulation), cloves (warming), coriander, ginger (usually used for intestines, but also improves circulation), daikon radish cut up and steamed or boiled (said to break up fat deposits throughout the body and improve circulation).

To improve the health of the heart, exercise is also recommended. Walking, tai chi chuan, and dance are among the best exercises because they are mild, aerobic, and do not overly tax the heart.

Other foods that heal the heart are any whole grains that contain water-soluble fiber that binds with cholesterol and eliminates it from the body. Although oat bran has received the most publicity, the fibrous grain that is most effective at reducing cholesterol is brown rice.

Fiber also improves bowel function, which is the body's most efficient means of eliminating cholesterol. (Up to 100 milligrams of dietary cholesterol can be eliminated through the feces in a single bowel movement. This will prevent a great deal of cholesterol from getting into the blood.)

Use small to moderate amounts of polyunsaturated oils, such as sesame, corn, and safflower oil. Also use olive oil, which is a monounsaturated oil, but is highly effective at lowering cholesterol.

Excessive use of polyunsaturated oils has been linked to cancer. Therefore, moderation in the use of all oil is recommended.

Salmon, cod, haddock, scrod, and other cold-water fish contain omega 3 polyunsaturated oils, which studies show reduce blood cholesterol level.

Vitamin E is an antioxidant, meaning that it prevents tissue decay from fatty acids turning rancid within the body. Vitamin E is available in whole grains, leafy green vegetables, and sea foods.

Limit red meat, dairy foods, eggs, the skin of poultry (which is higher in fat), coconuts, avocado, and olives, all of which contain high levels of fat.

Reduce blood cholesterol level to below 160 mg/dl, which will gradually eliminate cholesterol plaque from arteries and tissues throughout the body.

According to Ayurvedic healers, the heart is most influenced by the vata dosha, or the force of kinetic energy. Foods that balance the vata dosha include the following:

- *Grains:* Rice, wheat, oats.
- *Vegetables:* All cooked vegetables, especially asparagus, beets, carrots, cucumber, onion, okra, garlic, potato, zucchini.
- *Beans:* Mung beans, tofu, black and red lentils.
- *Fruit:* Apricots, berries, cherries, figs, grapefruit, oranges, plums.
- *Tastes:* Pungent increases vata and pitta; is warming, light, and dry. Bitter increases vata, tones, and increases appetite.

Science continues to search for ways of improving the health of the heart through drugs and surgery, but the best medicine remains food, herbs, exercise, and joy. Therefore, have a good meal and put a smile on your face. It may be the best first step to a healthy heart.

Herbs for the heart:

BLACK COHOSH: For angina.

CACTUS: For angina with irregular heartbeats.

ALFALFA: Lowers cholesterol.

HAWTHORNE BERRIES: For cardiac problems, high blood pressure.

CHAPTER 15

THE LUNGS

"OH, EAST IS EAST, and West is West, and never the twain shall meet," said Kipling. But lately the "twain" has been inching closer and closer. Sometimes, there are even magical moments of understanding that seem to unify the two worldviews, like a bridge suddenly thrown across the chasm. A journey into the world of the lungs offers a glimpse of this unifying perspective.

Many of us think of the lungs as balloons of air. We know that the body needs oxygen, but how many of us realize why we need it? The short answer is energy. Oxygen is essential in the process by which blood sugar is burned as fuel. Without oxygen, cells are deprived of energy and consequently die.

In the West, we think of food as energy, not oxygen. But food would be useless as a fuel without oxygen. It would be inert. Oxygen brings it to life; it makes the fuels that are derived from food reactive and life-sustaining (see respiration, below). In short, both food and oxygen are essential in the process by which energy is created.

Our need to get food has defined the American highway. But in fact, we need more oxygen than we do food, and we need it a

If we cultivate the habit of keeping the air pure and of breathing only fresh air, we can save ourselves from many a terrible disease.

MAHATMA GANDHI

Most of the muscles of the respiratory system are connected to the cervical and lumbar vertebrae and breathing therefore affects the stability and posture of the spine, while conversely the position of the spine will affect the quality and speed of breathing. Good breathing therefore also means good posture, just as good posture means good breathing.

MOSHE FELDENKRAIS

whole lot faster. People have fasted for up to sixty days and lived to tell about it. But if you suddenly hold your breath, your body will demand that you resume breathing in less than sixty seconds. The brain can last about four minutes without oxygen before it is damaged, but it can last as many as fifteen minutes without glucose, or blood sugar, before damage occurs. Without oxygen, cells die and organs stop.

On the hierarchy of needs, oxygen is first. The reason is simple: Oxygen is energy, and energy is life.

Oriental culture elevated this understanding into a realm in which science and religion become one. In the East, energy is understood in religious terms. In India, it's called prana, or the vital life force. According to Swami Rama, coauthor of the book *Science of Breath* with Drs. Rudolph Ballentine and Alan Hymes, the word *prana* is derived from the syllables *pra,* meaning the first unit, and *na,* meaning energy. Prana is the original cosmic energy that has brought everything else into being.

"All the diverse forms of this universe are sustained by the energy of prana," says Swami Rama. This energy is available to all. And it can be understood and controlled for human development. "One who has learned to control prana has learned to control all the energies of this universe—physical and mental," writes Swami Rama. "He has also learned to control his body and his mind."

Swami Rama was the first Indian Yogi to demonstrate under scientific conditions the ability to control various involuntary functions, including stopping his heart and emitting various brain waves at will. Many of these experiments were conducted at the Menninger Foundation in Topeka, Kansas. Swami Rama, who is the recipient of the Martin Buber award for service to humanity, has been among the most influential figures to demonstrate the authenticity of yoga to Western science.

According to the yogic tradition, the breath is the vehicle of prana. Prana enters the body when we inhale. How we breathe—whether it is shallow or deep, hurried or slow—controls how prana affects the body, that is, how it influences the body and mind. Indian yogis have long taught that to control the breath means to control the universal energy within, which is to say, to control the physical health and state of mind.

Studies have shown that people who breathe in a shallow and hurried way tend to be nervous and emotional, while those who

166

The Lungs

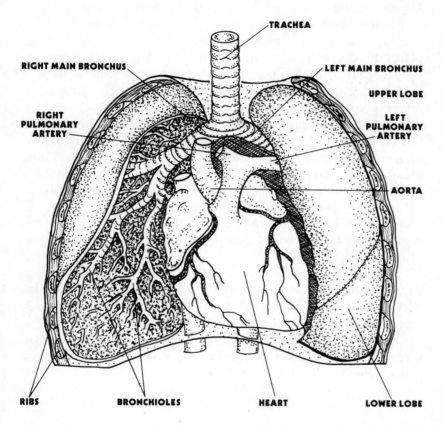

TRACHEA

RIGHT MAIN BRONCHUS

LEFT MAIN BRONCHUS

UPPER LOBE

RIGHT PULMONARY ARTERY

LEFT PULMONARY ARTERY

AORTA

RIBS

BRONCHIOLES

HEART

LOWER LOBE

The body's main organs of respiration, the lungs work closely with the heart and blood to take in energy in the form of oxygen and eliminate waste in the form of carbon dioxide.

breathe rhythmically and deeply—into the abdomen—tend to be more emotionally balanced, centered, and less affected by changes in their environment.

"All breathing exercises—advanced or basic—enable the student to control his mind through understanding prana," says Swami Rama.

One of the unique properties of breathing is that it is both an involuntary and a voluntary action. Breathing is normally controlled by the respiratory center of the brain, but it is brought under voluntary control at will. According to yogic tradition, the breath is a gateway to the deeper physical and psychological recesses of our being. The reason it has such powers of influence is

167

because the nervous system works in both directions: If you are breathing unconsciously, the state of your mind will control your breathing, which will serve to reinforce your current attitudes and belief system. But if you begin to control your breath by making it deeper and more rhythmic, the opposite effect takes place: this deeper rhythm and greater abundance of life force re-shapes your attitudes and strengthens your health. Thus, the breath is a gateway to the involuntary systems and the deeper recesses of your nature.

But this is just the beginning. Yogic breathing techniques are not only designed to influence various parts of the body, but to awaken levels of consciousness, to illuminate the soul. Thus, breath is regarded as more than a gateway to the inner being; it is a door to the divine within each of us. In the East, the science of breath is ultimately a religious path. "The human body is sustained by the same prana that sustains the universe," said Swami Rama. It is entering each of us between ten and fourteen times per minute.

To a Westerner who breaths an average of 20,000 times per day, perhaps without considering a single breath, such speculation about oxygen, life energy, and the divine must surely represent final proof that "never the twain shall meet."

But at this very moment, deep within each of us, trillions of tiny cells are embracing an equal number of tiny atoms of oxygen, each one bearing the gift of life.

THE PATH OF AIR

The lungs are the main organs of respiration. They supply the body with oxygen, which is essential for energy. The lungs also eliminate carbon dioxide waste. There are two lungs, one on each side of the thorax; together they weigh about two and a half pounds and stretch from the bottom rib to just below the collar bone. In childhood, they are pink, but for most adults they become gray. In men and women who smoke or are exposed to highly polluted air, the lungs often turn black.

Each lung is surrounded by a protective, double-membraned sack called a pleura. It allows the lungs to expand and contract inside the chest wall.

The respiratory system begins in the mouth and nose, where

we take in and exhale air. From there, it travels down the trachea, or windpipe, a long tube that divides into two smaller tubes, called bronchi, which enter the lungs. Once inside the lungs, the bronchi further divide into many smaller branches called bronchiolies, which lead to tiny grapelike air sacs called alveoli.

Most of the air we breathe is nitrogen (about 78 percent); the rest is oxygen (21 percent), with minute quantities of carbon dioxide (CO_2), trace gases, and water vapor. Once the air is inside the alveoli, the oxygen separates from the other gases and diffuses along the walls of these tiny sacs. There it seeps through the alveoli and into surrounding capillaries, and makes its way into the bloodstream. At the same time, the carbon dioxide inside the blood seeps into the alveoli, from which it is breathed out when we exhale.

Once oxygen is inside the blood, it binds with hemoglobin, the iron-rich part of the red blood cell. The blood is then pumped to the left side of the heart, and then on to tissues throughout the body.

Each quantity of oxygen-rich blood eventually reaches a part of the body where it surrenders its load of O_2 and receives the carbon dioxide waste from the cells. Onward it flows, back to the right side of the heart, which pumps the carbon-dioxide–rich blood into the lungs and down into the tiny alveoli.

There the CO_2 seeps past the walls of the capillaries and into the tiny alveoli, which expel the CO_2 when we exhale. In exchange for the CO_2, the blood receives oxygen.

The act of breathing requires a well-coordinated effort among the muscles of the rib cage and the diaphragm, a dome-shaped muscle system located between the thorax and the abdomen. The diaphragm pulls downward, while muscles within the rib cage expand. This causes the lungs themselves to expand and open. During relaxed breathing, the downward movement of the diaphragm is about two-thirds of an inch, which only minimally opens the lungs. But during deep breathing the diaphragm will descend as much as three inches.

Our experience of breathing is actually an illusion. It seems as if we are drawing or sucking air inside us, but in fact the air is being forced into us. It works like this: The lungs are in contact with the air outside the body through the nose, mouth, trachea, and bronchial tubes. As long as the pressure inside the lungs is

He lives most life whoever breathes most air.

ELIZABETH BARRETT BROWNING

169

According to natural medical philosophers, breath is not the lungs as such or the air moved by them but a divine emana-tion of potentiality, carrying the essence of every human faculty at its beginning and making it manifest in the various physical organs as it circulates through the body.

HAKIM G. M. CHISHTI

equal to that outside, there will be no movement of air between the lungs and the outer atmosphere. The balance is analogous to putting your palms together and maintaining equal pressure in both arms; the hands will remain stationary.

By expanding our lungs, we have caused the air molecules already inside the lungs to be spread out over a larger area. This causes the relative pressure within the lungs to drop.

Outside the body, molecules of air are packed together much more densely than they are now inside the lungs. So, the relative air pressure is greater outside the lungs than inside, which causes the high-pressure air to rush through the nose (or mouth) and down into the low-pressure zone of the lungs.

To go back to the metaphor of the two hands pressed against each other, the act of expanding the lungs is like reducing the pressure in one hand; the other hand suddenly advances.

When we breathe out, the reverse takes place: the diaphragm pushes upward and the rib cage collapses, thus applying pressure to the lungs that forces air outside of us.

The amount of air breathed into the lungs depends upon the oxygen demands of the body. During relaxation, an adult breathes in about ten to fourteen times per minute. Each breath takes about four to six seconds and draws into the lungs about nine to twelve pints of air per minute. During exercise, that same adult breathes at a rate of about one breath per minute, and takes in about twenty gallons of air per minute. An adult breathes in about 3,300 gallons of air per day, on the average.

The brain will signal changes in respiration due to a variety of conditions, including the following:

- Higher concentrations of carbon dioxide in the blood will increase the rate of our breathing. Conversely, lower concentrations of oxygen, such as when traveling at higher altitudes, will cause an increase in the rate of breathing.
- Higher body temperatures, such as fever, increase the respiration rate; lower temperatures reduce it. High blood pressure reduces the rate of breathing, while lower blood pressure increases it.
- Exercise increases the rate of breathing to meet the body's demands for oxygen, while resting and sleeping causes a reduction in the rate of breathing.

At any moment, we can voluntarily control our breathing, causing it to become deeper or shallow. However, if our oxygen demands do not go up, and we force more oxygen into the body (a condition typically called hyperventilation), the brain will usually compensate for the additional oxygen by slowing the breath or stopping it for a period of forty to sixty seconds in order to re-establish the oxygen and carbon dioxide balance in the bloodstream.

We tend to think of respiration as limited to breathing in and out, but the act of respiration includes the burning of fuel, which is the reason we breathe at all. Once the oxygen reaches the cells, it is combined with blood sugar, or glucose, to cause tiny combustion reactions within the cells. These reactions cause the release of energy which the cells use to maintain life. We might reasonably ask ourselves why we don't burn up in this combustion process, or why we don't breathe out smoke. The reason, in a nutshell, is that our internal combustion is slow and small.

According to Alan Hymes, M.D., coauthor of *Science of Breath*, "All living organisms can be thought of as meeting their energy needs from a slow-burning furnace. This furnace releases energy from a constant supply of fuel by slowly combining it with oxygen."

Hymes points out that in rapidly burning systems, intense heat and light are released, along with carbon dioxide and water vapor. The amount of light and heat released during combustion depends upon the speed with which the fuel is burned. A fire burns fuel at a rate fast enough to emit a visible light and palpable heat; an explosion consumes fuel at an even faster rate, and thus emits even greater amounts of light and heat.

However, if the burning of fuel occurs at a very slow rate, there may be no visible light at all, says Hynes. "Biological systems (i.e., all living organisms) are essentially burning fuel at a very slow rate."

Through a very complex chain reaction, this combination of blood sugar and oxygen oxidizes within a particular part of the cell, called the mitochondria. From there, the energy is stored in a molecule called adenosine triphosphate, or ATP, which is found in living systems throughout nature. When energy is needed, ATP has the capacity to provide it to the cell.

As with other forms of combustion, carbon dioxide and heat

are given off. This heat contributes to a normal body temperature of 98.6 degrees Fahrenheit. The carbon dioxide is released into the blood in exchange for oxygen.

This brings us to why we breathe: energy. The lungs and the digestive tract (which provide carbohydrates) provide the body with the raw materials of combustion, which produces energy. With that energy, the cells can do their work, which is to keep the body alive.

ILLNESSES OF THE LUNGS

Asthma may occur when the muscles wrapping the bronchial tubes contract, or when the membranes that line the tubes' interior expand, or when excess mucus is secreted by the mucous glands inside the bronchial walls. These actions prevent air from passing freely to and from the lungs. Asthma is often brought on by an allergic reaction to pollens, fungus, animal dander, and other substances. Standard medical treatment usually includes the use of such drugs as epinephrine, ephedrine, and atropine, which cause the autonomic nervous system to relax the muscles within the bronchial tubes, allowing the air passages to open. Like all drugs, these pharmaceuticals have side effects.

Infections of the lungs include:

- *Bronchitis:* swelling of the bronchial tubes caused by infectious organisms (bacteria), or chemical agents.
- *Croup:* Usually found in children, croup is caused by infectious organisms. Antibiotics are usually administered as treatment.
- *Pneumonia:* inflammation of the lungs, including the bronchial tubes, bronchiolies, and alveoli. Numerous agents can cause the infection, including bacteria, viruses, and fungi. Treatment includes antibiotics.

Lung cancer causes more deaths among men in the U.S. than any other killer disease. It is the second leading cause of death among women, topped only by breast cancer. The principal cause is cigarette smoking. Remarkably, the number of people afflicted with lung cancer continues to increase, despite the fact that, overall, fewer people smoke cigarettes today than a decade ago. Passive or secondary smoking, that is, breathing the fumes from someone else's cigarette, has been shown to cause lung cancers as well. Other causes include highly polluted air, especially air filled with car exhaust fumes.

Emphysema results when the walls of the alveoli begin to break down, thus reducing the area in which oxygen can be passed to the blood. Those with emphysema always seem to be struggling for breath because more breaths are needed to fulfill the body's oxygen requirements. Emphysema can be caused by chronic asthma, bronchitis, or cigarette smoking.

BREATHING IN THE LIFE FORCE

The lungs and the large intestine form the Metal Element in the Five Element Theory. They are associated with the fall, when the seasons provide the lungs with their maximum quantity of energy or life force. It is during the period from late September to December 21 that the lungs can be healed of many problems— or conversely, manifest disease, particularly if they have been abused in the past. During the day, the lungs receive their optimal amounts of qi between the hours of 3 A.M. and 5 A.M. Insomnia during these hours tends to be a symptom of lung imbalances.

As in all of Oriental medicine, the lungs are considered the recipients of the life force, or qi. The rhythm and depth of a person's breathing shapes the qi; the breathing gives the qi definition and behavior which in turn influences the body. If the breath is nervous, shallow and rapid, that same quality of energy will move like an erratic electrical current through the entire body. The personality, shaped by that person's own physical vibration, will be shallow, nervous, and weak. He or she will feel a greater sense of personal frailty, insecurity, and weakness.

On the other hand, if the breath is deep, rhythmic, and strong, the quality of the qi will have the same depth and vitality when it moves through the system. Consequently, a person's life will be rich, deep, and orderly. That person will experience a greater sense of personal security and calm.

In the Five Element schematic, the lungs pass qi onto the kidneys and bladder; control the qi in the liver; and receive qi from the spleen and stomach. They are controlled themselves by the heart and small intestine. While all of these relationships are important in healing, the relationship between the heart and lungs is key.

The heart is regarded as the Fire Element. A balanced heart is associated with joy, while an imbalanced Fire Element is associated with hysteria. The Chinese maintain that if the heart becomes imbalanced, the Fire Element will control the Metal Element excessively. Whenever our emotions go out of control, such as during hysterical moments, the lungs react with wild and irregular breathing. The heart can be seen as controlling the lungs. The lungs therefore take in qi and send it through the body in wild and chaotic waves. In this way, the heart's imbalance influences every system within the body by controlling the lungs and the qi energy they take in.

The system that is immediately affected is the kidneys. The imbalanced and erratic qi passed from the lungs to the kidneys, or Water Element, will inspire fear and a loss of will. Consequently, the Oriental teachers counseled that the way to control the mind and heart (or emotional nature) was to maintain control of the breath in all situations. When highly emotional, angry, or afraid, breathe deeply and rhythmically. The breath acts as a tether on the emotional and psychological realm, say the sages, much as a leash controls an animal.

The kidneys are responsible for drawing the breath deeply into the body. Weak kidneys are associated with chronic stress, nervousness, and shallow breathing. Strengthening the kidneys will deepen the breath and improve the lungs.

The lungs and large intestine are associated with the emotions of sadness and grief. People who hold on to sadness and grief often suffer from lung imbalances. This holding on will weaken lung energy. Conversely, weak lungs will have a tendency to maintain a condition of sadness and grief. Those who have strong lungs will release the past and maintain a balanced emotional perspective.

The Chinese maintain that the lungs control the animal spirit within humanity. This is illustrated best by the lung's relationship with the liver. The liver, or Wood Element, is the ruler of anger. If anger is allowed to run its course, it will become abusive and violent—in short, animalistic. Grief controls anger. A person grieves a loss of control. If the lungs are strong enough, grief will act in advance to limit a person's anger, and thus act as a governor on the animal nature. If the lungs are weak and the liver excessive, however, the lower nature will dominate and anger will have no limit.

The lungs are associated with mucus, and lung imbalances usually result in increased mucus production. The lungs also nourish the skin and hair; they give it luster and brilliance. You can observe strong lung qi as healthy, pinkish skin, while weak lungs can be seen in pale skin. Caucasians with weak lungs can easily be identified by their excessively pale or white faces, often with drawn and hollow cheeks. Such people often appear to radiate a sense of grief or sadness, as if they were carrying a great emotional burden.

The lung meridian runs from a point on the chest, two inches above the nipple, down the inside of the arm and wrist, over the great muscle of the thumb, to the end of the thumb.

The lungs can be injured by too much cold. Therefore, during winter, the chest must be well protected, say the Chinese.

The Chinese heal the lungs in part by treating the large intestine. Problems affecting the large intestine also will affect the lungs. Mucus increases if the lungs are irritated by the presence of toxins or excessive lung qi. Poisons not eliminated by the intestinal tract will remain in the bloodstream and infiltrate the lungs. Poor elimination or constipation will often manifest in the lungs as chronic mucus discharge. Poor intestinal health also can be a contributing cause of asthma. Whenever lung problems emerge, the Metal Element in general is troubled and both organs must be treated, say the Chinese. (See chapter on the large intestine.)

As described above, the lungs are a dense network of capillaries, which are often smaller than the red blood cells. Red cells pass through the capillaries by bending and folding in half. When you consume high-fat foods, however, microns of fat (called chylomicra) infiltrate the bloodstream and adhere to the red cells, causing them to stick together like rolls of coins. These sticky rolls of cells prevent individual cells from absorbing and carrying oxygen. They also prevent the cells from folding and passing through the tiny capillaries. So less oxygen enters the bloodstream, and the lungs become sites of cholesterol plaque, or atherosclerosis.

We must therefore understand that when we administer medicine, we administer the whole world: that is, all the virtue of heaven and earth, air and water. Because if there is sickness in the body, all the healthy organs must fight against it, not only one, but all. For one sickness can be death to them all.

PARACELSUS

175

Many lung problems quickly clear up when people eliminate dairy foods, eggs, and high-fat meats from their diets.

The spleen and Earth Element provide qi to the Metal Element or lungs. Excess sugar can weaken the spleen and therefore diminish the qi flowing to the lungs. When the lungs are troubled, all refined sugars, spicy and acidic foods should be avoided until the symptoms pass. Sing loudly to strengthen spleen and lungs! (See chapter on the spleen.)

To strengthen the lungs, the grain that has the strongest herbal effect on the lungs is rice. The taste that stimulates lung qi is pungent. In general, leafy green vegetables have a strong healing effect on the lungs.

The following foods and herbs are considered healing to the Metal Element.

- *Grains:* Brown rice and sweet brown rice.
- *Vegetables:* Mustard greens, turnip greens, celery, daikon, carrot, lotus root, onion, turnip, watercress, cabbage, cauliflower, Chinese cabbage, cucumber.
- *Animal foods:* Cod, haddock, scrod, flounder, halibut.
- *Herbs:* ginger, garlic, horseradish, dill, cinnamon, coriander, licorice, fennel, nutmeg, basil, black pepper, bay leaf, and cardamom.
- *Fruit:* pears, tangerines.

As a physical stimulant for the lungs, massage acupuncture point Lung 1. To find acupuncture point Lung 1, move your hand to the clavicle bone on the front of the chest, right where the bone bends forward, directly below the front of the neck. Drop down an inch and find a sensitive point in the muscle tissue, about two inches from the sternum bone in the center of the chest. By pressing this point in a circular manner, you can stimulate lung energy. Lung 1 is used to treat a variety of lung ailments, including colds, coughs, and asthma.

Ayurvedic healers say that the lungs are most influenced by the vata dosha, which is strengthened by eating the following foods and herbs:

- *Grains:* Oats, rice, and wheat.
- *Vegetables:* Cooked green leafy vegetables, asparagus, beets, carrots, cucumber, green beans, okra, onion, radishes.

- *Fruit:* Apricots, avocado, cherries, berries, grapefruit, plums, lemons.
- *Herbs:* Garlic, ginger.

Naturopaths say that chronic lung problems, such as asthma, are associated most often with hypoglycemia, or low blood sugar, and a variety of food allergies. Asthmatics tend to consume excess sweets and dairy products, and often overeat. They are often overweight or have high fat-to-muscle ratios. They may have allergies to milk, wheat, and/or chemical toxins in the home, such as from rugs, paints, or sealants.

Foods to eat include whole grains, a wide variety of vegetables, especially carrots, yellow squash, broccoli, and leafy greens, fruit, especially stewed fruits, and seaweeds, especially kelp. Supplements:

- Liquid chlorophyll, to strengthen lungs and immune system.
- Calcium and magnesium supplements, for immune system.
- Zinc, for immune system.
- B complex, for immune system.
- Vitamin A, for immune system.
- Herbs: garlic tablets, licorice root, coltsfoot.

Herbs for the lungs:

OREGANO and MARJORAM: To promote perspiration and treat colds, flu, and fevers. Can be used in baths and inhalations to clear the lungs and bronchial passages.

REED GRASS: Used for inflammation of lungs with acute symptoms of yellow phlegm, cough, expectoration, gastritis, belching, and vomiting.

EUCALYPTUS: For the treatment of coughs, colds, flu, croup, pneumonia, and asthma. Combine with olive and sesame oil to make an ointment to rub on the chest or make a tea from the leaves and drink it.

CHAPTER 16

THE SKIN

Health is a temporary, dynamic state of balance that has to break down periodically in order to reform as conditions change.

ANDREW WEIL

$\mathcal{P}$ERHAPS THE MOST famous skin problem belonged to Job, whose flesh was covered from head to foot with sores and worms, which was probably universal eczema. Others have been equally afflicted, but anyone who has suffered from acne knows the existential pain behind Job's lament: "My flesh is covered with worms and a crust of dirt; my skin hardens and runs."

While some skin disorders can indeed be life-threatening, most are merely ego-bruising. Even the occasional blemish or outbreak of acne exacts a seemingly disproportionate emotional toll, which is all the proof we need to show how important the skin is in our lives.

THE LARGEST ORGAN

The skin is the body's largest organ, responsible for an array of essential bodily functions, including breathing oxygen; eliminating carbon dioxide and other forms of waste; acting as a shield against toxins from outside the body; and helping to maintain body temperature. The skin is continually repairing and renewing itself. It responds almost instantly to sudden changes in emotions. It is also the body's main organ of sexual attraction, showing shape, texture, and allure.

The skin is composed of two layers: an outer epidermis, and a lower dermis, which includes even deeper tissue that some think of as a third layer. The epidermis, or upper layer, is covered with a thin sheath of dead cells, called the stratum corneum, which are continually being pushed up to the surface from below. If the dead cells are not removed, they can mitigate against the skin's effort to breathe and eliminate waste.

At the surface lies a slightly acidic coating of oil, called the "acid mantle," which can protect the skin against some bacteria. This mantle varies in acidity, though typically it has a pH of about 5. (pH, or potential hydrogen, measures the relative acidity of a substance. On the pH spectrum, 7 is balanced; anything above 7 is alkaline, anything below 7 is acidic.)

Below the epidermis is the dermis, a complex of sweat and oil glands, hair follicles, blood vessels, nerves, and muscle tissue. These are held together by a tough connective tissue called collagen, which runs in strands or fibers. The relative health of your collagen determines the contour of your skin, how wrinkled and lined it is. Healthy collagen is often called "soluble collagen," because it can absorb and hold moisture.

Diagram of the Skin

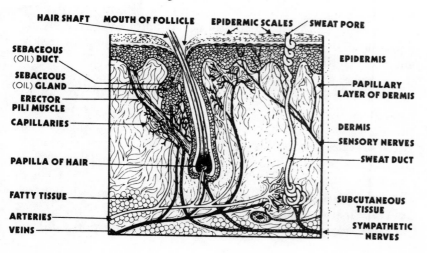

HAIR SHAFT **MOUTH OF FOLLICLE** **EPIDERMIC SCALES** **SWEAT PORE**

SEBACEOUS (OIL) **DUCT**
SEBACEOUS (OIL) **GLAND**
ERECTOR PILI MUSCLE
CAPILLARIES

PAPILLA OF HAIR

FATTY TISSUE
ARTERIES
VEINS

EPIDERMIS

PAPILLARY LAYER OF DERMIS

DERMIS
SENSORY NERVES
SWEAT DUCT

SUBCUTANEOUS TISSUE

SYMPATHETIC NERVES

The body's largest and in some ways most diverse organ, the skin takes in oxygen, eliminates carbon dioxide and other forms of waste, shields the body from toxins, helps to maintain body temperature, manufactures vitamin D, and constantly renews and repairs itself, among various other functions.

179

Below the collagen is a layer of fat and muscle, which also provides some contour and acts as a cushion and an insulating layer.

Aging of the skin occurs when collagen becomes hard and crosslinked with neighboring collagen fibers. This prevents it from holding water and plumping up. Instead, it collapses on itself, binds with other collagen fibers, and forms a kind of fish net below the surface of the skin, which we perceive as wrinkles.

The cause of this crosslinking is a process called oxidation or "free radical formation." What actually happens is the atoms of human tissue begin to decay, or lose electrons. Once an electron is lost, the atom attempts to regain its electrical balance by stealing one or more electrons from neighboring atoms. This stealing creates a chain reaction in which atoms are changing their structures and forming bonds that would not otherwise occur. The net effect is a chaos of crosslinking collagen fibers, revealed on the skin's surface as wrinkles.

Studies have shown that certain nutrients can stop free radical formation. Foods rich in beta carotene (the vegetable source of vitamin A) and vitamins E and C donate electrons to imbalanced atoms, thus restoring health and harmony to tissues throughout the body. Conversely, diets rich in fat, artificial ingredients, and chemical pollutants stimulate free radical formation, and thus contribute to aging and illness.

Natural cosmetic companies place an abundance of these nutrients, called antioxidants, in many of their skin care products, including cleansers, toners, and moisturizers. Skin specialists report that the depths that such products penetrate vary widely, depending on the size of the molecule, the temperature of the skin, and other factors.

Science has established that these nutrients do indeed stop free radical formation—whether they are taken in the diet or applied directly to the skin. But scientists are quick to point out that if people really want to take good care of their skin and slow the aging process, they will watch what they eat. Diets rich in antioxidants provide these substances to the bloodstream, thus getting to tissues throughout the body, including the deeper reaches of the skin. Most agree, therefore, that both diet and appropriate skin care are essential.

Acne occurs when oil, called sebum, blocks the pores and hair follicles at the skin's surface, thus preventing the skin from eliminating oil and waste. This, of course, causes waste to accumulate in the pores, resulting in pockets of infection that manifest as red sores, boils, and pimples. Acne does not occur when the pores remain unblocked.

Adolescents get more acne than adults because they experience a rapid increase in the production of the male hormone androgen—present in both sexes, but more abundant in males. Androgen causes the body to produce more sebum, which results in a greater number of blocked pores and blemishes.

CARING FOR THE SKIN

Skin care specialists maintain that before using any specific product for aging or acne, everyone should follow three skin care steps. The first is to properly clean the skin. Most of us have grown up using ordinary soap to wash with, but the skin experts recommend that we avoid soap because of its high pH, which dries skin and diminishes its life expectancy.

A healthful skin cleanser should be composed of vegetable oils; it should also have a balanced pH, and contain no animal fats, or mineral oils. Skin cleansers, also known as sufectants, can contain a number of different vegetable oils, including coconut, sesame, or palm oils. These are safe and effective cleansers and have a relatively low or balanced pH. Stearic acid, used in some natural skin care products to provide a pearly firmness, is a fatty acid derived from vegetable oils. These cleansers will dissolve sebum; water will dissolve and rinse away dirt.

Seaweeds are increasingly used as skin cleansers, as well. Their high mineral content stimulates circulation, helps eliminate toxins imbedded in the skin, and leaves the skin feeling smooth. Seaweeds can, to some extent, remineralize the skin, thus strengthening its immune and healing functions.

The next step in thoroughly cleaning the skin, especially if your skin tends to be oily, is to wash it regularly with a facial scrub that contains a mild abrasive. These abrasives vary in coarseness, ranging from a very mild base of oatmeal or ground almonds, to coarser materials, such as silica (a finely ground sand) or the shells of almonds or walnuts.

Studies have shown that men's skin tends to be smoother and less blemished than women's. The reason, say scientists, is that men exfoliate their skin every day by shaving. That is, they take off the top layer of dead cells with their razors, allowing their skin to breathe and eliminate waste much more efficiently. Skin care specialists recommend that women use a mild abrasive, such as a skin scrub made of crushed almond or walnut shells. Such exfoliants are widely available in natural foods stores.

While it is considered manly to slap alcohol on your face after shaving, alcohol dries the skin and thus harms the soluble collagen below.

Witch hazel turns up in a lot of natural skin care products, especially toners. Witch hazel has a strong astringent effect, but can dry out the skin somewhat if it is used in high quantities. Most natural cosmetics companies use only small amounts of witch hazel and combine it with moisturizing herbs—such as vitamin E, geranium, or honey—that balance its drying effects. Other common herbs in toners are lemon, ivy, sage, nettle, and burdock.

The third step that most skin care specialists advise is to use a moisturizer on your face after you've washed it thoroughly. Moisturizers, also known as humectants, attract moisture to the skin's surface and hold it there; moisturizers make the skin softer and prevent it from drying and chapping, thus slow the aging process.

Effective and widely used humectants include jojoba oil, vitamins A and E, sorbitol (derived from plants), honey, aloe vera, and iris.

Aloe vera is one of those plants that seems to have been designed by nature to treat human skin. Since ancient times, it has been used effectively to treat everything from dry skin, burns, and insect bites, to skin irritations, acne, cuts, and abrasions. Like many of the herbs mentioned in this article, aloe is surrounded by a great folklore that goes back to ancient Egypt, and a lot of research still needs to be done to investigate all its properties.

Iris is another plant that has remarkable moisture-controlling properties. Despite the fact that the iris grows in hot, dry climates, the plant itself is surprisingly moist, even watery. The secret seems to lie in the rhizome's ability to store water and release it in quantities that balance the prevailing atmospheric conditions.

Avoid moisturizers that include mineral oils, however. Mineral oil, used in many mass market skin care products, including the most popular cosmetic on the market, Oil of Olay, is a petrochemical that can dry the skin, block pores, and prevent it from breathing and eliminating waste.

Skin Cancer

The number of new cases of skin cancer is more than 600,000 a year, according to the American Cancer Society (ACS). That figure is so high that the ACS does not include it in its annual cancer totals, which the Society now says is more than one million new cases per year.

Skin cancers are now reaching epidemic proportions, according to a study published in an October 1989 issue of the *Journal of the American Medical Association.* Since the 1960s, malignant melanoma has increased 3.5 times in men and 4.6 times in women.

Scientists tell us that the vast majority of skin cancers are caused by the sun's ultraviolet rays. Today, the amount of ultraviolet radiation being showered down upon all of us is increasing dramatically because the ozone layer is growing thinner each year. The ozone layer is a thin, protective covering of ozone gas in the upper atmosphere of the earth. It was formed more than three billion years ago by algae that, among other things, were capable of breathing carbon dioxide and releasing oxygen. Those tiny plants filled the earth's atmosphere with oxygen. Gradually, the oxygen rose into the stratosphere and interacted with the sun's UV light, causing a chemical reaction that formed the ozone molecule, composed of three oxygen atoms.

The ozone layer made advanced life on earth possible. Without it, those first marine animals that crawled up on the shore would have died of skin cancer, a fact we may be relearning today.

As the ozone layer becomes thinner and more diffuse, greater amounts of ultraviolet radiation make their way down to your skin. These ultraviolet rays are highly toxic to you, as well as to animal and marine life. Consequently, skin cancer rates are expected to continue to climb rapidly.

UV light also causes cataracts and harms the immune system, which makes a variety of cancers more likely. Dr. Darrell Spencer Rigel of New York University, who has studied the effects of

The placebo is the doctor who resides within.

NORMAN COUSINS

183

ultraviolet rays on skin, reported recently that it is particularly important to protect children and young people under the age of twenty from sunburn.

Young people are far more sensitive to cell aberrations caused by overexposure to UV radiation. "Our studies have shown that the twenty-year-old break point is critical," said Rigel. "There's no such thing as a safe tan, and there's no good thing about sunburn. But sunburn is much worse under the age of twenty."

Rigel reports that there are several other risk factors involved that offer clues to who gets skin cancer. Those risk factors include the following:

- Being blond or red-headed;
- Having abundant freckles on the upper back;
- Having a tendency to develop a red, bumpy rash called actinic keratosis after exposure to the sun;
- Having at least three blistering sunburns before the age of twenty;
- Having at least one relative with malignant melanoma.

Common suggestions for protecting against skin cancer include the following:

- Protect children from overexposure from the sun by using a hat, protective clothing, and a good sunscreen. Adults also should use an effective sun block, especially if they are planning to spend any length of time in the sun's direct rays.
- Avoid commercial skin lotions or moisturizers, especially those containing mineral oils, a substance that dries the skin, blocks pores, and causes the skin to heat up in the sun or indirect light. That heat is actually cooking the skin, causing cell aberrations and possible skin disease.
- Use a vegetable-based skin cleanser that will not dry the skin, or block pores. Soaps are highly alkaline; they dry the skin and cause it to age faster. Gentle cleansers will leave the skin moist and the pores open, allowing oils and blood to circulate freely.
- Eat foods rich in antioxidants: beta carotene, and vitamins E and C. Rich sources of beta carotene are carrots, squash, broccoli, and collard greens. Vitamin E is abundant in whole grains and seafoods. C can be found in leafy greens and fruit.

Those foods prevent free-radical formation (the basis of most cancers, including those of the skin, as well as aging) and restore health to tissues throughout the body.

- Reduce fat in the diet. Fat causes free radicals to increase throughout the body, including the skin, which raises the likelihood of cancer and other illnesses.
- Eat foods low on the food chain and rich in nutrition, such as whole grains, vegetables, beans, seaweeds, and fish, which are abundant in nutrients that support the immune system. Cancer is an immune deficiency disease, too. A healthy immune system can deal with the sun and toxins in the environment, as long as we're not poisoning ourselves every day with our food.

Sweating therapy can be used for restoring circulation. It will raise body heat and metabolism, burn off toxins, and relieve congestion.

Herbs for the skin:

SASSAFRAS TEA: Excellent for most kinds of skin eruptions.

PLANETARY BITTERS TEA: Helps chronic skin problems.

THE BRAIN

THE BRAIN IS a vast and mysterious frontier, a universe within a hardened shell. The great constellations of that universe are marked by names that, for most of us, are vaguely familiar: cerebellum, cerebrum, cerebral cortex, frontal lobe, limbic system, and hypothalamus. Even if we know the function of these regions, they nevertheless stir in us wonder and awe.

To paraphrase F. Scott Fitzgerald, the brain is not like other organs. There is something about it that is beyond biology, indeed, beyond science. It is the altar of the body, the root of the mind. It is the place where the visible and invisible meet, where flesh and blood mingle with thoughts, emotions, instinct, and spirit.

Buried deep within lie the secrets of our souls, a record of our days, any one of which can be called forth unexpectedly by the right odor—a stroll past the local bakery, for example; the right face, even a stranger's; a piece of music; a pair of well-thumbed theater tickets.

In our reductionist age, it's tempting to think of the brain as a computer, and a person's worth as measured by the size of his or her brain. Mary Shelley's *Frankenstein: The Modern Prometheus*

(1817) offered up an answer to such thinking when her character, Dr. Frankenstein, installed a dead man's brain inside the head of a cadaver and then jumpstarted the beast with a streak of lightning. When Frankenstein's creation turned out to be a monster, Shelley provided an object lesson that grows more relevant with every passing decade: It takes more than gray matter and electricity to make a human being.

Opening the skull to cure headaches and other ailments, including brain tumors, dates back some four thousand years before Christ. The leading practitioners of cranial surgery were the ancient Peruvians, who successfully conducted hundreds of such operations as far back as the Stone Age. Researchers have proven that many of the patients survived these operations, as evidenced by the fact that bone tissue had clearly mended the original wound. Ancient skulls with plum-sized openings and saw-blade markings have been found throughout Europe, Asia, and North Africa.

In 500 B.C., a Greek living in Italy named Alcmaeon stated that intelligence is associated with the brain. His more famous contemporary, Empedocles, rejected the notion and taught that intelligence was found in the blood. Empedocles's teachings carried the day. Gradually, the brain would be associated with the intellect, but it remained an untouched mystery well into the modern age.

The first real breakthrough in understanding the brain came in 1861, when Dr. Paul Broca performed an autopsy on a man who, while living, could not speak in whole sentences. Broca, a Frenchman, discovered that a section of the left hemisphere of the man's brain was shriveled up in scar tissue. Broca named this part of the brain the speech center.

Broca's discovery stimulated further research on animals. Researchers used electric probes to stimulate parts of the brain, which in turn triggered distinct physical reactions. Gradually, a map of the brain was established showing where many specialized centers of learning and physical capabilities were located.

In the 1970s and 1980s, Dr. Roger Sperry pioneered the study of the left and right hemispheres of the brain. Sperry studied a group of epileptics who had undergone a radical form of surgery that involved severing the corpus callosum, the thick band of nerve fibers that connect the left and right hemispheres. Despite earlier research, many scientists still believed that the brain was largely an undifferentiated mass in which the entire organ was responsible for many specialized tasks. The corpus callosum, they believed, was a useless bundle of nerves.

Sperry discovered that the left and right hemispheres have distinct functions: the left side specializes in speech, analytical, sequential, and logical thinking; the right in spatial relationships, holistic, artistic, and intuitive thinking. The corpus callosum mediates between the two hemispheres, like a traffic cop at a busy corner. Without it, the two sides of the brain perceive life independently, and the person perceives himself as having two minds.

Today, we know that the right side of the brain controls the left side of the body, and vice versa. Interestingly, the left side of the brain is dominant in the Western world, and right-handedness is more abundant than left. This preference is evidenced in our language. The Latin word for left is *sinistra*, from which "sinister" is derived; the Celtic word for left meant "weak," and the French means "gawky" (*gauche*). Meanwhile, the words for the right side mean "dextrous" (Latin), "strong" and "straight" (Celtic), and "law" (French).

There is a growing body of evidence showing that left-handed people do not live as long as right-handers. A study done by researchers at the California State University at San Bernardino and the University of British Columbia found that left-handed baseball players, on the average, died nine months sooner than right-handed players. Other research examining non-baseball players has consistently supported the finding that left-handers experience more accidents and illness and die sooner than righties.

Interestingly, the population of left-handers exhibits greater extremes in intelligence: There are higher percentages of retardation and intellectual giftedness among lefties than among righties, who tend to gravitate toward the middle ranges of intellectual ability. Left-handers also may experience greater communication between the brain's hemispheres than right-handed people do. Theories abound as to why we culturally prefer right-handedness, and why differences in mortality rates exist. But science is still mystified.

During the late '70s and early '80s, researchers started to recognize the differences between the brains of men and women. Like other significant parts of the body, the sexes are different here, too. Scientists discovered that while men tend to have larger brains overall, women usually have larger corpus callosums than men do. This has led to speculation that women enjoy greater communication between the left and right hemispheres, a trait that might explain why women tend to score better on verbal and linguistic tests. Scientists also note that women often are better able to put their emotions into words, perhaps another benefit of the larger corpus callosum. Men, on the other hand, usually score better on tests that require perception of spatial relationships. Researchers speculate that the smaller corpus callosum may encourage greater specialization of the brain among men, more reliance upon the right hemisphere, and a comparatively weaker ability to put their intuitions and feelings into words.

Still, scientists are quick to point out that no one knows for sure what these differences in brain structure mean, if anything, and that the variances between the sexes may be more socially regulated than biological.

It's instructive to remember that most of us use only a tiny percentage of our brain's capacity, no matter which sex we are. In fact, scientists maintain that the brain's six capabilities reach far beyond our current usage, prompting the late author Arthur Koestler to say, "In creating the human brain, evolution has wildly overshot the mark."

Indeed, the brain remains more mysterious than understood. Take memory, for example. Scientists still cannot figure out where it is located in the brain—if at all—and by what mechanism we are able to recall information at will. No one knows what the basis of feelings and thoughts are; how we are able to discern and appreciate musical harmony from chaotic sound; how artistic ability, proven synchronistic events, and extrasensory perception are mediated by the brain; and how relatively tiny parts of the brain, such as the hypothalamus, are involved in so many complex and varied tasks.

Sages and poets make convincing arguments for the unity of body, mind, and spirit. The body, they say, is the physical manifestation of mind and spirit. Humanness, with all its marvelous capabilities, resides as much in the ether that surrounds and permeates the body, as it does in the organism itself. If science ever discovers that unity among the mind, body, and spirit, it will likely come from its explorations of this wondrous organ.

The probability that human consciousness and our infinitely complex universe could have come into existence through the random interactions of inert matter has aptly been compared to that of a tornado blowing through a junkyard and accidentally assembling a 747 jumbo jet.

STANISLAV GROF

189

THE MULTIPURPOSE ORGAN

The brain has six general functions, as follows:

1. It is the regulating center of the body. The brain receives a continual stream of information from the body in the form of sensory impulses. It evaluates this information, and provides an integrated biological response by activating or inhibiting an array of functions, including the endocrine system, muscles, heartbeat, and respiration, as well as conscious and unconscious thought processes. Most of these functions go on unconsciously, that is, without our being aware of them.

2. It is the center of consciousness. Consciousness, as defined by Edwin B. Steen and Ashley Montagu in *Anatomy and Physiology, Vol. 2,* "is the state of awareness of time, place, person, and, in greater or lesser degree, the activities of the body."

3. It is the receiver and interpreter of the senses. It receives and interprets sensory impulses from every point within the body, and from sensory organs that perceive information coming from outside the body. Our capacities for sight, sound, smell, taste, and touch originate at points distant from the brain, but must be processed by the brain before we experience such information. (See chapters on individual senses, Part Three.)

4. It initiates voluntary action. Every conscious act is initiated, coordinated, and processed by the brain.

5. It is the mediating organ for all emotion, urges, drives, and instincts. These emotional responses are processed and dealt with in the brain.

6. It is the seat of all intellectual activity, and the organ of intelligence. Perception, recognition, judgment, reasoning, memory, and learning are the basis for intelligence, and all are processed in the brain.

The brain, located in the cranium, is the main organ of the central nervous system. The spinal cord is its counterpart. (See chapter on the nervous system.) In the average adult, the brain can weigh anywhere from just over two pounds to just under four. Brain size and weight tends to vary between the sexes: the average man's brain is slightly larger than the average woman's—2.9 pounds for men compared to 2.6 for women. No one knows what, if anything, these differences mean. The size of the brain is one of the indicators of overall intelligence, but not the only one. Scientists point out that the largest brains found in humans tend to be those of retarded adults. Nevertheless, as Steen and Montagu state, "In general, the weight of the brain of persons of eminence tends to be slightly above the average."

The basic cellular unit of the brain is the neuron, a microscopic cell shaped like an octopus, with one particularly long tendril, called an axon. The axon terminates on other neurons and in this way makes it possible for nerve signals to travel from one cell to the next. When a nerve impulse is generated from the center of the neuron and then travels to the tip of the axon, it causes the release of a chemical called a neurotransmitter. That neurotransmitter is released from the axon into the spaces between neurons; once it touches the neighboring neuron, it causes the nerve to fire an impulse along its own axon, thus causing another neurotransmitter to be released, which in turns sets off another nerve impulse in the adjacent neuron. In short, neurons communicate with one another according to a basic bucket-brigade strategy. And just like the bucket brigade, healthy brain function depends upon the brain having sufficient chemical neurotransmitters. This, as we will see later, has become a growing problem, particularly among people suffering from Parkinson's disease.

There are different chemical neurotransmitters, and each one causes different reactions inside the brain. Serotonin gives rise to feelings of well-being and relaxation. It enhances our ability to focus our thoughts, and causes deeper and more restful sleep. Dopamine encourages greater alertness and aggression. It is often secreted by the brain when we face some difficulty and need a heightened sense of awareness. Acetylcholine, another transmitter, helps the brain to maintain coordinated motor activity. When acetylcholine levels diminish, a person can suffer from jerky, uncoordinated movements that, when acute, can be crippling.

As we will see later, the availability of these neurotransmitters is highly sensitive to the foods we eat. According to Dr. John D. Fernstrom of the Massachusetts Institute of Technology, "It is becoming increasingly clear that brain chemistry and function can be influenced by a single meal."

The Brain

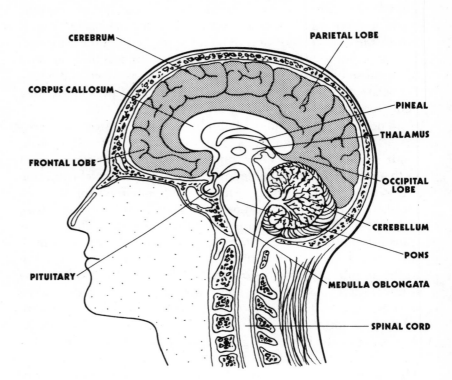

CEREBRUM

PARIETAL LOBE

CORPUS CALLOSUM

PINEAL

THALAMUS

FRONTAL LOBE

OCCIPITAL LOBE

CEREBELLUM

PONS

PITUITARY

MEDULLA OBLONGATA

SPINAL CORD

Despite recent medical and scientific advances, the brain remains more mysterious than understood. It stores memory, receives and evaluates a continual stream of sensory input, acts as the center of consciousness, initiates and coordinates voluntary action, mediates emotions, urges, drives, and instincts, and serves as the seat of all intellectual activity, including perception, recognition, judgment, reasoning, and learning. It does this all in a manner and with a speed that transcend any imaginable computer model.

A MARVEL OF INTEGRATED CIRCUITRY

While the brain is highly specialized, it is also fundamentally interdependent. Nerve impulses fire across the brain in fractions of an instant, linking and coordinating the relatively distant and disparate brain structures so that the body can function properly. In short, the brain is a marvel of integrated circuitry. It is also a supreme paradox in that it is highly specialized, but at the same time awesomely unified.

The brain can be divided into three main structures: the brain stem and cerebellum—the two oldest parts of the brain, in evolutionary terms—and the cerebrum, the most recent and most highly developed aspect of the organ. Within the cerebrum are four main lobes, or regions, in which specific functions take place.

Located in the base of the brain, the brain stem forms a tube-like structure that connects the spinal cord with the corpus callosum and the cerebrum. In general, the brain stem is responsible for connecting the higher and lower centers of the brain. It assists in involuntary movement, communicates sense information, and helps sustain physical balance. The specific functions of the brain stem reside in its four parts. The medulla oblongata controls the heartbeat, breathing, and blood pressure. The pons, an oval-shaped bulb that connects the medulla to the upper parts of the brain, contains sensory and motor nerves that communicate physical movement commands and sense information back and forth from the higher centers in the brain to the spinal cord. The midbrain, which helps maintain equilibrium, is responsible for many reflex actions, receives nerve impulses from the retina and other sense organs, and passes them along to the higher parts of the brain. The hypothalamus is a tiny organ, weighing only four grams—about three-thousandths of the brain's total weight—but its responsibilities are mind-boggling. Through nerve impulses and secretion of hormones, the hypothalamus acts like a great railway engineer, sending signals throughout the body's systems, like trains along various tracks, which in turn set other effects in motion. The hypothalamus performs the following tasks:

1. Controls involuntary organs, such as the heart and intestines, through the autonomic nervous system, over which we have no conscious control.
2. Controls many general involuntary functions, such as body temperature, appetite, thirst, and sex drive.
3. Controls the emotions, including feelings of pleasure, pain, fear, and anger, through creating endorphins, which are morphinelike substances that stimulate moods and provide pain relief.
4. Translates emotional states into physical symptoms, or so-called psychosomatic illnesses. Stress or fear affect hypothalamic function, which in turns influences the nervous, endocrine, immune, cardiovascular, and respiratory systems, and the gastrointestinal tract. If adversely influenced, these systems can manifest an array of symptoms, anything from nervous tension or indigestion, to heart attack or tumors.

All you have to do is rest. Nature herself, when we let her, will take care of everything else. It's our impatience that spoils things. Most men die of their cures, and not of their diseases.

JEAN MOLIÈRE

5. Coordinates the nervous and endocrine systems by releasing hormones that stimulate production of other hormones. The nervous system acts with hormones to affect blood pressure, heartbeat, and respiration. This occurs during times of acute stress, such as the moment you see a bear in the woods, or pleasure, such as when you are playing a game or are sexually excited.

6. Controls sleep. The hypothalamus activates parts of the brain that bring about the transition from sleep to wakefulness, and suppresses these brain capabilities when fatigue requires you to go to sleep.

(Other glands found in the brain, such as the pineal and the pituitary, are described in the chapter on the endocrine system.)

The cerebellum, which sits above the brain stem and extends behind it, is composed of two lobes that are striated with many small folds. The cerebellum is the old brain, the primitive part of the nervous system that is responsible for many instinctual and highly complex involuntary movements.

To perform these complex movements, the cerebellum has built-in programs that coordinate an array of muscles, nerves, and bones. For example, the simple act of raising your hand to your face requires the coordination of more than fifty muscles moving thirty bones in the arm and hand alone. You experience this motion as a smooth flow, yet it requires a complex orchestration of events, each with its own job and duration.

The cerebellum also helps to maintain posture, equilibrium, and muscle tone. It is essential to all motor activity, especially complex and instantaneous movements, such as those performed by athletes and performing artists, such as dancers.

The cerebrum is what you think of when you picture a brain: a large, spongy mushroom cap that is permeated with soft folds and fissures, called gyri and sulci, respectively. These folds and indentations give the brain a surface area of approximately 400 square inches. The cerebrum represents five-sixths of the total brain. It is divided from front to back into two hemispheres. It is further divided into lobes, described below.

The surface area, called the cerebral cortex, varies in thickness but averages about an eighth of an inch. Composed of the celebrated "gray matter," associated with intelligence, the cerebral cortex is where many highly advanced intellectual activities occur. These functions are rooted within the four main lobes of the cerebral cortex: the frontal, parietal, temporal, and occipital lobes.

The frontal lobe is the largest lobe, extending from the middle of the brain and emanating forward like a giant outcropping or cliff, to form the entire frontal area. In a band that stretches laterally over the very top of the lobe, or the top of the head, is the motor cortex, which is responsible for controlling all muscle movements of the body. The muscles that control everything from the mouth, tongue, face, eyes, arms, fingers, legs, and toes are controlled by this center.

In a small area in the left hemisphere of the frontal lobe is the word-meaning center, the part of the brain that deciphers word sounds. The frontal lobe also houses your ability to plan and create mental imagery.

However, much of what is in front of the motor center—the largest part of the brain—remains a mystery to scientists. In his book *The Body*, Anthony Smith reports that great portions of this area have been cut away by surgeons, yet patients emerge with only minor changes in behavior. They are highly sensitive to criticism, show little drive, and lack the concentration they enjoyed before. Otherwise they seem fine. However, if you scratch the motor area of the brain, paralysis will result.

The parietal lobe is located behind the frontal lobe. It is responsible for controlling all sensations, such as touch, pressure, temperature, and body position.

The temporal lobe is located on the sides of the brain, near what would be the area of the ears. It is responsible for hearing and discerning the origin of sounds. The left side of the temporal lobe controls the left ear, the right oversees the right ear. The temporal lobe is also the site of the part of the brain that helps us sound out words before we speak them.

Smith points out that the area involved in hearing is quite small, causing scientists to wonder what the rest of the temporal lobe is up to. Some believe it is involved in memory.

The occipital lobe, located in the back of the brain, is responsible for controlling sight. Like the temporal lobe, vision for the right eye is controlled by the right hemisphere's occipital lobe, while the left hemisphere controls the left eye. In the occipital lobe is located the word-reading center, the part of us that discerns

Our bodies are not made up of organ systems presided over by an authoritarian brain that is separate from our hearts, emotions, and spirits. We are instead a complex physical manifestation of our thoughts, dietary choices, relationships, parents, communities, hopes, and dreams.

CHRISTIANE
NORTHRUP

words and then sends the information forward to be interpreted by the frontal lobe.

The limbic system, among the most primitive parts of the brain, is located at the back of the brain stem and plays an important role in experiencing emotions. An emotion involves a two-fold reaction: first, an internal subjective feeling, and second, a response to that feeling, some kind of judgment about the emotion—whether we like it or not—and associations with it. Both of these reactions take place within the limbic system.

The limbic system is also closely associated with the ability to smell. The experience of smell is very much tied up with your associations to stimulating odors or fragrances. Consequently, smell is closely linked with memory (see chapter on smell). Those with injuries to the limbic system exhibit marked changes in emotion, either the diminution or extremes of fear, anger, aggression, passivity, pain, pleasure, and sexual drive.

Brain Activity and Food Choices

Researchers at the Massachusetts Institute of Technology have discovered that brain chemistry and function are greatly influenced by dietary choices. According to MIT's Dr. Judith Wurtman, a leader in this research, three groups of foods seem to cause relatively quick and impressive changes in brain activity:

- Carbohydrates (found in whole grains, vegetables, and refined sugars) promote calm, reduce anxiety and stress, and help the mind focus better;
- Proteins (found especially in animal foods) promote brain chemicals that stimulate and energize the body;
- Caffeine has an effect similar to protein foods.

Consumption of whole grains, such as brown rice, corn, barley, buckwheat, and oatmeal (including whole wheat bread and pasta) and vegetables will increase blood and brain levels of an amino acid called tryptophan, says Wurtman. Tryptophan will, in turn, stimulate production of a brain neurotransmitter called serotonin, which produces a heightened sense of calm, reduces stress and anxiety, and aids in inducing sleep.

"Those who eat calming foods consistently report feeling more relaxed, more focused, less stressed, less distracted after their meal," says Wurtman. "Tests confirm the volunteers' subjective assessments of their moods."

The stimulating agent in grains and sugar is glucose. Once in the body, the glucose found in carbohydrates is converted to blood glucose when it interacts with insulin, a hormone produced by the pancreas during digestion. Fruit sugar, which contains fructose, is gradually converted to glucose in the blood. But, according to Wurtman, the process is too slow to produce noticeable changes in brain chemistry and mood.

Further research at MIT has shown that some obese people use sugar as a sedative and to maintain a sense of well-being. When the sugar wears off, however, anxiety returns. The use of sugar—simple carbohydrate, as compared to the long chains of complex carbohydrates found in whole grains—may be counterproductive in the long run. Sugar causes wild swings in blood sugar levels, which may result in lower levels of glucose in the brain. Depleted brain levels of glucose may cause brain fatigue and diminished function. This condition, known as hypoglycemia, is associated with lower levels of blood sugar, cravings for sweets, wide mood swings, depression, and anxiety.

Protein foods, on the other hand, stimulate production of the neurotransmitters dopamine and norepinephrine. These cause people to "think more quickly, react more rapidly to stimuli, and feel more attentive, motivated, and mentally energetic," says Wurtman. "Problems, even big ones, often seem more manageable because of heightened 'brain power.'"

Wurtman counsels people to avoid high-fat sources of protein because fat diminishes the alertness response from protein and also causes an array of other serious illnesses. "It is important to choose protein foods that contain only small amounts of fats and/ or carbohydrates when you want to shift quickly into a more alert, energetic, and motivated state," she says.

Caffeinated beverages, such as tea and coffee, stimulate the production of dopamine and norepinephrine. Performance tests on volunteers have shown consistently that reaction times, vigilance, and mental alertness are all enhanced after one or two cups of coffee. Wurtman recommends that people do not exceed two cups.

Illnesses of the Brain

Brain disorders can be grouped into various categories, including congenital defects, injury, tumors, infections, and impaired blood supply.

Genetic disorders: These include a wide variety of disorders that arise during gestation and manifest before or after birth. They include Tay-Sachs disease, a progressive illness associated with blindness, brain deterioration, and death, usually during childhood, and Down's Syndrome, a genetic defect causing mental handicap and characteristic facial features which usually causes death between teenage years and middle age.

Infections: Encephalitis, which is a brain infection, is usually caused by viruses, the most common of which are rabies and herpes simplex. Meningitis, which affects the membranes or meninges surrounding the brain, is caused by bacterial infection.

Degeneration: Multiple sclerosis is an illness in which the myelin sheaths of nerves are gradually destroyed. (See nervous system.)

Alzheimer's disease is characterized by a progressive degeneration or shrinking of brain tissue. People with Alzheimer's disease gradually lose brain function and body control. The illness is responsible for more than 75 percent of all dementia among adults sixty-five and older. At present, scientists do not know the exact cause of the disease. Many believe that aluminum poisoning may play a role in the onset of Alzheimer's. There is no known cure.

Parkinson's disease is a degenerative illness affecting part of the motor function of the brain, located in the basal ganglia. It causes muscle tremors, trembling, rigid posture, and imbalanced walking. It too has no known cure.

Cerebrovascular disease: A diet rich in fat and cholesterol causes atherosclerosis, or cholesterol plaques, to form in the arteries leading to the brain. As the plaque grows larger, the artery passage narrows, thus diminishing the brain's supply of blood, oxygen, and glucose. Eventually, this illness can cut off blood and oxygen to the brain, thus suffocating a part of the organ and causing a stroke. Strokes can be fatal or disabling, depending on where they take place and which parts of the brain are affected.

Before such an event takes place, however, the diminished blood and oxygen to the brain can reduce brain efficiency, vitality, alertness and overall function. Oxygen can be reduced to the brain by progressive atherosclerosis and by reducing the blood's ability to carry oxygen. This occurs when dietary fat and cholesterol causes red blood cells to adhere to one another, thus preventing efficient oxygen carrying. (See circulatory system and rouleaux effect.) Consequently, the brain becomes fatigued. Eventually, atherosclerosis can cause senile dementia.

For many years, Nathan Pritikin, a pioneer of a low-fat, low-cholesterol, high-complex-carbohydrate diet, maintained that brain function is enhanced by avoiding foods rich in fat and cholesterol. Pritikin pointed out that the brain's demands for oxygen and glucose are so sensitive that diminished quantities of either oxygen or glucose will reduce brain efficiency dramatically.

To prove his point, Pritikin conducted before-and-after performance tests on people coming to his Pritikin Longevity Center in Santa Monica, California. The tests consisted of elementary arithmetic problems conducted during a two-minute period. Pritikin found that people scored far higher after they had been at the center more than two weeks—during which they were eating a low-fat diet and exercising daily, thus promoting optimal circulation to the brain.

Though we knew the connections of every tickling thread of every single axon and dendrite in every species that ever existed, together with all its neurotransmitters and how they varied in its billions of synapses of every brain that ever existed, we could still never—not ever—from a knowledge of the brain alone, know if that brain contained a consciousness like our own.

JULIAN JAYNES

"A CURIOUS ORGAN"

The Chinese regard the brain as one of the "curious" organs, the others being the bone marrow, uterus, blood vessels, bones, and gall bladder. Except for the gall bladder, there are no specific approaches to the curious organs, per se. Rather, the Chinese understand the brain in terms of how other organs influence its function. They also view it from the general standpoint of yin and yang.

The brain can be seen as a command center, but other organs in the body provide it with raw data, specific abilities, and even emotions, according to the Chinese. In order for the brain to function properly, the body must be healthy and balanced. The brain responds to general bodily states, according to Eastern medicine, rather than initiating them.

For example, clear and focused thinking, viewed in the West as a function of the brain, is seen as dependent upon healthy intes-

[The brain is a] great ravelled knot.

SIR CHARLES
SHERRINGTON

tinal function in the East. Constipation causes blocked or dull thinking—the inability to move thoughts freely—while diarrhea causes scattered, disjointed, or "spaced out" thinking. Spastic colon causes extremes in behavior—mood swings, rapid insights alternating with blocked thinking. Consistent intestinal health results in clearheadedness.

Good memory depends upon healthy liver function, while a weak liver will diminish one's recall. This may be related to the liver's role in purifying the blood and maintaining immune function. The liver must "remember" the antidotes to many thousands of toxins, bacteria, and viruses that enter the body, and come up with a remedy for each. Also, the liver is associated with the eyes and with sight. Being able to identify what is seen is, in part, a function of memory, and is therefore assisted by a well-working liver.

"The liver has the function of a military planner who excels in his strategic planning," says the Yellow Emperor. So the brain's ability to plan or strategize is dependent upon the liver. Those who have trouble planning ahead have weak livers, say the Chinese. This is probably related to the fact that the liver holds so much blood at any one time, which might be regarded as an enormous resource, and which must be treated carefully and parceled out appropriately.

As we have already seen, emotions and various mental states have their original source in specific organs. Joy and hysteria are related to the heart and small intestine; understanding and sympathy to the spleen and stomach; sadness and grief to the lungs and large intestine; fear and will to the kidneys and bladder; anger to the liver and gall bladder. When these organs are strong and the overall system is balanced, emotional and psychological harmony is maintained, say the Chinese. When these organs are balanced, the mind is balanced and emotional life is more stable. When these organs are imbalanced or in turmoil, the emotional and psychological life is also in turmoil.

Therefore, treatment for mental clarity and many psychological problems is focused on the body, which can be seen as the soil of the brain. Also, many physical problems related to the head and brain are seen as having their origin in the body's various organs.

Serious illnesses associated with the brain, such as stroke, are related to other organ systems, as well. In the case of stroke, the cause lies in the cardiovascular system and the development of atherosclerosis, in which cholesterol plaque builds within the arteries. Ultimately, such plaque can cut off blood and oxygen to the brain, which causes a stroke by killing part of the brain. The underlying cause of both stroke and heart attack is atherosclerosis. However, the place where the illness manifests most acutely depends upon an imbalance between yin and yang. Let's have a look.

The head and brain region can be seen as relatively yang in comparison to the rest of the body. They occupy the upper part of the body, which corresponds with heaven. The feet, on the other hand, can be seen as yin, or the lower part of the body, and correspond with the earth.

The Meridian Origin of Headaches

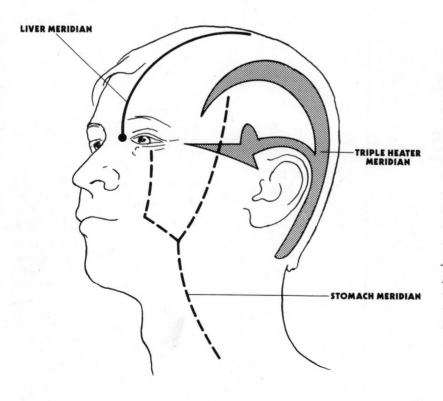

LIVER MERIDIAN

TRIPLE HEATER MERIDIAN

STOMACH MERIDIAN

Where a headache is located may indicate the origin of the imbalance, according to traditional Chinese healers. They diagnose headaches by whether the pain is along the triple heater meridian (which runs in an arc just above each ear and then to the temple), the stomach meridian (which begins at a point just below each eye and runs down to the jawline and then back up to a point just above the temples), or the liver meridian (which runs behind the eyes to the back of the neck).

201

In general, too many expansive foods, drinks, and activities will manifest as problems in the head region, because their influences naturally flow upward and outward, affecting the head. For example, alcohol, which is very expansive, has a profound effect on brain function. Drugs, which are even more expansive—sometimes referred to as mind-expanding—have an extreme effect on brain function. Drugs disorient and change our perception of reality. Foods such as sugar and spices, both less extreme than alcohol and drugs, also influence brain function. Sugar increases the level of serotonin in the brain, making the mind more relaxed, focused, while enhancing one's sense of well-being.

From either perspective, East or West, the brain is still the most mysterious of organs. Yet, experience tells us that it is also the one most dependent upon the rest of the body. If you haven't had enough sleep, enough to eat, or you're feeling ill, the brain's acuity is diminished. This prompted Orientals to offer sage advice: take good care of the body, and the mind will function well.

PART THREE

The Senses

THOSE OF US who have been brought up in the West have been trained to think of our senses as essentially objective sources of information. Indeed, even our sciences are based upon what can be *observed* in a laboratory. We Westerners use the senses to inform us of what is happening *outside* the body. The eyes see the world; the ears hear it; the tongue tastes it; the nose smells it; the skin touches it. We then take this information and quantify it—that is, we break it up into measured units, such as inches, ounces, decibels, or atoms. The result is that we see reality as more or less constant. We use the senses to deliver that outer world to our inner selves. If reality were not objective, a Westerner would argue, life would be reduced to chaos. We couldn't drive down the street without killing each other; we couldn't communicate; we couldn't observe and respect laws. Society would collapse.

In the Orient, the tables are turned. The most important aspects of reality are inward and subjective. Of course, an Oriental healer would agree that the senses deliver information from the outer environment, but your capacity to perceive what is truly happening around you depends entirely upon your inner state. Ten people can witness the same event and report ten very different experiences, as expressed so eloquently in the film *Rashomon*. Experience, in the end, is a subjective reality, say the Orientals.

Even more, the senses can be used to change the inner world, and thereby alter your ability to perceive more information. For example, certain smells can trigger memories and alter moods; certain colors can awaken sensitivities and heighten alertness; certain tastes can be used to strengthen or weaken individual organs; sound, as everyone knows, can transform us.

The senses alter the body and mind. They play with the soul. What you perceive in any moment powerfully affects your inner state, and thereby enhances or diminishes your capacity to further perceive that event. You may walk in a forest or along a beach and experience a tremendous heightening of awareness. Or you may be shocked by terrible violence and experience a state of dull apprehension. In both cases, your ability to sense is altered. Certain music may inspire you, while other sounds may depress or frighten you. In sensing the world, we interact with it, and in the process we are changed.

This mysterious truth is used by the Oriental practitioner as a means of healing. The senses are tools to the inner you. Therefore, what you sense can be used to strengthen your health, or weaken it. As we will see, Oriental and alternative healers have developed elaborate systems for healing based upon the senses alone.

We want this book to be an attempt at bridge-building, or unifying two worldviews. We wish to understand and recognize the contributions of both East and West. But in reality, these contrasting ways of looking at life represent different aspects of human experience. Each of us experiences both the objective and subjective forms of reality. When it comes to contrasting East and West, we are really talking about how cultures emphasize one way of looking at life over another. But both are already present inside each of us.

Let's look closer at the human senses, and examine the evidence supporting each of these contrasting worldviews that already exists inside ourselves.

CHAPTER 18

SMELL

Smell is the most sensitive of our senses, and perhaps the most primitive. We can distinguish literally thousands of odors and fragrances, and somehow remember them for the rest of our lives. Studies have shown that infants can identify their mothers on the basis of smell, and that mothers also can pick out their babies on smell alone. It requires only four scent-bearing molecules for us to recognize a particular smell, yet scientists still do not know exactly how odors are discerned or remembered.

Much, if not all, of our experience is associated with smell, even when we are unconscious of those smells in our environment. Consequently, memories and their related emotions can be called forth instantly by the right odor or fragrance. We can be consumed by our immediate problems while walking to work one day when suddenly, after passing a bakery or a candy store, we are enveloped in childhood memories by the smell of bread baking in the oven, or that of candy wafting innocently before our noses.

The reason that smell evokes such powerful memories and emotions is that our olfactory sense is linked directly with the brain's limbic system, one of the most primitive parts of the

In a general way I should like to raise the question whether the inevitable stunting of the sense of smell as a result of man's turning away from the earth, and the organic repression of the smell-pleasure produced by it, does not largely share in his predisposition to nervous diseases.

Sigmund Freud

central nervous system. The limbic system plays a central role in our ability to experience emotion and retain those experiences. It is literally a storehouse of memories, emotions, and their related odors, any set of which can be released by the right fragrance.

Smell also can arouse us sexually. Indeed, smell is among the most powerful of aphrodisiacs. After a long campaign on the battlefield, Napoleon wrote back to Josephine: "Home in three days. Don't wash."

One of the reasons that smell affects us sexually is that scent-bearing molecules also can carry hormones, called pheromones, which are received through the olfactory nerves. Research has shown that pheromones affect the behavior of sex organs. A 1971 study of Harvard women showed that, after spending sufficient time together, close friends and roommates all experienced their menstrual cycles at the same time of the month. It has long been known that animals communicate on the basis of smell, but this was the first evidence that humans were affecting one another on the basis of odors.

Later research, conducted at the Monel Chemical Senses Center in Philadelphia, showed that men help to regulate the fertility of their sex partners through their release of pheromones from their armpits. (We can only wonder if the deodorant industry isn't secretly contributing to our growing rates of infertility.) The Monel Center is now studying the efficacy of using human smells as a kind of "fingerprint" system in law enforcement and security.

Clearly, personal odor is one of the aspects of our humanness with which we are least comfortable, at least in the West. Perfume is a $4 billion industry alone. We are a people who like to be neutral-smelling, or emit mass-produced fragrances. To be identified with some unique odor is, as the TV commercial says, "uncivilized."

Recently, Madison Avenue has decided that we are olfactorily deprived and has begun scenting everything from shopping malls to magazines. You cannot pick up a copy of *Cosmopolitan* or *Esquire* without being slapped in the nose by fragrance (some would say odor).

Our capacity to identify a substance before we put it in our mouths has spared humanity much suffering and death. Eighty percent of what we perceive as taste is actually smell, though our

Nothing is more indisputable than the existence of our senses.

JEAN LE ROND
D'ALEMBERT

olfactory nerves get little of the credit. Much of what we crave from food is actually smell. According to Duke University researcher Dr. Susan Schiffman, each of us must be olfactorily sated before we actually feel satisfied by a meal. Many people are "seeking the pleasure of the odor of the food," says Schiffman. "The food doesn't tell a person to stop eating; even when they've met their caloric needs, they will go on eating until they have satisfied their hunger for smell, taste, and texture of the food."

Schiffman has been applying this principle to help obese people lose weight. She uses sprays to strengthen the fragrance of food, which in turn creates greater flavor and satiety from less volume of food. She treated a man who weighed 400 pounds who had previously said that he would rather die than give up pizza. She had a food spray created that would give the taste of pizza without the calories and fat. The man eventually lost 180 pounds with the help of the taste sprays. When food chemists and flavorists examine the world's cuisines, they point out that the typical American diet carries its flavors and fragrances in fat molecules, while the Oriental diet bears its fragrances in water.

Dr. Charles Weiner, a food chemist at International Flavors and Fragrances, and one of twenty-five senior flavorists in the U.S., says that the Oriental diet succeeds in satisfying taste without the harmful side effects. "The Oriental diet is delightfully aromatic, but there's less guilt associated with it because it's low in fat and cholesterol." Weiner says that such diets are the future. "The bland foods of twenty years ago—the meat and potatoes—are gone," says Weiner. "The demand is going up dramatically for aromatic foods and for highly seasoned foods. Twenty years ago, we didn't have so many Thai, Mexican, and Oriental restaurants. The baby-boomers want natural and healthful foods. The demand is going up for less synthetic additives and less fat, but more taste." Which really means, more smell.

The efficiency of absorption of therapeutic substances into the bloodstream by the nasal route has probably not received sufficient attention. Plant estrogens are known to exert a powerful influence upon animal behavior; the estrus of many species is triggered by the presence of plant estrogens in pasture in springtime, probably not by ingestion but by inhalation.

GERMAINE GREER

In Search of Scents

Just as the ear traps sound, the nose draws odors and fragrances to itself by inhalation. At the roof of the nose, just below the eyes, lies a closely bunched set of specialized nerve endings called smell receptors. These olfactory nerves protrude downward into the

The Sense of Smell

Inhaling air through the nose allows specialized olfactory nerves called smell receptors to begin a process that ultimately can distinguish an amazing array of odors and fragrances. As yet scientists are unable to determine any microscopic difference in the smell receptors, and thus are stymied at how smells can be differentiated.

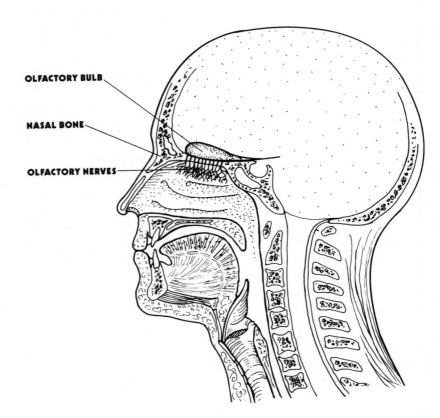

OLFACTORY BULB

NASAL BONE

OLFACTORY NERVES

nose canal. The tips of these nerves are swollen and have tiny hairs, called cilia, extending from them. A mucous membrane covers the surface of the nerves and serves to dissolve molecules that carry scent, thus making the odor accessible to the nerves.

The scent-bearing molecules stimulate the cilia, which pass sensory information onto the nerves. The nerves pass information upward to the olfactory bulbs, which are larger smell receptors that transmit the sensory information onto the olfactory nerve, which leads to the brain. The smell centers in the brain are located in the limbic system, just above the brain stem, and the frontal lobe. So far, scientists have not been able to determine any microscopic distinctions in the smell receptors. So, no one knows how smells can be differentiated.

The ability to smell varies widely among people. Some have a talent for smells, while the capacity to smell in others is relatively dull. Neither end of the spectrum is regarded as a disorder, but rather a genetic trait. However, loss of smell can occur temporarily or permanently; in both cases, our ability to taste is greatly diminished. The causes of temporary or permanent loss of smell vary widely. Swelling of the mucous membranes in the nasal passage and the development of scar tissue or lesions in the pathways or olfactory receptors can dull or even eliminate our ability to smell. Finally, disorders of the rhinecephalon or the limbic system can either diminish our ability to smell, or make it even more sensitive than normal.

SENSITIVITY AND THE SPLEEN

According to Chinese medicine, our ability to smell is governed largely by the spleen and lungs. As the Yellow Emperor says, the spleen opens in the nose, the lungs in the mouth. Since the lungs are responsible for taking in the breath through the nose, they play a major role in our ability to smell. But it is the spleen that is seen as most often responding to smells, largely because of its incredible sensitivity and its relationship to appetite and digestion. Some smells alone stimulate our hunger; others can give us indigestion. To the Chinese, this indicates the relationship between smell and the Earth Element (spleen and stomach).

When smell is weak, therefore, the Chinese recommend treating both the Metal (lungs and large intestine) and Earth Elements. (See chapters on the lungs and spleen.) In general, however, the loss of smell is regarded as a general loss of sensitivity and therefore suggests lack of circulation, fat and cholesterol plaques accumulating in the nasal passages, and a generalized weakened condition.

The Chinese also use body odor as one of the principle methods of diagnosis. Each smell corresponds to a particular element within the Five Element System, and reveals specific imbalances. According to Kiiko Matsumoto and Stephen Birch, authors of *Five Elements and Ten Stems,* the five smells and their corresponding organs are as follows: A greasy, oily odor, "like rotting flesh," indicates a liver imbalance (the Wood Element). A scorched or burnt odor indicates heart (Fire). Sweet odor points to spleen (Earth). An odor like raw fish or fat, which "clings to the nose," indicates lungs (Metal). Rancid or rotting odor "like decayed meat" is kidney (Water).

"A patient's odor is one of the things that is relevant if it is particularly noticeable," say Matsumoto and Birch. "Since these features become apparent very quickly, it will not be necessary to spend a great deal of time scrutinizing them."

FRAGRANCES THAT HEAL

Just as the word implies, aromatherapy uses fragrance to heal. The fragrances are drawn from plants in the form of essential oils. Each of these oils has its own distinct odor, which stimulates an array of emotional, psychological, and physical responses. Some arouse, excite, create alertness, or heighten sensuality; others relax, cool, and soothe. Aromatherapists say that the emotional and psychological states that these fragrances give rise to create physical responses—changes in pulse rate, respiration, perspiration, and immune response—which in turn can heal the body.

The use of fragrant oils to heal goes back 4,000 years to the Egyptians, and was later used by both the Greeks and the Romans. But it has recently begun to catch on again. Elizabeth Taylor and Princess Diana are only two of its more glamorous proponents.

The secret of aromatherapy lies in human experience—that is, how we relate fragrance to specific experiences. The odors present in a forest, a meadow, a room, or anywhere else are recorded, often unconsciously, and thus related to experience itself. To encounter that odor again will recall the emotions associated with the specific experience, even if we cannot recall the details of that experience. Aromatherapists maintain that within the fragrance lies the conditions under which the plant grew, as well. Each plant grows in specific geographical locations; it has specific characteristics; it responds to the sun, the moon, the earth, and the rain in different ways. These characteristics are also implicit in the essential oil and fragrance, say proponents of aromatherapy.

The rosemary flower, for example, is nestled deeply among its branches, close to the earth, and sends out a strong and stimulating fragrance to the entire plant. The flower has a kind of charisma all its own. It draws the sun toward itself, like a magnet, and then radiates its odors outward. Thus, rosemary offers the same characteristics to those who use it as an essential oil: it is said to stimulate, invigorate, and awaken the entire organism. It also imparts an earthly allure, drawing life toward you. For these reasons, rosemary is often found in morning lotions, day creams, or skin cleansers. Traditionally, it has been used as a purifying, warming, and decongesting herb, as well.

Lavender is just the opposite. Its flower lifts away from the plant—"almost like a cloud or a dream," says Weleda President Christine Murphy, whose company has been producing natural cosmetics and aromas for healing since her grandfather started the company with philosopher Rudolf Steiner more than sixty years ago. "Lavender leaves you feeling relaxed and light. It's wonderful after a stressful day."

Aromatherapists examine how each plant behaves in nature to discover the effects of its essential oils. Below is a short list of popular and evocative essential oils commonly used in a wide variety of natural body care products:

- *Pine:* The tree remains unaltered by the most severe winters or harshest summers, and therefore provides one of nature's greatest examples of constancy, stability, and duration in the face of life's vicissitudes. Pine is used to stimulate these same qualities, to balance the breathing, and refresh and stimulate the entire organism. As an herb, pine is used to decongest the lungs and arouse sensuality.
- *Olive:* The tree grows and produces fruit under the intense Mediterranean sun. Olive warms and soothes, creates circulation, and contains a certain fiery quality.
- *Arnica:* The plant grows high in the mountains, where the sun is pure and the air clean. It has been used traditionally as an herb for bruises and other injuries; it promotes healing, creates warmth, stimulates circulation, and moistens the skin. It arouses the senses, restores vitality, and awakens the mind and spirit.
- *Geranium:* Refreshes and arouses sensually and sexually. It lifts the mood and invigorates the senses.

When from a long distant past nothing subsists, after the people are dead, after the things are broken and scattered, still, alone, more fragile, but with more vitality, more unsubstantial, more persistent, more faithful, the smell and taste of things remain poised a long time, like souls, ready to remind us, waiting and hoping for their moment, amid the ruins of all the rest; and bear unfaltering, in the tiny and almost impalpable drop of their essence, the vast structure of recollection.

MARCEL PROUST

- *Cassia:* The tree grows in India and Southeast Asia. Its oils and fragrance are exotic, seductive, warming, and relaxing.
- *Eucalyptus:* One of the oldest traditional herbs, eucalyptus has been used to purify and decongest the lungs, as well as cool the overall condition. The essential oil has the same effects on the skin—it cleanses, purifies, and soothes and heals blemishes. It has a dispersing effect; it also enhances breathing.
- *Coriander:* Warms, relaxes, deodorizes, and soothes.
- *Chamomile:* One of the most widely used herbs and essential oils, chamomile soothes, relaxes, refreshes, and calms the overall condition.

Other evocative and popular essential oils are comfrey root, horse chestnut, lettuce, nettle, elm, tangerine, strawberry, magnolia, and sage. All of these essential oils have been used traditionally as healing herbs. Consequently, they influence the body directly, as medicinal compounds, as well as create their own atmospheres.

Essential oils are worth studying and experimenting with, especially on occasions when you want to change the mood, or heighten the senses.

CHAPTER 19

TASTE

TASTE IS PERHAPS the most immediately gratifying sense, and the one that gets us into the most trouble. The paradox of taste is that it also can be a powerful healing tool.

By itself, taste is the least refined of our senses. It relies heavily upon its sibling, smell, to compensate for its undeveloped nature. In fact, flavorists and food chemists point out that about 80 percent of what we perceive as taste is actually smell. Taste gets the credit for your gratified palate, but smell delivers most of the experience.

Humans perceive a multitude of tastes—everything from Cajun cookin' and Indian curry, to Japanese sushi and southern fried chicken seems to have its own unique spectrum of flavors. But the tongue allows us to experience only four distinct tastes: sweet, salty, sour, and bitter. All others flavors are provided to us by smell. We often hear people complain that they lose their sense of taste when they suffer from a cold or flu, but what they've really lost is their sense of smell, which dramatically reduces the ability to appreciate food.

Other factors that have little to do directly with taste play a role in our ability to taste food. These include the food's tempera-

The palate, like the eye, the ear, or touch, acquires with practice various degrees of sensitiveness that would be incredible were it not a well ascertained fact.

T. G. SHAW

ture (whether it is hot, cold, or warm), its texture (crunchy, soft, creamy), and our saliva, which helps to dissolve food and make the taste more accessible.

Taste has saved us much suffering and dying, too. Evolution has trained us to avoid certain tastes, especially bitter flavor, because it is the most common flavor carried by poisons. Conversely, we prefer sweet foods, which long experience has taught us are nutritious and especially rich in carbohydrates or energy. We also prefer salty flavor because of the presence of sodium, which is essential for proper pH balance. Children have been known to chew leather when necessary to obtain sufficient quantities of sodium.

Sometimes, we find ourselves craving certain tastes or foods, which may reflect nutritional needs. In a two-part article for the *New England Journal of Medicine* (May 26 and June 2, 1983; vol. 308, nos. 21 and 22), Duke University researcher Dr. Susan Schiffman pointed out that even infants will respond to certain foods on the basis of their perceived nutritional content. "It is clear that the ability to identify sodium chloride properly by taste in order to correct salt deficiency is innate," wrote Dr. Schiffman. "However, preferences for specific foods containing other basic nutrients, including other minerals, appear to be learned through the associations of taste with the state of need. In addition to sodium chloride, specific appetites have been reported for thiamine, calcium, potassium, and sugar in response to nutritional and metabolic imbalances."

Taste, therefore, is more than mere caprice. Indeed, at the Massachusetts Institute of Technology, researchers have identified the changes in brain chemistry that take place after a single meal consisting of protein or carbohydrates. The scientists point out that people often crave foods on the basis of their effects on brain chemistry, and the resulting mood changes that are evoked.

The next time we crave a particular food, we might ask ourselves what specifically we are looking for. Are we looking for a certain taste—sweet or salty; a certain texture—crunchy or luscious? The range of sweet foods runs from squash and fruit to apple pie and banana splits. Protein foods can be beans, fish, or beef. Calcium- and mineral-rich foods can be leafy greens (collard, kale, or mustard greens, for example), roots, or milk products. What we begin to recognize is that we have choices. Some are healthful, others not.

Beyond meeting certain biological needs, taste is a learned response to food. Parents can predispose their children to obesity, say scientists, by feeding them too many sweet-tasting foods, especially if such foods come as reward for behavior, or when a child is feeling depressed. Children also mimic their parents' food choices, even when those choices are repulsive to children. For example, Mexican parents often enjoy hot peppers that contain an irritant called capsaicin. Mexican children will eat those peppers in great quantities and suffer accordingly, because they associate the peppers with family. Eventually, the children acquire a taste for the hot peppers and even adapt to the capsaicin, but not before the peppers cause considerable pain and indigestion.

Herein lies a health secret: foods that promote health and well-being can be just as enjoyable and satisfying as unhealthful foods, if we are willing to retrain our palate. If a child can be taught to enjoy a food that burns his mouth, adults can learn to enjoy foods that are initially foreign and exotic, especially if the rewards are increased vitality, better health, and longer life.

THE FOUR TASTES OF THE WEST

Ten thousand specialized receptors, called tastebuds, give us the ability to perceive the four basic flavors: sweet, salty, bitter, and sour. These tastebuds are located mostly in the tongue, but also in the soft palate and throat. The lifespan of a tastebud is ten to twelve days.

The surface of the tongue, when magnified by a microscope, looks like a densely populated forest that's been cut down to stumps. Thousands of shoots, all closely crowded together, form what looks to the naked eye like a flat, slightly irregular surface. These tastebuds do not rest on the surface of the tongue, as many of us believe, but between crevices or pores created by these stumps, which are called papillae. Some papillae are wide (fungiform papillae), while others are narrow (filiform papillae). There are 200 to 300 tastebuds surrounding each of the papillae.

The tastebuds themselves are barrel-shaped. At one end of this taste receptor is a small opening, called a taste pore. Here, a tiny hair emerges, called a taste hair. At the other end of the tastebud is a nerve. When we chew food, saliva mixes with the food particles and dissolves them, making them accessible to the taste-buds. Molecules of food, latent with their own characteristic taste, stimulate the taste hair, which in turn triggers a nerve impulse that travels to the taste center in the brain, located in the parietal lobe.

The four tastes are located in specific parts of the tongue: the front of the tongue provides the sweet taste; the sides, near the front, respond to sour taste; further down along the sides of the tongue are located the salty taste receptors; and in the back of the tongue, near its root, are the receptors for bitter taste. Though there are regions for each taste, the tastebuds themselves are non-specific, according to Dr. Lloyd Beidler, a taste researcher at Florida State University. No one knows exactly how food triggers flavors, or how these tastebuds identify the four basic tastes.

Specific parts of the tongue are mostly responsible for certain tastes, with the front of the tongue providing the sweet taste, the sides near the front sour, the sides near the back salty, and the very back of the tongue the bitter taste. Though there are regions for each taste, the tastebuds themselves are nonspecific, and scientists don't know exactly how these tastebuds identify the four basic tastes. Researchers are not even sure exactly how food triggers flavors at all.

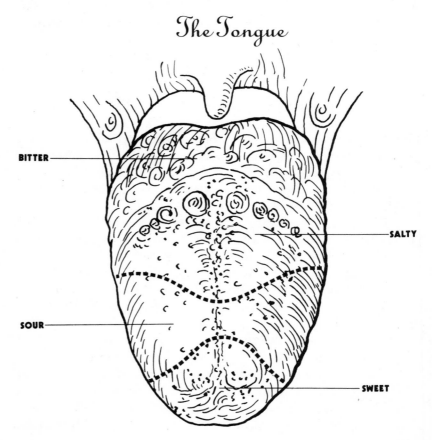

The Tongue

BITTER

SALTY

SOUR

SWEET

What scientists do know is that taste receptors adapt quickly to flavor, so that they need to be restimulated—either by moving the food around in our mouths or by taking another mouthful—in order for the enjoyment of food to endure.

The Five Tastes of China

In Chinese medicine, taste is used medicinally to heal specific organs and restore balance to the overall system. Taste is understood within the context of the Five Element system. The five tastes, according to the Chinese Five Element system, are sour, bitter, sweet, pungent (or spicy), and salty. In moderation, each will enhance and assist the function and healing of specific organs. If all tastes are consumed in moderation, they will create balance and health. Excesses of individual tastes will excite certain organs, while controlling and diminishing others. Let's take a closer look at the effects of each of these tastes. (See chapters on specific organs for more information on the foods related to each organ and taste; see the chapter on Chinese medicine for more information on the Five Elements.)

Sour: In moderation, sour taste will help to heal the liver and gall bladder (the Wood Element) by stimulating circulation in the liver. It eliminates stagnation and thus enhances liver activity. Sour stimulates blood cleansing, and thus helps to eliminate toxins in the blood. By moving blood and qi through the liver, it balances and reduces anger. In excess, sour will cause constriction of the liver and prevent it from eliminating waste. The liver's blood-cleansing function can become stagnant. Such stagnation can cause explosions of emotion, especially anger.

Since the Wood Element controls the spleen and stomach (Earth), it will diminish the stomach and digestive functions, causing the spleen to become deficient. This will lead to lung problems and constipation. A mildly sour taste has a slight sweetness to it. Excesses cause astringency.

Bitter: Moderate amounts of bitter taste strengthen the heart and small intestine (Fire Element). Bitter tastes will improve circulation, nutrient assimilation, and digestion. Bitter taste is cleansing and stimulating. By enhancing the Fire Element, it will increase our sense of joy and wonder about life. Since the Fire Element nourishes the Earth Element (spleen and stomach), mild bitter taste enhances digestion and assists the lymph system (spleen).

Excessive bitter taste will overstimulate the heart and small intestine, causing palpitations, racing heart, or erratic small intestine function. As the Fire Element becomes excessive, the Metal Element (lungs and large intestine) will be overly controlled, causing a deficient Metal Element function. Shallow breathing, shortness of breath, and constipation can occur. Imbalances in the heart and small intestine can predispose people to hysteria.

Sweet: Balanced sweet taste strengthens the spleen and stomach (the Earth Element). It enhances digestion—hence its appeal after a meal—and improves mood (it gives people a sense of calm and stability, like the earth). Well-chewed carbohydrates provide the ideal sweetness for the spleen and stomach because the food is well-mixed with saliva, which also enhances spleen function. The spleen mediates many immune cells. It functions best when our food is well chewed, infused with saliva, and consequently slightly alkaline. Excess sweetness and acidic foods cause excessive acidity in the stomach and unbalance the spleen. The result is heartburn, gas, and stomach disorders.

Since the spleen nourishes the large intestine and lungs, spleen imbalances lead to a variety of bowel disorders. Those who eat a lot of sweets usually suffer from chronic constipation or diarrhea.

The emotion associated with the Earth Element is sympathy or understanding. Excess sweet taste causes an excess of sympathy, to the point of being maudlin. Excess sweet taste overly stimulates the Earth Element and constricts the Water Element (kidneys and bladder). This results in excessive urination, urinary tract infections, and excessive fear and anxiety.

Pungent (or spicy): Moderate amounts of pungent taste, such as that from ginger or mild spices, enhance the function of the lungs and large intestine. It cleanses the system, stimulates healthy bowel function and circulation in the lungs. Small amounts of ginger or mild spices also can help to eliminate accumulated waste in the large intestine. It promotes the elimination of grief and sadness (the emotions related to the Metal Element) and the letting go of the past.

Excesses of pungent taste overly stimulate the bowels and lungs, causing diarrhea, and rapid and shallow breathing. Since the Metal Element controls the Wood (liver and gall bladder), excesses of pungent flavor will cause the constriction of the liver function, resulting in liver stagnation and a tendency toward anger.

Salty: Moderate amounts of salt strengthen the kidneys and bladder. Salt stimulates the kidney function. It supports the kidneys in their effort to eliminate waste from the blood and maintain a balanced pH in the body. Sea salt, which contains sodium and trace minerals, also supports the immune function and alkalizes the spleen and digestive tract. By assisting these blood-cleansing and elimination organs, salt makes the kidneys' job easier. Enhanced kidney function provides a person with courage and a strong will.

Conversely, excessive amounts of salt cause the constriction of the kidneys. Tight, contracted kidneys prevent optimal circulation within the organs, which can dramatically raise blood pressure and lead to hypertension. People with kidney imbalances suffer higher-than-normal amounts of stress and fear. They also lack a strong will.

The Six Tastes of India

One of the great healing tools within the Ayurvedic system is the use of taste to balance and enhance each of the three doshas—vata, pitta, and kapha.

Metabolic processes release all three dosha forces, causing them to become more active and dominant. A balance of all six tastes can moderate and balance the doshas, restoring harmony and peace to the body. Imbalances of certain tastes over others, however, can increase one or two doshas, while decreasing one or two. If such imbalances are sustained, sickness can arise.

It's important to keep in mind that all of these flavors should be eaten in moderation. Mild taste is healing; extremes are weakening and unhealthful. The six tastes are as follows:

Sweet: Increases kapha, and decreases pitta and vata. It cools, relaxes, and comforts. By increasing kapha, sweet encourages the desire to be mothered and passive. In extremes, it can be counterproductive to getting anything done.

Sour: Increases kapha and pitta, and decreases vata. Sour encourages elimination, and enhances appetite and digestion.

Once I had recognized the taste of the crumb of madeleine soaked in her decoction of lime flowers which my aunt used to give me . . . immediately the old gray house upon the street, where her room was, rose up like the scenery of a theater.

MARCEL PROUST

Excesses can contribute to stagnation and the inability to get things done and can inspire jealousy of others. Excesses of sour can inspire anger because of its tendency to increase expectations (kapha and pitta) without encouraging sufficient movement and action (vata) to fulfill those expectations. A person can "sour" on life.

Salty: Increases kapha and pitta, and decreases vata. Salty increases elimination, encourages cleansing, especially of lymph, kidney, and bowels, and stimulates appetite.

Excesses can encourage rigidity of thinking, loss of creativity, fear of change, and overindulgence in food and drink.

Pungent (such as ginger, peppers, and spicy foods): Increases pitta and vata, and decreases kapha. Pungent is highly activating; it is a stimulant. Hence, it eliminates waste and burns fat (which, as potential energy, is kapha). Excesses can keep the system from relaxing, inspire greed, anger, and anxiety or nervous tension.

Bitter: Increases vata, and decreases pitta and kapha. Bitter is cooling and drying. It causes contraction. It purifies the blood, balances the system, and cleans the palate. It also increases appetite. Excesses can inspire unrealistic expectations, workaholism, and aggression. Unfilled expectation can lead to "bitterness" and grief. (There is very little balance or perspective emanating from excess bitter flavor.)

Astringent: Increases vata and decreases pitta and kapha. Astringent contracts organs, reduces all secretions (such as saliva and bile acids), and reduces the activity of the liver. Excesses can dry a person up, turn off the "juices," make one introverted and fearful.

Taste is an exotic realm, and like all exotic worlds it can lead us to self-destruction or liberation.

CHAPTER 20

HEARING

HE MOST WIDELY understood and appreciated connection between human beings is sound. We speak, and our words are
heard. But hearing is more than words. It is the rapturous sound
of music; the chirping of birds; the hurry of the wind; a slap-
happy river; the crash of the ocean. Hearing is an early warning
system that alerts us to the needs of a baby, and the danger of an
oncoming car. It is discerning the layers of information within
the same sound; the emotion in another person's voice; the happiness of bells; and the cry of an alarm. Hearing awakens us to
worlds where eyes cannot venture, worlds of power and soul, to
the farthest reaches of spirit, to the intimacy of the breath.

Sound itself is composed of waves of energy moving through
a medium, such as air, water, or solid matter. These waves move
molecules very short distances—just far enough to transfer the
energy to the neighboring molecule. The process is not unlike a
line of billiard balls all slightly touching one another. When the
first ball is struck by a cue ball, all the balls move just enough to
transfer the energy down the line, yet no ball will move very far,
except the last one. This movement of energy through a medium
is understood as "vibration."

*The eye takes a person into
the world. The ear brings the
world into a human being.*

LORENZ OKEN

A slight sound at evening lifts me up by the ears, and makes life seem inexpressibly serene and grand. It may be in Uranus, or it may be in the shutter.

HENRY DAVID
THOREAU

Sound travels at different speeds, depending on the medium. It moves through air at about 1,125 feet per second; through water at 4,856 feet per second; and through iron at 10,627 feet per second.

Technically, sound is understood as wave cycles per second, meaning the number of complete waves (from peak to peak) that occur in a single second. One cycle—a single wave—per second is called a Hertz.

Humans can hear sounds that range from 16 cycles per second, or 16 Hertz (Hz), to about 20,000 Hz. A 16 Hz sound is very low and barely audible. A person feels the vibration more than he or she actually hears it. At the other end of the spectrum is a high-pitched whistle or a shriek. A dog's hearing ranges from about 12 Hz to better than 40,000 Hz. A bat hears from 1,000 Hz to greater than 200,000 Hz; a whale, from about 120 Hz to greater than 250,000 Hz. Bats and whales navigate by sound. They send out a signal that bounces off of objects ahead and then returns to them, giving the bat or whale information about what lies up ahead and how far off that object might be.

Humans determine distances by the relative loudness of sound. Loudness is measured in decibels, or tenths of a Bel, a unit named after Alexander Graham Bell, who improved the telephone. A soft whisper can register about 30 decibels; a normal conversation usually takes place at about 60 decibels, unless you offend your friend, in which case the shouting can reach about 90 decibels. A busy street can reach 80 decibels, and an orchestra can reach 90. We start to feel discomfort and even pain at about 110 decibels, and at 120 we can suffer damage to the inner ear. Upon take-off, a Boeing 707 has a decibel level of 130, or about ten trillion times greater than the lowest whisper you can hear. A loud rock group can play between 120 and 140 decibels, which explains why some people lose hearing after a rock concert. The Saturn booster rocket can reach 180 decibels. At these ranges, hearing is not only painful, but probably shortlived.

The sounds that we listen to change our inner world. We need only contrast the inner effects of a jackhammer going full throttle with the peaceful sounds of a forest or an inspirational melody to have all the proof we need. Sound enters our inner world and changes it, leading some therapists to use sound as a tool to heal.

For the past thirty years, Dr. John Diamond, a psychiatrist in

Valley Cottage, New York, has been using classical music to heal all manner of psychological and physical distress. Diamond maintains that sickness stems from an inner conflict that prevents life energy from flowing smoothly and efficiently through the body. Without life energy, cells degenerate and ultimately die. "Life energy is what makes a wound heal, what makes a flower grow," says Diamond. "I don't see how anyone can doubt that there is this quality of vitality in an individual."

Music, especially the work of the great composers, frees the body of inner conflict and thus allows life energy to flow freely again, according to Diamond. The emotional response that music evokes is a symptom of the physical changes that have occurred. Diamond, a musicologist, has studied between 30,000 and 40,000 musical recordings, as well as the lives of their composers and the background of their works.

"A composer composes to externalize his problems," says Diamond. "The composer in essence says to the audience, 'I have a problem I want to solve, and I want to tell you about it because I know that as I work my way through the ramifications of the problem, if I tell them to you step by step, I will be unstressed and energized by the process, and I will probably solve the problem, and you will also benefit.'"

Diamond maintains that all great musical compositions present both conflict and resolution. Listeners also experience the stress of these inner conflicts and also the resolution of the conflict, and are thereby healed in the process. This is the basis for the inspiration that music gives us, Diamond says.

He urges people to listen to the works of Mozart, Beethoven, Bach, and other great composers, especially when confronted with psychological or physical illness. Life's struggles and triumphs are all described in the music of these and other composers, says Diamond. Their triumph over difficulties of all kinds is found in the compositions they have left behind.

VIBRATION AND ELECTRICITY

Hearing is made possible by the ear, which also serves to maintain physical balance. The ear is composed of three parts: the outer ear, the middle ear, and the inner ear. The outer and middle ears trap sound and channel it into the inner ear, where the sound is transformed from vibration to electrical nerve impulses.

The horn we typically think of as the ear is called the pinna, or auricle. It is composed of cartilage and folds of skin arranged in a kind of spiral that leads to an opening. That opening is the entrance to the ear's canal, also known as the meatus. The skin that lines the outer reaches of the canal is able to secrete wax, which is used to trap dust, small particles, and even bugs that fly into the ear. The canal is about one inch long in adults and leads to a thin, fibrous wall called the tympanic membrane, or the eardrum. The eardrum marks the separation between the outer ear and the middle ear.

When sound travels along the ear's canal, it changes the pressure at the surface of the eardrum. This causes the eardrum to vibrate, which conducts the sound into the middle ear.

The middle ear is composed of three tiny bones that are linked, but still able to move. These three bones, collectively referred to as ossicles, transmit sound from the eardrum, across the middle ear, to the inner ear where the sound is converted to nerve impulses that travel to the brain.

The first of these ossicles is the hammer (also called the malleus), which connects the eardrum to a second bone, called the anvil (or incus). The anvil is connected to a third tiny bone, called the stirrup (or stapes). The stirrup, so named because it is shaped like a saddle stirrup, is attached to an oval opening, or window, in the bulb of the inner ear.

These three tiny bones vibrate with every sound wave and thereby transmit sound from the eardrum to the inner ear. By the time the sound has traveled from the outer ear to the inner ear, the sound has been amplified about ninety times.

Inside the middle ear is also found the eustachian tube, which connects the ear to the throat. The eustachian tube is normally closed, but opens when swallowing or yawning. You become aware of your eustachian tubes when taking off or landing in an airplane. Pressure increases in the tube until it is released by swallowing or maneuvering the muscles in the throat so that the passageway opens and the pressure is released through the nasal cavity or mouth.

The inner ear is a bulblike structure embedded inside the

The Ear

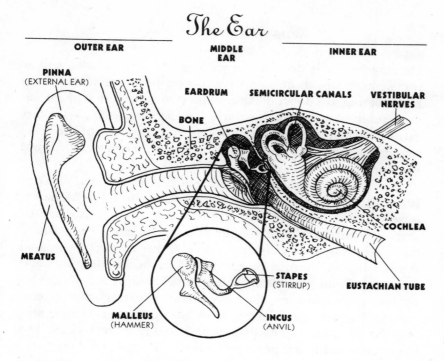

OUTER EAR   MIDDLE EAR   INNER EAR

PINNA (EXTERNAL EAR)

EARDRUM   SEMICIRCULAR CANALS   VESTIBULAR NERVES

BONE

MEATUS

COCHLEA

MALLEUS (HAMMER)

INCUS (ANVIL)

STAPES (STIRRUP)

EUSTACHIAN TUBE

The ear not only allows you to hear but orients your sense of balance and position in space. The outer and middle ears trap sound and channel it into the inner ear, where the sound is transformed from vibration to electrical nerve impulses. The semicircular tubes of the cochlea in the inner ear contain fluid and tiny hairlike nerve fibers that are sensitive to gravity, speed, posture, and the positions of the head. These nerve fibers serve as a kind of gyroscope, conveying information to the brain and allowing you to make appropriate physical adjustments to maintain balance and direction.

skull. Within this bulb is a maze of winding passages, known as the labyrinth. The front part of the bulb resembles a snail's shell, within which a tube winds in a circular motion. This part of the inner ear is called the cochlea and is involved in hearing. Inside the cochlea are nerve fibers that resemble tiny hairs. At the front of the cochlea, the nerves respond to high-frequency sound waves; at the rear, or deeper into the spiral, the nerves respond to lower-frequency sounds.

The cochlea nerves pass impulses along the auditory nerve to the temporal gyrus, the auditory part of the brain. (See chapter on the brain.) In back of the cochlea are three semicircular tubes, or canals, that rise out of the bulblike structure of the inner ear. They are set at right angles to each other. Inside these canals are fluid and tiny hairlike nerve fibers that are sensitive to gravity, speed, posture, and the positions of the head. These nerve fibers serve as a kind of gyroscope, conveying information to the brain about the body's current state of balance. The brain then orders appropriate physical adjustments to maintain balance and direction.

WHAT'S THAT YOU SAY?

He who has ears to hear sees!

JAKOB BÖHME

Hearing gradually deteriorates with age in the U.S. and much of the Western world. Studies have shown, however, that comparable hearing loss does not occur in traditional societies, or among industrialized people living on a low-fat diet. A high-fat diet causes atherosclerosis in the tiny vessels and arteries of the hearing mechanism, causing the inner ear to become dulled and hardened.

One study compared the hearing of citizens living in Wisconsin with that of the African tribespeople called the Mabaans. Researchers found that not one Mabaan—even at the age of seventy—suffered the hearing loss that the average Wisconsinite had suffered by the age of thirty-five. Other research compared the hearing of Finnish people with that of Yugoslavians and found that Finnish children begin to suffer hearing loss at age ten. By the age of nineteen, they have distinct hearing impairment, especially at the higher ranges of 16,000 to 18,000 cycles per second. No such hearing loss was found among Yugoslavians. The Finns have the highest per capita blood cholesterol level (290 mg/dl) of anyone in the world, and consequently the highest rates of heart disease in the world. The average cholesterol level among Yugoslavians is 180 mg/dl.

Ear infections are among the most common and painful ailments that afflict children. They occur most often in the ear canal or eustachian tubes, where the infection causes inflammation and pus to build. The result is stabbing pain and, in extreme cases, a punctured eardrum. Antibiotics are usually prescribed to kill a bacterial infection. Excess wax and pus are aspirated from the ear, as well. Ear infections can suggest a low immune function. (See the section on naturopathic remedies below.)

Tinnitus is the perception of hearing sounds, especially ringing or buzzing, when there is no sound emanating from the environment. It can be caused by excessive wax buildup, infection, osteosclerosis (the excessive buildup of bone that immobilizes the stirrup bone, the stapes), or poor blood circulation within the inner ear. Treatment usually includes the surgical removal of the stapes, which is then replaced by an artificial stirrup bone.

The Five Tones of Eastern Medicine

"The kidneys open into the ear," says the Yellow Emperor. "The kidney qi goes through the ear; if the kidney is harmonized the ear can hear the five tones." Because the kidneys provide life force or qi to the organs of the ear, hearing is dependent upon the healthy functioning of the kidneys. Diminished kidney qi will result in decreased life force to the ears, which will result in stagnation. The organs of the ear will begin to accumulate waste and toxins, such as plaque, and degeneration will proceed toward deafness. Diminished qi to the ears also can give rise to chronic ear infections.

When kidneys are deficient in qi, a person will suffer from poor circulation within the ear and possible ringing of the ears. He will suffer from poor sex drive, frequent urination, loss of hearing, and chronic earaches or infections. Conversely, excessive kidney energy can cause excessive qi to the ears, resulting in high blood pressure, excess wax in the ears, and highly sensitive hearing. Loud noises will be particularly painful.

To improve hearing, the Chinese maintain that the kidneys must become balanced and healed. Using the Five Element schematic, the kidneys and bladder are considered the Water Element. They are strengthened by mild salty flavor, beans, barley, and sea vegetables. Fat and cholesterol-rich foods clog the tiny kidney tubules and prevent blood from flowing smoothly through the kidneys, causing stagnation and degeneration. Excess sodium, which can injure the kidneys, also must be avoided.

The kidneys are controlled by the stomach and spleen (Earth Element) and nourished by the lungs and large intestine (Metal Element). Too many sweets and acidic foods cause the spleen to become excessive, which will control and limit kidney qi. For this reason, sugar and other sweet foods are often seen as the cause of ear infections and earache. They stimulate the spleen excessively, which dominates kidney qi and limits its flow to the ears and sex organs. (See chapter on the kidneys.) Consequently, all sweets should be avoided when ear infections or earache manifest.

At the same time, the lungs and large intestine should be strengthened. These Metal Element organs nourish the kidneys with life force. (See chapters on the lungs and large intestine.)

Finally, fear injures the kidneys and therefore plays a role in the flow of qi to the ears. For hearing to be healed, stress and fear must be effectively dealt with.

The five tones that the Yellow Emperor referred to above relate to the sounds associated with each organ system within the Five Elements. By listening closely to the voice, Chinese healers can recognize imbalances within specific organ systems. The greater the imbalance, the more pronounced these sounds are in a person's voice. Using the Five Element system, the five tones and their related organs are as follows:

Shouting: Associated with the liver and gall bladder (Wood Element). A person who shouts even when he or she is speaking normally, as on the telephone or when conducting routine business affairs, suffers from a liver imbalance. Chronically shouting in anger further indicates a liver imbalance.

Laughter or hysteria: Associated with the heart and small intestine (Fire Element). The tone in the voices of some people can be characterized as laughing. There is a certain playfulness, a lightness, and even lack of seriousness in the voices of many people, no matter what they are talking about. When the heart and small intestine are extremely imbalanced, hysteria is implicit in the voice and requires very little to be evoked. Both conditions indicate a heart and small intestine imbalance.

Singing: Associated with the spleen and stomach (the Earth Element). Singing strengthens the Earth organs. A singing voice indicates excessive qi in the stomach and spleen that is being discharged by a singing tone in the voice. Weak or deficient qi in the spleen and stomach also can manifest in the voice as excessive sympathy, whining, and discernible weakness.

Weeping: Associated with the lungs and large intestine (Metal Element). The Metal Element organs are associated with the emotions of grief or sadness, which manifests in the voice as a weeping quality, as if tears are implicit in the voice.

Fear: Associated with the kidneys and bladder (Water Element). Weak kidneys and bladder will stimulate a greater sense of fear and timidity. The voice will be tentative and cautious, with a palpable sense of fear in it.

THE DIETARY FACTOR

According to naturopathic medicine, the sources of most ear infections, especially among children, are dairy foods and sweets.

Mucus-producing foods, such as milk, cheese, and yogurt, refined white flour products, sugar, and fatty foods block circulation in the ear, and cause accumulation of waste products, making the environment perfect for viral or bacterial growth. Excess sugar, fruit, and fruit sugars (from fruit juice) also depress immune function. Allergies to certain foods, such as dairy or wheat, also may play a role in the onset of ear infections and other ear-related disorders, including ringing in the ears. Finally, chronic ear infections suggest a depressed immune system.

Hear, and your soul shall live.

Isaiah

People with ear infections or earaches are urged to avoid those foods, while increasing the following foods, herbs, and supplements:

- *Foods rich in vitamin A* (beta carotene): collard greens, broccoli, brussels sprouts, squash, and carrots.
- *Foods rich in vitamin C:* broccoli (one of the richest sources of C); tangerines; leafy greens. Supplements may also be necessary for short periods.
- *Foods rich in zinc:* whole grains, shrimp, and pumpkin seeds. Short periods of supplementation may be necessary.
- *Garlic:* It is antifungal and antibacterial.
- *Mullein:* antibacterial; four drops in each ear, four times per day.
- *Chamomile:* Especially for children, as a tea. Will promote perspiration, and elimination of accumulated toxins. Take two to three times per day.

Homeopaths note that earaches and ear infections may arise as part of a generalized flu, virus, or upper respiratory infection. The eustachian tubes are connected to the throat, allowing viruses to migrate to the ears and cause infection. For earaches accompanied by colds and coughs, use the following homeopathic remedies:

Aconite: especially for earaches after a chill and exposure to cold.

Belladonna: especially for those with fever, sensitivity to light, and sore throat.

Pulsatilla: for those with yellow or thick mucus, stuffed nose, fever, chapped lips.

CHAPTER 21

SIGHT

Use the light that is within you to regain your natural clearness of sight.

Lao-tzu

THE EYES REVEAL the world to us and, for the keen observer, reveal each of us to the world. No other sense is so heavily relied upon to tell us what is happening outside of us. Conversely, no other organ is scrutinized more closely to reveal the inner workings of our soul.

The eyes catch light. They drink it in great drafts and send it hurtling to the nervous system and then to the brain, where the images are interpreted and, to greater and lesser degrees, understood. Their capacity to perform this task far exceeds our ability to actually grasp their magic: The eyes can perceive 10 billion gradations of light and 7 million shades of color. They give us the ability to focus on an image close at hand, dissolve it, and then refocus on another image at considerable distance within a tenth of a second. We can witness in fine detail the myriad colors of an autumnal forest and, in the proverbial blink of an eye, suddenly shift our gaze to the coarse gray hairs of a squirrel's tail.

In simple terms, sight is the happy marriage between light and the brain. To most of us, light is the neutral brightness that occurs when the sun comes up or when we throw a switch. We are lulled into thinking that light merely illuminates colors that were already in existence before the lights went on. But that's not entirely true: Light is color, or rather many colors locked together.

We are witness to these brilliant colors when light is refracted, or separated, by a prism, which then reveals the color spectrum as a beautiful rainbow. At one end of the spectrum are violet and blue, at the other end are orange and red. These colors appear when the prism divides light into its component parts: individual waves of electromagnetic energy.

Physical objects appear to us as colored because they possess pigmentation, chemical substances that absorb certain wavelengths of light, while reflecting others back at us. Pigment in skin makes it possible for an organism to hold energy from the sun's light and convert it to heat, thus sustaining body temperature. The mix of waves that is reflected back at us gives the world its color.

Sunlight is an incredible variety of electromagnetic waves that are moving, or radiating, from the sun itself. When spread out on a spectrum, some of these waves are revealed to be very short from crest to crest—as short as six quadrillionths of an inch (.000000000000006)—while other waves span eighteen miles from crest to crest.

Remarkably, we are able to perceive only a tiny fraction of all the electromagnetic energy that is around us. In fact, the extent of the spectrum that we can see is measured in billionths of a meter, distances referred to as nanometers. We are able to see exactly 300 nanometers, which, for those of us not on intimate terms with the metric system, is a microscopic fraction of an inch. The rest of the electromagnetic energy spectrum, which spans many miles, is hidden from us. Thus, we are blind to the vast majority of what is actually happening all around us.

Science has proven that many animals, such as rats and birds, see the ultraviolet rays of the spectrum, and are therefore able to "see the invisible." New theories of bird migrations maintain that birds are able to see light waves that are invisible to humans. By following these waves, birds are able to find their ways to exact locations, north and south, each year.

Despite our limited sight, our eyes nonetheless provide us with the most intense and immediate information about our world. It should come as no surprise that sight provides about 75 percent of what we perceive, unless our eyes are impaired, in which case other senses become more acute. That figure is determined in part by cultural bias, especially by our scientific orientation, which fosters the notion that "seeing is believing." Other senses could offer more information, and often do for those whose lives or professions demand that they develop greater sensitivity to touch, smell, hearing, or taste, but those senses are less obvious in comparison to the brilliance of sight.

Just as the eyes provide information, they also convey it. Intense emotions are revealed in our eyes, as well as most of our subtle feelings. The eyes laugh, cry, convey happiness and sorrow. They respond to many physical changes in the body, from the condition of the liver, heart, and kidneys, to the health of the endocrine and nervous systems. The eyes even reveal the amount of oxygen in our bloodstream (the pupils dilate when oxygen is depleted) and become irritated when the immune system is mobilized.

The eyes are "dim windows of the soul," as William Blake

The human eye is a highly complex organ. Anatomical estimates put its number of working parts at close to one billion. Its light receptors, the rods and cones on the retina, can perceive ten million gradations of light and seven million shades of color. The rods and cones themselves represent about 70 percent of the body's total sense receptors. The eye works by taking in light and transforming it into electrical impulses that are sent to the brain, where 90 percent of vision occurs.

The Eye

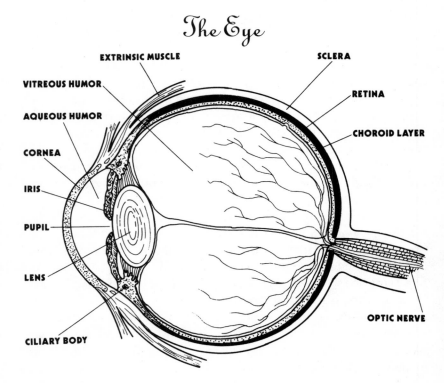

said. Indeed, the amount of information they convey seems limited only by our ability to decipher it.

An Inside Look at the Eye

Light enters the eye through the cornea, a clear convex window made of cells which permit light to pass without bending or scattering the electromagnetic waves. Immediately behind the cornea is the aqueous humor, a watery alkaline fluid that provides nutrition to the cornea and sustains just the right amount of pressure so that the cornea bulges slightly.

Behind the cornea is the pupil, the dark spot that expands and contracts to permit greater or lesser amounts of light to enter the eye. The pupil is controlled by the iris, the colored disc in the center of the eye. The iris is lined with muscle and autonomic nerves that control the opening or narrowing of the pupil. The parasympathetic nervous system causes the eye to contract, while the sympathetic nervous system causes it to expand.

The iris is colored by the presence of melanin, the pigment-giving substance that also colors the skin and hair. The amount of melanin determines the color of the eyes: greater quantities of melanin make the eyes brown; less makes the eye blue. Shades of green and gray are determined by greater and lesser amounts in between.

Behind the pupil is the crystalline lens, a bulblike structure that is shaped like a rounded diamond, with the wide end right behind the pupil, and the narrow near the center of the eye. The shape of the lens is continually being altered in order to focus on an object. This is called accommodation, meaning the ability of the lens to adjust to the distance from the object being focused on. Typically, the lens becomes less elastic and flexible with age, requiring eyeglasses for most older people. This loss of accommodation is more common in the West than among traditional peoples, however, a fact often referred to by many optometrists who argue that visual acuity is determined in large measure by lifestyle, attitudes, and overall health, as well as overuse of and overdependence on the eyes.

The lens changes shape, thus focusing on near and far objects, thanks to the ciliary body, a muscular ring that surrounds the

Two lights brighten our world. One is provided by the sun, but another answers to it—the light of the eye. Only through their entwining do we see; lacking either, we are blind.

Arthur Zajonc

235

lens. When the eye focuses on a near object, the ciliary body contracts, causing the lens to become more convex. When the eye
focuses on a distant object, the ciliary body expands, causing the
lens to relax. The ciliary body is connected to fibers of the autonomic nervous system, which allow the brain to tell the ciliary
ring to expand or contract, depending upon what the brain needs
in order to see the image clearly. Focusing the eye is thus an involuntary action.

Since muscles within the iris and the ciliary body focus the
eye, many leading eye therapists maintain that visual acuity is
largely a function of eye-muscle fitness. Indeed, numerous exercise programs have been developed that can successfully restore
visual acuity to those suffering from a wide variety of eye disorders.

The lens is surrounded by vitreous humor, a transparent jelly-
like mass that allows light to pass from the lens to the retina. The
vitreous humor makes up most of the mass of the eye and maintains the shape of the eyeball.

The retina is a tiny flap of nerves, no thicker than a postage
stamp, that catches the light. It sits at the very back of the eye and
surrounds much of the vitreous humor. The retina is composed
of photoreceptors, or light-sensitive nerve cells. These nerves are
divided into two groups, rods and cones. There are an estimated
120 million rods and 7 million cones in the human eye. The rods
detect low-intensity light; we rely upon them most heavily for
night vision. Rods tend to perceive light in shades of black and
white. Cones, so named because of their shape, respond to bright
light and are capable of perceiving color.

Rods and cones react to different degrees of light because of
their differing chemical natures. Rods contain the chemical rhodopsin, or visual purple. Cones contain a group of substances
called opsins, which are highly sensitive to the wavelengths of the
three primary colors, red, blue, and yellow.

When bright light hits the rods, rhodopsin bleaches, permitting the cones to become the dominant light-perceiving cells.
When the light is dim, rhodopsin increases in volume, thus causing the rods to become the dominant photoreceptors. Whether
the image we see is primarily black and white or full of color depends upon the degree of light available, and thus which nerves of
the retina—rods or cones—are employed. Inside the retina, both

rhodopsin and the opsins bind with vitamin A. When light hits the rods and cones, it interacts with vitamin A to create an electrical signal that flows from the retina to the vision center of the brain, thus allowing us to perceive images. It is this dependency upon vitamin A that created the folk wisdom—now known to be true—that carrots are good for the eyes.

Interestingly, the image that the retina receives is actually reversed, or upside down, due to the light being refracted or bent while it travels through the various layers of the eye. The brain corrects this error.

Your eyes are so coordinated that if you cover one eye and shine a light in the other, both pupils will contract. Motor nerves inside the brain and the eye manipulate six small muscles that surround each eye to coordinate their movements.

Because vision is so accurate at discerning the physical world, we tend to believe that the eyes serve as mere windows. On the contrary, the brain works more like a computer, putting together an incredible array of complex information to form its own picture, which corresponds with the outside world. This information is coordinated by the left and right hemispheres of the brain. For example, when you look at a baseball at rest, your right eye will perceive both the left and right sides of the ball; the left eye does the same. Hence, each eye will have left and right fields of vision. The brain treats the left and right fields of vision of each eye differently, however. The right field of vision for both eyes will be interpreted by the left hemisphere, while the left field of vision will be deciphered by the right hemisphere. The brain puts these four separate images together to form a coherent picture.

The eye is a master, the ear a servant.

JAKOB GRIMM

WHEN VISION IS LESS THAN PERFECT

Many illnesses of the brain, nervous system, and the eye will affect vision. Below is a review of the most common disorders affecting the eyes.

Nearsightedness occurs when light rays are focused at a point before they reach the retina. So, distant objects are blurred. What is actually happening is the eyes are over-focusing. The lens is not relaxing (or expanding) sufficiently, causing the image to be focused before it reaches the retina. The condition is corrected by

237

concave lenses, which expand the image and compensate for the exaggerated focusing action of the eyes.

Farsightedness occurs when the cornea and lenses are unable to focus (or contract) sufficiently, causing nearby objects to be blurred. Convex lenses are used to contract the image for the eye, thus correcting the distortion.

Glaucoma, one of the most common eye disorders, is a condition caused by excessive pressure within the eye, causing damage to the nerve fibers of the retina and the tiny blood vessels inside the choroid layer. The result is diminished vision and often total blindness. Orthodox physicians use drugs to lower the pressure, or several types of surgery to open a drainage canal so that the aqueous fluid can escape.

With cataracts, the lens loses its transparency and becomes increasingly opaque. This happens when proteins within the lens degenerate, forming white patches that move from the center of the lens to the periphery. Treatment usually involves the surgical removal of the lens and the insertion of a plastic artificial lens.

The Liver Connection

According to Chinese medicine, the eyes are nourished by the liver, meaning that the life force, or qi, flows from the liver to the eyes. The Yellow Emperor states that the liver "opens" into the eyes. "When the liver receives the blood it strengthens the vision," says the Yellow Emperor's Classic. A healthy liver will provide optimal qi to the eyes and therefore support visual acuity. Conversely, excessively yin or yang conditions of the liver will result in various types of eye disorders.

"When the liver is deficient (empty), then the eye becomes blinded and can no longer see," says the Yellow Emperor. Deficient qi flowing to the eyes will manifest as stages of illness, proceeding from small impairments of sight toward the gradual degeneration of the eyes until blindness sets in. An expanded or swollen liver will most often result in deficient liver qi, and thus inadequate qi to the eyes. The result will be an inability of the cornea and lens to contract, or focus on nearby objects (farsightedness).

Initially, an overly contracted liver will usually cause excessive

Oh thou most excellent eye, elevated above all that God created! What exalted praises are capable of expressing thy nobility? What peoples, what tongues, can describe thy abilities? Through the window of the eye the soul regards the world's beauty.

LEONARDO DA VINCI

liver qi because blood flow will likely be backed up inside the organ, causing a fiery condition. The eyes will therefore receive excessive life force, causing over-focusing or nearsightedness. However, as the condition in the liver worsens, a contracted liver also will result in diminished life force to the eyes, causing a variety of eye disorders, including glaucoma and cataracts.

Dim windows of the soul.

WILLIAM BLAKE

The reason: the liver provides life force to the eyes. Therefore, all cellular maintenance and metabolism within the eye depends upon the liver, which is the eyes' source. As the liver degenerates, the condition of the eyes also will worsen. Cellular reproduction and metabolism within the eye will become deformed, causing a buildup of waste within the eye (glaucoma) and cellular degeneration (cataracts).

According to Chinese medicine, the spleen also can be involved in eye disorders. The spleen nourishes the muscles, while the liver controls them (see chapters on the liver, spleen, and Chinese medicine). Muscle weakness within the eyes—which prevents the ciliary body from contracting and thus focusing on nearby objects—can be caused by both a liver and spleen imbalance. Whatever weakens the liver will ultimately affect vision, say the Chinese.

In the Five Element schematic, the liver is nourished by the kidneys (Water Element) and controlled by the lungs and large intestine (the Metal Element). The conditions and emotional states related to these organs also can play a role in the health of the liver and thus in visual acuity. For instance, the liver is associated with anger. Too much anger will injure the liver, often causing liver qi to become initially excessive, but eventually tired and lethargic. Hence, excessive or repressed anger, especially in childhood, can result in visual impairment.

The kidneys are associated with fear and the will. Kidney imbalances and excessive fear will cause the kidneys to become weak, thus preventing them from passing sufficient life force onto the liver. Without adequate qi from the kidneys, the liver condition will degenerate, thereby ultimately impairing vision.

When the qi of the lungs and large intestine is excessive, these organs will control the liver excessively, causing it to be deficient in life force, and thus diminishing the life force to the eyes. The lungs and large intestine are associated with grief or sadness. Consequently, these emotions, too, may play a role in how well or

Seeing is not a separate isolated function. It's a process involving the entire human organism. The child sees with his whole being; it is profoundly integrated with the total action system of the child—his posture, his manual skills and coordination, his intelligence, and his personality.

ARNOLD GESELL

how poorly we see. While the liver is the primary organ of concern with all eye-related problems, the health of other organs, especially the kidneys, lungs, and large intestine, also may be involved. Restoring healthy vision always begins with treating the liver, but these organs may be involved secondarily. (See chapters on the liver, spleen, kidneys, bladder, lungs, and large intestine for healing foods and herbs associated with these organs.)

Ayurvedic healers associate the eyes with the pitta dosha and the Fire Element of the Indian Five Element system. The pitta dosha serves to balance the more kinetic energies of vata, and the potential energy of kapha. Pitta is associated with both the Fire and Water Elements, creating harmony between these two opposites (and antagonists) within the body. When the pitta dosha is strong, the eyes see clearly. It is increased by sour, salty, and pungent tastes, and is decreased by sweet, bitter, and astringent flavors.

The following foods are said to promote the pitta dosha:

- *Grains:* barley, oats, rice, and wheat.
- *Vegetables:* cabbage, broccoli, brussels sprouts, asparagus, cauliflower, green beans, leafy greens, lettuce, mushrooms, okra, parsley, peas, sprouts, zucchini.
- *Beans:* All beans are considered supportive, except lentils.
- *Animal foods:* shrimp, chicken, turkey, egg whites.
- *Fruit:* apples, grapes, oranges, pears, prunes, raisins.
- *Seeds and nuts:* All nuts are considered harmful. Sunflower and pumpkin seeds are considered healthful in small amounts.

BODY-MIND RELATIONSHIPS

During the past fifty years, a new school of optometrists has emerged. These men and women, who refer to themselves as behavioral optometrists, believe that visual acuity is a learned response to the environment and that various emotional and psychological factors play a role in how well or how poorly we see. Also, physical capabilities, especially coordination, dexterity, and confidence, play fundamental roles in how well our eyes perform. Because all the physical senses, and indeed the body at large, develop together, vision is a whole-body function. Certain behavioral optometrists maintain that particular body types and personalities are associated with specific visual disorders, including nearsightedness and farsightedness. Others maintain that particular physical characteristics, especially lack of physical coordination, poor concentration, or poor self-awareness, conspire to bring about eye disorders.

Behavioral optometrists use a wide variety of exercises for the eyes and the whole body, such as relaxation techniques and mental imaging methods, to improve sight. Behavioral optometry has its roots in the work of pioneer vision therapist Dr. William Bates, who developed exercises to improve vision. The Bates Method was used successfully by many young men who wanted to be fighter pilots during World War II, but were unable to pass the eye exam at the first try. Among the most common practices: lie on a bed and trace the outline of your room where the walls meet the ceiling at a steady and rapid pace. You are rotating your eyes and thus exercising the muscles that focus the eye. Bates also encouraged reading for short periods—ten to twenty minutes—without the use of glasses. When the eyes get tired, rest them, and then read again for as long as possible until they tire again. This time stop. Bates encouraged people to do as much as possible without the use of eyeglasses, which tend to weaken the eyes by making them dependent upon the corrective lenses.

Nathan Pritikin was an expert on the eye and vision. He maintained that both high-fat and high-protein diets contribute to eye disorders by causing fat, cholesterol, and protein by-products (such as uric acid crystals) to infiltrate the eye from the choroid layer. These substances can migrate into both the vitreous humor and aqueous humors of the eye. They also can block the filter meshwork and canal of Schlemm, thus preventing optimal elimination of waste products from the eye. As the filter meshwork and canal of Schlemm become less efficient, aqueous fluid is prevented from flowing out of the eye and thus causes interocular pressure to build, resulting in glaucoma.

Who would believe that so small a space could contain the images of all the universe?

Leonardo da Vinci

241

CHAPTER 22

TOUCH

The human body is the best picture of the human soul.

LUDWIG
WITTGENSTEIN

WE ALL NEED to be touched and to touch one another. There is abundant scientific evidence showing that touching the skin, especially the skin of infants, promotes the development of life-sustaining systems, such as the nervous, respiratory, lymph, and circulatory systems. Breast-fed babies seem to possess a variety of superior physical characteristics, including enhanced immune and gastrointestinal functions, which scientists point out are not entirely attributable to breast milk alone. Studies have shown that infants who are not sufficiently touched have lower immune function and suffer higher rates of infection and even mortality. Touching a child is essential for the healthy psychological status of both the infant and the mother. Even in adulthood, some people who are deprived of the touch of loved ones experience a variety of antisocial behaviors and even violence.

The same occurs with other members of the animal kingdom. Domestic animals typically lick their young. Studies have shown that this licking stimulates the development and function of the gastrointestinal and urinary tracts, as well as the sex organs. Other research has shown that when animals are deprived of this licking, they frequently die.

Touch is your most basic means of experiencing the physical world. It is your most immediate way of understanding the nature of things: their temperature, texture, weight, size, and shape. Humans touch other people to communicate affection, to satisfy the desire for sex, to show love, and to receive love in return.

Still, despite the necessity of laws and mores that regulate touching, few things are more healing and essential than the touch of love. Every culture has had its form of healing touch, whether it is the laying on of hands, massage techniques, or bodywork. Today, therapeutic touch is returning in many forms. In the past twenty years, there has been a veritable explosion of bodywork therapists in the U.S., Europe, and Japan. Many nurses and other health-care professionals are providing therapeutic touch in hospital settings.

After decades of repression in which doctors were loathe even to touch a patient, the power and importance of touch is now being reevaluated. It's a good thing, for who among us can live without the gentle awakening that comes when another human hand is received in peace?

THE SENSATIONS OF TOUCH

Your sense of touch is located in the skin, including the lips, tongue, eyes, nose, genitals, and scalp. Many thousands of specialized cells in the skin respond to external stimuli and communicate to your brain the characteristics of the things with which you come in contact. These characteristics include five specific sensations: touch, pressure, pain, heat, and cold. Secondary sensations, such as tickling and itching, are muted variations of touch and pain, and are conveyed by the same nerves that provide both of these more common experiences.

The body's parts possess varying degrees of sensitivity. Some parts of the body possess greater sensitivity to temperature than others. The feet are more sensitive to heat than the hands, for example. Other parts are more sensitive to pain. The cornea is several hundred times more sensitive to pain than the bottoms of the feet. Other parts of the body have selective sensitivity, such as fingertips, which have excellent powers of recognition but are not particularly sensitive to pain.

Like other senses, touch has greater potential for sensitivity than most of us will ever experience. People who lose one of the physical senses or whose professions demand that they develop their potential for touch demonstrate far greater perception and sensitivity than most of us. The blind read Braille with their fingers, for example, while a massage therapist may develop an ability to assess another person's health with his or her hands.

The skin contains many types of touch receptors. In general, these are divided into two main categories. One type is made of a long nerve fiber that may rest near the surface of the skin or attach itself to a hair follicle and respond when the hair is moved. The other possesses a specialized nerve ending, called an end organ, that is capable of reacting to a specific stimulus, such as pressure or pain. These are more common in nonhairy parts of the skin, such as the lips and fingertips.

Touch receptors pass electrical nerve impulses from the point of origin (the fingertips, for example) to sensory nerves that flow to the spinal cord. The spinal cord then passes the information on to the thalamus in the brain, and from there to the sensory cortex, where it is interpreted and often made conscious. We are not aware of much of the physical stimuli that our nervous systems process. For example, you are probably unconscious of the interaction between your buttocks and your chair, or the feeling of this book in your hands, or even of the smell in the room. We remain unconscious of much of the information available to us.

The specialized touch receptors that are embedded at various depths within the skin provide information about specific sensations. Each group of receptors has its own responsibility and nature. Also, several types of touch receptors may be involved in the same chore. For example, touch and light pressure are conveyed to us by several types of specialized nerves, including Meissner's corpuscles, long tentaclelike nerves with round, flat nerve endings that look like tennis rackets; Merkel's discs, which are multiple branches of nerves that spring from a single stem; free nerve endings, which look like trees with many long limbs; and hairroot plexuses, which collect around hair follicles and respond when hairs are stimulated. Most of these nerves are right below the surface of the skin and respond to slight touch.

Deep pressure is conveyed by a type of nerve fiber called Pacinian corpuscles, which look like elongated donuts with a long string attached to them. Pacinian corpuscles are deep within the skin. You need to press on something before they are stimulated. Cold is communicated via the end bulbs of Krause, which possess a circular end organ with many thin stringlike fibers inside the circle. Heat is communicated by the end organs of Ruffini, which look like inverted umbrellas on long handles. Pain is conveyed by free nerve endings, which are very fine branches with knobs at their ends. Free nerve endings are distributed throughout most tissues, but especially just below the surface of the skin.

There are two types of pain. Somatic pain involves the external parts of the body, while visceral pain occurs in internal organs. Somatic pain can occur superficially, at the surface of the skin, or deep within the tissues, such as at the bone, tendons, muscles, and ligaments. Generally, pain is described as pricking, burning, or aching. Pricking occurs at the surface of the skin from a pin prick, a cut, or a pinch; burning pain is experienced from excessive heat or scraping the skin; aching or throbbing is a deep and persistent pain, often of low intensity.

Pain usually arises from disease, disorder, or injury. It is among the most important and primitive sensations of the human body. It alerts the conscious mind of danger. It informs you that remedial action or change is necessary and must be made immediately. The kinds of actions to be taken depend upon the source of the pain. It may require nothing more than moving your hand away from a flame, or more long-term actions, such as altering habits and lifestyle. Unlike other senses, such as taste or smell, adaptation to pain does not occur easily. Pain persists and will be perceived consciously until appropriate action is taken.

Pain is a symptom, a means of communication, caused by some underlying disorder. It is essentially a teaching mechanism. It is the body's way of telling you about its immediate condition, and instructing you on the effects of your behavior. It is this latter function that guides you in your understanding of which behaviors support health and life, and which are destructive. In this sense, pain is essential for continuation of life.

Pain is often seen as an inconvenience in modern society, hence the success of the analgesic industry. Painkillers cover up pain by eliminating your ability to feel it. They do nothing for the underlying cause of the pain, however. Consequently, the underlying problem may grow worse until a crisis manifests and you are forced to undergo more radical action.

FROM SHIATSU TO ACUPRESSURE

In the Orient the value of touch has been explored and elevated to highly evolved healing and spiritual disciplines. Touch is among the most important methods of healing in the East. It an important means of transmitting the life force from one person to another.

The healthful and efficient functioning of the human form depends upon the presence of optimal amounts of qi or prana. Traditional health care in the East is essentially the promotion and maintenance of the life force within the body. For the Oriental, we are literally standing in the midst of infinite energy. Our health and fulfillment depend upon our being receptive to this universal energy.

The oldest tradition that combines this understanding with the body is Indian yoga. Yogic tradition sees the body as the physical manifestation of the mind and spirit. All three are interrelated as one unit. Consequently, your consciousness, the way you feel about yourself, about others, and your world, is manifest in your physical body in a variety of ways. Those aspects of you that are developed, evolved, and at peace will be reflected as flexibility, strength, and vitality in your body. Those aspects that are in conflict will be reflected in your body as places of tension, rigidity, and structural abnormalities. Thus, to heal the body is also to heal the mind and spirit. Yoga employs postures and exercises to free the body of unnatural or abnormal restrictions that arise from past trauma and delusions.

Healing is the act of balancing the life force within the body to restore the overt biological functions to normalcy. The human body receives life force from the environment at large. It utilizes this life force to maintain its own health; at the same time, the body—if strong enough—can also transmit qi to others. Healing touch is the healer's act of transferring universal energy from the environment at large to the patient, by using his own body as a conductor.

Healing touch, such as the laying on of hands and various kinds of massage therapy, especially acupressure and shiatsu, are methods of transferring healing energy to another human being. The laying on of hands is a less specific way of transferring qi to another person. The premise is to enrich another person's overall life force, which, it is hoped, will help him or her to overcome illness.

Acupressure and shiatsu, just two of many Oriental disciplines, are massage techniques for transferring qi to specific acupuncture points and meridians. Rather than use needles, which work as antennae to draw qi into the body at specific points and along certain meridian lines, healing touch is used to stimulate qi and unblock meridians. This results in the reestablishment of the life force and the restoration of health.

Reflexology is also based upon the concept of meridians and life energy. Foot reflexology is the therapeutic massaging of the feet at energy points that are said to correspond to specific organs and systems.

The Bible is full of references to healing through touch. So, too, are the Dead Sea Scrolls. Indeed, the laying on of hands has been one of the oldest and primary means of restoring health in the Western world.

During much of this century, these traditions were practiced only among a few esoteric therapists. But since the 1960s, healing touch emerged as if from below ground in the form of a variety of bodywork therapies. These practices concentrate on places of tension and restriction in the body, and also on movement and posture. Among the most widely practiced bodywork therapies today are the Hellerwork, Rolfing, Feldenkrais, and Alexander techniques. While the techniques differ somewhat, the basic principles are essentially the same: the body, mind, and spirit are a unified entity, and by healing the body, one frees the mind and spirit of conflicts, distress, and illness.

Among the pioneering practitioners of bodywork in the West is Dr. Alexander Lowen, who has been exploring for decades how emotional conflicts in childhood keep people from experiencing their feelings. The failure to feel deeply is transferred to the body, which also becomes numb. The result is a parallel degeneration among the body, mind, and spirit.

"You grow up as a child with so many traumas," says Lowen,

"so much unfulfillment, so much pain and despair, that you can't stand it and the only way to stand it is to numb yourself. So you have to numb your body, because that's where feeling is. Then you can't function in a healthy way anymore because there's numbness. You're not sensitive to other people, you're not sensitive to your own needs."

The results, says Lowen, are a wide variety of physical distortions, changes in breathing, and ultimately disease. Lowen, who is the author of several important books on the relationship between the mind and body, including *Language of the Body* and *Love, Sex and Your Heart,* says that by working on the body, by "softening it" and removing its "armor," health can be restored.

He describes the process of going from sickness to health this way: "Health is aliveness, spontaneity, gracefulness, and, especially rhythm. We describe the process of getting well in three stages. First, the person has to become self-aware. You've got to feel yourself, know yourself, before you can work through. The second step, after you learn to know yourself, is to learn how to express yourself. You've got to be able to cry, to get angry, to feel sad or frightened. To be free to express feelings. The third step is self-possession, which means you have to have all your feelings available to know exactly how to use them." Lowen, who terms his work *Bioenergetics,* says that by working with the body, all three of these steps can be accomplished.

PART FOUR

The Systems

THERE ARE NO Oriental approaches to the body's systems, per se. An understanding of the nervous and endocrine systems, for example, is possible only with the help of the modern sciences, such as biochemistry and electricity. The fact that we know such systems exist at all is due exclusively to the work of Western medicine.

Yet, the Oriental systems, particularly the Chinese, do have their own classification of illnesses that are diagnosed today as diseases of the nervous or endocrine systems. What is recognized today as Parkinson's disease, an illness affecting the nervous system, was once diagnosed as an imbalance of the triple heater, for example. Swollen glands, a disorder of the lymph system, was seen in Chinese medicine as related to a spleen imbalance.

While you are reading these chapters, keep in mind the basic yin-yang dialectic used by the Chinese. Though the Chinese knew nothing of these systems, their most essential tool for understanding the human body—the premise that the body functions by virtue of a polarity between pairs of opposites—is consistently in evidence in the physiology of the systems.

We provide some of these crossover relationships, but also offer a variety of other alternative approaches to common illnesses that afflict these systems. In many cases, the alternatives are grounded in traditional understandings of health care. For example, we offer some of the cutting-edge insights into such illnesses as multiple sclerosis, diabetes, and osteoporosis. The approaches we describe often are grounded in the existing scientific evidence, as well as the ancient healing traditions of the East and West.

CHAPTER 23

THE CIRCULATORY SYSTEM

THE CIRCULATORY SYSTEM is well-known today because, in most industrialized nations, it is the part of the body most likely to fail in a way that causes death. In fact, there have been few epidemics in world history as deadly as cardiovascular disease. Today, sixty-six million Americans suffer from illnesses that afflict the heart and arteries, including coronary heart disease, high blood pressure, and stroke. Some 800,000 Americans die annually from these diseases, accounting for half of all deaths in the U.S.

The cost, not only in lives but in dollars, is staggering. Americans spend nearly $100 billion a year on medical care and lost wages from cardiovascular disease. Much of the medical bill goes to surgery, such as coronary bypass operations. Some 350,000 coronary artery bypass surgeries are performed annually, about 70 percent of them on men, at an average cost of about $20,000 apiece.

Ironically, cardiovascular disease is almost unheard of in the Third World and among Orientals living on traditional diets. The reason is simple: the diets of traditional peoples tend to be low in fat and cholesterol, and rich in whole grains, vegetables, and fish. That diet protects them from many illnesses, but especially from heart disease.

The rule of the artery is supreme.

ANDREW STILL

251

Drugs and surgery are all too often given as substitutes for understanding and changing what I believe are the primary underlying causes of coronary heart disease: harmful responses to emotional stresses, a high-fat, high-cholesterol diet primarily based on animal products, and cigarette smoking.

DEAN ORNISH

New research has shown, however, that such traditional diets not only prevent cardiovascular disease, but also cure it. In November 1989, Dr. Dean Ornish, director of the Preventive Medicine Research Institute in Sausalito, California, reported a study showing reversal of the cholesterol plaque (known as atherosclerosis) that clogs the arteries to the heart and is the underlying cause of cardiovascular disease. He cured the illness by having patients follow a program that included meditation and a diet low in fat and cholesterol. Ornish's research is the first to show that diet and lifestyle alone can reverse atherosclerosis in the coronary arteries in humans. Unlike other studies that demonstrated reversal, Ornish's study used no cholesterol-lowering drugs.

What is unfortunate is that the circulatory system is known for what goes wrong with it, rather than what it actually does. Your circulation provides every cell in your body with what it needs to stay alive right this instant: oxygen, nutrition, immune protection, and the elimination of waste.

A TALE OF TWO CIRCUITS

Human circulation is essentially a two-circuit system. Systemic circulation brings oxygen-rich blood to cells throughout your body, while pulmonary circulation returns carbon dioxide–rich blood to the lungs. Let's take a closer look at each, beginning with the first circuit.

After your blood receives oxygen in the lungs, it flows to the upper chamber, called the left atrium, of the heart, and then down into the left ventricle, the lower chamber. There, a powerful contraction of the heart muscle forces the blood out of the heart and into the main artery, the aorta, which runs down the center of the body and branches off into smaller arteries, called arterioles. These arterioles flow to organs and muscle tissue.

Inside the organ or muscle, the arterioles branch into a network of capillaries. Capillaries are made of semipermeable membranes that allow oxygen and nutrients in the blood to pass through the capillary wall to the cells that surround the tiny vessel. At the same time, carbon dioxide and other forms of waste can pass from the cells through the capillary wall and into the blood. While this exchange is taking place, the blood turns from

The Circulatory System

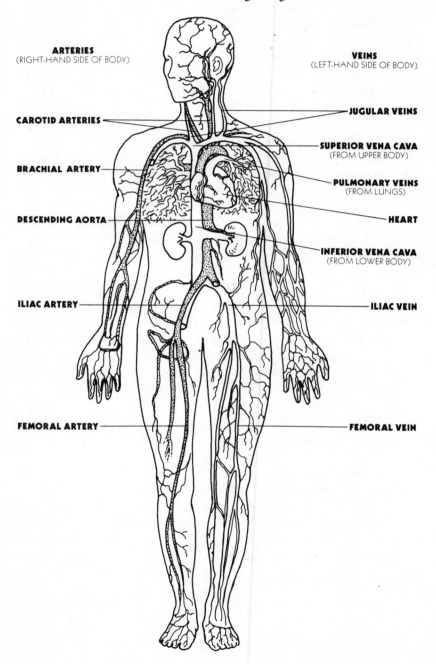

ARTERIES
(RIGHT-HAND SIDE OF BODY)

VEINS
(LEFT-HAND SIDE OF BODY)

CAROTID ARTERIES

BRACHIAL ARTERY

DESCENDING AORTA

ILIAC ARTERY

FEMORAL ARTERY

JUGULAR VEINS

SUPERIOR VENA CAVA
(FROM UPPER BODY)

PULMONARY VEINS
(FROM LUNGS)

HEART

INFERIOR VENA CAVA
(FROM LOWER BODY)

ILIAC VEIN

FEMORAL VEIN

The human body's dual circulation system brings oxygen-rich blood to cells through the arteries and returns carbon dioxide–rich blood to the heart and lungs through the veins. A series of interlinked loops ensures that all parts of the body are infused with nutrients and essential constituents, and that blood is constantly cleansed by the liver and kidneys.

253

*With advances in modern
medicine, and especially
transfusion technology, blood
is losing much of its sacred and
symbolic meaning, and instead
is often being seen and treated
as little more than an increasingly valuable commodity
in the medical marketplace.
Currently, blood is the most
commonly sold human
body "product."*

ANDREW KIMBRELL

its bright red, oxygen-carrying color, to a reddish purple, its color
while carrying carbon dioxide (CO_2).

After the blood has received the CO_2, it flows from the capillaries to small veins, called venules. These small veins flow to
larger veins that eventually join with one of two venae cavae that
flow into the heart. The superior venae cavae flows into the right
atrium of the heart from above; the inferior venae cavae flows into
the same atrium from below.

The heart pumps blood into the lungs via the pulmonary artery. In the lungs, the blood flows into another network of tiny
capillaries that join with millions of tiny sacs, called alveoli. Here,
the blood gives up its carbon dioxide load and receives oxygen.
Once again, the blood flows to the left atrium, then to the left ventricle, and then to the aorta.

The heart pumps blood with considerable pressure, but that
pressure is diminished on its way back to the heart, especially in
the legs and arms. Circulation is assisted by a valve system within
the veins which prevents blood from flowing backward.

The circulatory system is actually a series of loops within the
body that ensures the blood will pass through specific parts of the
body such as the neck and head and then back to the heart. Once
blood returns to the heart, it goes to the lungs again for oxygen,
and then back to the heart, and then onto another loop.

For the blood to nourish cells, it must receive adequate supplies of nutrition. It does this by passing from the aorta to the
stomach, intestines, spleen, and pancreas. These organs provide
the blood with vitamins and minerals, blood sugar (glucose), immune cells, and various other blood constituents. From there, it
passes to the liver.

The liver receives blood from two sources. The hepatic artery
carries oxygenated blood to the liver, while the portal vein carries
nutrient-rich blood from the digestive organs and spleen. The
liver cleanses the blood of impurities, infuses it with thousands of
enzymes and immune cells, and obtains the nutrients essential for
its health. From the liver, the blood goes back to the heart, where
it receives a new supply of oxygen and then flows to the next loop,
the kidneys, where it will be cleansed and nutrients will be balanced. From the kidneys, the blood returns to the heart, and then
onto another circuit, the lower extremities. Because all the loops
within the system are linked, the blood is always being infused

with nutrients and essential blood constituents, and being cleansed by the liver and kidneys. Thus, no part of the body is deprived.

High blood pressure, or hypertension as it is also called, is the most common cardiovascular illness in the U.S. It can lead to heart attack, kidney damage, pancreatic disease, and disorders of the eye. High blood pressure often results in aneurysms, "blowouts" of arteries leading to the brain that result in a stroke. Blood pressure is considered high when it exceeds 140/90. Many insurers will not carry a policy on someone when the lower number of the blood pressure scale exceeds 85.

Blood pressure is caused by the expansion and contraction of the heart. The diastolic phase occurs when the heart relaxes and opens, allowing blood to flow into the chambers. The systolic phase occurs when the heart contracts, causing blood to be pumped into the arterial system and throughout the body.

Contrary to what many people believe, elevated blood pressure is not an inevitable consequence of aging. Blood pressure increases with age in the U.S. and much of the Western world, but in populations that still follow traditional diets, blood pressure tends to remain within the healthy range throughout life.

The three principal causes of high blood pressure are atherosclerosis, excessive salt intake, and kidney disease. Atherosclerosis raises blood pressure by narrowing the passageways within arteries. This causes pressure to build behind the blood that is backed up. The effect is analogous to pinching a hose to increase the pressure of the water that flows out.

Excessive salt intake causes edema, which increases the plasma or liquid portion of the blood. Greater quantities of plasma mean increased blood flow within arteries and veins that have distinct limits. Salt also causes the tiny renal arteries in the kidneys to contract, which causes blood to back up behind the kidneys and thus increases pressure.

Sweating therapy can be used to restore circulation. It will raise body heat and metabolism, burn off toxins, and relieve congestion.

You can lower blood pressure simply by reducing the amount of fat in your diet. In most cases, blood pressure will be reduced even if salt is kept at a constant.

Ornish's study proved conclusively that by lowering fat and

Blood will tell, but often it tells too much.

DON MARQUIS

255

cholesterol, even advanced atherosclerosis can be cured. Ornish enlisted the cooperation of forty-eight men and women, all of whom had coronary artery disease and were scheduled for angiograms, a test used to determine the amount of atherosclerosis clogging the coronary arteries. All forty-eight people showed significant closure of the coronary arteries after their angiograms.

The test subjects were divided into two groups of twenty-four. The control group was given the standard medical advice for heart disease: they were encouraged to adopt a 30 percent fat diet, stop smoking, and do aerobic exercise three times per week.

The experimental group was placed on a vegetarian diet that derived only 8 percent of its calories from fat. The foods that the experimental group ate were primarily whole grains and vegetables. They also received instruction in stress management, yoga, and aerobic exercise. All of the members of the experimental group stopped smoking, as well.

The two groups were followed for one year. Before they began receiving their treatment, the average blood cholesterol level in the experimental group was 213 mg/dl. At the end of the year, their cholesterol levels fell to an average of 154 mg/dl. The control group started out with an average cholesterol level of 251 mg/dl, and managed to bring that down to 230 on the 30 percent fat diet.

Doctors also performed angiograms once again on the remaining participants of both groups. (Seven had dropped out of the study, two from the experimental group and five from the control group. Interestingly, compliance was better among the experimental group than the controls, who received the less demanding program.) Of the twenty-two remaining participants in the experimental group, eighteen members showed reversal of atherosclerosis in the coronary arteries. That is, the atherosclerotic plaque in the arteries leading to the heart got smaller, making the passageway within the artery larger. In the control group, ten of the remaining nineteen members showed a worsening of the atherosclerotic plaque. Three members remained the same, and six got slightly better.

After reviewing the study, Dr. Claude L'Enfant, director of the National Heart, Lung and Blood Institute, stated, "This is a tremendously important study in the control of coronary artery disease without pharmaceutical intervention."

Ornish's work and other recent studies suggest that heart dis-

Americans and Europeans are literally eating themselves to death, gorging on marbled beef and other grain-fed animal products, taking into their bodies massive amounts of saturated fats and cholesterol. The fatty substances are building up in the blood-stream, clogging arteries, lining cell walls, blocking passages, triggering metabolic and hormonal changes, stimulating cell growth, and rupturing organs. The "good life" promised by the beef culture has metamorphosed into a cruel joke as Americans, overweight and plagued by the diseases of affluence, suffer from their own excesses.

JEREMY RIFKIN

ease is much more than a pump in need of repair. In addition to being fed a healthful diet, your heart requires emotional and spiritual sustenance. According to Ornish, "Many people are in pain, spiritually and emotionally. Without addressing that pain, it's hard to get any further. But when it is addressed and when you show people ways of dealing with that, the transformations can in many cases be dramatic."

For the blood is the life.

DEUTERONOMY

Ornish points to the case of a volunteer in his study who had reduced his cholesterol level from 271 to 192, an admirable reduction but not yet sufficient, Ornish thought, to cause reversal of arterial blockage. An angiogram revealed, however, that the man's arteries had indeed opened. Ornish attributed the surprising success to the man's eagerness to open himself to a higher power, to explore his feelings of isolation and loneliness and do something about them, and to avoid the factors Ornish says are "most toxic to the heart": excessive self-involvement, hostility, and cynicism.

Much more than a pump, the heart is a symbol of love, compassion, affection, and spirit, as has been recognized by various societies throughout the world. By keeping it healthy, you can keep the rest of your body well, and also contribute to the overall health of friends, partners, family members—indeed, all those with whom you come in daily contact.

CHAPTER 24

THE MUSCULAR SYSTEM

Exercise is more than burning up calories. Movement is more than stretching. The presence of a mind in our person, and all that this means, from sensation to higher forms of reasoning, is paradoxically most obvious in the way our bodies move.

TED KAPTCHUK

USCLES ARE MOVEMENT. Muscles are Michael Jordan soaring across a basketball court and descending on a rim. They are José Canseco driving a baseball out of a stadium with an awesome swing of the bat. They are the physical comedy of Steve Martin, the sensuality of Madonna. Muscles provide much of the power and beauty of the human body.

Though the word *muscle* shares a Latin derivation (*mus*) with the word *mouse* (from the perceived resemblance between the movements of a mouse and a muscle), muscle also has come to mean sheer power and brute force. To "muscle in" is to be able to make one's way or take control by strength or force. Was it an accident that the 1980s, a decade that admired corporate "strong-arming" and business bullies, was the decade of pumping iron, Arnold Schwarzenegger, and the bodybuilding craze? What is it about muscles and the body's muscular system that inspires such varied views?

There are some 656 muscles in the body. Each works by pulling, thus drawing bones closer to one another. For this to happen, muscles must be coordinated; as one set pulls, another relaxes and stretches. Thus, when you lift something heavy with your arms, your bicep muscles contract while the tricep muscles (located in the back of the arm) relax and stretch. Conversely, when you want to extend your arms, your tricep muscles contract while the biceps relax. In this way, all movement occurs: your leg is straightened or bent, your head is turned, your eyes are opened. Healthy, well-toned muscles provide strength and endurance.

But their utility is only half the picture. Muscles are the foundation of human beauty. They are expressions of poised power. In their motion lies our capacity for physical grace, agility, speed, force, and flight. In the sculpture of ancient Greece and the painting of Renaissance Italy can be found perhaps the fullest expressions of the muscular system's archetypal beauty. Among God's most wondrous creations is the muscular body, said the Italian sculptor and painter Michelangelo.

An Inside Look at Muscles

Muscles and bone are joined by tendons, and are so closely wedded that many consider them one musculoskeletal system. Indeed, if we fail to use one, both will atrophy into nonexistence. A third dimension is often considered, as well. Muscles are coupled to nerves in a neuromuscular system. Bones, muscle, and nerves form the trinity of movement within the body, each one dependent upon the other, none fully understood without the other two.

There are three types of muscle: smooth, cardiac, and skeletal. Smooth muscles, which are located in the digestive tract and the walls of organs and blood vessels, are controlled by the autonomic nervous system and are largely involuntary. They serve four functions: to propel materials, such as food and waste, along the digestive tract; expel body fluids from organs, such as bile from the gall bladder and urine from the bladder; regulate the size of openings, such as the sphincter muscle of the anus or the pupil of the eye; and close blood vessels and other passages, such as bronchial tubes.

Cardiac muscles are found in the wall of the heart. Fibrous and striated, and arranged in parallel bundles, these muscles are made of cells that rhythmically expand and contract. The cells and bundles of muscle tissue function as one, partly by virtue of the coordinated electrical impulses fired by specific nodes within the heart.

Screw up the vise as tightly as possible—you have rheumatism; give it another turn, and that is gout.

ANONYMOUS

The skeletal muscles are what we typically think of when we picture muscles. They control posture, locomotion, and the movement of the head, neck, torso, back, limbs, and fingers. The skeletal muscles are long, cylindrically shaped, and composed of many striated fibers that lie parallel to one another. These fibers are grouped in bundles, called fasciculi, and enclosed in membranes called perimysium. The entire muscle is enclosed in a sheath called the epimysium. Sheets of connective tissue, called fascia, separate individual muscles.

Skeletal muscles are capable of both expansion and contraction. They work by stretching and shortening. The elasticity gives them the ability to regain their original form once their work is done and they relax. Muscles move thanks to nerve impulses which are triggered by a variety of stimuli, among which are changes in temperature and pressure. A weak stimulus causes a less intense response of shorter duration; a strong stimulus results in a more intense response that usually lasts longer. Continual stimulus results in sustained contraction, called tetanus.

When muscles are exercised they require more fuel in the form of oxygen and glucose. Thus, circulation is increased dramatically to muscle tissues. As tissue is changed into energy and waste products, new cells form, making the muscles stronger, bigger, and more efficient. Meanwhile, waste products that have been stored in the muscles are released into the blood stream and eliminated from the body. Fat, surrounding muscle tissue, is burned as fuel, causing muscle tone to be enhanced. As skeletal muscles become stronger and more fit, they act as auxiliary hearts, pumping blood more efficiently throughout the body and taking stress off the heart.

All muscles except the heart are susceptible to cramping, or sustained contraction, which can be painful. Inefficient and out-of-shape muscles are far more susceptible to cramping than well-toned muscles. Overall, muscle efficiency is dependent upon the frequency of exercise.

MUSCLES IN CHINA AND INDIA

In Chinese medicine, the spleen and liver control muscle condition and development. The Yellow Emperor says that the liver

The Skeletal Muscles

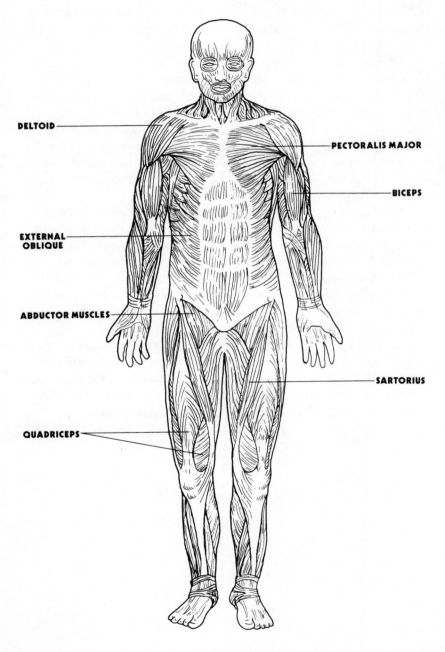

DELTOID

PECTORALIS MAJOR

BICEPS

EXTERNAL OBLIQUE

ABDUCTOR MUSCLES

SARTORIUS

QUADRICEPS

The long, cylindrically shaped skeletal muscles control posture, locomotion, and movement by expanding and contracting, stretching and shortening. This elasticity gives them the ability to regain their original form once their work is done and they relax.

controls the muscles and muscle activity. But it is the spleen that sends qi to the muscles and is responsible for muscle tone. (See chapters on liver and spleen for information concerning these organs and the foods and herbs that will strengthen muscle development and tone.)

From the point of view of Ayurvedic healers, all three doshas come into play in the utilization and maintenance of muscles. Vata controls all body movements, and therefore plays a central role in muscle activity. It is responsible for making glucose and other nutrients available to muscles, and for moving waste from muscle tissue. Kapha ensures that muscles have potential energy, sustains their essential form, and lubricates and cleanses the muscles with lymph. Pitta provides the fire that burns the glucose as energy.

Each of the three archetypal constitutions is revealed through a specific body type. Kapha has excellent muscle development, tone, and coordination. The kapha type is the most likely to be athletic, yet is prone to being overweight. The pitta constitution will have moderate muscle development, good athletic abilities, and will likely remain thin or moderately built. The vata type has the least muscle development, has little interest in athletics, and may appear to be wasting away.

Kapha types need vigorous exercise of any type and regular activity because their muscle development is potentially the greatest of the three constitutional types, and therefore the one most in need of continual attention to maintain balance. Pitta types are attracted to competitive sports and can sustain long periods of exercise. A vata person needs light exercises, such as yoga and tai chi, because he or she easily becomes exhausted.

CHAPTER 25

THE SKELETAL SYSTEM

HUMANS WOULD BE a race of odd-shaped worms if not for the skeleton. You owe your ability to stand upright to your bones, which also, along with the muscles, allow you to walk, run, and dance. In addition bones protect and support the organs within the body, especially the brain, encased in the skull; the spinal cord, encased in the vertebrae of the spine; and the heart, lungs and other thoracic organs within the rib cage. Some 99 percent of the body's calcium is stored in the skeleton. Bones are the stones of the human body, the mineral world within.

Bones are composed of several layers, the first of which is a thin membrane, the periosteum, which contains blood vessels and nerves. Beneath this outer layer is the hard dense shell that we typically think of as bone. Below that is the spongy marrow, which contains tissues that produce red and white blood cells. Calcium and phosphorus act as mortar to make bones hard, while collagen, a protein, forms a latticelike connective tissue upon which calcium and phosphorus accumulate.

As we have seen in virtually every other part of the human body, the bones remain healthy by virtue of opposing functions within them. In this case, these opposing functions arise from

The human body is an instrument for the production of art in the life of the human soul.

ALFRED NORTH
WHITEHEAD

263

two types of bone cells. Osteoblasts build bone tissue by causing calcium to be added to the collagen foundation, while osteoclasts break down bone by causing calcium to be removed from the bone and added to the blood.

New bone tissue is continually being formed within the bone, while old bone is being broken down in the paradoxical functions of metabolism and catabolism. Endocrine glands determine which of these functions is more active. Growth hormone from the pituitary, estrogen or testosterone from the sex organs, and calcitonin from the thyroid stimulate osteoblasts to form more bone, while parathyroid hormone encourages osteoclasts to remove calcium from bone tissue and increase blood levels of calcium.

The Skull

The skull is made up of twenty-nine mostly hollow bones, thus keeping the head light and maneuverable. The various cavities and holes in the skull allow it to hold such vital organs as the brain, mouth, eyes, and nose, and allow the entrance and exit of nerves, blood vessels, and the brain stem.

PARIETAL

TEMPORAL

FRONTAL

NASAL

OCCIPITAL

MASTOID PROCESS

MANDIBLE

A Jigsaw Puzzle of Bones

Most people possess 206 bones, though some have an extra vertebrae while others are missing a digit in a finger or toe. The skeleton also consists of ligaments, which are fibrous tissues that hold bones together at the joints and also connect organs to one another, and cartilage, which covers the ends of bones at the joints and serves as the foundation for some of the body's structures, such as the ears and nose.

The bones of most people do not reach their maximum density until around the age of thirty-five. After that, all of us experience some degree of bone loss, usually about 1 percent per year on the average.

There are four types of bones: long, found in the limbs; flat, in the skull, ribs, and sternum; short, in the wrist and ankle; and irregular, found in the spine and skull. The skeleton can be divided into general categories: the axial and the appendicular. The axial consists of eighty bones that make up the skull, spine, ribs and sternum (or breastbone).

The skull is made up of twenty-nine bones, all of them flat or irregular. Many of them are hollow and thus lighter, making it easier for you to move your head. Small bones within the skull include the hyoid, located in the back of the tongue, and three tiny bones in each middle ear. There are also various cavities and holes in the skull. The cavities hold the brain and form the mouth, eyes, and the nasal hole. The holes allow nerves and blood vessels to enter and exit, and allow the brain stem to enter from below.

The skull rests on the top vertebra of the spine, called the atlas, that allows extensive though limited movement of the head. The spine contains twenty-six bones, all of them small vertebrae. They are the seven cervical bones (or the upper section of vertebrae); the twelve thoracic (middle section); five lumbar (found in the small of the back); the sacrum (lower end of the spine); and the coccyx or tailbone.

There are 126 appendicular bones, including sixty-four bones in the shoulders and upper limbs. Your body has two collarbones (clavicles), two shoulder blades (the scapulas) capping each upper arm (the humerus), forearm bones (the radius and ulna), eight short bones in the wrist (carpals), five shorter bones in each hand (metacarpals), and fourteen bones in the digits of each hand (the phalanges, two in each thumb and three in each finger).

The lower extremities are composed of sixty-two bones, including the hip or pelvis, one bone in each thigh (the femur), a kneecap (the patella), the inner side shin (tibia), the outer side shin (fibula), seven short bones in each ankel (tarsals), five short bones in each foot (metatarsals), and fourteen bones in the digits in each foot (two in each big toe and three in each of the other toes).

WHEN BONES BECOME BRITTLE

Osteoporosis, a disease in which bone tissue becomes more porous and thus prone to fracture, afflicts approximately 25 million Americans. Fractures occur most commonly in the forearm, various spinal vertebrae, the hip, the pelvis, and the femur. Osteoporosis afflicts more women than men, and more Caucasians and Orientals living in the U.S. than African-Americans, who tend to have greater bone mass. It is more prevalent in the Western, industrialized world than in poorer Third World nations, a fact that many scientists point to when making the argument that lifestyle plays a significant role in the onset of the illness.

Osteoporosis is a controversial illness, with leading scientists and physicians disagreeing about the best methods for preventing and treating it. Some doctors maintain that diet and lifestyle should be given greater emphasis in both the prevention and the treatment of the illness, while others say that the singular treatment for osteoporosis is hormone replacement therapy. Much is still unknown about the illness. Though it has been diagnosed for centuries, it was only in 1984 that the National Institutes of Health termed the disease a major threat to public health. Regardless of whatever disagreements exist, both sides agree that all women should know the risk factors for contracting the illness.

In addition to gender and race, the other important risk factors for osteoporosis are:

- *Diet:* The scientific evidence demonstrates that the availability of certain nutrients increase bone mass, while too much of others contribute to bone loss.

The more I have studied the medical literature, the harder it has gotten for me to listen to the dairy industry's promotion of "milk for strong bones." In spite of its high calcium content, milk, because of its high protein content, appears actually to contribute to the accelerating development of osteoporosis. The occurrence of this condition has reached truly epidemic proportions in the United States, and the promotion of dairy products as an "answer" to the suffering of millions seems to me to be not only self-serving, but even criminal.

JOHN ROBBINS

- *Exercise:* Like muscle tissue, bones grow stronger with physical exercise, and atrophy from inactivity.
- *Smoking:* Nicotine and tars in cigarettes prevent calcium assimilation and bone development, and smoking has been shown to lower estrogen levels in women.
- *Alcohol:* The leading cause of osteoporosis among men, alcohol causes male sex organs to produce lower levels of testosterone.
- *Certain pharmaceutical drugs:* Prednisone, commonly prescribed for asthma and inflammation, is among the most destructive medications to skeletal health available on the market today.
- *A family history of osteoporosis.*
- *Blood levels of vitamin D.*

Once a woman reaches menopause, her rate of bone loss increases dramatically because she loses most, though not all, of her ability to produce estrogen. After menopause, the ovaries stop producing eggs and secrete far less estrogen. The adrenal glands compensate somewhat by producing additional hormone, but the total quantity of estrogen in a woman's body decreases sharply after menopause.

Estrogen in women and testosterone in men are essential for producing and maintaining bone tissue, though scientists still do not understand exactly how these hormones perform such tasks. Since men do not undergo menopause, their rate of osteoporosis is far lower than that of women. However, men can reduce the amount of testosterone their bodies produce by consuming too much alcohol, which will substantially decrease the male hormone and consequently diminish bone mass.

Women experience the sharpest decline in bone mass during the first five years after menopause, when they can lose anywhere from 2 to 6 percent of bone mass per year. Subsequently, bone loss tends to level off to an average of 1 percent per year. How that loss affects the overall health of the skeleton depends a great deal on how much bone reserve the woman has accumulated during her first thirty-five years. According to Jeffrey S. Bland, publisher of *Complementary Medicine,* a journal for health professionals, "All women after menopause lose bone, but they will not necessarily develop demineralization diseases of bone such as osteoporosis. If bone density is high before menopause and the rate of loss after menopause is slowed, the onset of bone demineralization disease may not clinically appear until the individual is 150 years old."

Once a woman reaches menopause, many doctors prescribe estrogen replacement therapy to prevent osteoporosis, even to women whose bodies are still producing some estrogen, because the hormone slows the rate of bone loss and encourages replacement of bone tissue. The effectiveness of hormone therapy has made it the principal line of defense against osteoporosis for many physicians, despite studies showing an increased risk of cancer.

Robert Lang, who taught medicine at Yale University Medical School for a decade and is an expert in osteoporosis, is a prominent proponent of diet and lifestyle as a means for both preventing and treating the disease. Lang argues that estrogen therapy, though essential for many patients, is not necessary for all women suffering from osteoporosis. "Medication, when it is needed, must be more individualized to the person's risk factors," says Lang. "Some people can do well without estrogens." He says that physicians should be more cautious in prescribing estrogens. Lang encourages women to follow a healthful diet to prevent and treat osteoporosis. He recommends:

- Between 40 and 50 percent of the total diet should be made up of whole grains such as brown rice, whole wheat, bulgur, corn, millet, barley, and oats.
- Women should eat large quantities of leafy greens, preferably twice a day, and a variety of other vegetables. Leafy greens are rich in calcium and other minerals essential for healthy bones. Among the most nutritious greens are collard, kale, mustard greens, and cabbage. Also include broccoli, squash, carrots, turnips, and other vegetables. In addition to vegetables, various seaweeds such as arame, hijiki, and nori and sardines with the bones still intact are excellent sources of calcium.
- Avoid or limit foods rich in fat and cholesterol, and if you crave dairy products, eat those low in fat, such as skim milk. In place of fatty animal foods, eat low-fat fish such as had-

Even your body is not really your own. It belongs to life, and it is your responsibility to take care of it. You cannot afford to do anything that injures your body, because the body is the instrument you need for selfless action.

EKNATH EASWARAN

dock, cod, flounder, scrod, and sole, and, if you crave it, small amounts of chicken.
• Avoid sugar, caffeinated beverages, and salt.

Contrary to popular opinion, the high rate of osteoporosis in the U.S. is not due exclusively to insufficient calcium consumption. In perhaps the most comprehensive study of diet and disease patterns ever undertaken, in 1990 Cornell University and Chinese researchers reported that rates of osteoporosis, cancer, and heart disease are low in China, even though the population consumes a diet that is far lower in calcium than the average American's. After examining the nutrient intake of 6,500 people living in China, the researchers found that the Chinese consume an average of 544 mg of calcium per day, as opposed to an American average of 1,143 mg per day. The U.S. recommended daily allowance (RDA) ranges between 1,000 mg to 1,500 mg, with older adults being urged to consume the higher amount.

Research on other cultures, such as the Bantus of Africa, has shown that native populations often consume small amounts of calcium yet have little evidence of osteoporosis. Why the discrepancy? Scientists have known for years that an excess of certain nutrients, especially protein, promotes bone loss. The reason, say researchers, is that protein metabolism increases the acid levels in the bloodstream. This causes the body to secrete more calcium, an alkalizing substance, to neutralize or buffer it, a task that takes place in the kidneys.

"The component in protein which is affecting the calcium loss is the sulfur-containing amino acids," says Robert Heaney, a specialist in osteoporosis at Creighton University in Omaha, Nebraska. Those amino acids "are converted to sulfate in the body and then excreted in the kidney," says Heaney. "The sulfate load tends to wash some calcium out with it. In a sense, it is kind of the endogenous equivalent of the acid rain problem."

There is also considerable evidence that animal proteins have a more harmful effect overall on the body than vegetable proteins, though scientists are still uncertain if animal proteins interfere with calcium metabolism more than vegetable proteins do.

Not only do the Chinese consume far less protein than Americans (an average of 64 grams per day compared to 91 grams for the Americans), but the vast majority of the Chinese protein comes from vegetable sources (60 grams, as compared to 27 for the Americans). Heaney notes, "Vegetarians get less protein than carnivores, and more calcium."

Dairy products contain relatively large amounts of protein and therefore are not ideal sources of calcium. On the other hand, leafy green vegetables are rich in calcium but low in protein. Protein, however, is not the only problem with dairy foods. Milk, eggs, and meat contain phosphates, which research suggests may inhibit the body's absorption of calcium.

Not all leafy greens are good sources of calcium, however. Popeye's panacea, spinach, contains calcium but also has oxalic acid, which binds with calcium and prevents its absorption by the body. Beet greens, rhubarb, sorrel, and Swiss chard also contain oxalates, which makes these vegetables less desirable for people concerned about osteoporosis.

Like protein, sodium promotes calcium loss through the kidneys. It also increases parathyroid hormone and thus contributes to bone loss.

Finally, vitamin D is essential to healthy bone metabolism. While only twenty minutes of sunlight twice a week will provide adequate vitamin D to maintain healthy bone, deficiencies of D often occur among the elderly who are shut-ins, undergo lengthy indoor convalescence, or are hospitalized. Physicians recommend that even if people are unable to walk, they should sit outdoors and get some sun periodically.

While Lang emphasizes the importance of a healthful diet, he encourages those who need calcium supplements to take one that combines calcium and magnesium. Researchers have established that magnesium promotes the body's ability to utilize calcium. "Ten years ago, health food stores were promoting supplements that combined calcium and magnesium, but doctors didn't think much of the research supporting that recommendation," comments Lang. "Now, there's good evidence to show that magnesium does promote better calcium utilization."

Finally, certain drugs can interfere with calcium metabolism and bone health. Of primary concern are the corticosteroid group, the most common of which is prednisone, prescribed for inflammation and asthma. For many, it wreaks havoc on bone tissue.

In light of the evidence showing how humans age, and how bone mass accumulates during the first half of life, exercise has become an increasingly important part of the formula for healthy bones. Two types of exercise are essential. Weight-bearing exercises, such as walking, stimulate the bone-forming osteoblast cells to create new bone. Consequently, people who exercise have denser bone at all ages, from the very young to the very old. Also, weight-bearing exercise speeds the rate of bone turnover. Old bone is broken down and eliminated and new, healthier bone replaces it.

"All of us experience micro-fractures," says Lang. "However, when bone turnover is low, these micro-fractures accumulate and become major breaks." Exercise makes muscles stronger and better able to carry body weight, thus taking the stress off bone tissue.

Stretching exercises are also important because they reduce cramping and muscle spasm. Lack of activity makes muscles contract and become shorter, causing them to apply more tension to the bone. Such contractions can cause fractures by themselves.

Every part of a bone she [nature] makes bone, every part of the flesh she makes flesh, and so with fat and all the rest; there is no part she has not touched, elaborated, and embellished.

GALEN

JOINT PROBLEMS

There are several kinds of arthritis, the most common of which are osteoarthritis, rheumatoid arthritis, and gout. All of them are characterized by swelling, pain, stiffness, and redness in the joints. The illness may involve many joints, or be concentrated in just a few, such as the hands.

Osteoarthritis, the most common form of the illness, usually afflicts older people. It is a degenerative condition in which the cartilage in the joints becomes deformed and enlarged. These bony outgrowths, called osteophyte, cause pain and prevent normal movement in the joint. Three times as many women as men contract osteoarthritis. The illness is treated with painkillers, anti-inflammatory drugs, physical therapy, and sometimes corticosteroid drugs (which also treat inflammation). Surgery also may be used to replace joints or immobilize them. The cause is unknown.

Rheumatoid arthritis is an autoimmune disorder in which the body's immune system attacks the tissue lining the joints, especially in the hands, feet, and arms. Like osteoarthritis, it affects two to three times as many women as men. Treatment includes painkillers, anti-inflammatory drugs, immunosuppressant drugs, and antirheumatic drugs, including gold and penicillamine, which may slow the growth of the disease. The underlying cause is unknown.

Gout occurs when uric acid accumulates in the body and migrates to the joints, where it forms crystals that cause inflammation and pain. The illness is associated with kidney stones and, when sufficiently advanced, kidney failure. It is extremely painful. Gout is treated with anti-inflammatory drugs, pain relievers, and changes in diet to reduce the level of protein, which causes higher levels of uric acid.

Traditional people the world over who live on diets low in fat and protein show few signs of any type of arthritis. Conversely, arthritis is epidemic among people living in affluent industrialized countries living on high-protein, high-fat diets. Gout, for example, was especially prevalent among the aristocracy of seventeenth-century England, who ate a diet rich in meat.

Nathan Pritikin, the pioneer nutritionist, theorized that arthritis is caused by an increase in uric acid and purines. The uric acid crystals and the purines stimulate an immune response, which views the uric acid crystals and purines as foreign substances. White blood cells attempt to consume uric acid crystals in the cell's acid-rich stomach. But the crystal cannot be digested by the white cell and, instead, may puncture a hole in the cell, causing the acid to spill out onto the joints and sensitive joint tissues. This gives rise to the associated pain, swelling, and stiffness of arthritis. Pritikin contended that by eliminating high-protein foods, especially animal foods, gout can be eliminated.

Other forms of arthritis are often relieved in the same way. Animal proteins, of course, come with fat, which reduces circulation and oxygen levels in joints. Blood and oxygen are essential for tissues to function properly. As fat and cholesterol increase in the blood, red blood cells become sticky and begin to adhere to one another, a condition called "rouleaux formation." These cells clump together and thus are unable to pass through smaller capillaries. This prevents blood and oxygen from getting to cells, thus causing cells to suffocate and die. Another effect is edema, or swelling within the joints, caused by rouleaux formation within the bloodstream.

CHAPTER 26

THE NERVOUS SYSTEM

*T*HE HUMAN NERVOUS SYSTEM is the most advanced communications network on earth. At every instant it receives untold bits of information, prioritizes them, and offers a range of appropriate responses—everything from forming words, to changes in internal chemistry, to beautifully coordinated movements. It governs a universe of cells, glands, and organs within us. At the same time, it allows us to experience life in orderly patterns and gives us the ability to respond to those patterns so that we can meet our needs and those of others around us.

At this very moment, every color, shape, and smell within your environment, every physical thing that touches your body, the very taste in your mouth, are all vying for your attention. The book you are holding, the words on this page, the sounds in the background, the faint smells in the air, the clothes you wear, and the chair on which you sit are all sending signals to your brain. You could be overwhelmed, but your nervous system's ability to organize this profusion of stimuli, and prioritize it according to your needs, makes the environment seem both calm and innocuous, at least most of the time.

Suddenly, a bee nears. Before you see the bee, you hear it

The environment is considered a candidate for healing along with the individual person.

DAVID J. HUFFORD

The nervous system has a fundamental characteristic: We cannot carry out an action and its opposite at the same time. At any single moment the whole system achieves a kind of general integration that the body will express at that moment. Position, sensing, feeling, thought, as well as chemical and hormonal processes, combine to form a whole that cannot be separated out into its various parts. This whole may be highly complex and complicated, but is the integrated whole of the system at that given moment.

MOSHE FELDENKRAIS

buzzing. The sound is recognized and given priority over all other forms of information. Your eyes search for the bee. You notice that it is coming at you! In the blink of an eye, your heart and respiration rates quicken. Your bloodstream is filled with adrenaline, giving you lightning-quick reflexes. You drop the book and swat at the bee. Though you miss it, your flailing motion is enough to dissuade the bee's curiosity. It's gone.

Now your priorities change. The words on the page draw your attention once again and sounds exist in the background of consciousness. Without your awareness, your nervous system is working furiously to slow your heart and breathing, lower your blood pressure, relax your muscles, and change the hormonal composition of your blood. It performs these tasks while it observes the words on the page, translates the symbols into meaning, remembers important facts, and relates the information sequentially so that each paragraph makes sense in light of its predecessor. In short, it is miraculous.

The nervous system is a symphony of billions of instruments that, in health, never miss a beat. It rules an infinite series of events so complex and so varied that no computer—no matter how big—could duplicate its abilities.

An Electrical and Chemical Marvel

Both the nervous and endocrine systems coordinate, integrate, and control all bodily functions. The nervous system operates largely through electrical and chemical mechanisms, while the endocrine system functions through chemical (hormonal) means. They are so interdependent that they are sometimes referred to as the neurohumoral system.

The nervous system, of course, is the seat of consciousness, intelligence, and memory. It is the physical tool for all higher mental activities, such as reasoning, thinking, judgment, and emotion. Much is known about how the nervous system works, yet much remains a mystery. Scientists do not fully understand how nonphysical events such as thoughts and emotions trigger physical changes in nervous function. Nor do they understand where memory is stored and how such information is called forth when needed.

Interestingly, many of your thoughts have specific effects on nervous and endocrine function. This is the basis for the relatively new science of psychoneuroimmunology, the study of how thoughts and emotions change the kinds of messages and chemical responses experienced by the nervous and endocrine systems.

There are two main physiologic divisions of the nervous system: the central nervous system, consisting of the brain and spinal cord, and the peripheral nervous system, which is made up of the nerve fibers that infuse the sense organs, skin, muscles, internal organs, and glands. The peripheral nervous system is connected to the central by twelve pairs of cranial nerves at the brain, and thirty-one pairs of spinal nerves at the spinal cord.

Sense organs send information from outside the body to the central nervous system. At the same time, receptor nerves within the peripheral nervous system monitor internal organs such as the heart, lungs, and bladder, and relay that information to the central nervous system. The central nervous system then decides what kind of response is necessary and orders a range of reactions that usually involve muscles, internal organs, and glands. Such reactions translate into human behavior, everything from external speech and physical movement to internal hormonal and biochemical changes.

There is also a functional division within the nervous system, known as the autonomic and the somatic (or voluntary) nervous systems. The autonomic nervous system works automatically or unconsciously. It regulates internal organs and performs reflex responses. All smooth muscle functions, which include digestion, respiration, and circulation, are controlled by the autonomic nervous system. When your body changes the size of your pupils, constricts and dilates blood vessels in the scalp, secretes hormones, or creates goose pimples on the skin, it is due to responses controlled by the autonomic nervous system.

The somatic or voluntary nervous system is under your conscious control. It performs the tasks that you consciously order at a particular moment: eating, drinking, scratching your head. The somatic or voluntary nervous system works by translating thoughts into physical responses. It does this by controlling skeletal muscles, such as those in the arms and legs, neck and feet, and face and mouth. Inside the brain and spinal cord are programs that coordinate specific muscular and skeletal activities so that orderly

The Nervous System

The body's many nerves are part of either the central nervous system, consisting of the brain and spinal cord, or the peripheral nervous system, made up of the nerve fibers that infuse the sense organs, skin, muscles, internal organs, and glands. The peripheral nervous system is connected to the central by twelve pairs of cranial nerves at the brain, and thirty-one pairs of spinal nerves at the spinal cord.

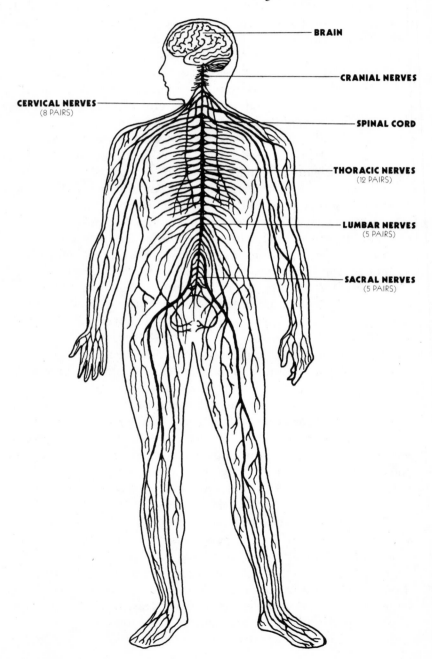

BRAIN

CRANIAL NERVES

CERVICAL NERVES
(8 PAIRS)

SPINAL CORD

THORACIC NERVES
(12 PAIRS)

LUMBAR NERVES
(5 PAIRS)

SACRAL NERVES
(5 PAIRS)

movement occurs. Consequently, when you want to, say, lift a piece of bread from a plate and bring it to your mouth, you experience the act as a fluid motion and not as a series of commands. Your nervous system is, however, in fact directing a series of individual commands, which were learned and perfected in childhood. Each of these commands must be performed at precise moments so that you can reach out, grasp the bread with your fingers, bring it to your face, bite off a small piece, and, while chewing the bread, return it to the plate. This simple act can involve as many as fifty muscles and thirty bones, all acting as one unit.

Such actions are made possible by billions of individual units within the nervous system called neurons. While individual neurons vary somewhat in shape, they are usually star-shaped with several short "arms" or projections emanating from the cell body, and a single long projection. The short arms are called dendrites; the long radiant is called an axon.

A nerve impulse occurs when an electrical signal is fired from the cell body and down along the axon. The impulse causes the tip of the axon to release a chemical called a neurotransmitter. This chemical neurotransmitter passes over a space called a synapse between the axon and the neighboring neuron. One of the dendrites on the neighboring neuron, or the cell body itself, will catch the neurotransmitter, which in turn will stimulate another electrical impulse within that cell body. The newly triggered electrical charge will trigger an electrical charge to flow along that cell's axon and cause the release of another neurotransmitter at the axon's tip. That chemical will breach the synapse and trigger another electrical impulse in an adjacent cell. In this way, nerve impulses are transmitted through the nervous system. And it all happens in the blink of an eye.

Each resting neuron is a polarized cell, meaning that the outside of the cell is surrounded by positively charged particles (or ions), which come from sodium. Inside the cell are negatively charged particles, which come from potassium. When the neuron is stimulated, such as the moment you touch something, the positively charged particles enter the cell and combine with the negative particles to release a flow of electrons which streak down the axon to stimulate the production of a neurotransmitter.

The chemical neurotransmitter then stimulates another electrical impulse in a neighboring neuron, but causes a specific re-

A state of "dis-ease" in the body is always a reflection of conflict, tension, anxiety, or disharmony on other levels of being as well.

SHAKTI GAWAIN

277

sponse within the tissues of that part of the body. For example, some neurotransmitters cause muscles to contract. Others cause muscles to relax, while still others cause hormones to be released from glands.

Neurons cannot be replaced after the nervous system has been fully developed in fetal life because individual neurons lose their ability to reproduce. Radiation, infection, aging, lack of oxygen, and poisoning, such as from drugs or alcohol, cause neurons to die. Depriving the body of oxygen for more than about four minutes can cause irreparable damage to the central nervous system.

Nerve cells are covered with an insulating tissue called a myelin sheath, which is composed of proteins and lipids (fats) that keep the nerve impulse conducted along its proper path and prevent it from stimulating adjacent fibers. The speed with which the nerve impulse fires through the body is awesome. Depending upon the size and thickness of the nerve cell, and whether it is covered with the insulating myelin sheath, the speed can vary from about three feet to 400 feet per second.

Like the brain, the central nervous system is composed of both gray matter and white matter. In the brain, the cerebral cortex is composed of gray matter, which makes possible all the higher functions: thinking, reasoning, perception, judgment, and emotional experience. Within the central nervous system, gray matter is found deep within the spinal cord. Nerve impulses are received by the gray matter. The information is analyzed and organized, and a response is initiated. White matter is found beneath the cerebral cortex, in the peripheral nervous system, and in the outer or surrounding portions of the spinal cord. Its primary role is to conduct nerve impulses.

THE YIN AND YANG OF THE NERVOUS SYSTEM

Though the Chinese do not have a concept for the nervous system, as such, it is revealing to consider it in terms of polarity and opposition: the autonomic versus the voluntary, the parasympathetic and the sympathetic systems. For instance, the parasympathetic can be seen as restrictive, contracting, and yin. The sympathetic system works on the overall system to excite, quicken, expand vessels, and create a fiery or yang effect. Also,

How the Nerves Work

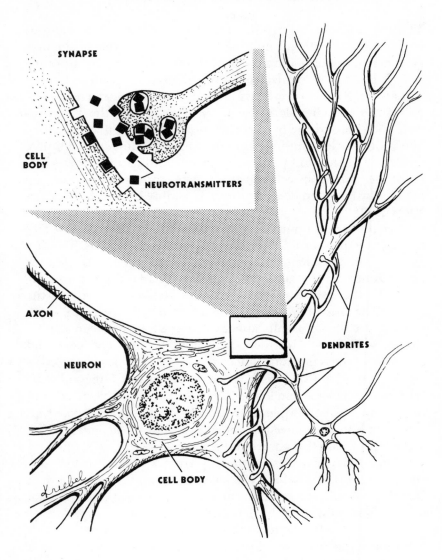

Nerves send their messages to the brain with the help of billions of neurons. These tiny, star-shaped units have short arms called dendrites, and usually a single longer one known as an axon. A nerve impulse occurs when an electrical signal is fired from the cell body and down along the axon. The impulse causes the tip of the axon to release a chemical called a neurotransmitter. This chemical neurotransmitter passes over a space called a synapse between the axon and the neighboring neuron. One of the dendrites on the neighboring neuron, or the cell body itself, will catch the neurotransmitter, which in turn will stimulate another electrical impulse within that cell body, triggering another electrical charge and release of neurotransmitters. In this way, nerve impulses are transmitted through the nervous system.

the function of individual neurons is made possible by the presence of positively (yang) and negatively (yin) charged particles. These particles create polarity, which make an electrical charge possible. Thus, the nervous system, too, can be seen in the larger dialectical terms of the East.

279

Attack of the Immune System

Multiple sclerosis is a progressive disease of the central nervous system in which the immune system attacks sections of the myelin sheath, the insulating cover of the nerve fibers. The immune system actually recognizes parts of the myelin sheath as foreign substances. Patches of scar tissue form, thus preventing nerve impulses from flowing along the nerve tissue. Often, the degeneration goes beyond the myelin sheath to the white matter below. Symptoms include numbness in the tips of the fingers and limbs, weakness in the limbs, spastic and uncoordinated movements, stiffness, slurred speech, unsteady gate, incontinence, vertigo, pain in the face, and double vision. The cause of the illness is unknown.

Scientists point out that both environmental and genetic factors seem to play a role in the onset of multiple sclerosis. The disease is more prevalent in temperate climates than in tropical or desert zones. At the same time, those with a family member afflicted by the disease are eight times more likely to contract the illness. The ratio of women to men affected by the disease is three to two. The illness usually attacks young adults between ages of twenty and forty. Treatment generally includes corticosteroid drugs to suppress immune function.

According to Roy Swank, at the University of Oregon Medical School, a low-fat and low-cholesterol diet could be effective in the treatment of multiple sclerosis. His studies in the 1960s and 1970s led him to believe that fat and cholesterol adversely affect the myelin sheath that covers nerve fibers.

After reviewing the scientific literature, Nathan Pritikin concurred, but offered a diet even lower in fat and cholesterol than Swank's. Like Swank, Pritikin maintained that exercise was vital to the improvement of the nervous system. Pritikin urged those with multiple sclerosis to walk daily. The person afflicted with MS should walk as far as he or she could, said Pritikin, rest for as long as necessary, and then walk home.

People with MS who have followed Pritikin's suggestions have improved somewhat. Laura Ornstein of New York City was counseled by Pritikin for several years. She reported that after following the program for several months, she was able to improve her walking distance from a hundred feet to a half-mile without assistance. Her right eye had begun to drift prior to adopting the Pritikin program, but after following Pritikin's recommendations she experienced an improvement in her vision and the correction of her right eye.

Naturopath Ross Trattler has suggested that in addition to improvement in exercise and dramatically lowering fat and cholesterol, the person with MS must abstain from all animal foods, artificial ingredients, and pesticides. He cites studies showing a link between MS and exposure to heavy metals, such as lead. Trattler's recommendations include taking supplementary vitamin A, B complex, C, D, E, and the minerals calcium, magnesium, manganese, selenium, and zinc.

CHAPTER 27

THE ENDOCRINE SYSTEM

Nature is liberal to provide for the necessities of the poor and has sent forth many matters of medicaments, that they may be found everywhere and with little art may be prepared.

NICHOLAS CULPEPER

ORMONES SUCH AS TESTOSTERONE, estrogen, and thyroxine are ghostly substances that we often associate with moods and behavior—or, rather, misbehavior. These strange chemicals move in the blood and lymph and affect people in powerful but sometimes bizarre ways. Often, when a coworker or family member experiences a sudden mood change, someone will say derisively, "It must be hormones." The word itself has become synonymous with unpredictable change. Yet, contrary to popular perception, hormones are among the most consistent performers in human biology. So important are they in health and development that if they were not so dependable, there would be scarcely any consistency in human anatomy and physiology.

The word *hormone,* from the Greek for "to stimulate" or "excite," was not used in connection to the body until 1905, when these strange and powerful chemical substances were discovered. Scientists soon learned that only some of these endocrine chemicals excite, while others inhibit physical reactions. Consequently, the word *chalone,* from the Greek "to slacken," was originally used to designate those inhibiting substances within body tissue. In time, the word *hormone* came to be applied to both the exciters and the inhibitors, and *chalone* is no longer used. Since 1920, knowledge of the endocrine system has steadily accumulated, but endocrinology is still considered a young science and much about the hormonal system is still unknown.

Hormones are produced by endocrine organs, called glands, and transported through the blood and lymph. Every organ that produces hormones can be considered an endocrine gland. These include the pituitary, thyroid, parathyroid, adrenals, pancreas, testes, ovaries, thymus, pineal, skin, kidneys, and intestines. Hormones can be targeted to specific organs or tissues, or have a general effect on the overall body.

The chemical composition of hormones varies. Some are made up of amino acids (the building blocks of proteins). Others are composed of whole proteins. Some are steroids, a classification of chemicals produced by the adrenal glands and sex organs, or fatty acids. Still others are peptides (fragments of proteins, made of two or more amino acids).

Whatever their composition, hormones are uniformly powerful. Tiny amounts of adrenaline, also known as epinephrine, will trigger rapid increases in respiration, heart rate, and energy consumption, for example. Once a hormone reaches its target, it effects some type of change in the organ, tissue, or blood. When the job is done, excesses of the hormone are broken down by the liver and turned into bile, or excreted by the kidneys.

Hormones control virtually every fundamental human function, including growth and development, maturation, reproduction, and most of human behavior. "Much of a person's behavior and most of the traits that collectively constitute personality depend on the normal functioning of the endocrine glands," write Steen and Montague in *Anatomy and Physiology*.

Endocrine glands work in harmony with one another, and with the constituents that make up the blood, which determines how much of a particular hormone is released by a gland. For example, the amount of blood sugar present determines how much insulin is released by the pancreas. Or the quantities of calcium in the blood determine how much parathyroid hormone is released by the parathyroid gland. In other words, endocrine glands are continually responding to the current conditions within the bloodstream, and to what the other glands are doing, as well. As we will see below, dietary factors greatly influence how particular

Burgeoning research on relations between the nervous, endocrine, and immune systems has revealed the body's great redundancy of healing (or homeostatis-maintaining) process. Because of this redundancy, particular kinds of physiological repair or mood alteration can be mediated in more than one way.

MICHAEL MURPHY

glands work, and how effective certain hormones—especially insulin—are.

Other important endocrine glands include the testes, ovaries, and mammary glands, all of which are dealt with in the chapter on the reproductive system. Let's have a look at the primary endocrine glands and their functions.

THE MASTER GLAND

Located in the base of the brain, within the brain stem, the pituitary is a pea-sized gland sometimes referred to as the "master gland" because it regulates the activities of other endocrine glands. The pituitary is itself controlled by the hypothalamus, which influences the pituitary function through its own hormones and a series of nerve fibers. (See hypothalamus in the chapter on the brain).

The pituitary gland, also called the hypophysis, is made up of three lobes, each of which has its own distinct functions. Like the hypothalamus, the pituitary gland seems to have a finger in virtually every important aspect of human physiology. Indeed, the hormones produced by the pituitary regulate the following functions of human behavior:

- Physical growth and development, made possible by growth hormone.
- Milk production in lactating women, made possible by the hormone prolactin.
- Regulation of the adrenal glands, which, among other things, accelerate reflexes in emergency situations (such adrenal responses are made possible by the pituitary's production of adrenocorticotripic hormone [ACTH]).
- Maintenance of metabolism through the production of thyroid-stimulating hormone (TSH).
- Healthful function of male and female sex organs, through the production of luteinizing hormone (LH) and follicle-stimulating hormones (FSH).
- Skin color, made possible by the production of melanocyte-stimulating hormone, which causes skin pigmentation.
- Proper water balance in the bloodstream, through the production of antidiuretic hormone (ADH), which signals the

The Endocrine System

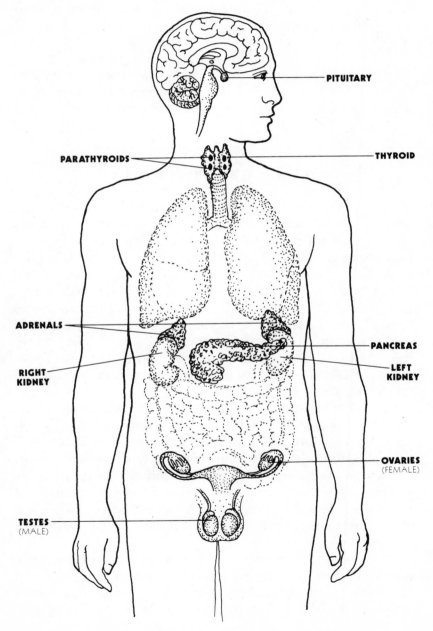

PITUITARY

PARATHYROIDS

THYROID

ADRENALS

PANCREAS

RIGHT KIDNEY

LEFT KIDNEY

OVARIES (FEMALE)

TESTES (MALE)

The endocrine system regulates the body's production and use of hormones, ghostly substances that intimately affect your moods and behavior. While much about the hormonal system is still unknown, scientists have identified a number of endocrine organs, including the pituitary, thyroid, parathyroid, adrenals, pancreas, testes, ovaries, skin, and kidneys.

kidneys to retain more water and decrease urination, and thus increases the water content of the blood.
- The ability of a woman's uterus to contract during child-birth and expel milk from her breasts, through the production of oxytocin.

That this little gland is involved in so many fundamental and vital functions boggles the mind. But perhaps the pituitary demonstrates best how powerful and important hormones really are. Tiny quantities of these chemicals enact life-altering changes in the body's biochemistry.

Your Body's Metabolism Cop

The thyroid gland is found at the base of the neck, toward the front. It is composed of two lobes, one on each side of the windpipe or trachea. The thyroid is responsible for regulating metabolism, the term used to describe the many processes that take place in the body. Metabolism is divided into two categories: catabolism, which is the breaking down of substances into still smaller parts; and anabolism, in which the body uses smaller substances to build larger structures, such as using minerals to produce bone tissue, or amino acids to create proteins. Catabolic processes release energy, while anabolic actions consume it. The rate of such metabolic processes depends to a great extent on the activities of the thyroid gland.

The thyroid produces two primary hormones, thyroxine and calcitonin. For the most part, thyroxine promotes catabolism. It regulates respiration and oxygen consumption by cells, as well as the body's utilization of carbohydrates and fat for energy. It's also essential in the promotion of protein synthesis. That is, it helps join amino acids so that the body can form proteins and thus build and replace tissue. In this way, the thyroid assists in normal growth and development. In addition the thyroid helps maintain the central nervous system.

Calcitonin, on the other hand, promotes anabolism, using calcium to form bone tissue. When blood levels of calcium are high, calcitonin is secreted by the thyroid to promote absorption of calcium and the formation of bone matter. It does this by promoting the activities of osteoblasts, the cells that produce bone, and depressing the activities of osteoclasts, the cells that break down bone tissue. Calcitonin performs the opposite task of parathyroid hormone, which is secreted by the parathyroid to increase calcium levels in the bloodstream.

The thyroid is dependent upon iodine, which is derived from foods such as iodized salt, fresh saltwater shellfish, seaweeds, and foods grown in iodine-rich soil. Deficiencies of iodine result in a range of disorders, including insufficient production of thyroxine and the creation of a goiter, which is the swelling of the thyroid gland.

Illnesses associated with the thyroid generally fall within two categories: hypothyroidism, the underproduction of thyroid hormones, and hyperthyroidism, the excess production of thyroid hormones. Tumors can form in the thyroid and lead to malignant cancers. Exposure to radiation is among the most common causes of thyroid cancer.

Traditional Chinese healers consider the thyroid gland part of the Fire Element within the Five Element system, and clearly thyroxine possesses all the characteristics of the Fire Element: catabolic, scattering, and heat-producing. Fire Element foods are used to enhance the thyroid function, especially when it is deficient, though such foods should not be considered a substitute for thyroxine for people with diagnosed hypothyroidism.

Naturopaths and other alternative healers often recommend various foods, vitamins, and minerals to help alleviate disorders of the thyroid, including vegetables such as radishes, mushrooms, watercress, collard and other leafy greens, squash, carrots, and broccoli; grains such as corn, wheat, and millet; garlic; shiitake mushrooms; vitamins A, B6, and E; and the minerals zinc and copper.

DISTINGUISHING SELF FROM NOT-SELF

Western medical scientists have only recently begun to appreciate the thymus. Only a few decades ago, doctors believed it was a useless organ, especially in adulthood, because it usually begins to shrink after puberty. Today, scientists know that the thymus gland is essential to a healthy immune system.

Located in the upper part of the chest just below the breast bone, the thymus is slightly smaller than a fist, with two lobes that are packed with tiny immune cells called lymphocytes. The function of the thymus gland is to produce lymphocytes and to train them to distinguish self from not-self, or one's own cells from disease cells. The thymus also trains the cells to act appropriately in the face of disease by either tagging diseased cells with an antigen, or by attacking the cell and destroying it. Once trained, these lymphocytes are called thymus cells, T-cells for short.

The thymus is essential to healthy immune function. Children whose thymus glands are impaired suffer higher rates of infection and severely impaired immune function. The thymus gland also influences the behavior of the immune system once the lymphocytes leave the thymus.

Studies have shown that the thymus gland shrinks and its functions are impaired as a consequence of chronic stress. Exposure to radiation and chemical pollutants also cause the thymus to shrink. In addition, the absence of various minerals in the diet, especially zinc, has a detrimental effect on both the thymus and the overall immune system. On the other hand, there's evidence that positive emotions and a more optimistic attitude toward life cause thymus function to be enhanced.

Like the thyroid gland, the thymus is considered part of the Fire Element in traditional Chinese medicine and is therefore supported by Fire Element foods, herbs, and medicinal preparations. Not surprisingly, the Fire Element is associated with joy and is suppressed or controlled by the Water Element, whose associated emotion is fear. Increased joy and a diminution of fear enhance thymus function, from the Chinese point of view. A diet rich in minerals, and Fire, Wood, and Earth Element foods and herbs, is essential to the healthy functioning of the thymus gland.

KEEPING BLOOD SUGAR IN BALANCE

The pancreas is a narrow organ, shaped like a horn of plenty, located in the center of the abdomen directly behind the stomach. The wide end of the pancreas is at the right and narrow end near the spleen, on the left. The pancreas serves two essential functions. It secretes digestive juices into the duodenum, thus assisting digestion, and it produces hormones (most notably, insulin) that make possible the utilization of blood sugar as fuel.

Most of the organ is composed of tissues that produce and secrete alkaline digestive juices (see chapters on the stomach, small intestine, and gall bladder). These enzymes are secreted directly into the small intestine where they help break down food particles.

Nestled among these tissues, however, are the endocrine cells that produce hormones. These cells, called the islets of Langerhans, are of two types: alpha and beta cells. The beta cells produce insulin, a hormone that promotes the uptake and utilization of blood sugar by the cells, especially those of muscle and liver cells. In the liver, blood sugar (also known as glucose) is changed to glycogen, the stored form of energy. In the muscles, the blood sugar is burned as fuel.

How insulin promotes the utilization of glucose is not completely known. It is believed that insulin coats the cell membrane, causing it to become more permeable. This greater permeability allows sugar to enter the cell and thus be burned as fuel.

To illustrate, picture the cell as a room in which there are many doors. These doors or insulin receptor sites are the places that allow blood sugar to enter, but only with the assistance of insulin, which somehow makes the doors open. When you eat a food that contains carbohydrates, your blood sugar levels increase, and your pancreas secretes insulin so that blood sugar can be used by the cells.

The pancreas's alpha cells provide the opposite effect on blood sugar. They produce glucagon, which increases blood sugar by promoting the conversion of glycogen (sugar stored in the liver) into glucose, or blood sugar. When you are in need of more fuel in your bloodstream but are unable to eat, the pancreas will secrete glucagon, which will raise your blood sugar level.

Glucose levels in the blood increase when we eat foods rich in carbohydrates. The rate of increase, however, is dramatically different among complex carbohydrates, such as those found in whole grains, beans, vegetables, and many fruits, and simple carbohydrates, such as those in white sugar and refined sweets. This is because refined sugars are small molecules that are able to enter the bloodstream immediately upon touching the tongue and other tissues in the digestive tract. This causes a quick and dramatic increase in blood sugar levels. The pancreas responds to this rapid rise in blood sugar by secreting quantities of insulin, which makes the glucose available to cells as fuel. This interaction of insulin and blood sugar gives you an immediate rush of energy. That fuel is quickly spent, however, leaving you with depressed energy levels. You may also experience a depression in mood, a rise in anxiety and nervous tension, and a hunger for more sweets to bring sugar levels back up. Such a low blood sugar state is called hypoglycemia.

On the other hand, the complex carbohydrates found in whole grains and vegetables are long chains of atoms that must be broken down slowly by enzymes in the mouth and small intestine. The body responds to these long chains by metabolizing them slowly as energy is demanded by the body, causing the person to experience long and enduring flows of energy. Complex carbohydrates thus provide ongoing supplies of energy and endurance, without the depression and anxiety normally experienced by people with hypoglycemia.

Doctors distinguish between two types of diabetes. Type I, or juvenile diabetes, is a genetic disorder in which the pancreas fails to produce insulin, thus preventing the body from metabolizing blood sugar. Juvenile diabetics usually experience rapid weight loss and require insulin in order to survive. Type II, or adult-onset diabetes, is a condition in which the pancreas produces adequate amounts of insulin—in some cases, even more insulin than is necessary—but cells are still unable to absorb glucose. It usually occurs later in life, and it is the much more common type of diabetes, counting among its victims 11 million of the 12 million Americans with diabetes. Both types of diabetes are associated with a number of other serious illnesses, including cardiovascular disease, blindness, gangrene, progressive loss of hearing, impotence, and palsy.

Adult-onset diabetes is among the most serious and misunderstood illnesses today. For decades, doctors believed that adult-onset diabetics were unable to produce sufficient quantities of insulin to sustain health. Consequently, doctors gave these patients insulin injections or oral medication. In addition, patients with adult-onset diabetes were told to avoid all carbohydrates, even complex carbohydrates from whole grains, vegetables, and fruits. These foods were believed to be harmful to diabetics because carbohydrates are sugars, which the diabetic cannot metabolize. Instead, doctors recommended that diabetics consume a high-protein, high-fat diet, consisting mainly of red meats, dairy products, and eggs.

And then, in 1970, new information began to surface. Or, to put it more accurately, old information surfaced again. That year, scientists recognized that adult-onset diabetics were in fact producing insulin—sometimes even more insulin than non-diabetics. But the insulin could not make glucose available to cells. Something was preventing the insulin from working. As researchers looked more carefully at the existing scientific evidence, they unearthed a cache of studies demonstrating that the problem for adult-onset diabetics was not the insulin but a high-fat diet that was preventing the insulin from working.

As far back as 1935, Dr. H. P. Himsworth had discovered that a healthy person could be made to test diabetic by placing him or her on a high-fat diet for as short a time as one week. Remarkably, Himsworth also found that he could reverse the process and restore health by placing the same person on a low-fat diet. Other researchers corroborated Himsworth's discovery, but it failed to gain the recognition it deserved until almost four decades later.

One of the first people to recognize Himsworth's work in the modern era was Pritikin, who theorized that dietary fat covers the cells and prevents insulin from attaching to the insulin receptor sites, preventing glucose from entering the cell and thus giving rise to diabetes. Consequently, the cells cannot obtain fuel and die. (Scientists have demonstrated that dietary fat and cholesterol coat immune cells, as well.) Pritikin demonstrated that most adult-onset diabetics could be cured with the use of a low-fat, low-cholesterol diet made up primarily of whole grains and vegetables.

Recent research done during the 1970s and 1980s by James Anderson at the University of Kentucky Medical School proved Pritikin's hypothesis. Anderson demonstrated that a high-fat diet does indeed give rise to a diabetic state, and that a low-fat, high-fiber diet can reverse adult-onset diabetes and restore blood sugar levels to normal. Anderson showed that soluble fiber, such as that found in brown rice, barley, and oats, binds with the fat and cholesterol and eliminates it from the body.

Other researchers confirmed Anderson's findings, which

caused the American Diabetics Association to reverse the standard dietary advice for diabetics. The ADA now urges diabetics to eat a diet low in fat and cholesterol and rich in whole grains, vegetables, and fiber. Doctors still prescribe insulin and oral medication for adult-onset diabetics, though for many patients dietary and lifestyle changes offer the hope of eventually discontinuing insulin intake. The diet also helps to prevent such diabetes-related illnesses as atherosclerosis, blindness, and gangrene.

Meanwhile, the Pritikin Longevity Center's success in treating adult-onset diabetes is well-documented. Loma Linda University researchers who conducted a study reviewing the effects of the Pritikin Program found that of those attending the Center who were taking insulin, half left the Center after a thirty-day program off insulin and free of all diabetic symptoms. Of those who arrived on oral medication for adult-onset diabetes, 80 percent left the Center symptom-free and off all medication.

In Chinese Medicine, the pancreas is considered part of the Earth Element and, therefore, supported by Earth and Fire foods, herbs, and activities (see chapters on the spleen and stomach). It is balanced by moderately sweet foods, round vegetables (especially squash), millet and sweet corn, and certain herbs, such as liquorice. On the other hand, it is injured by excessively sweet foods. (People with pancreatic problems, including diabetes, should follow the dietary recommendations outlined in the chapter on the spleen.)

The Stress Glands

There are two adrenal glands, each one triangular-shaped and sitting on top of a kidney. Each adrenal gland can be thought of as having two functional units. The cortex, or outer region, secretes groups of hormones, some generally referred to as corticosteroids and others as mineralocorticoids. These play a vital role in protein metabolism, mineral balance, immune response, and the health of bones. The cortex also secretes sex hormones. The interior region of the adrenals, called the medulla, secretes another set of hormones, most notably adrenaline.

The corticosteroids include hydrocortisone and cortisone, both of which assist in protein formation and metabolism. These hormones also have anti-inflammatory properties and, when released in excess, depress the immune system. The mineralocorticoids include aldosterone, which regulates the body's water balance and maintains sodium and potassium balance. Other hormones released by the cortex cause inflammation of tissues, especially when the body is experiencing an allergic reaction.

Adrenaline increases heart rate, respiration, and blood pressure. It also causes smooth muscles to relax and bronchial passages to contract, thus explaining how adrenaline can play a role in the onset of allergies or an asthma attack. The medulla also secretes dopamine, a neurotransmitter that triggers heightened alertness and aggression. Together, these hormones and neurotransmitters cause virtually instant release of energy. They also stimulate the sympathetic nervous system to provide quick reflex muscle reaction, the so-called "flight or fight" reaction.

The adrenals are highly susceptible to stress. During stressful situations, the pituitary gland secretes ACTH, which signals the adrenal glands to secrete hydrocortisone and adrenaline, which in turn can suppress immune function, create inflammation, and increase susceptibility to illness.

Traditional Chinese healers consider the adrenals part of the Water Element. The glands are, therefore, supported and enhanced by foods, herbs, and therapies grouped under the Water and Metal Elements (see chapters on the kidneys, bladder, lungs, and large intestine). Like the kidneys and bladder, the adrenals are highly vulnerable to fear and stress.

THE THIRD EYE GLAND

The pineal gland is a tiny cone-shaped organ in the brain stem. It grows only from gestation to puberty, but continues to function for the rest of your life. According to the *Atlas of Human Anatomy,* by Samuel Smith and Edwin B. Steen, "Some evidence suggests that it is a vestigial organ, the remnant of a third eye." For centuries, the pineal was regarded strictly in spiritual or religious terms. The seventeenth-century French philosopher René Descartes maintained that it was the seat of the soul. Until recently, scientists believed that the pineal gland had no function because, in adults, it became infiltrated with calcium deposits or "brain sand." New research, however, is showing that the pineal gland has a range of vital functions, including the maintenance of biorhythms, brain chemistry, and mood.

The pineal produces the hormone melatonin and the neurotransmitter serotonin. Increased blood levels of melatonin are associated with depression, irritability, lethargy, and the need for more sleep. The pineal produces more melatonin at night and in darkened environments, but stops producing melatonin when the eyes are exposed to sunlight. The sun stimulates nerve fibers in the eyes that send impulses to the pineal, via the optic nerve, to cease production of melatonin.

This research has explained the medical basis for the depression and lethargy suffered by millions of people living in northern climes during the fall and winter months. Scientists now refer to this condition as SAD, or seasonal affective disorder. People with SAD feel depressed and withdrawn when there is less sunlight, and they also overeat and crave foods rich in carbohydrates.

According to research conducted at the Massachusetts Institute of Technology, carbohydrates stimulate production of serotonin, a neurotransmitter that promotes deep and restful sleep, feelings of well-being, and the ability to focus the mind on a desired subject. Thus, melatonin and serotonin appear to have opposite effects on brain chemistry and mood. Also, carbohydrate cravings may be the body's way of counteracting melatonin production. Research suggests that melatonin can be created from serotonin, and that as melatonin levels increase, serotonin levels decrease.

Curing SAD is simple enough: expose the eyes to full-spectrum bright light, either from the sun or from special, high-intensity full-spectrum fluorescent lights, for up to thirty minutes per day. Studies have shown that 60 to 80 percent of people with SAD lose their symptoms when they are exposed to that much full-spectrum light per day.

"People who talked of hating winter all of a sudden become big fans of winter," notes Dr. Martin Teicher, chief of the chronobiology laboratory at McLean Hospital in Belmont, Massachusetts. "They take up skiing. They love Christmas. The holidays are no longer a matter of conflicted memories."

More than two dozen studies have demonstrated that light has antidepressant qualities. Light also has been shown to reduce the

A sleeping man can have an intuition of disease and can distinguish, from among all substances, those which contribute to his preservation and cure.

FRANZ ANTON
MESMER

rates of violence among prisoners who had previously been confined to cells that allowed little or no natural light to enter. Interestingly, studies also have shown that blood-cleansing organs,
especially the liver, function better when the body is exposed to
more sunlight than when it is kept in darkened quarters.

The scientific finding that the pineal is sensitive to light adds
to—and indirectly supports—the widespread traditional view

The Chakras

According to a number of spiritual traditions, the body contains a chain of seven spheres
or "chakras" of energy aligned
down the middle of the body.
Each energy center corre-
sponds with particular bodily
functions and characteristics.
The pineal corresponds to
the third eye chakra located
in the middle of forehead, seen
as the source of intuition and
the ability to perceive
universal truth.

that the pineal bears some relevance to human spirituality. Light has traditionally been seen as the medium of the soul and the higher spiritual realms. Ancient spiritual traditions, especially the Hindu, have conceived of the body as being a chain of seven spheres of energy. These spheres, called chakras, are aligned down the middle of the body at specific points: the top of the head, midbrain (or third eye), throat, heart, solar plexus, sacral (known in Japan as the hara), and sex organs. Each energy center corresponds with particular human characteristics. The pineal corresponds to the third eye chakra, the source of intuition and the ability to perceive universal truth.

CHAPTER 28

THE REPRODUCTIVE SYSTEM

*I*N ANCIENT TIMES, and especially in the East, sex was seen in an altogether different context than it is today. Rather than being the great temptation, the surest road to hell, it was considered a path of spiritual development, and thus a way toward greater intimacy with the divine.

That divinity is seen as a state of wholeness and completeness that is implicit in all of us. In the traditions of the East (especially in Taoism of China and Tantra of Tibet), man and woman represent opposite halves of that universal whole. Each is an earthly manifestation of the two cosmic creative forces, whose intermingling bring forth all phenomena. When man and woman unite in sex, heaven and earth are joined. The sexual experience offers a glimpse of that wholeness within. It is thus one of the great gifts of humanity, offering a relatively accessible experience of peace and harmony, and thus serving as a metaphor for the larger purpose of life. That purpose, said the sages, is to achieve peace and harmony through unification of opposites. Look around you, Lao Tzu might say, and recognize man and woman as yet another expression of the same cosmic duality that creates day and night, winter and summer, positive and negative, north and south, heaven and earth. Bring together these opposites and the world collapses in spiritual ecstasy, say the Taoist teachers.

We tend in this "scientific" age to explain human sexuality only in terms of anatomy and physiology. That might cover the matter well enough for rabbits, but human beings are vastly different.

BENJAMIN SPOCK

"In man and woman are found all the materials and experiences of the world," writes Ehud C. Sperling in his publisher's preface to *Sexual Secrets,* by Nik Douglas and Penny Slinger. "When they unite, these experiences and materials can be distilled into a vision of and a harmonization with the dynamic unity underlying all of reality. For centuries this vision of unity has been obscured by individuals and institutions that have promoted a schism between body and mind, between religious feelings and sexuality."

As Douglas and Slinger point out, sex is a powerful form of human energy that can be channeled and utilized for many purposes. "Tantra is a philosophy, a science, an art and a way of life whereby sexual energy is consciously and creatively utilized," write Douglas and Slinger. "The mystical treatises known as the Tantras contain a broad spectrum of practical techniques for enhancing sexual awareness and achieving transcendence. The hidden potency of the sexual act is the seed of all creativity. Through an understanding of the practical teaching of Tantra, a whole new experience of life opens up."

This same teaching is implicit in the mystical writings of the Egyptian, Hebrew, Greek, and Arab cultures. Each tradition understood sex as a gateway toward greater self-knowledge, personal health, power, and the experience of the divine.

Through most of its history, the West has focused primarily on the dark side of sex. Today, we are suffering the terrible consequences of our attitudes. At the same time, we stand at a crossroads in our maturity, in which it is possible to explore our sexual dimension in new and exciting ways.

Just as our disease patterns have forced us to change our dietary habits, and our environmental crisis causes us to alter our relationship with the earth, AIDS is forcing us to reexamine sex. AIDS challenges us to better understand ourselves, our potential, and our natural limits. Hence, another paradox: there may be a gift in our collective nightmare, yet.

THE ORGANS OF SEX

The male sexual anatomy is made up of two testes; a penis; the prostate gland; and a duct system that connects the testes, prostate, and penis, thus allowing sperm and seminal fluid to pass out of the penis during ejaculation.

The Male Reproductive System

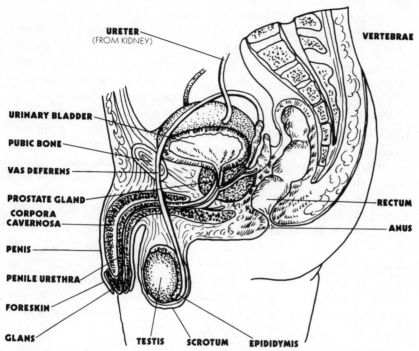

URETER (FROM KIDNEY)

VERTEBRAE

URINARY BLADDER

PUBIC BONE

VAS DEFERENS

PROSTATE GLAND

CORPORA CAVERNOSA

RECTUM

ANUS

PENIS

PENILE URETHRA

FORESKIN

GLANS

TESTIS SCROTUM EPIDIDYMIS

A man's two testes produce sperm, the male sex cells. During ejaculation, the sperm make their way upward to the penis by first passing into a canal called the epididymis and then into the vas deferens, tubes that run from the testes to the prostate gland at the root of the penis. Ducts within the prostate allow sperm to mix with seminal fluid and then to pass into the urethra and down through the erect penis.

The testes produce spermatozoa, the male sex cells, and sex hormones, called androgens, which convert to testosterone. The testes are suspended in a sac, called the scrotum. This sac is capable of expansion or contraction, allowing the testes to rise or fall, and thus draw closer or farther away from the body. This maintains and regulates the temperature of the testes to ensure a harmonious environment for sperm production.

The inner body of the testes is divided into lobules, or chambers, which contain tiny tubules, called seminiferous tubules. It is here, in these tiny tubules, where sperm is produced. The sperm makes its way upward to the penis by first passing into a canal called the epididymis, and then into one of two primary tubes that run from the root of the penis to the testes, called the vas deferens. The vas deferens run to the prostate gland. During ejaculation, sperm travels up from the testes and is mixed with prostate fluid. This seminal fluid is slightly alkaline, and made of zinc, magnesium, acid phosphatase, and numerous enzymes.

Ejaculation occurs at the height of sexual excitement, causing rapid contractions which pump sperm from the testes to the prostate, where it is joined with seminal fluid. From there, the sperm and seminal fluid passes down through the urethra and out the tip of the penis. An average ejaculation produces between 200 million and 400 million sperm. Each sperm has a long tail that it uses in a whipping motion to swim. Sperm can remain active for several days, but can fertilize an ovum for only twenty-four hours.

The female sexual anatomy consists of two ovaries, two Fallopian or uterine tubes, a uterus, vagina, and external genitalia. Breasts, or mammary glands, are considered accessory sex organs.

The ovaries produce reproductive cells, called ova, and the female hormones, estrogen, progesterone, and relaxin. They also create specialized cells called follicles, or groups of cells, that surround the ovum and assist in its development. About 200,000 follicles are present at birth and gradually decrease in number until no more remain at menopause. In a mature, premenopausal woman, an ovum and follicle develop together until they emerge from the ovary, at which time the ovum is released—a process called ovulation. Ovulation is assisted by various hormones that are under the direction of the pituitary gland. In health, ovulation takes place every twenty-eight days. Only one ovum is produced every twenty-eight days.

Once the ovum leaves the ovary, it enters the uterine tube. If there are no sperm present, it will gradually degenerate and leave the body during menstruation. Menstruation is the process in which the uterine wall becomes engorged with blood, caused by the cyclical death of tissues and blood vessels within the uterine wall. This part of the uterus, the outer layer, is called the endometrium, and is shed every twenty-eight days. An unfertilized ovum is released with the flow of blood, which usually lasts four to six days.

If sperm are present in the tube and the ovum is fertilized, the fertilized ovum, or zygote, will move from the uterine tube to the uterus, where it will attach itself and begin to develop. This movement requires four to five days and is assisted by cilia (tiny hairs inside the uterine tube) and muscles within the walls of the tube. The fertilized ovum draws nourishment from the endometrium, which would otherwise have been shed had not fertilization occurred.

The Female Reproductive System

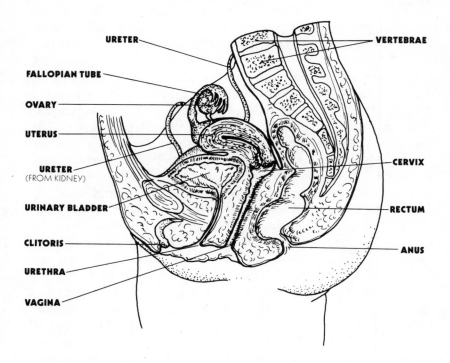

URETER

FALLOPIAN TUBE

OVARY

UTERUS

URETER
(FROM KIDNEY)

URINARY BLADDER

CLITORIS

URETHRA

VAGINA

VERTEBRAE

CERVIX

RECTUM

ANUS

A woman's ovaries produce a reproductive cell, or ovum, every twenty-eight days or so. With the help of various hormones, at ovulation the ovum leaves the ovary and enters the uterine or Fallopian tube. If there are no sperm present, it will gradually degenerate and leave the body during menstruation. If sperm are present in the tube and the ovum is fertilized, the fertilized ovum, or zygote, will move from the uterine tube to the uterus, where it will attach itself and begin to develop. This movement requires four or five days and is assisted by tiny hairs inside the uterine tube and muscles within the walls of the tube.

Just outside the vagina, toward the front of the pubis, is the clitoris, which is a small erectile structure containing many highly sensitive nerve endings. The clitoris is the homologue of a man's glans penis. Stimulation of the clitoris and vagina results in female orgasm. Unlike the vast majority of men, women can have multiple orgasms in close succession.

THE TAO OF LOVE AND SEX

The most advanced Eastern approaches to sex are those of China (Taoism), Tibet (Tantra), and India (yoga). The Tantric practices of Tibet are based on both Taoism and yoga. All highly developed Oriental philosophies, including those of Japan, are based upon these three essentially similar philosophies.

In the traditions of both Taoism and Tantra, sex is considered the aspect of humanness from which all creativity flows. All our desires and abilities to create flow from our sexual nature, whether it be art, music, literature, or fashion. It is our sexual energy that makes creativity possible, according to Taoist and Tantric traditions. Procreation is but one aspect of that creativity.

The words sex and creativity might be interchangeable in this context; however, by saying sex we better identify a source of those creative energies within us.

For a full presentation of Taoist and Tantric practices, you will have to turn to other books devoted entirely to the subject of sex. Among the best of these are *Sexual Secrets,* mentioned earlier, *The Art of Sexual Ecstasy* by Margo Anand, and *The Tao of Love and Sex* by Jolan Chang. However, all Taoist and Tantric sexual practices begin from certain common and fundamental tenets. The first is that the body is the temple of the divine, and therefore must be treated with absolute care and respect. To abuse the body with unhealthful foods, drink, thoughts, or behavior is to destroy the very home of the universal spirit. Conversely, to respect and understand the body is to understand the universe itself, for the body is the microcosm of all that exists.

Second, the mind, body, and spirit are a single whole that is unified by a larger body of energy that permeates our physical form. This larger body of energy is itself arranged in a highly complex pattern. Among the most important parts of this energy pattern is a channel of energy that flows along the spine, beginning at the sex organs and running to the top of the head. Along this channel, or spiritual axis as it is sometimes called, are six energetic chakras, representing levels of consciousness, or aspects of our mind.

At the sexual center is located a pool of powerful energy, conceived of as a coiled snake, or a female deity, called kundalini. During sex, this powerful energy can be coaxed out of its potential state and made to move upward along the spiritual axis, causing each state of consciousness, represented by the specific chakras, to be transformed and illuminated. Ultimately, the kundalini reaches the head, in a place between the eyebrows, called the third eye, known in esoteric traditions of both East and West as the place of cosmic consciousness. When the kundalini energy unifies all the chakras and unites with the Third Eye, you experience "the joyous ecstasy of oneness with the universe, outside the limitations of time," write Douglas and Slinger in *Sexual Secrets.*

To tap the sacred power of sex, we have to give up trying to make it a known quantity. Instead of trying to make it fit some convenient mold—as a form of recreation, or as a separate compartment of our lives, something that only happens in bed—we must assume an attitude of beginner's mind in the face of its mysteries. Then we can begin to sharpen our awareness of its subtler qualities, seeing how they permeate the whole of our interaction with our partner.

JOHN WELWOOD

A great yogi, called Anandagiri, described the rise of kundalini this way: "The inner woman, entering the 'royal road,' takes rest at intervals in the secret centers. Finally She embraces the Supreme Lord in the lotus of the head. From that union flows an exquisite nectar that floods and permeates the body; then the Ineffable Bliss is experienced."

The way to stimulate the rise of the kundalini is through visualization during meditation and sex, and by controlling your breath. Breath is the single greatest tool in learning to prolong sex, control your inner energy, and, in the case of the man, forestall orgasm. Tantric and Taoist practices teach that breathing should be deep and abdominal. The stomach should move outward, and take the shape of a pot. Also, the breath should be held, anywhere from one to four counts, and then exhaled fully. As we describe in the chapter on the lungs, we take in life energy in the form of our breath. Every breath can revitalize us. The retention of the breath allows the qi to permeate the body and enrich health and inner power. On the inhalation, you can visualize the movements of the qi to specific organs. Retain this breath and see the qi revitalize your organs, and restore health and vitality. Breath retention is one of the keys to greater personal power, vitality, and wisdom. By controlling the breath, you control the mind, say yogis.

With the exhalation, you free yourself from all negative thoughts and feelings. Make the exhalation long. See the dark clouds of negative thoughts and emotions, of illness and dark attachments, leave the body and rejoin the earth, where they are purified.

By learning to control the breath, we learn to control our more subtle energetic, nervous, and muscle systems. This gives us greater body control, and thus allows us more fulfilling lovemaking. Tantric and Taoist practitioners also suggest that lovers learn to breathe together and to share their breath, in order to experience sex at a deeper and more intimate level.

In the Taoist, Tantric, and yogic traditions, sex is a means of self-development. Tantra says that such self-development cannot take place without love, trust, and commitment to one's partner. All the higher human values must be joined with sex in order to make it elevating and spiritually uplifting. In such a context, sex is a way to the ultimate center within.

CHAPTER 29

THE IMMUNE SYSTEM

States of health or disease are, at heart, the organism's success or failure at adapting to environmental challenges.

RENÉ DUBOS

*I*N 1981, a mysterious and chilling disease surfaced in the United States that rendered the human immune system powerless to fight against an array of deadly diseases. Initially, the illness appeared to be confined to homosexual men, a fact that prompted medical doctors to begin calling it "gay-related immune deficiency," or GRID.

A year later, the number of cases had increased significantly and the old acronym was changed to AIDS: acquired immune deficiency syndrome. At the time, the cause of the illness was still unknown. But in 1983 French scientists at the Pasteur Institute in Paris isolated the virus that was causing AIDS. The French called the organism human immunodeficiency virus, or HIV.

In 1984, U.S. scientists officially recognized HIV as the cause of AIDS. Scientists learned quickly that the illness was spread through the exchange of body fluids, primarily through sexual relations, intravenous drug use, or blood transfusions. It was also learned that a latency period existed between the moment HIV invaded the body, and the point at which it became sufficiently virulent to manifest as AIDS. One could carry HIV for as long as a decade before it became AIDS.

Despite the obvious dangers the disease posed, there was little if any public education concerning AIDS in the early 1980s. As Randy Shilts points out in his book *As the Band Played On: People, Politics and the AIDS Epidemic,* researchers were initially dissuaded from even investigating the AIDS virus because it was thought to be confined to homosexuals, and therefore did not warrant the serious attention of the scientific community. It was not until the French made important discoveries in AIDS research that American scientists began to investigate the illness with greater urgency.

The belief that AIDS was confined to the homosexual population also provided the American public with a false sense of security. That feeling of safety quickly evaporated in 1985 when Rock Hudson, a symbol of American manhood, contracted the disease. Hudson's subsequent decline and death provided a very public education, as much of the world looked on in horror. One of the most handsome faces in the world soon became a skull covered with paperlike flesh. By the time Rock Hudson died, everyone knew what AIDS did to people. But it was just the beginning.

Following Hudson's death, several people contracted AIDS from blood transfusions given at hospitals. Suddenly, the true nature of the illness was clear: This was not simply a "gay disease," but an illness that afflicted people regardless of their sexual preference.

The media turned their full attention to what was being called the "AIDS epidemic." By 1986, the word most often used to describe the public attitude towards AIDS was "hysteria." Education campaigns shifted into full throttle, warning everyone from the third grade onward of the dangers of "unsafe sex" and random use of intravenous drug needles.

By 1991, more than 160,000 men and women had contracted AIDS in the U.S., and more than 100,000 had died. That year Centers for Disease Control (CDC) officials estimated that more than 1.5 million Americans were infected with HIV, and that by 1994, more than 215,000 will have died of AIDS. The Hudson Institute, one of the world's leading think tanks, stated in 1989 that by the year 2002, 14.5 million Americans would be infected with HIV, and the vast majority of them would develop AIDS unless a cure was found.

Most of those who are afflicted with AIDS in the U.S. are young (between the ages of twenty-five and forty-four) homo-

Health is not equivalent to happiness, surfeit, or success. It is foremost a matter of being wholly one with whatever circumstances we find ourselves in. Even our death is a healthy event if we fully embrace the fact of our dying.

MWALIMU IMARA

sexual men or intravenous drug users. However, a growing proportion of those with AIDS are young women, who now represent nearly 10 percent of AIDS sufferers.

The U.S., of course, makes up only a fraction of the picture. AIDS is spreading most rapidly among black Africans. According to the World Health Organization, the more than 2 million African people with AIDS represents only the tip of the iceberg. In Uganda alone there are 800,000 cases of HIV infection, which represents 20 percent of the population and 88 percent of the prostitutes, who are among the principal sources of the illness within the population. Ugandan health officials estimate that by the year 2000, one out of every two Ugandans will be infected with HIV.

AIDS research is now one of the world's top medical and scientific priorities, but scientists maintain that a vaccine will not be ready in this century, and that a cure is even further off. The principal means of protection is prevention, specifically safe sex and, for drug users, sterilized needles.

The scourge of AIDS has awakened us in many ways, especially to the miracle of the body's defense system. We live in a world alive with microorganisms, chemical pollutants, radioactive waste, and simple dust. Many of these foreign substances are deadly. Yet despite the fact that we breathe them into our bodies in virtually every inhalation, we are able to destroy them without ever being aware that they existed in the first place. Such are the wonders of this marvelous system called immunity.

THE PHASES OF IMMUNE DEFENSE

The body's first wall of defense is the skin, which serves as a barrier against an onslaught of innumerable organisms and poisons that bombard us at every moment. Those foreign substances that penetrate the skin are dealt with initially by tears, sweat, and saliva, all of which neutralize and evacuate the foreign invader.

Nevertheless, diseases do get inside the body. When a virus enters a cell, it causes the cell to reproduce the virus many times over, making cells factories for disease. More times than not, however, the immune system destroys the virus and the virus-producing cells before we become aware that we are infected. The same is true of a cancer cell. From time to time, the DNA or genetic code of a cell becomes deformed and causes the cell to replicate uncontrollably. Nevertheless, the cancerous cells are usually destroyed by the immune system before they gain a foothold in the body. No matter what the problem—an environmental toxin, a virus, or a cancer cell—the immune system has an answer, most of the time.

The system responds to an invader in several phases: first, it recognizes the invading enemy as "not-self"; second, it creates a specific and effective response; third, it carries on a highly coordinated battle, using multiple approaches; finally, it determines that the war has been won and calls off the immune response, lest it consume the body itself. Having called the army to a halt, the immune system resumes its everpresent vigil, continually alert. Let's look a little closer at each of these stages.

Once a virus appears in the bloodstream or tissues, it is immediately encountered by a group of large white blood cells called macrophages or phagocytes. These cells are the body's neighborhood cops. They patrol the bloodstream looking for bad guys. The macrophage cells can respond to an invading virus or groups of virally-invaded cells in several ways: they can gobble up as many invaders as they can; or consume a portion of the cell's membrane, thus destroying the cell; or mark the cells that they cannot destroy with a sign, called an antigen, that will distinguish the invader as "not self." This is important because the body must be able to tell self from not-self throughout the course of the battle to keep immune cells from destroying healthy tissue.

The presence of the antigen serves to call out other immune cells, the first group of which are the helper-Ts or T-4 cells, so named because they are schooled to react to disease by the thymus gland before they are set free to roam the body. These T-4 cells, which like other helper-Ts are part of the general category of immune cells called lymphocytes, rapidly multiply and join the fray.

T-4 cells are the battlefield generals. They do not engage the invader themselves, but organize the body's response to the invading pathogen. Once set into action, the T-4 cells lock onto the virus and signal the macrophage to secrete a chemical called Interleukin-1, or Il-1, which scientists maintain allows the immune cells to "communicate" with one another.

The Interleukin-1 stimulates the body to produce fever and deep sleep. Scientists now speculate that fever may actually be an important first step in the body's efforts to destroy an enemy

We should love our disease because it is keeping us healthy. Without the disease we have, we might have a worse illness. Disease is always a creative attempt to solve problems. When we accept this, we can move toward wellness by thanking our disease and discovering in relationship with other people—a group or our doctor—other ways to solve the problems which the disease is addressing.

LEWIS MEHL

invader, perhaps raising the body's temperature to make the inner environment hostile to the invading organism. Sleep is induced probably in an effort to allow the body to direct its energies to the task of destroying the enemy.

T-4 cells then secrete another chemical, Interleukin-2, or Il-2, which activates another type of lymphocyte called killer-T cell. Killer-T cells destroy virally-infected cells by attacking their cell membrane. This keeps the virus from replicating.

While the killer-Ts attack the invading organism, the T-4 cells call out another arm of the immune system, the B-cells. B-cells make specialized antibodies, composed of proteins, to fight the virus. In an extraordinarily complex array of maneuvers, B-cells mutate and shuffle genes to create the unique antibody that will destroy the virus. B-cells are literally on-site laboratories. They are perhaps the most prolific chemists ever created, capable of creating more than one million kinds of antibodies. They are also capable of producing immunoglobulins, proteins that also serve as antibodies against illness.

While the B-cells are creating the right chemical agent, the T-4 cells help select the perfect antidote to the invader. Once it is found, the T-4 cells stimulate the B-cells to multiply and produce more antibodies.

Macrophages, helper-Ts, killer-Ts, B-cells, and antibodies— these are the main soldiers on the body's inner battlefield.

When the appropriate antibody is found, as it is in better than 99 percent of the occasions, the immune system "records and re-members" the formula. It is now capable of warding off the patho-gen the next time it is encountered. We are said to be "immune" to the measles, mumps, or chicken pox after we've been afflicted with them once. This means that whenever that pathogen is en-countered again, the immune system instantly whips up a batch of the effective antibody and force-feeds it to the illness, thus kill-ing it before we ever feel a sniffle or any other symptom. In this way, the immune system also acts like a giant computer that keeps genetic information on hand. The body's immune record is al-ways available. The immune system is vigilant and prepared the next time you or I breathe a familiar flu or chicken pox virus.

Once the battle is won, the immune system must call off the fight, lest it ultimately destroy healthy tissue and, indeed, the body itself. To call off the attack, suppressor cells, called T-8s, are called

There is no riches above a sound body.

APOCRYPHA

out. These cells literally suppress the immune response by sending out a chemical that tells T- and B-cells that the fight is over and that they are to shut down their activity. This allows the immune system to return to a state of balance, or restful surveillance.

Immune cells are involved in virtually every disease and healing process, including the onset and recovery of cardiovascular disease (see chapter on circulation), cancer, and arthritis, just to name a few.

The immune system is powerful and effective, but at the same time it is highly sensitive to how we think, how we feel, and what we eat. These factors often decide whether or not we become ill, and how quickly we recover. Let's have a closer look at how the mind and nutrition affect immune function.

MIND AND IMMUNE FUNCTION

It is now well established that the mind plays a vital role—sometimes even a determining role—in the efficacy of immune function. The evidence began to pile up in the 1940s when pioneer researcher Hans Selye determined that the mind could greatly influence how the body functioned. He found that stress can have immediate and accumulated effects on the body. The body has been trained through evolution to either escape danger or confront it. However, in the modern world, we are often forced to face a dangerous situation and resist both urges. For example, when a police officer orders you to stop your car because you failed to stop at a red light, your natural impulse is to press down even harder on the gas pedal and flee, or get out of the car and tell him to get off your back. Unfortunately, you can do neither. It may be the same with your employer, or the banker, or some other member of your circle with whom you have a difficult relationship. When this natural instinct is repressed, the accumulated tension can cause a wide range of negative physical reactions, including hormonal, respiratory, cardiovascular, and nervous system disorders. These imbalances, said Selye, could cause kidney damage, cardiovascular disease, and even death.

In the 1960s, Dr. Meyer Friedman and Dr. Ray H. Rosenman articulated the so-called type A and type B personalities. Type A is goal-oriented, driven by deadlines, and heavily invested in the outcome of events; type B is more centered in the moment, more

Healing is a matter of time, but it is sometimes also a matter of opportunity.

HIPPOCRATES

Your immune system is your interface with the environment. If it is healthy and doing its job right, you can interact with germs and not get infections, with allergens and not have allergic reactions, and with carcinogens and not get cancer. A healthy immune system is the cornerstone of good general health.

ANDREW WEIL

relationship-oriented, and less concerned about the outcome of events. These respective personalities, Friedman and Rosenman showed, have very different impacts on cardiovascular health. Type A behavior causes elevated levels of corticosteroid hormones, adrenaline, and blood cholesterol, and runs a much higher risk of heart disease and stroke than type B. The research of both Selye and Friedman-Rosenman demonstrated that stress has potentially devastating consequences. How effectively a person deals with stress can determine both the quality and length of that person's life.

From then on, mind-body research began to explore the behavior of immune cells themselves. It has been known for years that people who suffer the recent loss of a loved one are at greater risk of succumbing to disease and death than those who have not undergone such a trauma. This is typically referred to as dying of a broken heart. Scientists at Mount Sinai Medical Center found that bereavement sometimes has a deadening effect on lymphocytes. Dr. Stephen Schliefer and his colleagues found that the lymphocytes in some bereaved men sometimes fail to respond in the presence of a virus or foreign body. If the bereaved person survives long enough after the death of the loved one—usually about six months after—the lymphocytes mysteriously resume their normal behavior and function perfectly.

At Harvard University, Dr. John B. Jemmot found that the immune systems of type A students were weaker than those of type B students. The scientists studied the quantity of immunoglobulin A, or IgA, produced by the B-cells. During the rigors of the school year, especially during exams, the Type A students lost more IgA, and took longer to restore the IgA, than did the type B students. The research confirmed that Type A people tend to be more heavily invested in the outcome of events, often viewing such events as "life and death" situations. The Type B students were far less identified with the outcome of the tests. Therefore, their immune systems were not as depressed.

While negative emotional states have a harmful effect on immune response, scientists have found that positive thoughts and images can help restore immune function. The mind can be used intentionally to reinvigorate immune cells. Such cases as Norman Cousins, who used laughter and a positive attitude to prolong his life with a terminal illness; the work of O. Carl Simonton, an oncologist who has reported that visualization can help patients extend their lives and, indeed, overcome serious illness, including cancer; and the enormous body of evidence showing that people who maintain longstanding supportive relationships live longer and enjoy more fruitful lives, all point to the dramatic influence the mind has over the body.

New studies are showing that laughter has impressive benefits on hormones, respiration, and heart function. One showed that even smiling alters both mood and brain chemistry for the better. Finally, meditation and positive imagery routines have been shown to have a strengthening effect on immune function.

All of this research points to the need to maintain balance in life. People who are singularly focused and heavily identified with one aspect of life tend to have weaker immune responses than those who live more varied and balanced lives. Something in the human condition needs variety.

Here the unity of mind and body are unequivocal: health is an outcome of a balance among work, supportive relationships, and self-esteem.

DIET AND IMMUNE FUNCTION

Numerous studies have shown that dietary factors, such as fat and cholesterol, vitamins, minerals, and fiber content play important roles in the relative strength or weakness of the immune system. These studies show that by enhancing the diet and reducing the number and severity of the toxic influences on the body, the strength of the immune system can be recovered.

In general, scientists have long recognized that inadequate nourishment causes depressed immunity and vulnerability to a host of pathogens. Malnutrition has been associated with a wide range of illnesses, from scurvy to malaria to blindness. But research has demonstrated a far more specific and powerful relationship between the body's defenses and our daily eating habits.

Saturated fat has been shown to affect a macrophage by adversely changing the cell's membrane and reducing its sensitivity. Macrophages, or scavenger cells, depend on the sensitivity of their cell membranes to identify and destroy pathogens. Failure to identify a pathogen renders this first phase of the immune response ineffective.

Once inside the system, dietary fats oxidize or become rancid. These rancid fats further break down into substances called free radicals, highly charged molecules that are extremely reactive within the system. Free radicals destroy DNA and cause cell mutations.

Scientists have discovered that foods rich in beta carotene, such as broccoli, carrots, and squash, and vitamins C and E, are "free radical scavengers," or antioxidants. These foods donate electrons to imbalanced atoms, thus restoring stability to molecules and tissues. Foods rich in beta carotene and vitamins C and E have been shown to prevent free radical formation, and to stop the chemical changes that otherwise create havoc in human tissues and immune cells.

Beta carotene has been shown to have powerful protective properties against the onset of cancer, even among cigarette smokers. The National Research Counsel of the National Academy of Sciences has encouraged Americans to increase their intake of foods rich in beta carotene to reduce their chances of contracting cancer.

Deficiencies of vitamin A have been shown to reduce the size and number of T- and B-cells. Iron deficiency has been shown to decrease the effectiveness of white blood cells.

Minerals, such as zinc, selenium, manganese, magnesium, copper, and calcium, dramatically affect immune response. In a study published in the *American Journal of Clinical Nutrition* (March 1987), scientists reported that zinc deficiencies cause atrophy of the thymus gland and reduce antibody response to antigens. The scientists compared two groups of infants, one whose diets were supplemented with zinc, while the other was given a placebo. The scientists found that the zinc-supplemented group had lower rates of infection and higher blood levels of white cells than the group given a placebo. Scientists familiar with the evidence have maintained that diet does indeed have a role to play in the treatment of AIDS and other immune-related diseases.

Writing in *Nutrition Update,* Dr. Brian Leibovitz of the University of California's Department of Food Science stated, "Two very important areas of research are being neglected: the control of viral expression and the enhancement of immune response by nutritional means. It is my firm belief that these are the two most important areas to be studied with regard to AIDS."

A variety of new and exciting studies examining the relationship between nutrition and immune function are now being done. The early research seems to convince scientists that healthful eating is essential to a strong and optimal immune response.

AIDS: A MULTIPLICITY OF CAUSES

While it is now well-established that HIV infection is the prerequisite for the contraction of AIDS, scientists have found that a long series of insults to the immune system is necessary before HIV turns into full-blown AIDS. Such information is important because it demonstrates that lifestyle factors can help prevent AIDS from manifesting, even after HIV infection has occurred.

In one of its early studies, the Centers for Disease Control (CDC) discovered that gay men with AIDS had a history of heavy drug use. The CDC reported in 1982 that of the 87 men with AIDS studied, 97 percent said they used poppers, or amyl nitrate; 93 percent said they smoked marijuana; 68 percent used amphetamines; 66 percent used cocaine; 65 percent LSD; 59 percent Quaaludes; 12 percent heroin. The CDC also found that, as a rule, the men were multiple drug users, consistently using a variety of "street drugs," not just one.

Poppers and other drugs have long been known to depress the immune function and cause anemia, intestinal disorders, and liver damage. Some studies suggest that poppers may be directly associated with the onset of Kaposi's sarcoma. Drug addiction has long been known to depress immune function; heroin, for example, has been found to deplete the number of T-cells.

The introduction of sperm into the male body, especially through anal intercourse, has been known to suppress the immune cells. The walls of the intestines are only one cell thick. Researchers describe the thin intestinal lining, or mucosa, as having the strength of wet tissue paper. The intestinal wall is easily torn, allowing sperm and infection to spread rapidly into the bloodstream. (By contrast, the vagina is lined with a thick protective layer of mucosa cells that protect against the invasion of sperm and other substances directly into the bloodstream.)

Sperm is a concentrated protein containing purines, ammonia, and other chemicals that can be toxic to the blood and tissue. The introduction of sperm into the blood causes rapid de-

313

ployment of immune cells, which must be directed away from other infections.

The CDC also reported that 80 to 90 percent of the gay male population with HIV harbors intestinal parasites. Parasites are cited as a potentially important contributing factor in the onset of AIDS among heterosexuals in Africa and the U.S. Intestinal parasites have been dealt with by the gay community with the use of antibiotics. But research has shown that antibiotics have a depressing effect on the immune system. In 1982, W. E. Hauser and J. S. Remington reported in the *American Journal of Medicine* that antibiotics depress at least four immune components.

All of this is in addition to the fact that so many men with AIDS have been previously infected with a variety of sexually transmitted diseases, including syphilis, herpes, hepatitis B, gonorrhea, and amoebic dysentery. These diseases are also immunodepressant.

Meanwhile, scientists at Johns Hopkins University in Baltimore discovered that a minority of patients—about five in 2,000—test positive for HIV after exposure, but are discovered to be seronegative several months later. These people are apparently able to destroy the virus once it manifests in their bloodstreams.

AIDS and other immune deficiency illnesses, such as Epstein Barr and chronic fatigue syndrome, demonstrate both the power of the immune system, and its delicacy. Research is showing increasingly that the power of immune response is very much in our own control, but that oftentimes we unwittingly depress immune function and sometimes even destroy it.

For additional information regarding specific conditions, see the related organs, systems, and senses described throughout this book.

Foods that boost the immune system include the following:

- *Allium vegetables:* Vegetables such as onions, garlic, leeks, chives, and scallions are immune-enhancing and protect against stomach cancer. Fifty or more pounds per year of these vegetables can prevent gastric cancer, according to some studies.
- *The cabbage family:* Broccoli, cauliflower, brussels sprouts, cabbages, and kale. These vegetables protect against colorectal, stomach, and respiratory cancers. Cole slaw and sauerkraut are good substitutes and can be equally effective.

- *Fish:* Fish oils can increase the activity of white blood cells, which detect and attack foreign cells. They have been shown to prevent metastasis in early stages of cancer.
- *Miso:* Contains high levels of lecithin and linoleic acid, which break down fatty deposits. It coats the inner wall of the colon with beneficial flora of lactus bacillus; it also improves digestion and assimilation of nutrients. Miso creates an alkaline blood and intestinal environment.
- *Organic foods:* Farmers in the corn belt have the highest incidence of leukemia and prostate and pancreas cancer deaths. In 1945, chlorinated hydrocarbon pesticides became available in South Dakota, Iowa, Minnesota, New Hampshire, Arkansas, Nebraska, Kansas, Oklahoma, Oregon, and Washington, and this brought about the rise in these diseases. Wheat farmers, who use considerably less insecticide, don't show these problems. These synthetic insecticides put large numbers of farmers at risk after heavy exposure for prolonged periods and put the general public at risk also, but to a lesser extent. Some of these pesticides are passed through the water supply and the food chain. Avoiding foods that have been treated with such pesticides by eating organically-grown fruits and vegetables is a wise idea.
- *Sea vegetables:* Rich in calcium, iron, zinc, and other trace minerals. Sea vegetables gather heavy metals and strontium 90 from the body and create insoluble salts, which are flushed from the body.
- *Shiitake mushrooms:* Immune-enhancing and antitumor. The *U.S. Journal of Cancer Research* reported that six out of ten mice suffering from sarcoma (a type of virally induced cancer) and treated with shiitake extract over short periods of time had complete tumor regression. At higher concentrations all the mice showed tumor regression. Shiitake dramatically lowers blood cholesterol. Animal studies have shown a drop in blood cholesterol between 25 to 45 percent, in a few days. The impact is stronger when a whole mushroom is consumed. Five to six mushrooms a day lower cholesterol 12 percent in a week. They contain cortinelin, a broad-spectrum antibacterial agent, which kills a wide range of pathogenic bacteria. A sulfide compound purified from shiitake has been found to have an antibiotic effect

Be careful about reading health books. You may die of a misprint.

MARK TWAIN

upon ringworm and other skin diseases. Researchers at Japan's Yamagushi University School of Medicine have reported that shiitake extract had a "protective effect" that inhibits the cell-destroying effects of the HIV virus.

- *Whole grains:* They contain B vitamins essential for proper functioning of the immune system and fiber to enhance digestion and intestinal function. They are rich in complex carbohydrates for long-lasting energy and contain protein, a wide variety of vitamins, and minerals.
- *Zinc:* It is immune-enhancing and essential to production of thymic hormones, needed to foster maturation of immune cells. An excess of zinc also can depress immunity, so it is safer to get it in foods than to take supplements. Good sources: seafood, whole wheat, whole wheat flour, bulgur wheat, cashews, most beans, and black-eyed peas.

There are also nutrients that boost the immune system. These include:

- *Argenine:* An amino acid. Stimulates immune reponse in patients whose immune systems are undermined by drugs or surgery. In animal studies, adding this amino acid to the diet enhanced immune responses and preserved immune function in the face of malnutrition and advancing cancers. Found in fish, beans, and grains.
- *Beta carotene:* Beta carotene is immune-strengthening, acts as an antioxidant, and protects against cancer and heart disease. Sources: carrots, squash, broccoli, bean sprouts, collard greens, brussels sprouts, peaches, apricots, prunes, watermelon.
- *Calcium:* Regulates lymphocyte function and the synthesis and functioning of prostaglandins. Good sources: leafy greens, especially collard, kale, and mustard greens, and sea vegetables.
- *Chlorophyll:* Found in green vegetables, blue-green algae, and chlorophyll supplement drinks, it can help rejuvenate the immune system, rebalance the body's physiology, rejuvenate the thymus, and act as a powerful detoxifier.
- *Fiber:* Sources: Whole grains, vegetables, fruit. Protects against colon cancer and, some studies suggest, breast cancer.

Let thy food be thy medicine.

HIPPOCRATES

- *Selenium:* Essential for the formation of antibodies and enzymes that participate in immunity. It is found in seafood, whole grain cereals, and garlic.
- *Vitamin B complex:* Immune-enhancing. Deficiency reduces production and efficiency of B-cells and T-cells, and causes atrophy of lymph tissue, poor antibody production, and diminished activity of thymic hormone. B6 deficiency impairs cellular and hormone-regulated immunity. Good sources are greens, whole grains, legumes, potatoes, corn, nuts, avocados, green peppers.
- *Vitamin C:* Immune-enhancing. Vitamin C strengthens the body's general resistance to viruses and stimulates eliminative process. It has been shown to protect against cancer of the esophagus and stomach. Good sources are broccoli, cabbage, strawberries, oranges, grapefruit, cantaloupe, leafy greens, sauerkraut, squash, and red and green peppers. Rose hips and hibiscus tea are especially rich sources of C.
- *Vitamin E:* Immune-enhancing; it is a free radical scavenger, meaning it can penetrate cells, restore tissue, and stop decay resulting from oxidation; it can also protect against ozone-induced free radical damage and slow aging. Researchers estimate that dietary measures that control oxygen radical damage could add five or more years to life. Vitamin C can help to regenerate Vitamin E. Sources: whole grains, especially wheat and bulgur; seafood.

Herbs that boost the immune system including the following:

- *Echinacea:* Boil the root to use as a tea or place fifteen to thirty drops in water. It stimulates and strengthens the body's immune system, and acts as an antibiotic. Echinacea is one of the most powerful and effective herbs against all forms of infection.
- *Goldenseal:* Herbalist Michael Tierra reports in his book *Planetary Medicine* (Lotus Press, 1988) that goldenseal is "effective against flu, fevers, and infections of all kinds; and in treating hemorrhoids, vaginal yeast infection and as an eyewash for inflamed eyes." Tierra warns against long-term use of goldenseal as a preventive, however, because it can weaken the flora in the intestinal tract.

A NEW WORLDVIEW OF HEALTH AND HUMAN POTENTIAL

If any thing is sacred, the human body is sacred.

WALT WHITMAN

WHAT IS HEALTH? Simple questions, such as this one, are often the most difficult to answer. If we fully understood the meaning of health, we would better understand what it means to be human. We would see more clearly our human potential, and even get a glimpse of where we are headed in our evolution.

Perhaps because the question of health leads to such a mine-field of subject-areas, the American Medical Association doesn't even attempt to answer it. It defines health as the absence of physical and mental disease. Unfortunately, that's like defining sunlight as the absence of darkness. Such an answer doesn't tell us a thing about sunlight, or about health. We'd like to have some pictures. Or, to use the vernacular of Western medicine, we'd like to know the "symptoms" of health. Does a healthy person possess more energy than an unhealthy person, for example? How does a healthy person age? What kinds of work do healthy people do? Is a healthy person more likely to have supportive or destructive relationships? Does a healthy person better understand himself in relationship to life?

These are the kinds of questions that we want to have answered when we consider the meaning of health. They get us thinking in the right direction, because, at bottom, we are wondering if health better equips us to answer the questions that life presents. If that is true, then health has got to be more than merely the absence of disease, because life itself is a struggle against ignorance and confusion as much as against illness.

Our medical system's inability to define health is at the very core of our health care crisis. Ours is the only medical system ever to exist that offers no unified definition of health, or what causes it. Without such a broad understanding of health and illness, we have been unable to offer an integrated approach to disease prevention, or health enhancement. Medical doctors have not begun to understand how the body heals itself. No one knows what the underlying power is that motivates wounds to heal, or the body to rid itself of disease. Doctors can describe part of the process, but cannot explain what causes it. The fact that the body makes a concerted and valiant effort to achieve health itself suggests all kinds of things about the nature of life, but scientists haven't got a clue as to how the human body might be linked to the larger forces of the universe.

As medical doctor and author Andrew Weil says in his book *Health and Healing,* "Allopaths may say that health is the absence of disease, but they have no clear conception or theory of what disease is, nor any general concept of treatment . . . Lack of a coherent philosophy of the abstract notions of health as wholeness, perfection, and balance encourages allopaths to pay attention mostly to the concrete manifestations of illness."

The current Western medical system is founded exclusively upon material values. When medical doctors look for health, they examine the behavior of cells and organs. They consult machines to determine the condition of the body and the causes of disease. In other words, the current medical system focuses on the elements of the earth for the answers to questions of health and illness. Moreover, it sees health and illness as conditions that are often outside of human control. You breathe in a flu virus and, bingo, you've got a cold. You suddenly manifest a cancer cell and your life is in jeopardy.

Such thinking is the basis for genetic research because it is believed that by altering the most fundamental aspects of human biology, the genes, illnesses such as cancer, diabetes, heart disease, and other disorders might be averted. In genetic research, modern

"M.D." does not stand for "Medical Deity."

BERNIE SIEGEL

science has taken its materialistic values to an extreme, for it discounts behavior and spirit entirely. Rather, it focuses upon genetically redesigning the body.

In traditional medicine, health was defined to embrace virtually every aspect of human experience because the sages of East and West maintained that the body, mind, and spirit are a single unified whole. All three of these human aspects are harmonized by an underlying entity that the ancients called the life force, a kind of spiritual energy that permeates the universe and manifests as individual beings—you and me. When you are fully infused with this life force, the body and mind function optimally; that is, all of your cells, organs, and systems function at their full potential. In the same way that the whole is greater than the sum of its parts, you would fully realize your potential. All your talents and abilities would be available to you to express as you desired. Such a state, said the sages, brings with it an experience of unity with the ultimate reality, a harmony with the creator of life itself. This philosophy defined the methods used to maintain health and treat disease.

Thus, the path to health was, and is, a path of spiritual development. Through self-study, we come to understand ourselves so thoroughly that we come to know what supports our physical and spiritual health, and what detracts from it. Since humankind is directly linked with the natural environment, the fruits of that environment are relied upon to treat disease and restore health.

This "holistic" understanding of health is the one that humanity has held for the longest time. It is only in modern times, specifically the last 400 years, that we have redefined health to mean something strictly limited to the body. At the same time, we have steadily given up the notion that we control our health.

If we eliminate some of the extreme approaches, we are able to see the value of both systems. Our modern technology and science have benefited us greatly and are essential to our development. Yet, responsibility for health must ultimately lie with each of us and our own behavior. By recognizing the value and the need for both systems, we must confront an age-old question: Is there a bridge that links the material and spiritual? Is there a way of linking the modern with the ancient?

The refusal of modern medicine to accept the value of the ancient systems is the reason our society is unable to define health. If

I can compress what we have learned about the causes of these modern killers in three summarizing sentences: We are killing ourselves by our own careless habits. We are killing ourselves by carelessly polluting the environment. We are killing ourselves by permitting harmful social conditions to persist—conditions like poverty, hunger, and ignorance—which destory health, especially for infants and children.

JOSEPH CALIFANO

we accepted the traditional approaches, we would be forced to embrace the invisible aspects of life, and of healing. Yet, we already know that our thoughts, emotions, and psychological outlook—the invisible influences—either enhance or detract from our health. The realms of the mind and spirit play vital roles in how the physical body functions. To exclude such realms is both arbitrary and wrong. Moreover, the traditional methods of health care have been shown to work. Diet, massage therapy, acupuncture, and herbs all have powerful enhancing effects on health.

How can we understand East and West to unify them? How can we define health so that it can embrace the physical, the mental, and the spiritual?

Physician and author Deepak Chopra says that the body is characterized by intelligence that is not limited to the intellect or the head, but permeates every cell. In his book *Creating Health,* he writes, "All disease results from the disruption of the flow of intelligence. Intelligence is not simply in the head, though. Its expression may be at the subcellular level, at the cellular or tissue level, or at the level of the central nervous system." The myriad enzymes, genes, hormones, immune constituents, and nerves are all "expressions of intelligence," says Chopra. "They regulate essential functions with perfect know-how and do it at the body's far outposts, so to speak, far from where intellect is seated. Although all these expressions of intelligence can be located, intelligence itself cannot . . . it is all-pervasive in us and universal in nature."

How this intelligence guides cells in their selective activities is still unknown, but there are interesting theories, which we will get to shortly.

Organs that are made up of healthy cells behave in the same orderly and efficient ways as the cells themselves. They do not routinely become hyperactive, or hypoactive, and when they become ill, they are capable of throwing off disease in a relatively short period of time.

Illness, on the other hand, is disorderly. At the atomic level, sick atoms break up and rapidly decay, a phenomenon called free radical formation. These degenerative atoms cause new chemical bonds to form within the cells, which can give rise to a wide array of illnesses, from arthritis and heart disease to cancer and Alzheimer's. What is remarkable is that disorderly cells do not act in harmony with the overall body, but behave according to their own specific patterns.

At the other end of the spectrum, we know that disorderly behavior also causes disease. Erratic or chaotic sleeping patterns, eating habits, thoughts, and lifestyle all may lead to illness of one kind or another. Sickness can be understood as disordered behavior at the macroscopic and microscopic levels.

We use order to treat sickness. More rest, more balanced eating, calmer thoughts, and less stress all contribute to better health. Of course, order can become dogmatic, rigid, and stagnant. Stagnation leads to the refusal to grow and to sickness. Indeed, all growth is made possible by the breakdown of old tissues and old behavior patterns, which are then replaced by stronger tissues or new ways of acting. Change and evolution depend upon old systems giving way to disorder and the construction of a new system. Life itself is not stagnant, but ever moving, ever flowing.

Therefore, we face the paradox of life at its most basic level once again. We cannot escape the adventure of change, made possible by the paradox of order and disorder, or regeneration and decay. We can easily become blinded to this reality, that opposites make up the fabric of life. Indeed, the more we build up one side of life, the more we deny the other. As physicist Fred Alan Wolf says in *Taking the Quantum Leap,* "For nature is dualistic; she behaves according to the Principle of Complementarity. . . . The more we determine or define a system in terms of one of these complements, the less we know about the other. . . . There was always a hidden, complementary side to everything we experienced."

Order must be challenged, systems must change, if health is to exist on any level, whether it be in the physical body or in institutions. In the same way, health is achieved by balancing paradoxical influences, so that both can exist to appropriate degrees. Here we come to another fact about health: Balance is essential for health to exist. Health cannot exist when extremes of behavior of any kind rule a person's life. Regeneration and degeneration must exist in balance. Excessive work, rest, worry, or criticism—all excess of any kind is the basis for illness.

In *The Stress of Life,* pioneering stress researcher Hans Selye took up the question of aging and pointed out that no one dies of old age, but of a breakdown of one or more vital organs upon which the entire body depends. "Among all my autopsies (and I have performed quite a few), I have never seen a man who died of old age. In fact, I do not think anyone has ever died of old age yet. To die of old age would mean that all the organs of the body would be worn out proportionately, merely by having been used too long. This is never the case. We invariably die because one vital part has worn out too early in proportion to the rest of the body. Life, the biological chain that holds our parts together, is only as strong as its weakest vital link."

Selye's advice is to spread the wear and tear around in a process he called deviation. "The human body—like the tires on a car, or the rug on a floor—wears longest when it wears evenly. We can do ourselves a great deal of good in this respect by just yielding to our natural cravings for variety in everyday life. We must not forget that the more we vary our actions the less any one part suffers from attrition." In short, live a balanced life.

Paradox and balance were the basis for all traditional medical systems. Whether it was the yin-yang system of the Chinese, or the four humors of the Greeks, the Hindu trinity of Brahma (creation), Vishnu (maintenance), and Shiva (destruction), health depends upon balancing opposing forces that exist in the body, and in all of life.

The ancients understood that health is not a static state, but a fluid one that is continually adapting to its environment. Why is health a flowing or moving condition? Because opposites or paradoxes are continually present in your life, to which you must continually adapt. Sometimes you need more rest, sometimes less; sometimes more of these foods, other times less; today you place greater emphasis upon work, tomorrow on play.

Opposites create movement and energy, the basis of life. This was the underlying realization that unified East and West in the traditional world. Nothing was more basic, nor more useful in physical and spiritual questions.

According to these systems, healing was accomplished through the abundant presence of this flowing life energy. Whether the problem was a cut or a cancer, life energy was the underlying force that caused the cells to close the wound or eliminate the illness. This life energy flowed best in a balanced physical, emotional, and spiritual life. Hence, the path toward

Never let a surgeon take out a "functionless" organ unless it is really diseased. Functionless organs have a way of turning into very useful ones as soon as researchers admit the possibility of function and try to document it.

ANDREW WEIL

greatest health, vitality, and spiritual development emanated from balanced behavior. The healing systems of the Chinese and Greeks were based upon balancing opposite forces. The Doctrine of the Middle Way is the Buddhist ideal for spiritual development. The Logos, truth, is followed by balancing opposites in daily life, said Greek philosopher Heraclitus. Balance allows life energy to flow and thus brings forth the healing process.

THE ERA OF ENERGY MEDICINE

As foreign as a life energy may sound to some, a new medical science is now emerging that supports this very concept. The science is being called energy medicine, or the understanding of how electromagnetic energy flows within the body.

As we have seen throughout this book, the body is more than a chemical and mechanical machine; it is also an electrical unit. For the most part, science has maintained that these electrical events are localized to specific organ functions, such as the heart or the nervous system. But new research is demonstrating that electromagnetic energy flows along pathways analogous to the meridians described in Chinese acupuncture. Moreover, scientific research is showing that electromagnetic energy may well be the underlying power that triggers the healing process.

In his book *Cross Currents: The Promise of Electromedicine; The Perils of Electropollution,* Dr. Robert O. Becker scientifically documents the presence of an underlying electromagnetic life force that animates the body, and causes it to grow and heal. Describing his work with technology that can measure minute electromagnetic energy, Becker demonstrates that the human body is a complex web of electrical currents. These currents trigger cells to restore health, repair wounds, and promote growth. The electromagnetic energy is itself the stimulus to the healing process, Becker found.

By combining biology, chemistry, and physics, Becker formulated an hypothesis and eventually proved how this repair process works. He showed that an injury causes the brain to send a low-level electrical signal to the wound that stimulates repair. As the repair process progresses, this original "stimulating signal" diminishes in intensity. The lower stimulating signal in turn

The scientific basis for energy medicine is often poorly understood, and body energies are still considered by many practitioners to be mysterious, unknowable entities. If energy medicine is to assume its rightful place as an effective form of medical therapy, it must be based on established scientific principles and careful scientific experimentation.

ROBERT BECKER

slows the repair activity. Eventually, when the wound is fully healed, the stimulating signal stops, at which point the repair process also stops.

This was just the beginning. Becker also has shown that the electrical web of the body corresponds to Chinese acupuncture meridians. The points along these acupuncture meridians enhance or reinforce the electromagnetic current flowing in the body. He says, "We found that about 25 percent of the acupuncture points on the human forearm did exist, in that they had specific, reproducible and significant electrical parameters and could be found in all subjects tested. Next, we looked at the meridians that seemed to connect these points. We found that these meridians had the electrical characteristics of transmission lines, while nonmeridian skin did not. We concluded that the acupuncture

The Body's Energy Field

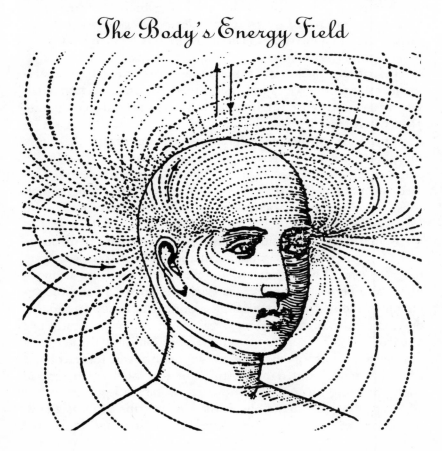

Scientists and alternative healers now envision the human body in not only chemical and mechanical terms, but as an electrical unit that both generates and is affected by electromagnetic fields. According to cell biologist Jim Oschman, "Parts of the whole may be interconnected by various types of energetic fields." Some scientists even speculate that electromagnetic energy may well be the underlying power that triggers the healing process.

system was really there, and that it most likely operated electrically. This system was quite likely the input route to the brain that transmitted the signal of injury."

Why doesn't a fingernail produce liver cells? What regulates DNA so that certain genes will be active while others remain dormant? Becker attempted to answer these questions by examining the ability of salamanders to regenerate. The salamander can regrow a leg in every detail. It can also regenerate an eye, ear, one-third of its brain, almost all of its digestive tract, and much of its heart. Remarkably, if you cut off a salamander's leg and remove the budding repair-cells of the leg and place them on a severed salamander tail, the salamander will grow a tail. If you cut off the tail and place it on a leg, the salamander will grow a new leg in every detail. Such experiments demonstrated to Becker that "there is some mechanism within the living salamander that contains an overall plan for the salamander's body and provides the information that instructs the blastema [newly formed cells] what tissue it should construct."

Essentially, Becker was asking how it is possible that the salamander's regenerative capacities act in so orderly a pattern, even when common sense might suggest that this would be the one place where disorder would reign.

Through rigorous scientific study, he demonstrates that these morphogenetic fields are actually electrical fields that permeate and surround the living organism. The fields contain complex information that directs the healing process and determines which cells will grow where. Such energetic fields are where intelligence may well lie.

Remarkably, the salamander is similar to humans in its skeletal and nervous systems. "The salamander's foreleg has the same bones, muscles, blood vessels, and nerves, in the same arrangement, as a person's arm," writes Becker. "The brain and the arrangement of nerves throughout its body are basically the same as ours, except that the thinking area of our brains is greatly expanded."

Becker, an orthopedic surgeon twice nominated for the Nobel Prize, has demonstrated that optimal amounts of electromagnetic energy flowing through the body determine the level of health. This discovery, he points out, is the basis for the birth of a new medicine—electromagnetic medicine.

A man laid on the operating table in one of our surgical hospitals is exposed to more chances of death than the English soldier on the field of Waterloo.

SIR JAMES YOUNG
SIMPSON

Electromagnetic medicine is essentially the enhancement or strengthening of the life energy within the body. Many ancient and modern healing techniques, including such diverse methods as shamanism and homeopathy, can enhance or strengthen the life energy within the body, Becker has shown. He has divided these many techniques into three groups.

The first is what he calls minimal energy techniques, which include visualization, placebo, shamanism, and hypnosis. The second is energy-reinforcement techniques, such as acupuncture, magnets, diet, homeopathy, herbs, and massage. The third is high-energy transfer techniques, which is the introduction of energy from outside the body. These include the use of machines that can transfer higher amounts of energy into the body and thus repair cells and restore health.

Proper use of these approaches works, says Becker, but much research remains to determine how they can be utilized best, especially the third category, high-energy transfer. Becker urges people to use caution in selecting practitioners of energetic medicine. The use of electrical acupuncture, for example, can be dangerous to cells, Becker points out, because only minute DC currents are active in the body. The introduction of excessive current can damage cells and create havoc. Though Becker is a pioneer in this field, many other scientists are now actively involved in developing electromagnetic medicine and its techniques, including scientists at the State University of New York Medical School, the University of California, and Syracuse University.

It may well be that electromagnetic medicine represents both the future of health care, and a bridge between East and West, ancient and modern, spirit and matter.

Healthy people look healthier and younger than unhealthy people. They're freer of disease and it shows. They're also happier, says Deepak Chopra. The reason: Health can exist only in an atmosphere of healthy thoughts. As the science of psychoneuroimmunology has demonstrated, thoughts profoundly affect the immune system and thus directly impact on health. Depression, chronic stress, anger, and loneliness weaken immunity and make the body more susceptible to a variety of illnesses, everything from the common cold to heart disease and cancer. Conversely, happy thoughts have health-enhancing effects on the body.

"It appears that happiness, which simply means having happy

The machine analogy has some plausibility in relation to adult organisms: machines, especially those containing feedback control systems, are indeed like artificial organisms or organs: airplanes are like birds, cameras like eyes, pumps like hearts, computers like brains. Machines, made by human beings to serve human purposes, reflect some of the organic, purposeful qualities of the people that make and use them. But the fact that machines are like artificial organisms does not mean that organisms are nothing but machines.

RUPERT SHELDRAKE

That true bible . . . the human body.

ANDREAS VESALIUS

thoughts most of the time, causes biochemical changes in the brain that in turn have profoundly beneficial effects on the body's physiology," says Chopra. "For every state of consciousness, there is a corresponding state of physiology. If you are having hostile thoughts, for example, they will be reflected in your mood, your facial expression, your social behavior, and how you feel physically."

In short, the condition we call health permeates every fiber of our being, every aspect of our lives. One of the best definitions of health, which also offers a glimpse of our potential, is offered by Michio Kushi. He defines health as having seven characteristics: experiencing abundant energy without fatigue, having an excellent appetite, enjoying deep and fully-restful sleep, having an excellent memory, never being angry, being ever joyous and alert, and having endless gratitude for life and other people.

Such a state describes someone fully equipped to enjoy life, and capable of realizing his or her full potential. That, said the great Swiss psychiatrist Carl Jung, is the purpose of life. For those willing to follow the path of life courageously and intelligently, life leads inevitably to one's own inner nature, the true center of being. Jung called such a path leading to self-knowledge the process of individuation.

"Individuation means becoming a single, homogeneous being, and, in so far as 'individuality' embraces our innermost, last, and incomparable uniqueness, it also implies becoming one's own self. We could therefore translate individuation as 'coming to selfhood' or 'self-realization.'"

That, said the ancients, is where health leads: to the knowledge of the inner you.

BIBLIOGRAPHY

Anatomy, Physiology, and Western Medicine:

The American Medical Association's Encyclopedia of Medicine. Random House, 1989.

Brody, Jane. *Jane Brody's New York Times Guide to Personal Health.* Times Books, 1982.

Gray, Henry. *Gray's Anatomy: Descriptive and Surgical.* Bounty Books, 1927.

Hooper, Judith and Dick Teresi. *The Three Pound Universe.* Jeremy P. Tarcher, 1986.

Juhan, Deane. *Job's Body: A Handbook for Bodywork.* Station Hill Press, 1987.

Steen, Edwin and Ashley Montagu. *Anatomy and Physiology,* vols. I and II. Barnes & Noble Books, 1985.

Early and Traditional Medical Systems:

Grossinger, Richard. *Planet Medicine: From Stone Age Shamanism to Post-Industrial Healing.* North Atlantic Books, 1987.

Preuss, Julius. *Biblical and Talmudic Medicine.* Trans. and edited by Fred Rosner, M.D. Sanhedrin Press, New York, 1978.

Thorwald, Jurgen. *Science and Secrets of Early Medicine*. Thames & Hudson, London, 1962.

Medical History:

Bettmann, Otto L., Ph.D. *A Pictorial History of Medicine*. Charles C. Thomas, Springfield, 1956.

Castiglioni, Arturo, M.D. *A History of Medicine*. Trans. from Italian and edited by E. A. Krumbhaar, M.D., Ph.D. Alfred A. Knopf, New York, 1947.

Clendening, Logan. *The Romance of Medicine: Behind the Doctor*. The Garden City Publishing Co., Inc., Garden City, New York, 1933.

Clendening, Logan, M.D. *Source Book of Medical History*. Dover Publications, Inc., New York, 1942.

Servetus, Michael. *A Translation of His Georgraphica, Medical and Astrological Writings*. Trans. by Charles Donald O'Malley. American Philosophical Society, Philadelphia, 1953.

Smith, Anthony. *The Body*. Viking Penguin, New York, 1986.

Chinese and Japanese Medicine:

Fierbrace, Peter, B.Ac. *Acupuncture: Restoring the Body's Natural Healing Energy*. Harmony Books, 1988.

Garvey, John W., N.D. *Introducing the Five Phases of Food: How to Begin*. Wellbeing Books, Brookline, Massachusetts, 1982.

Kaptchuk, Ted J., O.M.D., and Michael Croucher. *The Healing Arts*. Summit Books, New York. 1987.

Kaptchuk, Ted J. O.M.D. *The Web That Has No Weaver; Understanding Chinese Medicine*. Congdon and Weed, New York, 1983.

Kushi, Michio. *The Book of Macrobiotics*. Japan Publications, 1977.

Lu, Henry C., *Chinese System of Food Cures*. Sterling Publications Co., Inc., New York, 1986.

Matsumoto, Kiiko, and Stephen Birch. *The Five Elements and Ten Stems*. Paradigm Publications, Brookline, Massachusetts, 1983.

Muramoto, Naburo. *Healing Ourselves*. Avon Books, 1973.

Ohashi, Waturo, with Tom Monte. *Reading the Body*. Viking Penguin, 1991.

Von Durckheim, Karlfried Graf. *Hara: The Vital Centre of Man*. George Allen & Unwin, 1985.

Wing-Tsit Chan. *Chinese Philosophy, A Source Book.* Princeton University Press, 1963.

Wong, K. Chimin, and Wu Lien-Teh. *History of Chinese Medicine.* The Tientsin Press, Ltd., Tientsin, China, 1936.

The Yellow Emperor's Classic of Internal Medicine. Trans. with an introduction by Ilza Veith. University of California Press, Berkeley and Los Angeles, 1949.

Ayur-Veda:

Ballentine, Rudolph, M.D. *Diet and Nutrition.* The Himalayan International Institute, 1978.

Chopra, Deepak, M.D. *Creating Health: Beyond Prevention, Toward Perfection.* Houghton Mifflin, 1987.

Lad, Vasant, Dr. *Ayurveda: The Science of Self-Healing.* Lotus Press, Sante Fe, New Mexico, 1984.

Monro, Robin, Dr., et al. *Yoga for Common Ailments.* Fireside Books, 1990.

Svoboda, Robert E. *Prakruti: Your Ayurvedic Constitution.* Geocom, Albuquerque, New Mexico, 1989.

Naturopathy:

Trattler, Ross, Dr. *Better Health Through Natural Healing.* McGraw-Hill, 1988.

Homeopathy:

Panos, Maesimund B., M.D. and Jane Heimlich. *Homeopathic Medicine at Home.* Jeremy P. Tarcher, Inc., 1980.

Richardson, Sarah. *Homeopathy: Stimulating the Body's Natural Immune System.* Harmony Books, 1988.

Ullman, Dana. *Discovering Homeopathy: Medicine for the 21st Century.* North Atlantic Books, 1991.

Herbs and Supplements:

Hausman, Patricia, M.S. *The Calcium Bible.* Warner Books, 1985.

Hutchens, Alma R. *Indian Herbology of North America.* Shambhala, 1991.

Mairesse, Michelle. *Health Secrets of Medicinal Herbs.* Arco Publishing, 1981.

Mindell, Earl. *Vitamin Bible.* Warner Books, 1991.

Tierra, Michael. *Planetary Herbology.* Lotus Press, 1988.

Tierra, Michael, N.D. *The Way of Herbs.* Washington Square Press, Pocket Books, New York, 1983.

Greek Medicine:

Plato, Selections. Edited by Raphael Demos. Charles Scribner's Sons, 1927.

The Presocratics. Edited by Philip Wheelwright. The Odyssey Press, a division of Bobbs-Merrill Co., 1966.

The Republic of Plato. Translated by Frances MacDonald Cornford. Oxford University Press, 1975.

Alternative Approaches and Syntheses of East and West:

Becker, Robert O., M.D. *Cross Currents: The Perils of Electropollution; the Promise of Electromedicine.* Jeremy P. Tarcher, 1990.

Carlson, Richard, Ph.D., and Benjamin Shield, eds. *Healers on Healing.* Jeremy P. Tarcher, 1989.

Colbin, Annemarie. *Food and Healing.* Ballantine Books, 1986.

Diamond, John, M.D. *Your Body Doesn't Lie.* Warner Books, 1983.

Monte, Tom. *The Way of Hope.* Warner Books, 1989.

Samuels, Michael, M.D. *Healing with the Mind's Eye.* Summit Books, 1990.

Pearsall, Paul, Ph.D. *Super Immunity.* McGraw-Hill, 1987.

Price, Shirley. *Aromatherapy for Common Ailments.* Fireside, 1991.

Pritikin, Nathan, with Patrick McGrady. *The Pritikin Program for Diet and Exercise.* Grosset & Dunlap, 1979.

Pritikin, Nathan, et al. *Live Longer Now.* Grosset & Dunlap, 1974.

Sattilaro, Anthony J. and Tom Monte. *Living Well Naturally.* Houghton Mifflin, 1984.

———. *Recalled by Life: The Story of My Recovery from Cancer.* Houghton Mifflin, 1982.

Serinus, Jason, editor. *Psychoimmunity and the Healing Process.* Celestial Arts, 1986.

Weil, Andrew, M.D. *Health and Healing.* Houghton Mifflin, 1988.

INDEX

ABOUT THE AUTHOR

Tom Monte has written numerous books on health and environment. He coauthored *Recalled by Life: The Story of My Recovery From Cancer* and *Living Well Naturally,* both with Dr. Anthony Sattilaro (Houghton Mifflin, 1982 and 1984, respectively). He also wrote *Pritikin: The Man Who Healed America's Heart,* with Nathan Pritikin's widow, Ilene (Rodale Press, 1987); *The Way of Hope* (published by Warner Books, 1989); and *Reading the Body,* with Waturo Ohashi (Viking, 1991). Tom Monte's work has been published in many of the nation's leading magazines and newspapers, including *Life,* the *Saturday Evening Post, Runner's World, The Chicago Tribune, Natural Health, New Age Journal,* and many other well-known publications.

He is the former editor of *Nutrition Action,* a publication of Center for Science in the Public Interest and associate editor of *East West/Natural Health.*

He lives with his wife and three children in Amherst, Massachusetts.

ABOUT *NATURAL HEALTH* MAGAZINE

Natural Health: The Guide to Well-Being (formerly *East West Journal*) has been the leading national magazine on alternative health, herbalism, bodywork, personal growth, and natural foods for over two decades. *Natural Health* provides more than half a million readers in the U.S. and around the world with practical information on health and longevity. As a recent magazine review by *USA Today* noted, *Natural Health* "is far too splendid to be confined to a health-food store shelf."

The magazine's awards include the 1989 Alternative Press Award for Service Journalism. *Natural Health* is one of only three magazines listed under the Health and Nutrition Magazines category in *The New York Public Library's Desk Reference* of "The Ultimate One-Volume Collection of the Most Frequently Sought Information."

The editors of *Natural Health* have written numerous books on natural healing and whole foods cooking, including *Quick and Natural Rice Dishes; Meetings with Remarkable Men and Women: Interviews with Leading Thinkers on Health, Medicine, Ecology, Culture, Society, and Spirit; Sweet and Natural Desserts; Shopper's Guide to Natural Foods;* and *Natural Childcare.*

Natural Health is produced bimonthly in Brookline, Massachusetts. For subscription information write or call Natural Health, 17 Station St., P.O. Box 1200, Brookline Village, MA 02147; (617) 232-1000.